P9-ECA-705

TOWNSEND PRESS
SUNDAY SCHOOL COMMENTARY

International Bible Lessons for Christian Teaching

1999-2000

Seventy-ninth Edition

With Love
Moma

WRITER
Dr. William L. Banks

EDITOR
Rev. Ottie L. West

Published by
SUNDAY SCHOOL PUBLISHING BOARD
National Baptist Convention, U.S.A., Incorporated
Dr. E. L. Thomas, *Executive Director*

Copyright ©1999
Sunday School Publishing Board
N.B.C., U.S.A., Inc.

All rights reserved

Printed in the United States of America

No part of this book may be reproduced or transmitted in any form or any means, electronic or mechanical, including photocopying, recording or by any information storage or retrieval system, without permission in writing from the Sunday School Publishing Board, 330 Charlotte Avenue, Nashville, Tennessee 37201-1188.

The Commentary Lesson Expositions have been developed from the International Sunday School Lessons Series, Cycle of 1998-2004, copyrighted by the Committee on the Uniform Series and are used by permission.

Bible passages are from the King James Version unless otherwise noted.

Passages marked NRSV are from the New Revised Standard Version of the Bible, copyright 1999 by the National Council of the Churches of Christ in the U.S.A., and are used by permission.

ACKNOWLEDGEMENTS

This publication of the *Townsend Press Sunday School Commentary* on the International Bible Lessons for Christian Teaching is the centerpiece of the family of our church school literature designed to interpret the Word of God consistent with the divine purpose for living at all levels of human experiences with age-sensitive considerations. To accomplish the mission of providing enriched educational/inspirational resources to our constituency, a coterie of individuals were brought together to devote themselves to the task at hand. The expertise of these persons is enhanced by commitment to Jesus Christ as embraced and refined by biblical contents that require the worship of God through service to those for whom Christ died. It is within this context that this work is presented to all those who desire a more comprehensive treatment of the selected Scriptures than is provided in the Sunday school quarterlies.

Special commendation and gratitude is accorded Dr. Earl L. Thomas, Executive Director of the Sunday School Publishing Board, under whose leadership those who perform in various capacities at the Board have been endowed with a renewed sense of the larger purpose for which we exist. The contagious vision of the Executive Director has effected new perspectives of personal dignity as workers interface with one another and the corporate community wherein making a living is embellished by building a life that is consistent with the purpose of our creation.

With gratitude to God, we acknowledge the scholarly work of Dr. William L. Banks whose concern for clarity of exposition is marked by exegetical integrity of Scripture that relates the historical biblical setting to the human situation in which Christians are obliged to live. His concern that the Word of God impact the complexities of contemporary contingencies is reinforced by his personal commitment to the truth implicit in Scripture that is embraced by his personal credo within the community of faith.

Without question, Mrs. Kathlyn Pillow, Associate Director of Operations, has been the catalyst behind braiding the special contributions of the editor, typesetters, proofreaders, prepress, layout, and technical personnel as well as those in binding and mailing into a single mind-set to provide a high quality Commentary that addresses the need for a reader-friendly instrument to facilitate the transmission of the rich heritage of our faith to those who hunger for the Word of Life. Mrs. Pillow's attention to details with insistence on quality performance has resulted in this production for which we all take pride as a tribute to the grace of God working in and through us.

Finally, and most importantly, we acknowledge the faithfulness of our many readers for whom this publication has been prepared. It is our prayer that God will complement this effort with the work of the Holy Spirit to become the focus by which instructional strategies result in transformation in the lives of those with whom you interact in the process of teacher-student interchange. May God grant deeper understanding as we seek to model the Gospel that we proclaim in His name.

Ottie L. West
Editor

CYCLE OF 1998-2004

Arrangement of Quarters According to the
Church School Year, September through August

	1998-1999	1999-2000	2000-2001	2001-2002	2002-2003	2003-2004
Sep Oct Nov	God Calls a People to Faithful Living (Old Testament Survey) (13)	From Slavery to Conquest (Exodus, Leviticus, Numbers, Deuteronomy, Joshua) (13)	The Emerging Nation (Judges, 1, 2, Samuel [1 Chronicles], 1 Kings 1-11 [2 Chronicles 1-9]) (13)	Jesus' Ministry (Parables, Miracles Sermon on the Mount) (13)	Judgment and Exile (2 Kings 18-25 [2 Chronicles 29-36] Jeremiah, Lamentations, Ezekiel, Habakkuk, Zephaniah) (13)	Faith Faces the World (James, 1, 2, 2 Peter, 1, 2, 3, John, Jude) (13)
Dec Jan Feb	God Calls Anew in Jesus Christ (New Testament Survey) Christmas Sun. 12/20 (13)	Emmanuel: God With Us (Gospel of Matthew) Christmas Sun. 12/19 (13)	Good News of Jesus (Gospel of Luke) Christmas Sun. (12/24) (13)	Light for All People (Isaiah 9:1-7, 11:1-9; 40-66; Ruth, Jonah, Naham) Christmas Sun. 12/23 (13)	Portraits of Faith (Person-alities in the New Testament) Christmas Sun. 12/22 (13)	A Child is Given (4) (Samuel, John the Baptist, Jesus [2]) Lessons from Life (9) (Esther, Job, Ecclesiastes, Song of Solomon) Christmas Sun. 12/21 (13)
Mar Apr May	That You May Believe (Gospel of John) Easter (4/4) (13)	Helping a Church Confront Crisis (1, 2, Corinthians) Easter (4/23) (13)	Continuing Jesus' Work (Acts) Easter (4/15) (13)	The Power of the Gospel (Romans, Galatians) Easter (3/31) (13)	Jesus: God's Power in Action (Gospel of Mark) Easter (4/20) (13)	Jesus Fulfills His Mission (6) (Passion Narratives) Living Expectantly (7) (1, 2 Thessalonians, Revelation) Easter (4/11)
Jun Jul Aug	Genesis: Beginnings (Genesis) (13)	New Life in Christ (Ephesians, Philippians, Colossians, Philemon) (13)	Division and Decline (1 Kings 1-17, [2 Chronicles 10-28], Isaiah 1-39, Amos, Hosea, Micah) (13)	Worship and Wisdom for Living (Psalms, Proverbs) (13)	God Restores a Remnant (Ezra, Nehemiah, Daniel, Joel, Obadiah, Haggai, Zechariah, Malachi) (14)	Hold Fast to the Faith (8) (Hebrews) Guidelines for the Church's Ministry (5) (1, 2 Timothy, Titus)

*Parenthetical numerals indicate number of sessions.

PREFACE

The *Townsend Press Sunday School Commentary* on the International Bible Lessons for Christian Teaching is produced by the Sunday School Publishing Board of the National Baptist Convention, U.S.A., Inc. The contents herein are developed from curriculum guidelines of the Committee on the Uniform Series, Division of Education and Ministry, National Council of the Churches of Christ in the United States of America. The development and exposition of the lessons is provided by Christian scholars and theologians who themselves embrace the precepts, doctrines and positions on biblical interpretation that are consistent with what we have come to believe. The work is consistent with the subjects, selected Scriptures and Biblical Content Emphases as outlined in the Uniform Series and reflects the historic faith that we share within a rich heritage of worship and witness.

The Commentary's format is as follows: The Unit Title, General Subject with age-level topics, Devotional Readings, Historical Background of the lesson under discussion, Printed Parallel Texts from the King James and the New Revised Standard Versions of the Bible, Objectives of the lesson, Points to be Emphasized, Topical Outline of the lesson, Introduction to acclimate the reader to the context in which the lesson is discussed, Exposition and Application of the Scripture, Special Features that correlate the text with our own unique experiences as a people, a Concluding Word that anticipates the Biblical Content Emphases and the Home Daily Bible Readings designed to provide devotional continuity during the intervals of study.

The *Townsend Press Sunday School Commentary* is an instructional aid for Christian Teachers, Sunday School Workers, Christian Educational Leaders, and others whose desire is to gain a deeper understanding of the Word of God. While we affirm the autonomy of the individual soul before God, we also recognize that biblical truths find their highest expression within the community of believers whose corporate experiences serve as correctives that preserve the integrity of the Christian faith. Hence, the exposition and related materials presented are within the circle of concerns of those whose desire is not only to know God, but also to seek His will for their lives as indicated from the Holy Writ.

The presentation of the lessons anticipates the fact that some of the concepts and scriptural references do not lend themselves to meaningful comprehension by children. In instances wherein this is apparent, alternate passages of Scripture are employed along with content emphases designed to assist them in their spiritual development. Sensitivity to the various age groups allows this Commentary to be the centerpiece around which age-level quarterlies are developed in order that the Bible may be made plain. To this end, growth in Christian faith is realized and interaction with the Word of God results in a life that is transformed by His grace.

It must be clearly understood that encounters with God as experienced by persons whose names are part of the historical situation invite us to take that venture of faith that will draw us closer to Him. The eternal nature of God's Word is not eclipsed by the past, but speaks to the human condition as we surrender our lives to God in the dynamics of living.

INDEX OF PRINTED TEXTS

The Printed Scriptural Texts used in the 1999-2000 *Townsend Press Sunday School Commentary* are arranged here in the order in which they appear in the Bible. Opposite each reference is the page number on which Scriptures appear in this Commentary Edition.

CONTENTS

Fall Quarter
From Slavery to Promised Land

Winter Quarter
Studies in Matthew

Spring Quarter

Continuing Jesus' Work

Summer Quarter

New Life in Christ

PREVIEW OF CONCEPTS AND CHARACTERS

Aaron: The son of Amram and Jochebed, and the brother of Moses (and Miriam) who was known for his eloquence in speech (Exodus 4:14) in contrast to Moses who was "slow of speech." He was not only the principle communicator with the people of Israel and with Pharaoh, but also responsible for working many of the miracles of the Exodus (Exodus 4:30; 7:2). He failed in that he was not able to resist the demand of the people for a visible god to go before them, during the time when Moses was on the mountain with God, and made an image of God in the well-known form of Egyptian idolatry (Apis or Mnevis). He repented of his sin, and Moses gained forgiveness for him from God. In concert with his sister Miriam, he complained against Moses (Numbers 12:2), but in general he assisted Moses in the guidance of the people of Israel. Following his death at Mount Hor, his priestly authority along with his robe was transferred to his son Eleazer (Number 20:28).

Adultery: The sexual intimacy between a married woman or man with another who is not his or her mate. Whereas Israel is conceived as being married to God, adultery in the Old Testament is symbolic of Israel's infidelity to God. In the New Testament, "an adulterous generation" (Matthew 12:39) refers to a faithless and impious group of people who did not worship the One true God, but worshiped false gods instead.

Andrew: Was a native of Bethsaida in Galilee and brother of Peter. He was formerly a disciple of John the Baptist, and was instrumental in bringing Peter to Jesus pursuant to John's testimony regarding the person of the Christ (John 1:35, 36, 41).

Ark: A word adopted from the Egyptians meaning "chest." The ark of the covenant was an oblong chest of acacia wood, containing the Book of the Law, the covenant, and probably the pot of manna, and Aaron's rod (Hebrews 9:4). During the dedication of the temple, the ark contained only the two tables of stones. The ark symbolized the presence of God (1 Kings 8:9).

Bread: Bread was the term used for the whole meal. The best bread was made of wheat, ground and sifted, leavened and baked; the poorer kind of bread was made of barley, rye, beans and lentiles.

Burial: The dead were usually buried in tombs or graves whether they were rich or poor; even criminals were so buried (Deuteronomy 21:21-23).

Caleb: Of the Israelites who left Egypt, only Caleb and Joshua were allowed to enter the Promised Land. Caleb was the son of Jephunneh, the Kenezite (Joshua 14:14).

Cloud: The sign of the presence of God with the Israelite during their Exodus from Egypt (Exodus 8:21). As a cloud by day and fire by night, the cloud is not mentioned (or disappears) after the people of Israel crossed the River Jordan, but reappeared during the dedication of Solomon's Temple (2 Chronicles 5:13).

Crucifixion: Death by crucifixion was a common practice in the ancient east. A cup of stupefying liquor was often given to the victim just before the hand and feet were nailed to the cross. The body was often left to waste away naturally or to be eaten by birds and beasts, but the Jews were allowed to bury their dead out of respect for the law of Moses (Deuteronomy 21:22, 23).

Devil: The term used for the antagonistic, malicious, and perverse nature of the enemy of God and humans.

Exorcism: The ejection of evil spirits from persons or places that was usually accompanied by incantations and magical arts of various kinds. Those who did this are called exorcists. Jesus implied that such a power did exist, and might be employed after special preparation (Matthew 12:27; Luke 9:49).

Faith: Faith is the assent of the mind to the truth of God's will, whether it is historical—assent to the statements about the life and work of Jesus Christ and the apostles as historical truth; or, evangelical or saving faith—assent to the truth of revelation with trust and confidence in the character of God. Faith is essential for salvation as the mainspring of Christian life.

Frontlet: Something bound on the forehead, "between the eyes" and as a sign in the hand, possibly on a ring. Originally, it referenced keeping in memory the direction of the law—"bind them on the heart and tie them on the neck" (Proverbs 6:21). After the return from captivity, the Jews wrote the law out literally on bits of parchments called Phylacteries and tied on the forehead and left arm. The ribbon for tying them was purple in color as worn by the Pharisees for public display.

Jew: The short form of the word Jehudi (People of Judah). The word is first mentioned in 2 Kings 16:6 when the king of Syria drove the (Jehudim) Jews from Elath. The term Jew is frequently used by the prophet Jeremiah probably because the tribe of Judah constituted a large portion of the people who were taken into captivity. In the New Testament, the Jews were often cited as being determined opponents of Jesus, His gospel and His works.

Judah, Kingdom of: Emerged during the revolt of the ten tribes as a continuation of the kingdom of Saul, David, and Solomon that was considered to be divinely directed. Rehoboam, Solomon's son and successor, lost the ten tribes following his refusal to heed the advice of the older men of Israel (2 chronicles 1-19).

Kingdom of God: The divine kingdom of Jesus Christ. Matthew refers to it as the "Kingdom of Heaven" as the state of things to be expected at the coming of the Messiah.

Kiss: The kiss is used to denote: 1. Affection—on the lips; 2. Respect or salutation; 3. A symbol of charity in the early church (Romans 6:6; 1 Corinthians 16:20; 2 Corinthians 13:12; 4. Respect for old age or authority when placed on the beard; 5. Condescension when placed on the forehead; 6. Submission when placed on the back or palm; also to kiss the feet; A mark of respect when one kisses the ground; an act of worship when one kisses the hand of an idol (1 Kings 19:18; Hosea 13:2).

Law (Torah): The law of Moses, or Mosaic Law. A guide in the way of moral conduct. The Law of Moses depended on the Abrahamic covenant, which concerned the temporal promises, which were conditional on keeping the spiritual laws. The principles of the Law are universal but had special meaning for the Israelites and divided into civil, criminal, judicial, constitutional, ecclesiastical and ceremonial.

Lord's Prayer: The name of the prayer spoken by Jesus as a model to His disciples (Matthew 6:9-13; Luke 11:2-4).

Magi: (Wise men or magicians) were considered to be sacred scribes among the Jews as persons who were skilled in divining, and interpreting the hidden meaning of certain passages of Scripture.

Meat: Anything that may be eaten, but not used to refer to flesh-meat, except as it was included in a general sense as we now say food.

Messiah: (The anointed) The word is used in connection to the person that God has set apart for His own purpose. The Messiah was to be the son of David by the covenant (Psalm 59) who is described as "the mighty God, the Father of Ages, the Prince of Peace" (Isaiah 9:6).

Minister: One who serves another, and used to distinguish the person from the master. Note God's ministers (Romans 13:4-6); ministers of Christ (1 Corinthians 4:10).

Moses: The son of Amram and Jochebed of the tribe of Levi. Aaron was his brother and Miriam his sister. He was saved from Pharaoh's decree of death to all male infants born to the Hebrews by being placed in an ark (boat) of papyrus (bulrushes) and left among the reeds near the Nile bank where the daughter of the Pharaoh was in the habit of bathing. He was educated as an Egyptian in the priest's college at Helipolis, and was probably initiated into the sacred order of Priests (see Acts 7:22).

Mourning: The following customs were associated with mourning in the Bible: beating of the breast and body; weeping and screaming in an excessive manner; wearing dark-colored clothes/garments; songs and shouts of lamentation; funeral feasts; hired persons to mourn; the refusal to use perfumes, oil, and fine food, and the use of ashes, and coarse food and clothes. The period of mourning lasted from seven to thirty days.

Mystery: Truths that are hidden from the natural senses, and cannot be derives from human reason (1 Corinthians 13:2). In the New Testament, mysteries are truths hidden from the natural senses, but can be appropriated by the spiritual sense as indicated in Paul's instructions to the Colossians (see 2:2), and in Jesus' Words to His disciples (Matthew 13:11; Mark 5:11).

Ointment: The general term for perfume, ointment, oil or substances used for medicinal, sacred, or ceremonial purposes. Olive oil formed the bases for these ointments. There was a particular ointment used in consecration (see Exodus 30:23, 33; 29:7). The dead were anointed with both ointment and oil (see Matthew 26:12; Mark 14:3, 8; Luke 23:56).

Onesimus: A slave who had escaped from his master Philemon who was a resident of Colosse, and had fled to Rome where he was converted by Paul who recommended to Philemon that he be forgiven for having run away. Onesimus took the letter written by Paul to Philemon (Colossian 4:9).

Passion: refers to the suffering of our Lord and Savior Jesus Christ (Acts 1:3).

Passover: One of the three great annual festivals of the Hebrews that were held in the month of Nisan. The Passover dates from the Exodus wherein the death angel passed over the firstborn of the children of Israel, while the firstborn of the Egyptians suffered death. During the Passover, a lamb was roasted whole—not a bone was to be broken—and eaten in its entirety during the same night along with bitter herbs. The uneaten portion of the lamb was to be burnt.

Paul: Was a native of Tarsus, Cilicia, and a descendent of the tribe of Benjamin. He was born about A.D. 5 as a free Roman citizen. Paul was well read in the classical literature of his day, and received part of his education as a student of Gamaliel, who was a strict Pharisee. As a young man, Paul showed a great passion for the law of Moses (Judaism) and noted for holding the clothes of those who participated in the stoning of Stephen. The highlights of Paul's life were his conversion, ministry at Antioch; the first missionary journey in which he assumed the position as Apostle to the Gentiles, his visit to Jerusalem to settle the dispute between the Gentiles and Jewish converts, the introduction of the Gospel of Jesus Christ into Europe, the third missionary journey during which he wrote the four great epistles, his arrest and imprisonment, and his voyage to Rome where he died.

Pharaoh: The title given to the kings of Egypt. The Pharaoh mentioned during the Exodus may be described as impious and superstitious, and vacillated between right and wrong. He was as ready to promise as to break his promise, and his life came to an end when he and his army were destroyed in the Red Sea.

Pharisees: One of the three religious groups of Judaism during the time of Christ. Their origin dates back to about 150 B.C., and grows out of the concept of being separated for a special use. The name refers to all Hebrews who separated themselves from all kinds of impurity as indicated in the Mosaic Law of purity (Leviticus). The group had great influence both on the Sanhedrin and all Jewish society. They believed that God had given to all men alike the kingdom, the priesthood, and holiness; the members studied the law diligently in preparation for the office of Rabbi. Jesus referred to them as whited sepulchres or hidden graves, a charge that caused them to become His most determined enemies.

Sadducees: (Named from Zadok, the high priest) A religious sect of the Jews at the time of Christ who refused to accept that the oral law was the revelation of God to the people of Israel, and believed exclusively in the written law. They rejected belief in the Resurrection (Matthew 22:23).

Washing the Hands and Feet: Since no knives or forks were used at the table, washing the hands prior to and after meals was necessary. The dust and heat of the Eastern area mandated that the feet be washed upon entering the house and washing the feet was an act of respect. Washing the feet was performed by the master or head of the household as a special mark of respect and honor to the guests.

FALL QUARTER

September, October, November 1999

From Slavery to Promised Land

General Introduction

The Lessons for this quarter discuss the history of God's chosen people from the point of the Exodus through their entry into the Promised Land. The focus is on the process by which God saved Israel from slavery, entered into a covenant with them and fulfilled His historic promise to Abraham by establishing them in the land of Canaan. The scriptural basis for these lessons consists of selected passages from the books of Exodus, Leviticus, Numbers, Deuteronomy, and Joshua that are tied together with the themes of freedom, covenant, obedience, and faithfulness.

Unit I, *"Liberation and Covenant,"* consists of four sessions that survey the Exodus and the making of the covenant at Mount Sinai. The discussion begins with God's call of Moses, followed by the details involved in the children of Israel crossing the Red Sea. The third session reports the making of the covenant at Mount Sinai, and the unit concludes by describing the tabernacle and God's call to His people for unquestioned obedience.

Unit II, *"Wilderness Wanderings,"* is divided into five sessions. The first lesson describes how God led His people during their wilderness experience. Lesson two tells how the rebellion of the people became a factor in determining who would enter the Promised Land. With the realization that those who rebelled against God would not enter the Land of Promise, lesson three reports the attempt of the people to enter the land without God's support, which led to additional years of wanderings in the wilderness. The forth lesson of this unit focuses on the commandment to love God with all of one's heart, soul, and might. The final lesson puts forth a warning to the people not to forget God in their time of prosperity.

Unit III, *"Entering the Land,"* begins with a description of the death of Moses and God's promise to be with Joshua as the one whom He appointed to assume the leadership of the people of Israel. The second lesson in this unit is a report on the crossing of the Jordan River with commands and specifics instructions that not only affirmed God's presence, but also God's endorsement of Joshua as Moses' legitimate successor. After a discussion of the details surrounding the battle of Jericho, the unit ends with focus on the renewal of the covenant under Joshua's leadership.

While the various lessons are grounded in God's initiatives to establish Israel as His chosen people and their historic responses to God's action, there is a continuity of concerns that we in our day share with them as we affirm or reject God's will for our lives.

God Calls Moses

Unit I—*Liberation and Covenant*
Children Unit—*Relating to Others*

·····

Adult Topic—*Called to Involvement*

·····

Youth Topic—*Who, Me?*
Children's Topic—*Being a Helper*

·····

Devotional Reading—Exodus 6:2-8
Background Scripture—Exodus 3
Print—Exodus 3:1-12

PRINTED SCRIPTURE

Exodus 3:1-12 (KJV)

NOW MOSES kept the flock of Jethro his father-in-law, the priest of Midian: and he led the flock to the backside of the desert, and came to the mountain of God, even to Horeb.

2 And the angel of the LORD appeared unto him in a flame of fire out of the midst of a bush: and he looked, and, behold, the bush burned with fire, and the bush was not consumed.

3 And Moses said, I will now turn aside, and see this great sight, why the bush is not burnt.

4 And when the LORD saw that he turned aside to see, God called unto him out of the midst of the bush, and said, Moses, Moses. And he said, Here am I.

5 And he said, Draw not nigh hither: put off thy shoes from off thy feet, for the place whereon thou standest is holy ground.

6 Moreover he said, I am the God of thy father, the God of Abraham,

Exodus 3:1-12 (NRSV)

MOSES WAS keeping the flock of his father-in-law Jethro, the priest of Midian; he led his flock beyond the wilderness, and came to Horeb, the mountain of God.

2 There the angel of the LORD appeared to him in a flame of fire out of a bush; he looked, and the bush was blazing, yet it was not consumed.

3 Then Moses said, "I must turn aside and look at this great sight, and see why the bush is not burned up."

4 When the LORD saw that he had turned aside to see, God called to him out of the bush, "Moses, Moses!" And he said, "Here I am."

5 Then he said, "Come no closer! Remove the sandals from your feet, for the place on which you are standing is holy ground."

6 He said further, "I am the God

the God of Isaac, and the God of Jacob. And Moses hid his face; for he was afraid to look upon God.

7 And the LORD said, I have surely seen the affliction of my people which are in Egypt, and have heard their cry by reason of their taskmasters; for I know their sorrows;

8 And I am come down to deliver them out of the hand of the Egyptians, and to bring them up out of that land unto a good land and a large, unto a land flowing with milk and honey; unto the place of the Canaanites, and the Hittites, and the Amorites, and the Perizzites, and the Hivites, and the Jebusites.

9 Now therefore, behold, the cry of the children of Israel is come unto me: and I have also seen the oppression wherewith the Egyptians oppress them.

10 Come now therefore, and I will send thee unto Pharaoh, that thou mayest bring forth my people the children of Israel out of Egypt.

11 And Moses said unto God, Who am I, that I should go unto Pharaoh, and that I should bring forth the children of Israel out of Egypt?

12 And he said, Certainly I will be with thee; and this shall be a token unto thee, that I have sent thee: When thou hast brought forth the people out of Egypt, ye shall serve God upon this mountain.

of your father, the God of Abraham, the God of Isaac, and the God of Jacob." And Moses hid his face, for he was afraid to look at God.

7 Then the LORD said, "I have observed the misery of my people who are in Egypt; I have heard their cry on account of their taskmasters. Indeed, I know their sufferings,

8 and I have come down to deliver them from the Egyptians, and to bring them up out of that land to a good and broad land, a land flowing with milk and honey, to the country of the Canaanites, the Hittites, the Amorites, and Perizzites, the Hivites, and the Jebusites.

9 The cry of the Israelites has now come to me; I have also seen how the Egyptians oppress them.

10 So come, I will send you to Pharaoh to bring my people, the Israelites, out of Egypt."

11 But Moses said to God, "Who am I that I should go to Pharaoh, and bring the Israelites out of Egypt?"

12 He said, "I will be with you; and this shall be the sign for you that it is I who sent you: when you have brought the people out of Egypt, you shall worship God on this mountain."

KEY VERSE

And God said unto Moses, I AM THAT I AM: and he said, Thus shalt thou say unto the children of Israel, I AM hath sent me unto you.
—*Exodus 3:14*

OBJECTIVES

After reading this lesson, the student should be better informed about:

1. The significance of the burning bush;
2. The identification of the Angel of the Lord;
3. The compassion and concern of God for His own; and,
4. Learning the lesson of humility and service.

POINTS TO BE EMPHASIZED

Adult/Youth/Children

Key Verse: Exodus 3:14; Exodus 3:10 *(Children)*
Print: Exodus 3:1-12

—While tending Jethro's sheep near Horeb, Moses saw a bush burning that was not being consumed. (1-2)
—When Moses drew near to investigate this unusual occurrence, God called to him and Moses responded. (3-4)
—When God told Moses he was standing on holy ground and claimed to be the God of Moses' ancestors, Moses was afraid to look at God. (5-6)
—The Lord (YHWH) knew the plight of the Israelites and had come to deliver them from their oppression in Egypt. (7-9)
—The Lord called Moses to be an instrument in delivering the Lord's people out of slavery in Egypt. (10)
—In response to Moses' reluctance to undertake this mission, the Lord assured Moses that God would be with him and would bring him and the Israelites to this mountain to worship. (11-12)

(**Note**: Use KJV Scripture for Adults; NRSV Scripture for Youth and Children)

TOPICAL OUTLINE OF THE LESSON

I. Introduction

A. The Burning Bush
B. Biblical Background

II. Exposition and Application of the Scripture

A. Getting the Attention of Moses (Exodus 3:1-4)
B. Identifying the Holy God (Exodus 3:5-6)
C. A Compassionate Deliverer (Exodus 3:7-10)
D. God's Assurance to His Servant (Exodus 3:11-12)

III. Special Features

A. Preserving Our Heritage
B. A Concluding Word

I. Introduction

A. THE BURNING BUSH

What an extraordinary appearance! God came to Moses in a flame of fire out of the midst of a bush—a thorny bush, possibly a blackberry bush—and the bush was not consumed. Throughout the Bible, thorns are depicted as injurious. In fact, the first and last references to thorns in the Bible show that they are a curse. In the first mention of thorns, the ground was cursed: "thorns and thistles shall it bring forth" (Genesis 3:18). The last reference states "that which bears thorns and briers is rejected" (Hebrews 6:8).

In between these verses, there is nothing good said about thorns. They tear the flesh and are symbolic of desolated land. The failure of the Israelites to drive out the inhabitants of the land would cause those same people to become as "thorns in the side or eyes" of the Israelites. In the parable of the sower, the seed that fell among thorns and was choked symbolized God's Word falling upon hearts choked up with the cares of this world age and the deceitfulness of riches. Paul spoke of his malady as a "thorn in the flesh." Finally, recall that evil men platted a crown of thorns and put it on the head of Christ as they mocked Him.

But how could this bush burn and not be consumed? It is the very nature of fire to devour, eat up, consume, burn to ashes and destroy! The answer: God was in the bush! "God is in the midst of her" (Psalm 46:5). This is the secret of Israel's preservation. Throughout the centuries, the people of Israel have been hated, persecuted and killed, but not wiped out! Why? Because God has a program and no one permanently thwarts it. While it takes time to develop and mold the characters of those involved, when the Lord's time comes, He moves and accomplishes His purpose.

See then a picture of the nation Israel in its humiliation, a people hated by Satan, and despised by the world, of which Egypt, the "iron furnace" (Deuteronomy 4:20), is representative. Attempts to destroy the Jewish people—inquisitions, pogroms, holocaust—have failed. The bush is still preserved. God's promises to Abraham have never been completely, literally fulfilled. However, they shall be! So that the burning bush that was not consumed is a reminder that the Keeper (Preserver) of Israel neither slumbers nor sleeps (Psalm 121:4). Presently in apostasy, and temporarily set aside by God (Romans 11:25), the nation Israel faces yet another time of burning (Jacob's trouble: Jeremiah 30:7). But God remains in her midst and will not let her be consumed.

B. BIBLICAL BACKGROUND

After many years passed, the Egyptians no longer remembered how God had used Joseph to save Egypt and other nations from starvation. Fear of the increased numbers and influence of the Israelites then living in Egypt drove a new king to enslave the population of Israel. Infanticide was ordered by the Pharaoh, but by the providence of God the baby Moses was spared, and was reared in the palace as the son of the Pharaoh's daughter.

Moses lived there forty years. Then one day he saw an Egyptian beating an Israelite, and intervening, killed the Egyptian. He was forced to flee when the matter became known. Thus ended the story of the first forty years of his life.

Our lesson finds Moses forty years later (Acts 7:30) feeding the sheep of his father-in-law, Jethro, the priest of Midian. According to Josephus, Moses had been an astronomer, mathematician, and army general; and Stephen points out Moses "was learned in all the wisdom of the Egyptians, and was mighty in words and in deeds" (Acts 7:22). It is difficult then to conceive of this brilliant man now working as a shepherd. In search of better grazing land, he drove the flock through a desert area until he reached the pasture land on the west side. And so it was that at just such a moment, the Lord Jehovah came to Moses in a miraculous way, and called him into the Lord's service! "Ex" means "out"; and "odos" is a Greek word for "road, way." Jehovah was preparing a man to lead Israel in the Exodus or "way out" of the land of Egypt!

II. Exposition and Application of the Scripture

A. GETTING THE ATTENTION OF MOSES (Exodus 3:1-4)

NOW Moses kept the flock of Jethro his father-in-law, the priest of Midian: and he led the flock to the backside of the desert, and came to the mountain of God, even to Horeb. And the angel of the LORD appeared unto him in a flame of fire out of the midst of a bush: and he looked, and, behold, the bush burned with fire, and the bush was not consumed. And Moses said, I will now turn aside, and see this great sight, why the bush is not burnt. And when the LORD saw that he turned aside to see, God called unto him out of the midst of the bush, and said, Moses, Moses. And he said, Here am I.

Recall that Moses had married Zipporah, daughter of Jethro. His father-in-law is also called Reuel (Exodus 2:18) or Raguel (Numbers 10:29). Evidently, the Midianites, descendants of Abraham, still had some knowledge of the true and living God. The name Jethro was associated with his office as a priest of the Midianites. On this particular day, Moses led the flock to the west side of the desert. He came to the mountain of God, even to Horeb. Sinai and Horeb are names used interchangeably, and by calling it the mountain of God, consecration of the mountain is anticipated. Whereas Horeb is the name applied to the central group of mountains, Sinai is the name of one of the mountains composing the Horeb range. As we later learn, it was here that God gave the Law to Israel. This was in keeping with the promise made in Exodus 3:12.

As Moses tended the flock, suddenly the Angel of the Lord appeared unto him in a flame of fire out of the midst of the bush. This Angel of the Lord is the way in which the Old Testament speaks of the human encounter with God: called a Theophany or God-appearance. According to the biblical record, our Lord manifested

Himself in this way to Hagar, Jacob (Israel), Balaam, Gideon, Manoah (father of Samson), Elijah and David. We call this a pre-incarnate appearance, a before-He-became-flesh appearance, and it is one of the ways God made Himself known in the Old Testament.

In each instance, this visible manifestation of Deity was the second Person of the Godhead. Note that the "Angel of the Lord" in verse 2 is called "The Lord" and "God" in verse 4. Obviously, the Angel of the Lord is not some created angel whom God used merely to represent Him (as the Watchtower Society teaches)!

But now this was no ordinary sight, for the bush burned with fire but was not consumed. Ordinarily fire devours, eats up that which it touches, melts, destroys. Curious, Moses desired to see why this bush did not disintegrate, or burn to ashes. And when he turned to investigate, God called to him out of the midst of the bush, and said, "Moses, Moses." And he answered, "Here am I."

B. IDENTIFYING A HOLY GOD
(Exodus 3:5-6)

And he said, Draw not nigh hither: put off thy shoes from off thy feet, for the place whereon thou standest is holy ground. Moreover he said, I am the God of thy father, the God of Abraham, the God of Isaac, and the God of Jacob. And Moses hid his face; for he was afraid to look upon God.

Wherever the God of the Bible manifests Himself, shows His presence, that place is holy. Moses obeyed the command to take off his shoes. He showed respect for the very presence of the Lord. We too should show reverence when we enter the church, a place set apart for His glory and honor through worship and praise. In recent days, there has been a feckless accommodationism, a faddish trend to "come as you are" to the church. "Dress Up" has become "Dress Down," and may soon deteriorate into "Dress Less."

Of course, we are not required to remove our shoes before entering the church sanctuary. Our emphasis is upon heart attitude; we are concerned with the spirit of our hearts, not the soles of our feet. But, we do suggest that clothing which is slipshod, irreverent, "anything-goes," does not satisfy our concept of worshiping God in spirit and in truth. Here is the first place in the Bible that the word "holy" occurs. Moses stood on ground considered holy because of the very presence of God. Note, Moses was not given a choice! He was commanded to do so, and he obeyed.

Another argument for the deity of the Angel of the Lord is seen in verse 6. The speaker claims to be the God of Abraham, the God of Isaac, and the God of Jacob; and the word "father" is singular. Scholars seem to believe the reference is not to Amram the father of Moses (Exodus 6:20). Here is a title for God that reminds Israel of its relationship with the Lord, based upon His promise to the three patriarchs, for each had received directly from the Lord the promise concerning their descendants, the Hebrew people.

It is interesting that in Matthew 22:32, our Lord quoted this title to show the Sadducees who did not believe in a resurrection, that "God is not the God of the dead, but of the living." There is life after death. Man never ceases to exist. In the expression, "the soul that sins, it shall die" (Ezekiel 18:4), dying is not annihilation. The word "soul" represents the person, the whole being. Even after physical death, the soul exists. Our Lord confirms this in His speech to the Sadducees. If God is the God of Abraham, Isaac, and Jacob, whether in the day of Moses, or in the days of our Lord's flesh, it means that Abraham, Isaac, and Jacob were still in existence even as the Lord spoke.

Finally, in this section, we see that Moses hid his face, for he was afraid to look upon God. Thiessen suggests that when we observe our faces in the mirror, in a sense we see ourselves, yet in another sense we do not literally see ourselves. To see the reflection of God's glory was to see God. Although it is impossible to see God in His essence, yet in whatever way He manifests Himself, and we see that manifestation, we may truly say we have seen God.

C. A COMPASSIONATE DELIVERER (Exodus 3:7-10)

And the LORD said, I have surely seen the affliction of my people which are in Egypt, and have heard their cry by reason of their taskmasters; for I know their sorrows; And I am come down to deliver them out of the hand of the Egyptians, and to bring them up out of that land unto a good land and a large, unto a land flowing with milk and honey; unto the place of the Canaanites, and the Hittites, and the Amorites, and the Perizzites, and the Hivites, and the Jebusites. Now therefore, behold, the cry of the children of Israel is come unto me: and I have also seen the oppression wherewith the Egyptians oppress them. Come now therefore, and I will send thee unto Pharaoh, that thou mayest bring forth my people the children of Israel out of Egypt.

Here the God of all compassion informs Moses that He has seen Israel's affliction, heard her cry, known her sorrows, and identified her oppressors. We can rest assured the God of the Bible knows our burdens and wants. He is not an indifferent spectator of our suffering. Moses needed to know God would not allow Israel's intolerable situation to continue; time had come for redemption. Promise was made to deliver the Israelites from the slavery of Egypt, and then drive out the heathen nations and turn over their land to the Israelites.

A sovereign God has the right to do with sinners as He pleases. Besides, He had waited more than four centuries for any sign of repentance among the Canaanites; and there was none. The proverbial phrase "milk and honey" used to describe the land of Canaan signifies abundance; it speaks of the plenty, richness, fertility, and productivity of the land. "Milk and honey are the simplest and choicest productions of a land abounding in grass and flowers" (Keil and Delitzsch).

And so God informed Moses, "I am come down." This is God's way of expressing His condescension and concern. Moses had been away forty years and Israel was still in bondage. But the Lord had not forgotten; He was not deaf to her cries; nor had Jehovah fallen asleep. It was time for heaven's intervention, time for Divine Interference!

D. GOD'S ASSURANCE TO HIS SERVANT (Exodus 3:11-12)

And Moses said unto God, Who am I, that I should go unto Pharaoh, and that I should bring forth the children of Israel out of Egypt? And he said, Certainly I will be with thee; and this shall be a token unto thee, that I have sent thee: When thou hast brought forth the people out of Egypt, ye shall serve God upon this mountain.

Forty years earlier, Moses in self-will had offered himself as deliverer and judge. Now, he protested and made excuses not to return to Egypt. He no longer trusted in his own power, but pleaded his inadequacy. Forty years in Midian had humbled him. Now he must learn that whom God calls into service God also equips. Unfitness comes only when we seek to do God's work in our strength. When the Lord Jesus is with us, who we are is not important. God's grace is sufficient.

God assured Moses that when the Israelites are brought out, as surely they shall be, they would worship Him upon "this mountain." This would be the token or sign or proof which would further stimulate his faith; Jehovah would lead the people back to this mountain (Mount Sinai) to serve Him.

III. Special Features

A. PRESERVING OUR HERITAGE

Often it seems a waste of time to sit back and passively wait for certain things to happen. However, in the case of Moses, those forty years in Midian had not been wasted. He needed the discipline of waiting on the Lord. This is a lesson some of us still need to learn. Though no longer in slavery, subject to brutality, abuse, chains, and lynching, we still face racism and subtle efforts to deprive, denigrate and deny. The story of Moses and Israel encourages our hearts still, even as it did our slave foreparents. For we believe that God in Christ is in our midst. And He will not forsake His own.

The lesson does not suggest a do-nothing approach or attitude. Ask Pharaoh! But it teaches the necessity of the believer to wait on the Lord. A little boy asked his teacher how to spell "rat." "R-A-T", she replied. But the boy protested, "No, ma'am. I don't mean rat mouse, I mean rat now." And so God came to tell Moses, "Rat now is the time!" Forty years ago it was "rat mouse." This may be a difficult thing for Black Christians confronted by multitudes of Black (and White) unbelievers demanding instant change. What we learn is that God's timing is perfect. What we also learn is that God is faithful to His Word.

B. A CONCLUDING WORD

The words "Moses, Moses" (Exodus 3:4) remind us of God's earlier calling, "Abraham, Abraham" (Genesis 22:11); and a later call, "Samuel, Samuel" (1 Samuel 3:10). Our first observation in today's lesson is the fact that God simply does not use lazy people. When David was called, he too was busy minding the flock. Gideon was busy threshing wheat. Amos followed after the flock. Matthew was collecting taxes. Peter and the others who became disciples were either fishing or mending their nets. Why even Saul (Paul) was busy—on the road to Damascus!

Today, we see that the "harvest truly is plenteous, but the laborers are few." Surely, we need to pray the Lord of the harvest will send forth laborers into His harvest (Matthew 9:37-38). God grant that when He speaks to our hearts, we will answer, "Here am I; send me" (Isaiah 6:8).

HOME DAILY BIBLE READINGS FOR THE WEEK OF SEPTEMBER 5, 1999

GOD CALLS MOSES

Aug. 30 M. Exodus 2:1-10, Birth and Youth of Moses
Aug. 31 T. Exodus 2:11-15, Moses Flees to Midian
Sept. 1 W. Exodus 2:16-25, Moses Settles in Midian
Sept. 2 T. Exodus 3:1-12, Moses at the Burning Bush
Sept. 3 F. Exodus 3:13-22, Moses Called to Deliver Israel
Sept. 4 S. Exodus 4:1-9, Moses Empowered by God
Sept. 5 S. Exodus 4:10-20, Moses Responds to God's Call

Know Your Bible

- Moses was employed to keep his father-in-law's flock at the time when the Lord appeared to him out of the burning bush. (Exodus 3:1)
- The Lord proved to Moses that it was not by his own power and might that he would deliver the Israelites from Egypt, and the Lord demonstrated it by changing Moses' rod into a serpent and made his hand leprous, and restored them again. (Exodus 4:2-8)
- Moses was not an eloquent speaker, so the Lord selected Aaron his brother to be the spokesperson in the presence of Pharaoh. (Exodus 4:10-16)
- When Moses and Aaron demanded of Pharaoh that the Israelites be set free, they were accused for interfering with the people's work, and Pharaoh placed an even more difficult workload upon the Israelites. (Exodus 5:2-9)

Eternal God, our Father, grant that we may be sensitive to Your call and claim upon our lives. May we surrender to Your will that we shall become empowered to accomplish the task in Your name for Jesus' sake. Amen.

Crossing the Red Sea

Adult Topic—*Called to Deliverance*

•••••

Youth Topic—*Hope Out of Despair*

Children's Topic—*Being a Leader*

•••••

Devotional Reading—Psalm 106:1-12

Background Scripture—Exodus 13:17—14:31

Print—Exodus 13:17-22; 14:26-31

PRINTED SCRIPTURE

Exodus 13:17-22; 14:26-31 (KJV)

17 And it came to pass, when Pharaoh had let the people go, that God led them not through the way of the land of the Philistines, although that was near; for God said, Lest peradventure the people repent when they see war, and they return to Egypt:

18 But God led the people about, through the way of the wilderness of the Red sea: and the children of Israel went up harnessed out of the land of Egypt.

19 And Moses took the bones of Joseph with him: for he had straitly sworn the children of Israel, saying, God will surely visit you: and ye shall carry up my bones away hence with you.

20 And they took their journey from Succoth, and encamped in Etham, in the edge of the wilderness.

21 And the LORD went before them by day in a pillar of a cloud, to lead them the way; and by night in a pillar of fire, to give them light; to

Exodus 13:17-22; 14:26-31 (NRSV)

17 When Pharaoh let the people go, God did not lead them by way of the land of the Philistines, although that was nearer; for God thought, "If the people face war, they may change their minds and return to Egypt."

18 So God led the people by the roundabout way of the wilderness toward the Red Sea. The Israelites went up out of the land of Egypt prepared for battle.

19 And Moses took with him the bones of Joseph who had required a solemn oath of the Israelites, saying, "God will surely take notice of you, and then you must carry my bones with you from here."

20 They set out from Succoth, and camped at Etham, on the edge of the wilderness.

21 The LORD went in front of them in a pillar of cloud by day, to lead them along the way, and in a pillar of fire by night, to give them light, so that they might travel by

go by day and night:

22 He took not away the pillar of the cloud by day, nor the pillar of fire by night, from before the people.

.....

26 And the LORD said unto Moses, Stretch out thine hand over the sea, that the waters may come again upon the Egyptians, upon their chariots, and upon their horsemen.

27 And Moses stretched forth his hand over the sea, and the sea returned to his strength when the morning appeared; and the Egyptians fled against it; and the LORD overthrew the Egyptians in the midst of the sea.

28 And the waters returned, and covered the chariots, and the horsemen, and all the host of Pharaoh that came into the sea after them; there remained not so much as one of them.

29 But the children of Israel walked upon dry land in the midst of the sea; and the waters were a wall unto them on their right hand, and on their left.

30 Thus the LORD saved Israel that day out of the hand of the Egyptians; and Israel saw the Egyptians dead upon the sea shore.

31 And Israel saw that great work which the LORD did upon the Egyptians: and the people feared the LORD, and believed the LORD, and his servant Moses.

day and by night.

22 Neither the pillar of cloud by day nor the pillar of fire by night left its place in front of the people.

.....

26 Then the LORD said to Moses, "Stretch out your hand over the sea, so that the water may come back upon the Egyptians, upon their chariots and chariot drivers."

27 So Moses stretched out his hand over the sea, and at dawn the sea returned to its normal depth. As the Egyptians fled before it, the Lord tossed the Egyptians into the sea.

28 The waters returned and covered the chariots and the chariot drivers, the entire army of Pharaoh that had followed them into the sea; not one of them remained.

29 But the Israelites walked on dry ground through the sea, the waters forming a wall for them on their right and on their left.

30 Thus the LORD saved Israel that day from the Egyptians; and Israel saw the Egyptians dead on the seashore.

31 Israel saw the great work that the LORD did against the Egyptians. So the people feared the LORD and believed in the LORD and in his servant Moses.

KEY VERSE

And Moses said unto the people, Fear ye not, stand still, and see the salvation of the LORD, which he will show to you today: for the Egyptians whom ye have seen today, ye shall see them again no more for ever.—***Exodus 14:13***

OBJECTIVES

After reading this lesson, the student will have knowledge of:
1. The miraculous nature of the Red Sea deliverance;
2. The disastrous end of the enemies of God's people;
3. What it means to be lead by God; and,
4. The results of seeing the Lord's work of salvation.

POINTS TO BE EMPHASIZED

Adult/Youth/Children
Key Verse: Exodus 14:13
Print: Exodus 13:17-22; 14:26-31

—God led the Israelites out of Egypt, taking them by the way of the wilderness to avoid war with the Philistines. (13:17-18)

—In keeping with an oath between the Israelites and Joseph, Moses took with him the bones of Joseph. (19)

—God led the people by day in a pillar of cloud and by night in a pillar of fire. (13:21-22)

—God told Moses to stretch out his hand, and the empty sea through which the Israelites had traveled filled back up drowning the Egyptians. (14:26-29)

—Seeing how the Lord had miraculously saved them, the Israelites feared and believed in the Lord and believed in Moses. (30-31)

(**Note**: Use KJV Scripture for Adults; NRSV Scripture for Youth and Children)

TOPICAL OUTLINE OF THE LESSON

I. Introduction
A. Miracle at the Red Sea
B. Biblical Background

II. Exposition and Application of the Scripture
A. Journey From Egypt Resumed (Exodus 13:17-20)
B. Guided by the Pillar of Cloud and Fire (Exodus 13:21-22)
C. The Egyptians Drowned (Exodus 14:26-28)
D. The Israelites Delivered (Exodus 14:29-30)
E. God Feared and Believed (Exodus 14:31)

III. Special Features
A. Preserving Our Heritage
B. A Concluding Word

I. Introduction

A. MIRACLE AT THE RED SEA

We begin today's lesson with a study of the parting and crossing of the Red Sea. Because the event is so essential to the study of salvation, it is easy to see why the forces of antisupernaturalism array themselves against this event. First, there is the attack concerning location. There are scholars who would discount the miracle by claiming that the body of water cited in the Exodus passage was not the Red Sea, but the Sea of Reeds. We are told that the word "reed" was mistranslated. However, the Red Sea is mentioned more than a dozen times in the first five books of the Bible (Pentateuch); and another dozen times in the remainder of the Old Testament. But, these scholars suggest this Marsh Sea was in an area north of the Sea. They say that because the tide and wind conditions were favorable, and dried up the area, the Israelites were able to walk across it. When the Egyptians tried to cross, the wind suddenly changed directions. How they managed to drown is not revealed.

A second point of view attacks the nature of the event itself. Some years ago, a university scientist stated that the story of the parting of the Red Sea was a classic description of a desert mirage. Because the sun heats the desert ground which in turn heats the air, light passing through the temperature differences is bent (refracted), causing double images. But how did the Egyptians manage to drown? No problem replied the physicist. They only appeared to the Israelites to have drowned. Actually, the Israelites also appeared to the Egyptians to have drowned.

We recently read of computer calculations proving the possibility of the Red Sea parting precisely as the Bible describes it. Some Christians may be over-anxious to accept such scientific support for what they believe already. Of course, the ideal is to take God at His Word, believe what He says, whether or not evidence is found that corroborates the teachings of the Bible. It is amazing how some men who seek to eliminate the miraculous from the Bible would have us believe their theories which so often require a greater degree of credulity. Basic of course is their failure to accept the Bible as the Word of God.

If the Bible says all the Egyptians trying to cross the Red Sea died, why believe they did not die, but that it only appeared that they died? If the Bible describes powerful walls of water crashing in and drowning Pharaoh's army, why should we believe his army, horses and chariots became stuck in only two inches of mud, and thus allowed the Israelites to escape! May our hearts respond: We believe God!

B. BIBLICAL BACKGROUND

The events leading up to the actual crossing of the Red Sea may be summed up in one word: Judgment. Ten plagues befell the Egyptians. Recall, the number "ten" is used often in the sense of "many times." But "ten" also signifies perfection of order; it symbolizes God's complete outpouring of His wrath. The first three plagues have a repulsive, loathsome nature—water turned into blood, frogs, dust which became lice. Painful affliction characterizes the second triplet—swarms of flies, murrain (a highly infectious disease, like anthrax) upon the cattle, boils on the Egyptians and their animals. Then the final triplet of the nature plagues —hail, swarms of locusts, and thick darkness.

In spite of the increasing severity of each judgment strike, and in spite of the cumulative disastrous effect upon the people, the Pharaoh refused to liberate the Israelites. Pharaoh hardened or strengthened his own heart against the Lord. He refused to repent, and thereby reaped the consequences of having God harden the king's heart. Keep in mind also that each judgment plague was a strike against some god or goddess worshiped by the Egyptians. Jehovah demonstrated that the idol gods of Egypt were absolutely helpless.

Finally, there came stroke number ten, what A. C. Gaebelein calls, "the judgment of all judgments upon Egypt." The firstborn in the land—both human and cattle—were slain by Jehovah. Only those people with the blood of the Lamb smeared on the doorposts of their homes escaped the wrath of God. Without the shedding of blood, there is no remission, no forgiveness of sin.

II. Exposition and Application of the Scripture

A. JOURNEY FROM EGYPT RESUMED (Exodus 13:17-20)

And it came to pass, when Pharaoh had let the people go, that God led them not through the way of the land of the Philistines, although that was near; for God said, Lest peradventure the people repent when they see war, and they return to Egypt: But God led the people about, through the way of the wilderness of the Red sea: and the children of Israel went up harnessed out of the land of Egypt. And Moses took the bones of Joseph with him: for he had straitly sworn the children of Israel, saying, God will surely visit you: and ye shall carry up my bones away hence with you. And they took their journey from Succoth, and encamped in Etham, in the edge of the wilderness.

Pharaoh finally let the Israelites go. After all the misery wrought by divine judgment strokes, the king repented temporarily and freed the Israelites. And the journey started in Exodus 12:37 was resumed. However, the route taken was not the shortest and most direct to Canaan. The road up the seacoast past Gaza was the quick route (about two weeks travel time). However, God was in charge, and it was His determination not to lead them through the way of the land of the Philistines. Instead, He directed them through the way of the wilderness of the Red Sea.

The Lord had His reasons for going this way, and we are told in verse seventeen that He chose this direction, "Lest perhaps the people change their minds when they see war, and return to Egypt." Because the Philistines were very warlike, and the Israelites at this point unaccustomed to warfare, the first hint of opposition would have unnerved the Israelites. In short, the Israelites were not prepared for conflict, either militarily or psychologically; and they would have certainly expressed their desires to return to Egypt. Their possible reaction is seen in Exodus 14:10-12 in their expressions of fear when Pharaoh and his army approached them.

In our individual lives as Christians, we sometimes question the Lord's leading. For we do not always understand why He leads us through the wilderness and deserts of life. All too often, the shortcuts strongly appeal to us, and we step out of His will, only to learn the hard way His plan for our lives is best for us. Yea, the Holy Spirit gives assurance that even as Jehovah "led them forth by the right way" (Psalm 107:7), so He desires to lead us. Indeed, we believe He makes all things work together for our good.

And so the Lord made them turn around and head for the Red Sea via the desert. Thus, the children of Israel went up harnessed out of the land of Egypt. The precise meaning of the Hebrew word translated "harnessed" is not certain. NIV's and TEV's "armed for battle" is not appropriate; nor are "martial array," NASB, and "equipped for battle," RSV, acceptable. The Living Bible's paraphrase is to be utterly rejected: "Even though they had left Egypt armed." We believe the best translations, those in keeping with the context are: "in orderly array" (Moffatt) and "in orderly ranks" (NKJV). The Pilgrim Bible suggests they were "equipped for a long journey"; The New Bible Commentary: "organized." "Pre-

pared to march," states Keil and Delitzsch, "in contrast to fleeing in disorder like fugitives."

Finally, in this section of the lesson, we learn that Moses took with him the remains of Joseph's body which had been mummified and placed in a coffin. The Israelites had been made to promise to carry Joseph's bones to his homeland for burial. And now hundreds of years later, Joseph's will is carried out, for he had said: "God will surely visit you, and bring you up out of this land unto the land that he swore to Abraham, to Isaac, and to Jacob; you shall carry up my bones from here" (Genesis 50:24-26). Joshua 24:32, we learn that Joseph's bones finally were buried in Shechem, in a plot of ground which Jacob had bought many years before.

B. GUIDED BY THE PILLAR OF CLOUD AND FIRE
(Exodus 13:21-22)

And the LORD went before them by day in a pillar of a cloud, to lead them the way; and by night in a pillar of fire, to give them light; to go by day and night: He took not away the pillar of the cloud by day, nor the pillar of fire by night, from before the people.

As the Israelites journeyed from Succoth and camped in Etham at the edge of the wilderness, the Lord showed Himself in a miraculous, supernatural way. He went before them by day in a pillar of cloud, and by night in a pillar of fire. As long as the people continued in the wilderness, so long was this manifestation of the Lord's presence with them. There were not two different pillars alternately appearing, but one pillar of both cloud and fire (Exodus 14:24). The one God manifested Himself in two different ways. Basically, the cloud was a real, visible sign of God's presence with His people. It was a Theophany (God-appearance).

As a pillar of cloud by day, He guided the direction of their march. When the cloud stopped, the Israelites stopped. They rested during the hottest part of the day, protected by the cloud from the heat, sunstroke, pestilence, etc. As a pillar of fire by night, He continued to guide them, lighting up their path, for they also marched at certain times at night. The pillar served also at night as protection for the Israelites. It defended them from the terror "by night, the pestilence that walks in darkness," indeed, from all calamity.

The God of the Bible is a consuming fire. By fire, He answered Abel's sacrifice, spoke to Moses from a burning bush, with fire He devoured those who murmured and rebelled against Moses; answered Elijah's prayer on Mount Carmel, and later sent a chariot of fire and horses of fire to translate Elijah to heaven. He is the spirit of burning!

George Henderson (Studies in the book of Exodus) states the cloud occupied at least three different, distinct positions. First: the pillar protected the Israelites from their enemies at the Red Sea. Second: the pillar led them, accompanied them, guided them, backed them up, and protected them through their wilderness trek. Third: after the tabernacle was erected, the cloud covered the tent of the congregation; this same cloud of glory also filled the tabernacle. This three-fold work of the pillar illustrates the wonderful truth of God for us, God with us, and God in us. Since the resurrection of the Lord Jesus Christ, and the sending of the Holy Spirit at Pentecost, Christians are especially blessed to have the Holy Spirit living in their bodies (1 Corinthians 6:19).

C. THE EGYPTIANS DROWNED
(Exodus 14:26-28)

And the LORD said unto Moses, Stretch out thine hand over the sea, that the waters may come again upon the Egyptians, upon their chariots, and upon their horsemen. And Moses stretched forth his hand over the sea, and the sea returned to his strength when the morning appeared; and the Egyptians fled against it; and the LORD overthrew the Egyptians in the midst of the sea. And the waters returned, and covered the chariots, and the horsemen, and all the host of Pharaoh that came into the sea after them; there remained not so much as one of them.

The scene shifts now to the miraculous deliverance of the Israelites at the Red Sea. Approximately two million persons crossed over. Someone has said; "The Red Sea was a private road which God had opened up for His own family; Pharaoh had no business there." When Moses obeyed the Lord and stretched out his hand over the sea, the waters returned. Those Egyptians who had attempted to cross over dryshod as the Israelites did found themselves suddenly confronted with walls on both sides! What had been a threat to the Israelites, except for the mercy of God's restraining hand, became a disaster for the pursuing Egyptians. God allowed the waters of the sea to return in their full strength. With devastating force, the sea became their coffin. Every one of the Egyptians drowned!

D. THE ISRAELITES DELIVERED
(Exodus 14:29-30)

But the children of Israel walked upon dry land in the midst of the sea; and the waters were a wall unto them on their right hand, and on their left. Thus the LORD saved Israel that day out of the hand of the Egyptians; and Israel saw the Egyptians dead upon the sea shore.

God delivered Israel by a miracle, for the children of Israel walked upon dry land in the middle of the sea. The fact that the waters were a wall to them on their right hand and on their left destroys those arguments which claim the Red Sea was really the Reed Sea. The Hebrew word translated "saved" in verse 30 is *yasha.* It is the root of the name Joshua which is a contraction of the name, Jehoshua (Jehovah Saves, Jehovah is Salvation). The Hebrew name Joshua is Jesus in the Greek. Recall that He was so named because "He shall save his people from their sins" (Matthew 1:21).

E. GOD FEARED AND BELIEVED
(Exodus 14:31)

And Israel saw that great work which the LORD did upon the Egyptians: and the people feared the LORD, and believed the LORD, and his servant Moses.

Israel's deliverance laid the foundation for the nation's unity. But more important was the basis laid for their faith. The Israelites saw, feared, and believed. They saw the great work the Lord did in Egypt. They feared, reverenced, trusted the Lord. They believed or laid firm hold morally to what they had seen and heard. When God first commissioned Moses, unbelief of the people was Moses' first objection: "Behold, they will not believe me, nor hearken unto my voice" (Exodus 4:1). But now they believed Jehovah and His servant Moses. What happened to them was an excellent example of God's purpose in redemption. And in the story of Israel's redemption, we see a picture of that redemption provided us through the Lord Jesus Christ. We too have been delivered from Egypt, redeemed by power and blood—the blood of Jesus Christ our Lord.

III. Special Features

A. PRESERVING OUR HERITAGE

I remember as a boy hearing these words sung: "O Mary, don't you weep, don't you mourn, Pharaoh's army got drownded, O Mary, don't you weep." The entire story of Israel's deliverance from slavery in Egypt was long a favorite of our slave foreparents. It gave our people hope, for as Paul Laurence Dunbar put it, "de love he showed to Isrul wasn't all on Isrul spent" (An Ante-Bellum Sermon). Whereas Egypt represented the land of slaves, the exodus signified forging to freedom. Pharaoh symbolized oppression; the victory of Moses over Pharaoh was seen by Black American slaves as reference to their deliverance. And so they sang the very popular, "Didn't ol' Pharaoh get los', tryin' to cross the Red Sea." One version of "Go Down Moses" has this stanza: "Down came raging Pharaoh, Dat you may plainly see, Old Pharaoh an' his host, Got loss' in de Red Sea." God grant that we too appreciate the Christ who set us free and delivered us from Egypt!

B. A CONCLUDING WORD

May we desire and obey the leading of the Lord as He directs our paths in righteousness, beside the still waters, into all truth; and sets our feet upon a rock, establishes our goings, and guides us as we sing: "Sometimes 'mid scenes of deepest gloom, Sometimes where Eden's bowers bloom, By waters still, o'er troubled sea, Still 'tis His hand that leadeth me!" (J. H. Gilmore). May we sing: "Some thru the waters, some thru the flood, Some thru the fire, but all thru the blood; Some thru great sorrow, but God gives a song, In the night season and all the day long" (G. A. Young).

HOME DAILY BIBLE READINGS FOR THE WEEK OF SEPTEMBER 12, 1999

CROSSING THE RED SEA

Sept.	6	M.	Exodus 13:3-10, The Festival of Unleavened Bread
Sept.	7	T.	Exodus 13:17-22, Led by Pillars of Cloud and Fire
Sept.	8	W.	Exodus 14:1-9, Caught Between Pharaoh and the Sea
Sept.	9	T.	Exodus 14:10-18, Going Forward at God's Command
Sept.	10	F.	Exodus 14:19-25, Israel Crosses the Red Sea
Sept.	11	S.	Exodus 14:26-31, God Saves Israel from the Egyptians
Sept.	12	S.	Exodus 15:1-13, Moses Sings of God's Victory

Know Your Bible

- Before departing Egypt, God disposed the Egyptians to give the Israelites gold, silver and clothes which in a way compensated for the suffering that they had inflicted upon them. (Exodus 12:35-36, see also Romans 12:37-39)
- The Red Sea was the first obstacle that the Israelites faced when they left Egypt, and they immediately expressed to Moses that they had rather have stayed in Egypt. (Exodus 14:11-12)
- The Egyptians were separated from the Israelites by a pillar of cloud that kept the Egyptians in darkness and prevented them from moving during the night. (Exodus 14:20)

O God, when we face the difficulties of life, may we by Thy grace regard them as tests to purify our faith, and to strengthen our character and resolve to show our love for You. Amen.

The Covenant

Adult Topic—*Called to Covenant*

•••••

Youth Topic—*What Are the Limits?*
Children's Topic—*Following Rules*

•••••

Devotional Reading—Deuteronomy 4:32-40
Background Scripture—Exodus 19:1—20:21
Print—Exodus 19:3-6; 20:2-4, 7-8, 12-17.

PRINTED SCRIPTURE

Exodus 19:3-6; 20:2-4, 7-8, 12-17 (KJV)

3 And Moses went up unto God, and the LORD called unto him out of the mountain, saying, Thus shalt thou say to the house of Jacob, and tell the children of Israel;

4 Ye have seen what I did unto the Egyptians, and how I bare you on eagles' wings, and brought you unto myself.

5 Now therefore, If ye will obey my voice indeed, and keep my covenant, then ye shall be a peculiar treasure unto me above all people: for all the earth is mine:

6 And ye shall be unto me a kingdom of priests, and an holy nation. These are the words which thou shalt speak unto the children of Israel.

•••••

2 I am the LORD thy God, which have brought thee out of the land of Egypt, out of the house of bondage.

Exodus 19:3-6; 20:2-4, 7-8, 12-17 (NRSV)

3 Then Moses went up to God; the LORD called to him from the mountain, saying, "Thus you shall say to the house of Jacob, and tell the Israelites.

4 You have seen what I did to the Egyptians, and how I bore you on eagles' wings and brought you to myself.

5 Now therefore, if you obey my voice and keep my covenant, you shall be my treasured possession out of all the peoples. Indeed, the whole earth is mine,

6 but you shall be for me a priestly kingdom and a holy nation. These are the words that you shall speak to the Israelites."

•••••

2 I am the LORD your God, who brought you out of the land of Egypt, out of the house of slavery;

3 Thou shalt have no other gods before me.

4 Thou shalt not make unto thee any graven image, or any likeness of any thing that is in heaven above, or that is in the earth beneath, or that is in the water under the earth:

.....

7 Thou shalt not take the name of the LORD thy God in vain; for the LORD will not hold him guiltless that taketh his name in vain.

8 Remember the sabbath day, to keep it holy.

.....

12 Honor thy father and thy mother: that thy days may be long upon the land which the LORD thy God giveth thee.

13 Thou shalt not kill.

14 Thou shalt not commit adultery.

15 Thou shalt not steal.

16 Thou shalt not bear false witness against thy neighbour.

17 Thou shalt not covet thy neighbour's house, thou shalt not covet thy neighbour's wife, nor his manservant, nor his maidservant, nor his ox, nor his ass, nor any thing that is thy neighbour's.

3 you shall have no other gods before me.

4 You shall not make for yourself an idol, whether in the form of anything that is in heaven above, or that is on the earth beneath, or that is in the water under the earth.

.....

7 You shall not make wrongful use of the name of the LORD your God, for the LORD will not acquit anyone who misuses his name.

8 Remember the sabbath day, and keep it holy.

.....

12 Honor your father and your mother, so that your days may be long in the land that the LORD your God is giving you.

13 You shall not murder.

14 You shall not commit adultery.

15 You shall not steal.

16 You shall not bear false witness against your neighbor.

17 You shall not covet your neighbor's house; you shall not covet your neighbor's wife, or male or female slave, or ox, or donkey, or anything that belongs to your neighbor.

 **KEY VERSE**

Now therefore, if ye will obey my voice indeed, and keep my covenant, then ye shall be a peculiar treasure unto me above all people: for all the earth is mine. —**Exodus 19:5**

OBJECTIVES

After reading this lesson, the student should understand:

1. The significance of the Mosaic Covenant;
2. The interpretation of the Decalogue; and,
3. The dispensation of the Law.

Adult/Youth/Children
Key Verse: Exodus 19:5
Print: Exodus 19:3-6; 20:2-4, 7-8, 12-17

—On Mount Sinai, the Lord told Moses to remind the Israelites how the Lord had delivered them out of slavery in Egypt. (19:3-4)

—The Lord offered to make Israel God's treasured nation, set apart for service, if the people would obey the Lord and keep God's Covenant. (5-6)

—The covenant commandments required Israel to give exclusive allegiance to the Lord. (20:2-4)

—Revering the name of the Lord and dedicating a day of the week to the Lord were requirements of the covenant commandments. (7-8)

—The covenant commandments also contained expectations for living righteously in relationship with other people. (12-17)

(**Note**: Use KJV Scriptures for Adults; NRSV Scripture for Youth and Children)

TOPICAL OUTLINE OF THE LESSON

I. Introduction

A. Covenants and Dispensations
B. Biblical Background

II. Exposition and Application of the Scripture

A. The Fifth Dispensation and Covenant (Exodus 19:3-6)
B. The Decalogue: Our Love to God (Exodus 20:2-4, 7-8)
C. The Decalogue: Our Love to Others (Exodus 20:12-17)

III. Special Features

A. Preserving Our Heritage
B. A Concluding Word

I. Introduction

A. COVENANTS AND DISPENSATIONS

The word "covenant" has a root that literally means to convene, meet, come together, assemble, hence to agree, be suitable. Ordinarily, a covenant is a binding agreement between two or more parties; it is a mutual contract.

However, in the Bible, a covenant is a one-sided (unilateral), God-initiated pronouncement whereby God establishes a relationship of responsibility. God draws up the terms, makes them known, and guarantees their keeping. A covenant may be conditional or unconditional. If conditional, it may be broken, disrupted, because it depends upon human faithfulness. If unconditional, it cannot be broken since it places no dependence upon man. God, who says, "I will," carries out the terms of the covenant. Many conservative scholars hold to the existence of eight major covenants: Edenic, Adamic, Noahic, Abrahamic, Mosaic, Palestinian, Davidic, and New. Today's lesson establishes the Mosaic Covenant.

A dispensation is a period of history in which God deals with a people in a special way. Broadly speaking, if you believe that God does different things at different times, you are a dispensationalist! God Himself does not change, but His methods change. The Greek word translated dispensation is *oikonomia,* literally, "house rule." It means arrangement, stewardship, administration, order, oversight, plan, management. The word derived from Latin for "house rule" is economy. One who is economical rules his or her house well. Conservative scholars have distinguished at least seven Dispensations: Innocence, Conscience, Human Government, Promise, Law, Grace, and the Kingdom.

B. BIBLICAL BACKGROUND

In our last lesson, we saw how God delivered the Israelites from the armies of Egypt. The crossing of the Red Sea was miraculous. In subsequent chapters to today's lesson, we shall see how God provided Israel with water, manna, quails, etc. God gave them victory over Amalek. He gave to Moses the wise counsel of his father-in-law, Jethro. All these Divine exploits were calculated to serve one purpose of instruction—that of teaching the Israelites the power and loving care of the Lord God Jehovah.

II. Exposition and Application of the Scripture

A. THE FIFTH DISPENSATION AND COVENANT (Exodus 19:3-6)

And Moses went up unto God, and the LORD called unto him out of the mountain, saying, Thus shalt thou say to the house of Jacob, and tell the children of Israel; Ye have seen what I did unto the Egyptians, and how I bare you on eagles' wings, and brought you unto myself. Now therefore, if ye will obey my voice indeed, and keep my covenant, then ye shall be a peculiar treasure unto me above all people: for all the earth is mine: And ye shall be unto me a kingdom of priests, and an holy nation. These are the words which thou shalt speak unto the children of Israel.

While Israel encamped before Mount Sinai, Moses went up unto the Lord. There, God commanded Moses speak to the house of Jacob and tell the children of Israel to remember what they saw God do to the Egyptians, how He Himself delivered Israel from slavery. The phrases "house of Jacob" and "children of Israel" describe the same people. Indeed, "under his two names this personage Jacob or Israel is more frequently mentioned than any other in the whole of sacred history" (ISBE). Emphasis is not upon the patriarch himself, but upon the nation descended from him. The Mosaic Covenant, a covenant of works, the only one that is conditional, was established during the Dispensation of the Law. Composed of three parts—the commandments, the judgments, and the ordinances; all three forming the Law—this covenant governed Israel's behavior as a redeemed people.

From the time of Adam until Moses, there had been no direct law of God, for He dealt with His people primarily in grace. Law as law existed before Moses, but not as a test. Prior to this time, never before had the law been imposed upon any people or generation. In today's lesson, the Israelites are offered a conditional covenant of law. All that God does for mankind is a matter of grace, but we deal here with divine testing of man under grace rather than under law. The Dispensation of Law ended at Calvary. "For the law was given by Moses, but grace and truth came by Jesus Christ" (John 1:17).

Use of the word "if" in verse five provides us with the key to understanding the nature of this fifth Covenant and the fifth Dispensation. Obedience to God's voice and covenant would produce a peculiar people (a people for His own possession), a kingdom of priests, and an holy nation (1 Peter 2:5,9). Because of sin, Israel as a whole failed to be all that the Lord desired. And only by faith in the shed blood of Jesus Christ have we Gentiles become His priests and holy in His sight. This does not mean we (the Church) have replaced Israel. The promises God made to Israel remain to be fulfilled.

B. THE DECALOGUE: OUR LOVE TO GOD (Exodus 20:2-4, 7-8)

I am the LORD thy God, which have brought thee out of the land of Egypt, out of the house of bondage. Thou shalt have no other gods before me. Thou shalt not make unto thee any graven image, or any likeness of any thing that is in heaven above, or that is in the earth beneath, or that is in the water under the earth. Thou shalt not take the name of the LORD thy God in vain; for the LORD will not hold him guiltless that taketh his name in vain. Remember the sabbath day, to keep it holy.

"Decalogue" is a word derived from the Greek meaning "ten words"; it is another word for "Ten Commandments." The first four commandments deal with man's relationship with God; the last six concern man's relationship with man. Obviously, only if the vertical is right can the horizontal be right. Now the First Commandment (Exodus 20:3) forbids the worship of other gods. God hates idolatry. Because Jehovah is married to Israel, idolatry is adultery. Idolatry is spiritual polygamy.

Idolatry divides affection and allegiance. As our Lord said: "No man can serve two masters; for either he will hate the one, and love the other; or else he will hold to the one, and despise the other. Ye cannot serve God and money" (Matthew 6:24). One problem with having many gods is the need to decide which one rules at what time. Another problem: we become like our gods: "They who make them are like unto them; so is every one who trusts in them" (Psalm 115:8). Humans become like what they worship. Since idols are nothing, idolaters become vanity! Having other gods is a blatant disregard for the sovereignty of the true and living God. It is a denial of His rights. By seeking such denial, idolatry creates confusion. Failure to worship the true and living God results only in condemnation. From the very beginning then, the Lord warns He will not tolerate the worship of other gods—no matter what they are!

The Second Commandment forbids the making of images (Exodus 20:4). Some Israelites were guilty of manufacturing their own gods. In Judges 17, a man by the name of Micah made a silver idol and set up a private family cult around it. If all of us did this, the result would be absolute chaos! This Commandment enjoins us to worship the one God, and He is not to be represented by idol statues. The Third Commandment forbids taking God's name in vain (Exodus 20:7). It condemns talking about God with a familiarity that borders on irreverence, i.e., "Somebody up there likes me." Who is this Somebody? Perhaps He is the "Man Upstairs." Some years ago a film actress said, "And when you get to know Him you find He's a Livin' Doll." An eminent New York restaurateur rejoiced because the "Big Fellow Upstairs" helped him to run his "joint" successfully.

And how about, "Oh, my God!" expressed so often at the slightest provocation or mishap? Or worse, what about the highly theological language used by men who command God to damn or curse (in addition to consigning their enemies to the underworld)? Such vanity demonstrates men are religious, but lost. The Hebrew word translated "vain" (shav) has a primary meaning of emptiness, and designates "anything that is unsubstantial, unreal, worthless, either materially or morally" (Theological Wordbook of the Old Testament). It is perjury, falsehood, deception, and also designates worthless idols. Thus, Christians are not to lift up their minds or souls to idols or vanity (Psalm 24:4) nor take the Lord's name or reputation thoughtlessly, lighty, profanely or swear falsely in the Lord's name.

The Fourth Commandment states: "Remember to keep the Sabbath day holy" (Exodus 20:8). Of the Ten Commandments, this one is not set forth requiring Gentiles to observe it. There is no record in the New Testament showing that after the resurrection of our Lord that Christians worshiped on the Sabbath (Romans 14:5-7; Colossians 2:13-15). Bible Christians are not Sabbatarians or Seventh-Day Keepers. Such an observance is strictly Jewish. Furthermore, note the death penalty (Exodus 20:12-17).

C. THE DECALOGUE: OUR LOVE TO OTHERS (Exodus 20:12-17)

Honour thy father and thy mother: that thy days may be long upon the land which the LORD thy God giveth thee. Thou shalt not kill. Thou shalt not commit adultery. Thou shalt not steal. Thou shalt not bear false witness against thy neighbour. Thou shalt not covet thy neighbour's house, thou shalt not covet thy neighbour's wife, nor his manservant, nor his maidservant, nor his ox, nor his ass, nor any things that is thy neighbour's.

The Fifth Commandment exhorts the honoring of parents (Exodus 20:12), and is a key to social stability. Paul included this command in

Ephesians 6:2-3. Note in "Children, obey your parents in the Lord" that "in the Lord" refers to the children, not to the parents. So that the command is not to obey only if your parents are Christians, but for Christian children to obey, period. The Sixth commandment forbids murder (Exodus 20:13). The Hebrew word used, properly rendered "murder" rather than "kill," always indicates intentional slaying. The essential element in murder is the inner attitude, even as the real cause of all moral impurity is internal.

First John emphasizes this matter of hatred (1 John 3:11-15). Any man with hatred in his heart for another is a potential murderer. Black American Christians must not ever hold that capital punishment is immoral, for this would be the same as saying God is immoral, since the Bible is the Word of God. He is the One who established the rule for all mankind: "Whoso sheds man's blood, by man shall his blood be shed; for in the image of God made He man" (Genesis 9:6). We need justice in meting out the penalty! Never forget that Christ was made a curse for us (Galatians 3:13); and He who knew no sin became sin, and was smitten by God the Father. For the wages of sin is death! In other words, God the Father slew His Son, the Lord Jesus Christ! He was smitten of God (Isaiah 53:4).

The Seventh Commandment prohibits adultery (Exodus 20:14). With devastating results, sexual impurity breaks up homes, destroys marriages, produces feelings of guilt and shame, corrodes and dopes the conscience, dims the inner light, lowers spiritual life, makes slaves out of those who practice it, and is physically dangerous (Proverbs 6:26-35). Many things contribute to the increase of this evil today: Easy divorce, high degree of mobility, proliferation of hotels and motels, pornography, suggestive music, semi-nudity, the terrific influence of Hollywood, the availability of pills and contraceptives, consumption of alcohol, and the dearth of preaching about judgment.

The Eighth Commandment forbids stealing. Paul was led to write: "Let him that stole steal no more" (Ephesians 4:28). Stealing includes to defraud, bribe, swindle, embezzle, shoplift, pickpocket, extort, pilfer, loot, plunder, rob, burglarize, plagiarize, misappropriate, commit larceny, filch, abstract, smuggle—what an amazing number of variations of this evil! The Ninth Commandment prohibits false witnessing (Exodus 20:16), as well as malignant perjury, and all sin in words against our neighbor which injure his or her character and reputation. Many words describe false witnessing: Shameful lying, abuse, attributing motives, backbiting, base gossip of busybodies, calumny, censoriousness, contumely, defamation, depreciation, detraction, evil surmisings, falsehood, innuendo, insinuation, insolence, insult, jeers, jibes, lampoon, libel, malevolent spitefulness, misrepresentation, obloquy, personalities, railing, sarcasm, satire, scurrility, slander, slashing criticism, sneering, talebearing, tattle, taunting, vilification, vituperation, whispering—attest to the commonness, deadliness and variety of forms it takes (F. W. Farrar). False witnessing often leads to the physical hurt or death of the person lied against, e.g., Naboth (1 Kings 21:10-14), Stephen (Acts 6:8-15), Paul (Acts 25:1-12); our Lord Jesus Christ (Matthew 26:59).

In the Tenth Commandment (Exodus 20:17), the Hebrew word rendered "covet" means to desire, take pleasure in, in a bad sense of inordinate, ungovernable, selfish desire. In the New Testament a number of different words translated "covet," mean (1) to reach out, stretch (2) to desire, look for (3) a silver-lover (4) to have more, to overreach. There is a legitimate accumulation of earthly goods for which we thank God. However, to see something which does not belong to us, and which we do not have the means or right to secure, and then keep on wanting it until unsatisfied desire broods in our hearts and leads us to plot and scheme to get what we want—this is covetousness.

Covetousness is a PIG. It is Persistent. The covetous man is never satisfied. The more he gets, the more he wants. It is Internal. Covetousness is an insidious malady affecting the inward state of the heart. The breaking of this commandment easily leads to the breaking of the sixth, seventh, eighth and ninth commandments (murder, adultery, theft, false witness). It is Grievous, suggesting covetousness perverts life's purpose. We begin to think that what we own makes us what we are. We fail to even think of the question, "What shall it profit a man if he shall gain the whole world, and lose his own soul?" (Mark 8:36).

III. Special Features

A. PRESERVING OUR HERITAGE

The Hebrew word for eagle (nesher), meaning to "tear with the beak," is used both of eagles and vultures. Both birds eat carrion, but they also capture live prey (and even eat vultures). While vultures feed in flocks, eagles never eat flock. Many popular verses speak of the eagle: (Isaiah 40:31; Deuteronomy 28:49; Job 9:26; Psalm 103:5; Proverbs 30:19). They describe the power of its sustained flight, its swiftness or speed, long life, etc. One of the most popular verses preached by Black American ministers is Deuteronomy 32:11: "As an eagle stirs up her nest." Reference to bearing Israel on "eagles' wings" (Exodus 19:4, the first mention of the eagle in the Bible) indicates this majestic bird is able to carry heavy loads with its feet because of its powerful wings. The language denotes Jehovah's strong and loving care. It is easy to see how the eagle became a symbol of freedom and power. Saints of color rejoice in knowing that by the amazing grace of God, we were brought to Him on eagles' wings.

B. A CONCLUDING WORD

The love of money is a major sin in America. We are surfeited with credit cards, psychological advertisements, special sales, Santa Claus, fashion shows, etc. And Christians easily fall into covetousness. The remedy? Attend the school of Christ, and learn by experience to be content in whatever state we are (Hebrews 13:5). Christ's love for us enables us to love Him, and to realize that love stands as a sentinel against covetousness. Second, we can ask the Lord to regulate our desires. He has promised already to supply our needs. And whatsoever we ask, "we receive of him, because we keep his commandments, and do those things that are pleasing in his sight" (1 John 3:22).

HOME DAILY BIBLE READINGS FOR THE WEEK OF SEPTEMBER 19, 1999

THE COVENANT

Sept. 13   M.   Exodus 19:1-9, Israel Camps at Mount Sinai
Sept. 14   T.   Exodus 19:16-25, Israel Meets God at Mount Sinai
Sept. 15   W.   Exodus 20:1-11, Honor God, and Keep the Sabbath
Sept. 16   T.   Exodus 20:12-21, Commandments for Life in Community
Sept. 17   F.   Deuteronomy 4:1-8, Observe God's Statutes and Ordinances
Sept. 18   S.   Deuteronomy 4:9-14, Teach Obedience to Generations that Follow
Sept. 19   S.   Deuteronomy 4:32-40, Commandments, A Gift of God's Love

Know Your Bible

- The Israelites were fed during their wilderness wanderings by manna which is a small round thing like a frozen drop of dew, miraculously sent by God, and able to be made into bread. (Exodus 16:14, 15, 23, 31)
- The Israelites gathered the manna every day except the Sabbath day, but the day before the Sabbath they could gather a two-day's supply, or a double quantity of it. (Exodus 16:22-30)
- God delivered the Ten Commandments to Moses from the top of Mount Sinai, located near the Red Sea, amidst thunder and lightening, clouds and darkness. Moses went up into the thick darkness where God was and remained there for forty days and forty nights. (Exodus 19:20; 20:21; 24:18)
- Joshua was waiting on the side of the mount for Moses when he came down. (Exodus 32:17)
- When Moses came down from the mount with the Ten Commandments, he saw the people dancing around a golden calf that his brother Aaron had made at the request of the people. (Exodus 32:2-5, 19)

God of grace and God of glory, You have set Your love upon us to be committed wholeheartedly to Your way. Grant that we may never falter in our faith as we live that quality of life that is consistent with Your will. In Jesus' name. Amen.

The Tabernacle and Obedience

Adult Topic—*Called to Obedience*

•••••

Youth Topic—*A Point of Contact*
Children's Topic—*Remembering and Worshiping God*

•••••

Devotional Reading—Psalm 84
Background Scripture—Exodus 40:1-33; Leviticus 26
Print—Exodus 40:1-9; Leviticus 26:2-6, 11-13

PRINTED SCRIPTURE

**Exodus 40:1-9;
Leviticus 26:2-6, 11-13 (KJV)**

AND THE LORD spake unto Moses, saying,

2 On the first day of the first month shalt thou set up the tabernacle of the tent of the congregation.

3 And thou shalt put therein the ark of the testimony, and cover the ark with the vail.

4 And thou shalt bring in the table, and set in order the things that are to be set in order upon it; and thou shalt bring in the candlestick, and light the lamps thereof.

5 And thou shalt set the altar of gold for the incense before the ark of the testimony, and put the hanging of the door to the tabernacle.

6 And thou shalt set the altar of the burnt offering before the door of the tabernacle of the tent of the congregation.

7 And thou shalt set the laver between the tent of the congregation and the altar, and shalt put water therein.

**Exodus 40:1-9;
Leviticus 26:2-6, 11-13 (NRSV)**

THE LORD spoke to Moses:

2 On the first day of the first month you shall set up the tabernacle of the tent of meeting.

3 You shall put in it the ark of the covenant, and you shall screen the ark with the curtain.

4 You shall bring in the table, and arrange its setting; and you shall bring in the lampstand, and set up its lamps.

5 You shall put the golden altar for incense before the ark of the covenant, and set up the screen for the entrance of the tabernacle.

6 You shall set the altar of burnt offering before the entrance of the tabernacle of the tent of meeting,

7 and place the basin between the tent of meeting and the altar, and put water in it.

8 You shall set up the court all around, and hang up the screen for the gate of the court.

8 And thou shalt set up the court round about, and hang up the hanging at the court gate.

9 And thou shalt take the anointing oil, and anoint the tabernacle, and all that is therein, and shalt hallow it, and all the vessels thereof: and it shall be holy.

.....

2 Ye shall keep my sabbaths, and reverence my sanctuary: I am the LORD.

3 If ye walk in my statutes, and keep my commandments, and do them;

4 Then I will give you rain in due season, and the land shall yield her increase, and the trees of the field shall yield their fruit.

5 And your threshing shall reach unto the vintage, and the vintage shall reach unto the sowing time: and ye shall eat your bread to the full, and dwell in your land safely.

6 And I will give peace in the land, and ye shall lie down, and none shall make you afraid.

.....

11 And I will set my tabernacle among you: and my soul shall not abhor you.

12 And I will walk among you, and will be your God, and ye shall be my people.

13 I am the LORD your God, which brought you forth out of the land of Egypt, that ye should not be their bondmen; and I have broken the bands of your yoke, and made you go upright.

9 Then you shall take the anointing oil, and anoint the tabernacle and all that is in it, and consecrate it and all its furniture, so that it shall become holy.

.....

2 You shall keep my sabbaths and reverence my sanctuary: I am the LORD.

3 If you follow my statutes and keep my commandments and observe them faithfully,

4 I will give you your rains in their season, and the land shall yield its produce, and the trees of the field shall yield their fruit.

5 Your threshing shall overtake the vintage, and the vintage shall overtake the sowing; you shall eat your bread to the full, and live securely in your land.

6 And I will grant peace in the land, and you shall lie down, and no one shall make you afraid.

.....

11 I will place my dwelling in your midst, and I shall not abhor you.

12 And I will walk among you, and will be your God, and you shall be my people.

13 I am the LORD your God who brought you out of the land of Egypt, to be their slaves no more; I have broken the bars of your yoke and made you walk erect.

 KEY VERSE

*Ye shall keep my sabbaths and reverence my sanctuary: I am the LORD.—**Leviticus 26:2***

OBJECTIVES

After reading this lesson, the student should be better informed about:

1. The erection of the tabernacle;
2. The furniture in the tabernacle;
3. The spiritual significance of the tabernacle; and,
4. The blessings available through obedience.

POINTS TO BE EMPHASIZED

Adult/Youth/Children
Key Verse: Leviticus 26:2
Print: Exodus 40:1-9; Leviticus 26:2-6, 11-13

—The Lord instructed Moses to set up the tabernacle of the tent of meeting on the first day of the first month. (40:1-2)

—In the tabernacle, they were to place the ark of the covenant, screened by a curtain; the table; the lampstand and lamps; the altar for incense; the screen for the entrance; the altar of burnt offering; and the basin of water. (3-7)

—After the court was set up with a screen as the entrance, the tabernacle and everything within was to be consecrated by anointing with oil. (8-9)

—The Lord promised to bless the people with peace and bounty if they remained faithful and obedient. (26:2-6)

—The Lord promised to fulfill the covenant and to dwell among the people as their God. (11-13)

(**Note**: Use KJV Scripture for Adults; NRSV Scripture for Youth and Children)

TOPICAL OUTLINE OF THE LESSON

I. Introduction
   A. The Tabernacle and Typology
   B. Biblical Background

II. Exposition and Application of the Scripture
   A. The Command to Set Up the Tabernacle (Exodus 40:1-2)
   B. Placement and Description of the Furniture (Exodus 40:3-9)
   C. Conditions of Blessings (Leviticus 26:2-6)
   D. Further Rewards for Obedience (Leviticus 26:11-13)

III. Special Features
   A. Preserving Our Heritage
   B. A Concluding Word

I. Introduction

A. THE TABERNACLE AND TYPOLOGY

In the Bible, a "type" is a "divinely purposed illustration of some truth" (Scofield). Typology is the study of word-pictures. We use something we do understand in order to picture something that is difficult for us to understand. Types picture something far greater than themselves (Pilgrim Bible). A type is a symbol of something in the future, a prefiguration (Random House Dictionary), a foreshadow, something symbolized or represented prophetically. "Likeness" is one general common idea in typology. "A person, event or thing is so fashioned or appointed as to resemble another; the one is made to answer to the other in some essential feature" (ISBE).

With these definitions in mind, we turn to a study of the tabernacle or Tent of Meeting. The word translated "Tabernacle" means a dwelling place. We learn that the Tabernacle presents us with three types. First of all, it is seen as typical of the church. As God dwelt in the tabernacle, so He dwells in the church. Second, the tabernacle is a type of the believer. This is because the Holy Spirit lives in our bodies. Third, the tabernacle is a picture of things in the heavens (Hebrews 9:23-24). In other words, the tabernacle and its furnishings were copies or outlines of things in heaven. As a whole, the tabernacle is a type of the church, the believer, and of heaven, and therefore of the Lord Jesus Christ. Whereas our bodies are the temple of God, this concept should govern our behavior.

B. BIBLICAL BACKGROUND

At this point, Israel is a free nation, having escaped Egypt by the hand of God directing the hand of Moses. The pursuing Egyptians were drowned and the triumphant Israelites celebrated. As they continued their trek into the wilderness, God miraculously provided them with water, manna, and quails. The Sabbath was given to the nation. In their first conflict they fought with the Amalekites, and God gave Joshua the victory. Then we read of the visit of Jethro, Moses' father-in-law, who made valuable suggestions to Moses concerning his administration.

In the third month, when the Israelites had left Egypt, they came to Sinai and encamped there before the mount. Moses then went up the mount to receive the Ten Commandments. Thus, the Dispensation of the Law was established. Many other judgments were set concerning master and servant relationships; injuries to the person, property, and crimes against humanity; the land and the Sabbath, national feasts, and instructions and promises dealing with the conquest of the land.

This brings us to Exodus chapter 25, where we find that Moses remained in the mount forty days and forty nights. It was at this time God spoke of the tabernacle, and described the materials to be used in its construction, gave the measurements, and named all the articles to be placed within. Hence, God gave the form and contents of the tabernacle.

II. Exposition and Application of the Scriptures

A. THE COMMAND TO SET UP THE TABERNACLE
(Exodus 40:1-2)

AND THE LORD spake unto Moses, saying, On the first day of the first month shalt thou set up the tabernacle of the tent of the congregation.

Sometimes we gloss over the words, "the Lord spoke," "the Lord commanded," and "thus saith the Lord." Such words should remind us that the Bible claims to be the Word of God. They also remind us that Israel was to implicitly obey God's Word. It was now about a year after the Exodus, and eight and a half months after Israel arrived at Sinai. God commanded Moses to set up the tabernacle or dwelling place on the first day of the first month in the second year of the Exodus. Remember, "Exodus" means literally, going out. "Ex" means out; "odos" means road or way. And so this Greek word refers to Israel's going out of the land of Egypt.

In the chapters preceding our lesson, we see that the various parts of the tabernacle were already completed. Now they have to be put together; the furnishings must now be set in their respective places exactly as God ordered. The Israelites had to wait on the Lord's own time for this. The description of the tabernacle is found in chapters 25—31, and 35—40. Overall, see the tabernacle as a place where God dwelled and revealed Himself in the midst of a redeemed people. Today, God lives in the bodies of genuine Christians. And understand that by giving the tabernacle, the Lord intended to teach us that He has always desired that we worship Him His way, and not the way we think He should be worshiped.

B. PLACEMENT AND DESCRIPTION OF THE FURNITURE
(Exodus 40:3-9)

And thou shalt put therein the ark of the testimony, and cover the ark with the vail. And thou shalt bring in the table, and set in order the things that are to be set in order upon it; and thou shalt bring in the candlestick, and light the lamps thereof. And thou shalt set the altar of gold for the incense before the ark of the testimony, and put the hanging of the door to the tabernacle. And thou shalt set the altar of the burnt offering before the door of the tabernacle of the tent of the congregation. And thou shalt set the laver between the tent of the congregation and the altar, and shalt put water therein. And thou shalt set up the court round about, and hang up the hanging at the court gate. And thou shalt take the anointing oil, and anoint the tabernacle, and all that is therein, and shalt hallow it, and all the vessels thereof: and it shall be holy.

The first appointment mentioned is the ark of the testimony, located in the Holy of Holies, the innermost section of the tabernacle. This ark was a chest made of acacia wood (representing the humanity of the Lord Jesus), overlaid inside and outside with pure gold (representing the Deity of our Lord). The tables of stone which God gave to Moses with the Law written on them were the Testimony; these were kept within the chest or ark. By beginning here in the innermost part of the tabernacle, we learn that in revelation God begins from Himself. The veil (vail, Old English) covering the ark (verse 3) is the curtain that separates the holy place from the Holy of Holies. It was a cloth screen of blue, purple and scarlet, fine twined linen. This veil represents His body (Hebrews 10:19-20); it was split from top to bottom at the death of the Lord, thus giving us bold access into the very presence of God.

The table in verse four is the shewbread table. It was made of acacia wood, overlaid with gold, and crowned with two crowns of gold. Shewbread was placed upon this table. "Shew" (an old spelling) is pronounced "show," never "shoo." The word is derived from a verb meaning "to cause a person to see," or "a thing to be seen." "Presence-bread exactly gives the meaning of the Hebrew" (ISBE), and is called this because the twelve loaves were always on the table in God's presence. Also in verse four the lampstand (candlestick) was brought in. This article was beaten out of pure gold. With its six branches and seven lamps, it gave light in the holy place.

In verse five, we find the altar of gold was also made of acacia wood, overlaid with gold, and crowned with gold. Perpetual incense was burned upon this altar by the high priest, as well as the incense offered by the other priests. This gold altar of incense, placed in front of the ark of the testimony, was not kept permanently in the Holy of Holies, but was taken in on the Day of Atonement. Moses was also commanded to put the hanging of the door (the curtain at the entrance) to the tabernacle. This outer veil was a cloth screen composed of blue, purple scarlet, and fine twined linen. According to verse six, the altar of the burnt offering (this is the bronze altar), upon which all the sacrifices were burned, was placed in front of the entrance to the tabernacle.

From verse seven we learn that the laver or basin was set between the tent of meeting and the altar. Water was placed in this polished brass vessel so that the priests could cleanse their hands and feet (Exodus 30:19). The command comes in verse eight to set up the courtyard around the tabernacle and put the curtain at the entrance to the courtyard. This section closes with verse nine. Here, Moses is ordered to anoint and consecrate the tabernacle and its furnishings with oil; this will set it apart for God's use. We see then that each piece of furniture was to be placed where God appointed it.

C. CONDITIONS OF BLESSINGS
(Leviticus 26:2-6)

Ye shall keep my sabbaths, and reverence my sanctuary: I am the LORD. If ye walk in my statutes, and keep my commandments, and do them; Then I will give rain in due season, and the land shall yield her increase, and the trees of the field shall yield their fruit. And your threshing shall reach unto the vintage, and the vintage shall reach unto the sowing time: and ye shall eat your bread to the full, and dwell in your land safely. And I will give peace in the land, and ye shall lie down, and none shall make you afraid.

Prohibition against idolatry is coupled with the command to keep the

Sabbaths. The word "Sabbath" means cease, desist, rest. Modern-day Sabbath-keepers need to be reminded that this command was given only to the Israelites. "Reverence My sanctuary"—a reference to the tabernacle—is a specific command to the Israelites, pointing out that worship was accepted only in obedience to the sacrificial system which the Lord had set up for that nation.

In this chapter which deals with blessings and cursings, most of the conditions mentioned refer to the consequences of disobedience. Chastisement, distress, drought, wild animals, disease, famine, dispersion—these are the adversities God will use to lead Israel to repentance. It is not His purpose simply to inflict revenge. In our lesson, we study the blessings, for they are given first. In verse 4, rain is the first blessing for obedience. With abundant rainfall come fertility and the abundance of food. There were two rainy seasons, early (generally, November, December) and latter (March) (Deuteronomy 11:14) and Palestine depended greatly upon them. The safety of the people of Israel was likewise to be secured, and reinforced by the promise of peace.

D. FURTHER REWARDS FOR OBEDIENCE (Leviticus 26:11-13)

And I will set my tabernacle among you: and my soul shall not abhor you. And I will walk among you, and will be your God, and ye shall be my people. I am the LORD your God, which brought you forth out of the land of Egypt, that ye should not be their bondmen; and I have broken the bands of your yoke, and made you go upright.

Jehovah promised to dwell among the children of Israel and to be their God. With the erection of the tabernacle, He kept His promise to reside with them. No other nation on the face of the earth ever received such a promise. "My soul shall not abhor you," said the Lord God. "Abhor" is an English word with Latin roots. It means literally to shrink from, shudder away from, thus to reject. In Hebrew, the word translated "abhor" comes from a verb meaning to separate, be vilely cast away, loathe. Five times the hatred of God is expressed in this chapter (verses 11, 15, 30, 43, 44). What grace is shown to a sinful people like the Israelites! They deserved to be abhorred, but God's love prevented Him from despising them or casting them off permanently.

Once again, the Israelites are reminded of their deliverance from Egypt. God repeatedly brought to their minds the miraculous exodus. This served the purpose of assuring Israel that God would and could keep His promises. A two-fold aspect of their rescue is seen: (1) They were no longer slaves, the bands of their yoke were broken. The poles of a yoke were laid on the necks of beasts of burden in order to bend their necks and harness them for work. Egypt had put just such a yoke on the necks of the Israelites. God broke that yoke! (2) They were made to go upright, enabled to "walk with heads held high" (NIV). God struck the chains from their necks, the fetters from their feet, and caused them to walk with upright carriage as free men. Breaking the yoke symbolizes deliverance from severe oppression and affliction; walking upright symbolizes emancipation from slavery.

III. Special Features

A. PRESERVING OUR HERITAGE

See in the tabernacle—its architecture, furniture appointments, and ceremony—the spiritual truth that God lives with His own people. Moses was told to make the tabernacle after the pattern God showed him there on Mount Sinai. Has God given us a special pattern? With all due respect to White Americans, I do not think on the whole they have had the mountain-top spiritual experiences some Black Americans have had. To a degree, we have shared in their experiences, but because of our peculiar slavery situation, they have not had the insights and inspiration we have had. By no means are we espousing what is called Black Theology! And yet, how strange to talk of mountain-top experiences while living in the valley of servitude!

Will our spiritual eyes allow us to see as mountain-top experiences the deliverance from illiteracy and the fact that some states enacted laws making it a crime to teach slaves to read or write? Deliverance from the hypocrisy of religious whites that led us to accept not the white man's religion, but Jesus Christ, the God of the Bible? Deliverance from legal but immoral signs of segregation and Jim Crow? Deliverance from slavery to emancipation? We have come a long way! God grant that we see the hand of God in it all, and realize that one purpose He has is to give Black Christians a pattern for living grateful lives. We are encouraged to know that as we worship Christ in spirit and in truth, "according to the pattern," we shall reach even higher heights of joy, service and usefulness.

B. A CONCLUDING WORD

"The Tabernacle is the grandest of all Old Testament types setting forth the Lord Jesus Christ in His wonderful Person, and in His work of redeeming man" (Izetta A. Gamble). This is true, and the believer should see Christ in the tabernacle as a whole, as well as see Him in each piece of furniture in each part of the tabernacle. We noted earlier how the passage in our lesson (Exodus 40:1-9) begins within the tabernacle, and works its way out to the courtyard. "In the beginning God." See then in the tabernacle the Lord Jesus Christ in every aspect of His character, and in every phase of His redemptive work.

The first article mentioned is the ark of the testimony. Here Christ is the Son of man, located in the Holy of Holies. Christ is our ark of salvation and safety. The veil or curtain is the body or flesh of Jesus Christ that separates the holy place from the most holy. When it was torn top to bottom (Matthew 27:51), we gained access into the very presence of God the Father (Hebrews 10:19-20). As for the table of shewbread, the loaves represent our Lord as the Bread of Life (John 6:35), the Source of our sustaining life. Described next is the lampstand, which depicts Christ as the Light of the World. The altar of gold for the incense is mentioned next. It typifies Christ, our Intercessor.

As for the curtain at the entrance to the tabernacle, obviously, the priest had to enter through it in order to get into the holy place. This curtain also represents

Christ, the only way into fellowship with God. The brazen altar (altar of the burnt offering) is a type or symbol of the cross of Calvary. Since altar means "killing place," our minds are directed to Calvary. Next is the laver which signifies cleaning. We are cleansed by the Word daily. As the laver contained water for cleansing, so the Bible directs our attention to the fountain of the cleansing blood of Christ. The court, and the hangings (curtains) at the court gate, depending on their colors and material, variously represent Christ in His sufferings, humility, consecration, resurrection and glory. Finally, the anointing oil symbolizes the Holy Spirit whom Christ sent, and who now dwells in the bodies of all believers.

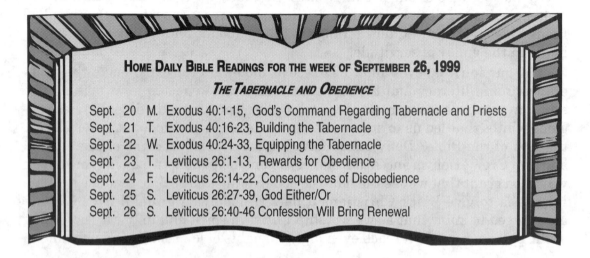

HOME DAILY BIBLE READINGS FOR THE WEEK OF SEPTEMBER 26, 1999

THE TABERNACLE AND OBEDIENCE

Sept. 20 M. Exodus 40:1-15, God's Command Regarding Tabernacle and Priests
Sept. 21 T. Exodus 40:16-23, Building the Tabernacle
Sept. 22 W. Exodus 40:24-33, Equipping the Tabernacle
Sept. 23 T. Leviticus 26:1-13, Rewards for Obedience
Sept. 24 F. Leviticus 26:14-22, Consequences of Disobedience
Sept. 25 S. Leviticus 26:27-39, God Either/Or
Sept. 26 S. Leviticus 26:40-46 Confession Will Bring Renewal

Know Your Bible

- Moses constructed the tabernacle according to the plan of God who gave to Moses the pattern while he was on the mount. (Exodus 25:9, 40)
- God especially endowed Bezaleel and Aholiab along with other wise-hearted men to perform the work of constructing the tabernacle according to the plan given by God. The women assisted in spinning. (Exodus 36:1, Exodus 35:22, 25, 26)
- Moses got the materials to build the tabernacle from the free offering brought by the people. (Exodus 35:21; 36:3-7)
- The princes of Israel offered gold and silver vessels and animals for sacrifice as gifts to the service of the tabernacle. (Numbers 7)
- The tabernacle was reared on the first day of the first month of the second year after the Israelites left Egypt (of their wanderings in the wilderness). (Exodus 40:17)
- The word "feast" does not necessarily mean a time of eating and drinking, but the meeting together for a holy and happy purpose. (Leviticus 23:4)

 *O God, may we come into Your presence with reverence and contrition. Grant that we may worship You with dignity and devotion. In Jesus' name. Amen.*

The Cloud and the Fire

Unit II—*Wilderness Wanderings*
Children's Unit—*Learning to Obey God*
Adult Topic—*Follow Day By Day*

•••••

Youth Topic—*Following Faithfully*
Children's Topic—*Following Directions*

•••••

Devotional Reading—Psalm 107:1-9
Background Scripture—Exodus 40:34-38;
Numbers 9:15-23
Print: Exodus 40:34-38; Numbers 9:15-19, 22-23

PRINTED SCRIPTURE

Exodus 40:34-38; Numbers 9:15-19, 22-23 (KJV)

34 Then a cloud covered the tent of the congregation, and the glory of the LORD filled the tabernacle.

35 And Moses was not able to enter into the tent of the congregation, because the cloud abode thereon, and the glory of the LORD filled the tabernacle.

36 And when the cloud was taken up from over the tabernacle, the children of Israel went onward in all their journeys:

37 But if the cloud were not taken up, then they journeyed not till the day that it was taken up.

38 For the cloud of the LORD was upon the tabernacle by day, and fire was on it by night, in the sight of all the house of Israel, throughout all their journeys.

•••••

15 And on the day that the tabernacle was reared up the cloud cov-

Exodus 40:34-38; Numbers 9:15-19, 22-23 (NRSV)

34 Then the cloud covered the tent of meeting, and the glory of the LORD filled the tabernacle.

35 Moses was not able to enter the tent of meeting because the cloud settled upon it, and the glory of the LORD filled the tabernacle.

36 Whenever the cloud was taken up from the tabernacle, the Israelites would set out on each stage of their journey;

37 but if the cloud was not taken up, then they did not set out until the day that it was taken up.

38 For the cloud of the LORD was on the tabernacle by day, and fire was in the cloud by night, before the eyes of all the house of Israel at each stage of their journey.

•••••

15 On the day the tabernacle was set up, the cloud covered the tabernacle, the tent of the cov-

ered the tabernacle, namely, the tent of the testimony: and at even there was upon the tabernacle as it were the appearance of fire, until the morning.

16 So it was always: the cloud covered it by day, and the appearance of fire by night.

17 And when the cloud was taken up from the tabernacle, then after that the children of Israel journeyed: and in the place where the cloud abode, there the children of Israel pitched their tents.

18 At the commandment of the LORD the children of Israel journeyed, and at the commandment of the LORD they pitched: as long as the cloud abode upon the tabernacle they rested in their tents.

19 And when the cloud tarried long upon the tabernacle many days, then the children of Israel kept the charge of the LORD, and journeyed not.

.....

22 Or whether it were two days, or a month, or a year, that the cloud tarried upon the tabernacle, remaining thereon, the children of Israel abode in their tents, and journeyed not: but when it was taken up, they journeyed.

23 At the commandment of the LORD they rested in the tents, and at the commandment of the LORD they journeyed: they kept the charge of the LORD, at the commandment of the LORD by the hand of Moses.

enant; and from evening until morning it was over the tabernacle, having the appearance of fire.

16 It was always so: the cloud covered it by day and the appearance of fire by night.

17 Whenever the cloud lifted from over the tent, then the Israelites would set out; and in the place where the cloud settled down, there the Israelites would camp.

18 At the command of the LORD the Israelites would set out, and at the command of the LORD they would camp. As long as the cloud rested over the tabernacle, they would remain in camp.

19 Even when the cloud continued over the tabernacle many days, the Israelites would keep the charge of the LORD, and would not set out.

.....

22 Whether it was two days, or a month, or a longer time, that the cloud continued over the tabernacle, resting upon it, the Israelites would remain in camp and would not set out; but when it lifted they would set out.

23 At the command of the LORD they would camp, and at the command of the LORD they would set out. They kept the charge of the LORD, at the command of the LORD by Moses.

KEY VERSE

For the cloud of the LORD was upon the tabernacle by day, and fire was on it by night, in the sight of all the house of Israel, throughout all their journeys.—Exodus 40:38

OBJECTIVES

After reading this lesson, the student should be able to appreciate:

1. The spiritual guidance God gives;
2. The significance of the Shekinah glory;
3. The necessity and wisdom of waiting on the Lord; and,
4. The challenge of obeying God's commandments.

POINTS TO BE EMPHASIZED

Adult/Youth/Children
Key Verse: Exodus 40:38; Exodus 40:36
Print: Exodus 40:34-38; Numbers 9:15-19, 22-23

—After Moses had set up the tabernacle as the Lord instructed, the cloud covered the tent of meeting and the glory of the Lord filled the tabernacle. (34-35)
—Under the Lord's command, whenever the cloud moved from the tabernacle, the Israelites were to break camp and follow. (36-37)
—Each day the cloud covered the tabernacle when it was set up, and at night the tabernacle was covered by a cloud of fire. (9:15-17)
—Even when the cloud of the Lord remained over the tabernacle many days, the Israelites obeyed God and rested in their tents until the cloud lifted from the tabernacle. (18-19)
—As the Israelites traveled, they obeyed only the command of the Lord that was spoken to them by Moses. (22-23)

(**Note**: Use KJV Scripture for Adults; NRSV Scripture for Youth and Children)

TOPICAL OUTLINE OF THE LESSON

I. Introduction

A. Shekinah
B. Biblical Background

II. Exposition and Application of the Scripture

A. God's Glory Filled the Tabernacle (Exodus 40:34-35)
B. Learning When to Stop; When to Go (Exodus 40:36-38)
C. Obedience to the Guiding Cloud (Numbers 9:15-19)
D. The Commandment of the Lord (Numbers 9:22-23)

III. Special Features

A. Preserving Our Heritage
B. A Concluding Word

I. Introduction

A. SHEKINAH

The word "Shekinah" (or Shekhinah) is a Hebrew word meaning, "That which dwells." It is derived from a verb that means to dwell, reside. Thus, it has to do with the dwelling or presence of God in the world. Now the word is not found in the Bible, but is first found in non-biblical Jewish writings, or what are known as Targums, translations of the Old Testament in Aramaic (ancient Semitic language). Shekinah is defined as the presence of God on earth, or a symbol or manifestation of His presence; a visible manifestation of the Divine Presence.

But more than a sign, symbol or manifestation of His presence, Shekinah also describes "the form" in which the Lord revealed Himself. For example, He showed His glory to Moses in the burning bush; and again at Mount Sinai where He descended upon it in fire. In today's lesson, God manifested Himself in the pillar of cloud and fire. In short, the Shekinah is another term for the glory of Jehovah, so often mentioned in the Old Testament.

This glory was visible evidence to man of the very presence of God. Allusions to this Shekinah are found at the announcement of our Lord's birth, when the glory of the Lord shone round about the country shepherds (Luke 2:9); in the Transfiguration scene, when a "bright cloud overshadowed" them (Matthew 17:5); and in the Kingdom age (Millennium), when the Lord's glory shall be seen: "The Lord shall arise upon thee, and his glory shall be seen upon thee" (Isaiah 60:2).

B. BIBLICAL BACKGROUND

In the chapters of Exodus (25—39) preceding today's lesson, we have the description of the tabernacle and its furnishings (the lesson taught last week). The thing that strikes our attention is the detailed nature of the description. It is as if God is saying, "This is exactly what I want in order for Me to dwell in your midst. See to it that you do according to all that I show you, after the pattern of the Tabernacle, and the pattern of all the furnishings thereof, even so shall you make it" (Exodus 25:9).

And so in the chapters that follow, the Israelites are instructed as to the materials for use in the construction of the tabernacle: metals, cloth, skins, oil, spices, gems, etc. The appointments are outlined: the ark of the covenant, table of shewbread, golden lampstand, curtains, coverings, boards, sockets, veils, altar, court, gate—the specific materials, colors, size or measurements, design, location, etc. Then the Lord led Moses to describe the priesthood: the garments to be worn by the priests— their color, material, accoutrements: ephod, breastplate, jewels, robe, crown, and other garments.

In addition, the consecration of the priests is outlined, calling for sacrifices of consecration, priests' food, offerings, etc. The point we make is this: consideration of the biblical background reinforces our awareness of God's desire and command that men obey Him, and worship Him the way He desires to be worshiped. Men discover that God makes Himself known in wondrous ways to those who obey Him.

II. Exposition and Application of the Scripture

A. GOD'S GLORY FILLED THE TABERNACLE (Exodus 40:34-35)

Then a cloud covered the tent of the congregation, and the glory of the LORD filled the tabernacle. And Moses was not able to enter into the tent of the congregation, because the cloud abode thereon, and the glory of the LORD filled the tabernacle.

Keep in mind that the book of Exodus is a history of Israel from the time of its deliverance from Egypt until the erection of the Tent of Meeting or Tabernacle. When Moses and the divinely gifted artisans finished erecting the tabernacle, and had set up all of the furnishings, a cloud covered the tent of the congregation (also called: the tabernacle of meeting: NKJV; the Tent of Meeting: NIV, RSV, NASB). God came down to sanctify by His visible presence all that was dedicated to Him. In the clause, "the glory of the Lord filled the tabernacle," the word for glory (kabod) is derived from a verb meaning to be heavy, weighty. This literal meaning is rarely used, but figuratively there is conveyed the idea of dignity, pre-eminence or majesty.

It is an easy step from the idea of someone in society who is "weighty," to someone who is honorable, impressive, has dignity, or is worthy of respect. Some forty-five times this form of the root word speaks of the visible form in which Jehovah revealed Himself. When "the glory of God" is mentioned, most of the occurrences refer to the tabernacle and to the temple. "The glory of Jehovah is clearly a physical manifestation, a form" (Exodus 33:18ff, ISBE). God wills to dwell with men, "to have His reality and splendor known to them" (Theological Wordbook of the Old Testament).

Of course, only through Jesus Christ is the glory of God fully portrayed (John 1:14, 17:1-5). The Holy Spirit living in the bodies of believers is likened to the Shekinah glory in the tabernacle. Our bodies are the temples of the Spirit of God, transformed from mere pieces of clay into holy temples, vessels with great treasure within, through faith in the shed blood of Jesus Christ. George Henderson (Studies in the book of Exodus) inquires: "How are we treating this Holy Guest?" Lives that are patterned according to God's plan indeed reflect God's glory. Now Moses was unable to enter into the Tent of Meeting. Here was visible testimony that God accepted their work. But the brilliance of His light was too much for Moses or any man to behold. We are reminded of Isaiah's experience (Isaiah 6:1-8). In his vision, he saw the Lord sitting upon a throne, high and lifted up, and the train of His robe filled the temple. Angels sang antiphonally, "Holy, holy, holy, is the Lord of hosts; the whole earth is full of His glory." No wonder the prophet cried: "Woe is me! . . .for mine eyes have seen the King, the Lord of hosts."

When the cloud covered the Tent of Meeting, God's glory filled the tabernacle. This indicates that God manifested Himself in both ways—cloud resting upon the tabernacle and glory filling the inside of the tabernacle. In other words, we make a distinction between cloud and glory, but only in form. Centuries later, at the dedication of the temple during the reign of King Solomon, we find "The cloud filled the house of the Lord," and this expression is synonymous with "the glory of the Lord" (1 Kings 8:10-11).

Just as the priests in Solomon's day could not stand to minister because of the cloud, so Moses could not enter. Aside from the very brilliance of that glory, and the realization that Moses' eyes could not look upon such bright resplendence, there is also the matter of holiness. Moses was a member of the tribe of Levi, and was authorized to perform the duties of a priest. Later his brother Aaron, and Aaron's sons, would be invested with this task. But Moses' inability to enter the tabernacle at this point is a reminder that men were forbidden to go directly into God's presence. Sin had erected a wall between a Holy God and unholy men. Later, the high priest would be given the privilege of entering the Holy of Holies once a year to make atonement for the sins of the people of Israel, and for himself. But not now!

B. LEARNING WHEN TO STOP; WHEN TO GO (Exodus 40:36-38)

And when the cloud was taken up from over the tabernacle, the children of Israel went onward in all their journeys; But if the cloud were not taken up, then they journeyed not till the day that it was taken up. For the cloud of the LORD was upon the tabernacle by day, and fire was on it by night, in the sight of all the house of Israel, throughout all their journeys.

When the cloud resting upon the tabernacle was taken up, it was the signal for the Israelites to move out. So long as the cloud remained upon the tabernacle, the Israelites were to stay encamped. When the cloud rose, the Israelites broke camp and proceeded on their journey. God provided them shade, and protected them. The visibility of the cloud gave assurance to the travelers that God was in their midst. Indeed, He was their guide. Our present passage emphasizes the cloud by day, but in verse thirty-eight mention is made also of the fire that was over the tabernacle by night. As has been noted earlier, the cloud and the fire were one. God's presence was likewise continuous. Whether cloud or fire, the house of Israel could see this manifestation of the presence of God. And He remained visible throughout all their journeys, a constant reminder that He was with them.

Today we have the Holy Spirit living in us. He is not seen, but His invisible presence is a reality nonetheless. Our bodies are His temple (1 Corinthians 6:19). The question comes: How do we treat this invisible Guest? Does He guide us as God led the Israelites? When He says stop, do we halt? When He says go, do we proceed? How do we know when He wants us to stay or go? How do we know His will in this our wilderness journey? Watchman Nee suggested we ask, "Is God's glory resting there? Discern that and you need wait for nothing further." He stated that corresponding to that which glorified God is the clue. Where God's glory rests, we need not ask the way. This is true, but not so easily accomplished. Yes, we are to walk by faith, not by the sight of a cloud or fire. But this faith-walk includes Bible study and memorization, giving the indwelling Holy Spirit something to work with as He works on, in, with, and for us. This faith-walk includes prayer, a spiritual sensitivity to our physical condition, circumstances, inner promptings, enlightened conscience, etc., for it is God's desire to lead us throughout all our journeys.

C. OBEDIENCE TO THE GUIDING CLOUD (Numbers 9:15-19)

And on the day that the tabernacle was reared up the cloud covered the tabernacle, namely, the tent of the testimony: and at even there was upon the tabernacle as it were the appearance of fire, until the morning. So it was always: the cloud covered it by day, and the appearance of fire by night. And when the cloud was taken up from the tabernacle, then after that the children of Israel journeyed: and in the place where the cloud abode, there the children of Israel pitched their tents. At the commandment of the LORD the children of Israel journeyed, and at the commandment of the LORD they pitched: as long as the cloud abode upon the tabernacle they rested in their tents. And when the cloud tarried long upon the tabernacle many days, then the children of Israel kept the charge of the LORD, and journeyed not.

The past tense is used as Moses relates Israel's history, and gives us a further description of the cloud and fire. On the day the tabernacle or Tent of the Testimony (Witness) was set up, the cloud covered the Tabernacle, while God's glory at the same time filled the Holy of Holies. At evening, the fire appeared and remained until the morning. In this way, the tabernacle was always covered, whether cloud by day, or fire by night. Here was one miracle the Israelites could see every day and every night! Sometimes such miracles become common place to us; we take them for granted. Or we hunger after the more spectacular (from our point of view)—the water from the Rock, the manna and quail from heaven!

Imagine! More than two million people traveling, stopping, settling down, getting up and traveling again in a waste, howling wilderness—with no compass, no maps, no highway signs, no guidebooks. All the Israelites needed was to obey the commandment of the Lord. There was to be no procrastination, only immediate response. When through the moving of the cloud or fire He said stop, or rest, pack up, rise, go, unquestioned obedience guaranteed them protection, safe passage, and an infallible guide. No matter how long or short the period, whether many days or not, the children of Israel obeyed. They kept the charge of the Lord, that is, they observed whatever Jehovah told them.

D. THE COMMANDMENT OF THE LORD (Numbers 9:22-23)

Or whether it were two days, or a month, or a year, that the cloud tarried upon the tabernacle, remaining thereon, the children of Israel abode in their tents, and journeyed not: but when it was taken up, they journeyed. At the commandment of the LORD they rested in the tents, and at the commandment of the LORD they journeyed: they kept the charge of the LORD, at the commandment of the LORD by the hand of Moses.

We have no record of how many "stops" and "goes" the Israelites experienced those forty years! Whether a rest period or travel period lasted overnight, or two days, a month, or a year, it did not matter. Repetition is calculated to impress our hearts with the importance of absolute dependence upon the Lord's guidance. And, in that guidance, we see the grace and loving care of God. Three times we read the words, "at the commandment of the Lord" in verse twenty-three. God stresses this matter. The repetition reinforces the importance of divine guidance, of being led by the Lord. What was the commandment of the Lord? It was the moving or settling of the cloud or fire.

III. Special Features

A. PRESERVING OUR HERITAGE

What are some of the ways Black Americans who are Christians may miss the blessings provided by obedience to the pillar of fire? First of all, we might think of returning to Egypt. This is highly unlikely; indeed, physically impossible for us to return to the slavery of yesteryear. There is danger, however, of a new enslavement to new masters: Welfare Mentality, or a Black Racism, or Love of Money, and the slavery that results when we make things our god.

Second, we could make up our minds to stay put even when the pillar of fire rises, and moves on. Some of us are content with the progress made as a race of people. I am reminded of church members in my first pastorate who said: "Don't worry about expanding; let's spend the money to 'fix up' what we have!" How terrible it would be to remain in darkness once the pillar of fire has removed.

Third, if the pillar remains too long, some of us become tired of waiting to move; we pack up and leave. We want to be faster than God. His ways are too slow! We think: if we don't go on and do something, everything will go to pieces! And so we run for the Promised Land ahead of the Promiser, the Lord Jesus Christ. In all three cases, we run smack dab into the world of darkness. The only antidote is found in John 8:12, where the Lord Jesus said: "I am the Light of the World; he that follows me shall not walk in darkness, but shall have the light of life." If we move when the Lord moves, and not one second before, we will do well. Don't let the continued racism in the United States rush us ahead of God. And remember: "Darkness about going is light about staying."

B. A CONCLUDING WORD

People depend upon many things for guidance. Horoscopes lead some folks, and they consult their "lucky stars" daily. They should be more concerned with their SIN than with their SIGNS. Christians are reminded that God hates astrology; it is an abomination to Him. Some people submit their lives to other human beings who are going astray themselves. How can the blind lead the blind? Still others idolize Hollywood stars, superathletes, rock musicians, et. al. And they allow their own eating habits, hair and clothing styles, brands of sneakers, conversation, etc. to be determined by these gods. Only the Christian has the right

Guide—the One who said, "I will guide you with my eye" (Psalm 32:8); the One who said, "I am the Way, the Truth, and the Life" (John 14:6). May this study of today's lesson cause us to sing with new meaning, "Where He leads me I will follow, I'll go with Him, with Him all the way" (Gospel Pearls, # 46).

HOME DAILY BIBLE READINGS FOR THE WEEK OF OCTOBER 3, 1999

THE CLOUD AND THE FIRE

Sept.	27	M.	Exodus 40:34-38, God's Glory Fills the Tabernacle
Sept.	28	T.	Numbers 9:15-23, Led by God's Cloud and Fire
Sept.	29	W.	Numbers 10:29-36, Journeying Away from Mount Sinai
Sept.	30	T.	Psalm 105:1-15, God Keeps Covenant Forever
Oct.	1	F.	Psalm 105:16-25, God Provided for Israel in Egypt
Oct.	2	S.	Psalm 105:26-36, God Sent Plagues Upon Egypt
Oct.	3	S.	Psalm 105:37-45, God Delivered Israel from Egypt

Know Your Bible

- Moses felt that the continued provocation of the Israelites was a great burden upon him as leader, so the Lord appointed seventy elders to assist him with his responsibilities. (Numbers 11:15-17)
- Although Miriam was the sister of Moses, and Aaron was his brother, they together made attempts to undermine Moses' authority by claiming equal authority with him. (Numbers 12:2)
- For Miriam's rebellion against Moses, God demonstrated His displeasure by making Miriam a leper. (Numbers 12:10)
- Aaron pleaded with Moses about the condition of Miriam, and Moses entreated God who removed her disease in seven days. (Numbers 12:11-15)
- The children of Israel were in the wilderness of Paran when Moses sent the twelve spies over to Canaan to search out the land. (Numbers 13:1-3)
- All of the twelve spies except Joshua and Caleb joined in giving a cowardly report about the inhabitants of the land of Canaan and the fortification of the cities. (Numbers 13:26-33)

O Thou who hast loved us with an everlasting love, may we be guided by Your Spirit as we journey through life. Grant that we may live in the constant expectation of Your intervention in our daily life. In His name. Amen.

The People Rebel

Adult Topic—*A Missed Opportunity*

••••••

Youth Topic—*Hitting the Panic Button*

Children's Topic—*Making Good Choices*

••••••

Devotional Reading—Numbers 14:5-19

Background Scripture—Numbers 12:1—14:25

Print: Numbers 13:1-3, 32—14:4, 20-24

PRINTED SCRIPTURE

Numbers 13:1-3, 32—14:4, 20-24 (KJV)	Numbers 13:1-3, 32—14:4, 20-24 (NRSV)
AND THE LORD spake unto Moses, saying	THE LORD said to Moses,
2 Send thou men, that they may search the land of Canaan, which I give unto the children of Israel: of every tribe of their fathers shall ye send a man, every one a ruler among them.	2 "Send men to spy out the land of Canaan, which I am giving to the Israelites; from each of their ancestral tribes you shall send a man, every one a leader among them."
3 And Moses by the commandment of the LORD sent them from the wilderness of Paran: all those men were heads of the children of Israel.	3 So Moses sent them from the wilderness of Paran, according to the command of the LORD, all of them leading men among the Israelites.
••••	••••••
32 And they brought up an evil report of the land which they had searched unto the children of Israel, saying, The land, through which we have gone to search it, is a land that eateth up the inhabitants thereof; and all the people that we saw in it are men of a great stature.	32 So they brought to the Israelites an unfavorable report of the land that they had spied out, saying, "The land that we have gone through as spies is a land that devours its inhabitants; and all the people that we saw in it are of great size.
33 And there we saw the giants, the sons of Anak, which come of the giants: and we were in our own sight as grasshoppers, and so we were in their sight.	33 There we saw the Nephilim (the Anakites come from the Nephilim); and to ourselves we seemed like grasshoppers, and so we seemed to them."
••••••	••••••
AND ALL the congregation lifted up	THEN ALL the congregation raised

their voice, and cried; and the people wept that night.

2 And all the children of Israel murmured against Moses and against Aaron: and the whole congregation said unto them, Would God that we had died in the land of Egypt! or would God we had died in this wilderness!

3 And wherefore hath the LORD brought us unto this land, to fall by the sword, that our wives and our children should be a prey? were it not better for us to return into Egypt?

4 And they said one to another, Let us make a captain, and let us return into Egypt.

.....

20 And the LORD said, I have pardoned according to thy word:

21 But as truly as I live, all the earth shall be filled with the glory of the LORD.

22 Because all those men which have seen my glory, and my miracles, which I did in Egypt and in the wilderness, and have tempted me now these ten times, and have not hearkened to my voice;

23 Surely they shall not see the land which I sware unto their fathers, neither shall any of them that provoked me see it:

24 But my servant Caleb, because he had another spirit with him, and hath followed me fully, him will I bring into the land whereinto he went; and his seed shall possess it.

a loud cry, and the people wept that night.

2 And all the Israelites complained against Moses and Aaron; the whole congregation said to them, "Would that we had died in the land of Egypt! Or would that we had died in this wilderness!

3 Why is the LORD bringing us into this land to fall by the sword? Our wives and our little ones will become booty; would it not be better for us to go back to Egypt?"

4 So they said to one another, "Let us choose a captain, and go back to Egypt."

.....

20 Then the LORD said, "I do forgive, just as you have asked;

21 nevertheless—as I live, and as all the earth shall be filled with the glory of the LORD—

22 none of the people who have seen my glory and the signs that I did in Egypt and in the wilderness, and yet have tested me these ten times and have not obeyed my voice,

23 shall see the land that I swore to give to their ancestors; none of those who despised me shall see it.

24 But my servant Caleb, because he has a different spirit and has followed me wholeheartedly, I will bring into the land into which he went, and his descendants shall possess it."

KEY VERSE

*If the LORD delight in us, then he will bring us into this land, and give it us; a land which floweth with milk and honey. Only rebel not ye against the LORD, neither fear ye the people of the land; for they are bread for us: their defense is departed from them, and the LORD is with us: fear them not. —**Numbers 14:8-9***

OBJECTIVES

After reading this lesson, the student should recognize that:

1. Murmuring is not acceptable Christian behavior;
2. Majority rule is not always right;
3. Forgiveness may not exclude penalty; but,
4. Obedience always pleases God.

POINTS TO BE EMPHASIZED
Adult/Youth/Children
Key Verse: Numbers 14:8-9; Proverbs 20:11 *(Children)*
Print: Numbers 13:1-3, 32—14:4, 20-24

—At God's command, Moses sent a leader from each of Israel's tribes to spy out the land of Canaan. (13:1-3)
—The majority of the spies brought back an unfavorable report of strong and intimidating residents in Canaan. (32-33)
—The Israelites were disheartened by the spies' report and demanded to return to Egypt. (14:1-4)
—Moses asked God to forgive the people, and the Lord granted his prayer, but said those who did not obey God would not live to see the Promised Land. (20-23)
—Caleb and his descendants would be brought into the Promised Land because he had trusted God. (24)

(**Note**: Use KJV Scripture for Adults; NRSV Scripture for Youth and Children)

TOPICAL OUTLINE OF THE LESSON

I. Introduction

A. Murmuring
B. Biblical Background

II. Exposition and Application of the Scripture

A. Sending of the Spies (Numbers 13:1-3)
B. Grasshoppers and Giants (Numbers 13:32-33)
C. Rebellious Reaction (Numbers 14:1-4)
D. Pardoned, but Not Possessing (Numbers 14:20-24)

III. Special Features

A. Preserving Our Heritage
B. A Concluding Word

I. Introduction

A. MURMURING

To murmur is to mutter, grumble, mumble, utter a low, indistinct, continuing whisper or confidential sound of complaint. The Latin root is probably imitative, and means to hum. One Hebrew word translated murmur suggests the malicious whispering of slander, and discontentment (Deuteronomy 1:27). Murmur in Numbers 14:2 means "to express resentment, dissatisfaction, anger, and complaint by grumbling in half-muted tones of hostile opposition to God's leaders and the authority which He has invested in them" (Theological Wordbook of the Old Testament); or the "semi-articulated mutterings of disaffected persons" (ISBE).

In the New Testament, the Greek word (gogguzo) translated murmur means to mutter, grumble, say anything in a low tone (Thayer). It includes the idea of secret debate, secret displeasure, querulous discontent and complaint (John 6:41, 43, 61; 7:12, 32). The first instance of murmuring occurred soon after the Israelites left Egypt. When only three days in the wilderness, they found no water. Upon arriving at Marah, they discovered the water there was bitter and they could not drink it. "And the people murmured against Moses, saying, What shall we drink?" (Exodus 15:22-24). Because the Lord had commissioned these leaders, their resentment actually was directed toward Jehovah.

Complaining sinners often seek to justify their behavior, and offer such reasons as thirst, hunger, impossible odds, fear of being captured or killed by enemy soldiers, etc. Obviously, there is behind all such murmuring a failure to believe God's Word, a failure made all the more reprehensible in light of the many divine miracles previously experienced. By expressing discontent with our lot in life, we judge God, bring Him down to our level, rob Him of His sovereignty, and deny His omniscience. God is told He should follow our opinions and directions. This is why the Lord considered murmuring a provocation, a testing, a scorning or despising (Numbers 14:11).

God graciously responded to Israel's murmuring with patience, and provided what they lacked—pure water, food, etc. However, in time, they paid for their expressions of discontent. Not only did they spend so many years in the wilderness, but many were put to death. Jehovah desires unconditional obedience to His voice, a waiting on Him, believing He will fulfill all His promises, whether we see how it is possible or not.

Christians are warned to beware of murmuring (1 Corinthians 10:10). It is dangerous to allow disappointments of our desires to lead us into expressions of discontentment. Christians are commanded (Philippians 2:14), "Do all things without murmurings and disputings." "Offer hospitality to one another ungrudgingly" (RSV), "Without grumbling" (NIV, NKJV), "Without grudging" (KJV). "Be hospitable to one another without complaining" (NEB, NASB).

B. BIBLICAL BACKGROUND

On the twentieth day of the second month, in the second year since leaving Egypt, the cloud was taken up from off the tabernacle, indicating the Israelites were to break camp and move on. Up to this time, they had encamped at Mount Sinai. Because of disobedience, the trip from Mount Sinai to the point at Kadesh-barnea, when the spies were sent out, was one in which God found it necessary to chasten Israel. Covering the period from Numbers 10:11 up to our lesson, we find the journey from Sinai to Kadesh-barnea took three days. Soon after their first stop, some of the people complained (we are not told the issue here), and fire from God burned up the malcontents (Numbers 11:1).

Next, the mixed multitude or "rabble" caused trouble. This group, composed of unbelievers who came out of Egypt with the Israelites (Exodus 12:38), expressed discontent because of their unfulfilled desire for the flesh-pots of Egypt. They remembered the fish, cucumbers, melons, leeks onions, and the garlic which they ate in Egypt freely. "But now our soul is dried away; there is nothing at all, besides this manna, before our eyes" (Numbers 11:5-6). God answered their lusting by sending quails into the camp. But then while the people had the meat between their teeth, before they chewed it, God smote them with a very great plague, and all those who lusted were buried (Numbers 11:33-34). Soon thereafter, Miriam and Aaron spoke against Moses. Miriam's name is put first because she instigated the murmuring against Moses because he had married an Ethiopian (Cushite) woman. Ethiopia means "burnt face," so you know what color she was. Miriam was stricken with leprosy for seven days; then God healed her (Numbers 12). Today's lesson describes an important pivotal point, for it portrays Israel as unready to enter the Promised Land.

II. Exposition and Application of the Scripture

A. SENDING OF THE SPIES
(Numbers 13:1-3)

AND THE LORD spake unto Moses, saying, Send thou men, that they may search the land of Canaan, which I give unto the children of Israel: of every tribe of their fathers shall ye send a man, every one a ruler among them. And Moses by the commandment of the LORD sent them from the wilderness of Paran: all those men were heads of the children of Israel.

God spoke to Moses and commanded him to send out men to search the land of Canaan. The Hebrew word rendered search means to go about, reconnoiter, spy out, seek. In preparation for conquest, the spies were to note whether the land was productive or not, wooded or barren, walled fortresses or a nomadic people living in tents, etc. They were to size up the people: how many, weak or strong, etc. "Careful examination" seems to capture the basic meaning of the root of the word (Theological Wordbook of the Old Testament). In Deuteronomy 1:22,

Moses rehearses Israel's history, and gives us additional facts. We are informed that the Lord yielded to the request of the Israelites that the territory be searched out.

Jehovah always wants us to use our own intelligence, yet recognize that He is our leader. And so twelve men, one from each tribe, were chosen for the expedition into enemy territory. Accept then both points: Spies were sent out because: (1) the Israelites asked, and (2) by the command of God. Their part in sending out the spies would later make their fearful rebellion all the more wicked. Remember that the Lord had told them already what the land was like—land He had prepared and promised, flowing with milk and honey. See in their request an element of unbelief. "We know what You said, Lord, but we want to see for ourselves!" God, of course, knew this in granting their request.

B. GRASSHOPPERS AND GIANTS (Numbers 13:32-33)

And they brought up an evil report of the land which they had searched unto the children of Israel, saying, The land, through which we have gone to search it, is a land that eateth up the inhabitants thereof; and all the people that we saw in it are men of a great stature. And there we saw the giants, the sons of Anak, which come of the giants: and we were in our own sight as grasshoppers, and so we were in their sight.

The twelve recognized leaders went out, reconnoitered, and returned. Ten of the twelve gave a negative report. Only Caleb and Joshua gave a positive report, recommending that the Israelites proceed to take over. In describing the statement of the ten faint-hearted spies as an "evil report," reference is made to defaming, infamy, perhaps whispered slander (Theological Wordbook of the Old Testament). It is used to describe Joseph's report concerning his brothers' behavior (Genesis 37:2). Evidently, the majority of the spy team started a campaign of speaking evil against Joshua and Caleb. But more important is the fact that the very evil of the evil was the attempt to leave God out of the report altogether!

Description of the land as one that "eats up the inhabitants" is variously interpreted. It does not mean the land was barren, poor, infertile, unproductive, unable to produce enough to support those who lived there. Neither is it a reference to the inclemency of the weather, or to pestilence. Nor does it mean the land was so difficult to cultivate that the farmers were worn out physically. More accurately the phrase refers to the fact that those living there highly valued the land, and fiercely resisted any who desired to conquer them. In other words, the present inhabitants would destroy any one attempting to settle there. Many people fought over the land because of its desirability, and these warring factions made life insecure (Scofield). As different countries fought over it, the inhabitants wasted away (Keil & Delitzsch). Because of the constant warfare that cursed Canaan at the time, the early death of the residents labeled the land as "devouring its inhabitants."

Another part of the majority report sought to discourage Israel by mentioning the presence of giants in the land (Deuteronomy 1:27-28). Rephaim is the general Hebrew name for giants. But the word used only in Genesis 6:4

and in Numbers 13:33 is Nephilim, derived from the verb meaning to fall. This signifies "tyrants, or those who make use of their power to cast down others" (Girdlestone). The Theological Wordbook of the Old Testament (TWOT) cautions that the word "may be of unknown origin and means heroes or fierce warriors." It recommends we play it safe: Do not translate giants, but simply transliterate, Nephilim, as is done in the RSV, NIV, NASB.

Giants were also known as the sons of Anak. They were a tribe of tall men ("longnecked") who dwelt on both sides of the Jordan prior to the coming of the Israelites. In Deuteronomy 2:10-11, the men are described as tall as the Anakim. Scholars are still not sure of the meanings and relationships of the words Nephilim, Anakim, Rephaim, and other names. Suffice it to say there is no doubt that men of giant stature existed. Goliath was six cubits and a span—approximately nine feet, nine inches (1 Samuel 17:4). The tallest man of whose measurements there is complete certainty was Robert P. Wadlow of Illinois, who lived from 1918 to 1940, and was 8 feet, 11 inches (Brewer's). No wonder their height caused the Israelite spies to exclaim: "We were in our own sight as grasshoppers, and so we were in their sight." Recall the eighth plague on Egypt (Exodus 10). Locust plagues throughout the centuries have threatened crops (Deuteronomy 28:38; Joel 1:4, 2:25), and devoured land (2 Chronicles 7:13). Locusts were eaten by John the Baptist (Leviticus 11:22; Matthew 3:4). Many references signify great numbers or multitude (Judges 6:5, 7.12: Jeremiah 46:23; Nahum 3:15). Finally, a grasshopper implies insignificance (Isaiah 40:22).

C. REBELLIOUS REACTION
(Numbers 14:1-4)

AND ALL the congregation lifted up their voice, and cried; and the people wept that night. And all the children of Israel murmured against Moses and against Aaron: and the whole congregation said unto them, Would God that we had died in the land of Egypt! or would God we had died in this wilderness! And wherefore hath the LORD brought us unto this land, to fall by the sword, that our wives and our children should be a prey? were it not better for us to return into Egypt? And they said one to another, Let us make a captain, and let us return into Egypt.

"Lifted up their voice—cried—wept—murmured." Note, voice is singular—they spoke as one! There is progression of volume from loud lamentation to soft murmuring. In despair, the Israelites blamed Moses and Aaron for their situation. And again, they cried the blues for Egypt. They quickly forgot the harsh enslavement and cruel treatment by their slavemasters (Exodus 2:23); the judgment strokes that befell Egypt; their miraculous deliverance crossing the Red Sea. Return to an Egypt still smarting from divine devastation, still grieving over the loss of their firstborn, and the destruction of their army?

How it must have hurt the heart of Jehovah to hear the congregation cry out, "Would God that we had died in the land of Egypt or even die in this wilderness!" Such expressions reek of ingratitude! And then to blatantly accuse the Lord—they murmured against Moses and Aaron in verse two, yet blame the Lord in verse three—of having brought them into the land to die by the sword and to have their wives and children perish. How often men use their families as an excuse to disobey the known will of God, and to cover their own unbelief! Such is the despair of all who transfer faith in God's judgment to faith in the judgment of men. In their madness, they are willing to depose the divinely appointed leader who brought them out of Egypt, and commission their own captain (head) to return them to that land.

D. PARDONED, BUT NOT POSSESSING (Numbers 14:20-24)

And the LORD said, I have pardoned according to thy word: But as truly as I live, all the earth shall be filled with the glory of the LORD. Because all those men which have seen my glory, and my miracles, which I did in Egypt and in the wilderness, and have tempted me now these ten times, and have not hearkened to my voice; Surely they shall not see the land which I sware unto their fathers, neither shall any of them that provoked me see it: But my servant Caleb, because he had another spirit with him, and hath followed me fully, him will I bring into the land whereinto he went; and his seed shall possess it.

Once again, Moses showed his love for Israel, and pleaded for pardon for the people. In loving-kindness, the living Lord showed mercy, and pardoned the rebellious Israelites. However, their sin demanded severe punishment. Instead of smiting all of them with pestilence and disinheriting them, the Lord decreed that their unbelief would prevent them from seeing the Promised Land. All God's decrees have His glory as their end (Isaiah 6:3). "They do not primarily aim at the happiness of the creature, nor at the perfecting of the saints, although both these things are included in His aims" (Thiessen). All those who left Egypt originally (twenty years old and upward) would perish in the wilderness (Hebrews 3:16-19). Through this judgment, God's glory would be seen. He would not have it otherwise, for the Israelites had provoked Him, and put Him to the test ten times. Some scholars make this number ten refer to the spies who brought the evil report. Others suggest that we should not take the number literally, for ten simply means a time of frequent testing. Still others say "ten" stands for completeness; this means a full measure of testing. Other say take the number ten literally; and point out the ten historical testings.

III. Special Features

A. PRESERVING OUR HERITAGE

In one of our spirituals we sing: "They crucified my Lord, they pierced Him in the side, The blood came twinklin' down, He bowed His head an' died, an' He never said a mumblin' word; Not a word, not a word, not a word." John Lovell (Black Song) considers these words "somewhat unbiblical." However, we must understand that the singular word represents more than just one word, even as we speak of the Bible as the Word of God. Furthermore, "mumblin'," or "mumbalin'," means murmuring. The Lord Jesus never complained or murmured the entire time on the Cross. Not even, "My God, My God, why hast Thou forsaken Me?" can be considered rebellious. May we as Christians learn never to blame God for what we consider the afflictions of life, but believe in our hearts that He is able to make all things work together for our good.

B. A CONCLUDING WORD

How sad that the generation delivered from Egypt forfeited their blessing. Pardoned by God for their sin of unbelief, yet they missed out on the rest Jehovah alone affords. Physical death was their lot. No mention is made of the loss of eternal salvation. What is stressed is the fact that disobedience (murmuring and rebellion) may cause the redeemed loss of present blessing and loss of future rewards. God grant that we will show a spirit similar to Caleb's, and follow the Lord Jesus Christ fully, with unswerving fidelity. May we look at the giants of adversity, hatred and racism not with the eyes of grasshoppers, but with Holy Spirit sight that gives us the confidence of Joshua and Caleb, and the assurance of David, conqueror of Goliath.

HOME DAILY BIBLE READINGS FOR THE WEEK OF OCTOBER 10, 1999

THE PEOPLE REBEL

Oct.	4	M.	Numbers 12:1-9, Aaron and Miriam Jealous of Moses
Oct.	5	T.	Numbers 12:10-15, Miriam Punished with Leprosy
Oct.	6	W.	Numbers 13:1-16, Twelve Sent to Spy Out Canaan
Oct.	7	T.	Numbers 13:17-24, The Spies Carry Out Moses' Orders
Oct.	8	F.	Numbers 13:25-33, Fearful Spies and a Negative Report
Oct.	9	S.	Numbers 14:1-12, Israel Rebels Against Moses and Aaron
Oct.	10	S.	Numbers 14:13-25, Moses Intercedes for Israel

Know Your Bible

- Pursuant to the belief of Joshua and Caleb that God would grant Israel the victory of conquering Canaan, God promised that they alone among the people who came out of Egypt would enter the Land of Canaan. (Numbers 14:30)
- God punished the ten spies who gave a fearful report by causing them to die of a plague, and caused those who believed the report to wander forty years in the wilderness until they too died. (Numbers 14:33, 37)

O God our Father, we are prone to wander and to go astray under the illusion that we know the way. Break the spirit of our rebellion that characterizes our living, and cause us to surrender totally and completely to Your will and way. In the name of Jesus Christ, we pray. Amen.

The Desert Years

Adult Topic—*In the Wilderness*

•••••

Youth Topic—*Paying the Price*

Children's Topic—*Obeying God*

•••••

Devotional Reading—Isaiah 35

Background Scripture—Deuteronomy 1:41—2:25

Print—Deuteronomy 1:41—2:8

PRINTED SCRIPTURE

Deuteronomy 1:41—2:8 (KJV)

41 Then ye answered and said unto me. We have sinned against the LORD, we will go up and fight, according to all that the LORD our God commanded us. And when ye had girded on every man his weapons of war, ye were ready to go up into the hill.

42 And the LORD said unto me, Say unto them, Go not up, neither fight; for I am not among you; lest ye be smitten before your enemies.

43 So I spake unto you; and ye would not hear, but rebelled against the commandment of the LORD, and went presumptuously up into the hill.

44 And the Amorites, which dwelt in that mountain, came out against you, and chased you, as bees do, and destroyed you in Seir, even unto Hormah.

45 And ye returned and wept before the LORD; but the LORD would not hearken to your voice, nor give ear unto you.

46 So ye abode in Kadesh many

Deuteronomy 1:41—2:8 (NRSV)

41 You answered me, "We have sinned against the LORD! We are ready to go up and fight, just as the LORD our God commanded us." So all of you strapped on your battle gear, and thought it easy to go up into the hill country.

42 The LORD said to me, "Say to them, 'Do not go up and do not fight, for I am not in the midst of you; otherwise you will be defeated by your enemies.'"

43 Although I told you, you would not listen. You rebelled against the command of the LORD and presumptuously went up into the hill country.

44 The Amorites who lived in that hill country then came out against you and chased you as bees do. They beat you down in Seir as far as Hormah.

45 When you returned and wept before the LORD, the LORD would neither heed your voice nor pay you any attention.

days, according unto the days that ye abode there.

.....

THEN WE turned, and took our journey into the wilderness by the way of the Red sea, as the LORD spake unto me: and we compassed mount Seir many days.

2 And the LORD spake unto me, saying,

3 Ye have compassed this mountain long enough: turn you northward.

4 And command thou the people, saying, Ye are to pass through the coast of your brethren the children of Esau, which dwell in Seir; and they shall be afraid of you: take ye good heed unto yourselves therefore:

5 Meddle not with them; for I will not give you of their land, no, not so much as a foot breadth; because I have given mount Seir unto Esau for a possession.

6 Ye shall buy meat of them for money, that ye may eat; and ye shall also buy water of them for money, that ye may drink.

7 For the LORD thy God hath blessed thee in all the works of thy hand: he knoweth thy walking through this great wilderness: these forty years the LORD thy God hath been with thee; thou hast lacked nothing.

8 And when we passed by from our brethren the children of Esau, which dwelt in Seir.

46 After you had stayed at Kadesh as many days as you did,

.....

WE JOURNEYED back into the wilderness, in the direction of the Red Sea, as the LORD had told me and skirted Mount Seir for many days.

2 Then the LORD said to me:

3 "You have been skirting this hill country long enough. Head north,

4 and charge the people as follows: You are about to pass through the territory of your kindred, the descendants of Esau, who live in Seir. They will be afraid of you, so, be very careful

5 not to engage in battle with them, for I will not give you even so much as a foot's length of their land, since I have given Mount Seir to Esau as a possession.

6 You shall purchase food from them for money, so that you may eat; and you shall also buy water from them for money, so that you may drink.

7 Surely the LORD your God has blessed you in all your undertakings; he knows your going through this great wilderness. These forty years the LORD your God has been with you; you have lacked nothing."

8 So we passed by our kin, the descendants of Esau who live in Seir.

KEY VERSE

*For the LORD thy God hath blessed thee in all the works of thy hand: he knoweth thy walking through this great wilderness: these forty years the LORD thy God hath been with thee; thou hast lacked nothing.—**Deuteronomy 2:7***

OBJECTIVES

After reading this lesson, the student should remember that:

1. We must fight sin God's way;
2. Presumptuousness displeases our Lord;
3. Disobedience creates further conflict; and,
4. God provides even in our wilderness wanderings.

POINTS TO BE EMPHASIZED

Adult/Youth/Children
Key Verse: Deuteronomy 2:7
Print: Deuteronomy 1:41—2:8

—Moses reminded the Israelites that when they had sought to enter Canaan against the will of God, He had told them not to fight or they would be defeated. (1:41-42)

—The Israelites were defeated by the Amorites because they failed to heed God's command to retreat into the wilderness. (43-45)

—After the Israelites' long stay in the wilderness of Seir, the Lord directed them to move northward and to respect and to deal openly with the descendants of Esau in the land. (1:46—2:6)

—Moses reminded the Israelites that the Lord had taken care of them for forty years. (2:7)

—The Israelites recognized their kin, the descendants of Esau, and passed by peaceably. (8)

(**Note**: Use KJV Scripture for Adult; NRSV Scripture for Youth and Children)

TOPICAL OUTLINE OF THE LESSON

I. Introduction

A. Presumption
B. Biblical Background

II. Exposition and Application of the Scripture

A. Determination Without God (Deuteronomy 1:41-43)
B. Defeat in Battle (Deuteronomy 1:44-46)
C. Description of the Journey (Deuteronomy 2:1-6)
D. Destitute for Nothing (Deuteronomy 2:7-8)

III. Special Features

A. Preserving Our Heritage
B. A Concluding Word

I.   Introduction

A. PRESUMPTION

Basically, there are three kinds of sins. There are sins of ignorance. The apostle Paul serves as an example of one who sinned ignorantly (1 Timothy 1:13). There are sins of weakness or infirmity. Simon Peter is an example of one who sinned this way (Luke 22:57-62). There are sins of presumption. David is an example of one who committed a presumptuous sin (2 Samuel 11; Psalm 19:13). Literally, the word "presumptuous" means to take before. The "pre" indicates something in front, a prefix! The verb root, sumere, means to take. Thus, to presume means to take in advance, to presuppose, foresee, assume. So to be presumptuous is to be excessively forward or confident; arrogant, too bold, daring too much, impudent, impertinent, audacious. One example of presumptuousness is seen in this story. On a very hot summer day, a mother warned her son not to go swimming in the nearby creek. When the boy came home, the mother felt the top of his head and discovered it was wet. "I thought I told you not to go swimming!" Whereupon the boy protested that he fell in! "But why aren't your clothes wet?" asked the mother. To which the boy replied, "Aw mom, I had a feeling I was going to fall in."

One way to define presumptuous sins is to study verses using the word, "presumption." For example, we are warned: "the soul that does anything presumptuously . . . reproaches the Lord; and that soul shall utterly be cut off from among the people" (Numbers 15:30). Here the two Hebrew words used and rendered "presumptuously"

mean with a high hand. To raise one's hand against Jehovah speaks of a spirit of proud defiance (Kirkpatrick); obstinate rebellion (TWOT). Pride is at the very center of this sin; he who acts presumptuously acts proudly. In Numbers 14:44, the Hebrew word used for "presumed" means to swell up, lift self up. Found only here in the Old Testament, it speaks of Israel's "rash and reckless attack on the Amalekites and Canaanites, following her lack of faith and great rebellion" (TWOT). "They went up heedlessly" (NASB); "dared to start" (Moffatt). In today's lesson, Moses told the Israelites at Kadesh-barnea not to go up to fight the Amalekites and Canaanites who dwelled there. "The Lord is not among you," the Israelites were told. They went anyway! The result: They were routed! They had run ahead of the Lord. Here the Hebrew word rendered "presumed" means to boil up (as water), to act proudly, to speak without authorization (ISBE); thus in the sphere of personality, to "act in a proud manner" (TWOT).

B. BIBLICAL BACKGROUND

The book of Deuteronomy begins with the words which Moses spoke unto all Israel on this side of the Jordan in the wilderness. From these words we are given insight into what follows. Even the Hebrew title of this last book of the Pentateuch, literally "words" directs our attention to the contents. Basically, Deuteronomy is a book of sermons, discourses or speeches, given to the children of Israel by Moses. We find the nation gathered on the east bank of the Jordan, there in the plain of Moab, just about ready to enter the Promised Land. Thirty-eight years had passed since their rebellion at Kadesh-barnea. Imagine! It had been a journey that ordinarily would have required only eleven days (Deuteronomy 1:2).

In his first message, Moses recounts Israel's history from Horeb. He reminds them of their failure to enter the land because of their murmuring at the report brought back by ten of the spies sent out to reconnoiter Canaan. Only Caleb and Joshua urged the Israelites to go on. God's anger was stirred. He predicted that only Caleb and Joshua would enter, along with the children; those who originally left Egypt would die. "Not one of these men of this evil generation shall see that good land" (Deuteronomy 1:35).

II. Exposition and Application of the Scripture

A. DETERMINATION WITHOUT GOD (Deuteronomy 1:41-43)

Then ye answered and said unto me, We have sinned against the LORD, we will go up and fight, according to all that the LORD our God commanded us. And when ye had girded up every man his weapons of war, ye were ready to go up into the hill. And the LORD said unto me, Say unto them, Go not up, neither fight; for I am not among you; lest ye be smitten before your enemies. So I spake unto you; and ye would not hear, but rebelled against the commandment of the LORD, and went presumptuously up into the hill.

Israel recognized that in their rebellion against Joshua and Caleb, they had "sinned against the Lord." The word for sin here (chata) means to miss the mark, to err. It is a word that signifies all wrong-doing is a failure or a coming short of that aim which God intended His own to reach (Girdlestone). But note this acknowledgement came after the Lord had commanded them to go back into the desert. True, they mourned bitterly their sin, but

you get the impression their new desire to go up and fight is only born out of their desire not to re-enter the wilderness. "We will go up!" they said, not realizing their new determination was in disobedience to Jehovah's command to turn and go back into the wilderness (Numbers 14:25; in Numbers chapter fourteen, you will find more information on today's lesson). In short, we shall learn that two wrongs do not make a right!

Not even waiting for an answer from the Lord through Moses, they girded on their weapons of war. Bow and sling and spear and sword for attack, and shield and helmet for defense would be the full equipment of the men called upon to fight. God then told Moses to tell them: "Don't go! Don't fight! For the Lord is not among you. You won't succeed! If you go, your enemies will defeat you. You will fall by the sword, for the Amalekites and the Canaanites are there to face you" (Numbers 14:41-43). Moses' plea fell on deaf ears. They heard but did not heed, and rebelled against this commandment of the Lord. In presumption, they climbed the hilltop to do battle. In Numbers 14:44, it is said they presumed—lifted themselves up, swollen in pride. In Deuteronomy 1:43, they boiled with pride! Two different words describe the same event. Surely pride leads to a downfall and shame (Proverbs 11:2, 16:18, 29:23). Their presumptuousness was motivated by pride. The Israelites' pride moved them to assert their own will in rebellion against the will of God who was in authority over them. They chose to fight rather than be right!

B. DEFEAT IN BATTLE
(Deuteronomy 1:44-46)

And the Amorites, which dwelt in that mountain, came out against you, and chased you, as bees do, and destroyed you in Seir, even unto Hormah. And ye returned and wept before the LORD; but the LORD would not hearken to your voice, nor give ear unto you. So ye abode in Kadesh many days, according unto the days that ye abode there.

Amorite is a name used in the Old Testament to denote the inhabitants of Palestine generally. Moses relates that the Amorites came out against the Israelites and chased them as bees do. This is the first time the word bee(s) occurs in the Old Testament. The Hebrew word for bee is "deborah," which has given us the name, Deborah. In Psalm 118:12, the psalmist states the nations "compassed me about like bees." In Isaiah 7:18, the bee signifies the kind of divine chastisement to be sent from Assyria upon Judah. The idea of swarming about, "as pertinaciously, as ferociously, and as numerously as bees" (ICC) is applied to the enemy soldiers who destroyed the Israelite soldiers.

And so their presumptuous, frivolous, rash attempt to force their way into the mountains of the Amorites ended in miserable failure. God was not with them, for the ark of the covenant of the Lord and Moses remained in the camp (Numbers 14:44). This is always the tragic consequence of willful sin. The beaten Israelites had failed in their hope to escape God's verdict against them. They returned, but their hearts had not changed. There was no true conversion to repentance for their rash disobedience or as a result of their defeat. There was only a fleshly repentance, and a sorrow that they lost the battle, but no remorse for having disobeyed Jehovah. And so they remained many days in Kadesh. Many days is a vague expression. It may mean many years, but also may signify many months or weeks. Mystery surrounds these years of barrenness spent at Kadesh and the nearby wilderness area.

C. DESCRIPTION OF THE JOURNEY (Deuteronomy 2:1-6)

THEN WE turned, and took our journey into the wilderness by the way of the Red sea, as the LORD spake unto me: and we compassed mount Seir many days. And the LORD spake unto me, saying, Ye have compassed this mountain long enough: turn you northward. And command thou the people, saying, Ye are to pass through the coast of your brethren the children of Esau, which dwell in Seir, and they shall be afraid of you: take ye good heed unto yourselves therefore: Meddle not with them; for I will not give you of their land, no, not so much as a foot breadth; because I have given

mount Seir unto Esau for a possession. Ye shall buy meat of them for money, that ye may eat; and ye shall also buy water of them for money, that ye may drink.

Moses continues describing the wilderness wanderings. Having turned and journeyed into the wilderness by the Way of the Red Sea, and having skirted Mount Seir for many days (i.e. many years), the Israelites were then commanded to no longer spend time making their way around the hill country, but to turn northward. Now the descendants of Esau lived in Seir. And because of their fear of the Israelites, not knowing what the intentions of the Israelites were, they were prepared for war. God warned the Israelites, "Watch yourselves carefully. Do not meddle with them," KJV (Do not provoke them to war, NIV; Do not contend with them, RSV).

Seir was the typical summit of the mountains of Edom, and the Edomites were the descendants of Esau, the brother of Jacob, who of course was the ancestor of the children of Israel. God had given the Edomites the land they now possessed (Genesis 36:6-8), and not a foot breadth—not one footstep (NKJV, NASB), not the sole of the foot to tread on (RSV), not enough to put your foot on (NIV)—would be given to Israel. From Numbers 20:17-21, we learn that Moses had requested permission to pass through Edom, but this was refused by the king of Edom, who said: "Thou shalt not pass by me, lest I come out against thee with the sword." The Israelites were willing to purchase food and water from them; however, they still refused. Thus Israel was compelled to turn away from them, turn back into the wilderness, and spend time in the area to the southwest of the Edomites.

D. DESTITUTE FOR NOTHING
(Deuteronomy 2:7-8)

For the LORD thy God hath blessed thee in all the works of thy hand: he knoweth thy walking through this great wilderness: these forty years the LORD thy God hath been with thee; thou hast lacked nothing. And when we passed by from our brethren the children of Esau, which dwelt in Seir.

Though some scholars suggest that in spite of the order of the king of Edom not to let the Israelites pass through their land, or to sell them food and water, some individuals did sell food and water to the Israelites. However, this is not certain. One thing that is sure: In their forty years out of Egypt, the Lord had taken care of them. Moses again reminds the Israelites of God's benevolence. Despite the fact their wandering was the execution of God's judgment, He provided all their needs. What grace! What mercy! The very people who disobeyed, insulted, provoked God, who murmured, complained, displayed ingratitude, and acted presumptuously against God— yet, He graciously supplied all their needs.

They were not destitute, abandoned, utterly lacking anything. Jehovah gave them food, clothing, shelter, protection, victory over their enemies, and miraculous evidence of His love. He knew their paths, every step of the way in the great wilderness was chartered, measured, observed. He knew "the works of their hands," a common expression in the book of Deuteronomy

(14:29, 16:15, 24:19, 28:12, 30:9, 31:29, 33:11). The phrase usually refers to their agricultural pursuits, the rearing of flocks and herds, all that they did for a living, sowing, reaping, selling, all their enterprises. It even includes their evil activities.

III. Special Features

A. PRESERVING OUR HERITAGE

Looking back at the history of our race in the United States, it is easy to consider our experience as that of a people on a wilderness journey. The brutality, lynching and dehumanization of African slaves and their descendants is well documented. Sow to the wind, and reap the whirlwind (Hosea 8:7) remains a fact today in the life of America. And yet, Black American Christians are not bitter. Holy Spirit discernment has enabled us to see the hand of the Lord Jesus Christ in all of life's episodes. Although racism has played and still plays a huge part in Americana, Christians recognize the role God has performed in preserving us in times of adversity. The contributions we have made in Music, Art, Sports, Entertainment, Inventions, Literature, and in Religion and the Church life of this country are tremendous. The very existence of the National Baptist Convention, U.S.A., Incorporated is proof of God's good hand upon us. When we look back over the Desert Years, we rejoice to see how far the Lord has brought us. Thank God for every blessing! But let us not lose sight of the fact that the United States is not our final destination. Whether we consider America still a desert wilderness or consider it the Promised Land, remember it is not heaven. We are still traveling to a city which has foundations, whose builder and maker is God (Hebrews 11:10).

B. A CONCLUDING WORD

The Israelites were physically ready to enter the Promised Land, but Moses was concerned about their spiritual readiness. This was still lacking. Their attempt to conquer the Amorites in disobedience to God's command demonstrated their spiritual immaturity. To think they could conquer anyone in their own strength showed their lack of spiritual growth. Here is a lesson we still need to learn and obey: Without God on our side, we fight a losing battle.

Sometimes we forget that there is a right way and a wrong way to fight evil. There are saints who believe it is permissible to fight evil any kind of way. No. We must recognize that the Lord is in charge. We are to move only when the pillar of cloud or fire moves, for God alone is our Leader. He is the Man of War (Exodus 15:3), the Hero of the battle! He is our General. He decides the strategy, and even picks the time and place we are to wage war. Why He even chooses the enemies we are to fight; recall His advising the Israelites to "meddle not with" the Edomites?

The weapons of our warfare are not carnal, but mighty through God to the pulling down of strongholds (2 Corinthians 10:4). We are therefore to wear the whole armor of God (Ephesians 6:10-17). May we remember that God will cause us to triumph in Jesus Christ, who has overcome the world (John 16:33).

HOME DAILY BIBLE READINGS FOR THE WEEK OF OCTOBER 17, 1999

THE DESERT YEARS

Oct. 11   M.   Deuteronomy 1:1-8, Moses Reminds Israel About Horeb
Oct. 12   T.   Deuteronomy 1:9-18, Tribal Leaders Were Appointed
Oct. 13   W.   Deuteronomy 1:19-33, Israel Refused to Obey God
Oct. 14   T.   Deuteronomy 1:34-45, Israel Was Punished for Disobedience
Oct. 15   F.   Deuteronomy 1:46—2:13, Israel Wandered in the Wilderness
Oct. 16   S.   Deuteronomy 2:13-25, A Generation of Warriors Passed Away
Oct. 17   S.   Deuteronomy 2:26-37, Israel Began the Conquest of Canaan

Know Your Bible

- Korah was a Levite who was found guilty of gathering sticks on the Sabbath day, and when it was brought to the attention of Moses, he was stoned to death at God's command. (Numbers 15:32-36)

- God had warned the people to keep the Sabbath holy, and that everyone who defiled this day shall be put to death and that his soul shall be cut off from among his people. (Exodus 31:14)

- Israel experienced a trial of faith in the desert of Zin because they had no water to drink, and they blamed Moses for the lack thereof. (Numbers 20:1-5)

- God commanded Moses to speak to the rock to bring forth water, but Moses dishonored God by striking the rock and speaking as if he himself was causing the water to flow. (Numbers 20:10-11)

- God punished Moses for his sin (arrogance) by not allowing him to enter the Promised Land. (Numbers 20:12)

- The Edomites were descendants of Esau who was called Edom "red" that references the red pottage that he received from Jacob in exchange for his birthright. (Genesis 36:1)

O Lord, while we live in a land of plenty, our souls are still impoverished by the lack of love, the failure to be concerned about others, and the belief that material things alone can satisfy our needs. Give us more of thyself and we shall come to know that peace that transcends the fleeting joys of the world. In Jesus' name. Amen.

The Great Commandment

Adult Topic—*Teach Your Children Well*

•••••

Youth Topic—*Link in the Chain*
Children's Topic—*Learning God's Greatest Rule*

•••••

Devotional Reading—Deuteronomy 30:11-20
Background Scripture—Deuteronomy 6
Print—Deuteronomy 6:1-9, 20-24

PRINTED SCRIPTURE

Deuteronomy 6:1-9, 20-24 (KJV)

NOW THESE are the commandments, the statutes, and the judgments, which the LORD your God commanded to teach you, that ye might do them in the land whither ye go to possess it:

2 That thou mightest fear the LORD thy God, to keep all his statutes and his commandments, which I command thee, thou, and thy son, and thy son's son, all the days of thy life; and that thy days may be prolonged.

3 Hear therefore, O Israel, and observe to do it; that it may be well with thee, and that ye may increase mightily, as the LORD God of thy fathers hath promised thee, in the land that floweth with milk and honey.

4 Hear, O Israel: The LORD our God is one LORD:

5 And thou shalt love the LORD thy God with all thine heart, and with all thy soul, and with all thy might.

Deuteronomy 6:1-9, 20-24 (NRSV)

NOW THIS is the commandment—the statutes and the ordinances—that the LORD your God charged me to teach you to observe in the land that you are about to cross into and occupy,

2 so that you and your children and your children's children may fear the LORD your God all the days of your life, and keep all his decrees and his commandments that I am commanding you, so that your days may be long.

3 Hear therefore, O Israel, and observe them diligently, so that it may go well with you, and so that you may multiply greatly in a land flowing with milk and honey, as the LORD, the God of your ancestors, has promised you.

4 Hear, O Israel: The LORD is our God, the LORD alone.

5 You shall love the LORD your God with all your heart, and with all your soul, and with all your might.

6 And these words, which I command thee this day, shall be in thine heart:

7 And thou shalt teach them diligently unto thy children, and shalt talk of them when thou sittest in thine house, and when thou walkest by the way, and when thou liest down, and when thou risest up.

8 And thou shalt bind them for a sign upon thine hand, and they shall be as frontlets between thine eyes.

9 And thou shalt write them upon the posts of thy house, and on thy gates.

.....

20 And when thy son asketh thee in time to come, saying, What mean the testimonies, and the statutes, and the judgments, which the LORD our God hath commanded you?

21 Then thou shalt say unto thy son, We were Pharaoh's bondmen in Egypt; and the LORD brought us out of Egypt with a mighty hand:

22 And the LORD showed signs and wonders, great and sore, upon Egypt, upon Pharaoh, and upon all his household, before our eyes:

23 And he brought us out from thence, that he might bring us in, to give us the land which he sware unto our fathers.

24 And the LORD commanded us to do all these statutes, to fear the LORD our God, for our good always, that he might preserve us alive, as it is at this day.

6 Keep these words that I am commanding you today in your heart.

7 Recite them to your children and talk about them when you are at home and when you are away, when you lie down and when you rise.

8 Bind them as a sign on your hand, fix them as an emblem on your forehead,

9 and write them on the doorposts of your house and on your gates.

.....

20 When your children ask you in time to come, "What is the meaning of the decress and the statutes and the ordinances that the LORD our God has commanded you?"

21 then you shall say to your children, "We were Pharaoh's slaves in Egypt, but the LORD brought us out of Egypt with a mighty hand.

22 The LORD displayed before our eyes great and awesome signs and wonders against Egypt, against Pharaoh and all his household.

23 He brought us out from there in order to bring us in, to give us the land that he promised on oath to our ancestors.

24 Then the LORD commanded us to observe all these statutes, to fear the LORD our God, for our lasting good, so as to keep us alive, as is now the case.

 KEY VERSE

*Hear, O Israel: The LORD our God is one LORD: And thou shalt love the LORD thy God with all thine heart, and with all thy soul, and with all thy might.—**Deuteronomy 6:4-5***

OBJECTIVES

After reading this lesson, the student should know:

1. The importance of teaching God's people God's Word;

2. The primary commandment is to love God;

3. The responsibility of belivers to teach their children; and,

4. The truth of the unity of the Trinity.

POINTS TO BE EMPHASIZED

Adult/Youth/Children

Key Verse: Deuteronomy 6:4-5

Print: Deuteronomy 6:1-9, 20-24

—Speaking through Moses, God gave the people of Israel a set of laws to guide and bless their lives in a new land. (1-3)

—The primary commandment was for God's people to love the Lord their God with complete fidelity. (4-5)

—The people were to keep continually the laws in their hearts and minds, to recite them to their children, and to post reminders of them on their person and in their households. (6-9)

—When the children asked the meaning of the covenant commandments, the Israelites were to tell them their story of slavery in Egypt and how the Lord delivered them and gave them the land in which they live. (20-24)

(**Note**: Use KJV Scripture for Adult; NRSV Scripture for Youth and Children)

TOPICAL OUTLINE OF THE LESSON

I. Introduction

A. One Lord

B. Biblical Background

II. Exposition and Application of the Scripture

A. God's Commandments (Deuteronomy 6:1-3)

B. The Essence of the Law (Deuteronomy 6:4-5)

C. Parental Instruction (Deuteronomy 6:6-9)

D. Deliverance From Egypt (Deuteronomy 6:20-24)

III. Special Features

A. Preserving Our Heritage

B. A Concluding Word

I. Introduction

A. ONE LORD

We learn that Israel stood for monotheism (one God) and against polytheism (many gods). Deuteronomy 6:4 states: "Hear, O Israel: The LORD our God is one LORD." The first word in this verse is Shema, pronounced Sh'mah. It comes from the Hebrew verb "to hear." Literally, the verse reads: "Jehovah our Elohim is one Jehovah." Now the word Jehovah is singular. But Elohim is plural. It is often translated "gods" when referring to the idols of the heathen. As used here in the Shema, it is the name of the one true and living God of creation. Some scholars see in the use of the plural what is called the plurality of majesty, an attempt to multiply the force of the title.

Of course, we cannot explain God; only God fully knows Himself. Man does not and cannot. We can, however, assert that the Bible teaches the One God exists in three Persons. We can prove by Scriptures that there is God the Father, that Jesus Christ is God, and that the Holy Spirit is God. Yet, the Bible teaches there is but one God. We are not asked to understand, but to believe. Trinity is a word we have made up and use to explain what we believe the Bible teaches. It is nonsense to say because the word "Trinity" does not occur in the Bible, therefore, there is no such thing. The combined words "Watchtower Society" are not found in the Bible either; nor will we find the words Sunday School!

Now the word for one is *echad*. This key word may signify that which is compounded out of unified parts, an integration of constituent parts. For example: It is said of Adam and Eve, "they shall be one flesh." This is why we recognize plurality within the Godhead. The word for one stands for compound unity. Both the unity and the trinity of the Godhead are taught in the Old Testament. Jehovah (LORD) stresses His oneness; Elohim (God) emphasizes His three persons. God is not divided into parts; His divine nature is indivisible. "Unity is not the same as a unit. A unit is marked by mere singleness" (Thiessen). There are three Persons in the Godhead, but one essence. To Jehovah alone rightfully belongs the name Jehovah.

B. BIBLICAL BACKGROUND

In his first discourse, Moses reviews the history of Israel after its deliverance from slavery in Egypt. In this first speech, the wilderness journey is recounted, and the trip from Horeb to Kadesh-barnea is described. He reminds them of their failure to enter the Promised Land because of disobedience and rebellion, and urges them to remember the great truths they were taught at Horeb. In his second speech, Moses rehearses and sums up the Law. The Ten Commandments are repeated in chapter five. This summary of the Sinaitic Laws reminds us of the title of the Book. The Hebrew title is literally, Words. But the Greek title, taken from the Old Testament translated into Greek (Septuagint) and from the Vulgate (Latin translation of the Bible) is made up of two words: "Deuteros" means second, and "nomos" means law. Today's lesson is part of this second discourse of Moses.

II. Exposition and Application of the Scripture

A. GOD'S COMMANDMENTS
(Deuteronomy 6:1-3)

NOW THESE are the commandments, the statutes, and the judgments, which the LORD your God commanded to teach you, that ye might do them in the land whither ye go to possess it: That thou mightest fear the LORD thy God, to keep all his statutes and his commandments, which I command thee, thou, and thy son, and thy son's son, all the days of thy life; and that thy days may be prolonged. Hear therefore, O Israel, and observe to do it; that it may be well with thee, and that ye may increase mightily, as the LORD God of thy fathers hath promised thee, in the land that floweth with milk and honey.

Nearly a dozen different words are used to describe the written Word of God. This is especially seen in Psalm 119 (also Psalm 19:7-9). Law, word, words, ordinances, judgments, way, commandments, precepts, testimonies, statutes, righteousness—these all have varying shades of meaning, and all provide us with peculiar insight into the beauty and excellency of the Scriptures. Our lesson opens with mention of three of these names: (1) Commandments are orders coming from God which are used as religious principles whereby men are to conduct themselves; (2) Statutes are decrees referring to civil and religious aspects of the law of Moses; and (3) Ordinances or judgments have to do with legal pronouncements; they are rules of divine administration.

It was the task of Moses to teach the Israelites to keep the commandments of the Lord, to implant in them "the spirit of true religion and dutiful obedience to" the will of God (ICC). They were to obey them in the land they were preparing to possess. Obedience meant Israel would receive many benefits. Keeping these statutes and ordinances laid a solid foundation for their future living in the Promised Land. Another purpose for obedience was that they might fear the Lord. This is not a servile, sycophantic ("boot-licking") fear, but an awe, respect, and reverence. It is reverential trust, and includes the hatred of evil (Scofield). Without it, the Bible labels a man a fool, for the "fear of the Lord is the beginning of knowledge, but fools despise wisdom and instruction" (Proverbs 1:7).

When taught the Word of God diligently, we begin to lose the fear of fear itself. In fearing God, we dismiss the fear of ungodliness. By mentioning the son and grandson, Moses passes from dealing with the nation to the individual Israelite. A third purpose of this teaching is the blessing of prolonged days (Proverbs 10:27). A fourth purpose is prosperity. God desired that it might be well with Israel materially, and that the nation might increase mightily (Deuteronomy 7:13). After all, the Promised Land flowed with milk and honey, "a proverbial description of the extraordinary fertility and loveliness of the land of Canaan. Milk and honey are the simplest and choicest productions of a land abounding in grass and flowers" (Keil & Delitzsch).

It is sometimes difficult to study the meaning of an English word when it is the translation of several Hebrew and Greek words. We may miss the shades and differences of meaning which, if known, would increase our knowledge and broaden our interpretation of the Scriptures. Such is the case with the word translated "teach." According to Girdlestone *(Synonyms of the Old Testament)*, twelve Hebrew words are used to explain the idea of teaching in the Old Testament. Note the shades of meaning in eight of the words: (1) One word translated teach is a verb connected with the first letter of the Hebrew alphabet; (2) to make or cause to understand; (3) to speak or to broach a subject; (4) to warn, hence to illuminate; (5) to make to know; (6) to chasten, instruct, often involving chastisement; (7) cast forth, show, hence direct or guide; and (8) cause to act wisely, or make wise.

In Deuteronomy 6:1, the word for teach (lamad) signifies to chastise. The name Talmud (ancient Jewish writings) is derived from this word. *Lamad* has the idea of training as well as educating. It is interesting to note that the training aspect can be seen in the fact that the term for "oxgoad" is derived from this word (TWOT). In Deuteronomy 6:7, the word for teach (Shanan) means to whet or sharpen (swords, arrows). Repetition is stressed here, a setting forth of the Word of God in its fullness, plying the Divine laws to and fro in the hearts of the children. So diligent instruction of children in the Word of God as meant here is to impress them (NIV, Moffatt); repeat them (NEB).

B. THE ESSENCE OF THE LAW
(Deuteronomy 6:4-5)

Hear, O Israel: The LORD our God is one LORD; And thou shalt love the LORD thy God with all thine heart, and with all thy soul, and with all thy might.

This great passage begins with one of the grand statements of Israel's belief in one God (monotheism). Their faith completely set them apart from the surrounding nations. The God of Israel is God; there is none else beside Him, no god with Him (Deuteronomy 4:35; 32:39). Paul the apostle reinforced this point of view when he stated that there is no other God but one, the Father of the Lord Jesus Christ. And the things which the Gentiles sacrifice, they sacrifice to demons, and not to God (1 Corinthians 8:5-6; 10:20). Biblical Christianity walks a narrow path!

One of the tremendous themes of Deuteronomy is the concept of love. Israel is commanded to love the Lord supremely, with its entire being, heart, soul and might. The heart is mentioned first because it is the seat of the intellect. There was to be no half-hearted, take it or leave it, lackadaisical attitude in this relationship. Love the Lord with all your soul follows. The soul (nephesh) is the seat of the affections, desires, emotions and will. It is the center of man's personality, his self-consciousness. Thus, devotion of the whole person to God is implied. The words "with all thy might" mean greatly, with all the force of body and soul.

It is out of this loving of the Lord that observance of the commands was to issue. When our Lord was asked, "Which is the great commandment in the law?", He referred to this text. And also when questioned, "What shall I do to inherit eternal life?", He gave this same text (Matthew 22:36-38; Luke

10:27). Here is the demand by Jehovah for exclusive and intense devotion to Himself. Man's sinful heart dictates love of self as primary, even if this self-love prefers some being other than God. We cannot truly, fully love anyone (not even ourselves) unless we first love the Lord—who first loved us! Our love for others must come out of our love for the Lord. Only faith in the shed blood of Jesus Christ enables us to overcome inherent, congenital selfishness, and attain agape love.

C. PARENTAL INSTRUCTION
(Deuteronomy 6:6-9)

And these words, which I command thee this day, shall be in thine heart: And thou shalt teach them diligently unto thy children, and shalt talk of them when thou sittest in thine house, and when thou walkest by the way, and when thou liest down, and when thou risest up. And thou shalt bind them for a sign upon thine hand, and they shall be as frontlets between thine eyes. And thou shalt write them upon the posts of thy house, and on thy gates.

Emphasis is placed upon the responsibility of believing parents to teach their children the Word of God. It is their duty to give religious training at home to their offspring. We read this every month at our communion service: "to religiously educate our children"—this is part of the church covenant in our churches. The passage states: "teach them. . . talk of them . . . bind them. . . write them." Reference is to the Word of God—His commandments, statutes, ordinances (judgments), words. These words are to be memorized, stored in the heart. The psalmist said that storing (hiding)

God's Word in his heart gave him strength to resist sin. The word for "teach" (to sharpen, to whet) here means to teach earnestly, incisively, impressively, and with frequency! This is God's command for parents to be consistently diligent teaching God's Word. There is to be no half-hearted, haphazard training here! The consistency and diligence is expressed in the verbs: sitting, walking, lying down, rising up at all times! Meditation upon God's Word was to take place day and night—though primarily oral training, note the command to write.

There was a time when men rejected this portion of Scripture because they believed that in Moses' day men could not write. However, it is believed Moses learned to write in Egypt (Acts 7:22). Furthermore, archaeologists found proof that in the time of Moses cuneiform and a primitive Hebrew alphabet were in use. The command to bind the words was taken literally by those orthodox Jews who wrote verses on parchment and put them in small boxes and bound them upon their foreheads and hands with leather strips. These little boxes are called phylacteries. They also nailed them near the doorways of their homes (they are called mezuzahs).

D. DELIVERANCE FROM EGYPT
(Deuteronomy 6:20-24)

And when thy son asketh thee in time to come, saying, What mean the testimonies, and the statutes, and the judgments, which the LORD our God hath commanded you? Then thou shalt say unto thy son, We were Pharaoh's bondmen in Egypt; and the LORD brought us out of Egypt with a mighty hand: And the LORD

showed signs and wonders, great and sore, upon Egypt, upon Pharaoh, and upon all his household, before our eyes: And he brought us out from thence, that he might bring us in, to give us the land which he sware unto our fathers. And the LORD commanded us to do all these statutes, to fear the LORD our God, for our good always, that he might preserve us alive, as it is at this day.

When an Israelite's son inquires as to the meaning of the testimonies, statutes and ordinances, the parent is to tell the story of Israel's redemption from the land of Egypt. The children of coming generations are to be taught in the source of the law now set before the nation. They had been slaves in that country, ill treated and afflicted, when God through Moses redeemed them with a mighty hand. "We were eye-witnesses. We saw the signs and wonders, the plagues which befell the Egyptians." The Lord "brought us out" that He might "bring us in," said Moses. Giving the law to Israel was for Israel's own good. If the people obeyed and walked in the path of righteousness, divine favor and blessing would be theirs from a merciful Lord. The purpose of this rehearsal of God's redemptive actions was to stir up love to the Lord in the hearts of the younger generation, and move them to desire to keep His commandments.

III. Special Features

A. PRESERVING OUR HERITAGE

The recounting by Moses of Israel's deliverance from slavery in Egypt had as its purpose the awakening of faith in the young people who heard the story. Awareness of the love of God would move them also to walk in the pathway of obedience. Responsibility for telling children about the goodness of God fell upon the parents. However, here is a good reason for having the testimony period in our local assemblies today. Years ago, when many of us had separate Communion services, not something just tacked on to the morning worship, testimony time was one of the highlights.

Talk about audience participation! We recognize how the Lord brought us as a race out of slavery, but the next step after redemption is sanctification. To hear the older saints tell how the Lord brought them through, broke the shackles of sin, opened doors, provided for their families, kept their health—to listen to their testimonies of thanksgiving and praise has been a blessing and encouragement to us all.

B. A CONCLUDING WORD

The commandments, statutes, ordinances, judgments, law, testimonies, precepts, way and word constitute the Word of God. As such, they are food for the soul, sweeter than honey. The Word is better than silver or gold, a sure foundation, able to make wise, profitable for doctrine, for reproof, for correction and instruction in righteousness. God's Word is a hammer, a lamp, a light, a fire.

Sharper than a two-edge sword, it is the power of God giving hope through patience and comfort. It shall all be fulfilled, never pass away. God's Word prepares us to meet the hardships and difficulties that face us as migrants, pilgrims, sojourners, pioneers and strangers passing through an unfriendly world. Martin Luther wrote:

"For feelings come and feelings go, And feelings are deceiving:
My warrant is the Word of God, Naught else is worth believing.
Though all my heart should feel condemned For want of some sweet token,
There is One greater than my heart Whose Word cannot be broken.
I'll trust in God's unchanging Word Till soul and body sever:
For though all things shall pass away, His Word shall stand forever."

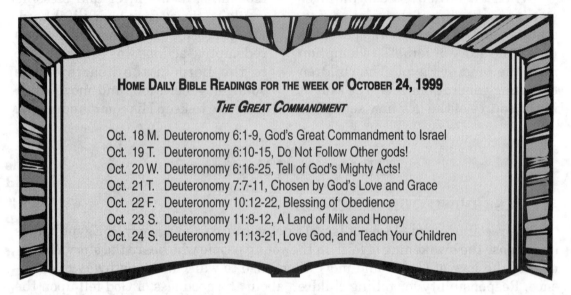

HOME DAILY BIBLE READINGS FOR THE WEEK OF OCTOBER 24, 1999

THE GREAT COMMANDMENT

Oct. 18 M. Deuteronomy 6:1-9, God's Great Commandment to Israel
Oct. 19 T. Deuteronomy 6:10-15, Do Not Follow Other gods!
Oct. 20 W. Deuteronomy 6:16-25, Tell of God's Mighty Acts!
Oct. 21 T. Deuteronomy 7:7-11, Chosen by God's Love and Grace
Oct. 22 F. Deuteronomy 10:12-22, Blessing of Obedience
Oct. 23 S. Deuteronomy 11:8-12, A Land of Milk and Honey
Oct. 24 S. Deuteronomy 11:13-21, Love God, and Teach Your Children

Know Your Bible

- The children of Israel had traveled to Moab when they encountered Sihon, and Og, both of whom were conquered and put to death. (Numbers 21:23-24, 33-35)
- Balak, king of Moab, was surprised and alarmed when he saw the children of Israel and sent for Balaam, a noted soothsayer, to curse the Israelites in order that he might have the upper hand. (Numbers 22:2-6)
- Balaam attempted to curse the Israelites, but was hindered by the command of God who allowed him to continue his journey, but to speak only that which God directed him to say. Balaam uttered a blessing instead of a curse. (Numbers 22:12-20; 23:8-10, 20-24)
- Joshua was of the tribe of Ephrain, one of Joseph's sons. (1 Chronicles 7:22-27)

Eternal God, You have shone us Your way through the power of Your Word. Fortify our spirits with Your presence. In the name and for the sake of Jesus Christ, we pray. Amen.

A Warning

Adult Topic—*Don't Lose Perspective*

•••••

Youth Topic—*Don't Forget*
Children's Topic—*Remembering God's Goodness*

•••••

Devotional Reading—Psalm 85
Background Scripture—Deuteronomy 8
Print—Deuteronomy 8:7-20

PRINTED SCRIPTURE

Deuteronomy 8:7-20 (KJV)

7 For the LORD thy God bringeth thee into a good land, a land of brooks of water, of fountains and depths that spring out of valleys and hills;

8 A land of wheat, and barley, and vines, and fig trees, and pomegranates; a land of oil olive, and honey;

9 A land wherein thou shalt eat bread without scarceness, thou shalt not lack any thing in it; a land whose stones are iron, and out of whose hills thou mayest dig brass.

10 When thou hast eaten and art full, then thou shalt bless the LORD thy God for the good land which he hath given thee.

11 Beware that thou forget not the LORD thy God, in not keeping his commandments, and his judgments, and his statutes, which I command thee this day:

12 Lest when thou hast eaten and art full, and hast built goodly houses, and dwelt therein;

13 And when thy herds and thy flocks multiply, and thy silver and

Deuteronomy 8:7-20 (NRSV)

7 For the LORD your God is bringing you into a good land, a land with flowing streams, with springs and underground waters welling up in valleys and hills,

8 a land of wheat and barley, of vines and fig trees and pomegranates, a land of olive trees and honey,

9 a land where you may eat bread without scarcity, where you will lack nothing, a land whose stones are iron and from whose hills you may mine copper.

10 You shall eat your fill and bless the LORD your God for the good land that he has given you.

11 Take care that you do not forget the LORD your God, by failing to keep his commandments, his ordinances, and his statutes, which I am commanding you today.

12 When you have eaten your fill and have built fine houses and live in them,

thy gold is multiplied, and all that thou hast is multiplied;

14 Then thine heart be lifted up, and thou forget the LORD thy God, which brought thee forth out of the land of Egypt, from the house of bondage;

15 Who led thee through that great and terrible wilderness, wherein were fiery serpents, and scorpions, and drought, where there was no water; who brought thee forth water out of the rock of flint;

16 Who fed thee in the wilderness with manna, which thy fathers knew not, that he might humble thee, and that he might prove thee, to do thee good at thy latter end;

17 And thou say in thine heart, My power and the might of mine hand hath gotten me this wealth.

18 But thou shalt remember the LORD thy God: for it is he that giveth thee power to get wealth, that he may establish his covenant which he sware unto thy fathers, as it is this day.

19 And it shall be, if thou do at all forget the LORD thy God, and walk after other gods, and serve them, and worship them, I testify against you this day that ye shall surely perish.

20 As the nations which the LORD destroyeth before your face, so shall ye perish; because ye would not be obedient unto the voice of the LORD your God.

13 and when your herds and flocks have multiplied, and your silver and gold is multiplied, and all that you have is multiplied,

14 then do not exalt yourself, forgetting the LORD your God, who brought you out of the land of Egypt, out of the house of slavery,

15 who led you through the great and terrible wilderness, and arid wasteland with poisonous snakes and scorpions. He made water flow for you from flint rock,

16 and fed you in the wilderness with manna that your ancestors did not know, to humble you and to test you, and in the end to do you good.

17 Do not say to yourself, "My power and the might of my own hand have gotten me this wealth."

18 But remember the LORD your God, for it is he who gives you power to get wealth, so that he may confirm his covenant that he swore to your ancestors, as he is doing today.

19 If you do forget the LORD your God and follow other gods to serve and worship them, I solemnly warn you today that you shall surely perish.

20 Like the nations that the LORD is destroying before you, so shall you perish, because you would not obey the voice of the LORD your God.

KEY VERSE

*Beware that thou forget not the LORD thy God, in not keeping his commandments, and his judgments, and his statutes, which I command thee this day.—**Deuteronomy 8:11***

OBJECTIVES

After reading this lesson, the student should be impressed that:

1. God's leading is a blessing;
2. God supplies our needs, even in the wilderness;
3. Prosperity may lead to ingratitude; and,
4. Ingratitude may lead to idolatry.

POINTS TO BE EMPHASIZED
Adult/Youth/Children
Key Verse: Deuteronomy 8:11
Print: Deuteronomy 8:7-20

—Moses advised the people to enjoy the good land the Lord was giving them and to bless God for the gift. (7-10)

—Moses warned the Israelites lest in their plenty they would fail to keep the Lord's Commandments. (11-13)

—Moses reminded the people that the Lord had brought them out of Egyptian bondage and provided for them in the wilderness. (14-16)

—Moses urged the Israelites to refrain from taking credit for their good fortune and to give due credit to the Lord. (17-18)

—Moses warned the people that if they turned away to follow other gods, they would perish like their enemies. (19-20)

(**Note**: Use KJV Scripture for Adults; NRSV Scripture for Youth and Children)

TOPICAL OUTLINE OF THE LESSON

I. INTRODUCTION

A. Prosperity
B. Biblical Background

II. Exposition and Application of the Scripture

A. Description of the Promised Land (Deuteronomy 8:7-9)
B. Danger of Ingratitude and Pride (Deuteronomy 8:10-14a)
C. Deliverance Forgotten (Deuteronomy 8:14b-17)
D. Destruction Caused by Disobedience (Deuteronomy 8:18-20)

III. Special Features

A. Preserving Our Heritage
B. A Concluding Word

I. Introduction

A. PROSPERITY

Today's lesson speaks to one of the issues brought up by those whom we label Prosperity Prophets. These are the radio preachers and televangelists who insist that all Christians should be rich in material goods. They argue: God is rich; God is in you; therefore you too should be rich; for the God who owns the silver and the gold, and the cattle upon a thousand hills, wants you to possess worldly goods as well. Failure (poverty), they say, is because of a lack of faith. We answer: What really is lacking is the ability to rightly divide (straight-cut) the Word of Truth. Furthermore, the philosophy of prosperity prophets seems to suggest God is an American. For surely what they espouse would not work among the multitudes of poverty-stricken genuine Christians living in various countries of Africa, Asia, and South America.

We learn from today's lesson that all too often material prosperity gets us into spiritual trouble. We wax fat and kick (Deuteronomy 32:15). Indeed, Moses predicted that Israel's material prosperity would lead to spiritual poverty. And throughout the Old Testament, God spoke to Israel through the prophets concerning this issue. In Jeremiah, we read that God had fed Israel to the full, the nation committed adultery (Jeremiah 5:7). In Hosea, it is stated that when filled from their pasture, Israel's heart was exalted; prosperity puffed them up (Hosea 13:6). Nehemiah likewise reminded Israel that once it ate, and was filled and became fat, it became disobedient, rebellious, despised the law and killed God's prophets (Nehemiah 9:25-26).

Perhaps, we should view material prosperity as a test. This is not to create ingratitude, but God wants to make us good stewards of whatever He gives us. It appears then that most of us are fruitful spiritually only in affliction (Genesis 41:52). The best attitude and the ideal answer to those who advocate prosperity by the "conceive it, believe it, achieve it" method is Habakkuk 3:17-18: "Although the fig tree shall not blossom, neither shall fruit be in the vine; the labor of the olive shall fail, and the fields shall yield no food; the flock shall be cut off from the fold, and there shall be no herd in the stalls; yet I will rejoice in the Lord, I will joy in the God of my salvation."

B. BIBLICAL BACKGROUND

Chapters seven through twelve of the book of Deuteronomy deal with the results of obedience and disobedience. First is the command to be separate. How harsh it sounds to the modern ear for God to command Israel to completely destroy the heathen nations before them. Make no covenant with them, show no mercy to them, do not intermarry with them. Utterly destroy their idols. Obey and God will bless you with victory over your enemies. This in essence is what Moses taught.

Furthermore, you "shall be blessed above all people" (Deuteronomy 7:14)—with many children, increase in flocks, sickness eliminated, deliverance from all your foes!—thus promised Jehovah. Finally, Moses reminds Israel how the Lord took care of them in the wilderness—manna, clothing that did not become old, feet that did not swell for forty years! With these things in mind, he exhorts them to obey God's commandments, walk in His ways, and reverence Him. This injunction has meaning with eternal significance.

II. Exposition and Application of the Scripture

A. DESCRIPTION OF THE PROMISED LAND (Deuteronomy 8:7-9)

For the LORD thy God bringeth thee into a good land, a land of brooks of water, of fountains and depths that spring out of valleys and hills; A land of wheat, and barley, and vines, and fig trees, and pomegranates; a land of oil olive, and honey; A land wherein thou shalt eat bread without scarceness, thou shalt not lack any thing in it; a land whose stones are iron, and out of whose hills thou mayest dig brass.

God is about to lead the Hebrews into a land where the naturally normal is a luxury compared to what Israel has experienced in the wilderness. Some fifteen aspects of the Promised Land are offered here: (1) It is described as a "good land." Use of the word "good" (TOB) includes practical, economic, and esthetic overtones (TWOT); (2) Brooks or streams of water. In a dry country, any perennial streams are highly valued; (3) Fountains or pools of water, along with; (4) Depths (waters under the earth) or springs that flow in the valleys and hills; (5) Wheat, a very valuable food commodity; (6) Barley, chiefly provender for horses and donkeys. A crop failure here would be a national disaster (Joel 1:11); (7) Vines; these are the grape vines. Grapes were eaten as fruit; cultivated as a source of sugar; and of course, wine was produced for drinking. Israel would inherit vineyards which they had not planted.

(8) Fig trees: figs were an important article of diet; (9) Pomegranates, one of the fruits the Israelites missed in the wilderness; (10) The cultivated olive tree, called "king of the trees" (Judges 9:8-9), was one of the most valued and useful trees in the land. Besides eating the olives, their oil was used for cooking, anointing, and illumination in their lamps; (11) Honey: in Old Testament times, honey was rare enough to be considered a luxury. The phrase "a land of olive trees and honey" has the same meaning as "a land flowing with milk and honey." It signifies a land filled with the abundance of good things; (12) Bread in the Old Testament stands for food in general. Bread is primary here, whereas in other parts of the world bread is considered only accessory. The promise is: Bread will not be scarce (NIV); (13) You will lack nothing (NI, RSV); (14) Next, the mineral wealth of the land is mentioned. Stones or rocks are iron; this ore was put to various uses: nails, axes, threshing instruments, weapons, fetters, armor, chariots, chisels, etc.; and (15) Copper is meant, for bronze or brass is an artificial product. That is, it is an alloy of copper and zinc (and/or tin). So the verse means: "You can dig copper out of the hills" (NASB, NIV, RSV). All of these items create a tremendous contrast with the dry, barren, unfruitful wilderness! It is obvious that the description of the Promised Land as a "good land" forms an important part of its message.

B. DANGER OF INGRATITUDE AND PRIDE

(Deuteronomy 8:10-14a)

When thou hast eaten and art full, then thou shalt bless the LORD thy God for the good land which he hath given thee. Beware that thou forget not the LORD thy God, in not keeping his commandments, and his judgments, and his statutes, which I command thee this day: Lest when thou hast eaten and art full, and hast built goodly houses, and dwelt therein; And when thy herds and thy flocks multiply, and thy silver and thy gold is multiplied, and all that thou hast is multiplied; Then thine heart be lifted up.

Gratitude is always in order, whether expressed for supernatural gifts like manna, or for the natural products like grapes and olives. In fact, believers are commanded to give God thanks in all things (1 Thessalonians 5:18). Failure to give God thanks is one of the first steps toward idolatry. The apostle Paul pointed this out in Romans 1:21: "neither were thankful, but became vain in their imaginations." When we have eaten and we are full, we should say, "Bless the Lord, O my soul, and all that is within me, bless His holy name" (Psalm 103:1).

Israel is exhorted to bless the Lord their God for the good land He has given them. Note, this is past tense used to express future certainty! Does it sound strange to speak of blessing God? The word *barak* literally means to kneel, suggesting some association between kneeling and the receiving of a blessing. Elsewhere it is rendered praise, salute. (Berachah Baptist Church is the Blessings Baptist Church). To bless God is to express thanksgiving and praise to Him because He has given out of the abundance of His life. "Where God is referred to, this word has the sense of 'praise'" (TWOT). Thus, Deuteronomy 8:10 in the NIV is: "When you have eaten and are satisfied, praise the Lord your God for the good land he has given you."

Moses continued with the warning that Israel take heed lest they forget the Lord. Such forgetfulness may be demonstrated by the failure to keep God's commandments, ordinances, and statutes.

Prosperity may make men forgetful, and forgetfulness leads to disobedience. One may define prosperity as: (1) A full belly; (2) Beautiful home, lofty, spacious mansion; (3) Multiplied herds and flocks; (4) Increased silver and gold; and (5) Increased possessions in general. Such luxury and ease have a way of blunting the edge of one's awareness and recognition of the hand of God. "Puffed-upness" suppresses the ability to recall the earlier days of slavery.

Pride is seen also as a lifting up of the heart. Such a heart is conceited, self-satisfied, one that depends not on God, but on itself, and gives self the credit for its prosperity. The heart includes the entire inner person: motives, feeling, emotions, affections, desire, will, aims, principles, thoughts and intellect (Girdlestone). The verb rendered "lifted" means to be high, lofty, to rise up. In this phrase, the height is used as symbolic of "negative notions such as arrogance and pride. Thus the high heart represents presumption or pride" (TWOT). Such a heart forgets the Lord.

C. DELIVERANCE FORGOTTEN
(Deuteronomy 8:14b-17)

And thou forget the LORD thy God, which brought thee forth out of the land of Egypt, from the house of bondage; Who led thee through that great and terrible wilderness, wherein were fiery serpents, and scorpions, and drought, where there was no water; who brought thee forth water out of the rock of flint; Who fed thee in the wilderness with manna, which thy fathers knew not, that he might humble thee, and that he might prove thee, to do thee good at thy latter end; And thou say in thine heart, My power and the might of mine hand hath gotten me this wealth.

Repeatedly, Israel is reminded of its deliverance from Egypt. God will not let the nation permanently forget what He did for them. Their lot in Egypt had been one of bondage; now, they were free from Pharaoh's whip. Moses then rehearses some of the events in which God delivered the Israelites while they were in the wilderness on their way to the Promised Land. With God's intervention in these and other ways, Israel's survival was guaranteed: (1) God led them in the wilderness wherein were fiery serpents and scorpions; (2) Where there was drought, no water, He brought water out of a rock of flint. The word flint, used only five times in the Old Testament, signifies here a hard tone; (3) He fed them manna; (4) He humbled them and; (5) Tested them; and (6) To do them good at their latter end. Keil and Delitzsch define the "latter end" as that time which follows some distinct point in life which is regarded as the end when it is contrasted with what happened before. Life in the Promised Land is the end; it is in contrast with the beginning—their life in Egypt and their wilderness journey.

These words remind us of Job. He lost most of his servants, as well as his sheep, goats, oxen, donkeys, camels; his seven sons and three daughters perished; he lost his health; he lost the compassion of his wife—but when the testing was over, the Lord "blessed the latter end of Job more than his beginning" (Job 42:12a). Surely, the God of the Bible is able to take a small beginning and cause the latter end to be greatly increased (Job 8:7). Yet after all these things, the time would come when Israel's heart would say, "Look what I have done."

By patting themselves on the back, they deny the Lord. Self-adulation enthrones self, not the Savior. "My power, the might of my hand has accomplished all this and gotten me this wealth." Immediately, we are reminded of the boasting of King Nebuchad-nezzar: "Is not this great Babylon, that I have built for the house of the kingdom by the might of my power, and for the honour of my majesty?" (Daniel 4:30). For his pride, his mind was taken away. For Israel's pride there was the threat of perishing!

D. DESTRUCTION CAUSED BY DISOBEDIENCE
(Deuteronomy 8:18-20)

But thou shalt remember the LORD thy God: for it is he that giveth thee power to get wealth, that he may establish his covenant which he sware unto thy fathers, as it is this day. And it shall be, if thou do at all forget the LORD thy God, and walk after other gods, and serve them, and worship them, I testify

against you this day that ye shall surely perish. As the nations which the LORD destroyeth before your face, so shall ye perish; because ye would not be obedient unto the voice of the LORD your God.

The command to remember is found often in Deuteronomy. For example: Israel is exhorted to remember they were slaves in the land of Egypt, and the Lord brought them out, redeemed them. Remember what the Lord did unto Pharaoh. Remember all the ways the Lord led them for forty years in the wilderness. Remember how they provoked God to wrath. Remember the day they came forth out of Egypt. Remember what Jehovah did to Miriam because of her rebellion against Moses. Remember what Amalek did to you!

The Hebrew word *zakar* means to imprint; it refers to inner mental acts. Remembering is contrasted with forgetting. Do remember, do not forget, the mercies, character and promises of God. Remembering the grace of God in our lives helps us to stay in His will. Truth in times of an empty stomach remains relevant in the times of a full stomach, so remember what you learned in the wilderness; it will come in good stead in the Promised Land. Do not forget that it is the Lord God who gives power to get wealth. He does this in order to establish His covenant which He swore to Abraham, Isaac, and Jacob. Warning is once again given that apostasy through idolatry would cause the destruction of the nation. The word perish is used twice in this closing warning. When used of persons it generally means physical death; used of nations, it speaks of their downfall, dissolution and desolation; it speaks of the devastation of crops; and the discouragement and dissipation of strength, hope, wisdom, knowledge, and wealth (Girdlestone). As God is faithful to His covenant, so Israel is exhorted to be faithful to the Lord. Obey His voice and be blessed! Praise Him for the abundance of all the good things He has provided.

III. Special Features

A. PRESERVING OUR HERITAGE

Study of Israel's subsequent history shows how necessary this warning was. The nation fell into idolatry, was conquered and taken into exile. To this day, Jews are scattered all over the world. Now what was written in the Old Testament is for our learning today (Romans 15:4). God's warning concerning prosperity and idolatry is a message to us. As a race, we too have increased in goods. The Black middle class has grown tremendously. But like all other people, prosperity is beginning to take its toll. Our wealth draws us to the casinos, and places of amusement. More wants more, so we are in great debt. Homicide still ranks high as the cause of death among young Black men. Evidently, church attendance is down; and the love, prayers and support so needed in this world's wilderness go lacking.

B. A CONCLUDING WORD

See in Jehovah's guidance of Israel a picture of His dealings with all believers. Spiritually, we were redeemed from slavery by the blood of Jesus Christ, but God has allowed us to remain in this wilderness world-system full of trouble. Through humiliation, afflictions, trials and testing, we move on. Christ interposes Himself, gives us strength for the journey, fights our battles, supplies our needs, and refreshes our souls. "Tho' sorrows befall us, and Satan oppose, Through grace we can conquer, defeat all our foes, God leads His dear children along. Some thro' the waters, some thro' the flood. Some thro' the fire, but all thro' the Blood; Some thro' great sorrow, but God gives a song, In the night season and all the day long" (G. A. Young; Gospel Pearls #53).

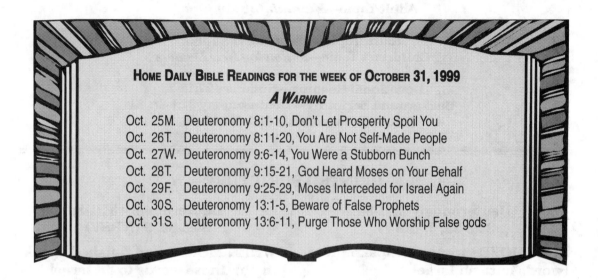

HOME DAILY BIBLE READINGS FOR THE WEEK OF OCTOBER 31, 1999

A Warning

Oct. 25M.   Deuteronomy 8:1-10, Don't Let Prosperity Spoil You
Oct. 26T.   Deuteronomy 8:11-20, You Are Not Self-Made People
Oct. 27W.   Deuteronomy 9:6-14, You Were a Stubborn Bunch
Oct. 28T.   Deuteronomy 9:15-21, God Heard Moses on Your Behalf
Oct. 29F.   Deuteronomy 9:25-29, Moses Interceded for Israel Again
Oct. 30S.   Deuteronomy 13:1-5, Beware of False Prophets
Oct. 31S.   Deuteronomy 13:6-11, Purge Those Who Worship False gods

Know Your Bible

- After Achan was punished for his sin, the Israelites attacked the city of Ai and destroyed it. (Joshua 8)
- Following the destruction of the city of Ai, Joshua performed a solemn act of obedience to the Lord by writing the law upon stone, and read its blessings and its curses on Mounts Gerizin and Ebal. (Joshua 8:30-35)
- When the Gibeonites heard of the victories of Israel, they deceived Joshua by sending messengers to him pretending that they did not live in the land of Canaan. (Joshua 9)
- The Gibeonites were spared because of a league entered into with Joshua that was confirmed by an oath. (Joshua 9:16-19)
- Because of their deception that was confirmed by an oath, the Gibeonites were forced to become hewers of wood and drawers of water. (Joshua 9:21)

O God, Thou hast set before us life and death as choices that are ours to make. We acknowledge that we are weak and inclined to choose those things that gratify our needs rather than glorify Thee. Direct our hearts and minds that we may choose You in whom there is life abundant. Amen.

Joshua Succeeds Moses

Unit III—*Entering the Promised Land*
Children's Unit—*Winning in God's Way*

•••••

Adult Topic—*Maintaining Continuity*

•••••

Youth Topic—*Receiving the Torch*
Children's Topic—*Following New Leaders*

•••••

Devotional Reading—Numbers 27:12-23
Background Scripture—Deuteronomy 31:1-8a, 34
Print—Deuteronomy 31:1-8; 34:5-8a, 9

PRINTED SCRIPTURE

Deuteronomy 31:1-8; 34:5-8a, 9, (KJV)

AND MOSES went and spake these words unto all Israel.

2 And he said unto them, I am an hundred and twenty years old this day; I can no more go out and come in: also the LORD hath said unto me, Thou shalt not go over this Jordan.

3 The LORD thy God, he will go over before thee, and he will destroy these nations from before thee, and thou shalt possess them: and Joshua, he shall go over before thee, as the LORD hath said.

4 And the LORD shall do unto them as he did to Sihon and to Og, kings of the Amorites, and unto the land of them, whom he destroyed.

5 And the LORD shall give them up before your face, that ye may do unto them according unto all the commandments which I have commanded you.

6 Be strong and of a good courage, fear not, nor be afraid of them;

Deuteronomy 31:1-8; 34:5-8a, 9 (NRSV)

WHEN MOSES had finished speaking all these words to all Israel,

2 he said to them: "I am now one hundred twenty years old, I am no longer able to get about, and the LORD has told me, 'You shall not cross over this Jordan.'

3 The LORD your God himself will cross over before you. He will destroy these nations before you, and you shall dispossess them. Joshua also will cross over before you, as the LORD promised.

4 The LORD will do to them as he did to Sihon and Og, the kings of the Amorites, and to their land, when he destroyed them.

5 The LORD will give them over to you and you shall deal with them in full accord with the command that I have given to you.

6 Be strong and bold; have no fear or dread of them, because it is the LORD your God who goes with

for the LORD thy God, he it is that doth go with thee; he will not fail thee, nor forsake thee.

7 And Moses called unto Joshua, and said unto him in the sight of all Israel, Be strong and of a good courage: for thou must go with this people unto the land which the LORD hath sworn unto their fathers to give them; and thou shalt cause them to inherit it.

8 And the LORD, he it is that doth go before thee; he will be with thee, he will not fail thee, neither forsake thee: fear not, neither be dismayed.

.....

5 So Moses the servant of the LORD died there in the land of Moab, according to the word of the LORD.

6 And he buried him in a valley in the land of Moab, over against Beth-peor: but no man knoweth of his sepulchre unto this day.

7 And Moses was an hundred and twenty years old when he died: his eye was not dim, nor his natural force abated.

8 And the children of Israel wept for Moses in the plains of Moab thirty days.

9 And Joshua the son of Nun was full of the spirit of wisdom; for Moses had laid his hands upon him: and the children of Israel hearkened unto him, and did as the LORD commanded Moses.

you; he will not fail you or forsake you."

7 Then Moses summoned Joshua and said to him in the sight of all Israel: "Be strong and bold, for you are the one who will go with this people into the land that the LORD has sworn to their ancestors to give them; and you will put them in possession of it.

8 It is the LORD who goes before you. He will be with you; he will not fail you or forsake you. Do not fear or be dismayed."

.....

5 Then Moses, the servant of the LORD, died there in the land of Moab, at the LORD's command.

6 He was buried in a valley in the land of Moab, opposite Beth-peor, but no one knows his burial place to this day.

7 Moses was one hundred twenty years old when he died; his sight was unimpaired and his vigor had not abated.

8 The Israelites wept for Moses in the plains of Moab thirty days.

9 Joshua son of Nun was full of the spirit of wisdom, because Moses had laid his hands on him; and the Israelites obeyed him, doing as the LORD had commanded Moses.

KEY VERSE

And the LORD, he it is that doth go before thee; he will be with thee, he will not fail thee, neither forsake thee: fear not, neither be dismayed.
—Deuteronomy 31:8

OBJECTIVES

After reading this lesson, the student will appreciate:

1. The role played by Moses in the life of Israel;
2. Moses' words of encouragement and warning to Israel;
3. Moses' words of encouragement to Joshua; and,
4. The smooth transition from Moses to Joshua.

POINTS TO BE EMPHASIZED

Adult/Youth/Children
Key Verse: Deuteronomy 31:8
Print: Deuteronomy 31:1-8; 34:5-8a, 9

—Moses informed the people of Israel that he would not enter the Promised Land with them. (31:1-2)
—Moses assured Israel that the Lord would bring them into the new land and give them victory. (3-6)
—Before all Israel, Moses told Joshua to be strong and bold for God had chosen him to lead and would go before him. (7-8)
—At age 120, Moses died and was buried in the land of Moab without having entered the Promised Land. (34:5-7)
—The Israelites mourned thirty days for Moses. (8)
—Having received the mantle of leadership from Moses, Joshua displayed the spirit of wisdom; and the Israelites followed him. (9)

(**Note**: Use KJV Scripture for Adults; NRSV Scripture for Youth and Children)

TOPICAL OUTLINE OF THE LESSON

I. Introduction

A. The Body of Moses
B. Biblical Background

II. Exposition and Application of the Scripture

A. The Last Words of Moses to Israel (Deuteronomy 31:1-6)
B. The Last Words of Moses to Joshua (Deuteronomy 31:7-8)
C. The Death of Moses (Deuteronomy 34:5-8a)
D. Joshua Succeeds Moses as Leader (Deuteronomy (34:9)

III. Special Features

A. Preserving Our Heritage
B. A Concluding Word

I. Introduction

A. THE BODY OF MOSES

In Numbers chapter twenty, we find the reasons why Moses was forbidden to enter the Promised Land. While gathered in Meribah-Kadesh, there was no water for the congregation. When the people murmured and contended with Moses and Aaron, the brothers went to the door of the tabernacle of the congregation, and there fell upon their faces. The glory of God appeared unto them, and the Lord instructed Moses to speak to the rock in front of the people, and it would gush forth its water, giving both people and beast the precious liquid. However, Moses said: "Hear now, ye rebels; must we fetch you water out of this rock?" He then lifted up his hand with the rod and struck the rock twice! And the water came out abundantly; all thirsts were quenched.

Consider what Moses did: First, when he said, "must we," he took credit for what God would do. Second, he disobeyed by striking the rock twice when he had been told to speak to it. Third, in unbelief, Moses and Aaron failed to sanctify the Lord in the eyes of the people. So God said: "Ye shall not bring this congregation into the land which I have given them" (Numbers 20:12). Aaron died first (Numbers 20:28), there atop Mount Hor. Moses was allowed to view the land as he stood on the top of Pisgah, over against Jericho, and then he too died. God buried him in a valley in the land of Moab, but no one ever discovered the burial place. We learn from the Letter of Jude, written centuries later, that the archangel Michael disputed with Satan about the body of Moses (Jude 9). We do not know why the dispute arose. Perhaps the Devil desired to build a shrine there, and cause the Israelites to fall into idolatrous worship of the bones of Moses. By keeping secret the burial place, this kind of idolatry and superstition was avoided. Whatever the nefarious purpose of Satan, he was thwarted. God, of course, was not finished using His servant Moses.

Later, Moses and Elijah would stand on the Mount of Transfiguration in Palestine, and talk there with the Lord Jesus Christ (Matthew 17:3). It is also believed that in the future, during what is called the Tribulation age, Moses (along with Elijah) will be one of the two witnesses working in earthly Jerusalem during the first half of that terrible period (Revelation 11). These are some of the answers offered as to why Satan was not allowed to confiscate the body of Moses. God intended returning Moses to finish his ministry. We believe when God buried Moses with His own hands, Moses' body escaped that corruption which normally sets in. Thus, Moses was put in the same category with "Enoch and Elijah."

B. BIBLICAL BACKGROUND

Having begun in Deuteronomy 1:5 the work of interpreting and enforcing the law, we find the work of legislation is brought to a close. The covenant had been renewed by the choice put before the congregation between blessing and curse, between life and death. But now as Moses' death approached, there remained still the task of leading the Israelites into Canaan. This leadership had to be provided by Joshua, whom Jehovah had appointed to succeed Moses. Furthermore, thorough completion of Moses' work included the completion of writing out the laws, and delivering to the priests the book of the law. Moses was also directed to recount Israel's history of rebellion and obstinacy; this was to be a witness against them. But also in teaching their history, they were reminded of the good hand of God in the life of the nation. To chapters thirty-one through thirty-two, chapter thirty-three is added, with its blessings upon the tribes in Moses' farewell to his beloved Israel. Finally, chapter thirty-four completes the Pentateuch with the recording of the death of Moses, a great servant of God in the house of Jesus Christ (Hebrews 3:1-6).

II. Exposition and Application of the Scripture

A. THE LAST WORDS OF MOSES TO ISRAEL
(Deuteronomy 31:1-6)

AND MOSES went and spake these words unto all Israel. And he said unto them, I am an hundred and twenty years old this day; I can no more go out and come in: also the LORD hath said unto me, Thou shalt not go over this Jordan. The LORD thy God, he will go over before thee, and he will destroy these nations from before thee, and thou shalt possess them: and Joshua, he shall go over before thee, as the LORD hath said. And the LORD shall do unto them as he did to Sihon and to Og, kings of the Amorites, and unto the land of them, whom he destroyed. And the LORD shall give them up before your face, that ye may do unto them according unto all the commandments which I have commanded you. Be strong and of a good courage, fear not, nor be afraid of them: for the LORD thy God, he it is that doth go with thee; he will not fail thee, nor forsake thee.

In beginning his charge to all the people, Moses makes known his age. It appears that his life's journey was divided into three parts. The first forty years were spent in the palace of Pharaoh, for Moses had been adopted by the king's daughter (Acts 7:23). The next forty years were lived in Midian with his father-in-law, Jethro (Acts 7:30). When commissioned to lead Israel out of the land of Egypt, he was eighty years old (Exodus 7:7). And now after forty years of a wilderness journey (Deuteronomy 29:5; Acts 7:36), he was one hundred and twenty years old! How interesting that it was Moses who wrote: "The days of our years are threescore years and ten; and if, by reason of strength, they be fourscore years, yet is their strength labor and sorrow" (Psalm 90:10).

Moses said: "I can no more go out and come in." Yet in Deuteronomy 34:7, we are told that when he died, "his eye was not dim, nor his natural force abated." The fact that he still retained the ability to work daily up to the very last moment of his life does not support the suggestion that he noticed he no longer had the stamina needed to lead Israel, especially in the military campaigns that were ahead. It is better to see the spiritual reason rather than seek any physical reason why Moses could no longer lead the Israelites. Thus, we are reminded that he was aware that God had forbidden him to go over Jordan into the Promised Land, even though able to do so physically. Moses had prayed that the Lord would let him go over and see the land that is beyond the Jordan; however, because of his disobedience at Meribah, the Lord refused his request; and told Moses not to speak to Him any more about this matter (Deuteronomy 3:25-26). Israel is given assurance that God will be their Vanguard, and will destroy the nations facing them, and make them Israel's possession. The nation is further informed that Joshua will be Jehovah's new mediatorial representative. Leadership of Israel is resigned into the hands of Joshua. Moses' parting words of encouragement to the people are: Be strong and of good courage. Do not fear, for God will fight for you; He will not fail you; He will not forsake you!

B. THE LAST WORDS OF MOSES TO JOSHUA (Deuteronomy 31:7-8)

And Moses called unto Joshua, and said unto him in the sight of all Israel, Be strong and of a good courage: for thou must go with this people unto the land which the LORD hath sworn unto their fathers to give them; and thou shalt cause them to inherit it. And the LORD, he it is that doth go before thee; he will be with thee, he will not fail thee, neither forsake thee: fear not, neither be dismayed.

Joshua, called Hoshea the son of Nun, and also called Jehoshua (Num-

bers 13:16), is first mentioned in Exodus 17:9, where he was made the leader of the army that defeated Amalek and his people with the edge of the sword. Now while both men stand together in Israel's sight, Moses personally gives Joshua the same charge as that given to Israel: "Be strong and of good courage." Jehovah Himself spoke these same words to Joshua; and likewise the people themselves encouraged Joshua's heart (Joshua 1:6, 7, 18). Joshua used these words to inspire the Israelites in their victory at Makkedah (Joshua 10:25). David's charge to Solomon recalls the words of Moses, as also the encouragement to build the temple (1 Chronicles 22:13; 28:20). Finally, hear king Hezekiah encourage the people to resist Sennacherib's invasion (2 Chronicles 32:7). God had promised this land to Abraham, Isaac and Jacob centuries earlier, and could not renege on His promise. As Jehovah would not fail or forsake Israel, so He would maintain Joshua. There was no need to be dismayed. The Hebrew word translated dismayed means to be broken. From this root is derived such ideas as to be abolished, be in panic, demoralized, terrorized, shattered. It was as if Joshua was told: "Be not dismayed, whate'er betide, God will take care of you."

C. THE DEATH OF MOSES
(Deuteronomy 34:5-8a)

So Moses the servant of the LORD died there in the land of Moab, according to the word of the LORD. And he buried him in a valley in the land of Moab, over against Beth-peor: but no man knoweth of his sepulchre unto this day. And

Moses was an hundred and twenty years old when he died: his eye was not dim, nor his natural force abated. And the children of Israel wept for Moses in the plains of Moab thirty days.

What a beautiful title, "servant of the Lord." The form of the Hebrew word *ebed* used here appears 799 times in the Old Testament (TWOT). Basically, it speaks of a slave, and is a title used of those who serve the Lord in very unique roles. This includes Abraham, Isaac, Jacob, Joshua, Caleb, David, Hezekiah, Eliakim, and Zerubbabel. God's prophets are also called servants. In the New Testament, two different words referring to Moses are used. In Hebrews 3:5, the word for servant is *therapon,* found only in the New Testament here: "Moses verily was faithful in all his house, as a servant. . . ." Trench states the *therapon* is the "performer of present services, with no respect to the fact whether as a freeman or slave he renders them. . . there goes with the word the sense of one whose services are tenderer, nobler, freer than those of the *doulos.*"

There is implied that he occupies a more confidential position, a freer service, a higher dignity, than that of a *doulos.* In Revelation 15:3, we read: "And they sing the song of Moses, the servant of God. . . ." Here the word for servant is *doulos.* This is the bond-man or bond-servant, one who is in permanent relation of servitude to another, "his will altogether swallowed up in the will of the other" (Trench). Moses was a model servant, one who made "as the Lord commanded" his life's motto.

Although at the age of one hundred and twenty when he died, we are impressed that Moses did not die of old age, but by the command of a sovereign God. In Psalm 90:10, Moses wrote that the normal life span was seventy or eighty years, but God allowed him to live beyond that. Two things are said about Moses' strength. First, his eye was not dim. Several different Hebrew words are used for the dimness of eyes, and have such meanings as: become dark, dazzled, heavy or weighty, stand still. But Moses' eyes are described as not becoming weak, or ineffective (TWOT). The idea of the eyes becoming weak in old age is prominent. Cataracts and degeneration of the retina caused senile blindness in Isaac, Jacob, Eli, and others. The frequency of senile dimness of sight made the case of Moses all the more remarkable, for at his age, his eye was not dim (ISBE). Second, we are told that "his natural force" did not abate. His vigor (NASB, NKJV), his strength (NIV) had not diminished. The Hebrew speaks of his moistness, freshness, greenness, newness! Thus, age had not reduced the "natural moisture and freshness of his body" (ICC).

D. JOSHUA SUCCEEDS MOSES AS LEADER (Deuteronomy 34:9)

And Joshua the son of Nun was full of the spirit of wisdom; for Moses had laid his hands upon him: and the children of Israel hearkened unto him, and did as the LORD commanded Moses.

Moses was commanded by God to lay his hand upon Joshua, and charge him in the sight of all the people (Numbers 27:18-13). Moses humbly did so. In Deuteronomy 31:14, Jehovah Himself directly gave the charge to Joshua. The laying on of hands symbolizes the bestowal of blessing; it points also to commissioning and conferring spiritual gifts. In the New Testament, Barnabas and Saul had hands laid on them (Acts 13:4); so did Timothy (1 Timothy 4:14), and others. After going through such a ceremony, we wonder if Joshua sang, "I know the Lord done laid His hand on me."

God described Joshua at that time as, "a man in whom is the Spirit." The Holy Spirit of wisdom dwelt in Joshua. Wisdom here is defined as a practical, administrative ability (ICC), showing itself in action. It was not until after the resurrection of our Lord that the Holy Spirit came to live in all believers, and make our bodies His temple. But in the Old Testament, we read that from time to time, the Spirit indwelt believers and gave them specific work to perform (Exodus 28:3). Bezaleel (Exodus 31:5), for example, was a "wisehearted", Spirit-filled craftsman, enabled by the Holy Spirit living in him to perform all kinds of manual skills, as well as "The intellectual wisdom and understanding essential to all art" (Scofield). Finally, it is suggested that Moses did not write his epitaph. Joshua probably wrote these final words; it is also possible that Eleazar or one of the elders added them. Having someone else record the death of Moses in no way alters the fact that Moses wrote the rest of the Pentateuch.

III. Special Features

A. PRESERVING OUR HERITAGE

The greatest hero of our slave foreparents was Moses, and the Spiritual, "Go Down, Moses," was extremely popular. Pharaoh, of course, represented the Devil. Some scholars believe the destruction of Pharaoh symbolized freedom from sin. Most experts in Negro Spirituals believe "Go Down, Moses" struck at the sinful institution of slavery. Thus, "Let My People Go" was the slaves' expression for freedom. It is said that Harriet Tubman used "Go Down, Moses" to call together those who were to be transported from the South. It is evident that there were those who hid behind Bible characters in their battle against slavery. Singing about Moses was intended to chide those who practiced or permitted such tyranny. By denouncing the Egyptian kings, they predicted the overthrow of oppression. What happened back in Moses' day could happen again! And so, "Go Down, Moses" was a song of hope. Note also in this Spiritual, the words, "No more shall they in bondage toil, Let them come out with Egypt's spoil." Reference is to Exodus 11:2-3, often used to support the demand to compensate (reparation) the descendants of Black Slaves. Now another hero was Joshua, Moses' successor. The slaves learned from Joshua's experience that they would have to continue to fight for their freedom. It was not just handed over to them on a silver platter. Joshua "fit" (fought) the battle of Jericho, and the walls (of slavery!) came tumbling down! Saints of color are encouraged to maintain not only our political freedom or civil rights, but more important, to stand fast in the freedom with which Jesus Christ has made us free, and not allow ourselves to be entangled again with the yoke of bondage which is legalism (Galatians 5:1). Remember: "Joshua was de son of Nun, He never would quit till his work was done."

B. A CONCLUDING WORD

Moses promised that the presence of God would go with Israel, and the Lord would destroy all their enemies, and help the nation possess the Promised Land. And so Israel was exhorted to be of good courage, and without fear. We learn that the power of the victorious life is in Jesus Christ. If we too will allow Him to work His way through us, we will learn that He will not fail us or forsake us. In Christ, we triumph over every foe.

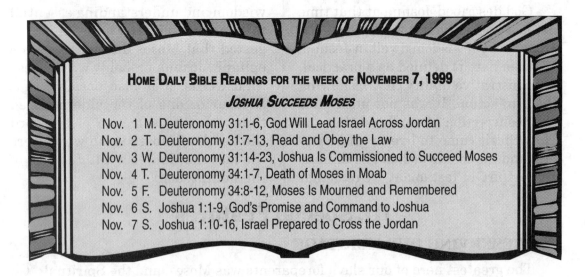

HOME DAILY BIBLE READINGS FOR THE WEEK OF NOVEMBER 7, 1999

JOSHUA SUCCEEDS MOSES

Nov. 1 M. Deuteronomy 31:1-6, God Will Lead Israel Across Jordan
Nov. 2 T. Deuteronomy 31:7-13, Read and Obey the Law
Nov. 3 W. Deuteronomy 31:14-23, Joshua Is Commissioned to Succeed Moses
Nov. 4 T. Deuteronomy 34:1-7, Death of Moses in Moab
Nov. 5 F. Deuteronomy 34:8-12, Moses Is Mourned and Remembered
Nov. 6 S. Joshua 1:1-9, God's Promise and Command to Joshua
Nov. 7 S. Joshua 1:10-16, Israel Prepared to Cross the Jordan

Know Your Bible

- Before God brought the final plague (the death of the firstborn) upon the Egyptians, God commanded the Israelites to have a Passover sacrifice and feast. (Exodus 12)
- Passover refers to the destroying angel "passing over" the homes of the children of Israel, who had sprinkled the lintels and the doorposts of their houses with the blood of the slain lamb. (Exodus 12:22-23)
- The special command given to Israel at the destruction of Jericho was that they should bring the silver and goal into the treasury of the Lord. (Joshua 6:18-19)
- Achan appropriated unto himself items that were to be dedicated to the Lord that resulted in the defeat of Israel in the battle with the men of Ai. (Joshua 7)
- For violating the command of the God not to take those things that were to be consecrated to the Lord, Achan and his family were put to death by stoning, and his goods were burned with fire. (Joshua 7:24-25)
- As soon as the land had rest from war, Joshua began to divide the land by lots in the presence of the Lord, and registered the various portions in a book. (Joshua 18:6-9)

O Thou who calls us to go forth although we cannot see our way, grant us the power to walk by faith as we surrender our lives in obedience and trust. In Jesus' name. Amen.

Israel Crosses the Jordan River

Adult Topic—*Going Forward in Faith*

•••••

Youth Topic—*Trusting Promises*
Children's Topic—*Trusting Others*

•••••

Devotional Reading—Joshua 4:15-24
Background Scripture—Joshua 3
Print—Joshua 3:7-17

PRINTED SCRIPTURE

Joshua 3:7-17 (KJV)

7 And the LORD said unto Joshua, This day will I begin to magnify thee in the sight of all Israel, that they may know that, as I was with Moses, so I will be with thee.

8 And thou shalt command the priests that bear the ark of the covenant, saying, When ye are come to the brink of the water of Jordan, ye shall stand still in Jordan.

9 And Joshua said unto the children of Israel, Come hither, and hear the words of the LORD your God.

10 And Joshua said, Hereby ye shall know that the living God is among you, and that he will without fail drive out from before you the Canaanites, and the Hittites, and the Hivites, and the Perizzites, and the Girgashites, and the Amorites, and the Jebusites.

11 Behold, the ark of the covenant of the LORD of all the earth passeth over before you into Jordan.

12 Now therefore take you twelve men out of the tribes of Is-

Joshua 3:7-17 (NRSV)

7 The Lord said to Joshua, "This day I will begin to exalt you in the sight of all Israel, so that they may know that I will be with you as I was with Moses.

8 You are the one who shall command the priests who bear the ark of the covenant, 'When you come to the edge of the waters of the Jordan, you shall stand still in the Jordan.'"

9 Joshua then said to the Israelites, "Draw near and hear the words of the LORD your God."

10 Joshua said, "By this you shall know that among you is the living God who without fail will drive out from before you the Canaanites, Hittites, Hivites, Perizzites, Girgashites, Amorites, and Jebusites:

11 the ark of the covenant of the Lord of all the earth is going to pass before you into the Jordan.

12 So now select twelve men from the tribes of Israel, one from

rael, out of every tribe a man.

13 And it shall come to pass, as soon as the soles of the feet of the priests that bear the ark of the LORD, the Lord of all the earth, shall rest in the waters of Jordan, that the waters of Jordan shall be cut off from the waters that come down from above; and they shall stand upon an heap.

14 And it came to pass, when the people removed from their tents, to pass over Jordan, and the priests bearing the ark of the covenant before the people;

15 And as they that bare the ark were come unto Jordan, and the feet of the priests that bare the ark were dipped in the brim of the water, (for Jordan overfloweth all his banks all the time of harvest,)

16 That the waters which came down from above stood and rose up upon an heap very far from the city Adam, that is beside Zaretan: and those that came down toward the sea of the plain, even the salt sea, failed, and were cut off: and the people passed over right against Jericho.

17 And the priests that bare the ark of the covenant of the LORD stood firm on dry ground in the midst of Jordan, and all the Israelites passed over on dry ground, until all the people were passed clean over Jordan.

each tribe.

13 When the soles of the feet of the priests who bear the ark of the LORD, the Lord of all the earth, rest in the waters of the Jordan, the waters of the Jordan flowing from above shall be cut off; they shall stand in a single heap."

14 When the people set out from their tents to cross over the Jordan, the priests bearing the ark of the covenant were in front of the people,

15 Now the Jordan overflows all its banks throughout the time of harvest. So when those who bore the ark had come to the Jordan, and the feet of the priests bearing the ark were dipped in the edge of the water,

16 the waters flowing from above stood still, rising up in a single heap far off at Adam, the city that is beside Zarethan, while those flowing toward the sea of the Arabah, the Dead Sea, were wholly cut off. Then the people crossed over opposite Jericho.

17 While all Israel were crossing over on dry ground, the priests who bore the ark of the covenant of the LORD stood on dry ground in the middle of the Jordan, until the entire nation finished crossing over the Jordan.

KEY VERSE

*Have I not commanded thee? Be strong and of a good courage; be not afraid, neither be thou dismayed: for the LORD thy God is with thee withersoever thou goest.—**Joshua 1:9***

OBJECTIVES

After reading this lesson, the student should have knowledge of:

1. The significance of the ark of the covenant;
2. The living God, the Lord of all the earth;
3. How God magnified Joshua; and,
4. The purpose of the miraculous crossing.

POINTS TO BE EMPHASIZED

Adult/Youth/Children
Key Verse: Joshua 1:9
Print: Joshua 3:7-17

—God promised to establish Joshua's leadership and gave him directions to give to the priests. (7-8)
—Joshua called the people together and told them that the crossing of the Jordan would be a sign of God's presence. (9-10)
—Joshua announced that when the priests bearing the ark of the covenant stood in the river, the waters would back up. (11-13)
—The priests bearing the ark of the covenant led the people into the river. (14)
—As the people moved toward the river, the priests stepped into the water, which then dried up while the people walked across Jordan. (15-16)
—The priests bearing the ark stood in the middle of the dry river bed until all the people had crossed the Jordan. (17)

(**Note**: Use KJV Scripture for Adults; NRSV Scripture for Youth and Children)

TOPICAL OUTLINE OF THE LESSON

I. Introduction

A. The Ark of the Covenant
B. Biblical Background

II. Exposition and Application of the Scripture

A. God's Plan to Magnify Joshua (Joshua 3:7)
B. God's Plan to Displace the Heathens (Joshua 3:8-10)
C. God's Command to Cross the Jordan (Joshua 3:11-13)
D. God's Miraculous Power Displayed (Joshua 3:14-16)
E. God's Command Obeyed (Joshua 3:17)

III. Special Features

A. Preserving Our Heritage
B. A Concluding Word

I. Introduction

A. THE ARK OF THE COVENANT

Seven times in today's lesson, the ark of the covenant is mentioned (verses 8, 11, 13, 14, 15-twice, 17); and ten times in the entire chapter of seventeen verses. God commanded the priests to bear the ark of the covenant of the Lord in front of the children of Israel. They were to carry the ark on their shoulders into the waters of the Jordan. As soon as their feet struck the Jordan, and their feet dipped in the brim of the water, the river would divide. And, the priests would find themselves standing on dry ground in the very midst of the Jordan, while all the people passed over. Now one truth that is significant is the central place held by the ark. It was carried before the people, so that all of them would have a clear view of the ark. We recognize that the ark symbolized the Lord Jesus Christ, who alone saves and keeps us saved. We are to keep our eyes upon Him, no matter what the test. "Turn your eyes upon Jesus, Look full in His wonderful face, And the things of earth will grow strangely dim, In the light of His glory and grace" (Helen H. Lemmel). A clear view of Him enables us to face the future, cross the un–crossable, and do the impossible!

Recall that in Exodus 25:10-16, Jehovah ordered Moses to build an ark of acacia wood. "They shall make an ark of acacia wood; it shall be two and a half cubits long, a cubit and a half wide, and a cubit and a half high. You shall overlay it with pure gold, inside and outside you shall overlay it, and you shall make a molding of gold upon it all around" (NRSV). Inside the ark, Moses was to place three things: (1) The tables of the law (Ten commandments), (2) The golden pot of manna, and (3) Aaron's rod that budded. Two cherubim were to be placed atop the ark. The ark was covered with gold inside and outside, and a gold molding all around. See then the ark as a symbol of the presence of God in the midst of His people (ISBE). This is the common teaching of the Old Testament. It strengthened, and comforted the believers, for the word "ark" implies safety.

B. BIBLICAL BACKGROUND

Our lesson is found in the midst of the preparation for entering the Promised Land. Joshua had been made the successor to Moses by God, and assumed command. Two spies were sent out to reconnoiter. News got out that spies were in the land, and the king of Jericho sent soldiers to Rahab's house to capture the Israeli spies, but Rahab had hidden them, and lied to the soldiers. Rahab had heard of the exploits of the Israelites; she knew that God had promised to give them the land, and she believed God. She had heard of Israel's miraculous deliverance from Egypt, and subsequent defeat of other enemies. So that faith, such as it was, moved her to request deliverance for her family and herself. Once the spies escaped, they returned to Joshua and gave a full report of their experiences and observations. The next day Joshua and the Israelites moved and came to Jordan, and lodged there. The assurance of the presence and power of God had empowered them with confidence.

II. Exposition and Application of the Scripture

A. GOD'S PLAN TO MAGNIFY JOSHUA (Joshua 3:7)

And the LORD said unto Joshua, This day will I begin to magnify thee in the sight of all Israel, that they may know that, as I was with Moses, so I will be with thee.

Jehovah spoke personally to Joshua, and promised to magnify him in the sight of all Israel. This was accomplished as recorded in Joshua 4:14, and caused Israel to fear (reverence) Joshua all the days of his life, even as they had feared (reverenced) Moses. The Hebrew word translated magnify is rendered exalt (NIV, RSV, NASB, NKJV), for the verb means to make or become great, or important, promote, make powerful, praise. It never refers to becoming numerous, but emphasizes greatness in the sense of importance. Inasmuch as God had chosen Moses, only God could replace him. Man cannot replace God's man. The same God who miraculously divided the Red Sea for Moses would soon accredit Joshua's leadership by opening the Jordan River.

What the Lord intended doing through Joshua would supersede what He had accomplished through Moses. And so there was about to begin a series of miracles which would serve to exalt Joshua in Israel's eyes as he fulfilled his office, and at the same time serve to put Israel in possession of the Promised Land. God intended making Israel aware of the fact that as He was with Moses, so He would be with Joshua. This action taken by God affirmed the continuity of His relationship with His chosen people.

B. GOD'S PLAN TO DISPLACE THE HEATHENS (Joshua 3:8-10)

And thou shalt command the priests that bear the ark of the covenant, saying, When ye are come to the brink of the water of Jordan, ye shall stand still in Jordan. And Joshua said unto the children of Israel, Come hither, and hear the words of the LORD your God. And Joshua said, Hereby ye shall know that the living God is among you, and that he will without fail drive out from before you the Canaanites, and the Hittites, and the Hivites, and the Perizzites, and the Girgashites, and the Amorites, and the Jebusites.

Having encouraged Joshua, the Lord then told him to tell the priests to bear the ark of the covenant to the edge of the water. Ordinarily, the Kohathites carried the ark (Numbers 4:15); Kohath was a son of Levi who was a son of Jacob (Israel). But on this occasion, the priests were to carry the ark. Joshua did as he was commanded, and the children of Israel gathered to hear God's Words. Driving out the inhabitants before the Israelites would be proof that the living God was indeed in Israel's midst.

The title, "the living God," occurs more than thirty times in the Bible. However, in the Old Testament passages, two different words for God are used. "El" is the word for God in Joshua 3:10, Psalms 42:2 and 84:2, and Hosea 1:10. In the other Old Testament verses, Elohim is used. God is said to be the "living God" in three ways: (1) Originally: He is life, the only source of life. He possesses life in Himself; (2)

Operatively: He alone gives life to all creatures: plants, insects, animals, humans, angels. He is God the Creator. From Him man receives natural, spiritual and eternal life; (3) Distinctively: in contrast to the dead impotent gods of the heathens, idols which cannot see, hear, or love, the God of the Bible is real, alive, and loving.

Israel was to learn that there was indeed a strong, living God in their midst, proven by the elimination or extermination of the Canaanites. In military operations, the verb rendered "drive out" signifies gaining control by conquering and expelling those people living in that area. Thus it came to mean dispossess, cast out, seize (TWOT). God promised to accomplish this dispossession without fail. The destruction of these nations is considered the purpose for God's miraculous guidance of Israel.

Now there are those who think that what is written concerning the elimination of these nations is too harsh, uncharacteristic of their concept of a God of love. They fail to see the sovereignty of God; they fail to see the moral basis of His acts. Four generations earlier, the Lord promised Abraham and his seed possession of this land. But the Amorites were allowed to continue in their sin until their cup was full, then God would dispossess them. Their idolatry, cruelty, immorality, witchcraft, child sacrifice—all ascended as a stench in the nostrils of God. Jehovah waited with longsuffering patience before He moved in judgment against the Canaanites, Hittites, Hivites, Perizzites, Girgashites, Amorites, and the Jebusites—"seven nations greater and mightier than" Israel (Deuteronomy 7:1-6).

C. GOD'S COMMAND TO CROSS THE JORDAN (Joshua 3:11-13)

Behold, the ark of the covenant of the Lord of all the earth passeth over before you into Jordan. Now therefore take you twelve men out of the tribes of Israel, out of every tribe a man. And it shall come to pass, as soon as the soles of the feet of the priests that bear the ark of the LORD, the Lord of all the earth, shall rest in the waters of Jordan, that the waters of Jordan shall be cut off from the waters that come down from above; and they shall stand upon an heap.

The title "the Lord of all the earth" is found twice here (verses 11, 13). It is suggested we translate verse eleven as follows: "Behold, the ark of the covenant. The Lord of all the earth is passing over before you into Jordan." In this way the ark represents the Lord. In other words, the ark containing the written law was the sign the Lord went in front of the people; He led the way against their enemies. By so doing, the Israelites could see that what they were getting into was not some manmade enterprise. Their God was in charge. True, the Israelites had to respond in faith. They had to walk; they had to present themselves; they had to step in the river—but without the leading of the Lord, they could not have crossed the Jordan dryshod. "Lord of all the earth" then is an appropriate title because it strengthened confidence in God's omnipotence.

D. GOD'S MIRACULOUS POWER DISPLAYED (Joshua 3:14-16)

And it came to pass, when the people removed from their tents, to pass over Jordan, and the priests

bearing the ark of the covenant before the people; And as they that bare the ark were come unto Jordan, and the feet of the priests that bare the ark were dipped in the brim of the water, (for Jordan overfloweth all his banks all the time of harvest,) That the waters which came down from above stood and rose up upon an heap very far from the city Adam, that is beside Zaretan: and those that come down toward the sea of the plain, even the salt sea, failed, and were cut off: and the people passed over right against Jericho.

As the people observed, the twelve men, one from each tribe, stepped into the water. Here, God's command was carried out. As the feet of the priests bearing the ark touched the water of the Jordan, a miracle took place. Water began to roll back; moved by the hand of God, the waters stood and rose up in one heap. This was all the more remarkable because at this time of year, the melting snows from Mount Hermon had caused the Jordan to overflow its banks. As the priests walked, the riverbed before them became dry. In fact, the waters were held back as far away as the city of Adam, the town on the same side of the Jordan as Zarethan, probably some twenty or thirty miles away! Even those streams south of the city of Adam, coming toward the sea of the Arabah (the Salt Sea) to the Jordan, were entirely cut off. The city of Adam is not mentioned elsewhere in the Bible.

E. GOD'S COMMAND OBEYED
(Joshua 3:17)

And the priests that bare the ark of the covenant of the LORD stood firm on dry ground in the midst of Jordan, and all the Israelites passed over on dry ground, until all the people were passed clean over Jordan.

Joshua commanded the people to pass over to where the ark of the Lord was held there in the midst of the Jordan (Joshua 4:5) by the twelve priests. All in one day, the Israelites made haste (Joshua 4:10), probably hundreds or thousands abreast, for there were approximately two and a half million Israelites at the time! It has been suggested that if the people stood a mile or more abreast, they could have crossed over in half a day (Keil & Delitzesh).

As the people followed the ark at a distance, they always kept it in view. Keeping the Lord Jesus Christ in view assures us of victory. The priests stayed in the middle of the riverbed until all Israel crossed over on dry ground opposite the city of Jericho. Attempts to explain what happened here as some natural occurrence all fail. Some scholars have suggested an earthquake took place.

The truth is, the God of the whole earth supernaturally opened a dry road through the Jordan river; His power arrested the flowing waters, made them rise "up in one heap," and remain that way until all of the children of Israel had safely passed over.

The story then is not some embellishment of the truth. Even as He used His power to open up the Red Sea, so now His omnipotence made a road through the Jordan. By His supernatural power, the Lord stabilized a wall of water until Israel's crossing was complete.

III. Special Features

A. PRESERVING OUR HERITAGE

The Jordan River was extremely popular to the slaves. It served as a "dividing line between time and eternity or between slave land and free land; a river chilly and cold that cannot stand still" (Lovell). Deep River, "one of the most deadly to the institution of slavery," refers to both free land and heaven after death: "My home is over Jordan, I want to cross over into Campground." See death, freedom, freedom in death, also in the Spiritual, "I Stood by de Ribber of Jordan." Sometimes heaven seemed so far away, when the slaves sang, "There's One Mo' Rive to Cross": "O, de river Jordan is so wide, One mo' river to cross. I don't know how to get on de other side; One mo' river to cross." Heaven is seen again in "Sin-Tryin' World": "Jordan's stream is chilly and wide, None can cross but the sanctified."

Again, the heaven theme appears in "Roll, Jordan Roll": "I wanter go to heav'n when I die, To hear ol' Jordan roll." Again, in "I Know de Udder Worl' Is Not Like Dis," we hear the words: "Jordan's river is a river to cross, I know de udder worl' is not like dis, Stretch yo' rod an' come across." Lovell states "Swing Low, Sweet Chariot," "very likely referred to free land" when it spoke of "home", although obviously Elijah was taken up into heaven: "I look'd over Jordan, an' what did I see, Comin' for to carry me home, A band of angels comin' after me, Comin' for carry me home."

Note this description of Jordan in "Stan' Still, Jordan": "Jordan river is chilly and cold. . . It will chilla my body, but not my soul." The converted slave had to tell it; he could not refrain from "letting out": "Lord, I can't stan' still." Finally, we National Baptists appreciate these words from another Spiritual (the title of which I did not find): "'Twas at the river of Jordan, Baptism was begun, John baptized the multitude, But he sprinkled nary one." Surely, there is good reason for us to continue singing about the Jordan River!

For some strange reason, the Promised Land became a picture of heaven. This is not an accurate assessment, however, for the following reasons: (1) There was fighting in the Promised Land. There will be no fighting in heaven. (2) The Israelites were twice dispossessed and then restored; but in heaven, "there'll be nobody there to put me out!" We learn then from the book of Joshua that Christians will always be involved in fighting evil if they sincerely seek to possess all of the abundant life God has promised us here on this earth (Scofield).

B. A CONCLUDING WORD

This was a momentous event in the history of Israel. We are reminded, however, that emphasis is not on heaven. Coming out of the wilderness and crossing the Jordan is not the same as leaving this earth and entering heaven. Canaan is not heaven, as we mentioned earlier in dealing with Negro Spirituals. Alan Redpath states: "The crossing of Jordan does not illustrate the passing of a soul into eternity, but rather does it illustrate the passing of a Christian from one level of Christian life to another." From our point of view, the river of impossibility lies between the life of wilderness wandering, grumbling, murmuring, fleshly effort, and, the life of faith, fighting as good soldiers of Christ, wearing His armor, and victorious living. The element of faith on the part of the priests who stepped into the flowing waters of the flooded river strikes us as something missing today in the lives of many professed Christians. We look at the river and feel it is impossible to cross. May our study of Joshua help us realize in a better way that with Christ all things are possible. In His will, there are no uncrossable rivers!

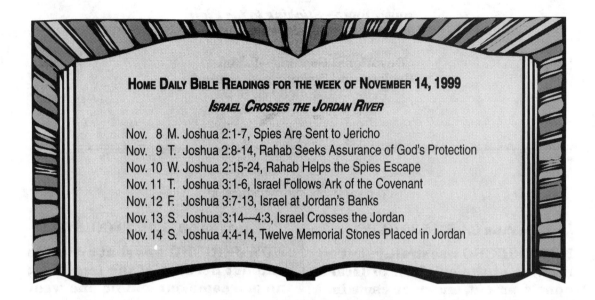

HOME DAILY BIBLE READINGS FOR THE WEEK OF NOVEMBER 14, 1999

ISRAEL CROSSES THE JORDAN RIVER

Nov. 8 M. Joshua 2:1-7, Spies Are Sent to Jericho
Nov. 9 T. Joshua 2:8-14, Rahab Seeks Assurance of God's Protection
Nov. 10 W. Joshua 2:15-24, Rahab Helps the Spies Escape
Nov. 11 T. Joshua 3:1-6, Israel Follows Ark of the Covenant
Nov. 12 F. Joshua 3:7-13, Israel at Jordan's Banks
Nov. 13 S. Joshua 3:14—4:3, Israel Crosses the Jordan
Nov. 14 S. Joshua 4:4-14, Twelve Memorial Stones Placed in Jordan

Know Your Bible

• The Lord ordered the destruction of the Canaanites because their wickedness and abominations had reached their heights. (Genesis 15:16; Deuteronomy 18:9)
• The hosts of warriors that fought against Joshua are described as numerous as the sand upon the seashore. (Joshua 11:4)
• Some of the Canaanites against whom the Israelites fought possessed chariots and horses, yet the Israelites completely conquered them because God was on their side. (Joshua 11:6-8; see also Romans 8:31)
• Joshua burned the city of Hazor with fire because it was the head of all the cities he had fought against, but this was not the last of his battles; he had many wars afterward until he had captured the whole land. (Joshua 11:15-23)

Eternal God, grant that our faith in You will be expressed in our willingness to follow Your command. May we regard the obstacles of life as opportunities to demonstrate our commitment, as we constantly depend upon You to undergird us with the consciousness of your presence and power. May we fulfil the high calling of God in Christ Jesus. Amen.

The Destruction of Jericho

Adult Topic—*Overcoming Obstacles*

•••••

Youth Topic—*Sticking to the Plan*
Children's Topic—*Solving Problems*

•••••

Devotional Reading—Psalm 47
Background Scripture—Joshua 6
Print—Joshua 6:1-5, 15-20

═══════════════════════════════

PRINTED SCRIPTURE

Joshua 6:1-5, 15-20 (KJV)

NOW JERICHO was straitly shut up because of the children of Israel: none went out, and none came in.

2 And the LORD said unto Joshua, See, I have given into thine hand Jericho, and the king thereof, and the mighty men of valour.

3 And ye shall compass the city, all ye men of war, and go round about the city once. Thus shalt thou do six days.

4 And seven priests shall bear before the ark seven trumpets of rams' horns: and the seventh day ye shall compass the city seven times, and the priests shall blow with the trumpets.

5 And it shall come to pass, that when they make a long blast with the ram's horn, and when ye hear the sound of the trumpet, all the people shall shout with a great shout; and the wall of the city shall fall down flat, and the people shall ascend up every man straight before him.

Joshua 6:1-5, 15-20 (NRSV)

NOW JERICHO was shut up inside and out because of the Israelites; no one came out and no one went in.

2 The LORD said to Joshua, "See, I have handed Jericho over to you, along with its king and soldiers.

3 You shall march around the city, all the warriors circling the city once. Thus you shall do for six days,

4 with seven priests bearing seven trumpets of rams' horns before the ark. On the seventh day you shall march around the city seven times, the priests blowing the trumpets.

5 When they make a long blast with the ram's horn, as soon as you hear the sound of the trumpet, then all the people shall shout with a great shout; and the wall of the city will fall down flat, and all

. . . . .

15 And it came to pass on the seventh day, that they rose early about the dawning of the day, and compassed the city after the same manner seven times: only on that day they compassed the city seven times.

16 And it came to pass at the seventh time, when the priests blew with the trumpets, Joshua said unto the people, Shout; for the LORD hath given you the city.

17 And the city shall be accursed, even it, and all that are therein, to the LORD: only Rahab the harlot shall live, she and all that are with her in the house, because she hid the messengers that we sent.

18 And ye, in any wise keep yourselves from the accursed thing, lest ye make yourselves accursed, when ye take of the accursed thing, and make the camp of Israel a curse, and trouble it.

19 But all the silver, and gold, and vessels of brass and iron, are consecrated unto the LORD: they shall come into the treasury of the LORD.

20 So the people shouted when the priests blew with the trumpets; and it came to pass, when the people heard the sound of the trumpet, and the people shouted with a great shout, that the wall fell down flat, so that the people went up into the city, every man straight before him, and they took the city.

the people shall charge straight ahead."

. . . . .

15 On the seventh day they rose early, at dawn, and marched around the city in the same manner seven times. It was only on that day that they marched around the city seven times.

16 And at the seventh time, when the priests had blown the trumpets, Joshua said to the people, "Shout! For the LORD has given you the city.

17 The city and all that is in it shall be devoted to the LORD for destruction. Only Rahab the prostitute and all who are with her in her house shall live because she hid the messengers we sent.

18 As for you, keep away from the things devoted to destruction, so as not to covet and take any of the devoted things and make the camp of Israel an object for destruction, bringing trouble upon it.

19 But all silver and gold, and vessels of bronze and iron, are sacred to the LORD; they shall go into the treasury of the LORD."

20 So the people shouted, and the trumpets were blown. As soon as the people heard the sound of the trumpets, they raised a great shout, and the wall fell down flat; so the people charged straight ahead into the city and captured it.

KEY VERSE

And it came to pass at the seventh time, when the priests blew with the trumpets, Joshua said unto the people, Shout; for the LORD hath given you the city.—**Joshua 6:16**

OBJECTIVES

After reading this lesson, the student should discern that:

1. Jericho was conquered God's way;
2. Spiritual battles are won with spiritual weapons; and,
3. God's judgment is according to truth.

POINTS TO BE EMPHASIZED

Adult/Youth/Children
Key Verse: Joshua 6:16
Print: Joshua 6:1-5, 15-20

—Israel laid siege to Jericho. (1)
—The Lord gave Joshua a plan for taking the city of Jericho. (2-5)
—Israel followed the plan, marching around the city with the ark of the covenant for six days. (6-14)
—On the seventh day the people marched around the city of Jericho seven times. (15)
—At the completion of the seventh encirclement of the city, Joshua ordered the people to shout and claim God's victory. (16)
—The Israelites were instructed to destroy certain vessels, give others to the Lord, and to spare only Rahab and her family. (17-19)
—As the Israelites shouted and the trumpets were blown, Jericho's wall collapsed, and the Israelites charged into the city and conquered it. (20)

(**Note**: Use KJV Scripture for Adult; NRSV Scripture for Youth and Children)

TOPICAL OUTLINE OF THE LESSON

I. Introduction
   A. Accursed
   B. Biblical Background

II. Exposition and Application of the Scripture
   A. God Calls Soldiers (Joshua 6:1-3a)
   B. God Chooses Strategy (Joshua 6:3b-5, 15-16)
   C. God Conquers Strongholds (Joshua 6:17-20)

III. Special Features
   A. Preserving Our Heritage
   B. A Concluding Word

I. Introduction

A. ACCURSED

In today's lesson, the word "accursed" (cherem, or charam) is used four times, and the word "curse," once (Joshua 6:17-18). Indeed, the word accursed is found more often in the book of Joshua than in the rest of the Bible combined. The root word means to separate, shut off. That which is separated to God's service is that which is irrevocably surrendered to Him. There are two ways of looking at that which is "devoted" to God. If the thing impedes or resists God's work, then it is considered accursed before the Lord. Jericho stood in the way of God's plan for Israel.

Whatever, if spared, would corrupt or contaminate Israel's religious life was considered "accursed." Whatever was hostile to the Theocracy was accursed. The policy was to exterminate people and destroy things which might "paganize" the unique religion of Israel. This was a sure way of preventing contamination. Consequently, idols, idolatrous persons and cities were banned. Wherever the cult of Baal flourished, those towns were destroyed: Jericho, Ai, Makkedah, Hazor, etc. The ban did not always apply to the silver, gold, or vessels of bronze and of iron. At times, these would be kept and put into the treasury of the house of the Lord (Joshua 6:21-24).

Now there are those who have problems with the ban. In the case of Jericho, the city was burned with fire, and all who lived there were destroyed: "Both man and woman, young and old, and ox, and sheep, and donkey, with the edge of the sword" (Joshua 6:21).

Would a God of Love exterminate "the innocent"? Consider the following: (1) The wages of sin is death. We are all sinners, all deserve to die. How we die, when, or where is up to a Sovereign God. He has the right to use one sinner or sinful nation to destroy another. It is absolutely essential to believe this in order to have some understanding of Divine Judgment; (2) The nations had been warned. But in filling up the measure of their cup of iniquity, their destruction at the hands of the Israelites was their just due. The moral perversity of the land called for Divine destruction. And we can be sure that the judgment of God is according to truth (Romans 2:2).

(3) What Israel did was at God's command. It was not Israel's responsibility, nor an effort to accomplish personal revenge; (4) Jericho's destruction was not for booty or plunder; the precious metals were devoted to God, and therefore accursed for man's use; (5) A holy and just God always avenges the right and punishes the evil. Anyone having problems with the extermination of the citizens of Jericho will also have problems with the Flood, the plagues of Egypt, the burning of Sodom and Gomorrah, and of course with the whole idea of eternal punishment in Hell; (6) Yes, God is Love, but He is also Holy. His love does not stop Him from maintaining His holiness; (7) Annihilation of the wicked inhabitants of Jericho was not done in order to satisfy Israel's desire for military glory. The Israelites from the beginning knew that Israel, the smallest of nations, would not be a super

power or conqueror in its own strength, but in the strength of the Lord; (8) Israel's triumph over their foes was not a meritorious reward from the Lord. After all, the wilderness journey was plagued with episodes of murmuring, complaining, and rebellion by the disobedient Israelites. If the Lord had not remembered His covenant promise, Israel would have perished there in the wilderness.

(9) The destruction of the Canaanites was needed as security against Israel's falling into idolatry and being spiritually demoralized; (10) Finally, it is suggested that instead of finding fault with God for meting out deserved punishment to the evildoers in Canaan, we ought to praise God for the grace shown in saving Rahab and her family. These points (some of them obviously overlapping) may not satisfy all hearts, for all too often we read Old Testament history with twentieth century eyes. And our values—westernized, Americanized, acculturated—uninformed by scriptural insight, create in us an unwillingness to see that

the God of the Bible is holy and righteous in all His deeds.

B. BIBLICAL BACKGROUND

Scholars are not sure when the conquest of Palestine began. The Scofield Bible note suggests about 1407 B.C; Eerdman's Handbook states, about 1240 B.C. Now three military campaigns were used to conquer the land. Joshua's first thrust was into the center of the country. He sought to drive a wedge between north and south. Thus, Jericho became his first target, so Joshua planned to divide and conquer. Later, there would be a southern campaign (chapters 9-10) and a northern campaign (chapter 11).

The first military foray consisted of two main engagements: one at Jericho, the other at Ai. Victorious at Jericho, the Israelites were temporarily defeated at Ai because of the disobedience and defiance of Achan who stole goods that should have been destroyed. Later Ai was captured. And eventually God's promise was fulfilled (Joshua 21:43-45).

II. Exposition and Application of the Scripture

A. GOD CALLS SOLDIERS
(Joshua 6:1-3a)

NOW JERICHO was straitly shut up because of the children of Israel: none went out, and none came in. And the LORD said unto Joshua, See, I have given into thine hand Jericho, and the king thereof, and the mighty men of valour. And ye shall compass the city, all ye men of war, and go round about the city once.

Jericho, the city of Palm trees (Deu-

teronomy 34:3), compared by our standards today, was a small city. It was apparently an important and wealthy city, a principal stronghold of the Canaanites. But this strongly fortified city stood directly in the way of Israel, so that is was absolutely necessary to conquer Jericho in order to advance in Palestine. The Canaanites had heard of Israel's deliverance from Egypt, and their victory over all opposition. Recall that Rahab had said earlier: "I know that the Lord has given you the land, and that your terror is fallen upon us, and that all the inhabitants of the land faint because of you" (Joshua 2:9).

It is understandable that the city was barricaded, so tightly shut up so that no one went out, and no one entered the walled city. However, their shut gates and high walls kept them in, but did not keep the Israelites out. God encouraged Joshua by assuring him that Jericho's fall was a done deal. Joshua simply had to carry out what the Lord had accomplished. Jericho's king and the mighty men of valor of his army were defeated already! Note that "all ye men of war" were to surround the city once a day. This suggests God did not require the entire population of Israel (nearly two and a half million) to march around Jericho—only the soldiers, the men of war, marched, accompanied by the seven priests. Under the law of Moses, all men became liable for military service "from twenty years old and upward, all who are able to go forth to war in Israel" (Numbers 1:3, 26:2). Of course, this was in preparation for entering the Promised Land.

There were exceptions to the conscription: (1) Levites were exempt (Numbers 2:33); (2) The man who recently built a home was exempt; and (3) The one who just planted a vineyard; and (4) Likewise the newly married man; and finally, (5) The fearful, fainthearted or timid (Deuteronomy 20:5-8). God determined who the soldiers would be; He was the One who called them. It is obvious that the Lord called Joshua (Joshua 1:1, 5); and thus Joshua assumed command of the armies of Israel.

B. GOD CHOOSES STRATEGY
(Joshua 6:3b-5, 15-16)

Thus shalt thou do six days. And seven priest shall bear before the ark seven trumpets of rams' horns: and the seventh day ye shall compass the city seven times, and the priests shall blow with the trumpets. And it shall come to pass, that when they make a long blast with the ram's horn, and when ye hear the sound of the trumpet, all the people shall shout with a great shout; and the wall of the city shall fall down flat, and the people shall ascend up every man straight before him. And it came to pass on the seventh day, that they rose early about the dawning of the day, and compassed the city after the same manner seven times: only on that day they compassed the city seven times. And it came to pass at the seventh time, when the priests blew with the trumpets, Joshua said unto the people, Shout; for the LORD hath given you the city.

Here is the plan put forth by the Lord for the conquest of Jericho. The soldiers are to go round the city silently once a day for six days, accompanied by the seven priests bearing seven (jubilee) trumpets of rams' horns. The priests are to blow the trumpets as they march and carry the ark of the covenant. Each night, they all return to their camp at Gilgal. On the seventh day, the soldiers, still in silence, are to march round Jericho seven times, still accompanied by the priests carrying the ark. On the seventh go-round on this seventh day, the priests are to make a long blast with the rams' horn, and when the people hear this sound of the trumpet, all the people are to shout with a great shout. This was God's strategy revealed to Joshua.

Several things come to our attention. Note the prominent role played by the priests, and the place of the ark of the covenant. God's presence in the very center of the march is symbolized. We see also the prominence of the number seven: priests, trumpets, days, etc. The number seven speaks of Divine perfection and completeness. It is embodied in the Hebrew word to swear. Thus to swear is to seven oneself, that is, make a thing binding by repeating the word or act seven times. God's perfect strategy is seen with respect to the destruction of Jericho. His judgment is complete!

Throughout the Bible, shouting was used as a war cry in the tumult of battle, a signal for war, victory over an enemy, alarm in case of attack. The shout was heard also in praise of God, acclamation of a king being enthroned, exaltation of the people, and in rituals of the tabernacle. Used eight times in Joshua chapter six, the primary meaning of the verb (rua) is "to raise a noise" by shouting or with an instrument, especially a horn (TWOT).

C. GOD CONQUERS STRONG-HOLDS (Joshua 6:17-20)

And the city shall be accursed, even it, and all that are therein, to the LORD: only Rahab the harlot shall live, she and all that are with her in the house, because she hid the messengers that we sent. And ye, in any wise keep yourselves from the accursed thing, lest ye make yourselves accursed, when ye take of the accursed thing, and make the camp of Israel a curse, and trouble it. But all the silver, and gold, and vessels of brass and iron, are consecrated unto the LORD: they shall come into the treasury of the LORD. So the people shouted when the priests blew with the trumpets: and it came to pass, when the people heard the sound of the trumpet, and the people shouted with a great shout, that the wall fell down flat, so that the people went up into the city, every man straight before him, and they took the city.

Once again, promise is made to deliver Rahab the prostitute, and all of her family. The Israelites are warned again not to take any of the riches of the city, for the city is accursed. However, the silver, gold, and vessels of bronze are to be consecrated unto the Lord and placed in the treasury of His house. Joshua and the Israelites did as Jehovah commanded. At the last march, at the sound of the trumpet, the people gave a shout, and the walls came crashing down!

Some liberal scholars have suggested there was nothing miraculous about all this. They claim the walls were old and crumbly, so that the vibrations from the trumpets and the shouting loosened the mortar and caused the walls to fall flat. Others say there was a providentially timed earthquake! Whatever caused the wall to collapse (fall in its place), it was by the hand of God. We see the supernatural; we see the miracle of timing and the completeness of destruction, we see the fulfilling of prophecy. We believe Hebrews 11:30: "By faith the walls of Jericho fell down, after they were compassed about seven days." And we hear again these words from the Negro Spiritual:

Up to de walls ob Jerico, He marched with spear in Han'.
"Go blow dem ram horns" Joshua cried, "Kase de battle am in my han'."
Den de lam' ram sheep horns begin to blow, trumpets begin to soun',
Joshua commanded de chillen to shout, An' de walls come tumblin' down.

III. Special Features

A. PRESERVING OUR HERITAGE

The Negro Spiritual, "Joshua Fit (Fought) de Battle ob Jerico," comes to our attention in today's lesson. In the minds of our slave ancestors, Jericho was the place of a famous battle where the forces of good defeat the forces of evil (Lovell). See in the Battle of Jericho the picture of a group of recently divinely emancipated slaves about to do battle with a well-equipped, superior army of Canaanites. These enemies must be fought, because they seek to keep the ex-slaves out of their Promised Land. It is necessary to fight for freedom, for the wicked enemy is deeply entrenched. Thus, we see slave "militancy disguised in religious imagery." No wonder Joshua is praised:

"You may talk about yo' king ob Gideon, You may talk about yo' man ob Saul,
Dere's none like good ole Joshua, At de battle ob Jerico."

Today's lesson encourages us to fight the Jerichos in our lives, all those things which would hinder us from conquering and celebrating the victory. Racism still confronts us, and seeks to detain, slow up, prevent us from possessing that which the Lord Jesus wants us to have and to richly enjoy. Thank God for the gift of faith, for Jericho city is too big, its army too powerful, its impregnable walls too high for us to conquer in our own strength. "By faith the walls of Jericho fell down. . ." (Hebrews 11:30). The Lord waits for that moment in our lives when we surrender to Him in order for Him to fight our battles. It is then in faith we have the assurance that "every Jericho in the world will fall" (Redpath).

B. A CONCLUDING WORD

If the called soldiers of Christ let God choose the strategy, and conquer the stronghold, they will indeed always celebrate the success. Let us not forget that God is in charge, that He is a Man of War, the Hero of the Hour. Jesus Christ is indeed the Captain of our Salvation, our Commander-in-Chief, the General who decides strategy. Sometimes, we presumptuously choose our own strategy and weapons. We start off wrong by selecting our own battlefield, even while singing, "I'm on the Battlefield for My Lord."

And what an extensive arsenal He has. At His bidding, there are grasshoppers available to devour, rivers to change their courses; a sun to stand still; seas and rivers to open up and provide dry paths. He can paralyze with a snow storm; flood the earth with rain from above and break up the deep beneath. He holds hurricanes in His fist, snaps His fingers and thunderbolts crash, blinks His eyes and lightning flashes, stomps His feet and earthquakes devastate the land. In

God's arsenal may be found worms that eat whatever commanded; the jawbone of a donkey, a small smooth stone for a slingshot, poisonous snakes that bite murmurers; blindness, confusion of tongues, etc.

In short, we learn that spiritual victories are won by means considered foolish by the world (Scofield). All that is thought too small, unsophisticated, insignificant, impotent, inadequate and naïve by men, God has in His stock of weapons. He will use what is deemed foolish by man to confound men who think they are wise. Surely, the destruction of Jericho encourages our hearts as we press on in the battle of life. Our JOSHUA, the Lord Jesus Christ, continues to lead us in triumph! (2 Corinthians 2:14).

HOME DAILY BIBLE READINGS FOR THE WEEK OF NOVEMBER 21, 1999

THE DESTRUCTION OF JERICHO

Nov. 15   M.   Joshua 5:10-15, The Passover Celebrated at Gilgal
Nov. 16   T.   Joshua 6:1-7, Israel Begins Conquest of Jericho
Nov. 17   W.   Joshua 6:8-14, Six-Day March Around Jericho's Walls
Nov. 18   T.   Joshua 6:15-20, Destruction of Jericho by Israel
Nov. 19   F.   Joshua 6:22-25, 27, Rahab and Her Family Are Spared
Nov. 20   S.   Joshua 8:30-35, Joshua Renews the Covenant
Nov. 21   S.   Psalm 44:1-8, A Sacred Song of Remembrance

Know Your Bible

- The Feast of Passover or Unleavened Bread began on the fifteenth day of the month (about March or April), and was observed by the sacrifice of a lamb, the use of unleavened bread and the offering of the first fruits of the early harvest. (Leviticus 23:5-6)
- While God fed Israel with manna during their stay in the wilderness, they ungratefully and discontentedly desired to change their food. (Numbers 11:1-6)
- The cowardly report concerning the people in the land of Canaan and the walled cities brought great distress to the Israelites, and they proposed to Moses that they return to Egypt. (Numbers 14:1-4)
- Caleb and Joshua, in their minority report to Moses, affirmed that the Lord was with Israel, and that they did not need to fear the inhabitants of the land of Canaan. (Numbers 14:6-9)

Eternal God, we have experienced the bitterness of oppression and have witnessed Your grace in breaking down the walls that separated us from You and from one another. We claim Your victory as we re-dedicate ourselves and that which we have to Your cause. Amen.

Choosing to Serve the Lord

Adult Topic—*Making the Right Choice*
•••••
Youth Topic—*Making Life's Choices*
Children's Topic—*Renewing Promises*
•••••
Devotional Reading—Joshua 24:14-24
Background Scripture—Joshua 24
Print: Joshua 24:1-2, 14-22, 25

PRINTED SCRIPTURE

Joshua 24:1-2, 14-22, 25 (KJV)

AND JOSHUA gathered all the tribes of Israel to Shechem, and called for the elders of Israel, and for their heads, and for their judges, and for their officers; and they presented themselves before God.

2 And Joshua said unto all the people,

•••••

14 Now therefore fear the LORD, and serve him in sincerity and in truth: and put away the gods which your fathers served on the other side of the flood, and in Egypt; and serve ye the LORD.

15 And if it seem evil unto you to serve the LORD, choose you this day whom ye will serve; whether the gods which your fathers served that were on the other side of the flood, or the gods of the Amorites, in whose land ye dwell: but as for me and my house, we will serve the LORD.

16 And the people answered and

Joshua 24:1-2, 14-22, 25 (NRSV)

THEN JOSHUA gathered all the tribes of Israel to Shechem, and summoned the elders, the heads, the judges, and the officers of Israel; and they presented themselves before God.

2 And Joshua said to all the people,

•••••

14 "Now therefore revere the LORD, and serve him in sincerity and in faithfulness; put away the gods that your ancestors served beyond the River and in Egypt, and serve the LORD.

15 Now if you are unwilling to serve the LORD, choose this day whom you will serve, whether the gods your ancestors served in the region beyond the River or the gods of the Amorites in whose land you are living; but as for me and my household, we will serve the LORD."

16 Then the people answered,

said, God forbid that we should forsake the LORD, to serve other gods;

17 For the LORD our God, he it is that brought us up and our fathers out of the land of Egypt, from the house of bondage, and which did those great signs in our sight, and preserved us in all the way wherein we went, and among all the people through whom we passed:

18 And the LORD drave out from before us all the people, even the Amorites which dwelt in the land: therefore we will also serve the LORD; for he is our God.

19 And Joshua said unto the people; Ye cannot serve the LORD: for he is an holy God; he is a jealous God; he will not forgive your transgressions nor your sins.

20 If ye forsake the LORD, and serve strange gods, then he will turn and do you hurt, and consume you, after that he hath done you good.

21 And the people said unto Joshua, Nay; but we will serve the LORD.

22 And Joshua said unto the people, Ye are witnesses against yourselves that ye have chosen you the LORD, to serve him. And they said, We are witnesses.

.....

25 So Joshua made a covenant with the people that day, and set them a statute and an ordinance in Shechem.

"Far be it from us that we should forsake the LORD to serve other gods;

17 for it is the LORD our God who brought us and our ancestors up from the land of Egypt, out of the house of slavery, and who did those great signs in our sight. He protected us along all the way that we went, and among all the peoples through whom we passed;

18 and the LORD drove out before us all the peoples, the Amorites who lived in the land. Therefore we also will serve the LORD, for he is our God."

19 But Joshua said to the people, "You cannot serve the LORD, for he is a holy God. He is a jealous God; he will not forgive your transgressions or your sins.

20 If you forsake the LORD and serve foreign gods, then he will turn and do you harm, and consume you, after having done you good."

21 And the people said to Joshua, "No, we will serve the LORD!"

22 Then Joshua said to the people, "You are witnesses against yourselves that you have chosen the LORD, to serve him." And they said, "We are witnesses."

.....

25 So Joshua made a covenant with the people that day, and made statutes and ordinances for them at Shechem.

KEY VERSE

And the people said unto Joshua, The LORD our God will we serve, and his voice will we obey. —Joshua 24:24

OBJECTIVES

After reading this lesson, the student should be aware that:

1. God desires worship in spirit and truth;
2. Man has many gods, but there is only one true God;
3. A jealous God will not tolerate idolatry;
4. Life is full of important choices; and,
5. The choices we make are witnesses against us.

POINTS TO BE EMPHASIZED

Adult/Youth/Children
Key Verse: Joshua 24:24
Print: Joshua 24:1-2, 14-22, 25

—Joshua gathered all the tribes of Israel at Shechem and spoke to all the people. (1-2)

—Joshua called the people of Israel to choose between the Lord and other gods, and he declared his intention to serve the Lord. (14-15)

—The people answered that they would serve the Lord, who brought them out of Egypt into a new land. (16-18)

—Joshua challenged the people on the seriousness of their pledge and warned them of the consequences of failing to keep it. (19-20)

—Joshua told the people that in choosing to serve the Lord they were witnesses against themselves; and the people agreed. (21-22)

—Joshua completed the covenant ceremony and specified the statutes and ordinances of the agreement. (25)

(**Note**: Use KJV Scripture for Adults; NRSV Scripture for Youth and Children)

TOPICAL OUTLINE OF THE LESSON

I. Introduction
A. A Jealous God
B. Biblical Background

II. Exposition and Application of the Scripture
A. The Call to Assemble (Joshua 24:1-2)
B. The Choice to be Made (Joshua 24:14-18)
C. The Challenge to Israel (Joshua 24:19-22)
D. The Covenant at Shechem (Joshua 24:25)

III. Special Features
A. Preserving Our Heritage
B. A Concluding Word

I. Introduction

A. A JEALOUS GOD

In his final words to the nation, Joshua reminded the people that Jehovah is "an holy God, he is a jealous God" (Joshua 24:19). Seven times the Bible informs us that the true and living God is a jealous God. It is in the Second Commandment (Exodus 20:5) that this characterization of God is first given, and in Exodus 34:14, we learn that this jealous God is also named, Jealous. Other Scriptures dealing with this matter are: Deuteronomy 4:24, 5:9, 6:15; and Nahum 1:2. The word "jealousy" brings to mind the human emotion we call envy, but envy plays no part whatever in God's makeup. What do we have that would make God jealous in this sense? He gave us all we have (1 Corinthians 4:7). Indeed, "the earth is the Lord's and the fulness thereof, the world, and they that dwell therein" (Psalm 24:1).

Another definition of jealousy comes to mind when we think of the relationship between husband and wife. Jehovah was married to Israel. God's love is compared to that of an ideal husband; it is a love that gives itself unreservedly, and expects an undivided love in return. When Israel worshiped idols, Israel was guilty of spiritual fornication. Her apostasy is called adultery; her idolatry is called whoremongering. This is strong language! Israel was to worship God and Him alone. He alone claimed Israel's love.

Our study reveals that holiness is also involved in the definition of Divine jealousy. His holiness will not tolerate adultery. It is at this point we bring in the word zealous for jealous. Jealousy becomes that zeal whereby God maintains His holiness and righteous government in the world, and preserves the purity of His people's worship. A jealous God fights for His own, that which belongs to Him. Not only does His jealousy affect Israel in covenant relationship when that nation sins, but it also operates against the enemies of Israel. Christ wants us to be jealous, zealous believers, to have a passionate, consuming zeal, focused on God and upon doing His will. Perhaps the word "separation" best sums up what a Jealous God should mean to us. We are not to be intimately entangled with nonbelievers (Exodus 34:12; 2 Corinthians 6:14-18). The Lord will not put up with having honor due Him transferred to false gods. Only the Lord Jesus Christ is to rule on the throne of our hearts.

B. BIBLICAL BACKGROUND

The farewell address of Joshua to Israel begins in chapter twenty-three, where he reminded the leaders of God's faithfulness. A key verse in this background is Joshua 23:14: ". . .not one thing has failed of all the good things which the Lord your God spake concerning you; all are come to pass unto you, and not one thing hath failed thereof." Awareness and acceptance of this truth demands courage for the future. They had no excuse for not finishing what Joshua had started. But they must remain loyal to the Lord's law, and keep separated from all evil, especially idolatry. Failure here would cause the good they had experienced to turn into terrible evil—snares, traps, scourges, thorns; and distress, drought, wild beasts, disease, famine, invasion, world-wide dispersion, persecution, and perishing! And so, the Israelites were warned that God would be as faithful in destroying them if they forget their covenant and fall into idolatry, as He was faithful in destroying the Canaanites.

The fact that none of God's words had failed does not mean that Israel occupied all the land God had promised. Jehovah had said He would not drive out at once all of the inhabitants, but it would be a gradual process, "little by little" (Deuteronomy 7:22). It is with these facts in mind that Joshua's second farewell address begins in chapter twenty-four.

II. Exposition and Application of the Scripture

A. THE CALL TO ASSEMBLE
(Joshua 24:1-2)

AND JOSHUA gathered all the tribes of Israel to Shechem, and called for the elders of Israel, and for their heads, and for their judges, and for their officers; and they presented themselves before God. And Joshua said unto all the people.

In the Old Testament written in Greek (called the Septuagint), and in the Arabic versions, instead of Shechem it reads Shiloh. It is true that a number of events mentioned in the latter part of the book of Joshua occurred at Shiloh (Joshua 18:1-10, 19:51, 21:2, 22:9, 12), for the national sanctuary (tabernacle) was located there. However, it appears that most scholars agree that Shechem is correct.

It is pointed out that: (1) Shechem was the place God appeared to Abraham and first made His covenant with him, promising Canaan to him; here also Abraham built his first altar; (2) Jacob settled here on his return from Mesopotamia; and called upon his household to put away their idol gods; (3) Shechem was an excellent area as a meeting place, because

of its sound (acoustical) qualities; (4) It was a regular meeting place (along with Mizpeh) for the tribes to gather. And so, Joshua gathered all the tribes of Israel to Shechem. Note the four groups he called for, as in Joshua 23:2. First, the elders. Literally, these were the old men, who acted on behalf of Israel on great occasions, whether civil or religious (Girdlestone). It is not clear exactly what age qualified one as an elder, although the Hebrew word means "bearded ones," and other Scriptures refer to the elders as having children and gray hair. Age sixty seems to separate the mature from the aged, although evidently the Levites retired at age fifty (Numbers 8:25). Second: Heads are mentioned: these are the leaders (NIV), the chief officers. Judges are listed third: these are the magistrates. Last are the Officers. Because the Hebrew word used here also means writers, it is believed these officials who were subordinate to the elders were probably originally trained as scribes (TWOT). These were all called together as a national assembly; they presented themselves before God and Joshua began to review Israel's history, starting with Abraham.

B. THE CHOICE TO BE MADE
(Joshua 24:14-18)

Now therefore fear the LORD, and serve him in sincerity and in truth: and put away the gods which your fathers served on the other side of the flood, and in Egypt; and serve ye the LORD. And if it seem evil unto you to serve the LORD, choose you this day whom ye will serve; whether the gods which your fathers served that were on the other side of the flood, or the gods of the Amorites, in whose land ye dwell: but as for me and my house, we will serve the LORD. And the people answered and said, God forbid that we should forsake the LORD, to serve other gods; For the LORD our God, he it is that brought us up and our fathers out of the land of Egypt, from the house of bondage, and which did those great signs in our sight, and preserved us in all the way wherein we went, and among all the people through whom we passed: And the LORD drave out from before us all the people, even the Amorites which dwelt in the land: therefore will we also serve the LORD; for he is our God.

Naturally, the "therefore" of verse fourteen is there for a reason. Because the Lord had done so much for Israel, through His servants Abraham, Isaac, Jacob, Moses and Aaron; and delivered them out of Egypt, and brought them into the Promised Land—there—fore, fear the Lord, serve Him, put away idols. The word for fear refers to reverential trust and faith in God and in His Word. It includes the hatred of evil and all that is contrary to God's will. Not only fear Him, but serve Him in sincerity. The Hebrew word rendered "sincerity" comes from a verb meaning to be complete, whole, finished; it is elsewhere translated, perfect, integrity. Israel was commanded to do that which is sound, wholesome, thus innocent, having integrity. It was a call to wholehearted loyalty and worship, a call to service without hypocrisy or show, but with simplicity of heart.

Note that sincerity is accompanied by truth. Men may be sincere in that which is evil, false, sinful. A man who starts out knowing that he preaches falsehood may be given up by God to believe his own lies. Who can be any more sincere than a man who believes what he preaches! But if what he speaks is a lie, then his sincerity makes him all the more dangerous! So, Joshua added the words, "and in truth." A third exhortation in verse fourteen is to put away the idol gods their fathers served on "the other side of the river." The word translated "river" is "flood" in the KJV, which may cause one to think of the days of Noah. However, the flood refers to the overflowing waters of the Euphrates river. Abram's family crossed the Euphrates upon leaving Ur of the Chaldees. Note that Abram and his family were idolaters (Joshua 24:2). Indeed, the moon god was the main deity there, but also present were shrines to many other gods as well. In short, Abram was a pagan, but by the sovereign grace of God, he was saved.

There were also many gods in Egypt which may have influenced some of the Israelites. Keil and Delitzsch point out that Joshua's appeal "does not presuppose any gross idolatry on the part of the existing generation." On the whole, the book of Joshua represents the Israelites as loyal to Jehovah. But yet, there were traces of idolatry still existing among them. They were not totally free of idols when in Egypt or in the wilderness. The natural heart constantly seeks to make idols, motivated by impure thoughts and desires.

The choice was before them. If the representatives of the nation were not willing or inclined to serve Jehovah, they were called upon to make a decision! Joshua's mind was made up already. As far as he and his family were concerned, they would serve the Lord! Idolatry offers many choices, for there are multitudes of gods. Yet, all of them put together cannot accomplish what the One True and Living God has done and is doing. In fact, the deliverance from Egypt was proof of the impotence of the heathen deities.

Thus Joshua made a strong appeal for the Israelites to remain loyal to the Lord. The people responded with a sincere heart commitment to serve Jehovah. They made known their awareness of the grace of God in the life of the nation—all that Joshua had reminded them of in verses three through thirteen—and repeated their promise to serve the Lord, their God.

C. THE CHALLENGE TO ISRAEL
(Joshua 24:19-22)

And Joshua said unto the people, Ye cannot serve the LORD: for he is an holy God; he is a jealous God; he will not forgive your transgressions nor your sins. If ye forsake the LORD, and serve strange gods, then he will turn and do you hurt, and consume you, after that he hath done you good. And the people said unto Joshua, Nay; but we will serve the LORD. And Joshua said unto the
people, Ye are witnesses against yourselves that ye have chosen you the LORD, to serve him. And they said, We are witnesses.

Joshua's shocking reply cramped their commitment: "You cannot serve the Lord!" These words have been variously interpreted. Their answer may have been glib, or their vow too easily made. Their present state of mind was not acceptable. The promise was made in their own strength, not by depending upon the Lord, or, said without any true repentance and faith. All of these thoughts could be true. They cannot serve God and idols at the same time, for God is a jealous, zealous God. He will brook (stand for) no rivals! Israel was warned that serving foreign gods would move the Lord to change His attitude toward the nation. In spite of previous blessings, the Lord would not hesitate to severely punish them. Once again, the people held to their vow.

D. THE COVENANT AT SHECHEM (Joshua 24:25)

So Joshua made a covenant with the people that day, and set them a statute and an ordinance in Shechem.

Finally, we see the solemn renewal of the covenant at the national assembly in Shechem, as Joshua brings his ministry to a close. As mentioned earlier, Shechem often had been consecrated as a sanctuary of God, so Joshua had no hesitation in choosing it now as a place for the renewal of the covenant. Because the people promised to serve Jehovah and obey His voice, a covenant was made, and a statute and an ordinance was set for them. In this way, the covenant was renewed and a granite stone was set up under the famous oak tree of Shechem (Genesis 35:2-4). This would remain a solemn witness of their avowed dedication to the Lord. To this, the Israelites also agreed. God grant that Christians who desire to serve, have first surrendered; and believers who would overcome, have first obeyed (Redpath).

III. Special Features

A. PRESERVING OUR HERITAGE

Joshua's assertion of loyalty are words that strike our heart: "But as for me and my house, we will serve the Lord" (Joshua 24:15b). Here is a principle that courses throughout the Scriptures, the fact that the God of the Bible delights in saving and blessing entire households. Of course, He is not willing that any should perish, but that all should be saved. He takes especial pleasure in "household piety" (Ironside). The record shows that the Lord invited Noah and all his house into the ark. He counted on Abraham commanding his children and his household after him to keep the way of the Lord. The priest in the holy place of the tabernacle was to make an atonement for himself, and for his household, and for all the congregation of Israel. Rahab and her father's household were saved from the destruction of Jericho. Lydia and all her household were baptized. The Philippian jailer was converted; and was baptized, he and all his, believing in God with all his house.

One of the things that comes to mind here is the family reunion. Though scattered all over the United States, Black Americans still have their family get-togethers. This is an event which continues to strengthen our family life. Even the National Baptist Convention meetings play a part in this family cohesiveness. Many of us have unsaved relatives. Let us stay in prayer for them; and continue to witness to them. What a joy it would be to know all the members of our families have faith in the shed blood of Jesus Christ, and when this life is over, we will be together for all eternity. Oh, to be able to say right now: "As for me and my house, we serve the Lord Jesus Christ!"

B. A CONCLUDING WORD

In this second farewell address, Joshua went all the way back to Abram, actually to Terah, Abram's father, in reminding the Israelites of God's goodness to them. By grace, Abraham came to know the Lord as "a personal, infinite, holy, and self-revealing God, as the Creator, preserver and governor of the universe" (Thieseen). Deliverance from Egypt is also mentioned as an example of Jehovah's special relationship with Israel. Defeat of the Amorites, frustration of Balak and Balaam in the desire to curse Israel, the crossing of the Jordan, capture of Jericho, victory over the nations dwelling in the Promised Land—all these things point to the mercies of God in Israel's history. The nation's besetting sin was idolatry. This is why there is such strong emphasis made against this evil. Because human nature is the same throughout the centuries, we find ourselves still confronted with idols. In every age, men are faced with gods and goddesses. Today, we are civilized, sophisticated pagans and refuse to put away the gods enthroned upon our hearts. Whatever we put before the Lord Jesus Christ in our lives is an idol. May Joshua's emphasis be ours, as we sing, "King of my life, I crown Thee now."

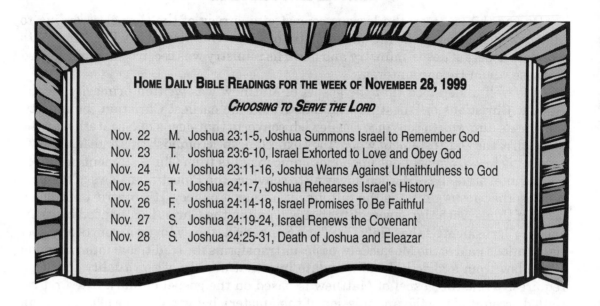

HOME DAILY BIBLE READINGS FOR THE WEEK OF NOVEMBER 28, 1999

CHOOSING TO SERVE THE LORD

Nov. 22	M.	Joshua 23:1-5, Joshua Summons Israel to Remember God
Nov. 23	T.	Joshua 23:6-10, Israel Exhorted to Love and Obey God
Nov. 24	W.	Joshua 23:11-16, Joshua Warns Against Unfaithfulness to God
Nov. 25	T.	Joshua 24:1-7, Joshua Rehearses Israel's History
Nov. 26	F.	Joshua 24:14-18, Israel Promises To Be Faithful
Nov. 27	S.	Joshua 24:19-24, Israel Renews the Covenant
Nov. 28	S.	Joshua 24:25-31, Death of Joshua and Eleazar

Know Your Bible

- The children of Israel traveled in the wilderness for three days before they found water, but the water was not suitable to drink (it was bitter). (Exodus 15:22-23)
- When Moses saw the people dancing around a golden calf, Moses broke the stone table, and destroyed the golden calf. (Exodus 32:19-20)
- The Ten Commandments were given a second time by God when Moses took two new tables of stone up to the mountain. (Exodus 34)
- During the second giving of the Commandments, Moses was on the mount for forty days and forty nights, but when he returned, his face shone so brightly that the Israelites were afraid to come near him. (Exodus 34:30; Deuteronomy 10:10)
- Aaron died at Mount Hor, and was honored at a ceremony wherein his priestly robe was removed and placed on his son Eleazar. This was followed by three days of mourning out of respect for him. (Numbers 20:22-29)

 *O God, in a world wherein men have raised the works of their hands to the level of praise and worship, grant that we may worship Thee alone as You have revealed Yourself to us in the person of Jesus Christ in whose name we pray. Amen.*

WINTER QUARTER

December, 1999, January, February, 2000

Studies in Matthew

General Introduction

During this quarter, the lessons consist of a survey of the Gospel according to Matthew with focus on the life and ministry of Jesus. Our attention will be limited to a certain aspect of Jesus' ministry and how His ministry was received and/or rejected by those whom He encountered.

It is well understood that the gospel of Matthew was written primarily for the Hebrew Christians of Palestine who constituted the earliest Christian community. Matthew's aim was to convince the Jewish converts that Jesus of Nazareth was the Messiah of the Old Testament whom they expected. To accomplish this end, Matthew's account is heavily dependent upon messianic insights from Old Testament prophecy and he interprets these in such a way as to convince the Palestinian Jews of the first century that Jesus Christ is the fulfillment of that prophecy. His contrast of the old order of things with the new reality that is found in the Christ is enhanced by references to Jerusalem as the "Holy City," the Sanhedrin, the synagogue courts and special citations paid to the Mosaic Law as Jesus transforms the traditional interpretation of the law from a strictly legal mandate into that quality of spirituality that God requires. While the gospel of Matthew is based on the gospel of Mark (the first recorded account of the life and mission of the Master), being a disciple of Jesus as an eyewitness afforded him the advantage of including various happenings and encounters that are unique to the book itself while maintaining its synoptic character.

The gospel of Matthew will be considered under three units.

Unit I, *"Beginnings: Birth and Ministry,"* consists of four sessions. The first introduces John the Baptist as the herald of Jesus' coming, followed by a recount of His temptations in the wilderness. The final two sessions center on the account of Jesus' birth and the visit of the wise men.

Unit II, *"Jesus' Teachings and Ministry,"* is presented in five sessions that include the calling of the twelve disciples, teachings on prayer, examples of Jesus' miracles of compassion, the growing opposition to Jesus, and the parable of the laborers in the vineyard.

Unit III, *"Fulfillment of Jesus' Mission,"* is a four-session unit that begins with the triumphal entry of Jesus into Jerusalem along with the symbolism implied in His mode and message. After the discussion on being prepared for the return of Christ, attention will be focused on Jesus' death, with the final session centered on His resurrection and the Great Commission to His followers.

While the gospel of Matthew is directed primarily toward the Palestinian Jews to indicate the continuity of the promises of God and the fulfillment of the same in Jesus as the Messiah, there is a point at which the message transcends historical circumstances and addresses the concerns of contemporary Christians. Our affinity with these lessons is based on the fact that we as a people have been enabled to endure all kinds of indignities because our ancestors were fortified by the hope of a better day.

King's Herald and Baptism

Unit 1—*Beginnings: Birth and Ministry*
Children's Unit—*God Sent a Savior*

•••••

Adult Topic—*Time of Preparing*

•••••

Youth Topic—*Fire and Water*
Children's Topic—*Jesus' Mother is Chosen*

•••••

Devotional Reading—Matthew 21:23-27
Background Scripture—Matthew 3
Print—Matthew 3:1-8, 11-17

PRINTED SCRIPTURE

Matthew 3:1-8, 11-17 (KJV)

IN THOSE days came John the Baptist, preaching in the wilderness of Judaea,

2 And saying, Repent ye: for the kingdom of heaven is at hand.

3 For this is he that was spoken of by the prophet Esaias, saying, The voice of one crying in the wilderness, Prepare ye the way of the Lord, make his paths straight.

4 And the same John had his raiment of camel's hair, and a leathern girdle about his loins; and his meat was locusts and wild honey.

5 Then went out to him Jerusalem, and all Judaea, and all the region round about Jordan,

6 And were baptized of him in Jordan, confessing their sins.

7 But when he saw many of the Pharisees and Sadducees come to his baptism, he said unto them, O generation of vipers, who hath warned you to flee from the wrath to come?

8 Bring forth therefore fruits meet for repentance:

Matthew 3:1-8, 11-17 (NRSV)

IN THOSE days John the Baptist appeared in the wilderness of Judea, proclaiming,

2 "Repent, for the kingdom of heaven has come near."

3 This is the one of whom the prophet Isaiah spoke when he said, "The voice of one crying out in the wilderness: 'Prepare the way of the Lord, make his paths straight.'"

4 Now John wore clothing of camel's hair with a leather belt around his waist, and his food was locusts and wild honey.

5 Then the people of Jerusalem and all Judea were going out to him, and all the region along the Jordan,

6 and they were baptized by him in the river Jordan, confessing their sins.

7 But when he saw many Pharisees and Sadducees coming for baptism, he said to them, "You brood of vipers! Who warned you to flee from the wrath to come?

8 Bear fruit worthy of repentance.

·····

11 I indeed baptize you with water unto repentance: but he that cometh after me is mightier than I, whose shoes I am not worthy to bear: he shall baptize you with the Holy Ghost, and with fire:

12 Whose fan is in his hand, and he will thoroughly purge his floor, and gather his wheat into the garner; but he will burn up the chaff with unquenchable fire.

13 Then cometh Jesus from Galilee to Jordan unto John, to be baptized of him.

14 But John forbad him, saying, I have need to be baptized of thee, and comest thou to me?

15 And Jesus answering said unto him, Suffer it to be so now: for thus it becometh us to fulfil all righteousness. Then he suffered him.

16 And Jesus, when he was baptized, went up straightway out of the water: and, lo, the heavens were opened unto him, and he saw the Spirit of God descending like a dove, and lighting upon him:

17 And lo a voice from heaven, saying, This is my beloved Son, in whom I am well pleased.

11 "I baptize you with water for repentance, but one who is more powerful than I is coming after me; I am not worthy to carry his sandals. He will baptize you with the Holy Spirit and fire.

12 His winnowing fork is in his hand, and he will clear his threshing floor and will gather his wheat into the granary; but the chaff he will burn with unquenchable fire."

13 Then Jesus came from Galilee to John at the Jordan, to be baptized by him.

14 John would have prevented him, saying, "I need to be baptized by you, and do you come to me?"

15 But Jesus answered him, "Let it be so now; for it is proper for us in this way to fulfill all righteousness." Then he consented.

16 And when Jesus had been baptized, just as he came up from the water, suddenly the heavens were opened to him and he saw the Spirit of God descending like a dove and alighting on him.

17 And a voice from heaven said, "This is my Son, the Beloved, with whom I am well pleased."

KEY VERSE

*I indeed baptize you with water unto repentance: but he that cometh after me is mightier than I, whose shoes I am not worthy to bear: he shall baptize you with the Holy Ghost, and with fire.—**Matthew 3:11***

OBJECTIVES

After reading this lesson, the student should have knowledge of:

1. The ministry of John the Baptist;
2. The spiritual nature of the Pharisees and Sadducees;
3. The Baptism of Jesus; and,
4. The doctrine of the Trinity.

POINTS TO BE EMPHASIZED

Adult/Youth
Key Verse: Matthew 3:11
Print: Matthew 3:1-8, 11-17

—John the Baptist preached repentance and the coming of the Lord. (1-3)
—Multitudes from Jerusalem and Judea went to hear John and to be baptized by him, confessing their sins. (4-6)
—John rebuked the Pharisees and Sadducees who asked for baptism, and admonished them to bear fruit worthy of repentance. (7-8)
—John said that he baptized for repentance but looked ahead to the One who would baptize with the Holy Spirit and fire and would separate the wheat from the chaff. (11-12)
—Jesus came to John and insisted on being baptized to fulfill all righteousness. (13-15)
—When Jesus came up from the water, the Spirit of God descended upon Him like a dove, and a voice from heaven confirmed His sonship. (16-17)

Children
Key Verse: Luke 1:30
Print: Luke 1:26-35, 38-40

—God sent the angel Gabriel to a virgin named Mary. (26-28)
—Mary was perplexed by the angel's greeting. (29)
—The angel announced to Mary that she would become pregnant with a son. (31)
—The baby Mary would have would be a great person. (32-33)
—Mary accepted the message from the angel, then the angel left. (38)
—Mary went to Elizabeth and Zechariah. (39-40)

(**Note**: Use KJV Scripture for Adult; NRSV Scripture for Youth and Children)

TOPICAL OUTLINE OF THE LESSON

I. Introduction
A. Baptism
B. Biblical Background

II. Exposition and Application of the Scripture
A. The Ministry of John the Baptist (Matthew 3:1-6)
B. The Message of Warning to the Religious Leaders (Matthew 3:7-12)
C. The Meaning of Our Lord's Baptism (Matthew 3:13-17)

III. Special Features
A. Preserving Our Heritage
B. A Concluding Word

I. Introduction

A. BAPTISM

A minister preached a sermon and sought to show that "in" and "into" did not mean immersion. He said: "John did not baptize Jesus in the Jordan, but close to, near by, round about Jordan. Philip and the Eunuch did not go down into the water, but close to, near by, round about." When he finished, a man rose and said: "Reverend, your sermon has comforted me by explaining many long perplexing mysteries. I never understood how Jonah lived in that great fish three days and three nights. Now I see that he was not in the fish, but close to, near by, round about, swimming in the water. I see now how the three Hebrews lived when cast into the fiery furnace. They were not actually in the furnace, but close to, near by, round about, warming themselves. As for Daniel who was cast into the den of lions, now I understand why he was not devoured. He was not in the den at all, but only close to, near by, round about where he could hear them roar and feel no harm. Then Reverend, I am a very wicked man and have long dreaded going to Hell. But you have relieved my apprehension. When the Bible says the wicked shall be cast into Hell with all nations that forget God, I shall henceforth interpret it to mean that I shall not actually go to Hell, but only close to, near by, round about."

In the printed lesson, the words Baptist, baptized, and baptism are found eight times. The verb *baptizo* means to dip, immerse; however, most English translations prefer to transliterate rather than translate its actual meaning. Kenneth Wuest states that baptism is "the introduction or placing of a person or thing into a new environment or into union with something else so as to alter its condition or its relationship to its previous environment or condition." As Baptists, we believe in immersion. However, we quickly add that the mode of baptism does not determine salvation. Identification is the key thought here. Baptism identifies us with Christ; it is proof that we mean business; it is evidence of a change; it is public identification with the local assembly.

B. BIBLICAL BACKGROUND

Here is a helpful outline in the study of the background for today's lesson: (1) The King's Ancestry: Matthew 1:1-17, (2) The King's Advent: Matthew 1:18—2:23, (3) The King's Announcer: Matthew 3:1-12, and (4) The King's Approval: Matthew 3:13—4:11. Matthew makes no mention of the interval of twenty-eight to thirty years between chapters two and three. During this time, the Lord Jesus was in the town of Nazareth, preparing for the work which lay ahead. These were years in which He performed no miracles, although men who are not content with the silence of this period of our Lord's life have made up all kinds of stories. "Lost Books" have been discovered dealing with our Lord's childhood. From the gospel of Luke, we know that as a child, He "grew, and became strong in spirit, filled with wisdom; and the grace of God was upon Him...and that He increased in wisdom and stature, and in favor with God and man" (Luke 2:40, 52).

II. Exposition and Application of the Scripture

A. THE MINISTRY OF JOHN THE BAPTIST (Matthew 3:1-6)

In those days came John the Baptist, preaching in the wilderness of Judaea, And saying, Repent ye: for the kingdom of heaven is at hand. For this is he that was spoken of by the prophet Esaias, saying, The voice of one crying in the wilderness, Prepare ye the way of the Lord, make his paths straight. And the same John had his raiment of camel's hair, and a leathern girdle about his loins; and his meat was locusts and wild honey. Then went out to him Jerusalem, and all Judaea, and all the region round about Jordan, And were baptized of him in Jordan, confessing their sins.

The words "in those days" are purposely vague, hiding the gap between the events closing chapter two, and the introduction of John the Baptist in chapter three. Recall that John's father was the priest Zacharias, and his mother, Elisabeth, who was a cousin of Mary, the mother of the Lord Jesus. Called and consecrated from birth to be the forerunner of Christ (Luke 1:15-17), John's task was to preach—he came preaching! The verb *kerusso* means to act as a herald, announce, proclaim. A herald does not create the message he proclaims. The one who sends the herald tells him what to speak. *Kerusso* calls our attention to authoritative proclamation. John came heralding and saying, "Repent."

The Greek noun, *metanoia*, means a change of mind (the transliterated Greek word, *paranoia*, beyond the mind, madness, demented). *Metanoia* does not stress feelings, but emphasizes the mind or purpose of the person who repents. Repent is a word with Latin roots meaning to be sorry, but Bible repentance is more than experiencing sorrow. Some folks are only sorry that they were caught! John called his audience to change their minds or purposes toward their sin. Repentance is far more than an intellectual change of mind, for its proof is seen in the fruits of a changed life.

"The Kingdom of heaven" (literally, heavens) is a phrase found only in Matthew's gospel. This is the spiritual kingdom of God in the hearts of men, entered into by the new birth; it is that sphere in which God's rule is acknowledged. It is seen in two ways: (1) the broad aspect includes all who profess to acknowledge God as Supreme Ruler, and (2) the narrow aspect, which includes only those who have been truly converted. Practically speaking, it is similar to "kingdom of God." Keep in mind, however, that it is not the Church. When Christ returns to establish His kingdom on earth, He will bring the Church with Him to help rule with a rod of iron. By not defining "kingdom of heaven," John and our Lord suggest they expected their audiences to understand its meaning in the light of Old Testament promises. We repeat: The Kingdom of Heaven refers to the millennial kingdom, that one thousand year earthly reign of Christ with headquarters in Jerusalem. John preached that this kingdom was near, "at hand," and the King was present among His people.

Some seven hundred years earlier, Isaiah predicted just such a person as John heralding the Messiah (Isaiah

40:3-5). John the Baptist was that "voice." He shouted: "Clear the way for the Lord in the wilderness; make smooth in the desert a highway for our God." In many ways, John resembled the prophet Elijah. Compare Elijah's sudden appearance on the scene (1 Kings 17:1) with the Baptist's appearance—"in those days came John the Baptist"! John's often harshly critical preaching also put him in the same category with Elijah's uncompromising messages.

John's physical appearance is likened to that of Elijah; he wore a rough coat of camel's hair, and had a leather belt around his waist (2 Kings 1:8). His diet was strange food to us, but Leviticus 11:22 approves of John's menu. The honey was wild, uncultivated. Altogether, John's zeal led him to disregard whatever comforts and pleasures of life were normal in his day. He was consumed by his calling and mission. His ministry was widespread, and many were baptized by him in the Jordan River, confessing their sins.

B. THE MESSAGE OF WARNING TO THE RELIGIOUS LEADERS
(Matthew 3:7-8, 11-12)

But when he saw many of the Pharisees and Sadducees come to his baptism, he said unto them, O generation of vipers, who hath warned you to flee from the wrath to come? Bring forth therefore fruits meet for repentance. I indeed baptize you with water unto repentance: but he that cometh after me is mightier than I, whose shoes I am not worthy to bear: he shall baptize you with the Holy Ghost, and with fire: Whose fan is in his hand, and he will throughly purge his floor, and gather his wheat into the garner; but he will burn up the chaff with unquenchable fire.

The word Pharisee comes from a Hebrew word meaning Separatist. In their desire to remind the Jews that they were the chosen people of God, separate from the Gentiles, this group sought to maintain reverence for the law among those Israelites who returned from the Babylonian captivity. The ministry of the post-captivity prophets had ended; and then during the time between the Old Testament and the New Testament, this sect was born. In time, the movement degenerated into a sect of ritualists who sought to abide by the letter of the law, but missed abiding in its spirit. For the most part, the Pharisees were Scribes, men learned in the Mosaic law and in the sacred writings. They were moral, zealous, self-denying, but were also self-righteous, "holier than thou," unaware of any sense of sin. Professing great devotion to the law of Moses, they were in many cases religious hypocrites, claiming their traditional interpretations were oral explanations God had given to Moses. To their shameful, bitter end, they were the number one persecutors of Christ from the beginning of His ministry. They saw both John the Baptist and this one (often in contempt they would not call Him by name) called Jesus as threats to "discredit their own teaching and self-opinionated piety" (Pilgrim Bible).

The Sadducees probably derived their name from Zadok, "who was high priest in the time of David and exhibited special fidelity to the king and his house (2 Samuel 15:24-29); hence, the posterity of this priest and all their adherents seem to have been called

Sadducees" (Thayer). They came into existence as a reaction against the Pharisees. Strongly entrenched in the Sanhedrin and priesthood, they were considered social aristocrats, religious skeptics, comparable to the rationalists of today. As antisupernaturalists, they denied miracles, the resurrection of the body, the existence of angels or demons, the immortality of the soul, and eternal punishment of future retribution.

Evidently, John was surprised that many of the Pharisees and Sadducees came to see him baptize. If they were so sure that they possessed the key to salvation, why bother with him? Undoubtedly, they were there because they feared that John's popularity and regard as a prophet might create a movement that would jeopardize their position. Note that these religious leaders were the objects of our Lord's scathing, unsparing denunciations (Matthew 12:34; 23:13-36). Here John opens up with an ironic tone of voice; he calls them a bunch of poisonous snakes, fleeing from a field being mowed or set on fire. He inquired: "Are you persuaded that God's wrath is near? Are you stirred up enough to try to avoid it? Well, if you really want to escape divine judgment, there is but one way possible: Repent, and behave like men who are really changed should conduct themselves!"

Fruit befitting true repentance is more than a few crocodile tears, a brief scare, or "a spasm of regret." John warned the religious leaders not to depend upon their physical relationship with Abraham for salvation (John 8:33-40). If God desired, He could create a new race possessing no such ancestry, and bestow upon them the blessings the disobedient sons of Abraham forfeited. Urgency and inevitability are seen in John's picture of the woodsmen already at work. Every life is like a fruit-bearing tree. Those that bear rotten fruit will be cut down and thrown into the fire. However, the Messiah will baptize and gather unto Himself those who are truly repentant and bearing good fruit. He will separate the repentant and the unrepentant. He will gather the repentant like wheat into a granary, but the unrepentant, like chaff, will be burned with unquenchable fire.

There is a difference of interpretation of the phrase, "He shall baptize you with the Holy Spirit, and with fire" (verse 11). Some scholars make the Holy Spirit and the fire identical, in which case the Holy Spirit burns up the junk that is in our lives. This then would not be hellfire judgment (Lenski), but that burning zeal within us. On the other hand, some scholars believe the fire baptism points to judgment. Christ thus consigns the impenitent to everlasting punishment, for fire speaks of judgment. The context and references to purging and burning appear to refer to judgment. If this latter is true, it plays havoc with the denomination known as The Fire Baptized Holiness Church.

C. THE MEANING OF OUR LORD'S BAPTISM
(Matthew 3:13-17)

Then cometh Jesus from Galilee to Jordan unto John, to be baptized of him. But John forbad him, saying, I have need to be baptized of thee, and comest thou to me? And Jesus answering said unto him, Suffer it to be so now: for thus it

becometh us to fulfil all righteousness. Then he suffered him. And Jesus, when he was baptized, went up straightway out of the water: and, lo, the heavens were opened unto him, and he saw the Spirit of God descending like a dove, and lighting upon him: And lo a voice from heaven, saying, This is my beloved Son, in whom I am well pleased.

When Christ came to be baptized, John at first would have hindered Him. But the Savior answered, "Permit it now." The question comes, "Why should He be baptized?" After all, John's Baptism was connected with the call to repentance. Christ of course had nothing to repent of, for there was no sin nature in Him. As a Jew, He obeyed all of the religious observances and duties; He had been circumcised, and presented in the temple. He thus identified Himself with those He came to redeem. By baptism, He inaugurated His public ministry as the Messiah; it symbolized that which He had come to earth to do.

In Old Testament times, before the high priest was anointed for service, he was washed (Exodus 29:4-7). So here, before Christ began His High Priestly office, He was washed symbolically in baptism, and anointed by the Spirit's descending upon Him like a dove. See the manifestation of what is called the Trinity. There is but One God, and He exists as Father, Son and Holy Spirit at the same time. God the Father spoke and said this was His Son in whom His pleasure rests. It was God the Son who was baptized, and God the Holy Spirit who descended like a dove (symbol of gentleness, meekness, innocence, peace, purity) and lighted upon Christ. Thus, the public ministry of our Lord was ratified or confirmed, and publicly proclaimed. On two other occasions, God the Father spoke from heaven in acknowledgment of His only Begotten Son (see Matthew 17:5; John 12:28).

III. Special Features

A. PRESERVING OUR HERITAGE

Years ago, we used to hear certain of our preachers claim that John the Baptist founded the Baptist Church, and that we were the first. We know of course that this is not historically true. And yet, though our numbers are dwindling in proportion to the total population, Baptists are still the largest denomination among Black Americans. And the National Baptist Convention, U.S.A., Incorporated, is the largest of all the Black Baptists.

There are a number of reasons why Black Slaves became Baptists. I don't think the idea that immersion appealed because of the importance of rivers in African life is an idea that holds "much water!" More important and solid are the suggestions that the slaves believed the Gospel heralded by the White Baptist preachers and then later that which came from the lips of anointed Black ministers. God used the evangelistic zeal of Baptist preachers. The emotionalism, fervor, freedom and autonomy, ease of ordination, inherent equality of the Gospel—these all helped to attract our ancestors to the Baptist denomination.

B. A CONCLUDING WORD

No doubt you have heard the words, "Dry Devil, Wet Devil." It is an expression that reminds us of the emphasis made by John the Baptist. Water Baptism means nothing if there is no heart change. Today, as Bible Christians, we know that the baptism that really counts is the one that comes as a result of faith in the shed blood of the Lord Jesus Christ—namely, where "by one Spirit were we all baptized into one body" (1 Corinthians 12:13).

HOME DAILY BIBLE READINGS FOR THE WEEK OF DECEMBER 5, 1999

KING'S HERALD AND BAPTISM

Nov. 29	M.	Matthew 3:1-6, John Preaches and Baptizes
Nov. 30	T.	Matthew 3:7-12, John Proclaims Jesus' Coming
Dec. 1	W.	Matthew 3:13-17, Jesus Is Baptized by John
Dec. 2	T.	Matthew 11:2-6, John Sends Messengers to Question Jesus
Dec. 3	F.	Matthew 11:7-11, Jesus Praises John the Baptist
Dec. 4	S.	Matthew 11:12-19, Jesus Admonishes the Crowd
Dec. 5	S.	Matthew 14:1-12, John the Baptist Is Executed

Know Your Bible

- John the Baptist was imprisoned because of his condemnation of Herod's unlawful marriage to his brother's Philip's wife (Herodias). (Mark 6:17)
- The people were amazed at Jesus' healing miracles because they knew Him only as the son of a Nazarene carpenter. (Luke 4:22)
- Our petitions to God are imperfect in their expression, but God still answers them because He knows what we are trying to say in our prayers. (Matthew 6:8)
- Jesus ate and drank with publicans and sinners because He came into the world "to seek" and "to save" the lost. (Luke 5:30-32; 1 Timothy 1:15)
- The blind men who came to Jesus to be healed proved their faith in Him because they acknowledged Jesus to be the Christ, the Son of David, and they prayed and persevered. (Matthew 9:27-30).
- Jesus rebuked the insincerity of the crowd that came in search of Him because they came expecting a repeat of the miracle of feeding. (John 6:26-27)

O Thou who art our Father, grant that we may anticipate Your intervention in our lives to the end that our total behavior will be consistent with Your redemptive will. Amen.

Temptations and Ministry

Adult Topic—*Time of Testing*

•••••

Youth Topic—*Temptation!*
Children's Topic—*An Angel Appears to Joseph*

•••••

Devotional Reading—Luke 4:14-21
Background Scripture—Matthew 4:1-17
Print—Matthew 4:1-14

PRINTED SCRIPTURE

Matthew 4:1-14 (KJV)

THEN WAS Jesus led up of the Spirit into the wilderness to be tempted of the devil.

2 And when he had fasted forty days and forty nights, he was afterward an hungred.

3 And when the tempter came to him, he said, If thou be the Son of God, command that these stones be made bread.

4 But he answered and said, It is written, Man shall not live by bread alone, but by every word that proceedeth out of the mouth of God.

5 Then the devil taketh him up into the holy city, and setteth him on a pinnacle of the temple,

6 And saith unto him, If thou be the Son of God, cast thyself down: for it is written, He shall give his angels charge concerning thee: and in their hands they shall bear thee up, lest at any time thou dash thy foot against a stone.

7 Jesus said unto him, It is written again, Thou shalt not tempt the Lord thy God.

8 Again, the devil taketh him up

Matthew 4:1-14 (NRSV)

THEN JESUS was led up by the Spirit into the wilderness to be tempted by the devil.

2 He fasted forty days and forty nights, and afterwards he was famished.

3 The tempter came and said to him, "If you are the Son of God, command these stones to become loaves of bread."

4 But he answered, "It is written, 'One does not live by bread alone, but by every word that comes from the mouth of God.'"

5 Then the devil took him to the holy city and placed him on the pinnacle of the temple,

6 saying to him, "If you are the Son of God, throw yourself down; for it is written, 'He will command his angels concerning you,' and 'On their hands they will bear you up, so that you will not dash your foot against a stone.'"

7 Jesus said to him, "Again it is written, 'Do not put the Lord your God to the test,'"

8 Again, the devil took him to a

into an exceeding high mountain, and showeth him all the kingdoms of the world, and the glory of them;

9 And saith unto him, All these things will I give thee, if thou wilt fall down and worship me.

10 Then saith Jesus unto him, Get thee hence, Satan: for it is written, Thou shalt worship the Lord thy God, and him only shalt thou serve.

11 Then the devil leaveth him, and, behold, angels came and ministered unto him.

12 Now when Jesus had heard that John was cast into prison, he departed into Galilee;

13 And leaving Nazareth, he came and dwelt in Capernaum, which is upon the sea coast, in the borders of Zabulon and Nephthalim:

14 That it might be fulfilled which was spoken by Esaias the prophet.

very high mountain and showed him all the kingdoms of the world and their splendor;

9 and he said to him, "All these I will give you, if you will fall down and worship me."

10 Jesus said to him, "Away with you, Satan! For it is written, 'Worship the Lord your God, and serve only him.'"

11 Then the devil left him, and suddenly angels came and waited on him.

12 Now when Jesus heard that John had been arrested, he withdrew to Galilee.

13 He left Nazareth and made his home in Capernaum by the sea, in the territory of Zebulun and Naphtali.

14 so that what had been spoken through the prophet Isaiah might be fulfilled.

Then said Jesus unto him, Get thee hence, Satan: for it is written, Thou shalt worship the Lord thy God, and him only shalt thou serve.
—Matthew 4:10

OBJECTIVES

After reading this lesson, the student will have a deeper knowledge of:

1. The nature of satanic temptation;
2. The use of God's Word in resisting temptation;
3. The impossibility of enticing Christ to do evil; and,
4. The importance of doing the will of God.

POINTS TO BE EMPHASIZED

Adult/Youth
Key Verse: Matthew 4:10
Print: Matthew 4:1-14

—Jesus, having been led by the Spirit into the wilderness to be tempted, fasted for 40 days and nights. (1-2)

—After Jesus' fast, the tempter suggested Jesus satisfy His hunger by turning stones to bread, but Jesus rebuked Satan, using Scripture about living not by bread alone, but also by God's Words. (3-4)

—The Devil placed Jesus on the pinnacle of the temple and suggested that He jump, but Jesus rebuked Satan, using Scripture that affirmed that people are not to put God to the test. (5-7)

—The Devil promised Jesus the kingdoms of the world if Jesus would worship him; Jesus rebuked Satan using Scripture about worshiping God alone. (8-10)

—Then the Devil left Jesus and angels ministered to Him. (11)

—When John was arrested, Jesus moved to Galilee and stayed in Capernaum, fulfilling Isaiah's prophecy. (12-14)

Children
Key Verse: Matthew 1:20
Print: Matthew 1:18-25

—Jesus' birth revealed His divine nature because Mary, a virgin engaged to Joseph, was with child from the Holy Spirit. (18-19)

—An angel appeared to Joseph in a dream and explained that Mary's child was conceived by the Holy Spirit and that Joseph should marry her. (20)

—The angel told Joseph to name the child Jesus, because He would save people from their sins. (21)

—Jesus' birth fulfilled a prophecy from Isaiah. (22-23)

—Joseph, fully convinced by the angel's words, married Mary, and when the child was born, Joseph named Him Jesus. (24-25)

(**Note**: Use KJV Scripture for Adult; NRSV Scripture for Youth and Children)

TOPICAL OUTLINE OF THE LESSON

I. Introduction
A. Impeccability
B. Biblical Background

II. Exposition and Application of the Scripture
A. The Setting of the Test (Matthew 4:1-2)
B. The First Temptation (Matthew 4:3-4)
C. The Second Temptation (Matthew 4:5-7)
D. The Third Temptation (Matthew 4:8-11)
E. Christ Begins His Public Ministry (Matthew 4:12-14)

III. Special Features
A. Preserving Our Heritage
B. A Concluding Word

I. Introduction

A. IMPECCABILITY

Applied to the Lord Jesus Christ, the word impeccability refers to the doctrinal teaching that He could not sin. Many Christians agree that He did not sin, but there are differences of opinion concerning His inability and incapability to sin. It is our belief that He could not commit any evil. First, note He was full of the Spirit (John 3:34), an absolute guarantee against failure. Second, He is God. And God cannot sin. It is absolutely impossible for God to stop being God, no matter what else He may become.

He cannot empty Himself of attributes which have to do with holiness, righteousness, and morality. What He emptied Himself of enabled Him to experience thirst, humility, pain, suffering, sorrow, death!—issues which did not affect His holiness. The mystery involved in *kenosis* (emptying) remains, for God cannot apostatize from Himself by committing evil. Even those self-imposed limitations, for specific reasons and occasions, were breached when we are told He knew men's thoughts, walked on water, changed water into wine, cast out demons, healed the blind, and raised the dead. It is therefore an error to claim that Christ "did not exercise His omniscience or omnipotence."

Third, He was Christ prior to the incarnation, taking on Jesus at the incarnation. His human nature was impersonal and never existed separately from His divine nature. Rather, He took on unfallen human nature, not to become two persons, but essentially one Person, indissoluble, inseparable, mystical—Jesus Christ, in whom all the fullness of the Godhead dwells in bodily form.

Fourth, born of a virgin, He had no old or adamic nature. This is why He could say that the Devil "Has nothing in me" (John 14:30). Fifth, the possibility of His sinning would have imperiled the plan of salvation. Sixth, impeccability in no wise makes it impossible for Christ to sympathize with us. Seventh, His inability to sin does not make the temptation story unreal or without purpose. In fact, the reality of it all is that the story proved His impeccability to us, and teaches us many lessons. Eighth, He was indeed human. The argument that true humanity includes the ability to sin is false. In our glorified bodies, we will still be human beings, but incapable of sinning. We will be more human than Adam ever was in his innocence.

B. BIBLICAL BACKGROUND

To rightly understand the significance of the temptation, we must realize that the basic meaning of the words translated tempt is to test or try, without any connotation of committing evil. Because men so often fail the test, the word tempt now connotes to solicit to evil, to seduce, to entice. It is unfortunate that the word testing has come to automatically include the incitement to evil. The thing to keep in mind is that the words rendered tempt do not automatically include solicitation to wickedness. They may mean simply to test. Keep this emphasis in mind for a proper interpretation of the original Greek and Hebrew words which are translated "test, tempt, or prove."

II. Exposition and Application of the Scripture

A. THE SETTING OF THE TESTING (Matthew 4:1-2)

Then was Jesus led up of the Spirit into the wilderness to be tempted of the devil. And when he had fasted forty days and forty nights, he was afterward an hungred.

The Holy Spirit played an active role in our Lord's conception and birth, baptism, anointing and empowering for service. Now we immediately note the role of the Holy Spirit in the Temptation. Having been led by the Spirit continuously the entire forty days, now we find our Lord brought up or led by the Spirit into the wilderness. He who had come to do the will of the Father was led by the Father through the Holy Spirit.

Do not picture Christ standing at the fork in the road, in a quandary over which way to go, or compelled to decide whether to obey His Father or pay attention to Satan's voice. In short, this episode was no accident. Our Savior was not an unwilling player in some evil plot of Satan. By adding the presence of wild beasts in this wilderness, Mark's gospel heightens the savage solitude there, adds to the general picture of terror, loneliness, and the awful circumstances under which the temptation took place.

In the Bible, the number forty represents penalty, a time of testing, confession, probation, chastisement, or punishment. This is seen first at the Flood; rain fell upon the earth for forty days and forty nights. Moses spent His first forty years in Egypt, the next forty years in Midian, and the last forty with Israel, wandering in the wilderness. Jonah announced, "Yet forty days, and Nineveh shall be overthrown." Elijah the prophet went forty days and forty nights unto Mount Horeb in the strength of the food God provided. Now in our Lord's life, we find that He fasted for forty days in the wilderness; and later we read of forty days that intervened between His resurrection and ascension (Acts 1:3).

Bible characters fasted for many reasons: calamity, disaster, despair, humility, spiritual power, repentance, testing, etc. With our Lord, as with Moses centuries before Him, absolutely nothing was eaten. Christ abstained from all food (double negative used in Luke 4:2: literally, "and not he ate nothing"). Naturally, when the time of fasting ended, He became hungry. Cleverly, at this point, the Devil came to do his worst. Satan recognized the Lord was conscious of hunger now that He was exhausted, and he figured this was the best time to catch Him at His weakest and overwhelm Him.

B. THE FIRST TEMPTATION (Matthew 4:3-4)

And when the tempter came to him, he said, If thou be the Son of God, command that these stones be made bread. But he answered and said, It is written, Man shall not live by bread alone, but by every word that proceedeth out of the mouth of God.

Just prior to the temptation, at the baptism of our Lord by John, a voice from heaven was heard to say, "This is my beloved Son, in whom I am well pleased" (Matthew 3:17). The word "if" is used to express a condition thought of as real or to denote assumptions relating to what has happened already (Arndt & Gingrich). Note two basic thoughts about the use of the word "if." First, it is seen that some scholars hold that the word "if" is to be taken as "since," suggesting that no doubt is implied or expressed. In other words, Satan calls on the Lord Jesus to prove that He is what God called Him at the baptism.

A second point of view suggests doubt in the Devil's mind. Perhaps he saw Christ only as a human being very closely related to God, more so than other men, and who has supernatural power, given by God, over the forces of nature. Thus Satan sought to have the Lord exercise that power, to use it selfishly. "Why go hungry when you have the power to change stones to bread and eat?"

Quoting from Deuteronomy 8:3, Christ answered: "It has been written, 'Man shall not live on bread alone, but on every word that proceeds out of the mouth of God.'" In Exodus 16, the Jews had complained about their food. So Jehovah sent down manna, and required the Israelites to go out and gather a day's portion every day. He wanted them to know that man does not live by bread alone. The Lord warns us not to let our attempts to satisfy our physical needs lead us to neglect our spiritual needs or despise our relationship with God.

C. THE SECOND TEMPTATION
(Matthew 4:5-7)

Then the devil taketh him up into the holy city, and setteth him on a pinnacle of the temple, And saith unto him, If thou be the Son of God, cast thyself down: for it is written, He shall give his angels charge concerning thee: and in their hands they shall bear thee up, lest at any time thou dash thy foot against a stone. Jesus said unto him, It is written again, Thou shalt not tempt the Lord thy God.

Satan transported Christ to the very center of Jewish national life, the temple in Jerusalem. Here was an ideal spot for the Lord Jesus to do what the Devil wanted. For the second time, the Tempter commanded, "Since you are God's Son, throw yourself down from here, this very moment!" This time the Devil quoted Scripture, but omitted the words, "in all your ways." Mishandling and deceitfully using the Word of God has ever been a device of the wicked. It is no marvel that their leader should do likewise. Psalm 91 speaks of a man who trusts God, but Satan sought to change the trusting into testing. In parrying Satan's thrust with "it is written," the Lord quoted Deuteronomy 6:16, and told His adversary that He was not to force a test on the Lord His God.

D. THE THIRD TEMPTATION
(Matthew 4:8-11)

Again, the devil taketh him up into an exceeding high mountain, and sheweth him all the kingdoms of the world, and the glory of them; And saith unto him, All these things will I give thee, if thou wilt fall down and worship me. Then saith Jesus unto him, Get thee hence, Satan: for it is written, Thou shalt worship the Lord thy God, and him only shalt thou serve. Then the devil leaveth him,

and, behold, angels came and ministered unto him.

Again transporting our Lord, Satan led him to a very high mountain. There the Enemy exhibited to Him all the power, wealth, and glory of the world's kingdoms, "all their magnificence, excellence, pre-eminence, dignity and grace" (Luke 4:6, Amplified) of the world-system within a moment of time. Because this took such a brief period of time, some scholars suggest the entire temptation story was all in the mind of Christ. However, it is best to hold to the literal interpretation of the entire event.

There are those who suggest that Satan lied when he offered "all these things" to Christ. But if he did not possess what he offered to give away, this third temptation would be pointless. NO. The offer was genuine, otherwise our Lord would have immediately branded it a lie. According to God's own plan and will, He permits the Devil to own, possess, usurp, deceive, seduce, afflict, influence, and rule over people, places, and things. What Satan has was given into his hands, delivered, entrusted or handed over to him. The authorities that be are ordained of God, but by no means has God abdicated. Satan and all his demons are under God's control, and Christ will have the last say.

See Satan's burning desire! More than anything else, he wants men to worship him (Isaiah 14:14). "Therefore if you worship before me, in my sight, in front of me—do homage and worship me just once!—all this domain and glory will be yours." But imagine! He whom the angels of God worship; whom the magi worshiped; whom a leper, Jairus, the disciples, a Canaanite woman, the demoniacs at Gadara, the two Marys, and the man born blind, all who worshiped Him; and of whom it is written that at His name every knee should bow—this One is told by the Devil to fall down and worship him! What gall!

Christ gave Satan his orders! "Begone!" is a present tense command or imperative, suggesting, "Go your way and keep on going!" And now for the third time the Lord used "it is written." This time, His answer came from Deuteronomy 6:13: "You shall worship the Lord your God, and serve Him only." Finally, after exhausting every kind of testing, having been at it the entire forty days, Satan left the Lord Jesus alone. But only for "a season" (Luke 4:13), only until an opportune or suitable time. Then angels came and were ministering to Christ. Exactly what they performed is not told; we assume they brought food and water, as was brought to the prophet Elijah centuries earlier (1 Kings 19:5-6).

E. CHRIST BEGINS HIS PUBLIC MINISTRY (Matthew 4:12-14)

Now when Jesus had heard that John was cast into prison, he departed into Galilee; And leaving Nazareth, he came and dwelt in Capernaum, which is upon the sea coast, in the borders of Zabulon and Nephthalim: That it might be fulfilled which was spoken by Esaias the prophet.

After the temptation, our Lord ministered in Judea for about a year. Matthew does not record this, and we have to fit it in between verses eleven and twelve of chapter four. Thus, the last three verses of our lesson begin with our Lord's Galilean ministry. After the arrest of John the Baptist, Christ returned to Galilee, resolved to do His main work there. John's imprisonment was seen by our Lord as a sign of His own rejection. Naturally, He went to Nazareth first, but did not stay there. After the enraged Jews sought to kill Him (Luke 4:29) for proclaiming salvation to the Gentiles, He migrated to Capernaum which became the headquarters of His Galilean work. This move to Galilee fulfilled Isaiah's prophecy (Isaiah 9:1-2) that Christ, the Light of the World, would become a great light to the ignorant, superstitious Gentiles sitting in darkness.

III. Special Features

A. PRESERVING OUR HERITAGE

The temptation story cautions us to avoid the emphasis upon materialism. It is interesting that certain black scholars have ridiculed the emphasis of black slaves on the future life, calling it "compensatory." But eschatology (the study of last things) properly held makes for a better life here and now. We are cautioned also to avoid the emphasis upon showmanship or what James would call "eyeball religion" (James 1:22-24). The entertainment factor is growing in our assemblies. The music we sing, the gowns and robes we wear, our preaching style—perhaps influenced by television—demonstrate our flair for spectacularism. Our temptation journey takes us from the physical to the emotional, finally to the spiritual. The third caution then is to avoid false worship—the worship of home-made idols like Power, Race, Blackness, Bigness, Money, etc.

We want to hold on to our wrestling against personal sins, vocally witnessing the shed blood of Jesus Christ, attending Sunday school, Sunday evening preaching or Bible teaching services, emphasizing evangelism, concern for missions, prayer meetings! But the victory is won only through the Word of God and that which is written!

B. A CONCLUDING WORD

What happened to Christ in the wilderness can be expected to befall the church in the world. As Satan attacked Christ, so now he attacks the corporate church and individual believers as well. So there is a lesson to be learned from the temptation story. Indeed, keep in mind that Satan's basic thrust was to get our Lord to act independently of God the Father. First, note the appeal to the Material, and realize that there is nothing immoral about changing stones to bread. But if it is not the Father's will for that time, place or purpose, it is sin. Second, note the appeal to the Spectacular. Again, Satan wanted our Lord to act independently of the Father. The element of presumption looms large here. Only foolish fanaticism deliberately and disobediently creates a dangerous situation and then asks God for deliverance. Such "faith" is folly. Third, note the appeal to the spiritual. By appealing to our pride and ambition, the Devil would bribe us, and lead us to take shortcuts to power, influence, prestige, position, acceptance, etc. Our answer to the enticements of Satan is the Holy Spirit led use of the Bible. With "IT IS

WRITTEN!" we can parry every thrust of the Devil, and discover the truth that God is faithful, and He will not permit us to be tempted above that we are able, but will, with the temptation, also make the way to escape, that we may be able to bear it (1 Corinthians 10:13).

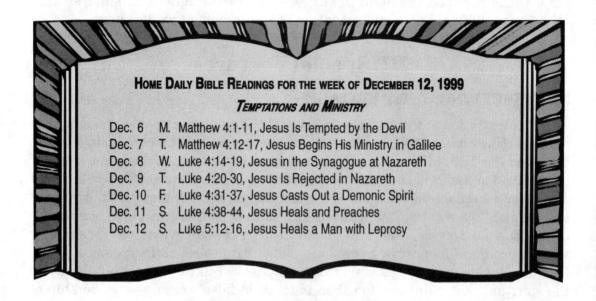

HOME DAILY BIBLE READINGS FOR THE WEEK OF DECEMBER 12, 1999

TEMPTATIONS AND MINISTRY

Dec. 6	M.	Matthew 4:1-11, Jesus Is Tempted by the Devil
Dec. 7	T.	Matthew 4:12-17, Jesus Begins His Ministry in Galilee
Dec. 8	W.	Luke 4:14-19, Jesus in the Synagogue at Nazareth
Dec. 9	T.	Luke 4:20-30, Jesus Is Rejected in Nazareth
Dec. 10	F.	Luke 4:31-37, Jesus Casts Out a Demonic Spirit
Dec. 11	S.	Luke 4:38-44, Jesus Heals and Preaches
Dec. 12	S.	Luke 5:12-16, Jesus Heals a Man with Leprosy

Know Your Bible

- Jesus spoke of His death and resurrection by referring to "raising up the temple in three days." (Mark 9:31; John 2:19-21)
- The "living who shall never die" are those Christians who are alive at the coming of the Lord. (John 11:25; 1 Thessalonians 4:16-18)
- We discover that we are precious in the sight of God by the joy that is created in heaven by just one sinner coming to God in repentance and faith. (Luke 15:7-10)
- We are not in our right minds when we are estranged from God, because our hearts and minds are willfully blinded and deceived, and the grace of God alone can bring us to ourselves (put us in our rightful minds). (Luke 15:17)
- The sinner who returns to God is described as "dead and lost" and then as "alive and found." (Luke 15:32)
- Christ receives all sinners who come to Him. (Luke 15:2)

Eternal God, our Father, as we face the various trials and tests that challenge our commitment to that which You have called us to do, may we recall the truth of Your Word as the appropriate response to each situation. In Jesus' name. Amen.

The Birth of Jesus

Adult Topic—*Time of Rejoicing*

•••••

Youth Topic—*A King is Born*
Children's Topic—*Jesus Is Born*

•••••

Devotional Reading—John 1:1-4
Background Scripture—Matthew 1
Print—Matthew 1:1-6, 18-25

PRINTED SCRIPTED

Matthew 1:1-6, 18-25 (KJV)

THE BOOK of the generation of Jesus Christ, the son of David, the son of Abraham.

2 Abraham begat Isaac; and Isaac begat Jacob; and Jacob begat Judas and his brethren;

3 And Judas begat Phares and Zara of Thamar; and Phares begat Esrom; and Esrom begat Aram;

4 And Aram begat Aminadab; and Aminadab begat Naasson; and Naasson begat Salmon;

5 And Salmon begat Booz of Rachab; and Booz begat Obed of Ruth; and Obed begat Jesse;

6 And Jesse begat David the king; and David the king begat Solomon of her that had been the wife of Urias.

•••••

18 Now the birth of Jesus Christ was on this wise: When as his mother Mary was espoused to Joseph, before they came together, she was found with child of the Holy Ghost.

19 Then Joseph her husband, being a just man, and not willing to make her a publick example, was

Matthew 1:1-6, 18-25 (NRSV)

AN ACCOUNT of the genealogy of Jesus the Messiah, the son of David, the son of Abraham.

2 Abraham was the father of Isaac, and Isaac the father of Jacob, and Jacob the father of Judah and his brothers,

3 and Judah the father of Perez and Zerah by Tamar, and Perez the father of Hezron, and Hezron the father of Aram,

4 and Aram the father of Aminadab, and Aminadab the father of Nahshon, and Nahshon the father of Salmon,

5 and Salmon the father of Boaz by Rahab, and Boaz the father of Obed by Ruth, and Obed the father of Jesse,

6 and Jesse the father of King David. And David was the father of Solomon by the wife of Uriah.

•••••

18 Now the birth of Jesus the Messiah took place in this way. When his mother Mary had been engaged to Joseph, but before they lived together, she was found to be with child from the Holy Spirit.

minded to put her away privily.

20 But while he thought on these things, behold, the angel of the Lord appeared unto him in a dream, saying, Joseph, thou son of David, fear not to take unto thee Mary thy wife: for that which is conceived in her is of the Holy Ghost.

21 And she shall bring forth a son, and thou shalt call his name JESUS: for he shall save his people from their sins.

22 Now all this was done, that it might be fulfilled which was spoken of the Lord by the prophet, saying,

23 Behold, a virgin shall be with child, and shall bring forth a son, and they shall call his name Emmanuel, which being interpreted is, God with us.

24 Then Joseph being raised from sleep did as the angel of the Lord had bidden him, and took unto him his wife:

25 And knew her not till she had brought forth her firstborn son: and he called his name JESUS.

19 Her husband Joseph, being a righteous man and unwilling to expose her to public disgrace, planned to dismiss her quietly.

20 But just when he had resolved to do this, an angel of the Lord appeared to him in a dream and said, "Joseph, son of David, do not be afraid to take Mary as your wife, for the child conceived in her is from the Holy Spirit.

21 She will bear a son, and you are to name him Jesus, for he will save his people from their sins."

22 All this took place to fulfill what had been spoken by the Lord through the prophet:

23 "Look, the virgin shall conceive and bear a son, and they shall name him Emmanuel," which means, "God is with us."

24 When Joseph awoke from sleep, he did as the angel of the Lord commanded him; he took her as his wife,

25 but had no marital relations with her until she had borne a son; and he named him Jesus.

*And she shall bring forth a son, and thou shalt call his name JESUS: for he shall save his people from their sins.—**Matthew 1:21***

OBJECTIVES

After reading this lesson, the student should be impressed that:

1. The advent of Christ was predicted by the prophet Isaiah;
2. Christ's genealogy includes Gentiles and immoral women;
3. Jesus Christ was born of a virgin; and,
4. His purpose for coming is revealed in His name.

POINTS TO BE EMPHASIZED

Adult/Youth
Key Verse: Matthew 1:21
Print: Matthew 1:1-6, 18-25

—Jesus Christ descended from Abraham and David, a family line that included women who were not Jews. (1-6)

—When Joseph found that Mary, to whom he was engaged, was with child, he decided to quietly end their relationship. (18-19)

—An angel appeared to Joseph in a dream and explained that Mary's child was conceived by the Holy Spirit and that Joseph should marry her. (20)

—The angel told Joseph to name the child Jesus because He would save people from their sins. (21)

—These events fulfilled Isaiah's prophecy that a virgin would bear a son named Emmanuel, which means, "God is with us." (22-23)

—Joseph, fully convinced by the angel's words, married Mary, and when her son was born, named Him Jesus. (24-25)

Children
Key Verse: Luke 2:11
Print: Luke 2:1-20

—While Joseph and Mary were in Bethlehem to be registered, the time came for Mary to give birth to her baby. (4-6)

—Mary gave birth to her firstborn son, wrapped Him in bands of cloth, and laid Him in a manger. (7)

—While shepherds were tending their sheep one night, an angel brought them good news. (8-10)

—After telling the shepherds that a Savior had been born in the city of David, the angel gave the shepherds a sign to help them find the Savior. (11-12)

—A multitude of angels appeared and praised God. (13-14)

—The shepherds found the child with Mary and Joseph, told others what they had seen and heard, and then returned glorifying and praising God. (19-20)

(**Note**: Use KJV Scripture for Adults; NRSV Scripture for Youth and Children)

TOPICAL OUTLINE OF THE LESSON

I. Introduction
A. The Virgin Birth
B. Biblical Background

II. Exposition and Application of the Scripture
A. The Roots of Our Lord (Matthew 1:1-6)
B. The Relationship with the Holy Spirit (Matthew 1:18)
C. The Role of Joseph (Matthew 1:19-21, 24-25)
D. The Revelation of Prophecy (Matthew 1:22-23)

III. Special Features
A. Preserving Our Heritage
B. A Concluding Word

I. Introduction

A. THE VIRGIN BIRTH

No man was involved in the conception and birth of Jesus Christ. Like all babies, His physical body and those elements which made up His blood were received from His mother. The conception was miraculous; the growth of the baby was like that of all other babies. We do not receive blood from our mothers, but we receive the elements which make up our blood by the process of osmosis.

The prediction of the Virgin Birth of Christ is seen first in Isaiah 7:14: "Therefore the Lord Himself will give you a sign: Behold, the virgin shall conceive and bear a Son...." The Hebrew word *(almah)* used here is the more general term, "the young woman," but does not exclude the meaning, "virgin." However, it would not be a "sign" for a virgin to do so. *Parthenos*, the Greek word rendered "virgin" has no other meaning. It is always translated "virgin" (Arndt & Gingrich). Obviously, Matthew was led by the Holy Spirit to use this word. And it remains a fact that the translators of the Old Testament into Greek (Septuagint) were correct in using the word *parthenos* for the word *almah*. In addition, Matthew points out that "before they came together," and Joseph "did not know her," Mary was found with child. To "know" means to have carnal knowledge, to know sexually. Recall that Mary said to Gabriel: "How can this be, since I do not know a man?" She was told: "The Holy Spirit will come upon you, and the power of the Highest will overshadow you; therefore, also, that Holy

One who is to be born will be called the Son of God" (Luke 1:34-35).

B. BIBLICAL BACKGROUND

It is important to know that there are two genealogies given of our Lord. In today's lesson, His genealogy begins with the founder of the Hebrew nation, Abraham, and concludes with Joseph, Mary's husband (Matthew 1:2-17). On the other hand, Luke's genealogy begins with Joseph (Mary's husband) and then goes all the way back to Adam (Luke 3:23-38). Though there are many similarities in the two genealogies, one major difference concerns the Son of David. Matthew traces our Lord's royal line through David's son, Solomon, and our Lord's foster father, Joseph. Note the angel called Joseph, "son of David" (Matthew 1:20). Matthew thus established our Lord's legal claim to the throne by way of ancestry through Joseph, His adopted father (Luke 4:22). Luke traces our Lord's true hereditary descent through His mother Mary, to Nathan, son of David.

Scofield suggests it is better to see Matthew presenting Joseph's genealogy and Luke giving Mary's genealogy—thus one through His father (adopted or legal), and one through His mother. There is no discrepancy between the two genealogies; actually each supplements the other.

Keep in mind that the gospel of Matthew was directed toward a Jewish audience, while the gospel of Luke focuses on Gentile Christians. Hence, the purpose of the various gospels impacts the presentation of their Christ.

II. Exposition and Application of the Scripture

A. THE ROOTS OF OUR LORD
(Matthew 1:1-6)

The book of the generation of Jesus Christ, the son of David, the son of Abraham. Abraham begat Isaac; and Isaac begat Jacob; and Jacob begat Judas and his brethren; And Judas begat Phares and Zara of Thamar; and Phares begat Esrom; and Esrom begat Aram; And Aram begat Aminadab; and Aminadab begat Naasson; and Naasson begat Salmon; And Salmon begat Booz of Rachab; and Booz begat Obed of Ruth; and Obed begat Jesse; And Jesse begat David the king; and David the king begat Solomon of her that had been the wife of Urias.

The word for "book" is *biblos*, which has given us such words as bibliography, Bible, etc. In Matthew 1:1, it means a scroll of papyrus, a "family roll." Jesus Christ is the title used most often of the Savior, and Matthew adds, "the Son of David." Much stock was put in genealogies by the Jews. To Jews who had become Christians, the Messiahship of the Lord Jesus depended on proof that He was indeed a descendant of David. The throne had been vacant for nearly six centuries. For anyone to claim to be the Messiah, he must first of all prove his royal descent.

Matthew thus connects our Lord with His royal heritage. We find this title often applied to our Lord, and it indicates more than mere physical relationship. He is the Son-immediate and rightful Heir of David's throne (Chafer). In other words, see in the title Son of David also One who fulfills the promises made by God in the Davidic covenant. And so our Lord's ancestry is traced to David. Reference to Son of Abraham is made second. After Israel's rejection of the Son of David, demonstrated at Calvary, we see His role as Son of Abraham completed by His sacrifice (an antitype or foreshadow of Isaac, Abraham's son). Understand then that Matthew's purpose was to show that the Lord Jesus was the Messiah, the direct descendant from David's royal house and of the seed of the patriarch, Abraham.

Verse two begins the first of the three groups set up to show the table of descent or "book of the generation." Matthew writes first of Abraham to the setting up of the kingdom under David (verses 2-6). The second group goes from David to the end of the kingdom when the Israelites were deported to Babylon (verses 6-11). And the third period is from the Babylonian Captivity to the birth of our Lord (verses 12-16). So verse two begins our series of "begots" or "fathered."

What strikes our attention here is the mention of the names of the women. It is unusual for women to be listed in Jewish genealogies. This suggests that Matthew purposely included these "questionable" women. The four are noteworthy of study. They are: Tamar, Rahab, Ruth, and Bathsheba. Tamar (verse 3) was a foreigner and woman of doubtful morality. She is mentioned in Genesis 38:6 as the wife of Er, Judah's son. God killed Er for his wickedness. Another son, Onan, then married her, but he too was slain by the Lord. Then Judah's wife, Shua, died. And Tamar, who had been told to wait until Shelah (another son of Judah) was grown in order to marry him, disguised herself as a prostitute. Judah saw her and thinking she was a prostitute had sex with her. Three months later, it was discovered that she was pregnant with twins, fathered by Judah whom she had seduced. Their names were Perez and Zerah.

Rahab (verse 5; Rachab in Hebrew) was a Canaanite harlot (Joshua 2:1; 6:25). There are scholars who do not believe this is the same Rahab mentioned in Joshua. However, Lenski, H. Morris, Alford, and other commentators, believe she is the harlot in Joshua. Matthew has her as the wife of Salmon, and thus an ancestress of David. Ruth, of whom there is no moral blot recorded, was a Moabitess. Recall that Moab was conceived in incest. Lot's daughters made Lot drunk and then lay with him; both became pregnant. One of the children born was Moab; the other, Ben-Ammi (Genesis 19:30-38).

Bathsheba is not mentioned by name but is called "her of Uriah." The translators filled in "who had been the wife" of Uriah. Perhaps it was put this way as a deliberate reminder that she is the one who committed adultery with David (2 Samuel 11-12). From this relationship resulted murder, the deaths of many soldiers, and the death of the first child. Later, after marrying David, she gave birth to Solomon.

Why are these women mentioned at all? Was it to defend against those who would slander Mary and detract from Christ? Was it done to show them their need to deal with these real "stains" in the ancestry of the Messiah? Did Matthew seek to disarm Jewish critics and those who hinted at the "irregularity" of the birth of Christ?

Expositor's believes it highly unlikely that Matthew would "condescend to apologize before the bar of unbelief." The fact is: irregular unions were blessed by God throughout the history of the legal ancestry of the Messiah. Imagine God using such characters with such blemishes in the bloodline of the Messiah! What condescension to include them as ancestors of His Son. Yea, what terrific examples of the grace of God! For all of these women could have been legally excommunicated from Israel or slain. Perhaps it is best then to see their inclusion as ancestresses of Christ as a "foreshadowing of the gracious character of the Gospel" of the Lord Jesus Christ.

Finally in this section, note in verse six that while David is called king, Solomon is not, nor are any of David's successors given this title. This may be to suggest that in the plan of God only Christ is the next king after David (Pilgrim Bible).

B. THE RELATIONSHIP WITH THE HOLY SPIRIT
(Matthew 1:18)

Now the birth of Jesus Christ was on this wise: When as his mother Mary was espoused to Joseph, before they came together, she was found with child of the Holy Ghost.

Three matters are cited to explain the birth of the Lord Jesus. First, His mother Mary was betrothed to Joseph. According to Jewish custom at the time, betrothed couples were called husband and wife. Marriage vows were said, a legal relationship was constituted. Custom decreed a time period, as long as a year, should intervene before the woman would live with the man. Usually she stayed with her father, and then the groom would come and get her and take her to his house.

Second: betrothed to Mary, and the betrothal a sacred relationship, Joseph found that she was with child. She was pregnant before they came together. The sexual act had not taken place to consummate their marriage. She was still a virgin. Third: Mary was pregnant with child of the Holy Spirit. That which was conceived in her was of the Holy Spirit (verse 20). Earlier, the angel Gabriel told Mary: "The Holy Spirit will come upon you, and the power of the Highest will overshadow you; therefore, also, that Holy One who is to be born will be called the Son of God" (Luke 1:35). No one can explain what took place here. It is a mystery. We can but read and believe. And understand that from His birth to His death, the Lord Jesus was in the care of the Holy Spirit. Note also the distinct personality of the Holy Spirit here. He is not a mere wind or influence. He is God!

C. THE ROLE OF JOSEPH
(Matthew 1:19-21, 24-25)

Then Joseph her husband, being a just man, and not willing to make her a publick example, was minded to put her away privily. But while he thought on these things, behold, the angel of the Lord appeared unto him in a dream, saying, Joseph, thou son of David, fear not to take unto thee Mary thy wife: for that which is conceived in her is of the Holy Ghost. And she shall bring forth a son, and thou shalt call his name JESUS: for he shall save his people from their sins. Then Joseph being raised from sleep did as the angel of the Lord had bidden him, and took unto him his wife: And knew her not till she had brought forth her firstborn son: and he called his name JESUS.

You can see the situation Joseph was in. For all practical purposes, as far as Joseph could determine, Mary had violated the solemn promise made before witnesses. Surely, fulfillment of the marriage contract (betrothal) was now impossible. And since Joseph was a just man, a God-fearing man, one who kept the Law, he could not just let it slip by and do nothing. In such a case, unfaithfulness was regarded as adultery. In times past, Mary could have been put to death by stoning.

Joseph's love for Mary is obvious. He could have charged her with adultery and made her a public example. Secretly divorcing her would have been no problem at all; that with the lax divorce laws common among the Jews at that time, He did not even have to tell why he divorced her.

In those days, it was not "No Fault," it was "Her Fault." He did not have to speak about indignities, incompatibility, infidelity or desertion. Certainly, any appeal to the courts would have exposed Mary to public ignominy, scorn and shame. Deep disgrace would have been heaped upon her, the child, and upon her family.

Naturally, Joseph thought about these things, and while he turned these matters over in his mind, God intervened. An angel of the Lord came to Joseph in a dream and told him not to be afraid to take Mary his wife. When Joseph awoke, he did as the Lord had told him; and did not know her till she had brought forth her firstborn son. The language used here safeguards the idea of the Virgin Birth. Mary later had children by Joseph. The Bible does not teach what is called the perpetual virginity of Mary (Matthew 12:46; 13:55-56; Mark 6:3; John 7:3,5; Acts 1:14; 1 Corinthians 9:5; Galatians 1:19).

D. THE REVELATION OF PROPHECY (Matthew 1:22-23)

Now all this was done, that it might be fulfilled which was spoken of the Lord by the prophet, saying, Behold, a virgin shall be with child, and shall bring forth a son, and they shall call his name Emmanuel, which being interpreted is, God with us.

What occurred here had been predicted by the prophet Isaiah (7:14). The paragraph containing this verse predicts deliverance from the impending war. However, it also goes beyond this, and points to that final deliverance given by God in the flesh. "Immanuel" means "God with us." The title not only signifies God's presence with His people, but also that by the Incarnation, God had become forever identified as one of the human family. According to Hebrew usage, the name Immanuel represents more of a characterization than it represents a title (Scofield). It certainly emphasizes our Lord's Deity (Isaiah 9:6).

III. Special Features

A. PRESERVING OUR HERITAGE

The inclusion of women like Tamar, Rahab, Ruth and Bathsheba suggests that the coming of the Messiah would bring salvation to all people. God so loved the world that He gave His only begotten Son. In Christ, the barriers of race and gender were torn down (Galatians 3:28). God's grace extends even to Gentiles! We often read about people who boast about the purity of their race. Even some White Gentile Christians are tinged with anti-Semitism, forgetful that Jesus Christ after the flesh was a Jew. Is it possible for Gentile bigots to fully love Jesus Christ, a Jew, and at the same time hate black people?—even Christian blacks? Such an attitude is contradictory, and unscriptural.

B. A CONCLUDING WORD

The angel that spoke to Joseph predicted Mary would bring forth a Son, and "you shall call His name Jesus, for He will (emphatic: He alone!) save His people from their sins." The name Jesus is a transliteration of the Hebrew, Joshua, which in turn is a contraction of Jehoshua. It means Jehovah is Salvation, or Jehovah Saves. By contracting Jehoushua to Joshua, emphasis shifts to the salvation aspect, stress falls upon the verb to save. Only the Lord Jesus Christ saves from sin. He alone was born of a virgin. He alone was born without a sin nature. As He had no mother in heaven, He had no father on earth. Only of Him did the prophet Isaiah predict some seven hundred years before time that they shall call His name Immanuel, "God with us." Only of Him did the prophet Micah foretell His birthplace.

"I know of a Name, A beautiful Name,
That angels brought down to earth.
They whispered it low, One night long ago,
To a maiden of lowly birth.
That beautiful Name, That beautiful Name,
From sin has power to free us!
That beautiful Name, That wonderful Name,
That matchless Name is Jesus" (Jean Perry).

HOME DAILY BIBLE READINGS FOR THE WEEK OF DECEMBER 19, 1999

THE BIRTH OF JESUS

Dec. 13	M.	Matthew 1:1-11, The Genealogy of Jesus the Messiah
Dec. 14	T.	Matthew 1:12-17, Jesus' Genealogy Completed
Dec. 15	W.	Matthew 1:18-25, The Birth of Jesus the Messiah
Dec. 16	T.	John 1:1-14, Jesus Christ, God's Eternal Word
Dec. 17	F.	Luke 1:26-38, The Angel Gabriel Visits Mary
Dec. 18	S.	Luke 1:39-45, Mary Visits Her Cousin Elizabeth
Dec. 19	S.	Luke 1:46-56, Mary's Song of Praise

Know Your Bible

- The principle by which the unjust steward acted was one that sought to make friends by any means possible, whether his conduct was good or bad. (Luke 16:1-10)
- Our judgment on human affairs is different from God's assessment of those same behaviors because God sees beyond that which is apparent to those hidden agendas that are at the basis of our actions. (Luke 16:15)
- The story of the rich man and Lazarus instructs the Christian to take care if he is rich and to make good use of his riches, but whether he is rich or poor, priority should be given to storing us treasures in heaven. (Luke 16:19-31)
- Obedience to God does not warrant self-exaltation on the part of the Christian. At best, obedience is that which we are required to do, because we can never repay God for all of His mercies toward us. (Luke 17:7-10)

Eternal God, our Father, as You did descend to us in the person of Jesus Christ, may we ascend unto Thee through the power of grace in that quality of life that depicts Your image and likeness, through Jesus Christ our Lord. Amen.

Coming of the Wise Men

Adult Topic—*Time of Worshiping*

·····

Youth Topic—*Search Until You Find*

Children's Topic—*Wise Men Look for Jesus*

·····

Devotional Reading—Psalm 98

Background Scripture—Matthew 2

Print—Matthew 2:1-12

PRINTED SCRIPTURE

Matthew 2:1-12 (KJV)

NOW WHEN Jesus was born in Bethlehem of Judaea in the days of Herod the king, behold, there came wise men from the east to Jerusalem,

2 Saying, Where is he that is born King of the Jews? for we have seen his star in the east, and are come to worship him.

3 When Herod the king had heard these things, he was troubled, and all Jerusalem with him.

4 And when he had gathered all the chief priests and scribes of the people together, he demanded of them where Christ should be born.

5 And they said unto him, In Bethlehem of Judaea: for thus it is written by the prophet,

6 And thou Bethlehem, in the land of Juda, art not the least among the princes of Juda: for out of thee shall come a Governor, that shall rule my people Israel.

7 Then Herod, when he had privily called the wise men, enquired of

Matthew 2:1-12 (NRSV)

IN THE time of King Herod, after Jesus was born in Bethlehem of Judea, wise men from the East came to Jerusalem,

2 asking, "Where is the child who has been born king of the Jews? For we observed his star at its rising, and have come to pay him homage."

3 When King Herod heard this, he was frightened, and all Jerusalem with him;

4 and calling together all the chief priests and scribes of the people, he inquired of them where the Messiah was to be born.

5 They told him, "In Bethlehem of Judea; for so it has been written by the prophet:

6 'And you, Bethlehem, in the land of Judah, are by no means least among the rulers of Judah; for from you shall come a ruler who is to shepherd my people Israel.'"

7 Then Herod secretly called for the wise men and learned from them the exact time when the star

them diligently what time the star appeared.

8 And he sent them to Bethlehem, and said, Go and search diligently for the young child; and when ye have found him, bring me word again, that I may come and worship him also.

9 When they had heard the king, they departed; and, lo, the star, which they saw in the east, went before them, till it came and stood over where the young child was.

10 When they saw the star, they rejoiced with exceeding great joy.

11 And when they were come into the house, they saw the young child with Mary his mother, and fell down, and worshipped him: and when they had opened their treasures, they presented unto him gifts; gold, and frankincense, and myrrh.

12 And being warned of God in a dream that they should not return to Herod, they departed into their own country another way.

had appeared.

8 Then he sent them to Bethlehem, saying, "Go and search diligently for the child; and when you have found him, bring me word so that I may also go and pay him homage."

9 When they had heard the king, they set out; and there, ahead of them, went the star that they had seen at its rising, until it stopped over the place where the child was.

10 When they saw that the star had stopped, they were overwhelmed with joy.

11 On entering the house, they saw the child with Mary his mother; and they knelt down and paid him homage. Then, opening their treasure chests, they offered him gifts of gold, frankincense, and myrrh.

12 And having been warned in a dream not to return to Herod, they left for their own country by another road.

KEY VERSE

*Where is he that is born King of the Jews? For we have seen his star in the east, and are come to worship him.—**Matthew 2:2***

OBJECTIVES

After reading this lesson, the student should know that:

1. The birthplace of the Messiah was predicted by Micah;
2. Magi from the East were supernaturally led to Jesus' place of birth;
3. Herod the Great was an exceptionally wicked man;
4. The magi, warned by God, wisely returned home another way; and,
5. While men may seek directions from those who are in positions of authority, our final guidance and instruction come from God Himself.

Adult/Youth/Children
Key Verse: Matthew 2:2
Print: Mathew 2:1-12

—After Jesus' birth, Magi from the East came searching for the newborn king. (1-2)
—Hearing of the Magi's coming, a frightened King Herod asked the Jewish religious leaders where the Messiah was to be born. (3-4)
—Asking the Magi to return and tell him where they found the child, Herod sent them to Bethlehem, where Micah has prophesied the Messiah would be born. (5-8)
—The Magi followed the star and joyfully found the place where Jesus was. (9-10)
—The Magi knelt before Jesus and gave Him valuable gifts. (11)
—Warned in a dream not to return to Herod, the Magi returned to their own country by another route. (12)

(**Note**: Use KJV Scripture for Adults; NRSV Scripture for Youth and Children)

TOPICAL OUTLINE OF THE LESSON

I. Introduction

A. The Magi or Wise Men
B. Biblical Background

II. Exposition and Application of the Scripture

A. Inquiry of the Wise Men (Matthew 2:1-2)
B. Inquiry of the Wicked Monarch (Matthew 2:3-4)
C. Response of the Religious Leaders (Matthew 2:5-6)
D. Response of the Evil Ruler (Matthew 2:7-8)
E. Reaction of the Wise Men (Matthew 2:9-12)

III. Special Features

A. Preserving Our Heritage
B. A Concluding Word

I. Introduction

A. THE MAGI OR WISE MEN

Magoi is a Greek word derived from the Persian, and in the present context, almost certainly means "astrologers" (Tasker). Used in a good sense, the Magi were learned astrologers; used in a bad sense, the term refers to those who practiced magical arts. Matthew used the term in the better sense.

Lenski calls them astronomers. Henry Morris states that in Persian society, the Magi were members of the priestly caste, and they were experts in astronomy and astrology; and well versed also in the Old Testament. More than likely, they were similar to the Chaldeans in Nebuchadnezzar's court (Daniel 2:2). It is quite possible that these Magi had come into contact with Jewish exiles, or with the prophecies of Daniel. It seems evident that although they were Gentiles, they did indeed possess some knowledge of Old Testament prophecies regarding the Messiah.

It is said that they were from the East; this may mean Arabia, but more likely, Persia or Babylon. There were probably more than three, but the number three came about because of the number of gifts presented to the Christ-child: gold, frankincense, and myrrh. And tradition has named them Caspar, Melchior, and Balthasar. There are no facts to confirm this tradition.

B. BIBLICAL BACKGROUND

In Matthew 2:6, the author cites Micah 5:2, which reads: "But you, Bethlehem Ephrathah, though you are little among the thousands of Judah, yet out of you shall come forth to Me the One to be Ruler in Israel, whose goings forth are from of old, from everlasting." It appears that Matthew used neither the Septuagint (Old Testament in Greek) nor the literal Hebrew translation of Micah 5:2. Several changes are noted. In the Septuagint, the word for ruler is shepherd. "Thousands" in Micah is changed into "princes" or "rulers." And because there were two Bethlehems in Palestine, the writer had to be careful in distinguishing which one is meant.

Bethlehem means "house of bread," a name signifying the fertility of the land. The Bethlehem in the north was about six miles southeast of Mount Carmel in the area belonging to the tribe of Zebulun. The Bethlehem which is the birthplace of our Lord is some six miles southwest of Jerusalem, in the district of Ephrathah (Aramaic: fruitful, fertile), within the tribal boundaries of Judah. This Bethlehem was also the birthplace of David; and it is implied that Christ will be another David, and consequently, be a true Shepherd of God's people, Israel.

God's Spirit moved upon the prophet Micah to predict seven hundred years before the birth of our Lord the exact place He would be born. Though Bethlehem was too small to have any prominence among the thousands of families of Judah, yet as the humble birthplace of the Messiah, and also the village of Christ's great ancestor, David, it was destined to be exalted throughout the world. Indeed, from this obscure little village would come forth the King of Kings.

The prophecy also points out both the Deity and Humanity of our Lord. As Man, He was born a baby in Bethlehem. However, as God, His "goings forth are from of old, from everlasting." Clothed in timeless dignity, His activities in creation, and His perpetual energy sustain and uphold "all things by the word of His power" (Hebrews 1:3). "The eternal preexistence of the Messiah is thus strongly resented" (Scofield). All of His redemptive activities, His preservation of His creation, His reincarnate appearances (Christophanies or Theophanies: Christ or

God appearances)—all point to this future Ruler as the One whose goings forth are from everlasting. In short, we see the remarkable fulfillment of the prophecy made in the eighth century by the prophet Micah concerning the exact, specific locality of the birth of the Messiah.

II. Exposition and Application of the Scripture

A. INQUIRY OF THE WISE MEN
(Matthew 2:1-2)

Now when Jesus was born in Bethlehem of Judaea in the days of Herod the king, behold, there came wise men from the east to Jerusalem, Saying, Where is he that is born King of the Jews? For we have seen his star in the east, and are come to worship him.

Scholars are not sure of the exact year of the birth of the baby Jesus. Estimates are about 6-4 B.C. (Note descending order). At any rate, He was born during the reign of Herod the Great. Herod was a very cruel man. He put to death his own wife and sons (Alford). He was a descendant of Esau, and thus a traditional enemy of the Jewish people. Needless to say, he was hated by the Jews.

After failing in his attempt to find the Christ-child through the aid of the Magi, in anger, he ordered the death of "all the male children who were in Bethlehem and in all its districts, from two years old and under" (Matthew 2:16). In this, Herod reminds us of the Pharaoh of Egypt who likewise practiced infanticide (Exodus 1).

Herod lied through his teeth when he told the Magi he wanted to worship the young Child also (Matthew 2:8). The very secrecy (verse 7) of his meeting with the wise men betrays his sadistic motive. About the only good thing to be said about Herod is that he died in 4 B.C., thus giving us the only evidence we have in Matthew's Gospel for dating the birth of the baby Jesus. It would appear that the Lord Jesus was born in the closing months of Herod the Great's reign. It is believed that Joseph and Mary brought Him back from Egypt soon after Herod's death. This is as specific as we can be (Tasker).

The Magi inquired: "Where is He who has been born King of the Jews?" They had seen His star and desired to prostrate themselves before Him in homage. Use of the word "worship" indicates they already regarded His Deity. But what is meant by "His star"? Was its appearance something extraordinary? Was it a supernatural or miraculous appearance? Did this star signify that Christ was born or about to be born? We do not know. The exact nature of this remarkable astronomical phenomenon is not revealed. But for the Magi, it was "His star" because they believed its appearance signified that the King also had appeared.

B. INQUIRY OF THE WICKED MONARCH (Matthew 2:3-4)

When Herod the king had heard these things, he was troubled, and all Jerusalem with him. And when he had gathered all the chief priests and scribes of the people together, he demanded of them where Christ should be born.

When Herod heard of the inquiry and statement of the Magi, he was stirred up. After all, he considered himself the "king of the Jews." All Jerusalem was likewise troubled. The fact that the coming of this baby so greatly agitated Herod and all Jerusalem betrays the bitter enmity of man's heart toward God. Ironside points out that the depravity of the human heart is shown when God's love is met with coldness, suspicion, and rejection; and God's grace is spurned.

Herod called together all the members of the Sanhedrin—the chief priests and scribes of the people. Most of the Pharisees were also scribes. The scribes' task was to make copies of the Scriptures. They classified and taught the principles of the oral law, and also kept accurate record of the written word. Surely, if anyone knew of the predicted coming of the Messiah, the teacher and interpreter of the divine law would know.

According to the historian Josephus, the Pharisees prophesied a revolution would take place at the coming of the Messiah. And so Herod made careful inquiry. He asked them what the Scriptures had to say about the birthplace of the Messiah. The attitude later shown by these Jewish religious leaders demonstrates that copying, guarding, teaching, and counting the Scriptures all mean nothing if the Word is not obeyed. What counts in life is letting God's Word control our lives. Failure here adds condemnation to the one so acquainted with Scriptures, but who does not yield to the Word. As Ironside stated, Herod and the religious leaders knew what the prophets said concerning the coming of the Christ, but they themselves had no room in their hearts for Him. They knew prophecy, but did not submit their hearts to the One of whom the prophets spoke.

C. RESPONSE OF THE RELIGIOUS LEADERS
(Matthew 2:5-6)

And they said unto him, In Bethlehem of Judaea: for thus it is written by the prophet, And thou Bethlehem, in the land of Juda, art not the least among the princes of Juda: for out of thee shall come a Governor, that shall rule my people Israel.

The response of the religious leaders to Herod was to point out to him the prophecy of Micah 5:2. As official interpreters of the Mosaic law, these leaders knew what Scriptures pertained to the Messiah. They were the religious scholars of their day; and they understood Micah 5:2 as predicting the place of the birth of the Christ. This passage gave the precise geographical location—Bethlehem of Judah.

This village would no longer be considered the least among the rulers of Judah. Why? Because (note the word for) out of it shall come a Ruler who will shepherd God's people. This was the reason for the new evaluation of Bethlehem. Insignificant among the many families of Judah, Bethlehem would be made famous as the birthplace of the Savior; from it would emerge the Ruler of Israel.

Tasker suggests that because Matthew 2:6 is not consonant with the Hebrew text of Micah 5:2, that we may assume Matthew put the Old Testament text in his own words, as he was led by the Holy Spirit. This made Micah's prophecy more pregnant with meaning than is apparent as written in the Old Testament. We see that the religious leaders knew that when the Messiah came, He would fulfill the prophecy of Micah 5:2.

D. RESPONSE OF THE EVIL RULER (Matthew 2:7-8)

Then Herod, when he had privily called the wise men, enquired of them diligently what time the star appeared. And he sent them to Bethlehem, and said, Go and search diligently for the young child; and when ye have found him, bring me word again, that I may come and worship him also.

Herod called a secret meeting with the Magi, and determined from them what time the star had appeared. The very privacy of the meeting shows the evil purpose of the king. He then sent them out, ordering them to diligently search for the young Child. Herod had no intention of worshiping the Christ-child. Mixed in with his hatred of the Jews was his fear that the coming of the Messiah might cause an uproar in Jerusalem, and jeopardize his standing with the authorities in Rome. He wanted the status quo to remain. He recognized that the presence of the Christ was a threat to his political kingdom. This is why he later ordered the killing of the male children two years old and under.

E. REACTION OF THE WISE MEN (Matthew 2:9-12)

When they had heard the king, they departed; and, lo, the star, which they saw in the east, went before them, till it came and stood over where the young child was. When they saw the star, they re-joiced with exceeding great joy. And when they were come into the house, they saw the young child with Mary his mother, and fell down, and worshipped him: and when they had opened their treasures, they presented unto him gifts; gold, and frankincense, and myrrh. And being warned of God in a dream that they should not return to Herod, they departed into their own country another way.

Understand that when the Magi were at home in their own land, they saw "His star in the East." They then traveled eastward to Jerusalem. And now, after hearing Herod's request, the Magi departed. As they left, behold, the star which they had seen in the East when they were in their own distant homeland went before them. Until this time apparently, it had not been seen in Jerusalem. It came and hovered over the entire village of Bethlehem—or more likely over that part of the village where the young Child was.

The crowd that had come to be registered was now gone. Evidently, the family had found suitable living quarters, and was no longer in the stable where Christ was born, or in the inn where lodging was first sought (Luke 2:7). This suggests that the visit of the Magi at this point took place several weeks or even months after our Lord's birth.

Upon entering the house, the Magi saw the young Child with Mary His mother. Joseph is not mentioned, probably because he was elsewhere at the time. It is significant that the visitors worshiped the Child, not His mother. When they opened their treasures (chests, trunks), they presented gifts to Him. The gold symbolized Deity and glory, the shining perfection of His Person. It also represented His future reign as King. The frankincense represented the fragrance of His purity and sinless perfection. The myrrh, a bitter herb, a spice used for burial, presaged the sufferings of Calvary, as He bore our sins upon Himself. It pointed then to His coming death. See then the gifts pointing to Christ as King, Son of God, and the One destined to die. Finally, warned in a dream by God not to return to Herod, the Magi departed for their own country another way. Having met the Messiah, they could not return the way they came, spiritually. Any encounter with the Lord Jesus transforms our lives.

III. Special Features

A. PRESERVING OUR HERITAGE

We are encouraged as a people by this story, for it shows that the God of the Bible is no respecter of faces or races in His development of the Salvation story. It demonstrates that people from unknown parts are included in honoring the Christ born in an insignificant village. It exhibits that grace of God that overcomes the cruelty of the human political leaders, and brings to naught their nefarious schemes to keep down those they consider no more than inferior subjects. In spite of all that has taken place in the United States in the lives of Black Americans, the Lord of History has seen to it that we are represented in that great number that shall fall down and worship Him. In every discouraging situation, it is the coming of Christ into our lives that changes things for the better.

B. A CONCLUDING WORD

Matthew alone records this story of the Magi. He was right on target as he portrayed Gentiles diligently seeking Christ, Herod planning to kill Him, the Jewish religious leaders indifferent, and the people of Jerusalem troubled. The fulfillment of prophecy is important proof of the divine inspiration of the Bible, of its God-breathed quality.

You can better understand now why Satan has always attempted to destroy the predictive quality of the Scriptures. He has assigned interpolations, postdating, errors in calculations, anachronisms, different authors, wishful thinking, etc. in his desire to undermine biblical prophecy. When the Bible was written, approximately a quarter of its contents was prediction; indeed, hundreds of prophecies were made in the Bible. Fulfillment served to prove that the Bible is not like any other book in the world. The minute accuracy in the prediction of the birth of Christ in Bethlehem Judah is a splendid example of the trustworthiness of the Scriptures.

Those who study the intricate relationship between obedience and disobedience within the history of Isreal will be equally impressed by God's promise of the consequences of disobedience and how the results of Israel's disobedience are realized consistent with that promise.

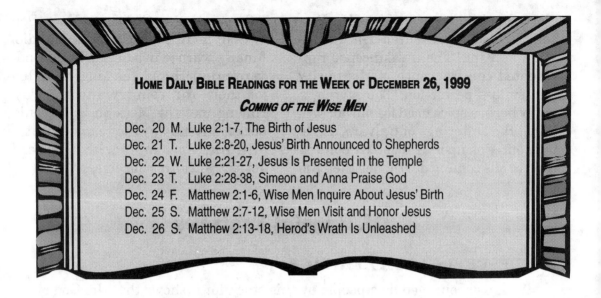

HOME DAILY BIBLE READINGS FOR THE WEEK OF DECEMBER 26, 1999

COMING OF THE WISE MEN

Dec. 20 M. Luke 2:1-7, The Birth of Jesus
Dec. 21 T. Luke 2:8-20, Jesus' Birth Announced to Shepherds
Dec. 22 W. Luke 2:21-27, Jesus Is Presented in the Temple
Dec. 23 T. Luke 2:28-38, Simeon and Anna Praise God
Dec. 24 F. Matthew 2:1-6, Wise Men Inquire About Jesus' Birth
Dec. 25 S. Matthew 2:7-12, Wise Men Visit and Honor Jesus
Dec. 26 S. Matthew 2:13-18, Herod's Wrath Is Unleashed

Know Your Bible

- The meaning of the kingdom of God being within us is the rule of God in the hearts of His people, producing righteousness, peace and joy in the Holy Ghost. (Romans 14:17)
- To be wealthy does not necessarily means that one is blessed, but wealth is always a temptation and a snare that can lead to ruin. (Luke 18:22-25)
- The parable of the householder teaches us that God is debtor to no one, but that God gives to each person that which He thinks is best for the person concerned. (Matthew 20:1-16)
- The tax-gatherers were known for the practice of receiving more taxes from the Jews than that which was due to the Roman government, and kept the excess for their personal use. (Luke 19:5-8)
- Some of the questions which were directed to Jesus were designed to bring Him into conflict with the Jewish or the Roman Law, depending on the way in which He answered them. (Mark 12:14-17)
- The difference between the long prayers of the Pharisees and the "pray without ceasing" that the apostle encouraged was that the prayers of the Pharisees were made as a pretence, to present a façade of being holy, while the apostle enjoined a constant spirit of prayer. (Matthew 23:14)
- The evidence that the Lord looks on the heart is illustrated by Jesus' commendation of the widow's mite, a gift that was made from sincerity of heart and purpose. (Mark 12:41-44)

O God, grant that we may search for Thee until You find us; then lead us into Your presence that we may worship You with sincerity of heart and purpose as we surrender our lives for Your service. In the name of Jesus Christ, we pray. Amen.

The Twelve Disciples

Unit 2—*Jesus' Teachings and Ministry*
Children's Unit—*The Ministry of Jesus*

.....

Adult Topic—*Thinking About Commitment*

.....

Youth Topic—*Follow Me*
Children's Topic—*Jesus Calls Twelve Disciples*

.....

Devotional Reading—Matthew 10:5-15
Background Scripture—Matthew 4:18-22; 9:9-12; 10:1-4
Print—Matthew 4:18-22; 9:9-12; 10:1-4

PRINTED SCRIPTURE

Matthew 4:18-22; 9:9-12; 10:1-4 (KJV)

18 And Jesus, walking by the sea of Galilee, saw two brethren, Simon called Peter, and Andrew his brother, casting a net into the sea: for they were fishers.

19 And he saith unto them, Follow me, and I will make you fishers of men.

20 And they straightway left their nets, and followed him.

21 And going on from thence, he saw other two brethren, James the son of Zebedee, and John his brother, in a ship with Zebedee their father, mending their nets; and he called them.

22 And they immediately left the ship and their father, and followed him.

.....

9 And as Jesus passed forth from thence, he saw a man, named Matthew, sitting at the receipt of cus-

Matthew 4:18-22; 9:9-12; 10:1-4 (NRSV)

18 As he walked by the Sea of Galilee, he saw two brothers, Simon, who is called Peter, and Andrew his brother, casting a net into the sea—for they were fishermen.

19 And he said to them, "Follow me, and I will make you fish for people."

20 Immediately they left their nets and followed him.

21 As he went from there, he saw two other brothers, James son of Zebedee and his brother John, in the boat with their father Zebedee, mending their nets, and he called them.

22 Immediately they left the boat and their father, and followed him.

.....

9 As Jesus was walking along, he saw a man called Matthew sitting at the tax booth; and he said to him, "Follow me." And he got up and

tom: and he saith unto him, Follow me. And he arose, and followed him.

10 And it came to pass, as Jesus sat at meat in the house, behold, many publicans and sinners came and sat down with him and his disciples.

11 And when the Pharisees saw it, they said unto his disciples, Why eateth your Master with publicans and sinners?

12 But when Jesus heard that, he said unto them, They that be whole need not a physician, but they that are sick.

.....

AND WHEN he had called unto him his twelve disciples, he gave them power against unclean spirits, to cast them out, and to heal all manner of sickness and all manner of disease.

2 Now the names of the twelve apostles are these; The first, Simon, who is called Peter, and Andrew his brother; James the son of Zebedee, and John his brother;

3 Philip, and Bartholomew; Thomas, and Matthew the publican; James the son of Alphaeus, and Lebbaeus, whose surname was Thaddaeus;

4 Simon the Canaanite, and Judas Iscariot, who also betrayed him.

followed him.

10 And as he sat at dinner in the house, many tax collectors and sinners came and were sitting with him and his disciples.

11 When the Pharisees saw this, they said to his disciples, "Why does your teacher eat with tax collectors and sinners?"

12 But when he heard this, he said, "Those who are well have no need of a physician, but those who are sick."

.....

THEN JESUS summoned his twelve disciples and gave them authority over unclean spirits, to cast them out, and to cure every disease and every sickness.

2 These are the names of the twelve apostles: first, Simon, also know as Peter, and his brother Andrew; James son of Zebedee, and his brother John;

3 Philip and Bartholomew; Thomas and Matthew the tax collector; James son of Alphaeus, and Thaddaeus;

4 Simon the Cananaean, and Judas Iscariot, the one who betrayed him.

 **KEY VERSE**

*And he saith unto them, "Follow me, and I will make you fishers of men"—**Matthew 4:19***

OBJECTIVES

After reading this lesson, the student should be better informed about:

1. The call of the first disciples;
2. The meanings of the terms disciples and apostles;
3. The significance of the healing ministry; and,
4. What it means to follow the Lord.

POINTS TO BE EMPHASIZED

Adult/Youth

Key Verse: Matthew 4:19

Print: Matthew 4:18-22; 9:9-12; 10:1-4

—Two sets of brothers (Peter and Andrew, James and John) obeyed the call to leave their vocation of fishing and to follow Jesus. (4:18-22)

—Matthew, a tax collector, responded to Jesus' call by leaving his business to follow Jesus. (9:9)

—Jesus ate dinner at Matthew's house along with many tax collectors and sinners. (9:10)

—When Pharisees criticized Jesus for eating with sinners, Jesus overheard and quoted a proverb that showed He spent His time with those who needed Him most. ((9:11-12)

—Jesus empowered His twelve disciples to cast out unclean spirits and to heal illnesses. (10:1-4)

Children

Key Verse: Matthew 4:19

Print: Matthew 4:18-22; 9:9-12; 10:1-5, 7

—Two sets of brothers (Peter and Andrew, James and John) obeyed the call to leave their vocation of fishing and to follow Jesus. (4:18-22)

—Matthew, a tax collector, responded to Jesus' call by leaving his business to follow Jesus. (9:9)

—Jesus ate dinner at Matthew's house along with many tax collectors and sinners. (9:10)

—When Pharisees criticized Jesus for eating with sinners, Jesus overheard and quoted a proverb that showed He spent His time with those who needed Him most. ((9:11-12)

—Jesus empowered His twelve disciples to cast out unclean spirits and to heal illnesses. (10:1-4)

—Jesus instructed the disciples to proclaim the Good News (10:7)

(**Note**: Use KJV Scripture for Adults; NRSV Scripture for Youth and Children)

I. Introduction

A. DISCIPLES AND APOSTLES

The word translated disciples means a learner or pupil. In our lesson, it is used of the twelve men our Lord called to follow Him. In addition, it is used with respect to all of His followers; it may also refer to Christians in general. A disciple is one who directs his mind, is engaged in learning, and binds himself to someone in order to acquire knowledge. There is thus implied a relationship to a teacher, a loyal following. True disciples of the Lord are those who know His doctrines and follow Him. They attach themselves to Him as their Teacher.

The word apostle, used in Matthew 10:2, is derived from the verb, *apostello*. The preposition *apo* means off, away; the verb *stello* means to send, place, set. An apostle is one sent out (with a commission), sent forth with orders, a delegate, envoy, messenger, "missionary."

The apostles are thus "sent ones." This word is especially applied to the twelve disciples Christ chose, out of the many of His adherents, "to be His constant companions and the heralds to proclaim to men the kingdom of God" (Thayer).

Today, we encounter men who call themselves "apostles," but technically speaking, they are not; there are none today. They all died. Furthermore, to qualify as an apostle in this technical sense, the following criteria are noted: One must be (1) directly chosen by the Lord Himself or by the Holy Spirit, (2) endowed with power to perform miracles, and (3) one must be an eyewitness, having actually seen the Lord. In conclusion: Our literature uses *apostolos* "predominantly for the apostles, a group of highly honored believers, who had a special function" (Arndt & Gingrich).

B. BIBLICAL BACKGROUND

Different factors are seen in the choices made by our Lord. From among a wide circle of men, He chose those representing a cross-section of humanity—of Jewish society at that time in that area. Many were fishermen; one was a tax collector. Their personalities varied. There was impetuous Simon Peter, with great leadership ability; pessimistic Thomas; ambitious James and John; Simon the Zealot, a former rebel; the deceitful purloiner, Judas Iscariot. All of them were busy, hardworking men, of average ability, but a few of outstanding intellect. They were all young men, probably in their twenties, with John the youngest.

What was outstanding about them was their relationship with Jesus Christ. Their commitment to Him is seen in their willingness to drop what they were doing and follow Him. It is good for young people to follow the Lord, for then they are most zealous, malleable, teachable and adaptable. More interested in quality than in numbers, Christ chose only twelve. Their task would be to evangelize, and win others to Him. In turn, those converted to the Lord would seek to win still others.

II. Exposition and Application of the Scripture

A. THE CALLING OF THE FISHERMEN (Matthew 4:18-22)

And Jesus, walking by the sea of Galilee, saw two brethren, Simon called Peter, and Andrew his brother, casting a net into the sea: for they were fishers. And he saith unto them, Follow me, and I will make you fishers of men. And they straightway left their nets, and followed him. And going on from thence, he saw other two brethren, James the son of Zebedee, and John his brother, in a ship with Zebedee their father, mending their nets; and he called them. And they immediately left the ship and their father, and followed him.

Walking by the Sea of Galilee, our Lord saw two brothers. One was Simon, nicknamed Peter by our Lord; the other, Andrew, Peter's brother. Simon is Greek for the Hebrew name meaning hearing. Peter or Petros means a stone. The Aramaic name, Cephas, also means a stone (John 1:42). His brother's name was Andrew, which means manly. Actually, these two were already disciples, having come to the Lord some months earlier, as recorded in John 1:40-41. Andrew had introduced Simon to the Lord. In today's lesson, their call is to service (Scofield). Their previous association was renewed and now made permanent (Wycliffe Bible Commentary).

Note they were busy, casting a net into the sea; for they were fishermen. The command, "Follow Me!" was a call for a constant companionship. Christ's desire was to make these fishermen "fishers of men." He would train them for the great work of reclaiming lost souls. Fishing for men, "taking men alive," leading men and women to accept the shed blood of Jesus Christ, is Holy Spirit work. It requires patience, prayer, and knowledge of the Scriptures—all applied in love. When believers are willing to learn at the feet of the Savior, and let Him "make" them, they become useful instruments in His hands, for His praise and glory.

The verb rendered "follow" means come behind, join, accompany. Among ancients, disciples were accustomed to literally accompanying their masters or teachers on their walks and journeys (Matthew 4:19, 20, 22; 9:9). On the other hand when the apostle Paul exhorted the saints to follow him, he used a verb which means to imitate, a verb from which we have derived the words "mime" and "mimic" (1 Corinthians 4:16, 11:1; Ephesians 5;1; 2 Thessalonians 3:7, 9).

The impact and influence of their earlier encounter prompted Peter and Andrew to immediately respond. There were no excuses, no putting off, no procrastination, no hesitation. They straightway reacted. And so they left their nets in the hands of their helpers and followed the Lord to fulfill a far greater calling. Continuing His walk, the Lord saw another pair of brothers, the sons of Zebedee, James and John. They too were busy, in the boat with their father, mending or getting their nets ready for use.

It appears from Luke's account (Luke 5:1-11) that the men were washing, mending and casting their nets when the Lord first approached. The Lord got into Simon's boat, and taught from it. Then, He caused the miraculous catch of fish, after which Simon and Andrew were called to follow Him. Upon landing on shore, James and John began to repair the nets broken by the great number of fish. At this point, the Lord also called James and John to follow Him.

Because there are three others by the name of James in the New Testament, this James the Apostle is never mentioned apart from his brother, John. He was one of the trio which enjoyed a special closeness with our Lord. We repeatedly read of "Peter, James and John" (see Mark 5:37, 9:2, 13:3, 14:33). Another apostle named James was the son of Alphaeus. Because he was of shorter stature than James son of Zebedee, he is also called James the Less (Mark 15:40).

Like Peter and Andrew, these brothers also dropped what they were doing, and immediately left their boat and their father, and followed the Lord. Sometimes when talking to men about a full-time ministry, they bring up the hardship it would cause their spouse and children. Our lesson clearly teaches that following the Lord may require giving up job, leaving spouse (Peter was married), and cutting family ties. Christ wants total heart allegiance. Such immediate response is an attitude of faith that pleases God. These two pairs of brothers formed the nucleus of the apostolic band (Tasker). Their immediate and sacrificial response led them to become able "fishers of men."

B. THE CALLING OF THE TAX COLLECTOR (Matthew 9:9)

And as Jesus passed forth from thence, he saw a man, named Matthew, sitting at the receipt of custom: and he saith unto him, Follow me. And he arose, and followed him.

This call is recorded after the healing of the paralytic man. As the Lord passed on from there, He saw a man named Matthew. Like the others whom the Lord called, he too was busy, but he was a publican, a customhouse officer, sitting at the tax office. Actually, it was a toll booth in the street, probably on the outskirts (ICC), set up to receive taxes. Jewish tax gatherers were despised by both their employers and by their own Jewish people. The Jews considered them traitors for working for the Roman government, which at the time dominated Israel. Note in Matthew 9:11, tax collectors and sinners are lumped together. Many of these publicans were dishonest. They demanded more than was required by the government, and pocketed the excess for themselves. Recall that of Zacchaeus it is said: "He was a chief tax collector, and he was rich" (Luke 19:2).

Despite Matthew's reputation and despised position in society, the Lord chose him. Matthew says very little about himself at this point. We are not told about his conversion. What is noteworthy is his immediate response. When Christ said: "Follow Me," Matthew arose from his desk and followed Him.

C. THE REBUKING OF THE PHARISEES (Matthew 9:10-12)

And it came to pass, as Jesus sat at meat in the house, behold, many publicans and sinners came and sat down with him and his disciples. And when the Pharisees saw it, they said unto his disciples, Why eateth your Master with publicans and sinners? But when Jesus heard that, he said unto them, They that be whole need not a physician, but they that are sick.

Matthew invited his former associates to his house to a feast arranged in honor of the Lord (Mark 2:15; Luke 5:29). It was his method of publicly confessing Christ. He also knew that his former acquaintances continued to live shabby lives and needed to meet the Messiah. Those who are called "sinners" were people considered immoral because their occupations were looked upon with disfavor by the religious leaders. They were folks who did not or could not observe the elaborate rules of the scribes and Pharisees.

When the religious leaders observed the Lord Jesus seated at the table with such outcasts, the Pharisees said to the disciples: "Why does your Teacher eat with tax collectors and sinners?" Upon hearing this, the Lord replied, "Those who are well have no need of a physician, but those who are sick." He struck at their self-righteousness. Their refusal to accept His healing meant that they had deluded themselves into believing they were morally well. How sick is the man who does not believe he is sick! Sin is deceptive.

D. THE SENDING FORTH OF THE TWELVE (Matthew 10:1-4)

And when he had called unto him his twelve disciples, he gave them power against unclean spirits, to cast them out, and to heal all manner of sickness and all manner of disease. Now the names of the twelve apostles are these; The first, Simon, who is called Peter, and Andrew his brother; James the son of Zebedee, and John his brother; Philip, and Bartholomew; Thomas, and Matthew the publican; James the son of Alphaeus, and Lebbaeus, whose surname was Thaddaeus; Simon the Canaanite, and Judas Iscariot, who also betrayed him.

Twelve disciples were chosen to represent the twelve tribes of Israel.

The disciples of verse one are appointed in verse two. Followers, learners, students, pupils, apprentices become "sent ones," envoys, missionaries. As Creator, Christ gave the men authority over unclean spirits (demons) and power to exorcise them. They also were enabled to heal all kinds of sickness and all kinds of disease. A miracle working ministry authenticated the Lord's claim as Messiah.

Their names are combined in pairs, probably because Christ sent them out on their first mission assignment "two by two" (Mark 6:7). A brief comment is made on each of the twelve apostles: (1) Simon, who is called Peter, is noted for his leadership, impetuousness and denial of the Lord. (2) Andrew, which means manliness, is Simon's brother. He introduced three persons to the Lord: Simon, the lad with the loaves, and certain Greeks (John 1:40-42; 6:8-9; 12:20-22). (3) James, son of Zebedee, was later beheaded by Herod Agrippa I (Acts 12:2). (4) John was also a son of Zebedee, and the brother of James. Both of them were members of the inner circle. John is the author of the gospel of John, the three Epistles of John, and the book of Revelation. (5) Philip: this name means lover of horses. He brought Nathanael to the Lord. (6) Bartholomew is generally believed to be Nathanael. (7) Thomas the Twin (Didymus) is often called "Doubting Thomas" because of his reluctance to believe the Lord had risen from the dead (John 20:24-29). (8) Matthew the tax collector or publican is also called Levi (Mark 2:14; Luke 5:27). Levi may have been his original name, changed after his conversion to Matthew (Tasker). Evidently, he knew Greek and was well-educated to hold this position (Lenski). (9) James the son of Alphaeus is also called James the Little or James the Less. (10) Lebbaeus means courageous. His surname was Thaddaeus, meaning breast. He is also called Jude or Judas, not Iscariot (John 14:22; Luke 6:16). (11) Simon the Canaanite. This does not mean he was a native of Canaan, but represents an Aramaic word meaning "zealous." He is thus called Simon the Zealot. He had been a member of a fanatical sect which sought to overthrow the Romans. (12) Purposely put last is Judas Iscariot, the son of perdition, who also betrayed the Lord. These are the names of the twelve apostles, "duly-empowered representatives of a higher official"— the Lord Jesus Christ!

III. Special Features

A. PRESERVING OUR HERITAGE

Opportunities for Black American Christians to be used of the Lord have increased tremendously. Positions as chaplains in hospitals, penitentiaries, the armed forces, institutions of higher learning, etc. have opened in a remarkable way. Missions organizations which were formerly lily-white (some still are) have opened their doors. Blacks now serve as doctors, nurses, teachers, translators, colporteurs, and evangelists across the globe. Of course, some colleges and seminaries were forced by Uncle Sam to open their doors to us, but thank God for

Uncle Sam! Even some Conventions eagerly recruit black membership! And believe it or not, there are denominations with churches that have not only opened their doors to black membership, but are willing—however few in numbers—to accept black pastors. Our lesson today persuades us to adopt an attitude which says: "Where He leads me, I will follow."

B. A CONCLUDING WORD

God has a work for each of us. And the work varies, for all of us are not called or fitted for the same task; the body has many different organs in it (1 Corinthians 12). But whoever yields himself or herself to the Holy Spirit for definite service discovers that the Lord directs, empowers, trains, equips, places and causes fruit to come forth. Farrar has described the disciple of Christ as: "One who believes His doctrines, rests upon His sacrifice, imbibes His spirit, and imitates His example." Whoever you are, He "will make you" what He wants you to be. What a glorious privilege to serve the Master! Life is lived at its fullest when we are surrendered to His will, and when we can truly say, "Thou art the Potter, I am the clay."

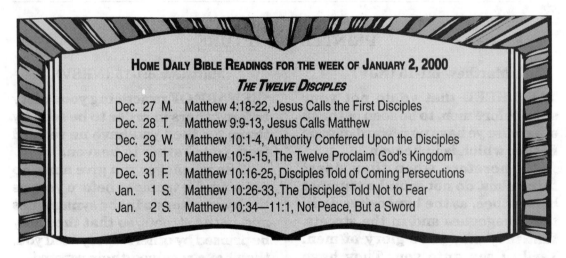

HOME DAILY BIBLE READINGS FOR THE WEEK OF JANUARY 2, 2000

THE TWELVE DISCIPLES

Dec. 27 M. Matthew 4:18-22, Jesus Calls the First Disciples
Dec. 28 T. Matthew 9:9-13, Jesus Calls Matthew
Dec. 29 W. Matthew 10:1-4, Authority Conferred Upon the Disciples
Dec. 30 T. Matthew 10:5-15, The Twelve Proclaim God's Kingdom
Dec. 31 F. Matthew 10:16-25, Disciples Told of Coming Persecutions
Jan. 1 S. Matthew 10:26-33, The Disciples Told Not to Fear
Jan. 2 S. Matthew 10:34—11:1, Not Peace, But a Sword

Know Your Bible

- The characteristic of humility is to be as willing to serve as to rule, and to be ready to render all types Christian service to those who are our brothers and sisters. (Luke 22:25-27)
- In order to participate in fellowship with Christ, all of our sins must be washed in His precious blood. (John 13:8)
- We may determine whether we are serving or rejecting Christ by our conduct toward His disciples. (Matthew 25:45)

Our Father, incline our hearts to become instruments in Your service. Teach us Your way so that our lives will model Your character as examples for those who struggle to know Your will for their lives. In the name of Jesus, we pray. Amen.

Teachings on Prayer

Adult Topic—*Thinking About Prayer*

•••••

Youth Topic—*Private Conversation*

Children's Topic—*Jesus Teaches About Prayer*

•••••

Devotional Reading—Luke 11:1-13

Background Scripture—Matthew 6:1-15

Print—Matthew 6:1-15

═══════════════════════════

PRINTED SCRIPTURE

Matthew 6:1-15 (KJV)

TAKE HEED that ye do not your alms before men, to be seen of them: otherwise ye have no reward of your Father which is in heaven.

2 Therefore when thou doest thine alms, do not sound a trumpet before thee, as the hypocrites do in the synagogues and in the streets, that they may have glory of men. Verily I say unto you, They have their reward.

3 But when thou doest alms, let not thy left hand know what thy right hand doeth.

4 That thine alms may be in secret: and thy Father which seeth in secret himself shall reward thee openly.

5 And when thou prayest, thou shalt not be as the hypocrites are: for they love to pray standing in the synagogues and in the corners of the streets, that they may be seen of men. Verily I say unto you, They

Matthew 6:1-15 (NRSV)

"BEWARE OF practicing your piety before others in order to be seen by them; for then you have no reward from your Father in heaven.

2 So whenever you give alms, do not sound a trumpet before you, as the hypocrites do in the synagogues and in the streets, so that they may be praised by others. Truly I tell you, they have received their reward.

3 But when you give alms, do not let your left hand know what your right hand is doing,

4 so that your alms may be done in secret; and your Father who sees in secret will reward you.

5 And whenever you pray, do not be like the hypocrites; for they love to stand and pray in the synagogues and at the street corners, so that they may be seen by others. Truly I tell you, they have received their reward.

6 But whenever you pray, go into

have their reward.

6 But thou, when thou prayest, enter into thy closet, and when thou hast shut thy door, pray to thy Father which is in secret; and thy Father which seeth in secret shall reward thee openly.

7 But when ye pray, use not vain repetitions, as the heathen do: for they think that they shall be heard for their much speaking.

8 Be not ye therefore like unto them: for your Father knoweth what things ye have need of, before ye ask him.

9 After this manner therefore pray ye: Our Father which art in heaven, Hallowed be thy name.

10 Thy kingdom come. Thy will be done in earth, as it is in heaven.

11 Give us this day our daily bread.

12 And forgive us our debts, as we forgive our debtors.

13 And lead us not into temptation, but deliver us from evil: For thine is the kingdom, and the power, and the glory, for ever. Amen.

14 For if ye forgive men their trespasses, your heavenly Father will also forgive you:

15 But if ye forgive not men their trespasses, neither will your Father forgive your trespasses.

your room and shut the door and pray to your Father who is in secret; and your Father who sees in secret will reward you.

7 When you are praying, do not heap up empty phrases as the Gentiles do; for they think that they will be heard because of their many words.

8 Do not be like them, for your Father knows what you need before you ask him.

9 Pray then in this way: Our Father in heaven, Hallowed be your name.

10 Your kingdom come. Your will be done, on earth as it is in heaven.

11 Give us this day our daily bread.

12 And forgive us our debts, as we also have forgiven our debtors.

13 And do not bring us to the time of trial, but rescue us from the evil one.

14 For if you forgive others their trespasses, your heavenly Father will also forgive you;

15 but if you do not forgive others, neither will your Father forgive your trespasses."

But Thou, when thou prayest, enter into thy closet, and when thou hast shut thy door, pray to thy Father which is in secret; and thy Father which seeth in secret shall reward thee openly.
—Matthew 6:6

OBJECTIVES

After reading this lesson, the student should be able to discern that:

1. True religion is not a show;
2. Prayer is not to be hypocritical or pagan;
3. We must be taught how to pray; and,
4. God hears, sees, rewards, and forgives.

POINTS TO BE EMPHASIZED

Adult/Youth/Children
Key Verse: Matthew 6:6
Print: Matthew 6:1-15

—Jesus cautioned against practicing piety to impress other people. (1)
—Jesus taught that giving alms should be done confidentially. (2-4)
—Jesus taught that prayer should be a personal and private matter. (5-6)
—Jesus taught that His followers should not use many empty phrases in their prayers because God knows what we need before we ask. (7-8)
—Jesus gave His followers a model prayer. (9-13)
—Jesus said that those who expect God's forgiveness should forgive others. (14-15)

(**Note**: Use KJV Scripture for Adults; NRSV Scripture for Youth and Children)

TOPICAL OUTLINE OF THE LESSON

I. Introduction

A. Hindrances to Prayer
B. Biblical Background

II. Exposition and Application of the Scripture

A. Motives and Methods for Good Deeds (Matthew (6:1-4)
B. Motives and Methods for Prayer (Matthew 6:5-8)
C. Model of Prayer (Matthew 6:9-13)
D. Matter of Forgiveness (Matthew 6:14-15)

III. Special Features

A. Preserving Our Heritage
B. A Concluding Word

I. Introduction

A. HINDRANCES TO PRAYER

We recognize that God deals with us where He finds us. This fact makes the teaching ministry imperative. We must be taught by God who would bring us from where He found us to where He wants us to be. Understand then that just because we are Christians, we must not assume that we automatically know how to pray. We do not. Consider then some of the hindrances to the kind of prayer life the Lord Jesus desires for us.

1. **Disregard for the poor:** "Whoever shuts his ears to the cry of the poor will also cry himself and not be heard" (Proverbs 21:13).

2. **Mistreatment of spouse:** "Likewise, you husbands, dwell with them with understanding, giving honor to the wife, as to the weaker vessel, and as being heirs together of the grace of life, that your prayers may not be hindered" (1 Peter 3:7).

3. **Selfish motives:** "You ask and do not receive, because you ask amiss, that you may spend it on your pleasures" (James 4:3). Include here from today's lesson those prayers which have as their motive to be seen and heard of men.

4. **Ingratitude:** This is one of the first steps towards idolatry (Romans 1:21). Unthankful (2 Timothy 3:1) for what we have, greed enters in, and we want more. Failing to remember "we brought nothing into this world, and it is certain we can carry nothing out" (1 Timothy 6:7), we fall in love with money and things. Failure to be content with such things as we have is one of the reasons the Prophets of Prosperity have gained such a following! Prayer life is adversely affected because of our ingratitude. The "gimmes" should be replaced by "thank You." God wants us to serve Him because we love Him, not just because we want something from Him.

5. **Broken fellowship:** "If I regard iniquity in my heart, the Lord will not hear" (Psalm 66:18). There should be no known, unconfessed sin in our lives. *Homologeo* is literally "to speak the same." Confession is to say the same thing God says about our iniquity. Keep the slate clean so you can enter boldly into His Presence. Don't let unconfessed sin clog up "the telephone line in your bosom."

B. BIBLICAL BACKGROUND

Apparently, our Lord taught what is called the Lord's Prayer on two separate occasions, and under different circumstances. Today's lesson, as part of the Sermon on the Mount (Matthew 5-7), is the first time it was given. Here He warns against "ostentatious formality in prayer" (Scofield). The second time we read what is termed the Lord's Prayer is in Luke 11:1-4. No name is given for the place of instruction, but the occasion was born when one of the disciples requested, "Lord, teach us to pray, as John also taught his disciples."

There are several differences or variations noted when the two prayers are compared. Matthew's "Give us this day our daily bread" becomes in Luke, "Give us day by day our daily bread." Matthew's "And forgive us our debts, as we forgive our debtors" is in Luke, "And forgive us our sins, for we also forgive everyone who is indebted to us." Then finally, Luke omits the ending that Matthew has: "For Yours is the kingdom and the power and the glory forever. Amen." Technically, it is not the Lord's Prayer. This is to say, He never prayed it. He knew no sin (2 Corinthians 5:21), and so could never pray for forgiveness. It is His in the sense that He is its Author. But the true Lord's Prayer is found in John chapter 17.

II. Exposition and Application of the Scripture

A. MOTIVES AND METHODS FOR GOOD DEEDS
(Matthew 6:1-4)

TAKE heed that ye do not your alms before men, to be seen of them: otherwise ye have no reward of your Father which is in heaven. Therefore when thou doest thine alms, do not sound a trumpet before thee, as the hypocrites do in the synagogues and in the streets, that they may have glory of men. Verily I say unto you, They have their reward. But when thou doest alms, let not thy left hand know what thy right hand doeth: That thine alms may be in secret: and thy Father which seeth in secret himself shall reward thee openly.

Righteous or charitable deeds are those acts of practical piety. Reference is to the religious life as expressed in the carrying out of religious duties (ICC). Such deeds are not to be done for self-glorification, to be seen by men, for such a motive vitiates the deed. In other words, our motive is not to seek the praise of men. Men may indeed see what we do, and glorify our heavenly Father (Matthew 5:16), but we are to avoid outward pretense of giving of alms or fasting in mere externalism and a spirit of vain show. All such is immediately judged by God the Father. Incidentally, the Father is mentioned eight times in today's lesson. A key though then is the believer's relationship with his or her Father.

Now there is nothing wrong with the deeds in themselves; they are called righteous. But we are not to parade our piety. What counts is the motive behind the method. Men may receive the applause of audiences, plaques (some of us are plagued to death with plaques in our churches!), citations, commendations, awards and fame—but if the motive for the service rendered is impure, there will be no heavenly reward. It is not denied that even with pure motives for righteous or charitable deeds, that we may still receive accolades of men. All human recognition is not inherently or necessarily wrong. But even here we must be careful lest we become puffed up.

We see then that the Lord does not reward hypocrisy (play-acting; stage-playing), ostentation, show, pretension. So when we perform a righteous act or good deed, we are not to sound a trumpet. This proverbial expression is not to be taken literally. It means to show off, "pat oneself on the back," practice self-laudation. It means to publicize, advertise. Some religious leaders of that day stood in the synagogues and on the street corners and drew attention to themselves when about to give their alms. People may say, "Oh my, what a religious man he is!" But this remark concerning his earthly reputation is the hypocrite's here-and-now full payment (meaning of the word, reward).

It is not taught that systematic giving is wrong. But there should also be a free and spontaneous nature to giving, as if uplanned. What the right hand gives is done so secretly that the left hand may not discover it. This implies simplicity, both of intention and act (Alford). The expression means to "give without self-consciousness or self-complacency, the root of ostentation" (Expositor's). However, what man cannot see is certainly observed by God. Man looks at the outward; God sees the inner recesses of the heart. What He sees in secret, He rewards openly.

B. MOTIVES AND METHODS FOR PRAYER (Matthew 6:5-8)

And when thou prayest, thou shalt not be as the hypocrites are: for they love to pray standing in the synagogues and in the corners of the streets, that they may be seen of men. Verily I say unto you, They have their reward. But thou, when thou prayest, enter into thy closet, and when thou hast shut thy door, pray to thy Father which is in secret; and thy Father which seeth in secret shall reward thee openly. But when ye pray, use not vain repetitions, as the heathen do: for they think that they shall be heard for their much speaking. Be not ye therefore like unto them: for your Father knoweth what things ye have need of, before ye ask him.

The first four verses center on the giving of alms as an example of a charitable or righteous deed. Verses 16-18 deal with fasting. The section we now study, verses 5-15, gives instructions concerning prayer. These three: almsgiving, praying, and fasting constitute the righteous deeds of verses 1-18. Once again, we encounter the word hypocrites. It is used to describe a religion that stresses ritual and external matters. Men can be hypocritical in the giving of alms (verse 2), in fasting (verse 16), and in prayer (verse 5). Hypocrisy observes no restrictions.

The very behavior and attitudes which the Lord rebukes help us to define hypocrisy—the act of men pray-

ing in such a manner that they show their desire to be seen and heard of men. The fact that the hypocritical religious leaders stood while praying in synagogues and on the street corners brings up the matter of posture in prayer. Our study reveals a variety of positions were used by believers. (1) Moses and Aaron fell on their faces (Numbers 16:22). So did Joshua (5:14), and David (1 Chronicles 21:16); Christ also prostrated Himself in prayer (Matthew 26:39). (2) Many Scriptures show believers knelt in prayer: Daniel (6:10); Paul (Acts 20:36); Christ Himself (Luke 22:41). "Oh come, let us worship and bow down, let us kneel before the Lord our Maker" (Psalm 95:6). (3) Solomon "Knelt down on his knees before all the assembly of Israel, and spread out his hands toward heaven" and prayed (2 Chronicles 6:13). (4) David prayed with his hands lifted up toward God's holy sanctuary (Psalm 28:2). We assume he was standing, as also in the case of the lifting up of holy hands in 1 Timothy 2:8, and as mentioned in Mark 11:25, and in today's lesson, Matthew 6:5. Solomon also stood and prayed with his hands spread out toward heaven (1 Kings 8:22).

Obviously, no one definitive prayer posture is given. David says he prayed in bed (Psalm 63:6). Most of us pray with our eyes closed. Yet at the tomb of Lazarus, the Lord Jesus looked up toward heaven with His eyes wide open (John 11:41). In my first pastorate, one of our deacons always stood praying with his eyes opened. I spoke to him about it, and he replied, "Reverend, the Bible says, 'watch and pray'" (Matthew 26:41). Because we have no set formula for posture in prayer, we are forced back to the main issue—motives, heart-attitudes, the inner person's relationship with the Lord. Evidently, standing was an ordinary or usual posture. But picking the most conspicuous spot to stand and pray aloud was hypocritical.

If a man prays in such a way that he shows his love of prominence, then his only reward is the prominence he gained. He will never take that to heaven. Public prayer of course is not prohibited. But private secret closet prayer is honored. The word rendered "closet" or "secret place" speaks of a storeroom in which one might keep treasures. We see that the "Bible encourages secret prayer, in the closet, away from all the disturbing elements around us" (Thiessen). It is often said that a man's public prayer reflects on his private prayer, for private prayer is seen as training ground for praying in public.

Properly defining the Greek word translated "vain repetitions" is made difficult because of its rarity. It is variously rendered: "use many phrases" (Knoc); "do not be saying idle things" (Syriac); "saying things irrelevant and senseless" (Alford); "babbling or speaking without thinking" (Parallel Bible Commentary); "empty phrases" (RSV); "heap up empty phrases" (NRSV); "meaningless repetition" (NASB); "like the involuntary repeats of a stammerer" (Expositor's); "babble, utter a lot of useless and superfluous words" (Lenski: who adds it has nothing to do with stammering).

Tasker states Tyndale's rendering, "babble overmuch" is probably as good as any other. A. T. Robertson wrote that it is used "of stammerers who repeat the words, then mere babbling or chattering, empty repetition." The etymology is uncertain, but is probably onomatopoetic like "babble." For further understanding, read of the heathen Baal worshipers at Mount Carmel (1 Kings 18:26), and of the sophisticated idol-worshipers of Diana who yelled out for about two hours, "Great is Diana of the Ephesians!" (Acts 19:34).

Christ does not condemn all repetition in prayer. Recall that He Himself "prayed the third time, saying the same words" (Matthew 26:44). He also spent entire nights in prayer. So long prayers are not in themselves forbidden. What is condemned is the idea that endless repetition will convince God of our sincerity. Or that many words are required to inform Him of our needs, or perhaps weary Him, overcome His will, and cause Him to grant our requests. Imagine attempting to tire out God! Such were the unworthy desires of the heathen in their prayers.

Finally, in this section, one may ask: "Why pray if God knows already what we need?" A straightforward answer would be: Pray because He tells us to do so! But He also desires that we express trust. Prayer demonstrates that we depend upon Him. Keeping within the context, we are commanded to pray because our heavenly Father knows our needs, and therefore we do not have to shout Him down, deluge Him with superfluous words, beat His eardrums with endless entreaty, or use "vain repetition."

C. MODEL OF PRAYER
(Matthew 6:9-13)

After this manner therefore pray ye: Our Father which art in heaven, Hallowed be thy name. Thy kingdom

come. Thy will be done in earth, as it is in heaven. Give us this day our daily bread. And forgive us our debts, as we forgive our debtors. And lead us not into temptation, but deliver us from evil: For thine is the kingdom, and the power, and the glory, for ever. Amen.

The words "in this manner" are not the same as "in these words." We have here a model for prayer that Christ gave His disciples. It was not intended to be a ritual prayer, although in many of our churches it is recited each Sunday. Throughout the Gospels, we find many other instructions for the prayer life of the present day believer. And in the Letters to the churches, we find further instruction.

Consider now the verses which constitute what is commonly called the Lord's Prayer. God is His name; the hundreds of titles in the Bible may all be rolled up into one, yet give us only an inkling of His character, attributes, personality, plans, purposes, acts, and power. His name is His self-revelation. His name expresses His essence, His character, what and who He really is. To hallow His name then means to sanctify, hold in reverence and awe, all that we know about Him, for He is holy.

The kingdom spoken of in verse ten is the Messianic kingdom. It is not the Church Age in which we presently live. It is that time when Christ shall rule the world with a rod of iron, with headquarters in Jerusalem. Christians yearn for the coming of the Lord to snatch up His own (the Rapture). There is, of course, a final kingdom to come, one beyond the Millennium (1 Corinthians 15:24-28). Rest assured His will shall be done on earth as it is in heaven. All be-

lievers want to see that day!

We learn here the principle of starting our prayers by acknowledging God's purpose for His creation. In this passage, we find the first mention made in the New Testament of His will. Verse ten then reminds us that His will is the most important thing in the world. We also make known our desire to be given that which is "indispensable" (Arndt and Gingrich), that bread required for the immediate future. We are reminded of the manna God made available for the Israelites in the wilderness (Exodus 16:4). They were to gather a certain amount each day.

All sin constitutes a debt to God (New Bible Commentary). Use of the word debts is a Jewish way of regarding sins, short-comings, viewed as moral and spiritual debts to God's righteousness. Now we must be careful here. These instructions on prayer are addressed to Jews looking forward to the Messianic kingdom. At this time they are not members of the church, for the church was not born until the Day of Pentecost. From a Christian perspective, no Christian can expect to be forgiven who does not himself forgive, but by no means should Christians think that we merit God's forgiveness because we first forgive others!

The petition of verse 13 does not contradict James 1:13: "Let no one say when he is tempted, 'I am tempted by God'; for God cannot be tempted by evil, nor does He Himself tempt anyone." He allows us to be tested and tried. We pass the test by acknowledging our inability to resist temptation or to succeed when tried. Here is a cry for daily salvation from sin, and from Satan, the evil one. Tasker puts it this way: "Give us the necessary strength so that life's trials do not become for us occasions of spiritual temptation." Chafer agrees: We desire to be spared from testing, but if in God's wisdom we must experience testing, then we pray for deliverance from flunking the test. We pray for salvation from the evil of demonstrating "unyieldedness and unfaithfulness."

D. MATTER OF FORGIVENESS
(Matthew 6:14-15)

For if ye forgive men their trespasses, your heavenly Father will also forgive you: But if ye forgive not men their trespasses, neither will your Father forgive your trespasses.

The passage throws further light on verse 12. It emphasizes the conditional nature of the matter of forgiveness. Recognize first of all that for the Christian, all sins have been forgiven already (Ephesians 4:32; Colossians 3:13). Through faith in the finished work of Calvary, we stand without condemnation. This aspect of forgiveness then is a once-for-all, settled matter. The fact is, though forgiven we still sin. Our trespasses (missteps, falling off to the side, going off of the right path) tend to break fellowship with God our Father. Confession is required, and forsaking of the sin in order to heal any brokenness. "If we confess our sins, he is faithful and just to forgive us our sins and to cleanse us from all unrighteousness" (1 John 1:9). Because of the grace of God in our lives—that grace whereby He forgives those already saved—we are encouraged to forgive others. For us, salvation is indicted through our spirit of forgiveness and our failure to forgive affects our fellowship with the Father.

III. Special Features

A. PRESERVING OUR HERITAGE

Today's lesson is one that should be taken to heart by many of our churches. All too often our public praying is unenlightened futility, loud, emotional, and at times full of "stock sentences and empty phrases." For example: How often do we hear what might be called, PREACHING PRAYERS? This may be excused as traditional, but when we preach prayer, is it directed to God the Father in heaven, or to our audience? How often do we hear folks pray private prayers in public? We hear "me, my, I" instead of "us, our, we." Some members even make announcements in their prayers. Henry Morris states: "All prayer, whether verbalized, sung or silent, should come from the heart and be addressed to God, not an audience." What happens when we apply this principle to church music, especially gospel? Surely, our musicians and singing groups need to take heed to what is said about prayer and transfer it to singing. Ostentation, showiness or theatricality, "showboating," seeking the applause of the audience—all such is not worshiping God in spirit and in truth. Expositor's admonishes: "Theatrical virtue does not count in the Kingdom of God. Right motive is essential there." Lord, teach us TO pray, and teach us HOW to pray! And while at it, Lord, teach us also how to sing!

B. A CONCLUDING WORD

Only one born again through faith in the shed blood of Jesus Christ has the right or authority to call God, Father. Our prayers are therefore in the name of Jesus Christ, a matter not touched on in today's lesson, for the instruction given to the disciples took place prior to Calvary. Again, because of Calvary, we come boldly to the throne of God (Hebrews 4:16, 10:19-20). Now the dispensational approach of L. S. Chafer very strongly reminds us of the kingdom nature of Matthew 6:1-18.

He states that the instructions on prayer basically appeal to "the faithfulness of Jehovah to His children in the kingdom," that age when Christ returns to the earth to rule for a thousand years. Disregarding this interpretation may lead to serious error concerning the prayer life of the Christian living in this present church age. Thank God for whatever principles we learn that we can apply for our use today. But, remember that we approach the Father on church ground, not on kingdom ground. We come to the Father only through the Lord Jesus Christ, believing that He "is able to do exceedingly abundantly above all that we ask or think, according to the power that works in us" (Ephesians 3:20).

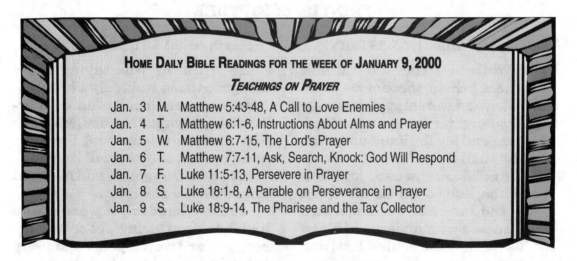

HOME DAILY BIBLE READINGS FOR THE WEEK OF JANUARY 9, 2000

TEACHINGS ON PRAYER

Jan. 3	M.	Matthew 5:43-48, A Call to Love Enemies
Jan. 4	T.	Matthew 6:1-6, Instructions About Alms and Prayer
Jan. 5	W.	Matthew 6:7-15, The Lord's Prayer
Jan. 6	T.	Matthew 7:7-11, Ask, Search, Knock: God Will Respond
Jan. 7	F.	Luke 11:5-13, Persevere in Prayer
Jan. 8	S.	Luke 18:1-8, A Parable on Perseverance in Prayer
Jan. 9	S.	Luke 18:9-14, The Pharisee and the Tax Collector

Know Your Bible

- Phylacteries were slips of parchment, with texts of Scripture upon them, which the Pharisees wore as charms. (See Numbers 15:38-39)
- The estimate of the amount of money for which Judas betrayed Jesus was the same as the compensation money for a servant who was killed by an ox. (Exodus 21:32)
- The love of the things of this world is incompatible with the love that we should have for Jesus Christ. (John 15:18-19)

O God, teach us how to pray as the means by which we commune with Thee. Grant that we may align ourselves with Your power, as we seek to accomplish Your will for our lives. Amen.

Miracles of Compassion

Adult Topic—*Thinking About Wholeness*

.....

Youth Topic—*Healing Touch*

Children's Topic—*Jesus Performs Miracles*

.....

Devotional Reading—Matthew 11:2-6

Background Scripture—Matthew 9:18-38

Print—Matthew 9:18-31, 35-36

PRINTED SCRIPTURE

Matthew 9:18-31, 35-36 (KJV)

18 While he spake these things unto them, behold, there came a certain ruler, and worshipped him, saying, My daughter is even now dead: but come and lay thy hand upon her, and she shall live.

19 And Jesus arose, and followed him, and so did his disciples.

20 And, behold, a woman, which was diseased with an issue of blood twelve years, came behind him, and touched the hem of his garment:

21 For she said within herself, If I may but touch his garment, I shall be whole.

22 But Jesus turned him about, and when he saw her, he said, Daughter, be of good comfort; thy faith hath made thee whole. And the woman was made whole from that hour.

23 And when Jesus came into the ruler's house, and saw the minstrels and the people making a noise,

Matthew 9:18-31, 35-36 (NRSV)

18 While he was saying these things to them, suddenly a leader of the synagogue came in and knelt before him, saying, "My daughter has just died; but come and lay your hand on her, and she will live."

19 And Jesus got up and followed him, with his disciples.

20 Then suddenly a woman who had been suffering from hemorrhages for twelve years came up behind him and touched the fringe of his cloak.

21 for she said to herself, "If I only touch his cloak, I will be made well."

22 Jesus turned, and seeing her he said, "Take heart, daughter; your faith has made you well." And instantly the woman was made well.

23 When Jesus came to the leader's house and saw the flute players and the crowd making a commotion,

24 he said, "Go away; for the girl

24 He said unto them, Give place: for the maid is not dead, but sleepeth. And they laughed him to scorn.

25 But when the people were put forth, he went in, and took her by the hand, and the maid arose.

26 And the fame hereof went abroad into all that land.

27 And when Jesus departed thence, two blind men followed him, crying, and saying, Thou Son of David, have mercy on us.

28 And when he was come into the house, the blind men came to him: and Jesus saith unto them, Believe ye that I am able to do this? They said unto him, Yea, Lord.

29 Then touched he their eyes, saying, According to your faith be it unto you.

30 And their eyes were opened; and Jesus straitly charged them, saying, See that no man know it.

31 But they, when they were departed, spread abroad his fame in all that country.

.....

35 And Jesus went about all the cities and villages, teaching in their synagogues, and preaching the gospel of the kingdom, and healing every sickness and every disease among the people.

36 But when he saw the multitudes, he was moved with compassion on them, because they fainted, and were scattered abroad, as sheep having no shepherd.

is not dead but sleeping." And they laughed at him.

25 But when the crowd had been put outside, he went in and took her by the hand, and the girl got up.

26 And the report of this spread throughout that district.

27 As Jesus went on from there, two blind men followed him, crying loudly, "Have mercy on us, Son of David!"

28 When he entered the house, the blind men came to him; and Jesus said to them, "Do you believe that I am able to do this?" They said to him, "Yes, Lord."

29 Then he touched their eyes and said, "According to your faith let it be done to you."

30 And their eyes were opened. Then Jesus sternly ordered them, "See that no one knows of this,"

31 But they went away and spread the news about him throughout that district.

.....

35 Then Jesus went about all the cities and villages, teaching in their synagogues, and proclaiming the good news of the kingdom, and curing every diseased and every sickness.

36 When he saw the crowds, he had compassion for them, because they were harassed and helpless, like sheep without a shepherd.

*When he saw the multitudes, he was moved with compassion on them, because they fainted, and were scattered abroad, as sheep having no shepherd. —**Matthew 9:36***

OBJECTIVES

After reading this lesson, the student should appreciate more deeply that:

1. The God of the Bible is a compassionate God;
2. The life of faith is a reality; and,
3. Christ Jesus is the source of all healing, physical and spiritual.

POINTS TO BE EMPHASIZED

Adult/Youth/Children

Key Verse: Matthew 9:36

Print: Matthew 9:18-31, 35-36; 9:18-34 *(Children)*

—Jesus and His disciples went with a leader of the synagogue who had asked Jesus to raise his daughter from the dead. (18-19)

—On the way, a woman who suffered from hemorrhages for twelve years touched Jesus' cloak, and because of her faith was healed. (20-22)

—At the Synagogue leader's house, Jesus restored the daughter to life. (23-26)

—As Jesus went on from there, He healed two blind men who believed in His power, and though He ordered them not to tell anyone, they went away and spread the news. (27-31)

—Jesus went about teaching, proclaiming the Good News, and curing diseases. (35)

—Jesus had compassion for the crowds and all their needs. (36)

(**Note**: Use KJV Scripture for Adults; NRSV Scripture for Youth and Children)

TOPICAL OUTLINE OF THE LESSON

I. Introduction

A. Death Seen as Sleep

B. Biblical Background

II. Exposition and Application of the Scripture

A. Healing the Woman's Issue of Blood (Matthew 9:20-22)

B. Raising the Ruler's Daughter (Matthew 9:18-19, 23-26)

C. Giving Sight to the Blind (Matthew 9:27-31)

D. Showing Compassion to the Multitude (Matthew 9:35-36)

III. Special Features

A. Preserving Our Heritage

B. A Concluding Word

I. Introduction

A. DEATH SEEN AS SLEEP

We study what is known as soul sleep because there are those who teach that when death comes, the deceased are immediately made unconscious. One may readily consider this as fact if the theme of the book of Ecclesiastes is ignored, and certain New Testament Scriptures omitted. However, statements like the "dead know nothing," and there is no knowledge" in the grave are points of view of man "under the sun" (Ecclesiastes 9:5, 10). God who dwells above the sun informs us that to be absent from the body is to be present with the Lord (2 Corinthians 5:8) and to depart and be with Christ is far better (Philippians 1:23).

Scriptures often represent death with the euphemistic term, sleep. This is because the body appears as if the dead person is asleep. Sleep is used only of the bodies of believers in this figurative sense for death: John 11:11-14; Acts 7:60; 1 Corinthians 15:6, 51; 1 Thessalonians 4:13-15; 2 Peter 3:4. According to the Scriptures, the dead are conscious. They know where they are, even as the rich man, Lazarus, and Abraham knew in the story (not parable) our Lord told in Luke 16:19-31. In today's lesson, scholars discuss the actual condition of the young girl at the time when her father came to the Lord. Some commentators say that she was not dead, but dying, "at the last extremity" (Alford), when Jairus approached Christ. It appears that she was dying when the father first left, but died while he was en route. Thus Matthew has the father state: "My daughter has just died." This is not an overstatement of a perturbed father.

However, Mark (5:23) has the father saying, "My little daughter lies at the point of death." And Luke 8:42 states "she was dying." The matter is easily resolved when we study all three of the Synoptics. We note that while the Lord was still talking to the woman healed of her issue of blood, "some came from the ruler of the synagogue's house who said, 'Your daughter is dead. Why trouble the Teacher any further?'" (Mark 5:35; Luke 8:49). At this point, the father said, as we read in Matthew 9:18: "My daughter has just died" (RSV). Thus as Tasker suggests, Matthew could have combined two separate appeals made by the father. The main issue that concerned the Gospel writers was the fact that when the Lord got to the home, He found that she was dead (Expositor's).

B. BIBLICAL BACKGROUND

As recorded in the book of Matthew, the following miracles were performed by Jesus prior to the events in today's lesson. Matthew 4:23-24 gives a general description of His early ministry in Galilee. He healed all kinds of sickness and all kinds of disease. Many miracles took place in Matthew chapter 8. He cleansed a leper, cured the servant of the centurion, healed Peter's mother-in-law of a fever; with a word cast out demons from those possessed. He rebuked the winds and waves on the stormy sea. Then He cast out the demons at Gergasa. Finally, in chapter 9, He cured the bed-ridden paralytic.

II. Exposition and Application of the Scripture

A. HEALING THE WOMAN'S ISSUE OF BLOOD
(Matthew 9:20-22)

And, behold, a woman, which was diseased with an issue of blood twelve years, came behind him, and touched the hem of his garment: For she said within herself, If I may but touch his garment, I shall be whole. But Jesus turned him about, and when he saw her, he said, Daughter, be of good comfort; thy faith hath made thee whole. And the woman was made whole from that hour.

Although in the lesson the ruler of the synagogue's plea is put first, we see later that our Lord's intention to take care of the father's request was interrupted by the woman with the issue of blood. In order to tell the story of the healing of the ruler's daughter without interruption, we have taken the liberty of relating the miracle that suddenly took place first. A woman who had a flow of blood for twelve years stood behind the Lord. Tasker states that her ailment, put in "modern medical terminology," was a menorrhagia, excessive menstrual discharge. According to Leviticus 15:19-27, such hemorrhage made her ceremonisously defiled or unclean. According to Mark, she "had suffered many things from many physicians," and had spent all of her money seeking a cure (Mark 5:26). Now she was broke and still deteriorating physically.

Having heard about the Master, she believed that she would be made whole if she touched His clothes. She did so, and immediately the fountain of her blood dried up. The Lord felt power had gone out of Him, and immediately inquired, "Who touched My clothes? Who touched Me?" This was no question of annoyance. He is never upset by our suddenness in coming to Him. He is always "poised, accessible and approachable" (MacDonald). Fearful and trembling, she fell down before Him, and in the presence of the crowd, told Him why she did what she did. He responded: "Be of good cheer, daughter (Usual address by a Rabbi); your faith has made you well." And so it was. She was made whole, saved from her misery for the first time in twelve years! Later, others were healed the same way (Matthew 14:36).

B. RAISING THE RULER'S DAUGHTER
(Matthew 9:18-19, 23-26)

While he spake these things unto them, behold, there came a certain ruler, and worshipped him saying, My daughter is even now dead: but come and lay thy hand upon her, and she shall live. And Jesus arose, and followed him, and so did his disciples. And when Jesus came into the ruler's house, and saw the minstrels and the people making a noise, He said unto them, Give place: for the maid is not dead, but sleepeth. And they laughed him to scorn. But when the people were put forth, he went in, and took her by the hand, and the maid arose. And the fame hereof went abroad into all that land.

While the Lord spoke about the cloth and wine skins (Matthew 9:16-17), a ruler of the synagogue, Jairus by name (Mark 5:22), came to Him, fell at His feet, and worshiped Him. Use of the word worship suggests that he recognized the Deity and authority of Christ. He had no fear of the scorn and contempt his associates would heap upon him for seeking the Lord's help. "My daughter is nigh to death. Come lay hands on her, heal her, so she will live." Then as Christ started to go, He was interrupted by the woman with the flow of blood. The woman was healed, and while the Lord talked with her, some men came and informed the ruler that his daughter had died.

The ruler then told the Lord, "My daughter has just died, but come and lay your hand on her and she will live." So Christ arose and followed the ruler, and the disciples did likewise. When the Lord came into the ruler's house, He saw the minstrels, flute-players hired to play their dirges in the homes where death occurred. Women were also hired to mourn and wail, moan, sob, and beat their breasts. Such was the nature of what someone has called "synthetic grief." It is said that "even the poorest in Israel will provide two flutes and a wailer" (ICC); this was incumbent upon the poorest man at the burial of a wife (Expositor's). Their presence left no doubt that this twelve-year old girl had died.

When Christ said, "The child is not dead, but sleeping," His statement brought forth ridicule. He was laughed to scorn. Well, she was indeed dead, but He knew He would bring her back to life again. The sleep of physical death of this only daughter was but temporary. Christ then asked them to leave, with all of their commotion and weeping. That left only Peter, James, John, and the girl's parents (Luke 8:51) with

Him. He took the dead girl by the hand and said to her, "Talitha cumi"—"Little girl, arise!" (Mark 5:41; Luke 8:54). Immediately, she arose and was given something to eat as the Lord commanded. And even though the Lord had charged them to tell no one what had happened, the news spread like wildfire throughout the land. Of the five persons restored to life as recorded in the New Testament, three of them were raised by Christ: Jairus' daughter in today's lesson; the young son of the widow of Nain (Luke 7:14), and Lazarus (John 11:43). Simon Peter was used by God to raise Dorcas (Tabitha, Acts 9:40); and God used Paul to restore the young man, Eutychus (Acts 20:9-12). It is also said that many saints were raised after the resurrection of Christ (Matthew 27:52-53).

C. GIVING SIGHT TO THE BLIND
(Matthew 9:27-31)

And when Jesus departed thence, two blind men followed him, crying, and saying, Thou Son of David, have mercy on us. And when he was come into the house, the blind men came to him: and Jesus saith unto them, Believe ye that I am able to do this? They said unto him, Yea, Lord. Then touched he their eyes, saying, According to your faith be it unto you. And their eyes were opened; and Jesus straitly charged them, saying, See that no man know it. But they, when they were departed, spread abroad his fame in all that country.

After this, two blind men followed Him, crying out and saying, "Son of David, have mercy on us!" The incident that follows is not mentioned in the other Gospels. Son of David is a title of honor, a Messianic title. They recognized Him as the Messiah. Though physically blind, they had better spiritual insight than the sighted religious leaders! Now the Lord said nothing and did nothing while on the street. When He entered the house, it may have been Matthew's (Parallel Bible commentary), the blind men came to Him. Lenski teaches that Christ preferred not to heal them in the street because He knew the title, Son of David, also had a political meaning for the Jews. He did not want to encourage any movement to make a political king.

Then, testing their sincerity, Christ said: "Do you believe that I am able to do this?", referring to healing them. Satisfied with their answer, "Yes, Lord," He touched their eyes, saying, "According to your faith be it unto you." Their faith was not to be disappointed (Knox). In an expression called an Hebraism (distinctive of the Hebrew language), we read: "And their eyes were opened." To the Jews, blind eyes were considered shut; seeing eyes were considered open.

Then came a stern warning not to tell anyone of their healing. They were straitly charged, austerely enjoined, commanded with threatening. Here is a verb used of horses snorting, men fretting and venting their anger. Its use here emphasizes that He emphatically commanded them not to speak of their healing. However, they disobeyed the Master's stern warning to remain silent. There is no doubt that Christ knew what they would do. Nonetheless, they should have obeyed. Doubtless, their broadcasting the miracle gave Christ another push toward Calvary by stirring up shallow curiosity,

and increasing the fear and hatred the religious leaders had for Him.

D. SHOWING COMPASSION FOR THE MULTITUDES
(Matthew 9:35-36)

And Jesus went about all the cities and villages, teaching in their synagogues, and preaching the gospel of the kingdom, and healing every sickness and every disease among the people. But when he saw the multitudes, he was moved with compassion on them because they fainted, and were scattered abroad, as sheep having no shepherd.

This section begins the Third Galilean Circuit. Continuous action is indicated by the original language. "He was going about in teaching, preaching, healing"—a tremendously active ministry! Two illustrations describe His concept of the crowds: They were shepherdless, neglected sheep, and they were a ripened harvest going to waste. Having observed their moral and religious situation, He saw their pitiful plight, and He was filled with compassion. It was believed the viscera (lungs, heart, liver, etc.) were the seat of such feelings as love, pity, etc., hence the term "bowels of compassion."

"They fainted" in the KJV is "were distressed" (ASV), "harassed" (NRSV). Robertson describes them as if rent or mangled by wild beasts. Tasker states that they were like sheep worried by dogs. Lenski pictures them as sheep wandering among brambles and sharp rocks, having their skin torn. "Hunted and tired out, exhausted, footsore and fleece-torn," states Expositor's. The original verb, to throw down, is rendered "scattered" in the KJV; "helpless" (NRSV), "lying on the ground unable to exert themselves" (Tasker). According to Robertson, the word denotes men cast down and prostrate on the ground, whether from drunkenness, or from mortal wounds. Such language paints a tremendous picture of the miserable spiritual condition of the multitude!

III. Special Features

A. PRESERVING OUR HERITAGE

Our hearts are made to bleed when we observe large numbers of Black Americans attending so-called Faith-Healing events. All too often, the men who operate these "healing" ministries, along with their accomplices, are phonies. Repeatedly, exposes have shown their methods questionable, their psychology exploitational, their use of electronic gadgets shameful, the mishandling of Scriptures deceptive, the misuse of funds and immoral lifestyles worthy of condemnation. The entire scene shows the continued need for prayerful Bible preaching and teaching.

B. A CONCLUDING WORD

The element of faith looms large in today's lesson. Faith in the Lord made well the woman with the issue of blood. The father of the restored daughter also had remarkable faith, for the Lord said to him: "Do not be afraid; only believe." Her healing revealed his faith. Likewise the blind men were questioned, "Do you believe that I am able to do this?" They answered in the affirmative. There is blessing in proportion to our willingness to trust Him. Let us, because of our faith in the finished work of Christ at Calvary, continue to grow with increased faith for daily living.

HOME DAILY BIBLE READINGS FOR THE WEEK OF JANUARY 16, 2000

MIRACLES OF COMPASSION

Jan. 10 M. Matthew 8:1-13, Jesus Continues His Healing Work
Jan. 11 T. Matthew 8:28—9:1, Jesus Heals the Gadarene Demoniacs
Jan. 12 W. Matthew 9:2-8, Jesus Heals a Paralytic
Jan. 13 T. Matthew 9:18-26, Jesus Gives Life and Healing
Jan. 14 F. Matthew 9:27-38, Jesus Heals the Blind and Mute
Jan. 15 S. Matthew 12:9-14, Jesus Heals a Man's Withered Hand
Jan. 16 S. Matthew 15:21-31, The Faith of a Canaanite Woman

O God whose compassion for us effected our redemption through Jesus Christ, grant that our concern for others will become full and complete as we model the life of Your Son, in whose name we pray. Amen.

Opposition to Jesus

Adult Topic—*Thinking About Jesus' Power*

•••••

Youth Topic—*Trouble!*
Children's Topic—*Jesus Meets Opposition*

•••••

Devotional Reading—Matthew 12:1-14
Background Scripture—Matthew 12:22-45
Print—Matthew 12:22-32, 38-40

PRINTED SCRIPTURE

Matthew 12:22-32, 38-40 (KJV)

22 Then was brought unto him one possessed with a devil, blind, and dumb: and he healed him, insomuch that the blind and dumb both spake and saw.

23 And all the people were amazed, and said, Is not this the son of David?

24 But when the Pharisees heard it, they said, This fellow doth not cast our devils, but by Beelzebub the prince of the devils.

25 And Jesus knew their thoughts, and said unto them, Every kingdom divided against itself is brought to desolation; and every city or house divided against itself shall not stand:

26 And if Satan cast out Satan, he is divided against himself; how shall then his kingdom stand?

27 And if I by Beelzebub cast out devils, by whom do your children cast them out? therefore they shall be your judges.

Matthew 12:22-32, 38-40 (NRSV)

22 Then they brought to him a demoniac who was blind and mute; and he cured him, so that the one who had been mute could speak and see.

23 All the crowds were amazed and said, "Can this be the Son of David?"

24 But when the Pharisees heard it, they said, "It is only by Beelzebul, the ruler of the demons, that this fellow casts out the demons."

25 He knew what they were thinking and said to them, "Every kingdom divided against itself is laid waste, and no city or house divided against itself will stand.

26 If Satan casts out Satan, he is divided against himself; how then will his kingdom stand?

27 If I cast out demons by Beelzebul, by whom do your own exorcists cast them out? Therefore they will be your judges.

28 But if it is by the Spirit of God

28 But if I cast out devils by the Spirit of God, then the kingdom of God is come unto you.

29 Or else how can one enter into a strong man's house, and spoil his goods, except he first bind the strong man? and then he will spoil his house.

30 He that is not with me is against me; and he that gathereth not with me scattereth abroad.

31 Wherefore I say unto you, All manner of sin and blasphemy shall be forgiven unto men: but the blasphemy against the Holy Ghost shall not be forgiven unto men.

32 And whosoever speaketh a word against the Son of man, it shall be forgiven him: but whosoever speaketh against the Holy Ghost, it shall not be forgiven him, neither in this world, neither in the world to come.

.....

38 Then certain of the scribes and of the Pharisees answered, saying, Master, we would see a sign from thee.

39 But he answered and said unto them, An evil and adulterous generation seeketh after a sign; and there shall no sign be given to it, but the sign of the prophet Jonas:

40 For as Jonas was three days and three nights in the whale's belly; so shall the Son of man be three days and three nights in the heart of the earth.

that I cast out demons, then the kingdom of God has come to you.

29 Or how can one enter a strong man's house and plunder his property, without first tying up the strong man? Then indeed the house can be plundered.

30 Whoever is not with me is against me, and whoever does not gather with me scatters.

31 Therefore I tell you, people will be forgiven for every sin and blasphemy, but blasphemy against the Spirit will not be forgiven.

32 Whoever speaks a word against the Son of Man will be forgiven, but whoever speaks against the Holy Spirit will not be forgiven, either in this age or in the age to come.

.....

38 Then some of the scribes and Pharisees said to him, "Teacher, we wish to see a sign from you."

39 But he answered them, "An evil and adulterous generation asks for a sign, but no sign will be given to it except the sign of the prophet Jonah.

40 For just as Jonah was three days and three nights in the belly of the sea monster, so for three days and three nights the Son of Man will be in the heart of the earth.

KEY VERSE

He that is not with me is against me; and he that gathereth not with me scattereth abroad.
—Matthew 12:30

OBJECTIVES

After reading this lesson, the student should be aware that:

1. The Lord Jesus faced tremendous opposition;
2. The miracles Jesus performed only hardened His enemies;
3. In opposing Christ, religious leaders blasphemed; and,
4. Jonah's experience predicted Christ's burial.

POINTS TO BE EMPHASIZED

Adult/Youth
Key Verse: Matthew 12:30
Print: Matthew 12:22-32, 38-40

—After Jesus healed a demoniac who was blind and mute, the crowds began to ask whether Jesus was the Messiah. (22-23)
—The Pharisees said that Jesus performed His miracles in the power of Beelzebub, the ruler of demons. (24)
—Jesus showed the folly of the Pharisees' accusation and claimed to cast out demons by the Spirit of God. (25-29)
—Jesus said that whoever is not with Him is against Him, and whoever does not gather with Him, scatters. (30)
—Jesus warned that blasphemy against the Holy Spirit will never be forgiven. (31-32)
—When some scribes and Pharisees asked Jesus for a sign, He responded that the only sign would be that of Jonah. (38-40)

Children

Key Verse: Matthew 12:30
Print: Matthew 12:22-32, 35-37

—After Jesus healed a demoniac who was blind and mute, the crowds began to ask whether Jesus was the Messiah. (22-23)
—The Pharisees said that Jesus performed His miracles in the power of Beelzebul, the ruler of demons. (24)
—Jesus showed the folly of the Pharisees' accusation and claimed to cast out demons by the Spirit of God. (25-29)
—Jesus said that whoever is not with Him is against Him, and whoever does not gather with Him, scatters. (30)
—Jesus warned that blasphemy against the Holy Spirit will never be forgiven. (31-32)
—Jesus taught that good people produce good things, evil people produce evil things, and every individual must give an account for every word spoken. (35-37)

(**Note**: Use KJV Scripture for Adults; NRSV Scripture for Youth and Children)

I. Introduction

A. BLASPHEMING THE HOLY SPIRIT

Here is a word we have taken right out of the Greek (transliterated), *blasphemeo, blasphemia*. Literally, it means to falsely speak. I would add, it is to "bad-mouth." According to Kittel, in secular Greek blasphemy is "abusive speech" (misuse of words). When one blasphemes deity, he mistakes the true nature, or violates or doubts its power. Furthermore, in the New Testament, the controlling thought is the violation of God's power and majesty. One may direct blasphemy against God, His Name, His Word, or against whoever is the bearer of the Word.

Now in today's lesson, the Lord informs the Pharisees that blasphemy or speaking against the Holy Spirit is an unforgivable, unpardonable sin. Just what then is the meaning of "blas-pheming the Holy Spirit"? It is to ascribe to Satan the Holy Spirit's work (Scofield). "It denotes the conscious and wicked rejection of the saving power and grace of God towards man" (Kittel). To give the Devil credit for the miraculous works of Christ is unforgivable. Can this sin be committed today? Scholars seem divided on this issue.

A. T. Robertson states it can be committed by men who give Satan credit for the work of Christ. Henry Morris would remind us that speaking against the Holy Spirit is the same as rejecting Jesus Christ. For such permanent rejection, there is no forgiveness (John 3:18, 36). MacDonald says it is reasonably doubtful that one today can commit the unpardonable sin. He believes that the unforgivable sin is not the same as rejecting the Gospel; nor is it equivalent to "backsliding." The basis for denying the possibility of men blaspheming the Holy Spirit today lies in the background of the lesson.

This is to suggest that, historically, such a sin was possible because the Lord was active in His earthly ministry. The religious leaders saw with their own eyes many of the miracles Christ performed, yet rejected the very clear witness of God. Since this specific scene can no longer be repeated— that is, no longer involves the physical bodily presence of the Lord Jesus— then it is no longer possible to sin again in this particular way.

This point of view would say that if you are concerned about such blasphemy, it means you have not committed it. Evidently, those guilty of such blasphemy were blind to their folly. In summary, Chafer teaches that since the Lord Jesus is not in the world as He was in New Testament times, it is no longer possible to commit this distinctive sin. More will be said about blaspheming in our exposition of Matthew 12:31-32.

B. BIBLICAL BACKGROUND

From the very beginning, the Lord faced opposition. The first instance of course was that of Herod the Great. A second instance of opposition was the temptation orchestrated by Satan (al-though Christ was led to the wilderness by the Holy Spirit). These instances are not harmonized with the other Gospels; I have limited the incidents to the gospel of Matthew, chapters 1 to 22:13. A mild form of opposition occurred when Christ allowed demons to enter the hogs there at Gadara. The whole city came out to meet the Lord. And when they saw Him, they begged Him to depart from their region.

Scribes accused our Lord of blasphemy because He forgave the paralytic of his sins. Pharisees questioned His eating with tax collectors and sinners. They said that He cast out demons by the ruler of the demons. Pharisees said His disciples violated the Sabbath by plucking heads of grain on the Sabbath and eating them. This brings us to the point where He healed the man with the withered hand on the Sabbath? Seeking to accuse Him, the religious leaders asked Him, saying: "Is it lawful to heal on the Sabbath?" Even though throughout early events of His ministry, our Lord sought to keep down the enthusiasm of the people and the broadcasting of His miracles, nonetheless, His fame spread abroad and increased the hatred and opposition of the religious leaders.

II. Exposition and Application of the Scripture

A. THE BLIND AND MUTE DEMONIAC HEALED
(Matthew 12:22-23)

Then was brought unto him one possessed with a devil, blind, and dumb: and he healed him, insomuch that the blind and dumb both spake and saw. And all the people were amazed, and said, Is not this the son of David?

The words "Possessed with a devil" are actually the translation of one Greek word. RSV and Moffatt thus simply call the man a "demoniac."

Throughout the New Testament, especially in the Gospels—as if the presence of the Lord stirred up Satan—we find people whose bodies demons had entered, causing those possessed to suffer all kinds of disease. Paralysis, deafness, epilepsy, melancholia, insanity, etc. are some of the afflictions encountered. In today's lesson, blindness and loss of speech prevail.

The word for the blindness the demoniac suffered means "to raise a smoke"; thus, the eyes are considered as darkened by smoke. The word for dumb is derived from a verb meaning to beat or pound, hence the tongue that is blunted or lame cannot speak. Incidentally, the ear that is blunted or dull in hearing is deaf (Matthew 11:5).

Christ proceeded to heal this man who was brought to Him. The result was threefold: (1) the demon was cast out; (2) the man spoke (became a speaker); and (3) he saw. The tense used means he became one who sees. Thus, he was speaking and seeing. The miracle amazed all the people. Matthew uses strong language here, for the word rendered "amazed" means to throw one out of his mind. Is this akin to the expression we sometimes hear today: "That blows my mind"? In their astonishment the question came, "Is not this the son of David?"

A negative answer is implied, indicating the people's predisposition to unbelief. NASB best shows this: "This man cannot be the Son of David, can He?" These folks may have wanted to believe our Lord was the Messiah, but with no guidance from the religious leaders, they hesitated. But the miracle just performed was breaking through their unbelief.

B. THE PHARISEES BLASPHEME THE HOLY SPIRIT (Matthew 12:24)

But when the Pharisees heard it, they said, This fellow doth not cast out devils, but by Beelzebub the prince of the devils.

When the religious leaders (this is the meaning of the phrase John's gospel so frequently uses when he speaks of "the Jews") became aware of the astonishment among the people, caused by the healing of the demoniac, they spoke against the Lord. They were especially concerned about the slightest suggestion the miracle healer was the son of David. "No way!" they said. Note once again the contempt they would heap upon the Lord by the highly derogatory practice of not calling Him by His name—which they knew—but by the words, "this fellow" (KJV: Matthew 26:61; Luke 23:2; John 9:29).

"This fellow" cast out demons only by Beelzebub, the prince of demons. Because of differences in various modern English translations, you will find the spelling either Beelzebub or Beelzebul. This latter spelling is closer to the Greek, Beelzeboul. The correct spelling and meaning are disputed (Kittel). As the Pharisees used it, Beelzebub is a name for the prince of demons. For Christ, all demons are under Satan, so the Lord tacitly substituted the name Satan for Beelzebub. The first time we meet this accusation is in Matthew 9:34.

After Christ healed two blind men, a speechless (dumb) man possessed with a demon was brought to Him. He healed the man and he regained his speech. When the multitudes marveled and said, "It was never so seen in Israel," the Pharisees retorted: "He casts out demons through the prince of demons." Whenever the crowds attempted to praise the Lord for performing a miracle, the religious leaders were antagonized.

Indignant, they were determined to check the growing conviction among the populace that this might indeed be the Messiah. A second mention of Beelzebub is found in Matthew 10:25. Here the Lord teaches the disciples that one of the costs of discipleship includes being called a tool of the Devil, even as their Master is called. Today's lesson is the third time Beelzebub is mentioned either directly or indirectly.

C. CHRIST'S RESPONSE: SATAN IS DIVIDED (Matthew 12:25-30)

And Jesus knew their thoughts, and said unto them, Every kingdom divided against itself is brought to desolation; and every city or house divided against itself shall not stand: And if Satan cast out Satan, he is divided against himself; how shall then his kingdom stand? And if I by Beelzebub cast out devils, by whom do your children cast them out? therefore they shall be your judges. But if I cast out devils by the Spirit of God, then the kingdom of God is come unto you. Or else how can one enter into a strong man's house, and spoil his goods, except he first bind the strong man? And then he will spoil his house. He that is not with me is against me; and he that gathereth not with me scattereth abroad.

Only God can read minds. We should never forget that He can. Knowing their thoughts, the Lord reminded them that divided kingdoms are brought to desolation. Every city or house divided against itself shall not stand. If Satan throws out Satan, it means he too is divided. Such rebellion is self-destructive. To be at variance with oneself is distracting, anxiety creating, schizophrenic. Satan does not willingly expel himself. Tasker said: "Satan is not engaged in committing suicide." After all, demon possession is a real feather in Satan's cap; for him it is a great achievement. Why should he mess it up?

"So now if I cast out demons by the power of Beelzebub, by whom do your sons exorcise them?" What a challenge Christ threw at them! These "sons" were fellow Jews, experts of their own guild who practiced exorcism. The religious leaders were proud of their own disciples, and attributed their exorcisms to the power of God. But when Christ cast out the demons, then the Pharisees ascribed a different source of power.

On the other hand, if the Lord cast demons out by the Spirit of God, then the religious leaders should recognize that God's kingdom is in their midst. Rejection of the divine nature of the miracles performed by the Lord means they were not aware that the kingdom of heaven had come in their midst. Indeed, the fact that He cast out demons means He has entered the adversary's home or territory. In God's own good time, Satan will indeed be bound (Revelation 20:2) and robbed. Snatching the demon-possessed out of Satan's power is but a foretaste of the robbing or spoiling to come.

Note the word "spoil" in Matthew 12:29. It means to rob, plunder, seize, snatch, carry off by force. It is used in 1 Thessalonians 4:17 with respect to what is called the Rapture (to rape, force), where the verb is rendered "caught up." This old earth will be spoiled, and we shall be snatched up to meet the Lord of glory. For Satan is a defeated foe, and his house is headed for destruction. Eventually, he will be thrown into the lake of fire, for hell was prepared for the Devil and his angels.

Finally, this section closes with the assertion that there is no fence walking when it comes either to salvation (Matthew 12:30) or service (Mark 9:40). Men are either with the Lord or against Him; either harvest or scatter. There is no middle ground, no neutrality. No fence-straddling. "Some things are not negotiable" (A. W. Tozer). The Pharisees showed, by their bad attitude, exactly where they stood.

D. THE UNPARDONABLE SIN (Matthew 12:31-32)

Wherefore I say unto you, All manner of sin and blasphemy shall be forgiven unto men: but the blasphemy against the Holy Ghost shall not be forgiven unto men. And whosoever speaketh a word against the Son of man, it shall be forgiven him: but whosoever speaketh against the Holy Ghost, it shall not be forgiven him, neither in this world, neither in the world to come.

Note how the Holy Spirit is related to the Son of Man. Both are Persons. Both may be blasphemed or spoken against, or slandered. But whereas men may be forgiven for speaking against the Son of Man, stern words warn that blasphemy against the Holy Spirit is unforgivable. Their moral vision is so blurred that no ophthalmologist can help them. Their doom is

forever settled and sealed. In Mark's account, the religious leaders kept accusing the Lord of having an "unclean spirit" (Mark 3:30). They thus saw the Devil where the Holy Spirit was busy. The words "it shall not be forgiven him, neither in this age, neither in the age to come" do not constitute a basis for believing in what is called, "purgatory." In other words, "the age to come" does not support any idea of some sins being remitted or forgiven later in the world to come.

E. THE SIGN OF THE PROPHET JONAH (Matthew 12:38-40)

Then certain of the scribes and of the Pharisees answered, saying, Master, we would see a sign from thee. But he answered and said unto them, An evil and adulterous generation seeketh after a sign; and there shall no sign be given to it, but the sign of the prophet Jonas: For as Jonas was three days and three nights in the whale's belly; so shall the Son of man be three days and three nights in the heart of the earth.

At this point, certain scribes and Pharisees expressed a desire to see a sign from the Master (Teacher). Their request was impudent, for why were they not impressed with all that He had done already? And so the Lord wasted no time setting these religionists straight. He called them sign-seekers, an evil and adulterous generation, idolaters all! Unfaithful to God! This accusation against the Jews was nothing new. Israel's great apostasy was idolatry, playing the part of a harlot, though married to Jehovah. James uses similar language in his warning: "Ye adulterers and adulteresses, know ye not that the friendship of the world is enmity with God? Whosoever, therefore, will be a friend of the world is the enemy of God" (James 4:4).

They had seen signs. They saw blind eyes opened, ears unstopped, paralysis eliminated, leprosy cleansed, the dead raised. But evidently these miracles held no weight, or not enough weight. The only sign that shall be given to such a generation is that of the prophet Jonah, who was swallowed by a great fish (or sea monster) and remained in the creature's belly for three days and three nights. This is clearly one of the most controversial stories in the Old Testament. Some men do not believe Jonah ever existed. They say the story is a myth, a folk tale made up to teach certain religious truths, but is not to be taken seriously or literally. And the reason Christ told it was because He was a Jew and had imbibed Jewish teachings. He was a product of His times. However, denials of an historical Jonah raise more questions than answers. It is especially the part about being swallowed by a great fish that stirs up the antisuper–naturalists.

Whatever it was they wanted to see, it required no faith, just sight. The word translated "sign" is the same word rendered "miracle." But man has no ability or authority to dictate to God the sign he wants or prefers. Reject Jonah, reject Christ. What more could the Lord do than He had done already to show the God-given nature of His miracles? And what about modern-day religious people who are forever looking for signs. They attend every Miracle Ministry that comes to town. They get healed; they are "slain in the spirit," or blessed financially, yet manage to show up at the next event, seeking the same things. How twisted it is that often these "sign-seekers" feel they are spiritually superior to the saints who are not "sign-seekers."

III. Special Features

A. PRESERVING OUR HERITAGE

America has allowed racism to divide it. Racism may not be an unforgivable sin, but it is highly insulting to God when a man despises another because of his race or skin color. And unfortunately, some of the opposition to accepting all people of all races is religious opposition. Religious evil is demonic, the worst kind of wickedness. For those in opposition are also those who claim that the Bible supports their concepts of segregation. Their foolish talk about miscegenation is in reality an insult to God and indicates they have much to learn about the grace of God.

B. A CONCLUDING WORD

Biblical Christianity cannot avoid stirring up opposition. All attempts to be what has come to be called "politically correct" are futile, and has led some Christians to become "spiritually incorrect." What is happening also is that the spirit of discernment is weakening. More and more people are less and less able to determine what is right. They see Bibles, they know Christians who live clean lives, they hear preaching—yet refuse to believe in the shed blood of Jesus Christ. How sad! For One greater than Jonah has come and He lives in the hearts of all believers.

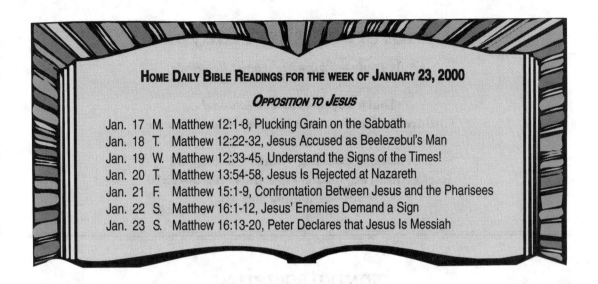

HOME DAILY BIBLE READINGS FOR THE WEEK OF JANUARY 23, 2000

OPPOSITION TO JESUS

Jan. 17 M. Matthew 12:1-8, Plucking Grain on the Sabbath
Jan. 18 T. Matthew 12:22-32, Jesus Accused as Beelezebul's Man
Jan. 19 W. Matthew 12:33-45, Understand the Signs of the Times!
Jan. 20 T. Matthew 13:54-58, Jesus Is Rejected at Nazareth
Jan. 21 F. Matthew 15:1-9, Confrontation Between Jesus and the Pharisees
Jan. 22 S. Matthew 16:1-12, Jesus' Enemies Demand a Sign
Jan. 23 S. Matthew 16:13-20, Peter Declares that Jesus Is Messiah

Know Your Bible

- The phrase, "Behold, the Bridegroom cometh!" means that instead of our Lord being faithfully looked for when He comes, His appearance will be generally unexpected by His followers. (Matthew 25:1-6)
- When Mary, the sister of Lazarus, poured a box of precious ointment on the head of Jesus, she anticipated His death. She probably elected to do at this point in time that which she might have not been able to do later. (Matthew 26:7 and John 12:3)
- Christians should not be surprised when the world is hostile toward them because the world first hated our Lord who Himself was perfect goodness and perfect love. (John 15:
- During period of trouble, Christian are consoled by the faith that Christ overcame the world, and that in Him we have peace, or a resolution of conflict. (John 16:33)
- Present-day Christians are included in Jesus' prayer because they are identified as those who would believe in the Christ as a result of the proclamation of the Word by the apostles handed down in the New Testament, and through the preaching and teaching of a succession of Christ's people from that point in time to the present day. (John 17:20)

God of grace and God of glory, grant that we may submit ourselves to Your transforming power. May we prove our faith in the midst of adversity that the world will know that we are children of a Living God. Amen.

Laborers in the Vineyard

Adult Topic—*Thinking About Rewards*

•••••

Youth Topic—*Turn It Around*

Children's Topic—*Jesus Teaches About Service*

•••••

Devotional Reading—Matthew 20:20-28

Background Scripture—Matthew 19:16—20:16

Print—Matthew 20:1-16

PRINTED SCRIPTURE

Matthew 20:1-16 (KJV)

FOR THE kingdom of heaven is like unto a man that is an householder, which went out early in the morning to hire labourers into his vineyard.

2 And when he had agreed with the labourers for a penny a day, he sent them into his vineyard.

3 And he went out about the third hour, and saw others standing idle in the marketplace,

4 And said unto them; Go ye also into the vineyard, and whatsoever is right I will give you. And they went their way.

5 Again he went out about the sixth and ninth hour, and did likewise.

6 And about the eleventh hour he went out, and found others standing idle, and saith unto them, Why stand ye here all the day idle?

7 They say unto him, Because no man hath hired us. He saith unto

Matthew 20:1-16 (NRSV)

"FOR THE kingdom of heaven is like a landowner who went out early in the morning to hire laborers for his vineyard.

2 After agreeing with the laborers for the usual daily wage, he sent them into his vineyard.

3 When he went out about nine o'clock, he saw others standing idle in the marketplace;

4 and he said to them, 'You also go into the vineyard, and I will pay you whatever is right.' So they went.

5 When he went out again about noon and about three o'clock, he did the same.

6 And about five o'clock he went out and found others standing around; and he said to them, 'Why are you standing here idle all day?'

7 They said to him, 'Because no one his hired us.' He said to them, 'You also go into the vineyard.'

8 When evening came, the owner

them, Go ye also into the vineyard; and whatsoever is right, that shall ye receive.

8 So when even was come, the lord of the vineyard saith unto his steward, Call the labourers, and give them their hire, beginning from the last unto the first.

9 And when they came that were hired about the eleventh hour, they received every man a penny.

10 But when the first came, they supposed that they should have received more; and they likewise received every man a penny.

11 And when they had received it, they murmured against the goodman of the house,

12 Saying, These last have wrought but one hour, and thou hast made them equal unto us, which have borne the burden and heat of the day.

13 But he answered one of them, and said, Friend, I do thee no wrong: didst not thou agree with me for a penny?

14 Take that thine is, and go thy way: I will give unto this last, even as unto thee.

15 Is it not lawful for me to do what I will with mine own? Is thine eye evil, because I am good?

16 So the last shall be first, and the first last: for many be called, but few chosen.

of the vineyard said to his manager, 'Call the laborers and give them their pay, beginning with the last and then going to the first.'

9 When those hired about five o'clock came, each of them received the usual daily wage.

10 Now when the first came, they thought they would receive more; but each of them also received the usual daily wage.

11 And when they received it, they grumbled against the landowner,

12 saying, 'These last worked only one hour, and you have made them equal to us who have borne the burden of the day and the scorching heat.'

13 But he replied to one of them, 'Friend, I am doing you no wrong; did you not agreee with me for the daily wage?

14 Take what belongs to you and go; I choose to give to this last the same as I give to you.

15 Am I not allowed to do what I choose with what belongs to me? Or are you envious because I am generous?'

16 So the last will be first, and the first will be last."

KEY VERSE

So the last shall be first, and the first last: for many be called, but few chosen.
—Matthew 20:16

OBJECTIVES

After reading this lesson, the student should remember that:

1. God is sovereign; He does as He pleases;
2. Calling God unjust is an act of ignorance;
3. Grumbling is symptomatic of ingratitude; and,
4. First and last are divine priorities

POINTS TO BE EMPHASIZED

Adult/Youth/Children
Key Verse: Matthew 20:16
Print: Matthew 20:1-16

—Jesus told a parable to illustrate that in God's kingdom the last will be first, and the first will be last.

—The landowner hired laborers at the day's beginning to work in his vineyard for a day's pay. (1-2)

—The landowner went out to the marketplace at nine o'clock, noon, three o'clock and five o'clock and hired other workers. (3-7)

—When evening came, the owner paid all the workers the usual daily wage, beginning with those hired at five o'clock. (8-9)

—Those hired first grumbled when they received the same wages as those hired later, even though they had worked longer in the heat. (10-12)

—The landowner replied that they were getting what they had agreed to, and that he was free to give all the workers the same wage if he chose to do so. (13-16)

(**Note**: Use KJV Scripture for Adults; NRSV Scripture for Youth and Children)

TOPICAL OUTLINE OF THE LESSON

I. Introduction

A. The Divine Standard of Morality

B. Biblical Background

II. Exposition and Application of the Scripture

A. The First Group of Laborers (Matthew 20:1-2)

B. The Second Group of Laborers (Matthew 20:3-4)

C. The Last Three Groups of Laborers (Matthew 20:5-7)

D. Payday (Matthew 20:8-10)

E. Complaints (Matthew 20:11-12)

F. The Landlord's Response (Matthew 20:13-16)

III. Special Features

A. Preserving Our Heritage

B. A Concluding Word

I. Introduction

A. THE DIVINE STANDARD OF MORALITY

"There is a way which seems right to a man, but its end is the way of death" (Proverbs 16:25, NASB). Men may be sincere in their desires to do what is right, but all too often the sin nature intervenes and distorts our ability to discern right from wrong. According to some men, might makes right. We are told by others that if gambling is legalized, then it is moral; it is permissible. And so is legalized prostitution, decriminalization of dope, euthanasia, abortion, etc. Man's desire to set up his own criteria for morality also leads him to judge the Word of God. And since God is His Word, we humans proceed to judge God.

One of the things that sticks in man's craw is the biblical concept of grace: the unearned, unmerited favor of God. Man wants the first to be first, and the last to be last, and stay that way. Why should men who work only an hour receive the same wages as men who work eight hours, bearing the "burden and the heat of the day"? Men cry, "It isn't fair." And God answers: "Am I not allowed to do what I choose with what belongs to me?" (Matthew 20:15, RSV). "Shall not the Judge of all the earth do right?" (Genesis 18:25). Remember then, "commercial concepts of morality are wholly irrelevant" (Tasker). God's thoughts are not our thoughts (see Isaiah 55:8).

B. BIBLICAL BACKGROUND

It is unfortunate that chapter 20 begins where is does. Actually, Matthew 19:27-30 should be the start of chapter 20, for it is in this passage that the parable in our lesson has its basis or reason for being. After the Lord's experience with the rich young ruler, and the expression concerning the difficulty rich people will have entering the kingdom of God, Simon Peter answered and said: "See, we have left all and followed You. Therefore what shall we have?"

The Lord assured the disciples that in the kingdom age (the Millennium), the disciples would be properly honored. In the millennium, the apostles would be the administrators over the kingdom of Israel. Isaiah 1:26 reveals the form of government that will exist when Christ rules the earth. He will give the apostles positions as judges, according to Matthew 19:28. Believers who have left family, friends, and possessions for the sake of Jesus Christ, "shall receive a hundred fold, and inherit eternal life."

The last verse, Matthew 19:30, is both different and the same as Matthew 20:16. "But many who are first will be last, and the last first" is really the same as, "the last will be first, and the first last."

Basically, the idea is: Many who began as members of the "IN" crowd will find themselves out of it; and many who at first were members of the "OUT" crowd will at last be in it. What may cause such a tremendous change? Wealth, self-complacency, pride, power, fame, privilege, etc. These thoughts set the stage for the parable of the laborers. See in this, therefore, an illustration of the definition of grace: It is not what we merit, but that which God gives.

II. Exposition and Application the Scripture

A. THE FIRST GROUP OF LABORERS (Matthew 20:1-2)

FOR the kingdom of heaven is like unto a man that is an householder, which went out early in the morning to hire labourers into his vineyard. And when he had agreed with the labourers for a penny a day, he sent them into his vineyard.

It is essential that we remember our Lord deals with Israel and the kingdom of heaven or the kingdom of God, as seen in what is called the Millennium or Kingdom Age. The Jews, the first called into the Lord's vineyard, are warned to beware of those things which would cause them to be rejected. In this parable, Christ reinforces His instructions concerning true Christian service, and illustrates the practical wisdom of Matthew 19:30. All genuine disciples will be rewarded, but it is the spirit in which one serves that the order of rewards is determined. In this parable, peculiar to Matthew, the householder is God. Apparently, it is the grape-gathering season (Expositor's), and many laborers are quickly needed; otherwise, there would be no need to hire men so late in the day as is done in verses 5 and 6 (Anchor).

The householder, or literally, housemaster or ruler, went out early to hire laborers for his vineyard. An agreement was reached with some men to work for a denarius a day. At this time, the denarius, a Roman silver coin (worth about seventeen cents) was the day laborer's wage. It was also the daily salary of the Roman soldier. It is said that the denarius was enough for an agricultural worker to provide the ne-

cessities of life for his family and for himself for that day. Such daily work heightens for us the meaning of the prayer, "Give us this day our daily bread" (Matthew 6:11). Evidently, the workers wanted a definite contract. Lenski calls this "a mercenary spirit." Was it a case of "No Contract, No Work!?" And so the master sent out those hired.

B. THE SECOND GROUP OF LABORERS (Matthew 20:3-4)

And he went out about the third hour, and saw others standing idle in the marketplace, And said unto them; Go ye also into the vineyard, and whatsoever is right I will give you. And they went their way.

Now we assume the "early in the morning" of verse one is before the sun rose or about six A.M. For this second contingent of workers, the householder went out about nine A.M. He saw some men in the marketplace (the agora) standing idle. According to Trench, the word translated idle involves blameworthiness. And so he said to them: "You also go into the vineyard, and whatever is right I will give you." Evidently, no labor management contract is offered this time. They are willing simply to work by faith, to take their employer's word to do right by them.

So no agreement was made concerning the fixed amount of money they would be paid. How much then is "whatever is right"? That which is "fair" does not mean whatever the landowner felt like or was pleased to give, "but a just proportionate wage" (Robertson). "Whatever is right" points to the justice of Jesus Christ. And so they went to work.

C. THE LAST THREE GROUPS OF LABORERS (Matthew 20:5-7)

Again he went out about the sixth and ninth hour, and did likewise. And about the eleventh hour he went out, and found others standing idle, and saith unto them, Why stand ye here all the day idle? They say unto him, Because no man hath hired us. He saith unto them, Go ye also into the vineyard; and whatsoever is right, that shall ye receive.

It seems that more workers were needed. To obtain them, the householder went out about twelve noon and about three P.M., and recruited more laborers. Then about five P.M., an hour before sunset, he again went out to hire more men. He found others standing idle. See God's grace here. They had not answered the want ads, or called for an interview. God the householder sought them, and He found them. That's grace! No matter what the timing may be, it is still God's grace in action. He said: "Why have you been standing here idle all day?" The word rendered idle is the same used in verse three; it may also be rendered, inactive, doing nothing, lazy, "shunning the labor which one ought to perform" (Thayer).

Watchman Nee speaks of the gambler's hand as unemployable; the swearer's tongue as unemployed. But once given over to Christ, they become instruments of righteousness to God (see Romans 6:13). To answer Christ's question with the words, "because no man has hired us," is to invite employment by the Lord in the most rewarding service there is. Such an answer

appears to weaken the thrust of the accusation that the men were lazy, street corner loungers. However, Trench reminds us that "all activity out of Christ, all labor that is not labor in His church, is in His sight a 'standing idle.'" And so the landowner hired them: "Go ye also into the vineyard; and whatsoever is right, that ye shall receive."

D. PAYDAY (Matthew 20:8-10)

So when even was come, the lord of the vineyard saith unto his steward, Call the labourers, and give them their hire, beginning from the last unto the first. And when they came that were hired about the eleventh hour, they received every man a penny. But when the first came, they supposed that they should have received more; and they likewise received every man a penny.

Now it is evening. According to Jewish law, a laborer who was hired for a limited time was to be paid as soon as his work was done. Leviticus 19:13: "The wages of him that is hired shall not abide with you all night unto the morning." Deuteronomy 24:15 exhorts do not let the sun go down on the hireling's wages. So the Lord of the vineyard instructed his steward (overseer, household manager) to call the workers together and pay them their wages, beginning with the last to the first.

Note this order, and ask yourself: "Which group would I have paid off first? Which group last?" Paying them off in this order gave the first hired the opportunity to see what the last hired received. The master's choice was to deal first with those who had no claims. Obviously, this order was calculated to cause exactly the response it did elicit, namely, grumbling and bitter resentment. Indeed, this order of payment was essential to the lesson taught here by our Lord.

They came when called, and each man received one denarius. In other words, the men hired about nine A.M., twelve noon, three P.M. and five P.M.—all receive the same wage, one denarius. The men who worked twelve hours also came. But they expected to received more than the later-hired workers. However, they too received only one denarius apiece.

E. COMPLAINTS
(Matthew 20:11-12)

And when they had received it, they murmured against the goodman of the house, Saying, These last have wrought but one hour, and thou hast made them equal unto us, which have borne the burden and heat of the day.

Upon receiving their pay, the members of this first-hired group started to murmur against the householder. Watching the others receive one denarius probably gave the first-comers false hopes of receiving more since they worked longer. Their hopes were dashed upon receiving the same as the others. So they began to grumble, and directed their anger towards the householder. From their point of view, they had been cheated, unfairly treated. They protested the "injustice," for: (1) they had worked longer, (2) had borne the burden, (3) and heat of the day, and (4) by receiving only one denarius were put on the same level with the late-comers.

They complained that the last group hired worked only one hour. "We worked twelve hours, and you're giving them what you gave us. This is rank injustice! They came to work in the cool of the day. We came early and worked in the burning, scorching sun at midday! It isn't fair!" The heat of the day is the burning heat of the sun, and refers to a "very dry, hot, east wind, scorching and drying up everything" (Thayer).

F. THE LANDOWNER'S RESPONSE (Matthew 20:13-16)

But he answered one of them, and said, Friend, I do thee no wrong: didst not thou agree with me for a penny? Take that thine is, and go thy way: I will give unto this last, even as unto thee. Is it not lawful for me to do what I will with mine own? Is thine eye evil, because I am good? So the last shall be first, and the first last: for many be called, but few chosen.

Their expressions of discontent are very strong. The Lord proceeded to answer, but He answered only one of them. Was this one the loudest protester? Had he been chosen as their spokesman? Expositor's states he answered just one man because it would have been undignified to address the entire gang, and by so doing take the situation too seriously. So one man was chosen and quietly spoken to, and addressed as, "friend." Study of the word rendered "friend" (*etairos*) reveals differences of opinion concerning its precise meaning. Matthew is the only New Testament writer who uses it (20:13, 22:12, 26:50). Now some scholars see the word used favorably. Thayer renders it, "My good friend." It may be used as a general form of address to someone whose name one does not know (Arndt and Gingrich). Since it also means comrade, it is a kindly reply (Robertson). "Familiar and kindly," says Expositor's. On the other hand, its use implies a rebuke (Anchor). Trench says, "Fellow" is the most accurate translation, but "contains too much of contempt in it." Lenski also renders it, "fellow" and agrees that there is an evil omen to the word.

After studying these remarks, I would settle for the comments of Kittel's Theological Dictionary of the New Testament. Here we learn that the word has been used for "one who is associated with another," the specific sense being determined by the context. Study then of its use in Matthew does not give the use of the word a positive ring. In all three passages in Matthew, the one called "friend" has a bad relationship with the speaker: (1) a grumbler, (2) one who insults, and (3) a traitor. "Fellow, I do you no wrong. I am not treating you unfairly. Did you not agree with me for a denarius? Is that not our contract? Take what belongs to you and go your way. I will (from the verb, to desire, wish, intend) give unto this last, even as unto you."

Here is the point of the parable, namely, the WILL of the householder. It was his money, his vineyard, and had he not asked their help, they would have remained idle. God has the right to do as He pleases. Because He is God, all He does is righteous. So no man has a valid reason to complain or reproach God, or accuse Him of injustice. If justice were allowed to have its way, we all would be in deep trouble. It is man's evil eye that moves him to falsely accuse God, to complain, murmur, mumble and grumble. An evil eye is one that is covetous, grudging, greedy, jealous, envious, resentful. Read Deuteronomy 15:9; Proverbs 22:9, 23:6, 28:22. It is the opposite of a liberal, bountiful eye or spirit. A person with an evil eye looks with malice at what he considers the "good fortune" of others. We see then the question, "Is your eye evil, because I am good?" means, "Are you envious because I am generous? Do you begrudge my generosity?" (RSV) is a good paraphrase. Their protest revealed the condition of their hearts.

III. Special Features

A. PRESERVING OUR HERITAGE

It is difficult not to think of the matter of reparation after reading this parable. However, I do not believe the United States owes me anything. I see naught but the hand of God's grace allowing me to be born here. Have you visited Haiti, Brazil, India, or one of the sub-Saharan countries on the continent of Africa? On the other hand, it is ironic that I should see African slaves in that first shift of workers. What do you think about all this? Discuss it in class. Ascertain what practical conclusions should prevail for the Christian concerning payment for the work done by our ancestors in America. But keep in mind always, the grace of God!

B. A CONCLUDING WORD

The protesters failed to reckon with the grace of God, whether in their own lives or in the lives of others. "Grace is better than justice" (Macdonald). The disciples needed to know that believers who came after them would also share in equal privileges in the kingdom. God is no respecter of persons, no receiver of faces or races, but is impartial, giving eternal life to all who believe in the Lord Jesus Christ. Rest assured that He is always fair, just, and righteous. What counts in the Lord's service is faithfulness to our opportunities. Only the God of the Bible is capable of adequately determining opportunities, motives, faithfulness, attitude, gratitude, etc. Judgments made by man based upon what man sees on the outside may well be wrong, false, erroneous. Only God is the proper Judge. He sees the internal also (1 Samuel 16:7). May the Lord grant that we serve Him with pure motives; not jealous of the gifts bestowed upon others; not begrudging God's grace; not questioning God's sovereignty, or attempting to second-guess His judgments; or being provoked to grumbling because of His generosity to others; or blinded because our thoughts are centered upon "our own ministries." From time to time, you encounter men who will seek to use you for their own praise and glory, for their ministry, even for their "tithe." Often, thoughts about being first get mixed up with pride and selfish ambition, and cause the worker to end up being last. Keep in mind then, this is a parable of the kingdom of God. And in that kingdom, the grace of God is the predominant factor.

HOME DAILY BIBLE READINGS FOR THE WEEK OF JANUARY 30, 2000

LABORERS IN THE VINEYARD

Jan. 24 M. Matthew 19:16-22, The Rich Young Man and Jesus
Jan. 25 T. Matthew 19:23-30, All Things Are Possible for God
Jan. 26 W. Matthew 20:1-7, Hiring of Laborers for the Vineyard
Jan. 27 T. Matthew 20:8-16, God's Grace Illustrated in a Parable
Jan. 28 F. Matthew 20:17-23, Jesus' Death and Resurrection Foretold
Jan. 29 S. Matthew 20:24-28, Jesus Teaches About Servanthood
Jan. 30 S. John 13:1-5, Jesus Demonstrates Servanthood

Know Your Bible

- In order for Christians to be successful in prayer, the spirit of forgiveness is indispensable. (Mark 11:25-26)
- The "Law" has reference to the Law of Moses and the writings of the prophets. (John 7:49)

 *O God, accept us by grace into Your service that Your work of redemption may truly become the desire of our hearts. Amen.*

Coming to Jerusalem

Unit III—*Fulfillment of Jesus' Mission*
Children's Unit—*Understanding Why Jesus Came*

·····

Adult Topic—*The Guidance of the Word*

·····

Youth Topic—*Greatness Through Humility*
Children's Topic—*Honoring Jesus*

·····

Devotional Reading—Luke 19:29-44
Background Scripture—Matthew 21:1-17
Print—Matthew 21:1-13

PRINTED SCRIPTURE

Matthew 21:1-13 (KJV)

AND WHEN they drew nigh unto Jerusalem, and were come to Bethphage, unto the mount of Olives, then sent Jesus two disciples,

2 Saying unto them, Go into the village over against you, and straightway ye shall find an ass tied, and a colt with her: loose them, and bring them unto me.

3 And if any man say aught unto you, ye shall say, The Lord hath need of them; and straightway he will send them.

4 All this was done, that it might be fulfilled which was spoken by the prophet, saying,

5 Tell ye the daughter of Zion, Behold, thy King cometh unto thee, meek, and sitting upon an ass, and a colt the foal of an ass.

6 And the disciples went, and did as Jesus commanded them,

7 And brought the ass, and the

Matthew 21:1-13 (NRSV)

WHEN THEY had come near Jerusalem and had reached Bethphage, at the Mount of Olives, Jesus sent two disciples,

2 saying to them, "Go into the village ahead of you, and immediately you will find a donkey tied, and a colt with her; untie them and bring them to me.

3 If anyone says anything to you, just say this, 'The Lord needs them.' And he will send them immediately."

4 This took place to fulfill what had been spoken through the prophet, saying,

5 "Tell the daughter of Zion, Look, your king is coming to you, humble, and mounted on a donkey, and on a colt, the foal of a donkey."

6 The disciples went and did as Jesus had directed them;

7 they brought the donkey and

colt, and put on them their clothes, and they set him thereon.

8 And a very great multitude spread their garments in the way; others cut down branches from the trees, and strawed them in the way.

9 And the multitudes that went before, and that followed, cried, saying, Hosanna to the son of David: Blessed is he that cometh in the name of the Lord; Hosanna in the highest.

10 And when he was come into Jerusalem, all the city was moved, saying, Who is this?

11 And the multitude said, This is Jesus the prophet of Nazareth of Galilee.

12 And Jesus went into the temple of God, and cast out all them that sold and bought in the temple, and overthrew the tables of the moneychangers, and the seats of them that sold doves,

13 And said unto them, It is written, My house shall be called the house of prayer; but ye have made it a den of thieves.

the colt, and put their cloaks on them, and he sat on them.

8 A very large crowd spread their cloaks on the road, and others cut branches from the trees and spread them on the road.

9 The crowds that went ahead of him and that followed were shouting, "Hosanna to the Son of David! Blessed is the one who comes in the name of the Lord! Hosanna in the highest heaven!"

10 When he entered Jerusalem, the whole city was in turmoil, asking, "Who is this?"

11 The crowds were saying, "This is the prophet Jesus from Nazareth in Galilee."

12 Then Jesus entered the temple and drove out all who were selling and buying in the temple, and he overturned the tables of the money changers and the seats of those who sold doves.

13 He said to them, "It is written, 'My house shall be called a house of prayer'; but you are making it a den of robbers."

KEY VERSE

*Tell ye the daughter of Zion, Behold, thy King cometh unto thee, meek, and sitting upon an ass, and a colt the foal of an ass.—**Matthew 21:5***

OBJECTIVES

After reading this lesson, the student should better recognize:

1. Who Jesus really is;
2. Why the religious leaders refused to recognize Jesus;
3. The place of Zechariah's prophecy; and,
4. God's house of prayer is not to become a den of robbers.

POINTS TO BE EMPHASIZED

Adult/Youth/Children
Key Verse: Matthew 21:5
Print: Matthew 21:1-13

—Jesus sent two disciples to secure a donkey to ride into Jerusalem, in order to fulfill the prophecy of Zechariah. (1-7)

—As Jesus entered Jerusalem, the crowd threw down their coats and branches along the road, and shouted praises to Him. (8-9)

—The people of Jerusalem were excited and asked about Jesus' identity. (10)

—The crowd replied that He was the prophet Jesus of Nazareth of Galilee. (11)

—Jesus entered the temple and overturned the money changers' tables, declaring that the Scripture says, "My house shall be called a house of prayer; but you have made it a den of robbers." (12-13)

(**Note**: Use KJV Scripture for Adults: NRSV Scripture for Youth and Children)

TOPICAL OUTLINE OF THE LESSON

I. Introduction
   A. Zechariah 9:9
   B. Biblical Background

II. Exposition and Application of the Scripture
   A. The Command to the Two Disciples (Matthew 21:1-3)
   B. Fulfillment of Prophetic Scriptures (Matthew 21:4-7)
   C. Reception by the Multitudes (Matthew 21:8-11)
   D. The Second Cleansing of the Temple (Matthew 21:12-13)

III. Special Features
   A. Preserving Our Heritage
   B. A Concluding Word

I. Introduction

A. ZECHARIAH 9:9

Matthew 21:4-5 refers to Zechariah 9:9, where the prophet predicted the Lord's entry into Jerusalem at His first coming. The verse begins with the exhortation for Jerusalem to rejoice or shout. Use of the word "daughter" signifies one who is acceptable to God, one who rejoices in God's peculiar care and protection. "Daughter of Zion (Jerusalem)" denotes collectively the citizens of that region; it means the "personified population of Jerusalem as a representative of the nation of Israel" (Keil and Delitzsch). In other words, all the believing inhabitants of the Holy City are bidden "to give unrestrained expressions of joy" (ICC). Why? Because the Promised Messiah King is coming to Jerusalem.

Note now three characteristics of this coming Monarch. First of all, He is just, that is to say, righteous. This first attribute is absolutely essential if there is to be any peace. Folks talk about peace these days but say very little if anything about righteousness. They see no connection between peace and righteousness. Second: He has the credential of possessing salvation, being endowed with, furnished with the assistance of God that is needed in order to carry on God's government. Third: He is lowly. The Hebrew word used refers not so much to meekness as it does to suffering, lowly or outward appearance with lowliness of soul.

We are to see one bowed down, miserable, suffering, brought low through adversity, yet one who is submissive to God and full of piety. The Messiah rode upon a lowly beast, the donkey, a symbol of humility. And this was literally fulfilled on Palm Sunday before His crucifixion. A colt is the young of a horse, zebra, donkey, etc., sometimes distinctively, a male foal (the young of an animal), as distinguished from a filly (a young female horse). And so rather than come in like some arrogant, proud man of war, a victorious general, seated on a prancing steed, the Lord Jesus Christ came in lowliness,

gentleness, peace. As Feinberg said, "Pride was as foreign to Him as it is common to the world's kings."

B. BIBLICAL BACKGROUND

God has a time schedule. There are specific events already programmed, "as definite as was His birth of a virgin in Bethlehem" (Chafer). This is evident in the predictions made by the Old Testament prophets. "When the fullness of the time was come, God sent forth his Son, made of a woman, made under the law" (Galatians 4:4). Everything was just right for the Lord Jesus Christ to be born into this world. Likewise, His earthly public ministry began "on time," even as John the Baptist heralded His coming forth. And now today's lesson teaches us that the time had come for Christ to publicly offer Himself as King. He knew, of course, what lay ahead, for He had repeatedly predicted His crucifixion. We see then that what is traditionally called a triumphal entry into the city of Jerusalem, recorded in all four of the Gospels, is actually one more step—a giant step—to Calvary. While our Lord appreciated the welcome given by the people in general, it was the evil spirit of the religious leaders that broke His heart. Surely, He had come unto His own, but His own received Him not (John 1:11). And the acknowledgement that He was the rightful heir of David's throne was but for a brief moment.

II. Exposition and Application of the Scripture

A. THE COMMAND TO THE TWO DISCIPLES (Matthew 21:1-3)

AND when they drew nigh unto Jerusalem, and were come to Beth-

phage, unto the mount of Olives, then sent Jesus two disciples, Saying unto them, Go into the village over against you, and straightway

ye shall find an ass tied, and a colt with her: loose them, and bring them unto me. And if any man say aught unto you, ye shall say, The Lord hath need of them; and straightway he will send them.

It is now the Sunday before Calvary (John 12:1). Having drawn near to Jerusalem, the Lord and His disciples came to Bethphage. This name means "House of unripe figs." Bethphage is mentioned nowhere else in the Bible except with regard to our Lord's entry into Jerusalem. It was a village near Bethany, near to and east of Jerusalem, and hid by the top of the Mount of Olives. Our Lord had lodged in Bethany earlier with Mary and Martha—and Lazarus, restored to life! Bethany is still known, but we are told that no trace of Bethpage remains. Sending out two of His disciples—their names are not mentioned—Christ gave them explicit instructions as to where, what, who, and when. In the village opposite them, they would find a donkey tied and a colt with her. He ordered: "Loose them and bring them unto me." This they did, apparently without asking anyone's permission for the animals.

It appears the owner of the beasts may have known the Lord, and on an earlier occasion had offered Him help. Perhaps he was a friend of the Master and His disciples. But then possibly we also have demonstrated here an example of "omniscience and supreme authority" (Macdonald). "If anyone says anything to you, you answer: 'The Lord has need of them,' and immediately he will send them." How the owner of the animals would interpret the title, "Lord," is not clear. The disciples were calling Him Lord, and He accepted the title and applied it to Himself. But now why ride a beast at all? Was He tired? Was it to draw attention to Himself? No, there was no such self-centeredness in Christ. Usually, He walked the distance, for it was no more than two miles to Jerusalem. However, there was a purpose in riding as He did.

B. FULLFILLMENT OF PROPHETIC SCRIPTURES
(Matthew 21:4-7)

All this was done, that it might be fulfilled which was spoken by the prophet, saying, Tell ye the daughter of Zion, Behold, thy King cometh unto thee, meek, and sitting upon an ass, and a colt the foal of an ass. And the disciples went, and did as Jesus commanded them, And brought the ass, and the colt, and put on them their clothes, and they set him thereon.

Here we discover the answer to the question posed earlier, why His entrance this way? "Now this is come to pass" in fulfillment of the Word of God spoken by the prophet Zechariah. The disciples were not aware of this prior to His resurrection (John 12:16). It had been predicted that He would enter the city this way. Indeed, in accord with Zechariah 9:9, He would make His final official offer of Himself as the Messiah King (Scofield). From Isaiah 62:11, we read: "Say ye to the daughters of Zion, Behold, thy salvation cometh...." This is incorporated in the first line of Matthew 21:5.

He deliberately entered the city riding on a donkey, even on the foal of a beast of burden. This animal had never been ridden before (Mark 11:2; Luke 19:30: "on which never man sat").

Both animals were brought together; separating them was purposely avoided, for the donkey was needed to calm the previously unridden colt. There would be no big show, no outward pomp on His part, none of that pretentiousness the proud, worldly-minded citizens of Jerusalem loved so well. He deliberately did not come mounted on a horse or riding in a chariot. It is predicted in Revelation 19:10 that Christ will return to earth seated upon a white horse. But for now, He came on a lowly beast, for meekness and humility characterized Him. His entrance demonstrated that He was none other than the Son of David, coming to claim the City of Zion as His own!

C. RECEPTION BY THE MULTITUDES (Matthew 21:8-11)

And a very great multitude spread their garments in the way; others cut down branches from the trees, and strawed them in the way. And the multitudes that went before, and that followed, cried, saying, Hosanna to the son of David: Blessed is he that cometh in the name of the Lord; Hosanna in the highest. And when he was come into Jerusalem, all the city was moved, saying, Who is this? And the multitude said, This is Jesus the prophet of Nazareth of Galilee.

The city was filled with Jews from many different places, all came to celebrate the Passover. But it is better to see, at the initial stage of His entrance, two different crowds here. Verse nine makes this clear; see a country crowd that was with Him; and see a city crowd that came out to meet Him. The country crowd consisted of many Galileans who knew who Jesus Christ was. They had heard Him preach, had eaten of the multiplied fish and bread, and had seen Him perform miracles. These were they who spread their garments in the way, an act which demonstrated submission combined with "the bestowal of highest honor" (Lenski). They cut down branches from the trees (Palm trees, John 12:13), and spread them upon the road. They were those who went ahead and that followed, crying, "Hosanna to the Son of David! Blessed is He that comes in the name of the Lord! Hosanna in the highest!" Transliterated from the Hebrew, "Hosanna" means "save now" (Psalm 118:25-26), and is a prayer for deliverance.

Previously, our Lord had avoided all such public displays. But now it is different. He knew the outcome of the tumultuous reception given Him; He knew the results of asserting His claim as Messiah, or of letting the people do so. It was all a matter of timing. The city crowd could not understand the stir created by His coming in this remarkable manner. And so they inquired, "Who is this Man?" They were confused, bewildered. To them, His identity was a mystery. He had purposely avoided Jerusalem during much of His ministry. Indeed, from this point on, questions would be asked: "Who is this who speaks blasphemies? Who is this that forgives sin also? Who are You? Who is this Son of man? Who are You, Sir?" You see why Tasker states the question was prompted by mixed feelings of surprise, indignation, expectation and contempt.

Who is this Man? For this one brief noisy moment the Lord Jesus was acknowledged as the rightful heir to the throne of David. But it was not the time for Him to assume the throne. Not yet. The Lion they sought must first come as a Lamb, the cross before a crown!

Furthermore, the religious leaders deeply resented the homage paid Him by the crowd on that historic Palm Sunday. Their displeasure grew by leaps and bounds. Eventually the crowd would scream, "His blood be on us, and on our children!" This crowd would cry, "Crucify Him! Crucify Him!"

People do not like their status quo upset. His preaching upset them because He preached with authority. His knowledge upset them, for they could not figure out its source. His popularity upset them, for the common people heard Him gladly. His miracles upset them because healing was performed on the Sabbath. His emphasis on hell upset them, for they thought they had the keys to heaven. His use of parables upset them, for they were befuddled in their spiritual blindness. His holiness upset them, for they could not convict Him of sin. They could not truthfully find any fault in Him.

Who is this that moves the city? The word translated "move" has given us the word, "seismic," used with respect to earthquakes. A. B. Bruce (Expositor's) said the city was "stirred with popular enthusiasm as by a mighty wind or by an earthquake." We are therefore tempted to ask, "Who is this that quakes our quo?" Who is this that agitates the minds of the citizens of Jerusalem?

Hear the answer the proud crowd kept giving to the questioners: "The One whom we have thus honored is Jesus, our countryman, the prophet of Nazareth of Galilee."

D. THE SECOND CLEANSING OF THE TEMPLE (Matthew 21:12-13)

And Jesus went into the temple of God, and cast out all them that sold and bought in the temple, and overthrew the tables of the moneychangers, and the seats of them that sold doves, And said unto them, It is written, My house shall be called the house of prayer; but ye have made it a den of thieves.

Our lesson closes with the second cleansing of the temple. Recall that at the very beginning of His ministry, the Lord drove out the commercialists from the temple area (John 2:13-16). The men there were guilty of charging exorbitant fees for the sacrificial animals and birds. Even the money changers charged excessive amounts for converting other currencies to be used by the Jewish worshipers to pay their temple tax (collected from every Jew twenty years and older: Exodus 30:11-16). This conversion of coins was required because only sacred coins could be used. The high priest (and his family) controlled the operation; they were guilty of extortion. Accept the fact that there were two cleansings, in spite of those who claim there was only one. Nearly a span of three years intervened, but it does not take long for men to return to their wicked ways, especially where money is involved.

Note then some of the differences between the two cleansings: (1) At the first, He was directly confronted by the authorities; at the second cleansing, in today's lesson, no one dared challenge Him. (2) At the first, He spoke to those in charge; at the second, He spoke to the mob He dismissed. (3) At the first, He rebuked and challenged in His own words; at the second, He gave a most scathing rebuke, and quoted Old Testament Scriptures. (4) Finally, at the first, the disciples remembered Psalm 69:9: "For the zeal of thine house hath eaten me up"; at the second, no mention is made of any recall by the disciples.

Combining the accounts, we see the physical action taken by our Lord! He used a scourge of small cords to chase the merchants and the animals out. Did He actually beat them in that first cleansing? He poured out their money, overturned ("most likely kicked over," Lenski) their tables, and would not allow any man to carry any vessel through the temple. How do you like that for the "gentle Jesus"? Rest assured the religious leaders were furious! This act of Christ renewed their determination to get rid of Him. Finally, we see the Author of the Word combining the prophets Isaiah and Jeremiah in His scathing denunciation of the profiteering there. He cited Isaiah 56:7: "Mine house shall be called an house of prayer for all peoples." From Jeremiah 7:11 came: "Is this house, which is called by my name, become a den of robbers in your eye?" This strong expression directs our attention to the greed and fraud of the traders. Imagine, robbers using God's Temple for a refuge! We can almost hear the sarcasm of Amos 4:4: "Come to Bethel (house of God), and transgress...."

III. Special Features

A. PRESERVING OUR HERITAGE

All too often in our churches, we hear preaching that is not Christ-centered. I recently heard a message entitled, "Don't Go Down to Moab" (Ruth 1:1-10). The preacher offered no cross in the message proper, but did manage to mention Jesus Christ and the Cross in the invitation. An audience should not have to ask, "Who is this?" Not if the preaching is Bible-centered. The strength of the black pulpit is Jesus Christ. We want to remain determined to preach Jesus Christ. No matter what text is taken, He is there—not as a tail that wags a dog, not as some afterthought, not as a form or fashion. But from Genesis to Revelation, the scarlet thread should be shown to every audience when the Gospel is preached. Perhaps too, some of our temples need to be cleansed, so that we might more clearly see the Lord Jesus Christ in all of His divine authority and righteousness. It would certainly help us to remember why He came to Jerusalem so long ago!

B. A CONCLUDING WORD

Who is this? Is He John the Baptist resurrected? Elijah, Jeremiah? The prophet predicted in Deuteronomy? Who is this? How often this question is found in the Scriptures. "Who are you?" asked Isaac (Genesis 27:18, 32). "Who is the Lord?" fumed the arrogant Pharaoh (Exodus 5:2). "Who are you?" inquired Joshua of the deceitful Gibeonites (Joshua 9:8). "Who is this King of glory?" asked David (Psalm 24:8, 10).

"Who are you?" the startled Boaz inquired (Ruth 3:9). "Who is the Lord?" may be asked in the vanity of prosperity (Proverbs 30:9). "Who is this who speaks blasphemies?" was the question put forth by the spiritually ignorant Pharisees (Luke 5:21). "Who is this that forgives sins also?" again inquired the religious leaders (Luke 7:49). "Who are you?" was the question of curiosity by the priests and Levites (John 1:19, 22); and one of puzzlement by the Pharisees (John 8:25). "Who is this Son of man?" responded the people when Christ spoke of being lifted up to draw all men unto Himself (John 12:32).

"Lord, who is it?" inquired John, desiring to know who would betray the Master (John 13:25). "Who are You?" a question the disciples dared not ask, knowing that it was the resurrected Lord who sat and ate with them (John 21:12). "Who are You, Lord?" are words that came from the quivering lips of Saul of Tarsus there on the road to Damascus (Acts 9:5).

Who is this? remains one of the most important questions in the world. In fact, it is an inescapable question. Taken out of the confines of our text, we discover the responsibility for answering correctly falls upon us today. Romans 10:9 states: "That if you confess with your mouth the Lord Jesus (Jesus is Lord), and believe in your heart that God has raised Him from the dead, you will be saved."

In other words, a personal confession is required from each of us. Not just words from our lips, but truth from convicted hearts. Thank God for the events of this week that led to Calvary. Because there He was crucified in our stead, that we might come to know who He is—our Lord and our God!

HOME DAILY BIBLE READINGS FOR THE WEEK OF FEBRUARY 6, 2000

COMING TO JERUSALEM

Jan. 31 M. Luke 9:51-56, Jesus Sets His Face Toward Jerusalem
Feb. 1 T. Matthew 21:1-11, Jesus Enters Jerusalem Amid Hosannas
Feb. 2 W. Matthew 21:12-17, Jesus Cleanses the Temple
Feb. 3 T. Matthew 21:23-27, Chief Priests and Elders Resist Jesus
Feb. 4 F. Matthew 21:33-46, Parable of the Wicked Tenants
Feb. 5 S. Matthew 22:23-33, A Question About the Resurrection
Feb. 6 S. Matthew 22:34-46, The Greatest Commandment of All

Know Your Bible

- The "snare" that was laid for Jesus was a question designed to bring an answer that would contradict either the Jewish or the Roman Law. (Mark 12:14-15)
- Worship that is acceptable to God is that worship that originates from the heart. (John 4:23-24)

Eternal God, our Father, may we come into Your presence with that posture of faith that will honor Your Name. Amen.

Watching for Christ's Return

Adult Topic—*The Joy of Being Prepared*

·····

Youth Topic—*Be Ready!*

Children's Topic—*Do Good At All Times*

·····

Devotional Reading—Matthew 24:36-44

Background Scripture—Matthew 24:1—25:13

Print—Matthew 24:45—25:13

PRINTED SCRIPTURE

Matthew 24:45—25:13 (KJV)

45 Who then is a faithful and wise servant, whom his lord hath made ruler over his household, to give them meat in due season?

46 Blessed is that servant, whom his lord when he cometh shall find so doing.

47 Verily I say unto you, That he shall make him ruler over all his goods.

48 But and if that evil servant shall say in his heart, My lord delayeth his coming;

49 And shall begin to smite his fellowservants, and to eat and drink with the drunken;

50 The lord of that servant shall come in a day when he looketh not for him, and in an hour that he is not aware of,

51 And shall cut him asunder, and appoint him his portion with the hypocrites: there shall be weeping and gnashing of teeth.

Matthew 24:45—25:13 (NRSV)

45 "Who then is the faithful and wise slave, whom his master has put in charge of his household, to give the other slaves their allowance of food at the proper time?

46 Blessed is that slave whom his master will find at work when he arrives.

47 Truly I tell you, he will put that one in charge of all his possessions.

48 But if that wicked slave says to himself, 'My master is delayed,'

49 and he begins to beat his fellow slaves, and eats and drinks with drunkards,

50 the master of that slave will come on a day when he does not expect him and at an hour that he does not know.

51 He will cut him in pieces and put him with the hypocrites, where there will be weeping and gnashing of teeth."

.....

THEN SHALL the kingdom of heaven be likened unto ten virgins, which took their lamps, and went forth to meet the bridegroom.

2 And five of them were wise, and five were foolish.

3 They that were foolish took their lamps, and took no oil with them:

4 But the wise took oil in their vessels with their lamps.

5 While the bridegroom tarried, they all slumbered and slept.

6 And at midnight there was a cry made, Behold, the bridegroom cometh; go ye out to meet him.

7 Then all those virgins arose, and trimmed their lamps.

8 And the foolish said unto the wise, Give us of your oil; for our lamps are gone out.

9 But the wise answered, saying, Not so; lest there be not enough for us and you: but go ye rather to them that sell, and buy for yourselves.

10 And while they went to buy, the bridegroom came; and they that were ready went in with him to the marriage: and the door was shut.

11 Afterward came also the other virgins, saying, Lord, Lord, open to us.

12 But he answered and said, Verily I say unto you, I know you not.

13 Watch therefore, for ye know neither the day nor the hour wherein the Son of man cometh.

.....

"THEN THE kingdom of heaven will be like this. Ten bridesmaids took their lamps and went to meet the bridegroom.

2 Five of them were foolish, and five were wise.

3 When the foolish took their lamps, they took no oil with them;

4 but the wise took flasks of oil with their lamps.

5 As the bridegroom was delayed, all of them became drowsy and slept.

6 But at midnight there was a shout, 'Look! Here is the bridegroom! Come out to meet him.'

7 Then all those bridesmaids got up and trimmed their lamps.

8 The foolish said to the wise, 'Give us some of your oil, for our lamps are going out.'

9 But the wise replied, 'No! there will not be enough for you and for us; you had better go to the dealers and buy some for yourselves.'

10 And while they went to buy it, the bridegroom came, and those who were ready went with him into the wedding banquet; and the door was shut.

11 Later the other bridesmaids came also, saying, 'Lord, lord, open to us.'

12 But he replied, 'Truly I tell you, I do not know you.'

13 Keep awake therefore, for you know neither the day nor the hour.

KEY VERSE

Watch therefore, for ye know neither the day nor the hour wherein the Son of man cometh.
—Matthew 25:13

OBJECTIVES

After reading this lesson, the student will know:

1. What it means to be a faithful servant;
2. What the behavior of an evil servant is like;
3. The meaning of the parables as they relate to the kindgom of heaven; and,
4. The need for diligently looking for the return of Christ.

POINTS TO BE EMPHASIZED

Adult/Youth/Children
Key Verse: Matthew 25:13; Exodus 24:7 *(Children)*
Print: Matthew 24:45—25:13

—Jesus told a parable about faithful and unfaithful servants to illustrate the importance of being prepared for His return. (45-51)
—In a parable about five wise and five foolish bridesmaids, Jesus emphasized being prepared for His return. (1-2)
—Five of the bridesmaids came with extra oil, and five did not; and when the bridegroom came later than expected, the foolish bridesmaids had to go buy more oil. (3-9)
—While the five bridesmaids were gone, the bridegroom came, and those who were ready went with him to the marriage feast and the door was closed. (10)
—The five bridesmaids returned asking that the door be opened only to hear that they were not known. (11-12)
—Jesus declared that one should be ready at all times because no one knows the time of His return. (13)

(**Note**: Use KJV Scripture for Adults; NRSV Scripture for Youth and Children)

TOPICAL OUTLINE OF THE LESSON

I. Introduction
   A. The Meaning of the Word, "Watch"
   B. Biblical Background

II. Exposition and Application of the Scripture
   A. The Faithful and Wise Servant (Matthew 24:45-47)
   B. The Evil Servant (Matthew 24:48-51)
   C. The Parable of the Ten Virgins (Matthew 25:1-13)

III. Special Features
   A. Preserving Our Heritage
   B. A Concluding Word

I. Introduction

A. THE MEANING OF THE WORD, "WATCH"

Perhaps the most famous watch in our churches is the Mizpah watch (Genesis 31:49): "The Lord watch between me and thee, when we are absent one from another." This verse is often used mistakenly as a benediction. Originally, it was far from a benediction. It was a sign of a kind of boundary between Jacob and his hostile father-in-law, Laban. Neither one trusted the other, so it would be necessary for the Lord to watch them. They both promised to keep the peace. The Hebrew verb rendered watch conveys "the idea of being fully aware of a situation in order to gain some advantage or keep from being surprised by an enemy" (Theological Wordbook of the Old Testament). The word for watch in Matthew 25:13 is *gregoreo*, from which is derived the name, Gregory (Watchman). This Greek verb means to be aroused from sleep, be vigilant (Young); be or keep awake (Arndt and Gingrich). Figuratively, the verb means give attention to, be cautious, active; take heed lest through negligence and laziness some disaster suddenly overtakes one (Thayer); be on the alert (Arndt and Gingrich). We would say, "Keep your eyes open!"

"O watch and fight and pray; The battle ne'er give o'er,
Renew it boldly ev'ry day. And help divine implore"
(George Heath #428, Baptist Standard Hymnal)

B. BIBLICAL BACKGROUND

Today's lesson forms part of what is called the Olivet Discourse, composed of Matthew chapters 24 and 25. Christ sat upon the Mount of Olives and proceeded to answer the questions His disciples had put to Him privately. Two questions were asked, but the second question has two parts which actually form one idea: His coming and the end of the world-age are combined. For analysis purposes, I have made two points out of the second question, giving three prongs to their query. (1) WHEN shall these things be? In the preceding chapter, He pronounced woes on the scribes and Pharisees, and predicted the coming fall of their great sanctuary. (2) WHAT shall be the sign of Your coming? (3) WHAT shall be the sign of the end of the world-age?

Well aware of the fact of the different interpretations of the Olivet Discourse, we offer what we believe is the accurate interpretation of what is one of the most important passages in the New Testament concerning things to come or last things (Eschatology). Today's lesson does not deal directly with the church. It is extremely important that this be kept in mind. Some applications of course may be made to the church and our present time, as is done in our Concluding Word. But suffice it to say here, the Scriptures under study cannot be assigned to the church. The Olivet Discourse is concerned with Israel; it is Jewish in scope, and no mention is made of the church or of the Rapture of the church. Christ deals with the faithful remnant within the nation of Israel, and they are exhorted to watch. See then today's lesson centering upon Christ's return to earth to establish His kingdom.

II. Exposition and application of the Scripture

A. THE FAITHFUL AND WISE SERVANT (Matthew 24:45-47)

Who then is a faithful and wise servant, whom his lord hath made ruler over his household, to give them meat in due season? Blessed is that servant, whom his lord when he cometh shall find so doing. Verily I say unto you, That he shall make him ruler over all his goods.

Consider first the servant (not a servant) described as faithful and wise. This man was placed by his master in a position of special responsibility, a ruler over his master's household. *Pistos* means trusty (Thayer); trustworthy, dependable (Arndt and Gingrich); it is used of one who shows himself faithful in carrying out business, discharge of duties, and execution of commands (Thayer). He or she is one who can be relied on. "The Lord commends faithfulness rather than ability" (Scofield). The apostle Paul said: "Moreover, it is required in stewards, that a man be found faithful" (1 Corinthians 4:2).

The word for wise (*Phronimos*) means intelligent, prudent, mindful of one's interests (Thayer); sensible, thoughtful (Arndt and Gingrich). This servant had the responsibility of providing food for the household, the other domestic servants, at the time appointed, "the right time." This servant, the one doing what he was told, is blessed when the master returns and finds the servant has been obedient. It pays to obey. Indeed (the word rendered verily or assuredly is amen), his reward is a promotion. He shall be made, appointed, or put in charge over all the property or possessions of the master as a result of his faithful performance.

B. THE EVIL SERVANT (Matthew 24:48-51)

But and if that evil servant shall say in his heart, My lord delayeth his coming; And shall begin to smite his fellowservants, and to eat and drink with the drunken; The lord of that servant shall come in a day when he looketh not for him, and in an hour that he is not aware of, And shall cut him asunder, and appoint him his portion with the hypocrites: there shall be weeping and gnashing of teeth.

Consider now the contrast. The evil servant is one who is morally bad; his mode of thinking, feeling and acting is wrong or wicked. He possesses a vicious disposition; for we are told his heart-thought. People often put on a front; they fix up their outside so as to disguise their inside. But when the right moment comes, the facade falls and their true nature shows itself. In this case, it is his master's absence that motivates his behavior. "When the cat's away, the mice will play." *Chronizo* (see the word for time, chronos) means to linger, delay, tarry (Thayer); take time, fail to come (or stay away) for a long time (Arndt and Gingrich). So this servant speaks in his heart, "My master is delayed" (RSV).

This demonstrates his "doctrinal defection." He then started to show his true colors, for bad doctrine leads to bad deeds. Right away he began to mistreat his fellow servants. The word for beat or smite is *tupto*; it means to strike (with a stick, whip, fist, the hand, etc.). From it is derived the word, type. A typewriter has keys which strike the paper through an inked ribbon. Instead of taking proper care of those servants under him, he abused them. He further flouted his employer's instructions by drinking and carousing with drunkards. He partied! Intoxicated with assumed power, he showed by his behavior that he was not ready for the kingdom.

The Lord warned that at the very moment this evil servant is not looking, and is completely unaware, the master will come. His sudden and unexpected coming will subject the evil servant to dreaded consequences. Some men think they are clever enough to stop their evil doings in time, and thus escape with impunity. But this is self-deception. Sin blinds. To cut in two or cut asunder is strong language "for severe and irrevocable punishment" (Filson). The verb *dichotomeo* (see the English word, dichotomy) means to cut into two parts. Thayer states this was a cruel mode of punishment used in those days, by which criminals and captives were sawn or cut in two. But inasmuch as the remainder of verse fifty-one has the wicked servant still alive, it is best to interpret the verb to mean, to "cut up by scourging, scourge severely."

Arndt and Gingrich state: "In the context of these two passages (Matthew 24:51; Luke 12:46), the meaning punish with utmost severity is possible, though no exact linguistic parallels for this meaning have been found." In addition, he is assigned a place with the hypocrites, where there is loud, audible grinding or chattering of teeth. Gnashing of teeth striking together denotes "the extreme anguish and utter despair of men consigned to eternal condemnation" (Thayer). "It simply denotes the despairing remorse which shakes their whole body" (Kittel). It signifies rage or sorrow (Acts 7:54; Mark 9:18).

Finally, to be assigned a portion with the hypocrites is to be put in terrible company. For the Bible teaches that the hope of the hypocrite shall perish with his death; his company will be barren, his joy but for a moment, for he stores up for himself the wrath of God (Job 8:13; 27:8; 15:34; 20:5; 36:13). From the New Testament, we learn that hypocrites have their glory from men, but no rewards from God. Blinded by the planks in their own eyes and unable to discern the signs of the times, they shall suffer seven (full, complete) woes (Matthew 6:2, 5, 16; 17:5; 16:3; chapter 23).

C. THE PARABLE OF THE TEN VIRGINS (Matthew 25:1-13)

THEN shall the kingdom of heaven be likened unto ten virgins, which took their lamps, and went forth to meet the bridegroom. And five of them were wise, and five were foolish. They that were foolish took their lamps, and took no oil with them: But the wise took oil in their vessels with their lamps. While the bridegroom tarried, they all slumbered and slept. And at midnight there was a cry made, Behold, the bridegroom cometh; go ye out to meet him. Then all those virgins arose, and trimmed their lamps. And the foolish said unto the wise, Give us of your oil; for our lamps are gone out. But the wise answered, saying,

Not so; lest there be not enough for us and you: but go ye rather to them that sell, and buy for yourselves. And while they went to buy, the bridegroom came; and they that were ready went in with him to the marriage: and the door was shut. Afterward came also the other virgins, saying, Lord, Lord, open to us. But he answered and said, Verily I say unto you, I know you not. Watch therefore, for ye know neither the day nor the hour wherein the Son of man cometh.

Literally, a parable is something thrown alongside; it is an illustration. This fact heightens the danger of pushing what is written to the point that we forget what the parable is intended to illustrate. Caution is certainly needed with respect to the Parable of the Ten Virgins. Beware of pushing or pressing parabolic teachings too far. This warning comes even with the realization that we may have violated this principle in today's lesson.

Therefore, we repeat the warning: Keep in mind that the major thrust of this parable is to exhort Israel to be prepared for the coming of their king, the Christ. The Lord (Bridegroom) is scheduled to return with His Bride (the church) to the earth where He is to rule and reign. The virgins are Jews; they represent Israel. Our Lord shows in this farewell word to Israel that many Jews will fail to enter the kingdom. So He warns the nation to expect the unexpected. There remains for Israel a great time of testing or tribulation. We have heard Jewish spokesmen assert, "Never Again!" with respect to the Holocaust. But the Bible predicts Jacob's trouble (Jeremiah 30:7) as a certainty. Therefore, it is important that Israel look for the Messiah's return.

The five and five is not to suggest fifty percent are wise, and fifty percent are foolish. Rather, it signifies there are two types of people. Some are foolish; the word used has given us "moron." It means stupid; imprudent, without forethought or wisdom, and is used to designate those who are "carelessly unprepared." Some are wise, prudent, mindful, provident. Now the supply of oil is what Trench (Parables) calls, "the turning point of the parable." In stating that they "took no oil with them," meant they had an insufficient supply. "They have some, but not enough" (Trench). The wise virgins took an extra supply in their receptacles in addition to the oil that was in their lamps (A. T. Robertson); they were prepared just in case the Bridegroom came later than expected. As was the custom then, marriages were celebrated invariably at night.

Sure enough, because the Bridegroom delayed, all of the maids fell asleep. The Bible says they "all slumbered and slept." Perhaps many of us think the words mean the same, since we often use them interchangeably. However, to slumber is to doze, nod, sleep lightly; the verb translated slept means to fall asleep or drop off to sleep, to sleep profoundly. Thus Lenski renders the phrase: they all nodded (past tense) and were sleeping (imperfect tense).

At midnight a cry awakened them and they prepared to go meet the Bridegroom. All of them had felt confident they would meet the Bridegroom whenever He came. But the foolish virgins were not justified in their security. We may be sincere, feel that we are capable, but flunk the test when it comes. We wake up to discover we have lamps but no oil; we profess but do not possess. Now there was no time for the wise virgins to do anything but trim their wicks, put in fresh oil, and light the lamps. However, the foolish virgins discovered their lamps only sputtered, flickered and smoked. They had no oil. "Our lamps are going out," they moaned.

Naturally, the foolish five requested that the wise virgins supply them with oil. They were refused. Do not ascribe selfishness to their refusal to give others of their oil. "Each tub must stand on its own bottom." "There can be no transfer of spiritual reserves or merit. Spiritual preparedness is an individual matter; no one can borrow the resource needed" (Filson). "Every man must live by his own faith" (Trench). The consequences of their folly could not be averted at the last moment (Plummer). It is a difficult lesson to learn, for we do not want to abide by the consequences of our own negligence. While they were going away to purchase oil, the Bridegroom came. Those who were prepared went in with Him, and the door was shut.

How solemn those words, "the door was shut." We read that after all had entered the ark of Noah's day, "the Lord shut him in" (Genesis 7:16). Thus the foolish virgins were locked out. For when they sought entrance to the marriage, crying: "Lord, Lord, open to us," He answered, "Verily, I say unto you, I know you not." How similar are these words to those recorded earlier in Matthew 7:21-23: "I never knew you; depart from me, ye that work iniquity."

The lesson closes with the major refrain: WATCH, THEREFORE! Ignorance of the time of the Lord's coming is not an excuse for neglecting to prepare for His return. The lack of oil is interpreted as being unprepared for the coming of the Bridegroom. And we see once again, according to Trench, that the purpose of the parable is to impress upon the hearer the need for vigilance.

III. Special Features

A. PRESERVING OUR HERITAGE

Unfortunately, some black scholars despise the other-worldliness of the Scriptures, and whatever is taught about things to come (Eschatology). One man calls it "compensatory." This is to say, because of our low economic status, we dream of the future when things will be better for us, especially once we are in heaven. Another scholar suggests the whole emphasis on things to come is irrelevant. Why? Because it overlooks our present concerns and needs. True, some people have indeed abused the doctrine of the Second Coming of Christ.

However, the proper grasp of such Scriptures actually is beneficial right now. The correct view of things to come helps us to live a better life right now! The warning is repeated: We must not allow our material progress to make us forget the doctrine of the Second Coming of Christ. We must not let our fight against racism in America blind us to the fact that as Christians, we have a better home.

B. A CONCLUDING WORD

By application, of course, we Christians of today's church-age should be prepared for the coming of Christ. According to our interpretation, He may come at any moment; His coming is imminent. And His coming is sudden. There will be no time to trim the lamp, for we will be changed in the casting of a glance. We need then to search our hearts to ascertain that a genuine work of the Spirit has been done. "Mere outward religion is found to have no illuminating power" (Plummer). Each generation has looked for our Lord's coming. This is as it should be, for there are no unfulfilled Scriptures that would prevent His coming for His blood-bought church. Watchman Nee inquires, "Can we wait and still be ready?" Some of us may have been ready several years ago, but suppose the Lord were to come right now! May the Lord preserve us from becoming foolish with the passing of the years. All genuine believers have the Holy Spirit living in them. He is our oil, our guarantee of salvation. For the church, the doctrine of the Second Coming of the Lord is a blessed hope, a purifying hope. Being watchful not only helps us to live a clean life in a dirty age, but if the Lord should tarry, we also discover that having waited for Him also prepares us for death.

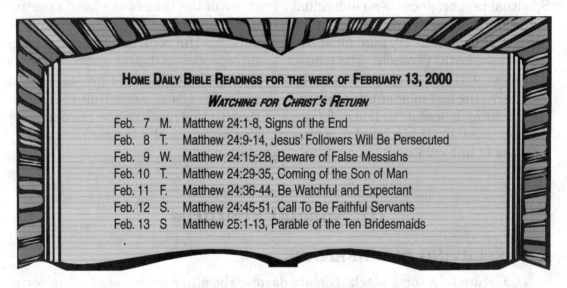

HOME DAILY BIBLE READINGS FOR THE WEEK OF FEBRUARY 13, 2000

WATCHING FOR CHRIST'S RETURN

Feb. 7   M.   Matthew 24:1-8, Signs of the End
Feb. 8   T.   Matthew 24:9-14, Jesus' Followers Will Be Persecuted
Feb. 9   W.   Matthew 24:15-28, Beware of False Messiahs
Feb. 10   T.   Matthew 24:29-35, Coming of the Son of Man
Feb. 11   F.   Matthew 24:36-44, Be Watchful and Expectant
Feb. 12   S.   Matthew 24:45-51, Call To Be Faithful Servants
Feb. 13   S   Matthew 25:1-13, Parable of the Ten Bridesmaids

Know Your Bible

- The universal success of the Gospel is not promised by Christ, the disciples were enjoined to proclaim the Gospel to all the world as a testimony to Jesus Christ. Faithfulness, not success, is the mandate. (Matthew 24:14)
- The sickness of the people of God is sometimes for the glory of God and not based on anything in the natural order of things. (John 11:4)

O God, grant that we may live in the consciousness of Your presence as we embody that quality of life that has eternal significance. In Jesus' name. Amen.

The Death of Jesus

Adult Topic—*The Death in Our Behalf*

·····

Youth Topic—*Darkness Before Dawn*
Children's Topic—*Jesus, the Son of God*

·····

Devotional Reading—John 19:16-30
Background Scripture—Matthew 27:32-61
Print—Matthew 27:38-54

PRINTED SCRIPTURE

Matthew 27:38-54 (KJV)

38 Then were there two thieves crucified with him, one on the right hand, and another on the left.

39 And they that passed by reviled him, wagging their heads,

40 And saying, Thou that destroyest the temple, and buildest it in three days, save thyself. If thou be the Son of God, come down from the cross.

41 Likewise also the chief priests mocking him, with the scribes and elders, said,

42 He saved others; himself he cannot save. If he be the King of Israel, let him now come down from the cross, and we will believe him.

43 He trusted in God; let him deliver him now, if he will have him: for he said, I am the Son of God.

44 The thieves also, which were crucified with him, cast the same in his teeth.

45 Now from the sixth hour there

Matthew 27:38-54 (NRSV)

38 Then two bandits were crucified with him, one on his right and one on his left.

39 Those who passed by derided him, shaking their heads

40 and saying, "You who would destroy the temple and build it in three days, save yourself! If you are the Son of God, come down from the cross."

41 In the same way the chief priests also, along with the scribes and elders, were mocking him, saying,

42 "He saved others; he cannot save himself. He is the King of Israel; let him come down from the cross now, and we will believe in him.

43 He trusts in God; let God deliver him now, if he wants to; for he said, 'I am God's Son.'"

44 The bandits who were crucified with him also taunted him in

was darkness over all the land unto the ninth hour.

46 And about the ninth hour Jesus cried with a loud voice, saying Eli, Eli, lama sabachthani? That is to say, My God, my God, why hast thou forsaken me?

47 Some of them that stood there, when they heard that, said, this man calleth for Elias.

48 And straightway one of them ran, and took a sponge, and filled it with vinegar, and put it on a reed, and gave him to drink.

49 The rest said, Let be, let us see whether Elias will come to save him.

50 Jesus, when he had cried again with a loud voice, yielded up the ghost.

51 And, behold, the veil of the temple was rent in twain from the top to the bottom; and the earth did quake, and the rocks rent;

52 And the graves were opened; and many bodies of the saints which slept arose,

53 And came out of the graves after his resurrection, and went into the holy city, and appeared unto many.

54 Now when the centurion, and they that were with him, watching Jesus, saw the earthquake, and those things that were done, they feared greatly, saying, Truly this was the Son of God.

the same way.

45 From noon on, darkness came over the whole land until three in the afternoon.

46 And about three o'clock Jesus cried with a loud voice, "Eli, Eli, lema sabachthani?" that is, "My God, my God, why have you forsaken me?"

47 When some of the bystanders heard it, they said, "This man is calling for Elijah."

48 At once one of them ran and got a sponge, filled it with sour wine, put it on a stick, and gave it to him to drink.

49 But the others said, "Wait, let us see whether Elijah will come to save him."

50 Then Jesus cried again with a loud voice and breathed his last.

51 At that moment the curtain of the temple was torn in two, from top to bottom. The earth shook, and the rocks were split.

52 The tombs also were opened, and many bodies of the saints who had fallen asleep were raised.

53 After his resurrection they came out of the tombs and entered the holy city and appeared to many.

54 Now when the centurion and those with him, who were keeping watch over Jesus, saw the earthquake and what took place, they were terrified and said, "Truly this man was God's Son!"

KEY VERSE

Now when the certurion, and they that were with him, watching Jesus, saw the earthquake, and those things that were done, they feared greatly, saying, Truly this was the Son of God.—Matthew 27:54

OBJECTIVES

After reading this lesson, the student will have a deeper understanding of:

1. The various role-players at the Crucifixion;
2. The supernatural events that occured at Calvary;
3. The fourth word from the Cross; and,
4. The significance of the darkness at Calvary.

POINTS TO BE EMPHASIZED

Adult/Youth/Children
Key Verse: Matthew 27:54; 1 John 4:14 *(Children)*
Print: Matthew 27:38-54

—When Jesus was crucified between two bandits, the people, chief priests, scribes, and the bandits mocked Him. (38-44)

—At about 3:00 P.M., after three hours of darkness, Jesus cried out the words of Psalm 22:1, but bystanders misunderstood what He said. (45-49)

—At Jesus' death, the curtain of the temple was torn from top to bottom, the earth shook, rocks were split, tombs were opened, and many of the saints who had died were raised. (50-53)

—The centurion and his soldiers saw what took place and testified that Jesus was God's Son. (54)

(**Note**: Use KJV Scripture for Adults; NRSV Scripture for Youth and Children)

TOPICAL OUTLINE OF THE LESSON

I. Introduction

A. The Fourth Word
B. Biblical Background

II. Exposition and Application of the Scripture

A. Reviled by Two Robbers (Matthew 27:38, 44)
B. Blasphemed by Passersby (Matthew 27:39-40)
C. Mocked by Religious Leaders (Matthew 27:41-43)
D. Forsaken by God (Matthew 27:45-50)
E. Testified to by the Dead and the Living (Matthew 27:51-54)

III. Special Features

A. Preserving Our Heritage
B. A Concluding Word

I. Introduction

A. THE FOURTH WORD

We study the Last Word given only by Matthew and Mark. The other six Words occur in Luke (first, second, seventh) and John (third, fifth, sixth). How do we interpret Matthew 27:46? Shall we ask: **Why** have You forsaken Me? Why have **You** forsaken Me? Why have You **forsaken** Me? Why have You forsaken **Me**? Whatever point of view you take, do not see the cry as a complaint. The word translated forsaken is very strong. It means to leave down in, leave in the lurch, abandon, desert, leave helpless. It is to thin out when things get too thick.

There is an incomprehensibility to it all. How could God abandon God? Indeed, here is a cry that "plumbs the depths of the atonement;" its full import "cannot be fathomed." Because Christ was hanged on a tree, He was accursed (Galatians 3:13; Deuteronomy 21:23). At Calvary, our sins were placed on Christ Who Himself bore our sins in His own body on the tree. He was smitten of God and afflicted.

Forsakenness involved tasting the wrath of God. Forsakenness is separation from God, and separation from God is hell. For Righteousness to be made Sin, for Life to be put to Death, for the Rock of Ages to be struck and shattered, for the Light of the World to be enshrouded in darkness—who can comprehend? What grips our heart is the fact that Christ took our place on the Cross, and endured God's punishment against sin.

B. BIBLICIAL BACKGROUND

In a brief study of Psalm 22, we find in the first verse the words uttered in Matthew 27:46. This desolate cry begins the vivid picture of our Lord's death. Although David wrote the words, the Lord Jesus used the language to express His own feelings and thoughts. God intended more by these words than David did. David perhaps thought only of his own persecutions, but Jehovah planned to use these words to confirm the Calvary event. God is the Author of the Bible and has the right to do with His Word as He pleases. Psalm 22:2 speaks of the night season and reminds us of the darkness of three of those crucifixion hours.

Verse 3 answers in part the Why of verse 1. Why should the sinless Son of God have our sins placed on Him? Because a Holy God enthroned in the praises of Israel cannot overlook or condone sin (Habakkuk 1:13). Wherever He finds evil, He must punish it. Psalm 22:6-8 describes the despisement, rejection, reproach, ridicule, contempt and mockery heaped upon Him whom men considered hardly a man— just a worm.

Hear the jeering crowd say: "He trusted in the Lord that He would deliver Him; let Him deliver Him, seeing He delights in Him!" Psalm 22:14-15 describes His physical suffering. The bone dislocations, weakness, unrelenting thirst, speak of excruciating pain. According to verses 16-17, the Roman soldiers, Gentile executioners, who had pierced His hands and feet, surrounded Him like a pack of vicious dogs. Psalm 22:18 predicts the casting of lots for His tunic (John 19: 23-24). We see the study of Psalm 22 gives tremendous insight into the Crucifixion Scene.

II. Exposition and Application of the Scripture

A. REVILED BY TWO ROBBERS
(Matthew 27:38, 44)

Then were there two thieves crucified with him, one on the right hand, and another on the left. The thieves also, which were crucified with him, cast the same in his teeth.

The word "robbers" is a better translation than "thieves." Greek uses two different words. *Klepto* (see this word in kleptomaniac) means to steal. A thief takes property by stealth (Thayer), appropriates what is not his by fraud and in secret (Trench). On the other hand, *lestes* is a robber, plunderer, brigand (Thayer); he takes what is not his by violence and openly. Trench goes on to state that these men "in all likelihood had belonged to the band of Barabbas" (Mark 15:7). Recall that Barabbas had been freed (Matthew 27:26), and the Lord was now on the Cross which would have held Barabbas. We learn also that the Lord Jesus was placed in the middle of these two robbers, and thus "numbered with the transgressors" (Isaiah 53:12).

Some scholars believe crucifying Him between two robbers was done purposely to insult the Jews. It was as if Pilate said: "Look at your King. See His two subjects! They are criminals, and He is the main miscreant. That's why He's in the middle!" Both of the robbers reproached the Lord with words similar to those spewed out by the religious leaders. And when He did not respond to their shouts to save Himself and them, the robbers rebuked Him. They "cast the same in his teeth," and expression which means to blame, reproach, throw reproof at someone, especially for something considered shameful.

B. BLASPHEMED BY PASSERSBY (Matthew 27:39-40)

And they that passed by reviled him, wagging their heads, And saying, Thou that destroyest the temple, and buildest it in three days, save thyself. If thou be the Son of God, come down from the cross.

"Wagging their heads" is an expression of derision (Thayer). Psalm 22:8 states: "they shake the head"; they arrogantly toss their heads (Tasker). This was a "sneering, mocking gesture" (Wycliffe), "mock commiseration, as they jeer at the fallen foe" (Robertson). To shake the head is to express disapproval and denial of His claims. They reviled (KJV), blasphemed (NKJV), derided (RSV, NRSV), railed (AS), were hurling abuse (NASB).

It seems the words our Lord uttered early in His public ministry were well remembered. He said: "Destroy this temple, and in three days I will raise it up" (John 2:19). There is no record that He repeated these words, but Leon Morris suggests the tenses used "point to a repeated claim by Christ. At the very least they do not look like a reference to a single, isolated saying." His antagonists recall His claim and mock Him (Matthew 26:61, 27:40). Surely if He could destroy and build the Sanctuary, He ought to be able to save Himself. They had taken Him literally, and missed altogether His meaning. He was their Sanctuary, their Temple, their Messiah.

God dwelled "in Him in a very special way" (Leon Morris). If the Jews reject Him, destroy Him, then He would raise Himself from death. They did not realize that if He saved Himself, as they taunted Him to do, the world would remain lost. And yet, by proceeding with the Crucifixion, the Jews brought about the very thing they had asked Him to do. His sacrificial death doomed the temple as a place for sacrificial offerings. They had grossly distorted and misrepresented His words. The whole scene is a sorry picture of man's depravity.

C. MOCKED BY RELIGIOUS LEADERS (Matthew 27:41-43)

Likewise also the chief priests mocking him, with the scribes and elders, said, He saved others; himself he cannot save. If he be the King of Israel, let him now come down from the cross, and we will believe him. He trusted in God; let him deliver him now, if he will have him: for he said, I am the Son of God.

Tasker labeled the passersby as "ignorant sinners." Now we deal with those tagged "religious sinners." In our outline, we looked first at those called "condemned sinners," the robbers. The religious leaders, members of the Sanhedrin, joined in the mocking, but their taunts and jeers were not made directly at the Lord, but shared among themselves and with the crowd. The word translated mocking means to play with, trifle with. They acted "like silly children" (Robetson). Like the passersby who urged Christ to save Himself, so in sarcasm these men exhorted Him to come down from the cross. They too, like the ignorant sinners, did not know that had He saved Himself then, He could not have saved anyone. But their ignorance was worse because it was "religious." Furthermore, contrary to their claims, they would not have believed in Him had He descended from the cross. Their falsity is seen in their attempt to cast suspicion on His claims of having performed any miracles at all. It was as if they said, "If you cannot save yourself from the predicament you are in, why should we believe you saved others? If you performed miracles for them, why not one for yourself? You are like a man dressed up in rags and without a penny in his pocket, telling us how to become millionaires."

Their promise to believe is the language of rationalistic unbelief. Liberals are great for shifting ground and coming up with new reasons for their unbelief. If they did not believe the cleansing of lepers, casting out of demons, healing the sick, and the raising of the dead, what would make them believe Him if He stepped down from the cross? "Christ will not give new proofs to the blind in heart" (Robertson). William Booth said: "They claimed they would have believed if He had come down; we believe because He stayed up."

Finally, we are reminded that faith based on sight alone is worthless. Who knows but that had they seen Him descend from the cross, there would have been an immediate outcry of fraud and deception. "He was not nailed there in the first place...His disciples bribed the Roman soldiers to make believe they crucified Him... Besides, Pilate never wanted to kill Him anyway. He has been toying with us!" Such is the deceptive way of the unregenerated heart.

D. FORSAKEN BY GOD
(Matthew 27:45-50)

Now from the sixth hour there was darkness over all the land unto the ninth hour. And about the ninth hour Jesus cried with a loud voice, saying, Eli, Eli, lama sabachthani? That is to say, My God, my God, why hast thou forsaken me? Some of them that stood there, when they heard that, said, This man calleth for Elias. And straightway one of them ran, and took a sponge, and filled it with vinegar, and put it on a reed, and gave him to drink. The rest said, Let be, let us see whether Elias will come to save him. Jesus, when he had cried again with a loud voice, yielded up the ghost.

Based on the Jewish reckoning of time, the sixth hour was twelve noon. The Crucifixion began the third hour, about nine A.M. Darkness covered all the land from noon until three P.M. Scholars are not agreed whether the darkness covered only Palestine (Tasker) or extended to include half the globe (Lenski). I accept the latter point of view, for as Lenski states, when the sun's light is hidden "the entire day-side of the earth will be in darkness." It has been speculated also that the darkness was caused by an eclipse of the sun. However, the time frame of three hours does not support a solar eclipse (Henry Morris). This was a supernatural darkness imposed by God so that man might not see the Savior becoming sin.

It is at this time we hear the middle Word of the Seven. The loudness of His voice (verses 46, 50) indicates the voluntariness of His death. "Eli Eli, lama sabachthani" is a mixture of Hebrew and Aramaic. Mark 15:34 uses the Aramaic, "Eloi, Eloi." Note the Lord did not cry out: "My Father, why have You forsaken Me?" These are fantastic words, coming at the end of the three hours of darkness. Here is where judgment and darkness came together, as sin's curse fell upon His human nature and He sensed the abandonment of God. Yet He calls aloud, "My God!" Here He experienced the separation that sin creates. We repeat: Separation from God is hell!

What took place in the midst of this darkness is not revealed to us. There was definitely more than physical pain involved. Christ suffered the infinite agony of being separated from the presence of God. Only love could move Perfect Man to suffer for imperfect men with such a great suffering. MacDonald states the eternal hell we deserve was compressed into those three hours of darkness. Those who stood nearby thought they heard Him call for the prophet Elijah.

Immediately one of them ran, filled a sponge with vinegar (Psalm 69:21), put it on a reed, and gave Him to drink. According to Arndt and Gingrich, what was given Christ "relieved thirst more effectively than water and, because it was cheaper than regular wine, it was a favorite beverage of the lower ranks of society, and of those in moderate circumstances." Though just prior to being nailed to the Cross, He had been offered sour wine mingled with gall to drink, but upon tasting it, refused to drink. He wanted no part of doped wine. And though repeatedly urged, He repeatedly refused (Matthew 27:34). But this time there was no dope involved. And so He drank. Others interrupted, "Leave Him alone! Let's see if Elijah comes to save Him." The Lord again cried with a loud voice of triumph then He died.

A variety of expressions describe our Lord's death: (1) At the Transfiguration scene (Luke 9:31), He spoke with Moses and Elijah about His **Decease**. The Greek is **exodus**, departure (2) In the Good Shepherd chapter (John 10:17-18), He said, "**I Lay Down My Life**." (3) In today's lesson, the phrase, **Yielded up the spirit** means to send away or forth, expire. (4) In John 19:30, the expression **Gave up the spirit** is literally, **Delivered up the spirit**. (5) Finally, in Mark 15:37, 39; Luke 23:46, "gave up the spirit" is literally, breathed His last (RSV, NASB, NIV). In the expression "giving up the ghost," the word *ghost* (Old English) is not more sacred than *spirit* (Latin). Both are translations of the same Greek word. In summary, we learn that His death was not one of slow exhaustion. Rather, with a loud victorious cry, He voluntarily died!

E. TESTIFIED TO BY THE DEAD AND THE LIVING
(Matthew 27:51-54)

And, behold, the veil of the temple was rent in twain from the top to the bottom; and the earth did quake, and the rocks rent; And the graves were opened; and many bodies of the saints which slept arose, And came out of the graves after his resurrection, and went into the holy city, and appeared unto many. Now when the centurion, and they that were with him, watching Jesus, saw the earthquake, and those things that were done, they feared greatly, saying, Truly this was the Son of God.

We next see the curtain (60 feet long, 30 feet wide), which separated the Holy of Holies from the Holy place, was rent from top to bottom. This tearing of the veil pointed to the hand of God. Man would have attempted to rend it bottom to top. The incident symbolizes the opening the way for all believers to enter directly into the presence of God. It is doubtful that the earthquake at this time was the cause of the splitting of the curtain. One of the amazing and puzzling miracles that took place was the opening of the graves, and the bodies of believers coming forth, going into the city and being seen by many people.

Keep in mind this took place after His resurrection. We are not told their bodies returned to the graves; nor are we informed that they were translated into heaven. Most of the scholars I read believe these saints were removed from the paradise or Abraham's bosom and were taken up to heaven to be with the Lord.

Finally, hear the words of the centurion (ruler of a hundred soldiers), and of those with him. It is useless to speculate whether this man became a believer or not, after having witnessed all he did. His sense of awe is evident; he certainly recognized that something supernatural had taken place.

In a larger sense, how often are persons confronted with the fact of God's activity, yet they are not led to a confession of saving faith? Experiences with the Christ must ensue in meaningful encounter in order for Him to be embraced as Lord and Savior.

III. Special Features

A. PRESERVING OUR HERITAGE

We repeatedly draw attention to the universality of the Gospel of Jesus Christ. Because all have sinned, all need a Savior. Any man who seeks to base God's salvation on race or skin color insults the God of the Bible. What Christ suffered on the Cross was not just for some specific race of people, but for the human race.

B. A CONCLUDING WORD

Jesus Christ suffered hell that we might forever enjoy heaven, for we are right now citizens of heaven. He paid the penalty of sin that we might forever hear the words, "There is therefore no condemnation." He was forsaken by God in order that we might never be abandoned. Yea, that we might ever enjoy the security found in the words, "He that comes to Me I will in no wise cast out." As we have studied the supernatural occurrences surrounding our Lord's birth in earlier lessons, and then the supernatural events that took place at His death, burial and resurrection, may our hearts consider the supernatural things that will happen at the coming of our Lord for His own.

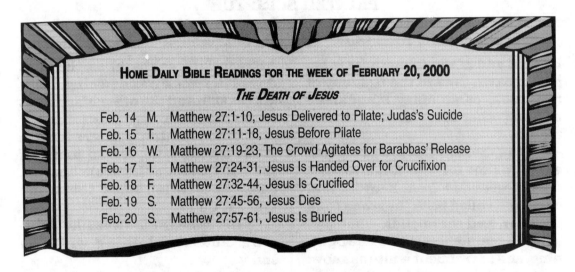

HOME DAILY BIBLE READINGS FOR THE WEEK OF FEBRUARY 20, 2000

THE DEATH OF JESUS

Feb. 14	M.	Matthew 27:1-10, Jesus Delivered to Pilate; Judas's Suicide
Feb. 15	T.	Matthew 27:11-18, Jesus Before Pilate
Feb. 16	W.	Matthew 27:19-23, The Crowd Agitates for Barabbas' Release
Feb. 17	T.	Matthew 27:24-31, Jesus Is Handed Over for Crucifixion
Feb. 18	F.	Matthew 27:32-44, Jesus Is Crucified
Feb. 19	S.	Matthew 27:45-56, Jesus Dies
Feb. 20	S.	Matthew 27:57-61, Jesus Is Buried

Know Your Bible

- The disciples could not cure the demoniac because of their lack of fasting and prayer. (Mark 9:18-29)
- The power of faith is seen in the promise that whatever we ask God that is according to His will shall be given to us. (Mark 11:22-24)

Eternal God, our Father, as You have demonstrated Your love for us in the death of Your Son for our salvation, may we by thy grace be empowered to live for Him who died for us, even Jesus Christ our Lord. Amen.

Resurrection and Commission

Adult Topic—*The Basis of Our Authority*

•••••

Youth Topic—*Being a Winner*

Children's Topic—*Telling Others About Jesus*

•••••

Devotional Reading—John 20:19-31

Background Scripture—Matthew 27:62—28:20

Print—Matthew 28:1-10, 16-20

PRINTED SCRIPTURE

Matthew 28:1-10, 16-20 (KJV)

IN THE end of the sabbath, as it began to dawn toward the first day of the week, came Mary Magdalene and the other Mary to see the sepulchre.

2 And, behold there was a great earthquake: for the angel of the Lord descended from heaven, and came and rolled back the stone from the door, and sat upon it.

3 His countenance was like lightning, and his raiment white as snow:

4 And for fear of him the keepers did shake, and became as dead men.

5 And the angel answered and said unto the women, Fear not ye: for I know that ye seek Jesus, which was crucified.

6 He is not here: for he is risen, as he said. Come, see the place where the Lord lay.

7 And go quickly, and tell his disciples that he is risen from the dead;

Matthew 28:1-10, 16-20 (NRSV)

AFTER THE sabbath, as the first day of the week was dawning, Mary Magdalene and the other Mary went to see the tomb.

2 And suddenly there was a great earthquake; for an angel of the Lord, descending from heaven, came and rolled back the stone and sat on it.

3 His appearance was like lightning, and his clothing white as snow.

4 For fear of him the guards shook and became like dead men.

5 But the angel said to the women "Do not be afraid; I know that you are looking for Jesus who was crucified.

6 He is not here; for he has been raised, as he said. Come, see the place where he lay.

7 Then go quickly and tell his disciples, 'He has been raised from the dead, and indeed he is going

and, behold, he goeth before you into Galilee; there shall ye see him: lo, I have told you.

8 And they departed quickly from the sepulchre with fear and great joy; and did run to bring his disciples word.

9 And as they went to tell his disciples, behold, Jesus met them, saying, All hail. And they came and held him by the feet, and worshipped him.

10 Then said Jesus unto them, Be not afraid: go tell my brethren that they go into Galilee, and there shall they see me.

.....

16 Then the eleven disciples went away into Galilee, into a mountain where Jesus had appointed them.

17 And when they saw him, they worshipped him: but some doubted.

18 And Jesus came and spake unto them, saying, All power is given unto me in heaven and in earth.

19 Go ye therefore, and teach all nations, baptizing them in the name of the Father, and of the Son, and of the Holy Ghost:

20 Teaching them to observe all things whatsoever I have commanded you: and, lo, I am with you always, even unto the end of the world. Amen.

ahead of you to Galilee; there you will see him.' This is my message for you."

8 So they left the tomb quickly with fear and great joy, and ran to tell his disciples.

9 Suddenly Jesus met them and said, "Greetings!" And they came to him, took hold of his feet, and worshiped him.

10 Then Jesus said to them, "Do not be afraid; go and tell my brothers to go to Galilee; there they will see me."

.....

16 Now the eleven disciples went to Galilee, to the mountain to which Jesus had directed them.

17 When they saw him, they worshiped him; but some doubted.

18 And Jesus came and said to them, "All authority in heaven and on earth has been given to me.

19 Go therefore and make disciples of all nations, baptizing them in the name of the Father and of the Son and of the Holy Spirit,

20 and teaching them to obey everything that I have commanded you. And remember, I am with you always, to the end of the age."

Go ye therefore, and teach all nations, baptizing them in the name of the Father, and of the Son, and of the Holy Ghost: Teaching them to observe all things whatsoever I have commanded you: and, lo, I am with you always, even unto the end of the world. Amen.—**Matthew 28:19-20**

OBJECTIVES

After reading this lesson, the student should know more about:

1. The early post-resurrection scene;
2. The effect of discovering an empty tomb;
3. Christ's first post-resurrection contacts; and,
4. The giving of the "Great Commission."

POINTS TO BE EMPHASIZED

Adult/Youth/Children
Key Verse: Matthew 28:19-20
Print: Matthew 28:1-10, 16-20

—When Mary Magdalene and the other Mary went to Jesus' tomb, the earth quaked, an angel opened the tomb, and the guards became like dead men. (1-4)

—The angel told the women that Jesus had been raised and instructed them to tell the disciples to meet Him in Galilee. (5-7)

—As the women joyfully hurried to tell the disciples, Jesus met them and encouraged them to tell the disciples to go to Galilee where they would see Him. (8-10)

—When the eleven disciples saw Jesus in Galilee, they worshiped Him, though some doubted. (16-17)

—Jesus declared that He had been given all authority in heaven and earth. (18)

—Jesus comissioned His followers to go and make disciples of all nations and baptize them in the name of the Father, Son, and Holy Spirit, and assured them of His eternal presence. (19-20)

TOPICAL OUTLINE OF THE LESSON

I. Introduction

A. Resurrection Defined
B. Biblical Background

II. Exposition and Application of the Scripture

A. The Women Discover the Empty Tomb (Matthew 28:1-7)
B. The Resurrected Savior Greets the Women (Matthew 28:8-10)
C. Christ Meets With the Disciples (Matthew 28:16-18)
D. The Great Commission (Matthew 28:19-20)

III. Special Features

A. Preserving Our Heritage
B. A Concluding Word

I. Introduction

A. RESURRECTION DEFINED

The Greek word for resurrection is *anastasis*. Literally, this means a rising or raising up. Often the words "from the dead" are added (Romans 1:4). At this point in history, Jesus Christ alone qualifies as One Who Has Been Resurrected from the dead, for there is a difference between resurrection and restoration. Those restored to life—Lazarus, the daughter of Jairus, Eutychus, and others—all died again, and await the resurrection of their bodies. Christ is called "the first fruits" (1 Corinthians 15:23). He presently has a glorified body, and will not, cannot die again. It is interesting to note that most passages dealing with His resurrection attribute it to God the Father (Romans 10:9). It is also true that the Lord Himself said, "I have power (authority) to lay down my life, and I have power to take it again," for He is the very Author of resurrection (John 10:17-18; 11:25). It also appears that the Holy Spirit took part in the resurrection of Christ (Romans 8:11). The truth is, the entire Godhead was involved in the Resurrection.

B. BIBLICAL BACKGROUND

Throughout His public ministry, the Lord spoke of His death and resurrection. But first, attention is drawn to Psalm 16:10: "For You will not leave my soul in Sheol, nor will You allow Your Holy One to see corruption." Here is the prediction of the resurrection of the King, the Lord Jesus. His body did not decompose or rot; it saw no corruption. Following A. T. Robertson's *Harmony of the Gospels*, we find the Lord stating: "Destroy this temple, and in three days I will raise it up" (John 2:19). This saying was used against Him when He was brought before Caiaphas and the Sanhedrin (Matthew 26:61), and again as He hung on the Cross (Matthew 27:40). Of course, these unbelievers had no idea whatsoever of the significance of the prophecy. But what is more perturbing is the fact that even the disciples did not grasp what the Lord told them. In Matthew 16:21, He foretold His death and resurrection, saying He would "be killed, and be raised the third day."

To Peter, James and John came the order to tell no one of the Transfiguration "until the Son of Man is risen from the dead" (Matthew 17:9). Still later, Christ again predicted to His disciples that He would be betrayed, condemned, delivered, mocked, scourged, crucified; but "the third day he will rise again" (Matthew 20:19). Finally, in foretelling Simon Peter's denial, the Lord said: "But after I have been raised, I will go before you to Galilee" (Matthew 26:32). After the Resurrection, we read in John 20:9: "For as yet they did not know the Scripture, that He must rise again from the dead." "The disciples never really believed He would rise until they saw the empty tomb and the risen Lord" (H. Morris).

II. Exposition and Application of the Scripture

A. THE WOMEN DISCOVER THE EMPTY TOMB (Matthew 28:1-7)

IN the end of the sabbath, as it began to dawn toward the first day of the week, came Mary Magdalene and the other Mary to see the sepulchre. And, behold, there was a great earthquake: for the angel of the Lord descended from heaven, and came and rolled back the stone from the door, and sat upon it. His countenance was like lightning, and his raiment white as snow: And for fear of him the keepers did shake, and became as dead men. And the angel answered and said unto the women, Fear not ye: for I know that ye seek Jesus, which was crucified. He is not here: for he is risen, as he said. Come, see the place where the Lord lay. And go quickly, and tell his disciples that he is risen from the dead; and, behold, he goeth before you into Galilee; there shall ye see him: lo, I have told you.

The regular weekly Sabbath began Friday sunset and ended Saturday sunset. So it was early Sunday morning, "as the first day of the week began to dawn," that Mary Magdalene and the other Mary (mother of James and John) went to the tomb. Other women went with them, but Matthew mentions the most prominent women. Gerhard gives five reasons why the Lord blessed the women to be the first to know about the Resurrection, and later to actually see, touch and worship Him: (1) It was God's choice to so use the weaker vessel; (2) Overwhelmed most by the sorrow of His death, now they were the first to experience the joy of His resurrection; (3) Their presence at the tomb made a lie out of the rumor that the disciples had stolen His body; (4) As death came by woman, so now women would announce salvation and life; and (5) God rewarded their love, devotion and loyalty.

The women were suddenly confronted with a violent earthquake! Behold!—this word bids the reader or hearer to attend to what is said (Thayer). God often used earthquakes to indicate His presence, and in the administration of grace or judgment. Earthquakes demonstrate His power and greatness, as He intervenes in the affairs of men, especially as the Righteous Judge speaking in His wrath. An angel of the Lord came from heaven, rolled back the stone from the grave, and sat upon the stone. Angels are evident throughout our Lord's earthly ministry. They were present at His birth; gave Him strength after the temptation in the wilderness; and again at His agony in the Garden of Gethsemane. And now here at the tomb. The stone was not moved in order for the risen Savior to escape. He was already gone. We do not know what language—what words—to use to describe Christ's exit. To say His living body "passed through the rock" does not satisfy us. Solid materials are no barrier at all for a glorified body "to go through."

The stone was removed so that the women could see that the tomb was empty. Luke (24:4) and John (20:12) mention two angels were present, but Matthew tells of the one who spoke.

There is no contradiction. If Matthew had said, "There was only one angel at the tomb," then we would have a problem with verbal inspiration. Note the angel's countenance or external appearance was like lightning, his clothes white as snow. The Roman guards, who had been stationed there to protect the tomb from disciples who might steal the body of their deceased Teacher, were so shocked with fear by what they saw and heard that they fainted. As Lenski states, the Roman authorities forgot to guard the tomb against Jesus Himself! Lying upon the ground, unconscious, they appeared as dead men. We know of course that they were not dead, for later they were bribed to tell a lie about what occurred (verses 11-15).

According to Mark, the women also were alarmed, but the angel immediately reassured them there was no need to fear: "Stop being afraid," he said. The angel calmed their fears with his gentle but positive statements. He knew the purpose of their coming was to embalm the body of their beloved Master. "He is not here, for He is risen, as He said." What thrilling words! God always keeps His promises. The women obeyed the angel's command to see the place where the Lord lay. "I know that you seek Jesus, who was crucified." They were looking for the "having-been-crucified-One." The verb tense used suggests a state of completion. He was crucified and will always be the One who was crucified, the eternal Lamb of God. We shall see the nail prints in His hands and feet. The women were ordered to go quickly and tell the disciples that the Master is not dead. Tell them that "He is going to precede you to Galilee."

B. THE RESURRECTED SAVIOR GREETS THE WOMEN
(Matthew 28:8-10)

And they departed quickly from the sepulchre with fear and great joy; and did run to bring his disciples word. And as they went to tell his disciples, behold, Jesus met them, saying, All hail. And they came and held him by the feet, and worshipped him. Then said Jesus unto them, Be not afraid: go tell my brethren that they go into Galilee, and there shall they see me.

With mixed emotions, the women obeyed and quickly left the tomb. The Greek word for tomb has in it the word for memory. Thus a tomb (or tombstone) is a remembrance, a memorial, that by which the memory of any person or thing is preserved. Imagine experiencing fear and joy at the same time. The presence of the angels had made them fearful, but the joy of knowing Christ was alive was a greater emotion. Their "great joy" indicates that joy predominated the fear (Lenski). "These mingled emotions of ecstasy and dread need cause no surprise when all things are considered" (A. T. Robertson).

Suddenly, there was the Lord Jesus in front of them. "All hail!" in the KJV becomes: "Good morning!" (LB), "Peace be with you" (TEV, JBP), "Hail!" (Moffatt, RSV), "Greetings!" (NIV, Lenski). Best bet: "Rejoice!" See the word spoken by the Lord as the common ordinary greeting to which they all were accustomed (Tasker). It is interesting to take note of those who worship Jesus Christ. The women came, held Him by the feet, and worshiped Him. They did not attempt to keep Him there, as did Mary Magdalene earlier; she was told,

"Stop clinging to me" (John 20:17). In every case where the Lord Jesus was worshiped, He accepted the worship. There is no suggestion in the Bible whatsoever that He received worship as Jehovah's Representative. No. He is God! And God alone is to be worshiped. He accepted what rightly belonged to Him. These women knew this. And recognizing His deity, fell at His feet and worshiped Him. Holding Him by the feet was their expression of submission to Him, their attitude of obeisance.

Christ closed His meeting with the women by first ordering them, "Stop being afraid." "Go and tell my brethren to go to Galilee, and there they will see me." My brethren? The men who deserted Him? Simon Peter who denied Him? Only John was close by when the Lord died. What grace! To call such a band of men, "Brothers." Prior to His death and resurrection, He had called them disciples, friends, servants—but now, brothers. Use of this intimate title suggests that they were forgiven for their lack of faith which was demonstrated when they abandoned Him in fear. It also indicates a new relationship of love and honor.

C. CHRIST MEETS WITH THE DISCIPLES (Matthew 28:16-18)

Then the eleven disciples went away into Galilee, into a mountain where Jesus had appointed them. And when they saw him, they worshipped him: but some doubted. And Jesus came and spake unto them, saying, All power is given unto me in heaven and in earth.

We do not know the exact location the disciples were to meet the Lord, but He had determined "a definite place on a certain mountain" (Lenski); the time

and place were arranged beforehand. And when they saw Him, they worshiped Him. The same word for worship is used as in verse nine. Matthew's gospel uses this particular word (*proskuneo*: Literally, kiss [the hand] toward) more than any of the other Gospel writers. A brief review of Matthew reminds us that the Magi, a leper, Jairus, the disciples in the storm, the Syro-Phoenician woman, the mother of Zebedee's sons, the women at the tomb—and now once again, the disciples worshiped Him. But some doubted. In Matthew 28:17, the word *distazo* means to stand divided, to waver (Thayer), to hesitate in doubt (Arndt and Gingrich). The "dis" means twice, in two, divided in mind. It is used only twice in the New Testament, both times in Matthew.

Recall Simon Peter walking on the water, then sinking. Christ stretched forth His hand, caught him, and said to him: "O you of little faith, why did you doubt?" (Matthew 14:31). Simon was pulled two ways—between trust in the power of Christ, and fear of the wind and waves. Lenski restricts the audience to the Eleven, stating they did not doubt the reality of the Resurrection, as was the case with Thomas, but doubted the identity of the One standing there. Living Bible paraphrases: "But some of them weren't sure it really was Jesus!" I prefer Robertson's interpretation. He makes the audience include not only the Eleven but also the nearly five hundred Paul later spoke of (1 Corinthians 15:6).

At any rate, the doubt soon vanished. And the Lord said: "All power (authority) is given to me in heaven and on earth." The disciples must realize in a more comprehensive way who He is. At the Cross, the power of all hostile forces was broken. Whatever power evil now wields, it does so with broken, shattered authority. At Calvary, Christ triumphed over (spoiled) all principalities and powers. God has His own time schedule, so that it remains to be fulfilled when at the name of Jesus every knee shall bow, and every tongue confess He is Lord. So the claim Christ made here was valid, legitimate, true, correct.

D. THE GREAT COMMISSION
(Matthew 28:19-20)

Go ye therefore, and teach all nations, baptizing them in the name of the Father, and of the Son, and of the Holy Ghost: Teaching them to observe all things whatsoever I have commanded you: and, lo, I am with you always, even unto the end of the world. Amen.

Literally, verse 19 is: "Having gone, therefore, teach!" The verb means to be or make a disciple of. Those who followed Christ and became His adherents were His disciples. As used here, all who confess Jesus as Lord, all Christians, are His disciples. At the very heart of this commission is the command that disciples turn others into disciples. This is not churchianity, seeking to make people members of our churches. Our task here is to bring people into a living relationship with a living Savior. All nations (ethnics, races) are to be taught. Obviously, the God of the Bible is no respecter of faces, races or places.

Those taught are to be baptized. The Greek word *baptizo* is transliterated. Baptists believe a conscious experience is implied in the making of disciples. Therefore, we do not baptize babies. We also believe that total immersion best represents and identifies the believer with Christ. God the Father put us into the Lord Jesus; He baptized us (1 Corinthians 12:13). We see that the word name is singular, not plural. The one God exists as Father, Son and Holy Spirit at the same time. Belief that Matthew 28:19 is a title is in error, for the same Greek word for "name" is used in Acts 2:38. Admittedly, the word Trinity is not found in the Bible. It is a word we invented to describe the doctrine the Bible teaches. See Colossians 2:9 and the use of the word, Godhead.

To baptize in the name of the Triune God means to publicly identify with all that God stands for. It means to recognize His authority and power, to be intimately connected with the Lord of glory. Finally, having been made disciples, and baptized, they are to be taught. Here the word to teach is not the same as that in verse 19. To make disciples as indicated in verse 19 is expressed in verse 20 in terms of to impart instruction, hold discourse with others in order to instruct them. Two different verbs are used. And the teaching is a continuous process. The tense of the verb "making disciples" is a once for all thing. But once a disciple, the teaching goes on and on. What are they to be taught?

To observe; the verb tense suggests to be observers of, to be keepers of whatsoever the Lord commanded. In other words, the disciple is to live under the direction of the Lord Jesus, and the guidance of the Holy Spirit. The Christian's lifestyle, his or her conduct, behavior, is one of obedience to the will of Jesus Christ. Finally, here is the wonderful promise to all who obey His command, carry out this commission. It includes all Christians who seek to win others to Christ: the evangelist, missionary, pastor—all Christians. We have this assurance: We are not left alone. And the more faithful we are in spreading the Good News, the more aware we will be of His presence. He promised never to leave us alone!

III. Special Features

A. PRESERVING OUR HERITAGE

Fulfilling the Great Commission focuses on our concept of Missions. What are our local assemblies doing? How many missionaries are we producing? Today's lesson impresses our hearts with the fact that winning souls to Christ is still the main work of the believer in the world. Aggressive personal disciplining, baptizing, and teaching, are still a major priority in the life of the church, and in the lives of its members. "Each soul saved represents mission prayers answered, a mission gift well-used, a mission witness come full circle. Each soul saved represents your faith in loving action" (Dr. Wm. J. Harvey, III). The Lord would have our churches busy "fishing for men."

B. A CONCLUDING WORD

Jesus Christ is not dead, hanging on a cross. We need no crucifixes in our Baptist churches! We believe in our hearts that God the Father raised Him from the dead, and so we confess Him with our mouths. May obedience to His command to evangelize be proof that He lives in our hearts today.

HOME DAILY BIBLE READINGS FOR THE WEEK OF FEBRUARY 27, 2000

RESURRECTION AND COMMISSION

Feb. 21	M.	Matthew 27:62-66, Pilate's Soldiers Guard Jesus' Tomb
Feb. 22	T.	Matthew 28:1-10, The Resurrection of Jesus
Feb. 23	W.	Matthew 28:11-20, Jesus Commissions His Disciples
Feb. 24	T.	Luke 24:13-27, Jesus and Travelers on the Emmaus Road
Feb. 25	F.	Luke 24:28-35, The Travelers Recognize Jesus at Table
Feb. 26	S.	Luke 24:36-43, Jesus Appears to His Disciples
Feb. 27	S.	Luke 24:44-53, Jesus Blesses the Disciples, and Ascends

Our Father in heaven, by Your grace we have become free from the power of sin and death. Grant that we may share the power implied in the Resurrection with a world that is estranged from Your will. Amen.

SPRING QUARTER

March, April, May 2000

Continuing Jesus' Work

General Introduction

Apostle Paul not only established churches as the direct results of the proclamation of the Gospel of Jesus Christ, but stayed abreast of the spiritual condition that was prevalent within many of these churches and expressed his concern via letters to them. Paul's letters to the church at Corinth that are the scriptural basis of our study during this quarter deal with matters that not only confronted the church at Corinth, but also behaviors that characterize deportment within a significant portion of the contemporary church community. This three-unit study, "Continuing Jesus' Work," provides a structure wherein some of the problems that are encountered in the church today can be addressed as the fellowship of faith endeavors to embody the mind of Christ.

Unit I, *"Christ the Basis of Unity,"* is presented in a four-session study taken from First Corinthians. Beginning with a session about Christian unity, our study continues as we focus on the role of the Holy Spirit as teacher, the leaders of the church as servants of Christ, and concludes with the need for discipline among members of the church.

Unit II, *"Unity in Human Relationships,"* is a continuation of our study of Paul's first letter to the Corinthians. In this, our attention will be focused on relationships: marriage, singleness, and family, and the necessity for love and knowledge to function in concert with each other. Following a discussion on spiritual gifts, we shall concern ourselves with the Resurrection (the Easter session) and the way in which Christians are mandated to live by the law of love.

Unit III, *"The Power of Christian Ministry,"* is a four-session presentation of Paul's second letter to the church at Corinth. The first and second lessons deal with the victory that Christians have through Christ in spite of the difficulties and trials that are part and parcel of the human situation. The third lesson puts forth directions concerning the nature of Christian giving. This unit concludes with an appeal by the apostle Paul to the Corinthians to live by the faith that they themselves had come to profess.

As we seek to understand the problems and possibilities among the membership of the church at Corinth, we can compare some of the concerns that Paul had with the various difficulties within the Christian community as many of their experiences intersect with patterns of behavior that pledge the church today. Hence, we can thrust ourselves into each lesson since the human condition remains relatively constant in spite of changing circumstances.

Helping a Church to Confront Crisis

Unit I—*Christ the Basis of Unity*

Children's Unit—*Growing Spiritually*

•••••

Adult Topic—*Appeal for Unity*

•••••

Youth Topic—*What Unites?*

Children's Topic—*Live Peaceably*

•••••

Devotional Reading—1 Corinthians 1:18-25

Background Scripture—1 Corinthians 1:1-17

Print—1 Corinthians 1:2-17

PRINTED SCRIPTURE

1 Corinthians 1:2-17 (KJV)

2 Unto the church of God which is at Corinth, to them that are sanctified in Christ Jesus, called to be saints, with all that in every place call upon the name of Jesus Christ our Lord, both theirs and ours:

3 Grace be unto you, and peace, from God our Father, and from the Lord Jesus Christ.

4 I thank my God always on your behalf, for the grace of God which is given you by Jesus Christ;

5 That in every thing ye are enriched by him, in all utterance, and in all knowledge;

6 Even as the testimony of Christ was confirmed in you:

7 So that ye come behind in no gift; waiting for the coming of our Lord Jesus Christ:

8 Who shall also confirm you unto the end, that ye may be blameless in the day of our Lord Jesus Christ.

1 Corinthians 1:2-17 (NRSV)

2 To the church of God that is in Corinth, to those who are sanctified in Christ Jesus, called to be saints, together with all those who in every place call on the name of our Lord Jesus Christ, both their Lord and ours:

3 Grace to you and peace from God our Father and the Lord Jesus Christ.

4 I give thanks to my God always for you because of the grace of God that has been given you in Christ Jesus,

5 for in every way you have been enriched in him, in speech and knowledge of every kind—

6 just as the testimony of Christ has been strengthened among you—

7 so that you are not lacking in any spiritual gift as you wait for the revealing of our Lord Jesus Christ.

8 He will also strengthen you to the end, so that you may be

9 God is faithful, by whom ye were called unto the fellowship of his Son Jesus Christ our Lord.

10 Now I beseech you, brethren, by the name of our Lord Jesus Christ, that ye all speak the same thing, and that there be no divisions among you; but that ye be perfectly joined together in the same mind and in the same judgment.

11 For it hath been declared unto me of you, my brethren, by them which are of the house of Chloe, that there are contentions among you.

12 Now this I say, that every one of you saith, I am of Paul; and I of Apollos; and I of Cephas; and I of Christ.

13 Is Christ divided? was Paul crucified for you? or were ye baptized in the name of Paul?

14 I thank God that I baptized none of you, but Crispus and Gaius;

15 Lest any should say that I had baptized in mine own name.

16 And I baptized also the household of Stephanas: besides, I know not whether I baptized any other.

17 For Christ sent me not to baptize, but to preach the gospel: not with wisdom of words, lest the cross of Christ should be made of none effect.

blameless on the day of our Lord Jesus Christ.

9 God is faithful; by him you were called into the fellowship of his Son, Jesus Christ our Lord.

10 Now I appeal to you, brothers and sisters, by the name of our Lord Jesus Christ, that all of you be in agreement and that there be no divisions among you, but that you be united in the same mind and the same purpose.

11 For it has been reported to me by Chloe's people that there are quarrels among you, my brothers and sisters.

12 What I mean is that each of you says, "I belong to Paul," or "I belong to Apollos," or "I belong to Cephas," or "I belong to Christ."

13 Has Christ been divided? Was Paul crucified for you? Or were you baptized in the name of Paul?

14 I thank God that I baptized none of you except Crispus and Gaius,

15 so that no one can say that you were baptized in my name.

16 (I did baptize also the household of Stephanas; beyond that, I do not know whether I baptized anyone else.)

17 For Christ did not send me to baptize but to proclaim the gospel, and not with eloquent wisdom, so that the cross of Christ might not be emptied of its power.

KEY VERSE

*Now I beseech you, brethren, by the name of our Lord Jesus Christ, that ye speak the same thing, and that there be no divisions among you; but that ye be perfectly joined together in the same mind and in the same judgment.—**1 Corinthians 1:10***

OBJECTIVES

After reading this lesson, the student will have a deeper understanding of:

1. The nature of church divisions;
2. Gratitude for spiritual gifts;
3. The danger of exalting human wisdom; and,
4. The place of water baptism.

POINTS TO BE EMPHASIZED
Adult/Youth
Key Verse: 1 Corinthians 1:10
Print: 1 Corinthians 1:2-17

—Paul greeted and pronounced a blessing on the saints in Corinth, affirming that they were one with all believers in Christ. (2-3)

—Paul thanked God that the Corinthian believers' spiritual gifts demonstrated God's grace to them. (4-7)

—God who is faithful will strengthen to the end those whom He has called. (8-9)

—In the name of Christ, Paul appealed for agreement that would end the quarrels and divisions in the church. (10-12)

—Paul stated that Christ is not divided and emphasized the importance of being baptized in Christ and not the importance of the humans by whom the baptismal rites were performed. (13-16)

—Paul stated that Christ sent him not to baptize, but to proclaim the Gospel in its simplicity so as not to obscure the power of the Cross. (17)

Children
Key Verse: 1 Corinthians 1:10
Print: Acts 18:1-4, 8; 1 Corinthians 1:10-15, 17

—When Paul went to Corinth, he found Aquila and Priscilla who had been forced to leave Rome. (Acts 18:1-2)

—Paul lived and worked with Aquila and Priscilla because all three were tentmakers. (3)

—Paul talked with Jews and Greeks, Crispus and his household and many others believed in Jesus and were baptized. (4, 8)

—When Paul left Corinth, he wrote a letter urging the people in the church to live peaceably. (1 Corinthians 1:10)

—The people were claiming to belong to the leaders who had baptized them. (11-13)

—Paul said God had sent him to preach the Gospel, not to baptize. (14-17)

(**Note**: Use KJV Scripture for Adults; NRSV Scripture for Youth and Children)

I. Introduction

A. DIVISIONS

A study of three words rendered "division" proves helpful here. First, there is *stasis*. This word means a standing up; it came to mean an insurrection, uprising, riot, revolt, rebellion; and then came the sense of strife, discord, disunion. It is most often translated, dissension (Acts 15:2; 23:7, 10). A second word is *dichostasia*. Note it also has the root *stasis* in it, but the prefix *dicho* means two. So literally, this word for division means two-fold standing, a standing apart (Romans 16:17; 1 Corinthians 3:3).

In our lesson, the word for division is *schism*. From it we have derived the English word, schism. Literally, it means a split, cleft, rent, tear, crack, as in a garment or in a stone (Matthew 9:16). Considered figuratively, it means division, dissension. As used in the New Testament, we first read of the division caused by the appearance of the Lord Jesus among His listeners. Their evaluation of His origin (John 7:43), deeds (John 9:16) and words (or sayings: John 10:19) caused division (Kittel).

Then we learn from the Corinthian Letters that the splits were not so much over doctrinal differences as they were over attachments to different leaders. In their distorted concepts of wisdom, the Corinthians sought to play off one leader against another in authority. It is interesting that even today the majority of the "splits" in Black Baptist churches is rarely over doctrinal matters, but over leadership personalities, which in turn may center on money, power, immorality, etc. As we shall see, the wrong concept of true wisdom was basic to the crises which arose in the church at Corinth.

B. BIBLICAL BACKGROUND

It was approximately 55 or 56 A.D. when this letter was written. Actually, Paul first set foot on Greek soil when on his second missionary journey. In response to a vision in Troas, he immediately endeavored to go into Macedonia, certain that God had called him to preach the Gospel there (Acts 16:9, 10). Eventually, he came to Corinth, a city which flourished commercially. Corinth was a natural trade center; ships from all over came to this great cosmopolitan center populated by native Greeks, Jews and Roman colonists.

As is common in a place where there is heavy transit and traffic, there was a high degree of restlessness. Corinth was notorious as a city wherein immorality was openly practiced. Cult, prostitution and idolatry were widespread. In fact, there came into existence the verb, "to corinthianize," meaning to play the part of a prostitute, to practice whoredom or immorality. This then was the place the Holy Spirit led Paul to proclaim the Good News of Jesus Christ. Knowledge of the pagan setting renders us more sympathetic; we see why the church was beset with problems of divisions, incest, fornication, lawsuits, etc. But we see too the power of God that snatched men out of darkness into eternal light; and we are led to ever thank the Lord for giving this Letter to us.

II. Exposition and Application of the Scripture

A. SALUTATION
(1 Corinthians 1:2-3)

Unto the church of God which is at Corinth, to them that are sanctified in Christ Jesus, called to be saints, with all that in every place call upon the name of Jesus Christ our Lord, both theirs and ours: Grace be unto you, and peace, from God our Father, and from the Lord Jesus Christ.

Paul wrote to "the church of God which is at Corinth." A friend sought to impress me with the fact that only "the church of God" was biblical, and that "Baptists" were not scriptural. I reminded him the Scripture says, "at Corinth," and not in Philadelphia. The concept of the church (the called-out ones) must not be limited to the visible church building and the organization thereof. The church invisible is made up of all who love Jesus Christ. Those who are "the having-been-set-apart-ones" are those "sanctified in Christ Jesus." Sanctification occurs the moment we accept Jesus Christ. Furthermore, all genuine Christians are "saints" or sanctified; sanctification has nothing whatsoever to do with denominations.

Note in verse two that the words "to be" are italicized. Omit them, and realize that we are "called saints," or as NASB puts it, "saints by calling." Incidentally, the phrase, "sanctified and holy," is redundant; both words mean the same. Not only was the church of God at Corinth composed of those sanctified in Christ Jesus, and called saints, but it was also composed of all who in every place call upon His name. This calling means praise, thanksgiving, worship; it implies confidence, trust, and dependence. Finally, note the order of the words grace and peace in this salutation. This order is never reversed. Peace comes only as a result of grace; no grace, no peace. In short, grace is the source of peace. Only by accepting the grace of God revealed in Jesus Christ, the Gift of God, is peace with God made available. The peace **of** God (Philippians 4:7) comes only to those who have peace **with** Him (Romans 5:1).

B. THANKSGIVING
(1 Corinthians 1:4-9)

I thank my God always on your behalf, for the grace of God which is given you by Jesus Christ; That in every thing ye are enriched by him, in all utterance, and in all knowledge; Even as the testimony of Christ was confirmed in you: So that ye come behind in no gift; waiting for the coming of our Lord Jesus Christ: Who shall also confirm you unto the end, that ye may be blameless in the day of our Lord Jesus Christ. God is faithful, by whom ye were called unto the fellowship of his Son Jesus Christ our Lord.

It was typical of Paul to begin with a statement of gratitude for the spiritual well-being of the saints. Paul was no ingrate; he had discovered that the more he thanked God, the more blessings he received for which to give God thanks. He was indeed grateful for the results of the Gospel preached in the city of Corinth. Those who experienced the grace of God in Christ were the richer for it. The purpose of that enrichment was to glorify God and be used by Him to enrich others. Paul

said: "He has enriched your whole lives, from the words (utterance) on your lips to the understanding (knowledge) in your hearts" (J. B. Phillips). Thus, the witness concerning Christ had been delivered, the Gospel preached, and by the power of God, the Lord Jesus in them had been established and made firm and strong.

What was the purpose of the testimony of Christ in them? That they would come behind in no gift. Whatever the Lord had called them to do, He made available the wherewithal to do it. As a church fulfills its calling, as it uses divine gifts according to God's will, it is to do so with a sense of expectancy! But expecting what? Eagerly awaiting what? The answer: the revelation of our Lord Jesus Christ. Do you realize that Jesus Christ may come back at any moment, that His coming is imminent?

Paul's point is that Christ will sustain them blameless (unimpeachable, unaccusable, irreproachable), until the day when the Lord comes for His own. The "day" of Christ is that time when all who love Him will appear before His judgment seat to be rewarded (2 Corinthians 5:10). Paul was certain that the Corinthian saints need have no fear of condemnation. Why? Not because **they** are faithful, but because their God is faithful. So far as our final salvation is concerned, the God of the Bible is completely trustworthy.

The fact that God is the One who called them should relieve them of the fear of being dismissed or dropped. God is faithful. "For the gifts and the calling of God are irrevocable" (Romans 11:29). He has a purpose in calling and is faithful to that plan and purpose. His calling qualifies. Indeed, His calling is a guarantee that those called shall enter into that fellowship of His Son. Those whom the Lord calls are not called in vain! In summary: Paul reminded the Corinthian Christians that they were called, enriched, given gifts, strengthened, established, guaranteed in Christ, to serve Him faithfully as they await His blessed return.

C. EXHORTATION TO UNITY
(1 Corinthians 1:10)

Now I beseech you, brethren, by the name of our Lord Jesus Christ, that ye all speak the same thing, and that there be no divisions among you; but that ye be perfectly joined together in the same mind and in the same judgment.

Paul now turned his attention to the divisions in the church. He had no desire to attempt to correct evils on his own or in his name. His appeal is made to the brethren "by the name of our Lord Jesus Christ." I counted the name of Christ mentioned some thirteen times in the Scriptures for today's lesson! Three requests were made as the apostle expressed his desire that a united front of testimony and witness be given to the unbelieving world. First, Paul desired that they all speak the same thing. Second came the desire that divisions among them would end. The verb *schizo* means to split, divide, separate, tear apart, tear off. It is seen in the word, schizophrenia, a common term used in psychiatry meaning, literally, split-mind. Third was the desire that they be mended, made complete, restored, perfectly joined together in mind and in judgment. True unity and harmony must begin in the mind and heart. Each

piece of a jig-saw puzzle is different either in size, shape, color or design, but when fitted together makes a beautiful picture. So Paul urged the Corinthian saints to demonstrate that unity which must begin in the heart and mind.

D. CONTENTIONS
(1 Corinthians 1:11-13)

For it hath been declared unto me of you, my brethren, by them which are of the house of Chloe, that there are contentions among you. Now this I say, that every one of you saith, I am of Paul; and I of Apollos; and I of Cephas; and I of Christ. Is Christ divided? was Paul crucified for you? or were ye baptized in the name of Paul?

The words "who are of the house" of Chloe are italicized, indicating they were supplied by the translators. In the original, it is simply "them of Chloe." Her name, which appears only here in the New Testament, means tender verdure, of trees, foliage, leaves; note it is from the same root as **chloros**. We are not sure who Chloe's people were: slaves, sons, relatives, freedmen, friends? There is no warrant for assuming that Chloe was a female minister, as *The Original African Heritage Study Bible* does (p. 1650). Evidently, they were Christians who were grieved by the splits in the church. It had been made clear to the apostle that strife, quarrelsomeness, dispute, wrangling were common in the church. This was not gossip or rumor, but fact. Contentiousness implies perversity of temper and persistence in dispute.

The four groups named in verse twelve were not actual parties formed within the church at Corinth. However, undue emphasis on allegiance and personal loyalty to human teachers can cause a bad spirit and lead to strife. Still today, there are those in our churches who exalt the messenger above the message. Basically, Paul, Apollos and Cephas (Simon Peter) agreed in doctrine; their messages were the same. But it appears one group upheld Paul's authority, and claimed to be guided solely by the words and deeds of Paul. Others stressed their loyalty to Apollos, who is first mentioned in Acts 18:24-28. The Cephas (rock) party pushed Simon as their leader. More difficult to explain is the "Christ" group. It may have been composed of people who actually had seen or known the Lord. Or a "Back to Christ" movement made up of folks claiming to be dependent upon Christ alone and not upon any mere human teacher.

Paul made it clear that the Corinthian saints owed their allegiance to Jesus Christ and to no one else. The apostle had not sought to glorify his own ministry, and start a Paul Party! The three questions in verse thirteen contain words in the original Greek which indicate that a negative answer is expected. NO, Christ is not separated; no, Paul was not crucified for you; no, you were not baptized into the name of Paul!

E. COMMISSIONED TO PREACH
(1 Corinthians 1:14-17)

I thank God that I baptized none of you, but Crispus and Gaius; Lest any should say that I had baptized in mine own name. And I baptized also the household of Stephanas: besides, I know not whether I baptized any other. For Christ sent me not to baptize, but to preach the gospel: not with wisdom of words, lest the cross of Christ should be made of none effect.

Paul was thankful that so few of them actually had been baptized by him. He recognized God's hand in this, for now no one could truthfully say he sought to start a following. Crispus (Acts 18:8) and Gaius (possibly the one mentioned in Acts 19:29, 20:4; Romans 16:23) were two men the apostle baptized. He was reminded also of having baptized the household of Stephanas (1 Corinthians 16:15-17). Paul was unable to remember whether there were others. After all, this was not his primary task or mission. Having said this, he is not to be accused of making light of or belittling baptism. Use of what is called the present infinitive in the original language "indicates a condition or process" (Dana and Mantey). Thus, he wanted it known that Christ did not commission him "to be a baptizer," but "to be a preacher of the gospel."

III. Special Features

A. PRESERVING OUR HERITAGE

Although waning in spiritual power, the "Black Church" continues to wield an enormous influence. Still every aspect of Black American life is touched. However, if the apostle were to visit us today, he would once again say: "There are contentions among you." There are many factors involved in the quarrelsomeness in our local assemblies, conferences, associations and conventions. Today's lesson has given us cause to consider a few possible solutions. For one thing, we must seek to honor our leaders in ways that please the Lord who has given them to us. Pastors who rule well, laboring in the Word of God and doctrine, are worthy of double honor (1 Timothy 5:17). But they are not to be worshiped.

A second thought: Pastors should realize that church business meetings can act as relief valves; the failure to have more than one meeting a year is like sweeping dirt under a rug, and then eventually tripping over the lump! A third thought: True unity comes by teaching the Bible, and giving the Holy Spirit in us something to work with as He works on us and in us. An inner doctrinal unity manifests itself in external ways. Discuss with your class other ways by which we may successfully confront crises.

B. A CONCLUDING WORD

Hatred for the newborn baby, the church, manifested itself in numerous ways. First, there is the Devil. The very fact that the early church—here illustrated by the church at Corinth—had many troubles suggests the strategy of Satan. His intention was to cause the visible church to fail in every way possible. We include here the world-system or kosmos which is also against the church. Remember, Satan is the prince of the world (John 12:31, 14:30, 16:11). We define the world-system (**kosmos**) as: That order or system whose center is man, which by its unbelief, air of independence, lack of realism, and spiritual blindness, demonstrates its evil opposition to God. It is composed of those people, pursuits, pleasures, purposes, and places where Jesus Christ is not wanted.

Second, there is man's old nature. Believers still have the old (adamic) nature in them. Though we are born again, indeed, new creatures in Christ, the old man in us is still kicking! Recall the apostle said in 1 Corinthians 6:11; "And such were some of you"—after listing such sinners as "fornicators, idolaters, adulterers, effeminate, homosexuals, sodomites, thieves, covetous, drunkards, revilers, extortioners." Well, the scars and pieces of the old life still remain. But thank God sin's power has been broken.

For nearly two thousand years, the church has been on earth. Millions of people have come to Christ. However, mankind has not improved morally. The adamic nature within believers has not improved just because we have grown in Christ. That nature ever seeks to show itself, and to "act up." And of course, there is no goodness in Satan upon which he may improve. Crises then are sure to continue to confront us.

Today's lesson provides some solutions for the problems we face: (1) Use the spiritual gifts bestowed by God upon His own; (2) Rely upon the strength of the Lord; (3) Be aware of the causes of strife in the church, and seek to avoid them; (4) Keep ever in mind that Jesus Christ is not divided; (5) Endeavor to keep the unity of the Holy Spirit (Ephesians 4:3); (6) Learn to follow leaders without making gods out of them; and (7) Proclaim the Gospel of the shed blood of Jesus Christ in all of its simplicity and power.

HOME DAILY BIBLE READINGS FOR THE WEEK OF MARCH 5, 2000

APPEAL FOR UNITY

February 28	M.	1 Corinthians 1:1-9, Paul Greets the Corinthians Christians
February 29	T.	1 Corinthians 1:10-17, Divisions Among Corinthian Christians
March 1	W.	1 Corinthians 1:18-25, God's Power and Wisdom in Christ
March 2	T.	1 Corinthians 1:26-31, Christ Jesus, Source of Our Life
March 3	F.	2 Timothy 1:3-14, Paul Encourages Timothy
March 4	S.	2 Timothy 2:1-13, Serve Jesus Christ Faithfully
March 5	S.	2 Timothy 2:14-26, The Ways of God's Servant

Know Your Bible

- Jesus' reference to the "things pertaining to the Kingdom of God" had to do with the prophecies concerning Himself, and the preaching of the Gospel "among all nations, beginning at Jerusalem." (Luke 24:45-49)
- The disciples of Jesus understood the "Kingdom of God" as "the restoration of the kingdom of Israel, with Christ as King." (Acts 1:3,6)
- The Day of Pentecost was fifty days (seven Sabbaths) from the Passover. (Luke 18:15,16)
- To be "pricked in the heart" is to have the conscience convinced of sin that ensues in the question, "What must I do to be saved?" (Acts 16:30)
- Members of the early church "had all things in common" which means that they voluntarily brought all their goods into one common stock or treasure. (Acts 2:44)
- The Sadducees did not believe in the resurrection of the dead. (Acts 23:8)
- The persecution of the Christians in Jerusalem caused the disciples to scatter to other places to preach the Word. (Acts 8:4)
- Paul's (Saul's) conversion on the road to Damascus was immediate in that he confessed Jesus as Lord, and asked, "what would you have me to do?" (Acts 9:5,6)
- Prior to becoming a Christian, Saul (Paul) was a student of the renown Jewish teacher named Gamaliel. (Acts 22:3)

O God, our Father, You have redeemed us as instruments of reconciliation. Grant us purity of motives as we face the problems and possibilities inherent in living within the fellowship of the forgiven. In Jesus' name, we pray. Amen.

The Holy Spirit
As Teacher

Adult Topic—*True Wisdom: A Basis for Unity*

•••••

Youth Topic—*In the Know*

Children's Topic—*Be Good Builders*

•••••

Devotional Reading—1 Corinthians 3:1-9

Background Scripture—1 Corinthians 2—3

Print—1 Corinthians 2:1-2, 4-13, 15-16

PRINTED SCRIPTURE

1 Corinthians 2:1-2, 4-13, 15-16 (KJV)

AND I, brethren, when I came to you, came not with excellency of speech or of wisdom, declaring unto you the testimony of God.

2 For I determined not to know any thing among you, save Jesus Christ, and him crucified.

•••••

4 And my speech and my preaching was not with enticing words of man's wisdom, but in demonstration of the Spirit and of power:

5 That your faith should not stand in the wisdom of men, but in the power of God.

6 Howbeit we speak wisdom among them that are perfect: yet not the wisdom of this world, nor of the princes of this world, that come to nought:

7 But we speak the wisdom of

1 Corinthians 2:1-2, 4-13, 15-16 (NRSV)

WHEN I came to you, brothers and sisters, I did not come proclaiming the mystery of God to you in lofty words or wisdom.

2 For I decided to know nothing among you except Jesus Christ, and him crucified.

•••••

4 My speech and my proclamation were not with plausible words of wisdom, but with a demonstration of the Spirit and of power,

5 so that your faith might rest not on human wisdom but on the power of God.

6 Yet among the mature we do speak wisdom, though it is not a wisdom of this age or of the rulers of this age, who are doomed to perish.

7 But we speak God's wisdom,

God in a mystery, even the hidden wisdom, which God ordained before the world unto our glory:

8 Which none of the princes of this world knew: for had they known it, they would not have crucified the Lord of glory.

9 But as it is written, Eye hath not seen, nor ear heard, neither have entered into the heart of man, the things which God hath prepared for them that love him.

10 But God hath revealed them unto us by his Spirit: for the Spirit searcheth all things, yea, the deep things of God.

11 For what man knoweth the things of a man, save the spirit of man which is in him? even so the things of God knoweth no man, but the Spirit of God.

12 Now we have received, not the spirit of the world, but the spirit which is of God; that we might know the things that are freely given to us of God.

13 Which things also we speak, not in the words which man's wisdom teacheth, but which the Holy Ghost teacheth; comparing spiritual things with spiritual.

•••••

15 But he that is spiritual judgeth all things, yet he himself is judged of no man.

16 For who hath known the mind of the Lord, that he may instruct him? But we have the mind of Christ.

secret and hidden, which God decreed before the ages for our glory.

8 None of the rulers of this age understood this; for if they had, they would not have crucified the Lord of glory.

9 But, as it is written, "What no eye has seen, nor ear heard, nor the human heart conceived, what God has prepared for those who love him" —

10 these things God has revealed to us through the Spirit; for the Spirit searches everything, even the depths of God.

11 For what human being knows what is truly human except the human spirit that is within? So also no one comprehends what is truly God's except the Spirit of God.

12 Now we have received not the spirit of the world, but the Spirit that is from God, so that we may understand the gifts bestowed on us by God.

13 And we speak of these things in words not taught by human wisdom but taught by the Spirit, interpreting spiritual things to those who are spiritual.

•••••

15 Those who are spiritual discern all things, and they are themselves subject to no one else's scrutiny.

16 "For who has known the mind of the Lord so as to instruct him?" But we have the mind of Christ.

KEY VERSE

Now we have received, not the spirit of the world, but the spirit which is of God; that we might know the things that are freely given to us of God.
—1 Corinthians 2:12

OBJECTIVES

After reading this lesson, the student will know that:

1. Preaching of the Gospel should be Christ-centered;
2. Preaching is to be empowered by the Holy Spirit;
3. Only the Holy Spirit reveals spiritual truths; and,
4. The Holy Spirit alone gives spiritual discernment.

POINTS TO BE EMPHASIZED
Adult/Youth
Key Verse: 1 Corinthians 2:12
Print: 1 Corinthians 2:1-2, 4-13, 15-16

—Paul proclaimed only Jesus Christ and Him crucified. (1-2)

—Paul's proclamation rested on demonstration of the Spirit and of power so that the believer's faith might rest not on human wisdom but on the power of God. (4-5)

—Among the mature believers, Paul spoke of God's wisdom revealed through the Spirit. (6-7, 9-10)

—The rulers of the present age did not understand God's wisdom or they would not have crucified Jesus. (8)

—The Spirit of God has bestwoed upon the believer the ability to understand the gifts of God (11-13)

—Those who receive God's wisdom will have the mind of Christ. (15-16)

Children
Key Verse: John 14:15
Print: 1 Corinthians 3:10-11; Matthew 7:24-27

—By teaching about Jesus, Paul laid a foundation for the people in Corinth to grow in Jesus. (1 Corinthians 3:10)

—Jesus Christ is the only foundation on which to build our lives. (10-11)

—Everyone who hears Jesus' Words and acts on them is like a man who builds his house on a foundation of rock. (Matthew 7:24-25)

—Everyone who does not act on Jesus' Words is like a man who builds on sand; the house is destroyed when storms come. (25)

(**Note**: Use KJV Scripture for Adults; NRSV Scripture for Youth and Children)

I. Introduction

A. GOD'S THOUGHTS

The question is put forth in 1 Corinthians 2:11: "For what person knows a man's thoughts except the spirit of the man which is in him?" (RSV). The answer is, "No one." One human being cannot read the mind of another. This is why it is necessary from time to time for us to give people a piece of our minds, to tell them off-so they will know what we are thinking! But if we do not know another person's thoughts, how can we know the mind of God? We cannot. He must reveal to us what He is thinking, for He said: "My thoughts are not your thoughts... they are higher than your thoughts" (Isaiah 55:8-9). Therefore, God has revealed His mind, and has given us the Bible, His Word. No Scripture ever came by the will of man, "but holy men of God spoke as they were moved by the Holy Spirit" (2 Peter 1:21). The Holy Spirit alone knows the things of God. And He alone makes known the thoughts of God.

B. BIBLICAL BACKGROUND

Paul believed that the underlying basis for the division at Corinth was the false concept of wisdom held by the Corinthians. This misconception showed itself in two areas. For one thing, they did not understand the nature and character of the Christian message. The Gospel of the Cross was to them foolishness, for it did not fit their preconceived ideals. The Cross stressed man's total dependence upon God. They did not know that true wisdom originates in the Lord (Job 28:28).

Secondly, the false concept of wisdom demonstrated that they misunderstood the Christian ministry. The very idea of pitting one preacher against another reveals this error. Their emphasis on oratory, the parade of "Knowledge," the speculation in philosophy —all showed their mistaken evaluation of human attainments. Human wisdom has so many starting points that it is no wonder there were contentions among the Corinthians.

II. Exposition and Application of the Scripture

A. PAUL'S PREACHING
(1 Corinthians 2:1-2, 4-8)

AND I, brethren, when I came to you, came not with excellency of speech or of wisdom, declaring unto you the testimony of God. For I determined not to know any thing among you, save Jesus Christ, and him crucified. And my speech and my preaching was not with enticing words of man's wisdom, but in demonstration of the Spirit and of power: That your faith should not stand in the wisdom of men, but in the power of God. Howbeit we speak wisdom among them that are perfect: yet not the wisdom of this world, nor of the princes of this world, that come to nought: But we speak the wisdom of God in a mystery, even the hidden wisdom, which God ordained before the world unto our glory: Which none of the princes of this world knew: for had they known it, they would not have crucified the Lord of glory.

Paul gave no encouragement to the divisions at Corinth. When he came to the city, he came with his mind made up to preach and solemnly proclaim the testimony of God. He reminded the brethren that he did not come with excellency (as a superior person) in speech or wisdom. There was no ostentatious display of oratory with him. Indeed, the apostle concentrated upon the Person and work of the Lord Jesus Christ. He was determined to know nothing but Christ crucified, buried and risen! This emphasis is not to be taken as belittling the value of other doctrines. He felt that the center, not the circumference, of his message should be emphasized. He knew that the Cross of the crucified Christ could conquer carnality in the church at Corinth.

Paul's message and method of delivery—what he had to say, and the way in which he said it—did not depend upon flowery language and clever expressions. Faith does not depend upon "enticing" (persuasive) arguments. Faith is the gift of God and we need not strive by our own eloquence to bring men to faith. The apostle knew that if a man's faith was based upon a preacher's oratory, it was upon shaky ground.

To Paul's mind, the most efficient method for winning men, women, boys and girls to Christ was to preach plainly and simply the Lord Jesus Christ and Him crucified. This simple message, unadorned with human philosophy and wisdom, was the Good News that saved the lost. Those who might think the Christian message is devoid of wisdom altogether are in error. There is wisdom in the Gospel. To whom then is it given? Paul answered: To them that are perfect. The word "perfect" does not mean absolute sinlessness. No man on the face of this earth possesses this. "Perfect" here speaks of having attained the end or purpose; completed. Thus, a perfect man or woman is one who is spiritually mature.

We learn here that there are deeper truths available for grown-up Christians. Because the wisdom of Christianity is not the wisdom of this present age, let no one think that Christianity is stupid. Look again at verse six. God's wisdom is not only NOT of this world-age, but it is not the wisdom of the princes of this world-age. These rulers are those in authority, men of prominence, men with significant positions. They are high officials, dignitaries. While it is true that the princes of this age refers primarily to human beings, it is also true that evil angelic spirits rule behind the scenes and influence the course of human history, as God permits. Without Christ, they all are doomed to destruction.

For the grown-up saint, God's wisdom existed before time began, destined for the glory of the believers. Such wisdom was not known to the unbelieving rulers of this age. They are woefully ignorant of Bible truths. Elemental truths about God in Christ are hid from the wise and prudent of this age, and are revealed to babes. Yea, the mysteries—things man could never discover—have been revealed only unto the grown-up believers. Verse eight closes with a wonderful title of Christ—the Lord of Glory (James 2:1; John 17:5). Christ is He to whom glory belongs! This title teaches us that Jesus Christ is Jehovah God Almighty.

B. GOD'S REVELATION
(1 Corinthians 2:9-12)

But as it is written, Eye hath not seen, nor ear heard, neither have entered into the heart of man, the things which God hath prepared for them that love him. But God hath revealed them unto us by his Spirit: for the Spirit searcheth all things, yea, the deep things of God. For what man knoweth the things of a man, save the spirit of man which is in him? even so the things of God knoweth no man, but the Spirit of God. Now we have received, not the spirit of the world, but the spirit which is of God; that we might know the things that are freely given to us of God.

So far as earthly matters are concerned, man's ability to see, hear and think is satisfactory. However, in the realm of the spiritual, in the things of God, man is an idiot. The human eye has not seen, the ear has not heard, nor have man's thoughts entertained the things which God has prepared for them that love Him (Isaiah 64:4). **Too often students stop here!** We should not overlook verse ten. These things are to be known and enjoyed in some measure through the Holy Spirit here and now. Paul spoke of present blessings, not future bliss in heaven.

Who can know the deep things of God? Only God. The Holy Spirit is God Almighty, and as God, He is omniscient. He searches (present tense) all things. He examines, investigates actively, thus implying accurate knowledge. He plumbs the ocean depths of truth and probes the outer space of understanding. He not only knows what He knows, but He is able to communicate, to share that knowledge. His ability to reveal to simple minds the transcendent truths of the only wise God leaves Christians with no excuse for spiritual ignorance.

Now even that which a man may know of himself is at best imperfect. Sin distorts even this knowledge of self. Sin beclouds and confuses the human spirit's estimation of itself. Furthermore, the human heart is tricky, deceitful and incurably sick. If man is inscrutable to his fellowman, if it is impossible to penetrate his mind and discover his thought, how can we humans know the mind of God? Only the Holy Spirit discerns the things of God. Thank God for the Bible! All who accept the shed blood of the Lord Jesus Christ have the Holy Spirit living in them. We did not receive the spirit of the kosmos, the world-system, that spirit of human wisdom which leads hell-bound men and women to emphasize the temporal, the materialistic, the visible, the tangible, the here and now.

Chafer said: "It is God's purpose that every one of all who are saved shall be instructed relative to those truths which can enter the human understanding only by divine revelation." See then the purpose of the Spirit of God to reveal to us the things that are freely given to us of God, things which are graciously given as a favor. And remember this: "He who did not spare his own Son, but delivered him up for us all, how shall he not with him also freely give us all things?" (Romans 8:32).

C. THE SPIRIT'S DISCERNMENT
(1 Corinthians 2:13, 15-16)

Which things also we speak, not in the words which man's wisdom teacheth, but which the Holy Ghost teacheth; comparing spiritual things with spiritual. But he that is spiritual judgeth all things, yet he himself is judged of no man. For who hath known the mind of the Lord, that he may instruct him? But we have the mind of Christ.

Because the indwelling Spirit makes known to us the things of God, we in turn are enabled to communicate or share the blessings of the Lord with others. Of course, physical, material sharing is included. However,

emphasis here is upon spiritual truths. We speak, we share what we know in words taught by the Holy Spirit. Note especially the words, "comparing spiritual things with spiritual." Because the Greek is somewhat ambiguous, several translations are possible. The verb rendered "comparing" also means to explain or interpret. Thus, we could render 1 Corinthians 2:13: "interpreting spiritual things to spiritual men or those possessing the Spirit" (RSV). Because the verb also means to combine, bring together, we could interpret: "giving spiritual truth a spiritual form." Or, "combining spiritual thoughts with spiritual words" (NASB). A third idea is to compare spiritual gifts and revelations which we have with those which we are to receive and thereby judge them. This interpretation also suggests the idea of comparing Scripture with Scripture.

What is meant by "he that is spiritual"? This is the Christian who attempts to see things from God's point of view. He that is spiritual knows that God has a plan and purpose, and that He makes all things work together for the good of the saints. In this way, the spiritual Christian is able to make eternity judgments and not simply time judgments. The text claims that he that is spiritual judges or discerns spiritual things. This is true only because the indwelling Holy Spirit is permitted to have His own way. The man or woman who is filled with God's Spirit walks in full communion with God.

He that is spiritual puts first things first. He remembers the exhortation to seek first the kingdom of God and His righteousness, and all other things that are needful will be added. This is why the spiritual man's values are different from those of the world. Too often today, we find values are twisted and distorted. He that is spiritual is enabled by the resident Spirit to put all things in their proper perspective and to view them in the light of truth. And yet, the lesson closes by informing us that the spiritual man is not judged or discerned or called to account by the natural man.

The natural man is "soulish." Use of the designation "natural" refers to the unspiritual, unregenerate, unsaved, unrenewed man. He is the old man, the old nature, the Adamic man in his completeness; he is the animal man without the presence of the Holy Spirit of God. It is suggested that every man who is not a Christian is a natural man. He may be intelligent, cultured, educated, sophisticated, eloquent, a good citizen, a regular guy, but because he has no relationship with the Holy Spirit, through faith in the Lord Jesus Christ, he is spiritually dead.

The natural man lives on a purely material, temporal plane, hemmed in by human thinking and ignorant of spiritualities. We are told that he does not receive the things of the Spirit of God because such things are foolishness, idiotic, stupid, and moronic to him. He simply is not moved by them. Such a description makes it imperative that ministers of the Gospel resist the pressures of the world. Resist following the demands of the carnal minded who clamor for the church to follow the agenda they have set up.

Spiritual folks don't need unbelievers telling them how to conduct church business. The world has a wisdom of course, but it is not the spiritual wisdom by which believers live, or by which the church operates. Christians should keep this in mind in these days when the unbelieving world so readily volunteers its advice and seeks authority over the church. The question asked by Paul comes from Isaiah 40:13: "Who has directed the Spirit of the Lord, or as His counselor has taught Him?" (cf. Romans 11:34). The answer of course is that no one knows God's mind! NO one instructs or counsels Him! Believers have the mind of Christ, for He has revealed it to us in His Word and by the Holy Spirit. If we then have His mind, why would we need the world's instruction? "No one can instruct, know, probe, judge us, in a word, evaluate aright what we are and have" (Lenski).

The last sentence in the scriptural text of our lesson is very emphatic. Literally, the Greek is: "But **we**, Christ's mind **we** have." Use of the pronoun "we" and then the verb ending showing it is plural makes the "we" emphatic. As the world criticizes us and considers our faith in the shed blood of Jesus Christ folly on our part, this portion of God's Word encourages us to remain unperturbed by the world's mockery. We are blessed by the God of the Bible who makes Himself known to us.

We have the *nous* (mind: God's infinite wisdom) which is so far superior to the world's judgment.

Therefore, let us never deviate from the mind of Christ. This calls for steadfastness on the part of all those who are "in Christ;" they must always remain categorically distinguished from the power structures of this world order.

III. Special Features

A. PRESERVING OUR HERITAGE

I sat down and wrote within a few minutes more than twenty white preachers I have heard over the years—such men as Barnhouse, McCartney, Lee, Stanley, Boice, Swindoll, Havner, Eldersveld, Graham, Greene, Galloway, Telford, Sweeting, Culbertson, Wiersbe, Lutzer, Schmidt, McIntire, Hoffman, et al. You may have others to add to the list. Few of them, as I recall, touch the oratory of many of the black preachers I have known. We have a tremendous heritage when it comes to sermon delivery and eloquence.

And yet, there is a danger inherent in such preaching, a peril that the apostle Paul warns of in today's lesson. The trap is the possibility of depending on the "excellence of speech" more than upon the Holy Spirit. There is always the danger of being more concerned with the method of delivery than with the message delivered.

B. A CONCLUDING WORD

Four words are offered in review of today's lesson. The first is *definition*. To this are added *revelation*, *inspiration*, and *illumination*, as proposed by MacDonald (Believer's Bible Commentary).

1. *Definition*: 1 Corinthians 2:1-2, 4-8. Here the apostle Paul made clear and distinct the difference between the wisdom of men and the wisdom of God. He described that wisdom which is of men, and of this world-age, as a wisdom that depends upon oratory, eloquence, excellency of speech, enticing or persuasive words. On the other hand, the wisdom of God is described as that which is demonstrated by the power of God, and totally dependent upon the Holy Spirit.

2. *Revelation*: 1 Corinthians 2:9-12. The word rendered "revealed" in verse ten comes from the verb *apokalupto* which means to uncover, disclose, lay open what has been veiled or covered up (Thayer). It is a word used of God revealing to men by the Holy Spirit things unknown to them. We have seen that if men cannot read the minds of other men, they certainly cannot know the mind of God. The things of God have to be supernaturally made known to us.

3. *Inspiration*: 1 Corinthians 2:13. Actually, the word translated "inspiration" in 2 Timothy 3:16 is literally, "God breathed." What we learn from verse thirteen is that the "revealed things are taught in **words** given by the Spirit" (Scofield). Note the verse speaks of **words**, not thoughts. Some scholars teach God gave the thoughts and left it up to men to express the thoughts in words of their own choosing. NO, what we are taught here is verbal (words) inspiration. The writers used the exact words given them by the Spirit of God.

4. *Illumination*: 1 Corinthians 2:14-16. To illuminate is to provide with light, thus to make understandable, clarify. The believer has the mind of the Lord. He is thus enabled by the Holy Spirit to understand those truths miraculously revealed. Such discernment makes unnecessary any help offered by unbelievers in spiritual matters.

HOME DAILY BIBLE READINGS FOR THE WEEK OF MARCH 12, 2000

THE HOLY SPIRIT AS TEACHER

March 6 M. 1 Corinthians 2:1-5, Proclaiming Christ Crucified
March 7 T. 1 Corinthians 2:6-16, The True Wisdom of God
March 8 W. 1 Corinthians 3:1-9, Put Away Quarrels and Jealousies
March 9 T. 1 Corinthians 3:10-15, Build on the Foundation of Jesus Christ
March 10 F. 1 Corinthians 3:16-23, We Belong to God through Jesus Christ
March 11 S. Romans 8:1-8, Life in the Spirit
March 12 S. Romans 8:9-17, We Are Children of God

Know Your Bible

- The meaning of "unclean" as used by Peter in his vision on the housetop referred to that which was forbidden to be eaten according to Jewish law. (Acts 10:9-16)
- Although the disciples were commissioned to preach the Gospel to all the world, they were astonished to experience the fact that God had granted repentance unto life to the Gentiles. (Acts 10:45; 11:18)
- The disciples were first called Christians at Antioch. (Acts 11:26)
- Christians may expect to endure trouble in this world because it is only "through much tribulation" that we can "enter into the kingdom of God." (Acts 14:22)
- The Jewish ceremonial law is referred to as a "yoke" that was difficult "to bear." (Acts 15:10)
- Humans do not have a natural inclination to receive the Gospel, God must first open the human heart and make it receptive to the message. (Acts 16:14)
- The Scriptures are the supreme authority in matters of faith as well as in matters of religious controversy. (Acts 17, 2, 3, 11; 18:28)
- On the Day of Pentecost, there were Jews in Jerusalem who came "out of every nation" because they had been scattered "among all people" as God had said they would be for their sins. (See Deuteronomy 28:64)
- The result of the preaching of the Gospel among the Gentile was their turning from darkness to light and this must be followed by works consistent with their belief in the saving power of the Christ. (Acts 26:18-20)

Eternal God, in a world of conflicting voices generated by personal preferences and priorities, atone our hearts and minds to the directive of the Holy Spirit so that we may walk in the path of Your righteousness. In the name of Jesus Christ, we pray. Amen.

The Church and
Its Leaders

Adult Topic—*Mature Leaders Bring Unity*

·····

Youth Topic—*Lead, But Serve*

Children's Topic—*Be Good Caretakers*

·····

Devotional Reading—1 Peter 5:1-11

Background Scripture—1 Corinthians 4:1-13

Print—1 Corinthians 4:1-13

PRINTED SCRIPTURE

1 Corinthians 4:1-13 (KJV)

LET A man so account of us, as of the ministers of Christ, and stewards of the mysteries God.

2 Moreover it is required in stewards, that a man be found faithful.

3 But with me it is a very small thing that I should be judged of you, or of man's judgment: yea, I judge not mine own self.

4 For I know nothing by myself; yet am I not hereby justified: but he that judgeth me is the Lord.

5 Therefore judge nothing before the time, until the Lord come, who both will bring to light the hidden things of darkness, and will make manifest the counsels of the hearts: and then shall every man have praise of God.

6 And these things, brethren, I have in a figure transferred to myself and to Apollos for your sakes; that ye might learn in us not to think

1 Corinthians 4:1-13 (NRSV)

THINK OF us in this way, as servants of Christ and stewards of God's mysteries.

2 Moreover, it is required of stewards that they be found trustworthy.

3 But with me it is a very small thing that I should be judged by you or by any human court. I do not even judge myself.

4 I am not aware of anything against myself, but I am not thereby acquitted. It is the Lord who judges me.

5 Therefore do not pronounce judgment before the time, before the Lord comes, who will bring to light the things now hidden in darkness and will disclose the purposes of the heart. Then each one will receive commendation from God.

6 I have applied all this to Apollos any myself for your benefit, brothers and sisters, so that you may

of men above that which is written, that no one of you be puffed up for one against another.

7 For who maketh thee to differ from another? and what hast thou that thou didst not receive? now if thou didst receive it, why dost thou glory, as if thou hadst not received it?

8 Now ye are full, now ye are rich, ye have reigned as kings without us: and I would to God ye did reign, that we also might reign with you.

9 For I think that God hath set forth us the apostles last, as it were appointed to death: for we are made a spectacle unto the world, and to angels, and to men.

10 We are fools for Christ's sake, but ye are wise in Christ; we are weak, but ye are strong; ye are honourable, but we are despised.

11 Even unto this present hour we both hunger, and thirst, and are naked, and are buffeted, and have no certain dwellingplace;

12 And labour, working with our own hands: being reviled, we bless; being persecuted, we suffer it:

13 Being defamed, we intreat: we are made as the filth of the world, and are the offscouring of all things unto this day.

learn through us the meaning of the saying, "Nothing beyond what is written," so that none of you will be puffed upon favor of one against another.

7 For who sees anything different in you? What do you have that you did not receive? And if you received it, why do you boast as if it were not a gift?

8 Already you have all you want! Already you have become rich! Quite apart from us you have become kings! Indeed, I wish that you had become kings, so that we might be kings with you!

9 For I think that God has exhibited us apostles as last of all, as though sentenced to death, because we have become a spectacle to the world, to angels and to mortals.

10 We are fools for the sake of Christ, but you are wise in Christ. We are weak, but you are strong. You are held in honor, but we in disrepute.

11 To the present hour we are hungry and thirsty, we are poorly clothed and beaten and homeless,

12 and we grow weary from the work of our own hands. When reviled, we bless; when persecuted, we endure;

13 when slandered, we speak kindly. We have become like the rubbish of the world, the dregs of all things, to this very day.

KEY VERSE

Let a man so account of us, as of the ministers of Christ, and stewards of the mysteries of God.—1 Corinthians 4:1

OBJECTIVES

After reading this lesson, the student should know that:

1. Faithfulness is a primary requisite for church leaders;
2. God's judgment of church leaders is more important than man's judgment;
3. Everything we possess was given to us; and,
4. Humility and patience are commendable attributes in church leaders.

POINTS TO BE EMPHASIZED

Adult/Youth

Key Verse: 1 Corinthians 4:1

Print: 1 Corinthians 4:1-13

—Paul asked that he and the other leaders be considered as servants of Christ and as truthstowthy stewards of God's mysteries. (1-2)

—Paul was not concerned about being judged by humans. (3-4)

—Believers must not pronounce judgment, but leave judgment and commendation to the Lord when He comes. (5)

—Paul used himself and Apollos as examples that believers have no reason to boast because everything they have received is a gift. (6-7)

—Paul contrasted the pride of the believers in Corinth with the humility and suffering of the apostles. (8-11)

—The apostles when reviled, blessed, when persecuted, endured, when slandered, spoke kindly. (12-13)

Children

Key Verse: Matthew 25:21

Print: 1 Corinthians 4:1-2; Matthew 25:14-23, 28-29

—Stewards of God's Word must be trustworthy. (1 Corinthians 4:1-2)

—Jesus told a parable about a man who went on a journey and gave his slaves money to use for him while he was away. (Matthew 15:14-15)

—The slave with five talents made five more, the one with two doubled his, and the last one buried his in the ground. (16-18)

—When the master returned, he demanded an accounting and praised the two slaves who had doubled their talents by giving them more responsibilities. (19-23)

—The persons who use their talents will be given more, those who do not will lose what they have. (28-29)

(**Note**: Use KJV Scripture for Adults; NRSV Scripture for Youth and Children)

I. Introduction

A. MINISTERS, STEWARDS, AND APOSTLES

A study of these three kinds of leaders in the early church will prove helpful in better understanding today's lesson. In verse one is found the title, Minister. This is rendered servants by most of the other versions (NKJV, RSV, NIV, NASB, Moffatt); underlings (NEB). Literally, it means "under-rower." Ancient ships were moved by wind power and sails, and augmented by man power at the oars. On a warship, sometimes there were one to three banks of men pulling oars. The bottom row of men were the under-rowers or under-seamen. Later, the word came to mean any subordinate official, assistant. His sole function was to take orders and at once without question execute them. His will was only that of his master.

Also in verse one is found the title, Steward. When you hear the Greek word translated "steward," the word economy immediately comes to mind, for the Greek is *oikonomos*, literally, house ruler or house manager. In Paul's day, a steward was a man entrusted with the management of the affairs of a house. He handled the money, servants, food, young children, property, etc.

Finally, in verse nine, we have the word Apostle. The verb *apostello* means to send off, send away. An *apostolos* is one sent forth with orders, with a commission; a delegate, messenger. In time, the word was especially "applied to the twelve disciples whom our Lord chose, out of the multitude of His adherents, to be his constant companions and the heralds to proclaim to men the kingdom of God" (Thayer). In this narrow, technical sense, there are no apostles today. As such, those who appropriate this title unto themselves are obliged to inform themselves of the historic meaning of its biblical usage.

B. BIBLICAL BACKGROUND

Inasmuch as the lesson teaches us that the judgment of the servants of Jesus Christ is not committed to men, we thought a word concerning judgments would be appropriate. There are many judgments mentioned in the Bible. Perhaps the most significant ones are: (1) the Cross; (2) believers, (a) self-judgment of believers, (b) judgment of our works by Christ; (3) Israel; (4) the Gentile nations; (5) Satan and his angels; and (6) the unsaved at the Great White Throne. God is in charge of all such judgments. Even hell is under His management, not that of the Devil. Satan will be a victim, not a supervisor.

Now in today's lesson, Paul makes it known that men are not the judges of the ministry of the servants of Christ. As the apostle asked in Romans 14:4: "Who are you to judge another's servant? To his own master he stands or falls." At the second coming of the Lord, believers will be judged by Christ. Rewards will be based upon what was done with what was given, as well as upon motives. "We must all appear before the judgment seat of Christ, that everyone may receive the things done in his body, according to that he hath done, whether it be good or bad" (2 Corinthians 5:10). A definite reward is promised for those who are faithful. Christ will judge the saints for their works. Rest assured that this judgment includes church workers!

II. Exposition and Application of the Scripture

A. WARNINGS AGAINST JUDGING (1 Corinthians 4:1-5)

LET a man so account of us, as of the ministers of Christ, and stewards of the mysteries of God. Moreover it is required in stewards, that a man be found faithful. But with me it is a very small thing that I should be judged of you, or of man's judgment: yea, I judge not mine own self. For I know nothing by myself; yet am I not hereby justified: but he that judgeth me is the Lord. Therefore judge nothing before the time, until the Lord come, who both will bring to light the hidden things of darkness, and will make manifest the counsels of the hearts: and then shall every man have praise of God.

Think habitually about the fact that the true preacher is the minister of Christ and God's steward. Since the New Testament church had no hierarchy, all preachers are ranked on the same level as subordinates (servants) of Christ. The minister is also the steward, manager or administrator of the mysteries of God. He is thus a trustee of the secrets of God. A mystery in the Bible is any truth undiscoverable by human wisdom and reason, and which must be revealed by God. It is not education, eloquence, oratory, personality or wisdom that is sought for, but faithfulness. Indeed, the Lord desires that all who serve Him should be faithful to their calling.

The cliques or parties within the church at Corinth were basically due to improper ideas about wisdom and about the Christian ministry. People who follow exclusively one preacher are quite prone to criticize the other preachers, and usually their criticisms are unfair. Keep in mind that the problem here is the pitting and exalting of one faithful minister against another faithful minister. At this point Paul says, "Your examination and judgment of me doesn't mean anything! It is a matter of supreme unimportance that I should be judged by you or any human judgment."

Paul included his own judgment of himself. Evidently, the steward of God cannot even trust himself to make a true and valid judgment and criticism of himself. Verse four is accurately rendered: "I am not aware of anything against myself" (RSV); or paraphrased: "For I might be quite ignorant of any fault in myself" (JBP). It was the fact that the Lord Jesus will be the One who will judge His stewards that made Paul feel independent of and even indifferent to the judgments and criticisms of the partyists or separatists at Corinth. Christ will judge (2 Corinthians 5:10)! And so, knowing that the Lord was his Judge, Paul considered man's judgment of him, and his own judgment of himself, were not important.

When the Lord Jesus Christ returns, everything shall be made plain. In the meantime, it was best for the Corinthian saints to suspend their judgments of God's faithful ministers. No one can judge another's motives, and since God alone is able to search out the motives of the heart, He therefore is a better Judge than men. "...For there is nothing covered, that shall not be revealed; and hid, that shall not be known" (Matthew 10:26). At that point, God will give suitable, fitting praise where it is due. Be assured that God's judgment is not only accurate, but final and decisive.

B. WARNINGS AGAINST BOASTING (1 Corinthians 4:6-7)

And these things, brethren, I have in a figure transferred to myself and to Apollos for your sakes; that ye might learn in us not to think of men above that which is written, that no one of you be puffed up for one against another. For who maketh thee to differ from another? and what hast thou that thou didst not receive? now if thou didst receive it, why dost thou glory, as if thou hadst not received it?

Paul cited Apollos and himself merely to illustrate to the saints their need to abandon all party pride. It was not necessary to name all of the teachers and leaders who were involved, for it was the principle that Paul sought to establish, namely, that the saints no longer attach themselves to some one teacher or leader to the detriment and disparagement of others. The word rendered "transferred" is *metaschematize*. This means to change the form of, to transform; or better yet, to change the outward expression. Paul gave this exhortation the outward form of an exposition about Apollos and himself; it was a truth taught by making application to Apollos and himself. "I have applied all this to myself and Apollos for your benefit, brethren..." (RSV). "I have used myself and Apollos above as an illustration" (JB Phillips).

His purpose in doing so was to prevent them from being "puffed up." The verb used means to blow up or puff, inflate, cause to swell up. When employed figuratively, it means to be proud or arrogant, to become conceited, pompous, or put on airs. Interestingly, the apostle used this verb seven times, and all instances are found in the Corinthians Letters! (1 Corinthians 4:6, 18, 19; 5:2; 8:1; 13:4; 2 Corinthians 12:20, where it is rendered, "swellings").

Now it is a fact that men and women differ in gifts and abilities. Paul did not dispute this. However, the question asked is not, "Do we all have the same gifts?" but rather, "Who makes you to differ from somebody else?" RSV: "For who sees any thing different in you?" Moffatt: "Who singles you out, my brother?" The 20th Century: "For who makes any one of you superior to others?" Arndt and Gingrich: "Who concedes you any superiority?" Berquist: "Who distinguished you, and set you apart, and made you so different."

The second question actually helps to answer the first question. Here is one of the most humbling verses in the Bible! It cuts the ground from under all boasting, bragging, puffedupness and foolish pride. What do you have that was not given to you? Now if something has been given to you, why boast (glory) as if it were something you had achieved yourself? Paul wanted the saints at Corinth to see the inconsistency of bragging about something given to them as if it had not been given.

C. EXAMPLES OF HUMILITY
(1 Corinthians 4:8-10)

Now ye are full, now ye are rich, ye have reigned as kings without us: and I would to God ye did reign, that we also might reign with you. For I think that God hath set forth us the apostles last, as it were appointed to death: for we are made a spectacle unto the world, and to angels, and to men. We are fools for Christ's sake, but ye are wise in Christ; ye are honourable, but we are despised.

At this juncture, Paul used irony and satire calculated to further convince them of the folly of their pride. The phrase, "Now ye are full" contains a verb meaning to satiate, to fill or have enough. It is as if Paul said: "Aha! Already you think you have all the spiritual food you need!" The folks at Corinth indicated by their actions that they believed they had arrived. He continued: "Now you are rich," using the Greek word for rich which is *ploutos* (plutocracy; rule or government by the wealthy). The third expression is: "Ye have reigned as kings without us." Evidently, the Corinthian saints suffered from delusion. They imagined themselves full, rich and reigning like kings! Compare with Revelation 3:17, 18, 22.

And indeed, Paul wished that it were true that they had achieved kingship, for that would mean that he would be reigning with them. "But look at the facts! Look at how the world is treating me," said Paul. "How then can you be reigning while we are still suffering?" You see how Paul was moved to employ the "pen" of satire and sarcasm to prick their balloon of conceit. He reminded them of the hardships of the apostles and said, "How could you Corinthians saints be full, rich and reigning as kings when your poor teachers and instructors are suffering and being persecuted?"

It was as if the Lord had exhibited the apostles last, referring to condemned criminals and others who were to fight in the arena. After the preliminaries were over and the crowd had been sated to the point of boredom, the main event then came on. The hapless victims were the last to come out, unarmed, to fight with wild beasts in what would prove to be their exit from this world. "We are made a spectacle (*theatron*); we are exposed to contempt, made a gazingstock (Hebrews 10:33), made sport of, mocked, made fun of by a cruel world, angels, and men. We are foolish ones (*moros*: morons) through (because of, for the sake of) Christ.

D. EXAMPLES OF PATIENCE
(1 Corinthians 4:11-13)

Even unto this present hour we both hunger, and thirst, and are naked, and are buffeted, and have no certain dwellingplace; And labour, working with our own hands: being reviled, we bless; being persecuted, we suffer it: Being defamed, we entreat: we are made as the filth of the world, and are the offscouring of all things unto this day.

In this last section of the lesson, Paul described not only his own experiences, but those of all the missionaries. Earlier, he wrote in general terms of being made spectacles, fools, weak, dishonored. Now a catalogue is given which is more specific in its description of the world's contempt for believers. Reading it is sure to prick our consciences. For there is little suffering for Christ's sake in our churches today. We have "celebration," and we emphasize dealing with the "whole man," but the spirit of entertainment does not allow us to say, " to the present hour, we suffer for Christ."

First is the combination HUNGERING AND THIRSTING. Figuratively, to hunger and thirst is to crave or seek with eager desire (Matthew 5:6). But here the apostle spoke of the lack of physical food and water. NAKED is rendered poorly clothed, ill clad, light clothing, or in rags. *Gumnos* (see the word gym here) points to the lack of sufficient clothing, especially during inclement weather (Lenski). BUFFETED is variously rendered: cuffed, beaten, knocked about, brutally treated, roughly handled. The verb does not refer to official beatings, but the uncalled-for striking of the bodies and faces with the fist. "We are roughly treated" (Arndt and Gingrich). NO CERTAIN DWELLING PLACE: Here is a verb (used only once in the New Testament) describing Paul's way of life as unsettled, homeless, a vagabond, vagrant, wandering about.

LABOR, WORKING WITH OUR OWN HANDS. The apostles were compelled to earn their own living by hard manual (hands) labor. Paul was by trade a tentmaker (Acts 18:3). Ordinarily, the apostle appreciated the personal independence of self-employment. But in this Letter to the Corinthians, such toil is calculated to show the puffedupness of the Corinthians. Such hard work shows up their ingratitude and lack of care for the needs of the Gospel messengers. REVILED, WE BLESS. Rising above their sufferings, the apostles met curses with blessings (Luke 6:28). From the world's perspective, failure to curse back is a mark of an abject spirit. The world would respond to insulting abuse with the same. PERSECUTED, WE SUFFER or endure: They held out, held on, held up; they "put up with it" (Moffatt). They submitted; "took it patiently" (JB Phillips). DEFAMED, WE ENTREAT. Although slandered, the apostles did not retort in kind. Instead, they continued to answer kindly, trying to conciliate.

Understand that all of these differences between the Corinthians and the apostles are calculated to show from the Corinthians' point of view their superiority, and the lowliness of Paul and his fellow laborers. The concluding statement summarizes this attitude, FILTH: Literally, the Greek word used means "cleanse all around" or "cleanse on all sides." It thus refers to dirt, refuse, trash. OFFSCOURING means to "wipe off all around, wipe clean." It is that which is removed by the process of cleanings; it is dirt rubbed off, scrapings. What patience is demonstrated here by the willingness to be treated in such a manner! To be considered the very scum of the earth, the refuse, rubbish of the world, the dregs of humanity! "The filth that one gets rid of through the sink and the gutter" (Expositor's). Strong language! But you can see through Paul's eyes the estimate the Corinthians (the world) had of the messengers of Christ.

III. Special Features

A. PRESERVING OUR HERITAGE

One of the things that attracted black slaves to the Baptist denomination was the doctrine that all human beings are equal in the realms of the social, political, economic, and civil rights. This is called Equalitarianism (or Egalitarianism). Many of the White Baptist preachers heralded a Gospel that treated blacks and whites as equals. Their rapport with the common people, their appeal to the poor, the downtrodden, white or black was one of the strong points of their early colonial witness for Christ.

Blacks were placed on a plan of equality by a Gospel with universalistic dimension that moved men to believe Christ died for them as individuals. However temporary this approach may have been in slave society, it is backed up by the eternal Word of God. In addition to the verses which stress the fact that the God of the Bible is no respecter of persons, today's lesson adds 1 Corinthians 4:7 to the arsenal of equality. This text reduces all men to size, for all we have was given to us. People who are puffed up because of their race, IQ, skin color, culture, and other things over which they had no say or control, fail to realize all they have was given them by God.

Therefore, the man who despises another because of his race is not only arrogant, but ignorant, One other thought. Even within the local assembly, church leaders need to keep in mind that they hold their positions only by the grace of God, Who deigns to use the democratic process in placing the powers that be within the local church, conference or convention.

B. A CONCLUDING WORD

Three characteristics of the Church Leader are seen. First, he must be *Fundamental in Creed* (verse 1). The Lord wants us to believe the right thing first, and doctrine is stressed (1 Timothy 4:6, 13, 16; 2 Timothy 3:16). We are to be good stewards of the mysteries of God. Second, the Church Leader should be a **Fool for Christ** (verse 10). Some church members cannot be fools for Christ because they think they are smart. They believe they know how to run the church; however, what they run they ruin. The fool (moron-fool) for Christ is humble, not puffed up; he is willing to sacrifice for the Savior. Third, the Church Leader should be **Faithful to Commitment** (verse 2). Stewards or house rulers (managers) are to be honest, trustworthy, dependable, faithful, recognizing that what they manage belongs to the Lord Jesus Christ.

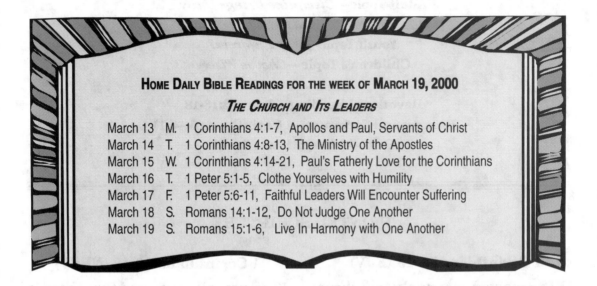

HOME DAILY BIBLE READINGS FOR THE WEEK OF MARCH 19, 2000

THE CHURCH AND ITS LEADERS

March 13 M. 1 Corinthians 4:1-7, Apollos and Paul, Servants of Christ
March 14 T. 1 Corinthians 4:8-13, The Ministry of the Apostles
March 15 W. 1 Corinthians 4:14-21, Paul's Fatherly Love for the Corinthians
March 16 T. 1 Peter 5:1-5, Clothe Yourselves with Humility
March 17 F. 1 Peter 5:6-11, Faithful Leaders Will Encounter Suffering
March 18 S. Romans 14:1-12, Do Not Judge One Another
March 19 S. Romans 15:1-6, Live In Harmony with One Another

Know Your Bible

- Samson was a member of the tribe of Dan whose remarkable birth as a Nazarite unto God, and deliverer of Israel from the Philistines was foretold by an angel of the Lord. (Judges 13:1-5)
- Samson's father (Manoah) and his wife knew that they had been visited by an angel by the words that the angel spoke, and by his ascending in the flame. (Judges 13:18-20)
- Samson's feats or exploits included the fact that he tore a young lion apart as if he were a kid (Judges 14:5,6); Samson killed thirty Philistines in single combat (Judges 14:19), and later slew one thousand (Judges 15:15); Samson carried away the gates of the city of Gaza (Judges 16:3); Samson broke the green withs and new ropes with which he had been bound as if they were mere threads (Judges 16:19); carried away the beam of a weaving machine to which his hair had been secured (Judges 16:14); and pulled down a large building by its two pillars on the heads of the Philistines (Judges 16:29-30)

O Thou who has loved us with an everlasting love, grant that we may embrace our responsibility as a trust from Thee. Amen.

The Need for Discipline in the Church

Adult Topic—*Discipline Brings Unity*

•••••

Youth Topic—*Who Enforces?*

Children's Topic—*Choose Wisely*

•••••

Devotional Reading—James 3:13-18

Background Scripture—1 Corinthians 5—6:11

Print—1 Corinthians 5:1-13

PRINTED SCRIPTURE

1 Corinthians 5:1-13 (KJV)

IT IS reported commonly that there is fornication among you, and such fornication as is not so much as named among the Gentiles, that one should have his father's wife.

2 And ye are puffed up, and have not rather mourned, that he that hath done this deed might be taken away from among you.

3 For I verily, as absent in body, but present in spirit, have judged already, as though I were present, concerning him that hath so done this deed,

4 In the name of our Lord Jesus Christ, when ye are gathered together, and my spirit, with the power of our Lord Jesus Christ,

5 To deliver such an one unto Satan for the destruction of the flesh, that the spirit may be saved in the day of the Lord Jesus.

1 Corinthians 5:1-13 (NRSV)

IT IS actually reported that there is sexual immorality among you, and of a kind that is not found even among pagans; for a man is living with his father's wife.

2 And you are arrogant! Should you not rather have mourned, so that he who has done this would have been removed from among you?

3 For though absent in body, I am present in spirit; and as if present I have already pronounced judgment

4 in the name of the Lord Jesus on the man who has done such a thing. When you are assembled, and my spirit is present with the power of our Lord Jesus,

5 you are to hand this man over to Satan for the destruction of the flesh, so that his spirit may be saved in the day of the Lord.

6 Your glorying is not good. Know ye not that a little leaven leaveneth the whole lump?

7 Purge out therefore the old leaven, that ye may be a new lump, as ye are unleavened. For even Christ our passover is sacrificed for us:

8 Therefore let us keep the feast, not with old leaven, neither with the leaven of malice and wickedness; but with the unleavened bread of sincerity and truth.

9 I wrote unto you in an epistle not to company with fornicators:

10 Yet not altogether with the fornicators of this world, or with the covetous, or extortioners, or with idolaters; for then must ye needs go out of the world.

11 But now I have written unto you not to keep company, if any man that is called a brother be a fornicator, or covetous, or an idolater, or a railer, or a drunkard, or an extortioner; with such an one no not to eat.

12 For what have I to do to judge them also that are without? do not ye judge them that are within?

13 But them that are without God judgeth. Therefore put away from among yourselves that wicked person.

6 Your boasting is not a good thing. Do you not know that a little yeast leavens the whole batch of dough?

7 Clean out the old yeast so that you may be a new batch, as you really are unleavened. For our paschal lamb, Christ, has been sacrificed.

8 Therefore, let us celebrate the festival, not with the old yeast, the yeast of malice an evil, but with the unleavened bread of sincerity and truth.

9 I wrote to you in my letter not to associate with sexually immoral persons—

10 not at all meaning the immoral of this world, or the greedy and robbers, or idolaters, since you would then need to go out of the world.

11 But now I am writing to you not to associate with anyone who bears the name of brother or sister who is sexually immoral or greedy, or is an idolater, reviler, drunkard, or robber. Do not even eat with such a one.

12 For what have I to do with judging those outside? Is it not those who are inside that you are to judge?

13 God will judge those outside. "Drive out the wicked person from among you."

KEY VERSE

Therefore let us keep the feast, not with old leaven, neither with the leaven of malice and wickedness; but with the unleavened bread of sincerity and truth.—1 Corinthians 5:8

OBJECTIVES

After reading this lesson, the student should be better informed about:

1. The danger of permitting known immorality in the church;
2. The need for enforcing church discipline;
3. How church factions create indifference to evil; and,
4. The value of the doctrine of separation.

POINTS TO BE EMPHASIZED
Adult/Youth
Key Verse: 1 Corinthians 5:8

Print: 1 Corinthians 5:1-13

—Paul reprimanded the Corinthians for failing to address a case of sexual immorality. (1-2)

—Paul demanded that the person be put out of the church because a little yeast leavens the whole batch of dough. (3-7)

—The believers needed to get rid of malice and evil and to live in sincerity and truth. (8)

—Paul realized that the believers would associate with sinful persons in the world, but told them not to recognize as brothers or sisters in Christ persons who refused correction of their sin. (9-11)

—Paul instructed the people of Corinth to enforce discipline in the church. (12-13)

Children
Key Verse: 1 Corinthians 6:10

Print: 1 Corinthians 6:12, 19-20; Daniel 1:8, 11, 12-15

—Some things that are lawful are not beneficial. (1 Corinthians 6:12)

—Our bodies are like a temple; God's Holy Spirit lives in us. (19)

—We belong to God; we are to care for our bodies in a way that glorifies God. (19, 20)

—Daniel decided not to eat or drink anything that God would not want him to have. (Daniel 1:8)

—Daniel drank water and ate vegetables. He was healthier than young men who ate rich food and drank wine. (12-15)

(**Note**: Use KJV Scripture for Adults; NRSV Scripture for Youth and Children)

I. Introduction

A. FORNICATION

In the Old Testament, the relationship between Jehovah and Israel is regarded as a marriage bond. When the nation fell into idolatry, it was said to have committed fornication (also adultery and whoremongering). "The usage was more easily understandable because many pagan cults (Astrate, Isis, et al) were connected with sexual debauchery" (Arndt and Gingrich). Used figuratively then, fornication speaks of idolatry, apostasy from God. However, in today's lesson, unlawful sexual immorality is the issue.

The Greek words *porne, pornos, porneia* refer to "every kind of unlawful sexual intercourse" (Arndt and Gingrich), and also may be used of adultery, incest, unchastity, or male and female prostitution. "Converts from among the heathen regarded this vice" leniently, and lightly indulged in it (Thayer). You see the English word *pornography* is derived from the Greek language. The words *fornication* and *fornicators* are used five times (1 Corinthians 5:1, 9, 10, 11), while there is also reference to the one who "has done this deed" (twice), "such an one," and, "that wicked person."

A brief study of the various *porn-rooted* words reveals that fornication is a work of the flesh (Galatians 5:19), is contrary to sound doctrine (1 Timothy 1:10), not once to be named among believers (Ephesians 5:3), for it is God's will that we abstain from it (1 Thessalonians 4:3). Fornication is to be put to death, mortified (Colossians 3:5), for our bodies are not for fornication. We are therefore exhorted to habitually run away from fornication (1 Corinthians 6:13, 18). Marriage is one way to avoid this sin (1 Corinthians 7:2). And finally, we are warned that those who **practice** fornication are excluded from the kingdom of God (1 Corinthians 6:9; Romans 1:29, 32; Galatians 5:19, 21).

B. BIBLICAL BACKGROUND

Just as Satan wasted little time entering the Garden of Eden, so he wasted little time entering the local assembly. However, this time the combination is not one of innocence and the Devil, but of the fallen, adamic nature of man and the Devil. Strife was stirred up from the very beginning of the church age. Thus, it became necessary for many Scriptures to be written, calling for discipline of transgressing church members. In obedience to the Bible then, it is absolutely necessary that church discipline be maintained. Matthew 18:15-17 gives a procedure which has been incorporated in the disciplinary manuals of many denominations and churches. It deals with the proper steps to take to settle personal aggrievances.

Repeatedly, the saints are told to withdraw, separate, ostracize, avoid fellowship with professed believers who are trouble-makers, disobedient, disorderly, holding to false doctrine, heretics, or divisive (Romans 16:17; 1 Corinthians 11:30; 2 Thessalonians 3:6; Titus 3:10). In 1 Thessalonians 5:14, the unruly are warned; while 1 Timothy 5:20 advises public rebuke of those church members who practice sin.

II. Exposition and Application of the Scripture

A. IMMORALITY REPORTED
(1 Corinthians 5:1)

IT is reported commonly that there is fornication among you, and such fornication as is not so much as named among the Gentiles, that one should have his father's wife.

In the last verse of chapter four, Paul mentioned the need for discipline in the church. Now in chapter five, we find a specific case for which some disciplinary action was needed, and the worst of it was that the church had done nothing. It was actually reported through various sources that one man, a professed Christian, was living with his own stepmother. Note the present tense, "a man **has** his father's wife." Use of the present infinitive here suggests some kind of a permanent union, not a spur of the moment thing. The word fornication is used instead of the world adultery, and this word seems to indicate that the father was dead (or possibly divorced). Either way, it was highly immoral. It was considered incest, and evil in God's sight and against Jewish laws, the Roman law, and a thing not commended even among the pagans that a man should have his own stepmother.

B. IMPENITENCE REBUKED
(1 Corinthians 5:2)

And ye are puffed up, and have not rather mourned, that he that hath done this deed might be taken away from among you.

Now the thing that really shocked Paul was that the man who practiced this immorality was permitted to remain in the church. He should have been "taken away from" them. Perhaps "expel" would be a good word to use here. Or excommunicated! But the church failed to remove this immoral man. They failed to mourn the deed he had done. There was no sorrow for the sin committed. Why? Because they were puffed up, or literally, "having been puffed up ones." The perfect tense indicates present results from past actions. They had been so inflated with their own wisdom and self-importance, so concerned with pushing their own parties, exalting their leaders, advancing their little cliques, they were indifferent to immorality right under their nose.

C. INDIFFERENCE REPRIMANDED
(1 Corinthians 5:3-5)

For I verily, as absent in body, but present in spirit, have judged already, as though I were present, concerning him that hath so done this deed, In the name of our Lord Jesus Christ, when ye are gathered together, and my spirit, with the power of our Lord Jesus Christ, To deliver such an one unto Satan for the destruction of the flesh, that the spirit may be saved in the day of the Lord Jesus.

Deeply upset by the church's toleration of the ungodly deed, Paul's mind as to what should be done was made up almost immediately. As far as he was concerned, there were no extenuating circumstances, no reason for hesitation. At the time he wrote this text, he was not in Corinth. But he assured the saints there that he was present in spirit. In verse four, the words rendered "are gathered together" are derived from the word *synagogue*, which means literally, "a gathering together, assembly."

We see that the church itself was to decide the case. The early church, the New Testament church, the apostolic church, had no hierarchical setup as some denominations have today. Thus, Paul could not take the matter out of the hands of the local church. He had made his judgment already as he felt led of the Lord, but the last say was not his. In fact, he reprimanded them for not having done the proper thing in his absence! However, he felt sure the church would concur with his judgment when next it met to take some action.

There are several interpretations given to verse five. Here is the first time we find the name Satan, a name derived from the Hebrew meaning adversary, slanderer, one who speaks against another, opposes another in purpose or act. To deny the existence of Satan is to deny the veracity of the Bible. For in twenty-four different Books of the Bible, and in forty-two different chapters, one hundred ten references to the Devil are made. To deny the existence of Satan is to reject the Word of God! But now one difficulty in interpretation lies in the fact that the word translated *destruction* is used only four times in the New Testament, and means ruin and death.

The flesh is the old, adamic unregenerate, carnal, self-nature of man. According to Trench, it covers the entire domain of our fallen nature; it is the whole region of that in man which is alienated from God and from the life in God. In just such a realm, Satan rules. Thus, Paul's recommendation was that this man be excluded from the fellowship and permitted to reap the consequences of the fleshly life. It is like saying, "Give the flesh enough freedom and it will destroy itself." While the word *flesh* here does not mean the body, the destruction of the flesh may well result in physical sickness and death. The flesh works out its own pay and defeats itself. And the purpose of it all? That the man might repent and be saved in that day when Christ snatches up His Church, and proceeds to evaluate our works (2 Corinthians 5:10).

D. INSTRUCTION RECOMMENDED
(1 Corinthians 5:6-8)

Your glorying is not good. Know ye not that a little leaven leaveneth the whole lump? Purge out therefore the old leaven, that ye may be a new lump, as ye are unleavened. For even Christ our passover is sacrificed for us: Therefore let us keep the feast, not with old leaven, neither with the leaven of malice and wickedness; but with the unleavened bread of sincerity and truth.

Leaven as used in the Bible symbolizes evil. The saying that "a little leaven leavens the whole lump" means that evil spreads surely and rapidly, no matter how small its beginning may be. Another way of putting this: One monkey in a house full of bananas can bring disaster. Martin Luther said: "A small piece of dust in the eye hurts the eye." The pride of the Corinthians had blinded them to this truth.

Note the verbs used by the apostle concerning this man. In verse two, he said that the man should be taken away; in verse three that he had already

judged him; in verse five, the offender was to be delivered unto the Devil. Taken away, judged, delivered—surely Paul was determined that this man be dealt with. Now comes the instruction, "Purge out the old leaven!" This shows that Paul is even more concerned about the spiritual condition of the church as a whole. The Greek word translated "purge" means to clean out or cleanse; it is used only twice in the New Testament: here, and in 2 Timothy 2:21.

Recall that in the Exodus account, the blood sprinkled upon the side posts and door posts was symbolic of the blood of Jesus Christ shed on the Cross of Calvary for our sins. Just as the lamb was slain, so God seeing the blood would pass over and not kill the firstborn, so the blood of Jesus Christ applied to the door posts of our hearts guarantees that the wrath of God in judgment shall pass over all who believe in Him. It is this passing over by the Destroyer, the Angel of Death, which is meant by the word Passover. The Lord ordered Israel to keep the day as a memorial. The Jews do, but have not as a people recognized that it points to Jesus as the Messiah. Exodus twelve goes on to say that the Israelites were to keep a feast (Unleavened Bread).

In Exodus 12:15-20, we see the significance of 1 Corinthians 5:6-8. Upon pain of being cut off, no leaven was to be found in the home or eaten during these seven days. The Israelites were to thoroughly search their homes and throw out every crumb of leaven. The apostle Paul made application of this. Christ is our Passover Lamb slain for our sins whose blood cleanses and delivers from the bondage wages of sin.

All who are cleansed are exhorted to live separated lives, holy and clean. We need therefore to search our lives and throw out all the crumbs. What is true of each individual Christian is true of each local church. Our churches need to be swept clean too! In the light of Christ's sacrifice for our sins, may we celebrate the feast with the unleavened bread of sincerity and truth.

E. ISOLATION REQUIRED
(1 Corinthians 5:9-11)

I wrote unto you in an epistle not to company with fornicators: Yet not altogether with the fornicators of this world, or with the covetous, or extortioners, or with idolaters; for then must ye needs go out of the world. But now I have written unto you not to keep company, if any man that is called a brother be a fornicator, or covetous, or an idolater, or a railer, or a drunkard, or an extortioner; with such an one no not to eat.

Here we deal with the limitation of Christian fellowship, especially with regard to a professed Christian (anyone named brother; identified as a believer) who is not living right. Carnality is a sad possibility for genuine believers. Paul reminded the Corinthians that he had written an earlier letter about this matter, in which he requested that they not continue to get themselves mixed up with fornicators, immoral people. The words "not to keep company with" come from a verb meaning to get oneself mixed up with, mingle, commingle, or associate with. Evidently, the people had misunderstood Paul. Whether through ignorance or purposely, we do not know. But it appears that his previous letter **was** misinterpreted, and some people thought Paul meant literally to have nothing to do with immoral people.

Verse ten makes it clear that he did not mean that they were to have no contact at all with the immoral people of this world. The idea of convents, cloisters and monasteries never entered Paul's mind (John 17:15). Indeed, to escape the presence of immoral, covetous men, people who are drunkards, extortioners and idolaters, it would be necessary to be shot out into space. The points is: We cannot avoid everyday contact with immoral people.

F. INTERNAL RESPONSIBILITY
(1 Corinthians 5:12-13)

For what have I to do to judge them also that are without? do not ye judge them that are within? But them that are without God judgeth. Therefore put away from among yourselves that wicked person.

In the Letters written by the apostle, those "without," on the outside, were the non-Christians, unbelievers in general; those who did not belong to the Christian brotherhood. Believers are ever urged to maintain a wholesome testimony before unbelievers. Because the unsaved watch us, the church should maintain discipline within its own walls. But those outside the church, those who are not Christians—God judges! The jurisdiction of the church does not extend that far. It is not the duty of the church as such to attempt to solve all of the problems, and straighten out all the ills, and correct all the errors of the unsaved. Plainly put: We are to judge those inside the church, not those outside the church. Our solemn responsibility is to keep our own selves unspotted from the world. Yes, judgment must begin at the house of God, and this immoral man should be put out! But if it starts with the church, what shall the end be of them that obey not the Gospel of the Lord Jesus Christ?

III. Special Features

A. PRESERVING OUR HERITAGE

My doctoral thesis was entitled: *A Survey of the Attitudes and Perceptions of Black Baptist Pastors of Philadelphia Regarding the Use of the Courts to Settle Intrachurch Disputes.* Our research discovered far too many Black Baptist churches in Philadelphia had no provision for scheduled review of their constitutions and bylaws. The majority of churches we studied had no reference to Matthew 18:15-17; or reference to 1 Corinthians 6:1-8 with respect to Christians taking Christians to court. The entire matter of church discipline was sadly lacking.

Baptists believe in the autonomy of the local church. Autonomy immediately becomes a reason for the different standards (or lack thereof) of discipline held. Each local church sets up its own rules. We often follow the rule that public sin requires public confession. But usually there are those in the congregation who oppose even this principle. It is too bad that many church members do not see the value of church discipline, and fail to cooperate in setting a standard for the local church that pleases its Head, the Lord Jesus Christ.

Basically, there's nothing wrong with this autonomous approach, for the members of a particular local assembly should know better than anyone else the nature, seriousness, potential harm of the offense, as well as have an intimate knowledge of the offenders. However, when taken to a secular court, it becomes difficult for the local church to legally show its motives were proper (J. A. Quine). Because of the investment we have in our churches, the entire matter of discipline becomes a complicated matter. The topic should create a lively discussion, as you explore discipline prevailing in your church!

B. A CONCLUDING WORD

It is suggested that there are three basic reasons for church discipline as given in the New Testament. Keep in mind that church discipline is not optional. It is God's will that all things in the church be done decently and in order (1 Corinthians 14:40). First is the matter of RESTORATION. Reconciliation is always in order. Sometimes repentance comes quickly and it is not necessary to punish the offender. Forgiveness, love, prayer should be exercised in the attempt to reconcile and restore. Incidentally, it is believed that this particular man repented and was brought back into the church (2 Corinthians 2:6-8). Discipline accomplished its purpose.

Second, discipline is needed to maintain the PURITY OF THE CHURCH. In other words, discipline is for the good of the local assembly (and for the church universal). Inasmuch as a little leaven seeks to leaven the whole lump, it may be necessary to "remove" the offender, to excommunicate him or her. After all efforts have been made to salvage the relationship, the fact remains that flagrant immorality cannot be allowed to remain unpunished in the church. Third, discipline also has as its purpose to DETER, discourage, prevent other church members from sin.

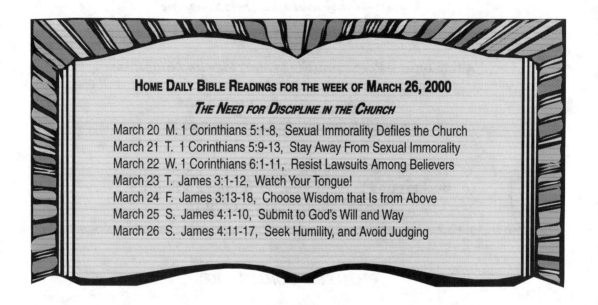

HOME DAILY BIBLE READINGS FOR THE WEEK OF MARCH 26, 2000

THE NEED FOR DISCIPLINE IN THE CHURCH

March 20 M. 1 Corinthians 5:1-8, Sexual Immorality Defiles the Church
March 21 T. 1 Corinthians 5:9-13, Stay Away From Sexual Immorality
March 22 W. 1 Corinthians 6:1-11, Resist Lawsuits Among Believers
March 23 T. James 3:1-12, Watch Your Tongue!
March 24 F. James 3:13-18, Choose Wisdom that Is from Above
March 25 S. James 4:1-10, Submit to God's Will and Way
March 26 S. James 4:11-17, Seek Humility, and Avoid Judging

Know Your Bible

- Eli angered God by only mildly reprimanding his wicked sons when he should have restrained them with the authority of a father. (1 Samuel 2:23, 24; 3:13,14)
- All of the men of Israel were required to appear before the Lord three times per year. (Exodus 23:17)
- The Feast of Passover (held at the end of March or the first of April) was attended by both men and women of Israel (Luke 2:41)
- God honors those who honor Him, but dishonors those who dishonor Him. (1 Samuel 2:30)
- God's presence as symbolized by the ark was conditional upon obedience of the children of Israel to God's instructions. (1 Samuel 14:11)
- Amos prophesied not only against the sins of Israel and Judah, but also against the sins of Syria, Philistia, Tyre, Edom, Ammon and Moab. (Amos 1—3)

Our Father and our God, grant unto us the grace to surrender to spiritual discipline. May Your law reform our lives as Your Spirit directs us toward that higher quality of living that is resident in Your Holy Word. Amen.

Counsel Concerning Marriage

Unit II—*Unity in Human relationships*

Children's Unit—*Getting Along With Others*

•••••

Adult Topic—*Responsibility in Marriage and Singleness*

•••••

Youth Topic—*Sex and Marriage*

Children's Topic—*Living in My Family*

•••••

Devotional Reading—1 Corinthians 7:25-35

Background Scripture—1 Corinthians 6:12—7:16

Print—1 Corinthians 7:1-5, 8-16

PRINTED SCRIPTURE

1 Corinthians 7:1-5, 8-16 (KJV)

NOW CONCERNING the things whereof ye wrote unto me: It is good for a man not to touch a woman.

2 Nevertheless, to avoid fornication, let every man have his own wife, and let every woman have her own husband.

3 Let the husband render unto the wife due benevolence: and likewise also the wife unto the husband.

4 The wife hath not power of her own body, but the husband: and likewise also the husband hath not power of his own body, but the wife.

5 Defraud ye not one the other, except it be with consent for a time, that ye may give yourselves to fasting and prayer; and come together again, that Satan tempt you not for your incontinency.

1 Corinthians 7:1-5, 8-16 (NRSV)

NOW CONCERNING the matters about which you wrote: "It is well for a man not to touch a woman."

2 But because of cases of sexual immorality, each man should have his own wife and each woman her own husband.

3 The husband should give to his wife her conjugal rights, and likewise the wife to her husband.

4 For the wife does not have authority over her own body, but the husband does; likewise the husband does not have authority over his own body, but the wife does.

5 Do not deprive one another except perhaps by agreement for a set time, to devote yourselves to prayer, and then come together again, so that Satan may not tempt you because of your lack of self-control.

8 I say therefore to the unmarried and widows, It is good for them if they abide even as I.

9 But if they cannot contain, let them marry: for it is better to marry than to burn.

10 And unto the married I command, yet not I, but the Lord, Let not the wife depart from her husband:

11 But and if she depart, let her remain unmarried, or be reconciled to her husband: and let not the husband put away his wife.

12 But to the rest speak I, not the Lord: If any brother hath a wife that believeth not, and she be pleased to dwell with him, let him not put her away.

13 And the woman which hath an husband that believeth not, and if he be pleased to dwell with her, let her not leave him.

14 For the unbelieving husband is sanctified by the wife, and the unbelieving wife is sanctified by the husband: else were your children unclean; but now are they holy.

15 But if the unbelieving depart, let him depart. A brother or a sister is not under bondage in such cases: but God hath called us to peace.

16 For what knowest thou, O wife, whether thou shalt save thy husband? or how knowest thou, O man, whether thou shalt save thy wife?

8 To the unmarried and the widows I say that it is well for them to remain unmarried as I am.

9 But if they are not practicing self-control, they should marry. For it is better to marry than to be aflame with passion.

10 To the married I give this command—not I but the Lord—that the wife should not separate from her husband

11 (but if she does separate, let her remain unmarried or else be reconciled to her husband), and that the husband should not divorce his wife.

12 To the rest I say—I and not the Lord—that if any believer has a wife who is an unbeliever, and she consents to live with him, he should not divorce her.

13 And if any woman has a husband who is an unbeliever, and he consents to live with her, she should not divorce him.

14 For the unbelieving husband is made holy through his wife, and the unbelieving wife is made holy through her husband. Otherwise, your children would be unclean, but as it is, they are holy.

15 But if the unbelieving partner separates, let it be so; in such a case the brother or sister is not bound. It is to peace that God has called you.

16 Wife, for all you know, you might save your husband. Husband, for all you know, you might save your wife.

KEY VERSE

*What? Know ye not that your body is the temple of the Holy Ghost which is in you, which ye have of God, and ye are not your own?—**1 Corinthians 6:19***

OBJECTIVES

After reading the lesson, the student should be aware that:

1. God instituted marriage;
2. There are divine regulations for married believers;
3. There are divine regulations for unmarried believers; and,
4. Sanctification is a part of the marriage relationship.

POINTS TO BE EMPHASIZED

Adult/Youth
Key Verse: 1 Corinthians 6:19
Print: 1 Corinthians 7:1-5, 8-16

—Outside marriage, a man and woman should not be sexually intimate. (1-2)

—Husbands and wives do not have authority over their own bodies, but are responsible for the intimate happiness of each other. (3-4)

—Husbands and wives are not to deprive one another of sexual intimacy, other than for spiritual reasons; and this should be for a limited time with the consent of both partners. (5)

—Paul advocated that unmarried persons and widows remain single if they can practice celibacy; otherwise they should marry. (8-9)

—As believers, Paul asserted that neither the husband or the wife should initiate separation or divorce; but should divorce occur, they should remain unmarried or be reconciled to each other. (10-11)

—In the case of marriage to an unbeliever, divorce is discouraged because the union may result in salvation for the unbeliever. (12-16)

Children
Key Verse: March 9:50

Print: Genesis 2:7, 18, 21-24; 4:1-2

—God formed man of dust from the ground and breathed into his nostrils the breath of life and man became a living being. (Genesis 2:7)

—God made a helper for man. (18, 21-23)

—God instituted marriage by proclaiming that a man should leave his father and mother and take a wife so that they might become one. (24)

—Adam and Eve had two sons, Cain and Abel. (1-2)

—Cain became jealous of Abel. (3-4)

(**Note**: Use KJV Scripture for Adults; NRSV Scripture for Youth and Children)

I. Introduction

A. THINGS THAT SATAN DOES

In 1 Corinthians 7:5, we learn that Satan is able to tempt married couples. This certainly is not all that he does or has done. He tempted Eve, inspired Cain, afflicted Job, provoked David, slandered Israel, disputed over the body of Moses, test our Lord, filled the hearts of Ananias and Sapphira to lie to God. Presently, he blinds the minds of unbelievers, deceives the nations, hinders God's servants, provides thorns in the flesh, works signs and lying wonders, seeks to devour, strikes fear of death in the hearts of men, binds with the spirit of infirmity, buffets, possesses, masquerades as an angel of light, and governs as the prince of this world-system, the god of this world-age. Today's lesson adds that he tempts married couples for their incontinence.

Literally, incontinence means the inability to contain, unable to hold together. The majority of Bible versions translates the Greek word (*akrasia*) lack of self-control. It means lack of sexual restraint. Matthew 23:25 translates the same word "excess" (KJV), "rapacity" (RSV), but it is better rendered, self-indulgence. Failure to come together again moves Satan to tempt married couples to find release outside of their marriage bonds, and to commit adultery.

B. BIBLICAL BACKGROUND

Corinth is called "the city of vice par excellence in the Roman world" (ISBE). The fact that there existed a verb to corinthianize, which means to play the part of a prostitute, to lead a debased life, well indicates the spiritual nature and condition of this metropolis. "It was notorious also for luxury and moral corruption, particularly the foul worship of Venus" (Thayer), the Roman goddess of beauty and sensual love. The city's lewd reputation was well-earned. "Because of the depraved religion of the people, it soon became the center also for the grossest forms of immorality" (MacDonald). Paul had to deal with sexual relationships; the immorality of the city called for it. It is no surprise then that the apostle, led by the Holy Spirit, spoke about such matters as fornication, the single life, adultery, homosexuality, harlotry, virginity and marriage (1 Corinthians 5:1, 9-11; 6:9, 13, 15-16, 18; 7:1-16, 25-40).

II. Exposition and Application of the Scripture

A. ONE WAY TO AVOID FORNICATION
(1 Corinthians 7:1-2)

NOW concerning the things whereof ye wrote unto me: It is good for a man not to touch a woman. Nevertheless, to avoid fornication, let every man have his own wife, and let every woman have her own husband.

The saints at Corinth had written Paul asking many questions. Naturally, the Gospel of Jesus Christ coming into a pagan society stirred up many things. New problems were created as old customs were torn down. Christianity has a way of lifting up moral standards, and there is always resistance to such edification. Now, one of the problems at Corinth concerned celibacy, the unmarried or single life—the state of not having a spouse, the abstention from sexual relationships. Celibacy's root idea is "to live alone." Evidently, one question was: is it a sin to remain unmarried? Paul answered, "No!" There is nothing wrong with celibacy. As the Amplified Bible puts it: "It is well, and by that I mean advantageous, expedient, profitable and wholesome, for a man not to touch a woman (to cohabit with her), but to remain unmarried."

Note that the word translated "good" means pleasing to God, morally good. The phrase "to touch a woman" is of course a biblical euphemism, a mild expression substituted for one which might offend (Genesis 20:6; Proverbs 6:29). It is not a sin to remain unmarried; celibacy is honorable, and has its advantages. Paul did not say it is **better** for a man not to touch a woman. In error some men have taught that the unmarried state is superior to the married state. Old Testament priests were not forbidden to marry. Jeremiah was told not to take a wife (Jeremiah 16:2); but Isaiah, Hosea and Simon Peter were married (Matthew 8:14-15; Mark 1:30). Paul also stated that those who taught compulsory celibacy were in league with the Devil (1 Timothy 4:3).

In the KJV, the words "to avoid" are italicized, indicating they were put there by the translators. While it was Paul's desire that the saints at Corinth avoid fornication, this is not the proper translation. Literally verse two states: "Because of immoralities everyone must have a wife for himself, and every one must have her own husband." The plural, immoralities, suggests the various ways of expressing immorality, and the many instances then current in Corinth. Understand that the words "have his own wife" and "have her own husband" are commands. Single Christians are told that if in their unmarried state they are tempted to satisfy their bodily desires by practicing immoralities, then it would be better for each saint to get married and have his or her own spouse. Stating that in the midst of so much immorality, marriage might act as an antidote by no means disparages marriage. Rather, it is a valuable piece of practical advice.

B. RULES FOR MARRIED COUPLES (1 Corinthians 7:3-5)

Let the husband render unto the wife due benevolence: and likewise also the wife unto the husband. The wife hath not power of her own body, but the husband: and likewise also the husband hath not power of his own body, but the wife. Defraud ye not one the other, except it be with consent for a time, that ye may give yourselves to fasting and prayer; and come together again, that Satan tempt you not for your incontinency.

The Bible teaches that when a man and woman marry, the two become one. This oneness is initially a physical unity, but as time passes, oneness of disposition, personality, and mind increases. It becomes more apparent that each belongs to the other; the husband to his wife, the wife to her husband. Each marriage partner has power (authority) over the other. This refers to conjugal rights or marital rights and duties. Conjugal means the sexual rights or privileges implied by and involved in the marriage relationship. The power or rule refers to the exclusive authority and control of the body. This is a mutual thing, and because it is, one marriage partner should do nothing with his or her body without an understanding with the other partner.

For example: the husband should not defraud the wife, nor the wife defraud the husband. Defraud here means to rob or steal; as used by Paul it means that one mate should not deprive the other of marital rights. This too is a command, a present tense imperative, indicating there were Christian husbands and wives who for ill-advised reasons deprived each other of marital rights. The tense of the Greek verb commands the Corinthian saints to stop doing something they were at the time doing. This means Paul says: "Stop it! No longer continue to live apart. Do not continue to defraud and deprive one another."

Furthermore, husband and wife are not to live separately except with consent (*sumphonos*). This means harmonious, accordant, agreeing; we have derived from it the word, symphony, to sound together, be in accord, match, fit in with or together. For husband and wife to live apart should not be the selfish decision of one partner; rather it is to be a mutual agreement. Furthermore, the separation is to be for a time, that is, temporary. In addition, this separation must have a purpose! Two things mentioned by Paul are prayer and fasting. However, the word "fasting" is not found in the better manuscripts. Prayer is to be the object, the goal for the temporary and agreed-upon physical separation.

The phrase "may give yourselves to" comes from a verb (*scholazo*) which means to have time or leisure, to devote oneself to something. We have derived the word "school" from this verb. A school is a place where teachers and students meet in order to devote themselves to something. In summary we learn: Marriage partners are to be mindful of each other's needs; there is to be no physical separation between husband and wife unless it is agreed upon, is temporary, and is for special prayer. When this has been accomplished, the couple is to come together again.

Failure to obey the rules given here leaves the door wide open to immorality. The Corinthians were warned that any physical separation between husband and wife contrary to God's will can lead to a weakened lack of restraint of sexual desire, and the Devil will take advantage of this lack of self-control. Satan will strive to get either one or both of the marriage partners to fulfill their desires in an unlawful manner. This leads to adultery and allows the Devil to triumph over the believer. This should not be, for victory belongs to us through Jesus Christ.

C. ADVICE TO THE UNMARRIED
(1 Corinthians 7:8-9)

I say therefore to the unmarried and widows, It is good for them if they abide even as I. But if they cannot contain, let them marry: for it is better to marry than to burn.

Once again using himself as an example (as he did in verse 7), Paul addressed his advice to the unmarried and widows. The word translated unmarried is *agamos*, and while used four times in this chapter, is not found elsewhere in the New Testament. Considering the words, "It is good for them if they abide even as I," we understand

that Paul's language by no means indicates that he had never been married. Conybeare and Howson state: "it is probable that his wife and children did not long survive, for otherwise some notice of them would have occurred...some allusion to them (would have been made) in the Epistles. And we know that if ever he had a wife, she was not living when he wrote his first letter to the Corinthians" (*Life and Epistles of Saint Paul*, p. 72). Dr. A. T. Robertson states that Acts 26:10 teaches, Paul was a member of the Sanhedrin. "If he had to be married, as was the custom (for membership in that august body), we have no evidence to the contrary" (*Epochs in the Life of Paul*, p. 33). I would add that Paul's insights in general with respect to husbands, wives, and the marriage and family relationships lend weight to the belief that the apostle spoke from experience.

He suggested that if they cannot "contain" themselves—that is, exercise self-control, self-discipline, temperance—in sexual matters, they should get married at once! (This is the force of the command used). Why? Because marriage is preferable to being **burned up**! He did not refer to hell. It is figurative language for being inflamed with passion, burning with sexual desire, inflamed with lust, "tortured by unsatisfied (ungratified) desire" (JBP, Amplified).

D. ADVICE TO THE MARRIED
(1 Corinthians 7:10-13)

And unto the married I command, yet not I, but the Lord, let not the wife depart from her husband; But and if she depart, let her remain unmarried, or be reconciled to her

husband: and let not the husband put away his wife. But to the rest speak I, not the Lord: If any brother hath a wife that believeth not, and she be pleased to dwell with him, let him not put her away. And the woman which hath an husband that believeth not, and if he be pleased to dwell with her, let her not leave him.

Now it must be made clear that the Bible teaches No Divorce! This is plainly taught in verses 10-11. For the Christian, divorce is not an option that pleases the Lord, the very One who instituted marriage (Genesis 2:22-24). Biblical Christianity does not encourage the dissolution of the marriage relationship. To teach otherwise is to misinterpret the Scriptures. Study now the following statements in 1 Corinthians 7:10, 12: "I command, yet not I, but the Lord...But to the rest speak I, not the Lord." Combine these with verses 6, 25, 41: "I speak this by permission, and not by commandment... I have no commandment of the Lord; yet I give my judgment... After my judgment." The key to understanding these verses is the fact that the Lord Jesus Christ gave special teaching on the matters of marriage, celibacy, separation and divorce.

Concessions granted by Moses because of the hardness of the hearts of the Israelites were rescinded by Christ. God's standard as announced in the Old Testament and set up at creation was restored by our Lord. Thus, only in what Christ taught is found authoritative revelation about marriage and divorce. So Paul referred to our Lord's commandment. However, some of the issues he faced at Corinth were not specifically addressed by our Lord, so Paul, as an apostle of Jesus Christ, expressed his own judgment. He used that authoritative revelation Christ taught. Where there was nothing else he could apply to the peculiar problems at Corinth, he expressed what he was led as an apostle to teach.

The problem occurred when a husband was saved and the wife was not; or a wife was saved and the husband remained unsaved. To answer this matter, Paul did not step outside of the Holy Spirit and speak of his own will. He simply stated that the Lord Jesus had left no special instructions, no direct command on this subject, that there is nothing recorded in the Gospels about the problem of "mixed marriages." Our Lord's earthly ministry was directed primarily to the spiritually enlightened Jew, who by that time knew better than to marry pagans. Thus, the problem Paul faced was practically new. His advice was for every man to abide in the same calling wherein he was called. In other words, if married before conversion, do not seek a divorce now because a mate is still an unbeliever.

Finally, note the words "be pleased to dwell with." They are important here. The Greek verb means to approve, agree to, consent to. So if the unbelieving partner consents to remain living with the Christian, then the Christian should not leave. The Christian is not to break up the marriage simply because his or her mate is an unbeliever. Incidentally, the present tense commands not to "put away" or "leave" in verses 12 and 13 indicate there were saints who had gotten rid of their unbelieving spouses. The command then is to no longer continue this; they were to stop doing what they were doing already!

E. UNEQUALLY YOKED RELATIONSHIPS

(1 Corinthians 7:14-16)

For the unbelieving husband is sanctified by the wife, and the unbelieving wife is sanctified by the husband: else were your children unclean; but now are they holy. But if the unbelieving depart, let him depart. A brother or a sister is not under bondage in such cases: but God hath called us to peace. For what knowest thou, O wife, whether thou shalt save thy husband? or how knowest thou, O man, whether thou shalt save thy wife?

Basically, sanctified means to separate, set apart. We learn that the unbeliever married to a Christian is influenced to some degree by the sanctity (consecration; set apartness) of the Christian. The sacredness of the Christian is in some measure extended to the unbeliever. The child's sin nature (uncleanness) is not removed, but the child is **set apart** because of the believing parent. Just as there is a sanctifying influence over the non-believing mate, so there is over the children. Thus, the Christian parent can be a great blessing in the life of the child.

But now, suppose the unbeliever, mad with God, the world, and his mate, desires to leave—what then? Paul states: "Let him leave!" The believer remains, for he or she is not obligated or slavishly compelled to seek to maintain the marriage relation. By no means does this suggest grounds for the Christian seeking a divorce. If the unbeliever's mind is made up to leave, no good cause is served by the believer trying to make him or her stay. For God has called us to peace, not that which results in sorrow, strife, conflict, contention, struggle. Do not misinterpret the words "not under bondage" to mean free to get a divorce and remarry. The phrase means the believer is not bound as a slave to attempt to keep the unbeliever from leaving. You have no assurance, no guarantee, no certainty whatsoever that your attempts will save the unbelieving spouse.

III. Special Features

A. PRESERVING OUR HERITAGE

Often this study on marriage brings up the matter of "mixed marriages." We immediately think of racial intermarriage; the lesson does not speak of this. In fact, the Bible has nothing to say about racial intermarriage. Unfortunately, there are Christians who sincerely believe and religiously believe that racial segregation is ordained of God, and who are strongly opposed to interracial marriage. But the Scriptures they usually cite for support are passages which forbade the Jews to marry heathen. The prohibitions were religious, not racial. Christians are likewise warned not to be "mismated with unbelievers" (RSV), or "unequally yoked together" with them. But those at Corinth who became Christians while already wed to unbelievers were advised to remain in the place of calling.

B. A CONCLUDING WORD

We learn that one thing which caused trouble at Corinth was the fact there were saints who thought becoming a Christian meant the immediate end of certain relationships. Paul was led by the Holy Spirit to inform the saints that the New Birth did not bring an end to the status quo. We are reminded that there is no greater human relationship than that of marriage, for in it we see a picture of our relationship with the Lord Jesus Christ. The church is His Bride; we are married to Him. He loved the church, and gave Himself for it (Ephesians 5:25).

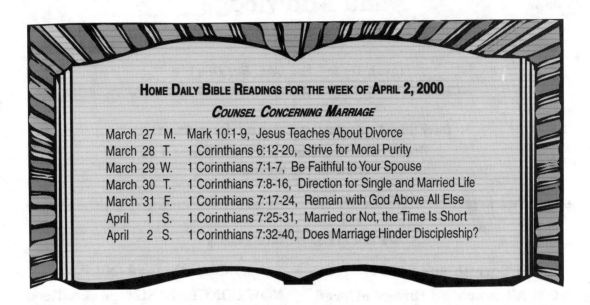

HOME DAILY BIBLE READINGS FOR THE WEEK OF APRIL 2, 2000

COUNSEL CONCERNING MARRIAGE

March 27	M.	Mark 10:1-9, Jesus Teaches About Divorce
March 28	T.	1 Corinthians 6:12-20, Strive for Moral Purity
March 29	W.	1 Corinthians 7:1-7, Be Faithful to Your Spouse
March 30	T.	1 Corinthians 7:8-16, Direction for Single and Married Life
March 31	F.	1 Corinthians 7:17-24, Remain with God Above All Else
April 1	S.	1 Corinthians 7:25-31, Married or Not, the Time Is Short
April 2	S.	1 Corinthians 7:32-40, Does Marriage Hinder Discipleship?

Know Your Bible

- Beth-shemesh was guilty of looking into the ark (1 Samuel 6:19), which was an expressed violation of the command of God that caused the death fifty thousand and seventy men. (Numbers 4:20)
- Saul, the first king of Israel, was very tall and very handsome. (1 Samuel 9:2)
- The children of Israel desired to have a king because Samuel was old, and his sons were unfit to help him or to succeed him as leader of Israel. (1 Samuel 8:5,20)
- God's test of obedience to Saul was that in fighting with the Amalekites Saul should destroy all their sheep and oxen (1 Samuel 15:3), but Saul saved the life of the best sheep and oxen. (1 Samuel 15:9)
- King Ahaz re-introduced the worship of Baal and the gods of Syria. (2 Chronicles 28:2, 23-35)

O Thou Who has created us to live in relationship, may our encounter with each other become the reflection of Your design as we strive for unity of plan and purpose within the context of Your transcending love. In the name of Jesus Christ, we pray. Amen.

Concerning Love and Knowledge

Adult Topic—*Let Love Lead*

. . . . .

Youth Topic—*You Can, But Don't!*

Children's Topic—*Accepting Differences in Others*

. . . . .

Devotional Reading—1 Corinthians 10:23—11:1

Background Scripture—1 Corinthians 8

Print—1 Corinthians 8

PRINTED SCRIPTURE

1 Corinthians 8 (KJV)

NOW AS touching things offered unto idols, we know that we all have knowledge. Knowledge puffeth up, but charity edifieth.

2 And if any man think that he knoweth any thing, he knoweth nothing yet as he ought to know.

3 But if any man love God, the same is known of him.

4 As concerning therefore the eating of those things that are offered in sacrifice unto idols, we know that an idol is nothing in the world, and that there is none other God but one.

5 For though there be that are called gods, whether in heaven or in earth, (as there be gods many, and lords many,)

6 But to us there is but one God, the Father, of whom are all things, and we in him; and one Lord Jesus Christ, by whom are all things, and we by him.

1 Corinthians 8 (NRSV)

NOW CONCERNING food sacrificed to idols: we know that "all of us possess knowledge." Knowledge puffs up, but love builds up.

2 Anyone who claims to know something does not yet have the necessary knowledge;

3 but anyone who loves God is known by him.

4 Hence, as to the eating of food offered to idols, we know that "no idol in the world really exists," and that "there is no God but one."

5 Indeed, even though there may be so-called gods in heaven or on earth—as in fact there are many gods and many lords—

6 yet for us there is one God, the Father, from whom are all things and for whom we exist, and one Lord, Jesus Christ, through whom are all things and through whom we exist.

7 It is not everyone, however,

7 Howbeit there is not in every man that knowledge: for some with conscience of the idol unto this hour eat it as a thing offered unto an idol; and their conscience being weak is defiled.

8 But meat commendeth us not to God: for neither, if we eat, are we the better; neither, if we eat not, are we the worse.

9 But take heed lest by any means this liberty of yours become a stumbling block to them that are weak.

10 For if any man see thee which hast knowledge sit at meat in the idol's temple, shall not the conscience of him which is weak be emboldened to eat those things which are offered to idols;

11 And through thy knowledge shall the weak brother perish, for whom Christ died?

12 But when ye sin so against the brethren, and wound their weak conscience, ye sin against Christ.

13 Wherefore, if meat make my brother to offend, I will eat no flesh while the world standeth, lest I make my brother to offend.

who has this knowledge. Since some have become so accustomed to idols until now, they still think of the food they eat as food offered to an idol; and their conscience, being weak, is defiled.

8 "Food will not bring us close to God." We are no worse off if we do not eat, and no better off if we do.

9 But take care that this liberty of yours does not somehow become a stumbling block to the weak.

10 For if others see you, who possess knowledge, eating in the temple of an idol, might they not, since their conscience is weak, be encouraged to the point of eating food sacrificed to idols?

11 So by your knowledge those weak believers for whom Christ died are destroyed.

12 But when you thus sin against members of your family, and wound their conscience when it is weak, you sin against Christ.

13 Therefore, if food is a cause of their falling, I will never eat meat, so that I may not cause one of them to fall.

If any man think he knoweth any thing, he knoweth nothing yet as he ought to know. But if any man love God, the same is known of him.
—1 Corinthians 8:2-3

OBJECTIVES

After reading this lesson, the student should have knowledge of:

1. The unreality of idols, the reality of the true God;
2. The meaning and work of the conscience;
3. The limitations of Christian liberty; and,
4. The Love that considers what others believe.

POINTS TO BE EMPHASIZED
Adult/Youth
Key Verse: 1 Corinthians 8:2-3
Print: 1 Corinthians 8

—When the church in Corinth raised the issue of Christians eating food sacrificed to idols, Paul stated that pride in intellectual superiority creates an arrogant sense of self-esteem while love creates a concern for others. (1-2)

—Faithful followers know that idols are unreal because there is only one God and one Lord Jesus Christ through whom all things exist. (4-6)

—Some seekers have serious concerns about the consequences of eating food that has been offered to idols. (7)

—Paul stated that the believers' liberty should not become a stumbling block to a weaker brother or sister. (9-11)

—Although eating meat offered to idols is not a sin, destroying the faith of a weak follower is; therefore, Paul's decision is not to eat such meat out of concern for the weaker brothers and sisters. (12-13)

Children
Key Verse: Romans 13:9
Print: 1 Corinthians 8:1; Luke 10:25-37

—Paul states that love builds understanding and good relationships. (1 Corinthians 8:1)

—Jesus responded to the lawyer's question by saying love God and love your neighbor as yourself. (Luke 10:26-27)

—Jesus told the story of the good Samaritan in response to the lawyer's question as to who is one's neighbor. (29-30)

—The lawyer understood that the man who had cared for the beaten man was the neighbor. (36-37)

(**Note**: Use KJV Scripture for Adults; NRSV Scripture for Youth and Children)

TOPICAL OUTLINE OF THE LESSON

I. Introduction
   A. Some Facts About Conscience
   B. Biblical Background

II. Exposition and Application of the Scripture
   A. Knowledge Puffs Up, Love Builds Up (1 Corinthians 8:1-3)
   B. Knowledge and Idolatry (1 Corinthians 8:4-6)
   C. Knowledge and Conscience (1 Corinthians 8:7-10)
   D. Knowledge and Love (1 Corinthians 8:11-13)

III. Special Features
   A. Preserving Our Heritage
   B. A Concluding Word

I. Introduction

A. SOME FACTS ABOUT THE CONSCIENCE

Literally, the word "conscience" means "with knowledge." It is "the awareness of a moral or ethical aspect to one's conduct together with the urge to prefer right over wrong" (*American Heritage Dictionary*). Our possession of a conscience is the result of the fall of Adam; consequently, all men universally have a conscience. The Bible describes the conscience in a number of ways: (1) **Good**: the faculty of judgment is clear and gives a good verdict (Acts 23:1); (2) **Pure**: sincere, free from every admixture of what is false (2 Timothy 1:3); (3) **Inoffensive**: so far as one's outward life of word and action is concerned, he or she has a desire to preserve a conscience clear of giving offense to anyone (Acts 24:16). (4) **Purged**: cleansed by the blood of Jesus Christ of sinful works and meaningless ceremony done without love as a motive (Hebrews 9:14); (5) **Seared**: the English word "cauterized" is derived from the Greek word use here. The idea of a burned out conscience may be what is meant by some people when they say a man "has no conscience." Such a person is capable of committing any degree of wickedness (1 Timothy 4:2). (6) **Evil**: "a mind conscious of wrong-doing" (Thayer: Hebrews 10:22). The following are taken from today's lesson, 1 Corinthians 8:7. (7) **Weak**: not fully enlightened, inadequately informed by knowledge; "not strong enough to distinguish clearly between things lawful for a Christian and things unlawful" (Thayer). It "cannot come to a decision" (Arndt and Gingrich). (8) **Defiled**: reproached by sin. Here the weak conscience becomes contaminated, soiled. Finally, from Romans 2:15, we learn that the conscience: (a) bears witness (b) has thoughts (c) accuses (d) and excuses.

B. BIBLICAL BACKGROUND

The Corinthian society offered meat sacrifices their gods. When the Gospel was preached there, some of these pagans were converted and saved from their idolatry. They had been accustomed to dedicating meat to their idol gods. A very small part of the meat was burned at the altar during the ritual. A small part of it was eaten by the priest at a solemn meal in the temple of the god or goddess. Perhaps the biggest portion of the meat was sold in the market place for money. In this way such meat would eventually find its way back to the supper table in some home. Now suppose you were a Christian and at mealtime discovered that meat placed before you had been offered to an idol? What would you do? This was the problem. Should a believer eat such meat? Some did ("strong"), and some did not ("weak"). Here was a new problem created in a pagan society by the advent, acceptance, and establishment of Christianity.

II. Exposition and Application of the Scripture

A. KNOWLEDGE PUFFS UP, LOVE BUILDS UP (1 Corinthians 8:1-3)

NOW as touching things offered unto idols, we know that we all have knowledge. Knowledge puffeth up, but charity edifieth. And if any man

think that he knoweth any thing, he knoweth nothing yet as he ought to know. But if any man love God, the same is known of him.

Knowledge alone puffs up; it may cause one to become conceited and put on airs. Knowledge alone may lead to an air of condescension, the spirit of argument, and the feeling of superiority. Puffedupness incapacitates; it blurs vision, distorts values, twists judgment and makes true discernment impossible. This is why God is not able to use a proud, haughty, know-it-all man. God resists the proud, but gives grace to the humble. On the other hand, without love, our knowledge is vain. Love builds up or edifies. The word "edify" (*oikodomeo*) means to build a house; it is to benefit, establish or strengthen.

Love combined with knowledge imparts something better than what knowledge alone can give. Love is not puffed up and does not puff up, but builds up constructively and permanently. Love moves us with concern and makes us think of the other person. It causes a desire to impart knowledge; this is the responsibility of knowledge. Without love, this responsibility becomes drudgery and no pleasure is found in it. The more we learn of God's Word, the more we are held responsible to practice what that Word teaches. Here then is the challenge! We are to translate our Bible study and Bible knowledge into the language of love.

As a whole, the Corinthians were proud people, especially proud of their knowledge and wisdom. They certainly would not have accepted the definition of knowledge as the "passing from a state of unconscious ignorance to a state of conscious ignorance" (Chafer). But belief in Christ had not eradicated their pride or their false concept of wisdom. The "we know-it -all" attitude often leads to sin; at Corinth, it led to strife in the church. A man might think that he has arrived, but he is ignorant of the one thing he really needs to know. And what is that? He ought to know that he is ignorant. If we become acquainted with God by love, we may rest assured that we are the special objects of His knowledge. He knows the way of the righteous (Psalm 1:6).

B. KNOWLEDGE AND IDOLATRY
(1 Corinthians 8:4-6)

As concerning therefore the eating of those things that are offered in sacrifice unto idols, we know that an idol is nothing in the world, and that there is none other God but one. For though there be that are called gods, whether in heaven or in earth, (as there be gods many, and lords many,) But to us there is but one God, the Father, of whom are all things, and we in him; and one Lord Jesus Christ, by whom are all things, and we by him.

We have seen how "knowledge breeds conceit, while love builds up character" (20th Century). This was Paul's way of saying the attitude of love would best solve the problems at Corinth. He agreed with the "strong" Christians that there was no need for getting so upset about eating meat offered to idols. Two reasons are then proffered why the more spiritual saints were not upset. First of all, an idol is nothing in the world. Certainly idols exist, but the deities they are said to represent have no corresponding reality or power. The only real person and power behind all idolatry is Satan. Throughout the Bible, we are taught that the gods and idols of the nations are vain things, lying vanities. The second reason given for the "nothingness" of idols is that there is no God but one. Polytheism or the belief in many gods is condemned throughout the Scriptures. **Biblical Christianity holds a very narrow view of all so-called world religions.** Read Ephesians 2:12; 1 Corinthians 10:20; 1 Timothy 2:5. Salvation comes by the grace of God only through faith in the shed blood of the Lord Jesus Christ.

C. KNOWLEDGE AND CONSCIENCE
(1 Corinthians 8:7-10)

Howbeit there is not in every man that knowledge: for some with conscience of the idol unto this hour eat it as a thing offered unto an idol; and their conscience being weak is defiled. But meat commendeth us not to God: for neither, if we eat, are we the better; neither, if we eat not, are we the worse. But take heed lest by any means this liberty of yours become a stumbling block to them that are weak. For if any man see thee which hast knowledge sit at meat in the idol's temple, shall not the conscience of him which is weak be emboldened to eat those things which are offered to idols.

The fact that idols are absolutely nothing in this world does not give the "strong" Christian license to do as he pleases with the consciences and feelings of other Christians! Yes, idols are absurd, and there can be no real meaning to the sacrifice of food to them. However, all of the saints at Corinth did not feel this way. These of course were primarily the Gentile believers. Some of them had been so steeped in idolatry that they could not fully dismiss from their minds the fact that the meat had been associated with an idol. Some of them may have felt that to eat such meat was to pay homage to the idol god. And having been snatched out of paganism and idolatry, they wanted absolutely nothing more to do with it.

Still others may have felt that these evil deities were present to accept the eating of the meat as an act of worship. The taint of the idol would still cling to their minds, making them extremely sensitive about the association of the meat and the idol. Certain attitudes, superstitions and feelings remained. Thus, while some saints were scrupulous about the eating of such meat, they were not adequately informed by knowledge. And those who knew the truth about the idols were not adequately motivated by love. This in essence was the problem.

The Greek word rendered "commendeth" here has a variety of translations: give, provide, prove, present, assist, stand by, yield, show, stand with, and put at one's disposal. As a technical legal term, it means "to bring before or stand before" a judge. If we apply this forensic meaning we would get: "Food will not bring us before the judgment seat of God" (Arndt and Gingrich). Perhaps this is the idea in J. B. Phillip's translation: "Now our acceptance by God is not a matter of meat." A still better idea is to have the verb mean being drawn closer to God. Moffatt said, "Now mere food will not bring us any nearer to God...." The 20th century Bible translated: "What we eat, however, will not bring us any nearer to God...." We believe this idea of drawing close or near to God is the best interpretation.

Here then is another phase of Paul's answer to the problem of eating food offered to idols. It in no way affects the Christian's status or relationship with God. Whether we eat or refrain from eating, there is no advantage or disadvantage, no loss or gain (Moffatt), and we are no better or worse (RSV). In short, there is no moral issue involved at all so far as eating such meat is concerned. What we need to keep in mind, however, is the effect upon others which such freedom of action may have.

The word translated "liberty" means "authority." At first this Greek word meant the power of choice or freedom to do as you desire. Then the idea of "right" and "power" developed. The saints who were "in the know"—the "strong" Christians—had the right, authority, or freedom to eat whatever they pleased. "But be careful," said Paul, "lest this liberty somehow becomes a hindrance to the weak or causes the weak Christian to stumble." Remember by "weak" is meant those who have scruples about eating meat that had been offered to idols. Sometimes people go out of their way to impress others with their sophistication and knowledge. Undoubtedly, these "strong" saints at Corinth were prepared to make a show of the fact that they were emancipated from any and all religious dietary restrictions. They were determined to let everybody know that they were an enlightened breed, and could eat as they pleased.

Paul was led by the Spirit to teach them another lesson. **There are times when Christians must accommodate themselves to the prejudices and weakness of other Christians.** Love motivated us to do this; without love in our hearts for others, it cannot be done. We must weigh our behavior in the light of its affect upon other. Never create opportunities for others to make a misstep. Let no man put a stumbling block or an occasion to fall in another believer's way. Remember that it is possible for a "weak" believer to see you doing something that he thinks is wrong, although what you are doing is not immoral, and he decides he will try it also. He is encouraged to go against his conscience. His imitating you was based upon good motives; his conscience was emboldened but not enlightened. He thus sins because he goes against his conscience. Whatever is not done of faith is sin. He imitated you not because he believed it was right, but because he saw you do it.

Perhaps you are thinking: "Well, that's his own fault. He's stupid. I didn't tell him to eat the food. He's a grown man with a mind of his own. How can I be held responsible?" Accept it or not, you are in some measure held responsible for whatever damage is done in the spiritual life of the weak Christian. The strong saint cannot disclaim how his actions affect others. In fact, no believer can claim this, for no man lives unto himself (Romans 14:7).

D. KNOWLEDGE AND LOVE
(1 Corinthians 8:11-13)

And through thy knowledge shall the weak brother perish, for whom Christ died? But when ye sin so against the brethren, and wound their weak conscience, ye sin against Christ. Wherefore, if meat make my brother to offend, I will eat no flesh while the world

standeth, lest I make my brother to offend.

The truth is, Christians who through their superior knowledge of the truth are strong Christians who are obligated by love to guard the weak. "Perish" in verse eleven does not mean loss of one's salvation. Though the language is strong, it means to cause damage, disaster, downfall or ruin. The strong saint's inconsiderate behavior could ruin the testimony of the weak saint—the believer who is over-scrupulous about trifles and amoral things. Shall we demonstrate our lack of love for another saint by parading our liberty, unwilling to exercise the least bit of self-denial? "To wound" is literally to strike, beat or smite, with a stick, a whip, the fist, hand, etc. Figuratively, it means to disquiet, cause anguish. A Christian is capable of wounding another's conscience by careless, unthinking behavior. We want to avoid that attitude that says: "What I do is my own business. I don't see why I should let his narrow-mindedness interfere with my pleasure!" Such an expression shows a lack of love for the weak brother. To sin thus against another Christian is to sin against Christ. It may well be that many church members never think this way because they are not aware of the full significance of Christian brotherhood. Paul made up his mind to be a vegetarian when necessary, rather than by eating meat offered to an idol leading a weak brother into doing something that brother considered wrong (Romans 14:21). As far as the apostle was concerned, eating meat offered to idols was too unimportant to risk the ruin of a fellow saint. The consequences were not worth it. Thus, Paul was determined to regulate his Christian liberty so as not to cause a Christian brother to fall.

III. Special Features

A. PRESERVING OUR HERITAGE

An expression we have heard often in our churches is: "Let your conscience be your guide." This is not good biblical advice; in fact, it can be dangerous. The peril exists because the conscience may be weak, defiled, evil, seared. It is true that to go against your conscience is sin; it is self-destructive. Our only infallible guide is the Word of God, and the Holy Spirit. However, I have often wondered what went through the minds of whites, who were professed Christians, when they saw "Colored Only" or "White Only" signs. Who knew that racism was evil: that race prejudice was an insult to the God of the Bible who is no respecter of persons? Did their consciences bother them? Even today, is it still pride (as it was for the Corinthians) that prevents Christians from practicing biblical brotherhood? Or is it the love of money, the "culture gap," fear, feelings of superiority, etc.?

B. A CONCLUDING WORD

There are still those today who would apply certain dietary laws, some under the pain of sin, lack of spirituality or bad health. For example: Some people hold to vegetarianism. Certain meats are forbidden, even though their claim for such restrictions is not religious but hygienic. Other groups state that the hog is poison, and that eating it decreases mental power. Evidently, these legalistic dieticians have overlooked Simon Peter's experience in Acts chapter ten. Jewish food laws were not to bind the Christian.

It is common sense to recognize that an improper diet affects the health both of believer and unbeliever. Our bodies are different and what agrees with one may not agree with another. We recognize this. But there is absolutely no biblical basis for declaring any food off limits for religious reasons. The apostle was led by the Holy Spirit to write: "For every creature of God is good, and nothing is to be refused, if it is received with thanksgiving; for it is sanctified by the word of God and prayer" (1 Timothy 4:4-5). And again: "For the kingdom of God is not eating and drinking; but righteousness and peace and joy in the Holy Spirit" (Romans 14:17). "Do not be carried about with various and strange doctrines. For it is good that the heart be established by grace, not with foods which have not profited those who have been occupied with them" (Hebrews 13:9). In other words, Christianity is not ritualism and ceremonialism. God's kingdom does not consist in eating or not eating certain foods. Do not make your diet your mark of identification as a child of God or a member of God's kingdom. And what is more important: do not let your attitude towards other Christians who disagree with you in amoral matters be an attitude that demonstrates a lack of love.

HOME DAILY BIBLE READINGS FOR THE WEEK OF APRIL 9, 2000

CONCERNING LOVE AND KNOWLEDGE

April 3 M. 1 Corinthians 8:1-6,   Knowledge Puffs Up; Love Builds Up
April 4 T. 1 Corinthians 8:7-13,   Don't Cause Another to Stumble
April 5 W. 1 Corinthians 9:1-12,   Love Has Priority Over "Rights"
April 6 T. 1 Corinthians 9:13-18,   Preaching the Gospel Is Reward Enough
April 7 F. 1 Corinthians 9:19-27,   Do Whatever It Takes
April 8 S. 1 Corinthians 10:1-13,   Learn From Lessons of the Past
April 9 S. 1 Corinthians 10:14-22,   Flee From the Worship of Idols

Father, as You have bestowed Your love upon us without any merit on our part, grant that Your grace may instruct us in our relationships with others regardless of their status or condition in life as we raise the level of communion and fellowship. In His name. Amen.

Spiritual Gifts

Adult Topic—*Work Together*

.....

Youth Topic—*Many Parts; One Body*

Children's Topic—*Sharing With Others*

.....

Devotional Reading—Romans 12:1-8

Background Scripture—1 Corinthians 12:1-30

Print—1 Corinthians 12:4-20, 26

PRINTED SCRIPTURE

1 Corinthians 12:4-20, 26 (KJV)

4 Now there are diversities of gifts, but the same Spirit.

5 And there are differences of administrations, but the same Lord.

6 And there are diversities of operations, but it is the same God which worketh all in all.

7 But the manifestation of the Spirit is given to every man to profit withal.

8 For to one is given by the Spirit the word of wisdom; to another the word of knowledge by the same Spirit;

9 To another faith by the same Spirit; to another the gifts of healing by the same Spirit;

10 To another the working of miracles; to another prophecy; to another discerning of spirits; to another divers kinds of tongues; to another the interpretation of tongues:

11 But all these worketh that one

1 Corinthians 12:4-20, 26 (NRSV)

4 Now there are varieties of gifts, but the same Spirit;

5 and there are varieties of services, but the same Lord;

6 and there are varieties of activities, but it is the same God who activates all of them in everyone.

7 To each is given the manifestation of the Spirit for the common good.

8 To one is given through the Spirit the utterance of wisdom, an to another the utterance of knowledge according to the same Spirit,

9 to another faith by the same Spirit, to another gifts of healing by the one Spirit,

10 to another the working of miracles, to another prophecy, to another the discernment of spirits, to another various kinds of tongues, to another the interpretation of tongues.

11 All these are activated by the

and the selfsame Spirit, dividing to every man severally as he will.

12 For as the body is one, and hath many members, and all the members of that one body, being many, are one body: so also is Christ.

13 For by one Spirit are we all baptized into one body, whether we be Jews or Gentiles, whether we be bond or free; and have been all made to drink into one Spirit.

14 For the body is not one member, but many.

15 If the foot shall say, Because I am not the hand, I am not of the body; is it therefore not of the body?

16 And if the ear shall say, Because I am not the eye, I am not of the body; is it therefore not of the body?

17 If the whole body were an eye, where were the hearing? If the whole were hearing, where were the smelling?

18 But now hath God set the members every one of them in the body, as it hath pleased him.

19 And if they were all one member, where were the body?

20 But now are they many members, yet but one body

.....

26 And whether one member suffer, all the members suffer with it; or one member be honoured, all the members rejoice with it.

one and the same Spirit, who allots to each one individually just as the Spirit chooses.

12 For just as the body is one and has many members, and all the members of the body, though many, are one body, so it is with Christ.

13 For in the one Spirit we were all baptized into one body—Jews or Greeks, slaves or free—and we were all made to drink of one Spirit.

14 Indeed, the body does not consist of one member but of many.

15 If the foot would say, "Because I am not a hand, I do not belong to the body," "that would not make it any less a part of the body.

16 And if the ear would say, "Because I am not an eye, I do not belong to the body," that would not make it any less a part of the body.

17 If the whole body were an eye, where would the hearing be? If the whole body were hearing, where would the sense of smell be?

18 But as it is, God arranged the members in the body, each one of them, as he chose.

19 If all were a single member, where would the body be?

20 As it is, there are many members, yet one body.

.....

26 If one member suffers, all suffer together with it; if one member is honored, all rejoice together with it.

KEY VERSE

Now there are diversities of gifts, but one Spirit... And there are diversities of operations, but it is the same God that worketh all in all.—
1 Corinthians 12:4, 6

OBJECTIVES

After reading this lesson, the student should realize that:

1. The Holy Trinity is the Source of all gifts;
2. The exercise of spiritual gifts constitutes true ministry;
3. The human body illustrates the relationships of gifts in the church;
4. Unity in diversity, and diversity in unity is the principle; and,
5. Christians must learn to work together.

POINTS TO BE EMPHASIZED
Adult/Youth
Key Verse: 1 Corinthians 12:4, 6

Print: 1 Corinthians 12:4-20, 26

—There are a variety of gifts, services, and activities, but one God is the source of all. (4-6)

—Paul lists the various kinds of gifts the Spirit gives to believers for service and to glorify the church. (8-10)

—The unity and diversity of the body of Christ, the church, can be compared to the unity and diversity of the human body; there is one body with many parts. (12)

—Parts of the human body illustrate how each spiritual gift works in relationship to the others; all members of the body are important and essential. (12-20)

—Since all members make up the body of Christ, if one member suffers, the whole body suffers; if one member is honored, all rejoice together. (26)

Children
Key Verse: 1 John 3:18

Print: 1 Corinthians 12:4-6; Acts 9:36-41

—Paul stated that there are varieties of gifts, services, and workings; but God inspires them all. (1 Corinthians 12:4-6)

—Dorcas, a disciple, who was full of good works and acts of charity became ill and died. (Acts 9:36-37)

—The disciples sent for Peter. (38)

—When Peter arrived, the widows were showing tunics and other garments Dorcas had made for them. (39)

—Peter sent the widows away and then knelt beside Dorcas' body and prayed. He then commanded Dorcas to rise. (40)

—Peter called the saints and widows to show them Dorcas was alive. (41)

(**Note**: Use KJV Scripture for Adults; NRSV Scripture for Youth and Children)

I. Introduction

A. THE BAPTISM OF THE SPIRIT

There is no reference to the baptism of the Spirit in the Old Testament. It is a New Testament event. Simon Peter informs us in Acts 11:15, 16 that the baptism of the Holy Spirit first occurred on the Day of Pentecost (Acts 2) in fulfillment of the Lord's promise in Acts 1:5. In today's lesson, the apostle Paul explains this baptism in 1 Corinthians 12:13, a passage that is important for a number of reasons.

First: It teaches the importance of positional (versus conditional) truths.

Second: It emphasizes the spiritual, rather than the physical or ritual baptism.

Third: It refutes all efforts to establish some sort of "second blessing" or second "baptism of the Spirit," claimed to be evidenced by speaking in tongues. The baptism of the Spirit is a truth that describes our position or standing in Christ. The believer is put into the body of Christ.

Fourth: There is no reference here to physical water, H_2O. Therefore, there is no particular method or formula to be used or spoken by the one administering baptism. The Holy Spirit, who is God, performs the baptism. This text does not refer to any emotional experience for which one must tarry, speak in tongues, fast, cry, pray, etc.

Fifth: What God does here is a once-for-all thing, never to be repeated. For those born again, this act is an accomplished historical fact; indeed, it takes place in the lives of all believers. The moment the finished work of Christ is accepted, the believer is put, placed, or introduced into the body of Christ.

B. BIBLICAL BACKGROUND

The apostle Paul was led to describe the gifts in three passages: Romans 12,

1 Corinthians 12, and Ephesians 4. He used the word charisma (plural: charismata), which means grace. Reference then is to a grace or gift, a God-given ability for service. In Romans 12:3-8, the gifts are contemporary, that is, they are designated for all believers during the church age, and not only for the apostolic or early church. Seven gifts are mentioned.

In Ephesians 4:7-16, emphasis is not upon gifts to individuals, but gifted individuals who are given by God to the church. They are spoken of them as spiritual offices. Jesus Christ **gave gifted gifts** to His body, the church. Four gifts are listed. Their purpose is to promote the growth of the body, both in quality and in numbers. The third group is found in today's lesson. They are gifts calculated to promote the unity of the body. It is believed these spiritual gifts were temporary. This is a highly debatable interpretation, but it is offered for your prayerful consideration as part of the exposition of the lesson believed to support this point of view.

II. Exposition and Application of the Scripture

A. THE TRINITY AND SPIRITUAL GIFTS (1 Corinthians 12:4-6)

Now there are diversities of gifts, but the same Spirit. And there are differences of administrations, but the same Lord. And there are diversities of operations, but it is the same God which worketh all in all.

Gifts differ. Not all gifts are the same, nor are the same gifts bestowed in similar degree. The point of varieties or diversities of gifts is stressed. Failure to accept and understand this truth often leads to distorted values, improper emphasis, ingratitude, envy, jealousy, lack of cooperation, conflict and strife. Furthermore, there are varieties or diversities (differences: KJV) of ministries, different kinds of service (NIV). Third: there are varieties of operations, results, effects and activities. There are diversities of working, but it is the same God who works all of the gifts in all who are gifted.

Note that verses 4, 5, and 6 imply the doctrine of the Trinity. In verse 4, there is the Holy Spirit; in verse 5, the Lord Jesus Christ; and in verse 6, God the Father. All of the gifts—the endowments, the services, the effectuating—come from the One God. It is His church. They are His gifts to be used as He sees fit for His glory. So they are distributed according to the will and good pleasure and purpose of God the Father, Son, and Holy Spirit. How wonderful it is to be saved by the precious blood of Jesus Christ, endowed with gifts by the Spirit, given opportunities of service by our Lord, and energized by God the Father.

B. SPIRITUAL GIFTS ENUMERATED
(1 Corinthians 12:7-11)

But the manifestation of the Spirit is given to every man to profit withal. For to one is given by the Spirit the word of wisdom; to another the word of knowledge by the same Spirit; To another faith by the same Spirit; to another the gift of healing by the same spirit; To another the working of miracles; to

another prophecy; to another discerning of spirits; to another divers kinds of tongues; to another the interpretation of tongues: But all these worketh that one and the self-same Spirit, dividing to every man severally as he will.

To every saint is given the disclosure, evidence, announcement, exhibition, and open proclamation of the Holy Spirit. This may mean two things: (1) something the Holy Spirit exhibits or demonstrates or makes known, or (2) the exhibition or evidence of the Holy Spirit Himself.

Nine different gifts are mentioned in this section. More than likely, there is no special significance to the order in which they are given. In fact, the very lack of arrangement would add to the emphasis desired, namely there is variety, yet all come from the one Holy Spirit. Two gifts are named in verse eight.

First is the **Word of Wisdom**: This is that divine wisdom which God imparts to those who are close to Him. It is from above, "pure, peaceable, gentle, willing to yield, full of mercy and good fruits, without partiality and without hypocrisy" (James 3:17). "Word" (*logos*) may be rendered "preaching" or "utterance." The word wisdom then is the Holy Spirit using a believer to speak of Christ in such a way as to convey to others an insight and illumination unto the truth and the Christian gospel. It is the art of speaking to the purpose about things pertaining to Divine wisdom.

The second gift is the **Word of Knowledge**. Knowledge and wisdom are often used interchangeably, but there are these distinctions: (1) Knowledge is all that the mind knows, from whatever source derived or obtained, or by whatever process; it is the aggregate of facts, truths, or principles acquired or retained by the mind. (2) Wisdom is the power of using knowledge in the best way. It is the right use of knowledge; wisdom indicates discernment based not only on factual knowledge but also on judgment and insight.

The third gift is **Faith**. It is not that faith in Jesus Christ whereby men are saved, for Paul deals with those who are already Christians. The faith spoken of here is something special, a miraculous wonder-working faith (Matthew 21:21; 1 Corinthians 13:2); mountain-removing faith that meets all emergencies head on and seemingly insurmountable obstacles vanish!

The fourth gift by which the Holy Spirit manifested Himself is that of **Healing**. It is believed that once the New Testament was completed, this particular supernatural gift was no longer needed as a sign to authenticate or validate a man's preaching or teaching. All attempts to make the Holy Spirit do today what He did 1900 years ago are in vain. It is not "Can God heal?"—of course He can and does—but "Is it His will?" (Hebrews 2:4).

The fifth gift is the **Working of Miracles**. Through believers, the Holy Spirit demonstrated mighty powers. Punishment of evildoers, control of the forces of nature, casting out demons, raising the dead—these are some of the things wrought through believers by the Holy Spirit. They were done primarily as signs or attestation to the spoken word. **Prophecy** is the sixth gift. The verb to prophesy means to speak forth, to proclaim; the prophecy or message thus spoken may or may not contain an element of prediction.

The seventh gift is the **Discerning of Spirits**. Some Christians seem unaware that there are different spirits. There is the one and only Holy Spirit who is God. There are good spirits; the angels of God are called ministering spirits (Hebrews 1:14). There are evil spirits. And there is the human spirit. Discernment is the ability to distinguish, separate, literally, to sift, and thereby determine the nature of the spirits. Getting the church started in the midst of paganism required this gift in large measure. Satan sought to thwart the establishment of the church by counterfeiting the deeds of the Holy Spirit as much as he possible could.

The eighth and ninth gifts are **Kinds of Tongues and Interpretations of Tongues**. Do not interpret the word tongues here to mean some type of ecstatic utterance or gibberish. That would be completely out of place, altogether incongruous with the nature and quality of the other gifts whereby the Spirit manifested Himself. **Tongues** here are languages.

The Spirit enabled believers to speak and interpret foreign languages which they had not learned or understood previously. It is only later that some people at Corinth counterfeited the language gifts, and pretended they were moved by the Holy Spirit to speak in another language, when in reality they gave out nothing but meaningless gibberish.

Paul looked at these gifts in the light of their purpose. The Holy Spirit knew just what the church needed to get it established, and so gave these gifts to the believers. He energized these various gifts in the believers. No man told Him what to do. Nor did the saints at Corinth choose or bargain with Him. No demands were made, but the Sovereign Spirit gave as He willed.

C. ONE BODY; MANY PARTS
(1 Corinthians 12:12-14, 20)

For as the body is one, and hath many members, and all the members of that one body, being many, are one body: so also is Christ. For by one Spirit are we all baptized into one body, whether we be Jews or Gentiles, whether we be bond or free; and have been all made to drink into one spirit. For the body is not one member, but many. But now are they many members, yet but one body.

Paul was led to use the human body as an illustration of diversity within unity. True unity is to be seen in the fact that all spiritual gifts come from the one Holy Spirit. The human body has many different organs and members, but together constitute one body. Similarly, the varied spiritual gifts operate within the one body, the church. There exists an organic relationship within the church, and although every member is different, yet each depends upon the other, each operates for the good of the body as a whole. So also is Christ, for the church is His body (Romans 12:4-5).

Our introductory remarks explain 1 Corinthians 12:13. We learn that the Holy Spirit makes no distinctions, but embraces the entire human race. He cares nothing about nationality, race, skin color, class, caste, and previous condition of servitude, political party, position, prestige, power or office. It does not matter to Him whether you are a slave or free. All former standings of the flesh and the world are done away with, and the believer is given a new standing. He is put into the one body of Jesus Christ. Just as the human body is composed of the skeleton, muscles, nerves, blood vessels, and the various organs and members—feet, hands, ears, eyes, for example, are mentioned in the lesson—so the church is composed of many different parts. There is but one true church, and it is the body of the Lord Jesus Christ.

D. MANY PARTS, DIVERSE FUNCTIONS
(1 Corinthians 12:15-19)

If the foot shall say, Because I am not the hand, I am not of the body; is it therefore not of the body? And if the ear shall say, Because I am not the eye, I am not of the body; is it therefore not of the body? If the whole body were an eye, where were the hearing? If the whole were hearing, where were the smelling? But now hath God set the members every one of them in the body, as it hath pleased him. And if they were all one member, where were the body?

Even as no member of the body should belittle himself or herself, so also no member of the body should depreciate others in the body. No matter what kind of work the Lord leads us into, we are not rid of our responsibility to the rest of the body. Can you imagine the foot saying, "Well, since I'm not a hand, I don't belong to the body"? Or the ear saying, "Well, since I'm not an eye, I don't belong to the body"? Do they automatically cease belonging to the body by their assertions? By no means! Paul said: "In lowliness of mind let each esteem others better than themselves" (Philippians 2:3). The

"I-have-no-need-of-you" attitude is very bad. Not even sinners can live unto themselves. No man is an island unto himself. Some may think their office or function makes them superior to others, but it does not. Indeed, said Paul, those parts of the body which seem naturally the weaker, or more delicate, are really indispensable.

Once we see that differences in function are not to be despised, once we learn each member is indispensable, then the whole body will be better off. When preachers think they alone are indispensable and their churches cannot do without them; when deacons become puffed up with pride; when trustees feel they alone are capable of running the church; whenever any one member or group or auxiliary overestimates its worth and importance, and begins to despise others, there will be trouble. The jealousies and mistrust that result soon lead to schism within the body.

E. ALL ONE, IN SUFFERING AND JOY (1 Corinthians 12:26)

And whether one member suffer, all the members suffer with it; or one member be honoured, all the members rejoice with it.

Finally, we learn that when one member of the local assembly suffers, all the members of that assembly suffer. When one Baptist church suffers, all Baptist churches suffer. And so it goes. The whole body suffers. It may be only an ingrown toenail, a splinter in the finger, and one little old toothache! But when you have it, you really wish it were not of the body. On the other hand, we rejoice to see the Holy Spirit accomplishing the will of Christ in the lives of our fellow Christians.

III. Special Features

A. PRESERVING OUR HERITAGE

When you read certain books on the history of the church in the United States, you get the impression that either there are no Black Christians in this country, or if there are, they have contributed little or nothing to the religious life of America. This is a false impression, one born of ignorance compounded by racism. The fact is: Black American Christians have contributed much by way of (1) Message (2) Music (3) Morality {pricking consciences} (4) Money (5) and Missions to the spiritual life of America—for such has been the grace of God who has bestowed so many gifts upon us. Through faith in the shed blood of Jesus Christ, we have been placed in the body of Christ, the body of One who is no respecter of faces or races. Indeed, one Spirit baptizes us all into one body, whether we be black or white, for the body of Christ transcends all races and nationalities. Though professing Christians have the legal right to segregate racially, they are immoral in doing so, for in the presence of God no flesh shall glory (1 Corinthians 1:29). Our hands have built church edifices; our feet have traveled the missionary trail; our lips have preached the Gospel; our tongues have sung spirituals, hymns, anthems and gospels; our eyes have seen the glory of God work in the lives of a downtrodden and mistreated race; our ears have heard and believed the Bible in spite of hypocrisy!

B. A CONCLUDING WORD

God the Holy Spirit sovereignly bestowed gifts for the mutual building up of the church. He gave to each saint what He desired. No one person has all gifts; no one person can do every ministry equally well, and no one person has been called to perform the entire work. The belief that the gift of miracles was temporary does not mean that there are no miracles today. What is implied is that saints today do not possess such gifts as the apostolic believers did, and that miracles no longer constitute God's main evidence for the truth or validation of the preached Word. Keep in mind that gifts are given with a purpose, for a reason.

This is more than evident when we study the use of miracles in the time of Moses, Elijah, and Elisha, and during the earthly ministry of our Lord and His disciples. God used miracles during these periods to authenticate the message preached by His prophets or apostles. Once this was met, it appears that such miracles were no longer common. All gifts were given to promote the unity of the church, to contribute to the growth of the body. And of course, to glorify Him who is Head of the Church, the Lord Jesus Christ.

The comtemporary church is replete with members who have expertise in various areas of ministry. Regardless of the individual efforts that we put forth to perfect ourselves in our occupation of choice, our faith gives God the credit not only for that which we have, but also who we are as persons; and we must embrace both as members of the family of God who are interrelated in special ways for the enrichment of the fellowship of the faithful.

HOME DAILY BIBLE READINGS FOR THE WEEK OF APRIL 16, 2000

SPIRITUAL GIFTS

April 10 M. 1 Corinthians 12:1-6, Understand the Source of Spiritual Gifts
April 11 T. 1 Corinthians 12:7-11, Many Spiritual Gifts, But One Spirit
April 12 W. 1 Corinthians 12:12-19, One Body, Many Members
April 13 T. 1 Corinthians 12:20-31, We Need One Another
April 14 F. Romans 12:1-8, Transformed by New Life in Christ
April 15 S. Romans 12:9-15, Marks of a Faithful Christian
April 16 S. Romans 12:16-21, Guidance for Living the Christian Life

Know Your Bible

- Jonathan affirmed his love for David by giving him his robes and some of his arms, though the sacredness of the arms had made them valuable items. (1 Samuel 13:22)
- Saul became very jealous and angry because after the battle with the Philestines, the women went to meet the conquerors in battle and greeted them with the song, "Saul has slain his thousand, and David his ten thousands." (1 Samuel 18:17)
- Michal, the wife of David and daughter of Saul, proved her love for David by letting him down from a window in order that David might escape the rage of Saul. (1 Samuel 19:12-17)
- When the Lord placed Saul in the power of David, David would not kill him or allow any of his men to harm him; Saul reacted to this act of mercy by weeping and speaking kindly to David. (1 Samuel 24:4-7, 8-22)
- David was returning to Ziklag when he received the news of the death of Saul and Jonathan. (2 Samuel 1:1)
- David expressed his love for Saul and Jonathan by composing a song of lamentation. (2 Samuel 1:17-27)
- Upon the death of King Saul, and after seeking direction from the Lord, David went to Hebron and was anointed king. (2 Samuel 2:1-4)
- The war between the house of Saul and the house of David continued for about two years (2 Samuel 2:10), but came to an end when Abner deserted Israel on account of a quarrel with Ishbosheth, and offering to make terms with David. (2 Samuel 2:6-20)

O God, we give You thanks because You have created us with individual significance. Grant that we may embrace our differences as spiritual gifts from Your hands. Amen.

Christ's Resurrection and Ours

Adult Topic—*What About the Resurrection?*

•••••

Youth Topic—*What's the Last Word?*
Children's Topic—*What Jesus Did for Me*

•••••

Devotional Reading—1 Corinthians 15:12-19, 50-57
Background Scripture—1 Corinthians 15
Print—1 Corinthians 15:20-27, 35-44

PRINTED SCRIPTURE

1 Corinthians 15:20-27, 35-44 (KJV)

20 But now is Christ risen from the dead, and become the firstfruits of them that slept.

21 For since by man came death, by man came also the resurrection of the dead.

22 For as in Adam all die, even so in Christ shall all be made alive.

23 But every man in his own order: Christ the firstfruits; afterward they that are Christ's at his coming.

24 Then cometh the end, when he shall have delivered up the kingdom to God, even the Father; when he shall have put down all rule and all authority and power.

25 For he must reign, till he hath put all enemies under his feet.

26 The last enemy that shall be destroyed is death.

27 For he hath put all things under his feet. But when he saith all things are put under him, it is manifest that he is excepted, which did put all things under him.

1 Corinthians 15:20-27, 35-44 (NRSV)

20 But in fact Christ has been raised form the dead, the first fruits of those who have died.

21 For since death came through a human being, the resurrection of the dead has also come through a human being;

22 for as all die in Adam, so all will be made alive in Christ.

23 But each in his own order: Christ the first fruits, then at his coming those who belong to Christ.

24 Then comes the end, when he hands over the kingdom to God the Father, after he has destroyed every ruler and every authority and power.

25 For he must reign until he has put all his enemies under his feet.

26 The last enemy to be destroyed is death.

27 For "God has put all things in subjection under his feet." But when it says, "All things are put in subjection," it is plain that this does

.....

35 But some man will say, How are the dead raised up? and with what body do they come?

36 Thou fool, that which thou sowest is not quickened, except it die:

37 And that which thou sowest, thou sowest not that body that shall be, but bare grain, it may chance of wheat, or of some other grain:

38 But God giveth it a body as it hath pleased him, and to every seed his own body.

39 All flesh is not the same flesh: but there is one kind of flesh of men, another flesh of beasts, another of fishes, and another of birds.

40 There are also celestial bodies, and bodies terrestrial: but the glory of the celestial is one, and the glory of the terrestrial is another.

41 There is one glory of the sun, and another glory of the moon, and another glory of the stars: for one star differeth from another star in glory.

42 So also is the resurrection of the dead. It is sown in corruption; it is raised in incorruption:

43 It is sown in dishonour; it is raised in glory: it is sown in weakness; it is raised in power:

44 It is sown a natural body; it is raised a spiritual body. There is a natural body, and there is a spiritual body.

not include the one who put all things in subjection under him.

.....

35 But someone will ask, "How are the dead raised? With what kind of body do they come?"

36 Fool! What you sow does not come to life unless it dies.

37 And as for what you sow, you do not sow the body that is to be, but a bare seed, perhaps of wheat or of some other grain.

38 But God gives it a body as he has chosen, and to each kind of seed its own body.

39 Not all flesh is alike, but there is one flesh for human beings, another for animals, another for birds, and another for fish.

40 There are both heavenly bodies and earthly bodies, but the glory of the heavenly is one thing, and that of the earthly is another.

41 There is one glory of the sun, and another glory of the moon, and another glory of the stars; indeed, star differs from star in glory.

42 So it is with the resurrection of the dead. What is sown is perishable, what is raised is imperishable.

43 It is sown in dishonor, it is raised in glory. It is sown in weakness, it is raised in power.

44 It is sown a physical body, it is raised a spiritual body. If there is a physical body, there is also a spiritual body.

KEY VERSE

But now is Christ risen from the dead, and become the firstfruits of them that slept...For as in Adam all die, even so in Christ shall all be made alive.—1 Corinthians 15:20, 22

OBJECTIVES

After reading this lesson, the student should be better informed about:

1. God's guarantee of the resurrection of the dead;
2. God's schedule of resurrection events;
3. The certain demise of Death; and,
4. The composition, glory, and nature of the believer's new body.

POINTS TO BE EMPHASIZED

Adult/Youth

Key Verse: 1 Corinthians 15:20, 22

Print: 1 Corinthians 15:20-27, 35-44

—Christ became the first to be raised from the dead; just as death came through a human being, so will the Resurrection. (20-23)

—After Christ destroys every ruler, and every authority and power—even death, the kingdom will be handed to God the Father. (24-27)

—In nature, the death of the seed is necessary for the life of the plant, which has a new body. (35-36)

—Just as God provided appropriate forms of all life, even so our resurrected bodies will be different but appropriate to their spiritual nature. (38-44)

Children

Key Verse: 1 Corinthians 15:20

Print: 1 Corinthians 15:20; Luke 24:1-10

—Paul stated that Christ had been raised form the dead. (1 Corinthians 15:20)

—When the women went to the tomb on the first day of the week, thy found the stone that sealed the tomb had been rolled away. (Luke 24:1-2)

—The women went into the tomb and found it empty. (3)

—While they stood utterly at a loss, all of a sudden two men in dazzling garments were at their side. They were terrified, and stood with eyes cast down, but the men said, 'why search among the dead for one who lives?' (4-5)

—Remember what he told you while he was still in Galilee, about the Son of Man: how he must be given up into the power of sinful men and be crucified, and must rise again on the third day.' Then they recalled his words. (6-8)

—The women remembered Jesus' saying and ran to the disciples to tell them what they had seen and heard. (9)

—The women were Mary Magdala, Joanna, and Mary the mother of James, and they, with the other women, told the apostles. (10)

(**Note**: Use KJV Scripture for Adults; NRSV Scripture for Youth and Children)

I. Introduction

A. RESURRECTION DEFINED

All who have been raised from the dead before Christ rose, died again. Only the Lord Jesus was raised from the grave never to die again. He is alive for evermore (Revelation 1:18). Technically then, we should call all of the other raisings, restorations. From the Old Testament, we find the bodies of the son of the Shunammite woman, and the dead man whose body touched the bones of the prophet Elisha were raised. From the New Testament, we find restored of life the bodies of the daughter of Jairus, the son of the widow of Nain, Lazarus, Dorcas, and Eutychus. They all were restored to life, but their bodies were the same kinds of bodies they had before they died. They were still mortal, and they all died again. However, when believers are raised from the dead at the return of Christ, they will receive new, glorified bodies that will never again taste death.

Now the word translated "resurrection" in the New Testament is **anastasis**. The feminine name Anastasia has been derived from this Greek word. Literally, it means to stand up, rise up. Our Lord was raised up when His lifeless body was glorified, made to leave the tomb, and reunite with His human spirit He had committed into the hands of the Father (Luke 23:46).

B. BIBLICAL BACKGROUND

Earlier, some of Paul's opponents had suggested there is no resurrection of the dead (verse 12). Paul then took the hypothesis that Christ did not rise, and showed its logical implications: Our preaching is a waste of time, our faith is futile, we are telling lies on God, and we are yet in our sins—if Christ did not rise from the dead. Yea, all those who died with faith in the Lord Jesus have perished. Such is the impossible position in which we are placed when the physical, bodily resurrection of Jesus Christ is denied.

Today's lesson teaches that there is no basis for thinking such thoughts. The truth is our preaching is not empty, our faith is not idle, we are not false witnesses of God, and we are not still in our sins! Indeed, it is with the joy of victory that we state this solid fact: Jesus Christ has been raised from the dead. He is the firstfruits of those who have fallen asleep. Christ promised to rise and He did. The empty grave is proof.

Thousands of lives have been transformed because of the belief that Jesus Christ lives. According to the record, Mary saw Him, the apostles saw Him, many disciples saw Him, Paul saw Him. Because the Bible is the Word of God, we believe their testimony, we believe the Gospel record. And then although we have not seen Him with our own eyes, we have met Him. We believe in our hearts that God the Father raised Him from the dead (Romans 10:9).

II. Exposition and Application of the Scripture

A. ALL THE DEAD SHALL BE RESURRECTED
(1 Corinthians 15:20-22)

But now is Christ risen from the dead, and become the firstfruits of them that slept. For since by man came death, by man came also the resurrection of the dead. For as in Adam all die, even so in Christ shall all be made alive.

Note the contrast that is set up between Adam and Christ. Through Adam sin entered into the world, and death by sin. By the same token, resurrection comes through a man, the man Christ Jesus. As flows the current of death through a man, so through the same channel must flow the counter current of resurrection. As came the tragedy, so also the triumph. In saying that "all are dying in Adam," it is meant that physical death was introduced to humanity through Adam. It is not taught that all men will die. We know from other Scriptures that when Christ returns for His church, believers then alive will never die. "We shall not all sleep" (1 Corinthians 15:51); "those alive and remaining until the coming of the Lord" shall not die, but will be plucked up, forced up to meet the Lord (1 Thessalonians 4:15, 17).

In contrast, note that in Christ all shall be made alive. Universalists have taken this to mean that eventually all men shall be saved. However, the "being made alive" refers to physical life; only bodily resurrection is meant here. The resurrection of Jesus Christ guarantees that all the dead shall be raised, so that He might judge the world in righteousness (Acts 17:31). Christ is the channel through which quickening power will be conveyed to all mankind. Do not limit this resurrection to believers only. Here we are taught that Jesus Christ is the channel through which all persons will be resurrected. We learn from John 5:25-29 that all the dead shall hear Christ's voice and will live. All will hear and be raised, but at different times.

B. THE ORDER OF THE RESURRECTIONS
(1 Corinthians 15:23-24)

But every man in his own order: Christ the firstfruits; afterward they that are Christ's at his coming. Then cometh the end, when he shall have delivered up the kingdom to God, even the Father; when he shall have put down all rule and all authority and power.

We must immediately understand that there will be two resurrections, and they will occur at different times. The word order means "that which has been arranged." God has a certain arrangement of the Resurrection and it will take place with military precision. Do **not** conclude from John 5:25-29 that there will be **one** big general resurrection of the dead. There will be two resurrections (Revelation 20:5-6). Christ is the firstfruits of this first resurrection, the Pioneer, the trail blazer, the beginning, the firstborn from the dead (Colossians 1:18). But included in the first resurrection are they that belong to Christ. No time element is given here, so we do not disobey the Scriptures by attempting to predict the date of our Lord's coming. All who have attempted to set dates for the Lord's return have been proven liars.

The words "then comes the end" do not directly refer to the second resurrection, but point to that end time when Christ shall have accomplished His specific work of subduing all the enemies of God and mankind. It is of course true that the wicked dead shall be raised last, but the "end" here is that time when the Lord Jesus Christ shall have vanquished the enemies of righteousness. "All rule" signifies the political organization of demonic powers; hostile spirits will be stripped of their evil influence. "All authority" also speaks of supernatural powers of evil. The third expression, "all power," speaks of demonic cosmic ability. All such shall be put down once for all, made powerless, inoperative.

C. THE DESTRUCTION OF OUR ENEMIES (1 Corinthians 15:25-27)

For he must reign, till he hath put all enemies under his feet. The last enemy that shall be destroyed is death. For he hath put all things under his feet. But when he saith all things are put under him, it is manifest that he is excepted, which did put all things under him.

Note the divine imperative—He must reign. Conquest of the enemies of God and mankind is a part of the task Christ came to fulfill. Just who are these enemies? They are: (1) Satan (Matthew 13:24-28, 39); (2) Unregenerate man (Romans 5:10); (3) The word-system. Remember, Satan is the head of this cosmos (John 15:18); and (4) Death is the last enemy to be destroyed (1 Corinthians 15:26). Until this is done, the work of Christ is not complete. Destruction here means rendering ineffective, setting at naught.

To put something under one's feet is to make that thing submit, give up.

All things are to be subjected to Christ. At this point, the matter of subordination of office is important. The Persons of the Godhead are one in essence but differ in office or function. This is in the interest of economy and efficiency, if I may put it that way. Throughout the Bible, we see that the Holy Spirit is subordinate to the Father and to the Son; the Son is subordinate to the Father only. The Father is always first, the Son second, and the Holy Spirit third. And this subordination is not of Person, but of office. We thus learn that within the Godhead there is an economy of function, a division of labor. Once Christ accomplishes the mediatorial and redemptive work appointed to Him by the Father, and all the enemies of God are subdued, this aspect of Christ's work is finished and the kingdom is delivered up to God the Father.

D. THE NATURE OF THE RESURRECTED BODY
(1 Corinthians 15:35-44)

But some man will say, How are the dead raised up? and with what body do they come? Thou fool, that which thou sowest is not quickened, except it die: And that which thou sowest, thou sowest not that body that shall be, but bare grain, it may chance of wheat, or of some other grain: But God giveth it a body as it hath pleased him, and to every seed his own body. All flesh is not the same flesh: but there is one kind of flesh of men, another flesh of beasts, another of fishes, and another of birds. There are also celestial bodies, and bodies terrestrial: but the glory of the celestial is one, and the glory of the terrestrial is another.

There is one glory of the sun, and another glory of the moon, and another glory of the stars: for one star differeth from another star in glory. So also is the resurrection of the dead. It is sown in corruption; it is raised in incorruption: It is sown in dishonour; it is raised in glory: it is sown in weakness; it is raised in power: It is sown a natural body; it is raised a spiritual body. There is a natural body, and there is a spiritual body.

First, consider God's design of the resurrected body (1 Corinthians 15:35-39). Those who rejected Paul's arguments for a physical bodily resurrection continued to ask their skeptical questions. It appears that questioning the method and manner, the how and what of the resurrection, showed a complete failure to accept the logic set forth earlier by the apostle. Looking with contempt upon those who raised such questions, Paul said: "You Fool," and used a word (*aphron*) meaning literally, without mind, without reason, senseless, stupid, ignorant. This is a strong term of reproach, for here is a skeptic suggesting that whatever he does not understand must not be possible, or cannot be true.

Paul does not imply that the resurrection may be proven by nature, but there are things which occur in nature which ought to open our eyes and at least remove some of the difficulties, and show by analogy that a certain process is not altogether impossible. The failure to see even that which nature teaches means a man is foolish to argue against that which God teaches. For example: When you plant a seed in the ground, it dies; this is to say, it disintegrates, breaks up. "The seed goes to seed!" That which arises anew is not exactly identical with that which died. The new plant is not the original seed. So the new resurrection body is not the identical body that died and was buried. All flesh is not alike. There is human flesh and it is different from animal flesh or fish flesh or bird flesh. They are all different. Each flesh has its own sphere in which to work and live and is not suited for any other. *Does this suggest that the attempts to transplant the organs of animals into the bodies of human beings are doomed to failure?*

Second, see the glory of the resurrected body (1 Corinthians 15:40-41). Looking into the sky, we see that the heavenly or celestial bodies also differ according to their places, purposes, and functions. In the terrestrial or earthly sphere, there also exists great variety and diversity. As for the celestial bodies, what astronomers call magnitude is called here glory. Each star has its own kind of splendor and a glory that differs from that of another star. In short, there are varying degrees of brightness among the different stars and planets in the universe; one surpasses or excels another. The point is that God is able to make whatever kind of body is needed for the occasion. He has power to create bodies that are different. And when the time comes, He will instantly, radically, perfectly change these limited bodies we now possess.

Third, we see the contrasts between the dead body and the resurrected body (1 Corinthians 15:42-46). Just as God has fitted all other bodies—celestial and terrestrial, heavenly and earthly—so He plans to raise the human bodies of believers out of death and the grave, and change them for life in His presence in heaven. Four things are said of "the seed that is sown," referring to our present bodies when they die and are buried in the ground. (1) At burial, the body is in a state of decay, decomposition, deterioration, rotting. It is sown in corruption. However, at the resurrection, the raised body will never rot again; it will be imperishable, incorruptible. (2) The dead body is sown in dishonor, that is to say, in disgrace, shame. This refers to the unseemliness and offensiveness of a dead body. A dead, decomposed body is not a pleasant thing to behold. Recently in the news, families had to exhume the bodies of loved ones because the cemetery had misplaced them. Seeing those bodies had a traumatic effect! But when Christ returns in the clouds, He shall change that body sown in humiliation and fashion it like unto His own body of glory. (3) Even in life the body is mortal, that is, dying, weak. But the weakness of verse forty-three is that which is characteristic of a lifeless body. It cannot hear, see, feel, move, or do anything; it is powerless. By contrast, our new bodies will be raised in power, possibly able to move at the speed of thought, free from aches and pains, disease and fatigue. (4) The dead body is buried a natural body. Since the word translated "natural" means soulish, it is suggested that the vital force which presently animates the body and shows itself in breathing is a soul-governed body. This is the nature of our present body which enables us to live here on this earth and it is full of animal life. By contrast, the resurrection body is described as one governed by the Spirit, a body thus perfectly suited to live in a new realm.

III. Special Features

A. PRESERVING OUR HERITAGE

In recent days, certain Black Americans have invented a holiday that they call Kwanzaa. The term is said to mean "the first" or "the first fruits of the harvest," in the East African language of Kiswahili. Swahili means "coast people," and points to a people living along the East Coast of Africa, from Somalia to Mozambique. However, in overwhelming numbers, the ancestry of African Americans is traced to the West Coast of Africa.

Actually, the technical term "firstfruits" is used with regards to religious sacrifices, so that the claim that Kwanzaa is not religious is false. In the Old Testament, two Hebrew words are translated "firstfruits." One word means the chief or principal part; the other word means firstborn and speaks of the earliest ripe of the crop or of the tree. The idea is that the fruits first ripe were to be offered to God as a thanksgiving for the harvest. Before the rest of the harvest could be put to secular use, the first ripe sheaf is an earnest, a sample consecrated to God in the hope and anticipation of the rest of the harvest.

The first sheaf of ripened grain was presented to Jehovah as a sample, proof, evidence, assurance, guarantee or pledge of the remainder of the harvest. Thus in the firstfruits is wrapped up the destiny of the fruits that would follow. In short, "firstfruits" is the offering to God in gratitude for all His gifts (ISBE). As Christians who happen to be Black American Baptists, let it be said that our joy is in knowing that the resurrection of Jesus Christ was the first of its kind. And because of our faith in His shed blood, we too shall be raised!

B. A CONCLUDING WORD

I looked at a picture taken during World War II that showed a group of us standing before a pile of scrap iron collected for the war effort. It came to mind that there is not a single particle of flesh or bone now on me that I had then. My physical body has undergone many complete changes since that photograph was taken. I am still the same person—heavier, taller, wiser! Though all of us look different as we have grown older, yet there is still an intimate and mysterious connection with that childhood body in the photographs of yesteryear.

You see, the resurrected body is the old body re-animated or restored. It is not the same one that shall go to the grave if the Lord tarries. Christians have been eaten by lions and sharks; and some have been blown to pieces. When I was a little boy, I thought that some particle of my dead body had to remain in order for the Lord to resurrect me. But nothing needs to be preserved. Decomposition and dissolution will not hinder God from resurrecting us. After all, He made us out of nothing to begin with. His resurrection work does not depend upon preserving the particles of the old body, no more so than the new plant must have the same material as the seed originally planted. God will give each kind of seed a body of its own.

Do not therefore be guilty of an ignorant, unobserving skepticism. Paul would say: "You believe in the harvest, believe also in the resurrection of the body." Rest assured, the Lord is going to change these bodies of humiliation and fashion them like unto His own glorious body (Philippiens 3:21). Rest assured that when we blood-bought children of God see Jesus Christ, we shall be changed. "Beloved, now are we the sons of God, and it does not yet appear what we shall be; but we know that, when He shall appear, we shall be like Him; for we shall see him as he is" (1 John 3:2).

HOME DAILY BIBLE READINGS FOR THE WEEK OF APRIL 23, 2000

CHRIST'S RESURRECTION AND OURS (EASTER)

April 17   Monday 1 Corinthians 15:1-11,   The Resurrection of Christ the Lord
April 18   Tuesday 1 Corinthians 15:12-19,   How Can You Deny the Resurrection?
April 19   Wednesday 1 Corinthians 15:20-28,   The Resurrected Christ Destroys Death
April 20   Thursday 1 Corinthians 15:29-34, The Dead Are Raised: Believe It!
April 21   Friday 1 Corinthians 15:35-41,   God Will Give the Glory
April 22   Saturday 1 Corinthians 15:42-49,   Raised a Spiritual Body
April 23   Sunday 1 Corinthians 15:50-58,   We Have Victory Through Jesus Christ

Know Your Bible

- After the defeat of the Philistines, David resolved to bring the ark from Kirjath-jearin (2 Samuel 6:2,3) and to place it in a tent on Mount Zion. (2 Samuel 7:1,3; 16:1)
- Michal, David's wife, was offended because of his dancing to the music before the ark, not understanding that David's action was an expression of religious joy and humble thanksgiving to God. (2 Samuel 6:20)
- David arranged his kingdom by making Joab commander-in-chief of his army; Johoshaphat the historian, Zadok and Ahimelech priests; and his own sons and others as judges and officers. (2 Samuel 8:15-18)

Eternal God, our Father, by Your grace we affirm that death is not a period that marks the end of life, but an exclamation point that intensifies the meaning of our earthly existence. You have given us a cause for which to live that is greater than life itself as we embrace the challenge to live as a resurrection people. In Christ's name. Amen.

The Way of Love

Adult Topic—*What's Real Love?*

•••••

Youth Topic—*What's Real Love?*

Children's Topic—*Showing Love for Others*

•••••

Devotional Reading—1 John 4:7-21

Background Scripture—1 Corinthians 12:31—13:13

Print—1 Corinthians 12:31—13:13

PRINTED SCRIPTURE

1 Corinthians 12:31—13:13 (KJV)

31 But covet earnestly the best gifts: and yet show I unto you a more excellent way.

•••••

THOUGH I speak with the tongues of men and of angels, and have not charity, I am become as sounding brass, or a tinkling cymbal.

2 And though I have the gift of prophecy, and understand all mysteries, and all knowledge; and though I have all faith, so that I could remove mountains, and have not charity, I am nothing.

3 And though I bestow all my goods to feed the poor, and though I give my body to be burned, and have not charity, it profiteth me nothing.

4 Charity suffereth long, and is kind; charity envieth not; chairty vaunteth not itself, is not puffed up,

5 Doth not behave itself unseemly, seeketh not her own, is not easily provoked, thinketh no evil;

6 Rejoiceth not in iniquity, but

1 Corinthians 12:31—13:13 (NRSV)

31 But strive for the greater gifts. And I will show you a still more excellent way.

•••••

IF I speak in the tongues of mortals and of angels, but do not have love, I am a noisy gong or a clanging cymbal.

2 And if I have prophetic powers, and understand all mysteries and all knowledge, and if I have all faith, so as to remove mountains, but do not have love, I am nothing.

3 If I give away all my possessions, and if I hand over my body so that I may boast, but do not have love, I gain nothing.

4 Love is patient; love is kind; love is not envious or boastful or arrogant

5 or rude. It does not insist on its own way; it is not irritable or resentful;

6 it does not rejoice in wrongdoing, but rejoices in the truth.

rejoiceth in the truth;

7 Beareth all things, believeth all things, hopeth all things, endureth all things.

8 Charity never faileth: but whether there be prophecies, they shall fail; whether there be tongues, they shall cease; whether there be knowledge, it shall vanish away.

9 For we know in part, and we prophesy in part.

10 But when that which is perfect is come, then that which is in part shall be done away.

11 When I was a child, I spake as a child, I understood as a child, I thought as a child: but when I became a man, I put away childish things.

12 For now we see through a glass, darkly; but then face to face: now I know in part; but then shall I know even as also I am known.

13 And now abideth faith, hope, charity, these three; but the greatest of these is charity.

7 It bears all things, believes all things, hopes all things, endures all things.

8 Love never ends. But as for prophecies, they will come to an end; as for tongues, they will cease; as for knowledge, it will come to an end.

9 For we know only in part, and we prophesy only in part;

10 but when the complete comes, the partial will come to an end.

11 When I was a child, I spoke like a child, I thought like a child, I reasoned like a child; when I became an adult, I put an end to childish ways.

12 For now we see in a mirror, dimly, but then we will see face to face. Now I know only in part; then I will know fully, even as I have been fully known.

13 And now faith, hope, and love abide, these three; and the greatest of these is love.

KEY VERSE

Now abideth faith, hope, charity, these three; but the greatest of these is charity.—1 Corinthians 13:13

OBJECTIVES

After reading this lesson, the student should realize that:

1. God gives gifts for a definite purpose;

2. All gifts are to be exercised in love;

3. Without love, our gifts and service are valueless; and,

4. Love is greater than faith and hope.

POINTS TO BE EMPHASIZED

Adult/Youth
Key Verse: 1 Corinthians 13:13
Print: 1 Corinthians 12:31—13:13

—Spiritual gifts and service have no value unless exercised in love. (1-3)
—Real love is characterized by patience, kindness, trust, hope, and endurance; it is free of arrogance, selfishness, and illwill. (4-7)
—When compared with other spiritual gifts, love supersedes them all. (8)
—Our best understanding is incomplete and unclear, but in God's hands we will arrive at clear and complete understanding that is rooted in love. (9-12)
—Faith, hope, and love are what will endure; and of the three the greatest is love. (13)

Children
Key Verse: 1 Corinthians 13:4
Print: 1 Corinthians 13:4; Ruth 1:16-18; 2:2-3, 8-9, 11-12

—Paul described Christian love. (1 Corinthians 13)
—When Naomi returned to Bethlehem, Ruth chose to remain with her. (Ruth 1:16-18)
—Ruth went to a field belonging to Boaz to gather grain for food for herself and Naomi. (Ruth 2:2-3)
—Boaz was kind to Ruth and offered her food and water. (8-9)
—Boaz praised Ruth for her kindness to Naomi and prayed God's blessings for her. (11-12)

(**Note**: Use KJV Scripture for Adults; NRSV Scripture for Youth and Children)

TOPICAL OUTLINE OF THE LESSON

I. Introduction
A. A Study of the Greek Words for Love
B. Biblical Background

II. Exposition and Application of the Scripture
A. Love is Primary (1 Corinthians 12:31)
B. Love is Profitable (1 Corinthians 13:1-3)
C. Love is Personified (1 Corinthians 13:4-7)
D. Love is Permanent (1 Corinthians 13:8-12)
E. Love is Pre-eminent (1 Corinthians 13:13)

III. Special Features
A. Preserving Our Heritage
B. A Concluding Word

I. Introduction

A. A STUDY OF THE GREEK WORDS FOR LOVE

Before considering the Greek words, note that we shy away form the use of the word **charity**. In the year 1611, the word charity (derived from the Latin) meant love of one's fellow men. It was defined as Christian love. Today, it has a different meaning. It stresses personal kindness or philanthropy shown to those who are poor and suffering. It involves providing help or relief to the poor; almsgiving.

Now the one Greek word for love that does not appear in the New Testament is *eros*, from which is derived the English word, erotic. It is used with regard to sexual yearning, love, or desire. Sensual passion is its emphasis. The second Greek word is *philos*. The verb *phileo* means to be fond of, to like, to be friendly to, delight in; it is a love between friends. The third Greek word is *agape*, form the verb, *agapao*. It means to love deeply, and is used of God's love. This is the word used in today's lesson. It denotes the "highest, most perfect kind of love, and implies a clear determination of will and judgment." William Evans (ISBE) said love, "whether used of God or man, is an earnest and anxious desire for, and active and beneficent interest in, the well-being of the one loved." Study John 21:15-17 to see how both words for love are used.

B. BIBLICAL BACKGROUND

We learned earlier that the human body is a type of the church. There is but one true church, one body of Christ, and it is composed of all true believers in Jesus Christ. As the heart, lungs, stomach, liver, kidneys, hands, eyes, and other organs and members of the human body vary, so the members vary in the body of Christ. We are individuals of different races, backgrounds, circumstances, languages, intellects, and from different denominations—but all having our sins washed away by the blood of Jesus Christ. We all belong to the one body.

As each member of the human body has a special work to do, so each saint has a special task to perform. Once this is realized, there is no despising other denominations, no ridiculing other saints, no need for jealousy, envy, scorn, or fighting for office and position. We learn that no one Christian has all the gifts and no one gift is given to all Christians. The Sovereign God bestows gifts and ministries as it pleases Him throughout the entire body.

II. Exposition and Application of the Scripture

A. LOVE IS PRIMARY
(1 Corinthians 12:31)

But covet earnestly the best gifts: and yet shew I unto you a more excellent way.

Usually when we hear the word covet, we think of the last of the Ten Commandments, "Thou shalt not covet" (Exodus 20:17). Here the word means to desire, delight in, take pleasure in; and it is used in the bad sense of inordinate, ungoverned and selfish desire. However, in 1 Corinthians 12:31, the original idea of the verb is to be hot, boil, seethe. It is used figuratively of the emotions of anger, love, eagerness, zeal to do good or evil. Our English word *zealous* (jealous) is derived from it.

So the words "covet earnestly" are not to be taken in the bad sense of inordinate selfish desire or wanting something forbidden. The good sense is "earnestly desire" (NKJV, RSV), "eagerly desire" (NIV), pursue, exert yourself, "strive for the more valuable spiritual gifts" (Arndt & Gingrich). Some of the saints at Corinth were impressed by the more spectacular manifestations of spiritual gifts which, as pointed out by Paul, were not always the most useful. It is therefore as if the apostle said, "Since you earnestly desire certain gifts, at least aim for the higher, more useful ones. Furthermore, beyond all of them, I will show you a path wherein to walk—the path of love, a gift which all may share."

B. LOVE IS PROFITABLE
(1 Corinthians 13:1-3)

THOUGH I speak with the tongues of men and of angels, and have not charity, I am become as sounding brass, or a tinkling cymbal. And though I have the gift of prophecy, and understand all mysteries, and all knowledge; and though I have all faith, so that I could remove mountains, and have not charity, I am nothing. And though I bestow all my goods to feed the poor, and though I give my body to be burned, and have not charity, it profiteth me nothing.

It appears that this chapter is placed parenthetically to show a way far better, far superior—the way of love. Without love governing and directing, the gifts of the Spirit are worthless. This is the message of these first three verses. Note that eloquence is first mentioned. The word "tongues" here refers to language, articulate speech. Some saints were so impressed by this gift of language that they sought to imitate it and succeeded only in speaking gibberish and nonsense, thus counterfeiting the gift.

There is no basis for suggesting angels have some special language which the saints might be enabled to speak. The gift of tongues was not given for men to communicate with angels, but to communicate with humans, that they might hear the Gospel and be saved and edified. It is therefore best to see in the phrase "tongues of men and of angels" a rhetorical way of saying, "all possible languages, and all powers of eloquence." Without love, all such speaking is nothing. Without love, the most splendid oratory becomes only noise—echoing brass, a noisy gong. Unless governed by love, this gift of eloquence is but shrill clashing, clanging, crashing noise!

In verse two, the gifts of prophecy and preaching are mentioned. Paul said: "If I had the gift of prophecy in its fullness and were able to understand the deep unfathomable secrets of God; and if I had the faith of doing, of accomplishment, or miraculous success, a wonder-working faith—without love, it all would mean nothing. If I succeeded in achieving that inward, indomitable assurance that no matter how difficult a project might be, that it could and would be accomplished successfully—but did not have love, I am nothing."

The words "the poor" are italicized in verse three. Though nothing is said about the poor, the verb rendered "to feed" means to nourish by putting a bit or crumb of food into the mouth. The "goods" signify those things at hand, thus one's possessions, property or substance. We could thus translate: "And if I give away bit by bit all of my possessions," but have not love, it profits me nothing. Paul goes a step further. This time he speaks of body-burning, a symbol of martyrdom. The God of the Bible has never called upon any man to immolate himself. Even such voluntary self-torture with its willingness to suffer for a conviction, faith or belief, is not a guarantee of sound spiritually or the presence of love.

C. LOVE IS PERSONIFIED
(1 Corinthians 13:4-7)

Charity suffereth long, is kind; charity envieth not; charity vaunteth not itself, is not puffed up, Doth not behave itself unseemly, seeketh not her own, is not easily provoked, thinketh no evil; Rejoiceth not in iniquity, but rejoiceth in the truth; Beareth all things, believeth all things, hopeth all things, endureth all things.

This section deals with the attributes of love. First is the quality of long-suffering. The Greek word means a "long holding out of the mind before it gives room to action or more generally, to passion." It means to set anger at a distance and thus exclude it; it is that self-restraint which does not hastily retaliate a wrong. It is opposed to wrath or revenge, and would rather patiently bear an injury or wrong.

The second attribute of love is its kindness. Love is not harsh, hard, sharp, bitter. J. B. Philips paraphrased: "Love looks for a way of being constructive." Third: Love does not envy. The word translated "envy" has a root which means to boil with heat, be hot. It is used figuratively of boiling anger, love, zeal for what is good or bad. In the good sense, to be zealous or jealous is to strive, desire, or exert oneself earnestly.

Do you "boil" over what other people have? Some church folks begrudge others their gifts and are grieved because another has more—materially, physically, mentally or spiritually. Saints on fire for the Lord don't boil with envy. A fourth virtue of love is that it vaunteth not itself. This means that love is not immodest; it does not call attention to itself. This is to say, it is not vain-glorious, boastful or a braggart. Moffatt says: "It makes no parade." J. B. Phillips paraphrases, "It is not anxious to impress."

Love is not puffed up. Used figuratively, it means to blow up, puff, inflate, cause to swell up, be proud or arrogant, to become conceited, pompous, to put on airs. Puffed-upness was characteristic of the Corinthians. Misusing and desecrating the special spiritual gifts they received, they became proud and boastful. But love, stated Paul, is never conceited or arrogant, never inflated with a sense of its own importance, never swell-headed, swollen with vanity.

In verse five, we learn that love does not behave itself unseemly, that is, not according with established standards of good form or taste; unbecoming, indecent. Thus love is not unmannerly or rude. The Greek word translated "behave...unseemly" means to behave disgracefully, dishonorably, indecently. Instead, love is polite and courteous. Another attribute of love is that it does not seek its own—things, advantage, profit, good wealth, etc. In other words, love does not ask, "What's in it for me?"

Our eighth attribute is: Love is not provoked (omit the word "easily"; it is not found in the original). Used favorably in Hebrews 10:24, provoke means to encourage or stir up one another in love. Love is not touchy or quick to take offence, carries no chip on its shoulder, and is not a bunch of nerves. Love is cool, calm and collected. Indeed, a touchy, temperamental person is one in whom the element of self predominates. But love ignores self and thinks of others.

The last clause in verse five teaches that love thinks no evil. Several ideas come out of the word translated "thinks." One thought is that love does not impute evil. This means if someone has done you wrong, love will forgive and never even suspect the wrong was done intentionally. A second idea is that love does not keep book on the evil done, it keeps no record on wrongs. Thus, there is no desire to get revenge. A tenth attribute of love is that it does not rejoice in iniquity. It takes no pleasure in the misfortunes and failures of others. Instead, it rejoices in the spread of the truth among men. And because it is not suspicious, always rejoices when truth triumphs.

From verse seven, we learn that love bears all things—it passes over in silence those things which displease. "By covering to keep off something which threatens, we actually bear up against it, or hold out against it and thus we endure or bear" (Thayer). Love

also believes all things. This is not naive credulity or a willingness to believe on the slightest evidence. Believe here speaks of the disposition to accept others without suspicion. Love creates within us the attitude which is trustful of others. The spirit of love bids us be eager to give the other guy the benefit of the doubt.

Love hopes all things. Hope is the expectation of good; fear is the expectation of evil. In the face of adversities, love does not become pessimistic. Holy optimism does not fade because of bad circumstances. Love has the assurance of final victory even when it finds no adequate ground for such hope. Finally, love endures all things. Patience is a rare quality today. Anybody can put on a show for a while, or put up a front. But love takes abuse; is no quitter; it sticks it out.

D. LOVE IS PERMANENT
(1 Corinthians 13:8-12)

Charity never faileth: but whether there be prophecies, they shall fail; whether there be tongues, they shall cease; whether there be knowledge, it shall vanish away. For we know in part, and we prophesy in part. But when that which is perfect is come, then that which is in part shall be done away. When I was a child, I spake as a child, I understood as a child, I thought as a child: but when I became a man, I put away childish things. For now we see through a glass, darkly; but then face to face: now I know in part; but then shall I know even as also I am known.

To say love never fails is to say it never disappears, becomes old-fashioned or obsolete. It never comes to an end, never fades out, never falls down on the job. However, there are at least three spiritual gifts which are not eternally abiding, things which eventually would pass off the scene. First on the list are prophecies, that spiritual gift whereby men were enabled to interpret and speak the will and purpose of God. This gift was a temporary endowment of the early church. Once the New Testament was complete, there was no longer any need for this gift.

The miraculous gift of tongues enabled a man to preach. Christ in a foreign language he had never studied before. This is what happened at Pentecost—a reversal of what occurred at the tower of Babel. Paul stated such a gift would cease, stop, be at an end. Tongues as signs stopped when the need for them ceased. The third gift is knowledge. This *gnosis* is not mere intelligence; it is the gift of discernment, a special illumination. It signifies a supernatural mystical knowledge. But it too shall vanish away or fail. These three spiritual gifts are found to be inferior to love. Paul predicted that in time, they will have fulfilled their function and passed away.

Verses nine and ten tell us why these spiritual gifts shall cease. Though the gifts were perfect and fully able to accomplish God's purpose, they were but the elementary first steps, the beginnings of God's program for the early church. Now that the whole is here, the "in part" is no longer needed.

We now have the complete written New Testament for the grown-up mature stage of the church age. Today, God uses the Scriptures—that which is perfect or complete. And He uses the native abilities of saints who surrender their talents to the Holy Spirit.

The time of the need for such gifts as the Corinthians so highly valued was likened to childhood, a time of immaturity. There is a stage of life wherein things are not too clearly understood. What we see in the mirror of life is at best obscure, faint, dim, puzzling, indistinct. This is the best these spiritual gifts can do for us now; however, the time will come when we shall see more clearly. As these gifts are destined to disappear, love is permanent, for the way of love is a grown-up stage of Christian discipleship.

E. LOVE IS PRE-EMINENT
(1 Corinthians 13:13)

And now abideth faith, hope, charity, these three; but the greatest of these is charity.

Finally, love is not only superior to these gifts which shall pass away, but it is also supreme among the graces which do not pass away, faith and hope! These are abiding elements of human life and not like the gifts over which the Corinthians made so much fuss. But love is greatest. All three abide: faith, hope and love. These are three great lasting qualities, but the greatest of these is love.

III. Special Features

A. PRESERVING OUR HERITAGE

The strength of what is called "The Black Church" lies not in its gifted ministers, its concern for social equality, or the soul-stirring singing of its choirs—but in its expressions of love. Where the Bible is preached and Jesus Christ is held central, the members learn more about the grace of God, and come to love Him more. Our love for Him who cleansed us in His own blood then overflows and moves us to love one another. Imagine a love that transcends convention affiliations, heals divisions, motivates the missions thrust, and enables us to have fellowship with one another (John 13:35). When Christians love one another, that love will overflow and begin to affect the lives of those who are not Christians. These three stages of love then—love God, love believers, love unbelievers—lie within the spirit of the church used by God.

B. A CONCLUDING WORD

From the very heart of our lesson, we learn that LOVE! (1) sets anger at a distance; (2) is usefully good; (3) does not boil with jealousy; (4) does not brag; (5) is not a conceited wind-bag; (6) is not rude and discourteous; (7) does not ask, "What's in it for me?" (8) carries no chip on its shoulders; (9) keeps no record of wrongs; (10) is not glad when others go wrong; (11) rejoices to see truth triumph; (12) bears up under all things; (13) is not suspicious of others; (14) is an optimist; (15) patiently sticks it out; and (16) never falls down on the job.

HOME DAILY BIBLE READINGS FOR THE WEEK OF APRIL 30, 2000

THE WAY OF LOVE

April 24 M. 1 Corinthians 13:1-7, The Gift of Love
April 25 T. 1 Corinthians 13:8-13, Love Is the Greatest Gift
April 26 W. 1 John 2:7-17, Love: An Old New Commandment
April 27 T. 1 John 3:11-17, Show Your Love for One Another
April 28 F. 1 John 3:18-24, Believe in Jesus, and Love One Another
April 29 S. 1 John 4:7-12, Let Us Love as God Loves
April 30 S. 1 John 4:13-21, We Abide in God If We Love

O Thou whom we know as love personified, grant that we may imitate You in all areas of our common existence. May our love be authentic as we reject the façade that prevents us from living that quality of life that is consistent with Your nature. In Christ's name, we pray. Amen.

The Christian March of Triumph

Unit III—*The Glory of Christian Ministry*
Children's Unit—*Joy in Ministry*

•••••

Adult Topic—*From Sorrow to Joy*

•••••

Youth Topic—*Discipline From Love*
Children's Topic—*The Joy of Serving*

•••••

Devotional Reading—2 Corinthians 1:3-11
Background Scripture—2 Corinthians 1—2
Print—2 Corinthians 2:4-17

PRINTED SCRIPTURE

2 Corinthians 2:4-17 (KJV)

4 For out of much affliction and anguish of heart I wrote unto you with many tears; not that ye should be grieved, but that ye might know the love which I have more abundantly unto you.

5 But if any have caused grief, he hath not grieved me, but in part: that I may not overcharge you all.

6 Sufficient to such a man is this punishment, which was inflicted of many.

7 So that contrariwise ye ought rather to forgive him, and comfort him, lest perhaps such a one should be swallowed up with overmuch sorrow.

8 Wherefore I beseech you that ye would confirm your love toward him.

9 For to this end also did I write, that I might know the proof of you, whether ye be obedient in all things.

10 To whom ye forgive any thing, I forgive also: for if I forgave any thing, to whom I forgave it, for your sakes forgave I it in the person of Christ;

2 Corinthians 2:4-17 (NRSV)

4 For I wrote you out of much distress and anguish of heart and with many tears, not to cause you pain, but to let you know the abundant love that I have for you.

5 But if anyone has caused pain, he has caused it not to me, but to some extent—not to exaggerate it—to all of you.

6 This punishment by the majority is enough for such a person;

7 so now instead you should forgive and console him, so that he may not be overwhelmed by excessive sorrow.

8 So I urge you to reaffirm your love for him.

9 I wrote for this reason: to test you and to know whether you are obedient in everything.

10 Anyone whom you forgive, I also forgive. What I have forgiven, if I have forgiven anything, has been for your sake in the presence of Christ.

11 And we do this so that we may not be outwitted by Satan; for we are not ignorant of his designs.

11 Lest Satan should get an advantage of us: for we are not ignorant of his devices.

12 Furthermore, when I came to Troas to preach Christ's gospel, and a door was opened unto me of the Lord,

13 I had no rest in my spirit, because I found not Titus my brother: but taking my leave of them, I went from thence into Macedonia.

14 Now thanks be unto God, which always causeth us to triumph in Christ, and maketh manifest the savour of his knowledge by us in every place.

15 For we are unto God a sweet savour of Christ, in them that are saved, and in them that perish:

16 To the one we are the savour of death unto death; and to the other the savour of life unto life. And who is sufficient for these things?

17 For we are not as many, which corrupt the word of God: but as of sincerity, but as of God, in the sight of God speak we in Christ.

12 When I came to Troas to proclaim the good news of Christ, a door was opened for me in the Lord;

13 but my mind could not rest because I did not find my brother Titus there. So I said farewell to them and went on to Macedonia.

14 But thanks be to God, who in Christ always leads us in triumphal procession, and through us spreads in every place the fragrance that comes from knowing him.

15 For we are the aroma of Christ to God among those who are being saved and among those who are perishing;

16 to the one a fragrance from death to death, to the other a fragrance from life to life. Who is sufficient for these things?

17 For we are not peddlers of God's word like so many; but in Christ we speak as persons of sincerity, as persons sent from God and standing in his presence.

Now thanks be unto God, which always causeth us to triumph in Christ, and maketh manifest the savour of his knowledge by us in every place.
—2 Corinthians 2:14

OBJECTIVES

After reading this lesson, the student should appreciate:

1. The fact that true repentance is not to be regretted;
2. The value of forgiveness in the church fellowship;
3. Awareness of the devices of the Devil; and,
4. The truth that God always leads us in victory in Christ.

POINTS TO BE EMPHASIZED

Adult/Youth

Key Verse: 2 Corinthians 2:14
Print: 2 Corinthians 2:4-17

—Paul previously wrote in anguish, not to cause pain, but to express love for the believers in Corinth. (4)

—Paul urged the church to forgive and love the one who had caused pain, lest he despair. (5-8)

—Paul and the church forgave so that Satan could not have his way, and cause division in the group and loss of the offender. (10-11)

—Paul tells of his anxious feelings when he went to Troas and did not find Titus there. (12-13)

—The witness of Christians can lead others to eternal life; rejection leads to destruction. (14-16)

—Believers are to serve Christ with sincerity and integrity. (17)

Children

Key Verse: 2 Corinthians 1:24

Print: 2 Corinthians 1:21-24; Acts 6:1-6

—Paul stated that God establishes us in Christ and puts the spirit in our hearts. (1 Corinthians 1:21-22)

—Paul did not want to tell the Corinthians what to believe; he wanted to work with them. (24)

—The disciples called the community of believers together to hear the complaint that the Hellenist widows were being neglected. (Acts 6:1-2)

—The disciples instructed the believers to choose seven men and appoint them to serve by taking the responsibility for the care of the widows. (3-4)

—The community of believers chose seven helpers and had the disciples bless them. (5-6)

(**Note**: Use KJV Scripture for Adults; NRSV Scripture for Youth and Children)

TOPICAL OUTLINE OF THE LESSON

I. Introduction
A. The Devices of the Devil
B. Biblical Background

II. Exposition and Application of the Scripture
A. A Sufficient Punishment (2 Corinthians 2:4-6)
B. An Exhortation to Forgive (2 Corinthians 2:7-11)
C. The Departure for Macedonia (2 Corinthians 2:;12-13)
D. A Triumphant Ministry (2 Corinthians 2:14-17)

III. Special Features
A. Preserving Our Heritage
B. A Concluding Word

I. Introduction

A. THE DEVICES OF THE DEVIL

One of the things which may hinder us from marching in triumph in the parade of life is ignorance concerning the strategies of Satan. Study of the Bible reveals the many methods used by the Devil. He blinds minds, accuses believers, chokes the Word, devours the unwary, deceives, counterfeits, corrupts, disguises himself as an angel of light, mixes error with truth, persecutes, murders, smites with disease, terrifies and enslaves with the fear of death, harasses, hinders, lies, divides and conquers, imitates, possesses bodies, robs, sows bad seed, creates discord and strife, sifts, uses great signs and lying wonders, and tempts mankind.

Today's lesson warns us to be on the lookout especially for his plan to move Christians to become unforgiving in their spirits. Cold, callous, self-righteous saints who forget that they were once slaves in the land of bondage tend to be legalistic instead of loving toward those who genuinely repent. Believers fall into the trap which ignores the exhortation, "Be ye kind one to another, tenderhearted, forgiving one another, even as God, for Christ's sake (in Christ) hath forgiven you" (Ephesians 4:32). Failure to forgive is to fall into Satan's snare.

B. BIBLICAL BACKGROUND

In 1 Corinthians 5:1; Paul dealt with the case of the church member who at that very moment lives in immorality with his stepmother, his father's wife. Folks in the church knew it, but elected to do nothing about it. Surely the condoning of known evil was certainly one reason for the divisions they suffered in the church. When Paul heard of this incident, he wrote that, in the name of Jesus Christ, disciplinary action be taken. The church agreed and acted accordingly.

Now in today's lesson, it appears that whereas the offender repented, there were those who declined to forgive him. Paul feared that such an unforgiving attitude would create despair that would bring spiritual disaster in the life of the church, not to mention what it would do to the penitent believer. Be aware of the fact that not all scholars relate today's lesson with the incident mentioned in 1 Corinthians 5. Plummer (ICC) doubts Paul refers to this case of incest.

Filson (Interpreter's) asserts it cannot have been the immoral man of 1 Corinthians 5. He claims Paul dealt with some other church member, one "prompted by intruders hostile to Paul," who led a revolt against the apostle. MacDonald (Believer's Commentary) states reference may be to the incestuous man, or to some other trouble-maker in the church at Corinth.

We will stick with the belief held by Mitchell (Parallel Bible Commentary) and Bernard (Expositor's Greek Testament) that it is the man in 1 Corinthians 5:1, and that Paul suppresses the man's name "with a rare delicacy of feeling." Henry Morris (as also Lenski, and Alford) believers Paul's rebuke of the sin of incest resulted in excommunication, and repentance, and now the apostle urges the church to forgive the man and restore him to the fellowship of the assembly.

II. Exposition and Application of the Scripture

A. A SUFFICIENT PUNISHMENT
(2 Corinthians 2:4-6)

For out of much affliction and anguish of heart I wrote unto you with many tears; not that ye should be grieved, but that ye might know the love which I have more abundantly unto you. But if any have caused grief, he hath not grieved me, but in part: that I may not overcharge you all. Sufficient to such a man is this punishment, which was inflicted of many.

The chapter begins with Paul's explanation of the reason for the postponement of his visit to Corinth. There is no record of this intermediate visit. And the letter mentioned in verse three does not exist. Some commentators assume the letter was First Corinthians. Others believe it was lost. At any rate, it appears the trip was postponed because he had no desire that the visit would be as painful as the previous one had been. When he wrote the first epistle, his state of mind was one of much affliction, anguish of heart, and many tears!

He had heard from Chloe's household about the bad situation of the church there in Corinth, and had been moved by the Holy Spirit to severely reprove them. Paul's love for the saints was very great, and he wanted them to know how he felt.

The church was reminded that to grieve Paul was to grieve the church. To attack one member was to attack the whole assembly. Such is our relationship with one another as Christians; we are members of the same body.

The apostle cautioned against punishing the offender too severely, and advised the church accordingly. Note the use of the word," by the majority" or "by the man" in verse six. Baptists see here a congregational polity or government, one of majority rule. Evidently, each local assembly had the power to carry out its own discipline. Each church was autonomous. Baptist churches still have autonomy, but it seems far too many have lost the desire to maintain the separation between church and state.

Some assemblies no longer enforce discipline. We live in an age of "anything goes," when church members do as they please. We see the lack of punctuality, "come as you are" dress codes, the spirit of entertainment that manifests itself in mime dancing. Nothing is said about having children out of wedlock, and some of our churches have even removed from their covenant the phrase, "to abstain from the sale and use of intoxicating drinks as a beverage."

There is no need to insist that the words "the many" should be interpreted to mean unanimous. On occasions in church meetings, we hear motions made to change a majority vote into a unanimous vote. This, of course, is an unnecessary measure, and meaningless even if passed. There is no need to seek unanimous support in order to claim the leading of the Holy Spirit. The period of disfellowship experienced by the immoral member was sufficient punishment whether voted upon by simple majority or unanimously.

B. AN EXHORTATION TO FORGIVE (2 Corinthians 2:7-11)

So that contrariwise ye ought rather to forgive him, and comfort him, lest perhaps such a one should be swallowed up with overmuch sorrow. Wherefore I beseech you that ye would confirm your love toward him. For to this end also did I write, that I might know the proof of you, whether ye be obedient in all things. To whom ye forgive any thing, I forgive also: for if I forgave any thing, to whom I forgave it, for your sakes forgave I it in the person of Christ; Lest Satan should get an advantage of us: for we are not ignorant of his devices.

Forgiveness is a great healer. Christians ought not forget to apply it. The word used (*charizomai*) means to give freely or graciously as a favor (Arndt & Gingrich); to remit, pardon; to show one's self gracious, kind, benevolent (Thayer). Along with forgiveness is mentioned comfort, a word meaning to encourage and strengthen by consolation. Failure to forgive and console could cause the repentant believer to be driven to despair—"swallowed up" in extreme sorrow, excessive grief. Paul thus discouraged chastisement that was too severe.

Keep in mind, however, that we are not dealing here with the forgiveness of personal wrongs. That's another matter, one which requires us to forgive the very moment the wrong is committed against us. Our lesson deals with wrongs against the church. A fallen and repentant church member who has sinned against the church is to be forgiven by the church in some formal congregation's resolution. Remember, it was by church vote that the offender was excommunicated or disfellowshiped (1 Corinthians 5:2, 13). Paul urged the saints to confirm or reaffirm (NIV) their love to the penitent believer. "Ratify to him love" (Lenski). Accepting him as a brother restored to the fellowship would constitute a public display of reaffirmation. Referring to his earlier letter, Paul said he desired to know more about their genuineness in order to see (test in order to approve) if they were indeed obedient to Jesus Christ in all things.

Uniting with them in their decisions, the apostle made known that whom they forgive, he forgives. Paul's relationship with the saints at Corinth was one "in the sight of Christ." The phrase signifies a consciousness of Christ being present and approving their actions. The Lord bound together Paul and the Corinthian church he founded, in order that they might not be taken advantage of by Satan. There is a definite article (the) before this name, making it **the Satan**. Later, the name came to be used regularly as a proper name, Satan. It is a word derived from the Hebrew and means adversary. Devil means slanderer, accuser. The Greek for Devil is *diabolos*; in Spanish we have, *Diablo*. Other names are dragon, serpent, Beelzebub, Belial, lucifer, the evil one, tempter, god of this age, prince (ruler) of this world-system, prince of the power of the air.

We are to realize that one of Satan's devices (thoughts, evil purposes, ideas, products of the mind) is to defeat a believer or an entire congregation in these two ways. One: move the saint to condone sin. Two: move the saint to refuse to forgive the repentant. Either way, the Devil seeks to cause disharmony in the church—to defeat, outwit, defraud, cheat, overreach, and gain control in the local assembly. By exercising forgiveness in love, we can defeat the Devil's design. "Let us then act promptly to prevent the Devil capturing the sorrowing penitent," exhorted Paul!

C. THE DEPARTURE FOR MACEDONIA
(2 Corinthians 2:12-13)

Furthermore, when I came to Troas to preach Christ's gospel, and a door was opened unto me of the Lord, I had no rest in my spirit, because I found not Titus my brother: but taking my leave of them, I went from thence into Macedonia.

Paul went to Troas, a seaport in the northwest section of what is today the nation of Turkey. From here he could depart for Macedonia. His purpose in going to Troas was to preach Christ's Gospel. A door had been opened for him by the Lord (or in the Lord). Servants of Christ are always amazed how the Lord creates opportunities for them to be used in His service. However, because he did not find Titus (his brother in the Lord) there, he still had no peace of mind. Indeed, his anxiety concerning what took place at Corinth was so great that Paul said good-bye to the saints at Troas, and headed on to Macedonia. Recall that some time earlier, Paul had sent Titus from Ephesus to Corinth to gather information about conditions in the church there. Paul's disappointment at not meeting Titus increased his concern about the problem in the Corinthian church. This is why he decided to leave Troas and proceed to Macedonia.

D. A TRIUMPHANT MINISTRY
(2 Corinthians 2:14-17)

Now thanks be unto God, which always causeth us to triumph in Christ, and maketh manifest the savour of his knowledge by us in every place. For we are unto God a sweet savour of Christ, in them that are saved, and in them that perish: To the one we are the savour of death unto death; and to the other the savour of life unto life. And who is sufficient for these things? For we are not as many, which corrupt the word of God: but as of sincerity, but as of God, in the sight of God speak we in Christ.

"But unto God thanks" is the way this verse begins in the Greek, thus emphasizing who gets the praise and credit. Paul is jubilant as he celebrates along with Titus and Timothy the victory at Corinth. Satan's dangerous efforts to destroy the church had failed. And all the credit goes to God in Christ. In the Lord, there is no defeat. No matter where the servant of Christ labors, he or she is led on "from place to place in the train of His triumph" (Conybeare). In Christ, we have the victory already, for we serve a risen, living Savior.

The translation *leads us in triumph* comes from a verb used twice by Paul. In Colossians 2:15, we read Christ "spoiled principalities and powers... made a show of them openly, *triumphing* over them in it." The verb comes from a word which was a festal hymn to Bacchus, also known as Dionysus, a Greek god of wine and giver of the grape. It came to be used of the Roman triumph. Whenever a victorious Roman general returned home safely, this high honor might be bestowed upon him. As word spread of the coming procession, people burned incense or sweet spices and toss them into the street. Flowers were tossed; folk sang and shouted as the procession approached. First in the procession were the magistrates and the senate.

They were followed by the trumpeters. Then came the spoils, arms, standards, statues, etc., all the booty; then the sacrificial animals, white oxen with gilded horns to be offered up in the temple of Jupiter. Then came the prisoners, the captives. After them came the victorious general himself, in a chariot drawn by four horses bedecked with laurel, and possibly contained his children or very close friends, and a slave holding a crown over his head. Last of all came the soldiers shouting and singing. Verse fourteen is placed here. "Leads us in triumph" is better than "causeth us to triumph." This verse is one of joy and victory, not of humiliation.

Paul and those with him are "in Christ," and it is this phrase which places them in the victory column. Evidently, the apostle had seen these processions and was impressed with the prisoners before the general and the soldiers behind the general's chariot. Regardless of position in the parade, the general was still the leader, the hero of the hour. "Thanks be to God, who always leads us (His soldiers) in the train of His triumph." It is the Christian who marches behind Christ in His triumph even "as the solders of the victorious army always did" (Ramsay).

The fragrance means different things to different people. To believers (those being saved), it is the aroma of everlasting life. To the enemies of Christ, the smell is one of defeat, retribution, death and destruction—the malodor, if you please, of perishing! "And who is sufficient for these things?" "And who is equal to such a task?" (NIV) "Who would think himself adequate for a responsibility like this?" (JBP). You might expect to answer, "No man." Indeed, of himself man cannot handle it. False prophets and phony teachers corrupt the Word of God. They are but hucksters and peddlers who make merchandise of the things of Christ, yea, who adulterate the Truth. Their mercenary motives move them to make money out of the ministry. However, Paul replies that the sincere servant of Christ realizes that sufficiency is from God, and from Him alone.

III. Special Features

A. PRESERVING OUR HERITAGE

As Black Baptists, we should treasure our heritage. Baptists believe in an autonomous church government. There are several intimations that early church assemblies were indeed autonomous, and not under some hierarchical set up. First of all, in 1 Corinthians 5, Paul does not demand by apostolic authority. He states that whatever action the church takes *when they are gathered together*, in the name of our Lord Jesus Christ, that it be done. In today's lesson, we again see the congregational aspect. In verse six, as noted in the Exposition, the punishment of the immoral member was meted out by the majority. "Each church had the power to carry out its own church discipline" (Thiessen).

Then in verse nine, the obedience is to Christ in every regard—and not to Paul. "Each congregation is autonomous but...is ever under Christ when it is exercising its autonomy" (Lenski). Paul's confidence in the congregation is expressed in verse ten. The church did not have to get Paul's approval for its action. The local assembly acted, the apostle agreed. They forgave the offender; Paul likewise had forgiven him. What the congregation did was indeed wise, for to have done otherwise would have allowed Satan to take advantage of them.

Black Baptists must work to maintain the autonomy of each local assembly. We must resist the inroads of the government at whatever level the state seeks to usurp authority over us. We must not sell our congregation souls for a pot of subsidized soup. Nor are we to allow self-appointed bishops to extend their **fulness** over us! Our orders come from Jesus Christ!

B. A CONCLUDING WORD

Never forget that Jesus Christ rose triumphant from the grave. And, we are in Him. Even when it seems we have lost the battle, rest assured the outcome of the skirmish does not determine the outcome of the war. We are on the winning side. And because we are, we must pay attention to the exhortation to be aware of Satan's attempts to discourage us. We are not to let ignorance of the "wiles" (methods) or "devices" (schemes) of the Devil allow this enemy of our souls succeed in any way to "achieve his perverted self-goals" (Lindsey). Whatever affliction or turmoil you may go through this day, remember the Lord Jesus Christ always leads us in victory!

HOME DAILY BIBLE READINGS FOR THE WEEK OF MAY 7, 2000

THE CHRISTIAN MARCH OF TRIUMPH

May 1 M. 2 Corinthians 1:1-11, God Consoles Us in Our Afflictions
May 2 T. 2 Corinthians 1:12-22, Sealed by God's Spirit
May 3 W. 2 Corinthians 1:23—2:4, Love Prevails Over Pain and Conflict
May 4 T. 2 Corinthians 2:5-11, Christian Forgiveness for the Offender
May 5 F. 2 Corinthians 2:12-17, The Gospel: The Fragrance of Life
May 6 S. 2 Corinthians 3:1-11, Good News Written on Human Hearts
May 7 S. 2 Corinthians 3:12-18, Freed and Transformed by the Spirit

Our Father, who has promised that we would encounter tribulations in this world, may we accept the toils and trials of our life as opportunities to purify our Christian character. Amen.

Trials and Triumphs of Christian Ministry

Adult Topic—*From Suffering to Triumph*

•••••

Youth Topic—*Power From Weakness*

Children's Topic—*The Joy of Telling Good News*

•••••

Devotional Reading—2 Corinthians 6:1-10

Background Scripture—2 Corinthians 4

Print—2 Corinthians 4:5-18

PRINTED SCRIPTURE

2 Corinthians 4:5-18 (KJV)

5 For we preach not ourselves, but Christ Jesus the Lord; and ourselves your servants for Jesus' sake.

6 For God, who commanded the light to shine out of darkness, hath shined in our hearts, to give the light of the knowledge of the glory of God in the face of Jesus Christ.

7 But we have this treasure in earthen vessels, that the excellency of the power may be of God, and not of us.

8 We are troubled on every side, yet not distressed; we are perplexed, but not in despair;

9 Persecuted, but not forsaken; cast down, but not destroyed;

10 Always bearing about the body the dying of the Lord Jesus, that the life also of Jesus might be made manifest in our body.

11 For we which live are always delivered unto death for Jesus' sake, that the life also of Jesus might be made manifest in our mortal flesh.

12 So then death worketh in us, but life in you.

2 Corinthians 4:5-18 (NRSV)

5 For we do not proclaim ourselves; we proclaim Jesus Christ as Lord and ourselves as your slaves for Jesus' sake.

6 For it is the God who said, "Let light shine out of darkness," who had shone in our hearts to give the light of the knowledge of the glory of God in the face of Jesus Christ.

7 But we have this treasure in clay jars, so that it may be made clear that this extraordinary power belongs to God and does not come from us.

8 We are afflicted in every way, but not crushed; perplexed, but not driven to despair;

9 persecuted, but not forsaken; struck down, but not destroyed;

10 always carrying in the body the death of Jesus, so that the life of Jesus may also be made visible in our bodies.

11 For while we live, we are always being given up to death for Jesus' sake, so that the life of Jesus may be made visible in our mortal flesh.

13 We having the same spirit of faith, according as it is written, I believed, and therefore have I spoken; we also believe, and therefore speak;

14 Knowing that he which raised up the Lord Jesus shall raise up us also by Jesus, and shall present us with you.

15 For all things are for your sakes, that the abundant grace might through the thanksgiving of many redound to the glory of God.

16 For which cause we faint not; but though our outward man perish, yet the inward man is renewed day by day.

17 For our light affliction, which is but for a moment, worketh for us a far more exceeding and eternal weight of glory;

18 While we look not at the things which are seen, but at the things which are not seen: for the things which are seen are temporal; but the things which are not seen are eternal.

12 So death is at work in us, but life in you.

13 But just as we have the same spirit of faith that is in accordance with scripture— "I believe, and so I spoke"—we also believe, and so we speak,

14 because we know that the one who raised the Lord Jesus will raise us also with Jesus, and will bring us with you into his presence.

15 Yes, everything is for your sake, so that grace, as it extends to more and more people, may increase thanksgiving, to the glory of God.

16 So we do not lose heart. Even though our outer nature is wasting away, our inner nature is being renewed day by day.

17 For this slight momentary affliction is preparing us for an eternal weight of glory beyond all measure,

18 because we look not at what can be seen but at what cannot be seen; for what can be seen is temporary, but what cannot be seen is eternal.

KEY VERSE

We are troubled on every side, yet not distressed; we are perplexed, but not in despair; Persecuted, but not forsaken; cast down, but not destroyed.
—*2 Corinthians 4:8-9*

OBJECTIVES

After reading this lesson, the student should be impressed that:

1. The Christian ministry is Christ-centered;

2. The godly suffer but are not destroyed;

3. Power for effective ministry comes from God alone; and,

4. Growth of the inner person is eternally important.

POINTS TO BE EMPHASIZED
Adult/Youth
Key Verse: 2 Corinthians 4:8-9
Print: 2 Corinthians 4:5-18

—The truth we proclaim is not ourselves, but Jesus Christ as Lord and ourselves as slaves for Jesus' sake. (5)

—God the creator of light has shone in the believers' hearts to let others know the glory of God in Jesus Christ. (6)

—Our power comes from God and not from ourselves. (7)

—We experience many difficulties and trials, but through God's power we are not destroyed in order that Jesus may be made known. (8-12)

—Our faith enables us to proclaim that God who raised Jesus will also raise us. (13-14)

—We can have hope and not despair because we know that our affliction is temporary and is preparing us for eternal glory. (16-18)

Children

Key Verse: 2 Corinthians 4:5
Print: 2 Corinthians 4:5; 5:14; Acts 8:26-31, 35-38

—Paul stated that he was not preaching about himself; he told about Jesus Christ. (2 Corinthians 4:5)

—Paul wanted others to know and respect God. (2 Corinthians 5:11)

—Philip encountered an Ethiopian on the road from Jerusalem to Gaza. (Acts 8:26-28)

—On hearing the Ethiopian reading from the book of Isaiah, Philip asked him if he understood what he was reading. (28-30)

—Philip shared with the Ethiopian the Good News about Jesus. (35)

—The Ethiopian requested that Philip baptize him. (36-38)

(**Note**: Use KJV Scripture for Adults; NRSV Scripture for Youth and Children)

TOPICAL OUTLINE OF THE LESSON

I. Introduction
A. Earthen Vessels
B. Biblical Background

II. Exposition and Application of the Scripture
A. The Preaching of Christ (2 Corinthians 4:5-6)
B. The Power of God (2 Corinthians 4:7)
C. The Perils of Ministry (2 Corinthians 4:8-12)
D. The Proclamation of Faith (2 Corinthians 4:13-15)
E. The Preparation for Glory (2 Corinthians 4:16-18)

III. Special Features
A. Preserving Our Heritage
B. A Concluding Word

I. Introduction

A. EARTHEN VESSELS

The word rendered *earthen* (*ostrakon*) means baked clay. Vessels made of clay were probably non-porous, heat-resistant, and were used for cooking and for boiling clothes. In Jeremiah 31:14, the deeds to the field of Hanamel, Jeremiah's cousin, were put in an earthen vessel for preservation, after the prophet paid for the land. Paul spoke of an earthen (ware) vessel, along with vessels of gold, silver and wood (2 Timothy 2:20).

Then there is the figurative use of the phrase, *earthen vessels*. In Jeremiah 19:1, 11, the potter's earthen flask symbolizes the nation, Judah. The prophet is told to smash the vessel in the sight of some of the elders of the people and priests, and thereby illustrate God's breaking Judah because of its idolatry (Isaiah 30:14). Breaking the earthen vessel symbolized the destruction of Jerusalem. In Lamentations 4:2, the clay pots signify commonness.

This figurative aspect is seen in today's lesson in 2 Corinthians 4:7. The vessel is our body. We humans are but mortal pieces of clay, dying daily and returning to mother earth. We are frail (Thayer), breakable (Arndt & Gingrich); diseased, subject to change, fragile, physically weak, and presently dwelling in a body of humiliation (Philippians 3:21). Of ourselves, by ourselves, and in ourselves, we can do nothing. We hear Christ our Lord saying: "Without me you can do nothing" (John 15:5).

The marvel of it all is that God neither needs our strength, nor is He hindered by our weaknesses. Our impotence does not detract from His omnipotence; indeed, His strength is made perfect in weakness (2 Corinthians 12:9). By His power the Gospel is preached, souls are saved, and saints are edified. All the praise belongs to Him! To glorify God is to magnify, exalt, adore, honor, worship and obey Him. Thanksgiving is one of the noblest offerings we can give to God's glory. All glory belongs to Him! For the excellency of the power is of God and not of us.

B. BIBLICAL BACKGROUND

A major thrust of Second Corinthians is the defense of Paul's apostolic authority. The Greek word for defense is *apologia*, from which is derived our word, apology. Literally, it means, "a word for," verbal defense, speech in defense. We also get the word *apologetics*, which is the branch of theology that is concerned with defending or proving the truth of Christian doctrine.

There were those at Corinth who accused the apostle of insincerity. Some people questioned whether he was really an apostle. Paul went on the speak of the joy in Christ even while unkind attacks were made against his character and behavior. Saints are able to use what they suffer for Christ to encourage others who also suffer for the Savior. Paul then went on to explain his failure to visit them; he explained the reason for the delay. Notice that Paul's commitment to the call of Christ empowered him to deal with the questions raised regarding his motivation for service. His devotion was unshaken by criticism.

II. Exposition and Application of the Scripture

A. THE PREACHING OF CHRIST
(2 Corinthians 4:5-6)

For we preach not ourselves, but Christ Jesus the Lord; and ourselves your servants for Jesus' sake. For God, who commanded the light to shine out of darkness, hath shined in our hearts, to give the light of the knowledge of the glory of God in the face of Jesus Christ.

In the opening verse of our lesson, three things are said about preaching. First, "It is not our practice to make ourselves the topic of our preaching," said Paul. The word translated *preach* means to proclaim, announce, cry as a herald, "always with a suggestion of formality, gravity and an authority which must be listened to and obeyed" (Thayer). Preachers are not to exalt themselves. The pulpit is not a stage; it is not a place for showing off or exhibiting gifts for self-glory. Second. We preach Christ Jesus as Lord—owner, possessor, master, controller, having power or authority to dispose of as He pleases. There is really no message other than the Lordship of Christ.

The desire "to see Jesus" should not be hindered because the preacher is in the way. Have you heard it said that, "If Christ is not Lord of all He is not Lord at all"? **This is false!** Those who say it mean well, hoping to emphasize the fact that we should be totally surrendered. However, Christ is Lord absolutely! It does not matter what our degree of surrenderedness is. Our failure to fully realize His claim to ownership does not lessen His Lordship. In fact, He still rules even in the area of our disobedience by chastening us!

Third. Because we are bondservants of the Lord Jesus, we are also the bondservants of all who belong to Him. Our service to Him should show itself in our dealings with others. We are slaves of Christ, and one aspect of His will for us is that we serve other Christians. We serve on account of Christ, because of Christ, for Christ's sake! With the proper motives, means, methods and message, our serving others is serving Him. Note that we Christians are also reflectors of God's light. We ought daily sing, "There is sunshine in my soul today" (Eliza E. Hewitt). Our conversion is defined as God's having shone in our hearts. He did so in order that we might make known to others "the knowledge of His glory in the face of Jesus Christ."

B. THE POWER OF GOD
(2 Corinthians 4:7)

But we have this treasure in earthen vessels, that the excellency of the power may be of God, and not of us.

Watchman Nee states that in this verse "we have possibly the clearest statement there is of the nature of practical Christianity." The glorious ministry of Jesus Christ is not limited by mere human weakness. Our bodies are weak, decaying vessels; our humanity is depicted in its brittleness. We are "common clay pots" (TEV), "jars of clay" (NIV), "perishable containers" (LB), "earthenware jars of pots" (JBP, NEB). Within us the conflict continues between the new nature and the old. Alford suggests the treasure is the preaching of the Gospel described in the preceding verses. Fortunately, the Gospel is not the product of man's genius or human strength.

What counts is not the condition of the vessel, but the degree to which our ministries point attention to the glory of God. Imagine committing such a valuable jewel as the Gospel of the shed blood of Jesus Christ to frail, weak earthen vessels! We are to remember then that the Lord measures our consecration. Dr. Wm. E. Kuhnle reminds us that "what we bear in these earthen vessels is called a treasure. It is not a bargain basement proposition. What we do with this treasure in effect determine our faithfulness to God."

C. THE PERILS OF MINISTRY
(2 Corinthians 4:8-12)

We are troubled on every side, yet not distressed; we are perplexed, but not in despair; Persecuted, but not forsaken; cast down, but not destroyed; Always bearing about in the body the dying of the Lord Jesus, that the life also of Jesus might be made manifest in our body. For we which live are always delivered unto death for Jesus' sake, that the life also of Jesus might be made manifest in our mortal flesh. So then death worketh in us, but life in you.

"Must I be carried to the skies On flow'ry beds of ease, While others fought to win the prize, And sailed thro' bloody seas?" This section of the lesson answers Isaac Watts' question and informs us that life is not necessarily easy for the vessels with the treasure within them. Paul used present participles to denote action in progress in the list of adversities and triumphs given in verses 8-10. Reading the list helps us to see better how

the Lord protects His earthen vessels!

There are four sets of contrasts established: (1) Troubled on every side, hardpressed, afflicted, harried, handicapped, YET not distressed, crushed, hemmed in, frustrated or broken; (2) Perplexed, puzzled, bewildered, sometimes in doubt, BUT not in despair or at wits' end, ready to give up and quit; (3) Persecuted, hunted down by many enemies, BUT not forsaken or abandoned, or never having to stand it alone, never without a friend; and (4) Cast down, struck down, badly hurt, BUT not destroyed or left to die. "Knocked down but never knocked out" (J. B. Philips).

We are always bearing about in the body of the dying of the Lord Jesus. This means we are identified with the death of our Lord, and also with His life. For it is impossible to show His life IN us unless we also recognize our death WITH Him. In other words, when he died, we died; when He rose; we rose (Galatians 2:20). These are basically positional truths, but may show conditional aspects as well. Not only is there physical suffering for Christ, but there is the mortifying (Colossians 3:5)—putting to death of the self life, the old nature, as well. "A true definition of the believers' cross-bearing has been given" (Chafer). The death that operates in us, whether physical or dying to sin, is for our benefit. "God uses our death to lead you to eternal life in Christ, as well as abundant life," said Paul.

D. THE PROCLAMATION OF
FAITH (2 Corinthians 4:13-15)

We having the same spirit of faith, according as it is written, I

believed, and therefore have I spoken; we also believe, and therefore speak; knowing that he which raised up the Lord Jesus shall raise up us also by Jesus, and shall present us with you. For all things are for your sakes, that the abundant grace might through the thanksgiving of many redound to the glory of God.

If you have faith at all, that faith desires to express itself. Faith in the Word of God is the comfort of the psalmist who wrote: "I believed, therefore have I spoken" (Psalm 116:10). There is to be then no mere silent witness, but a spontaneous articulate response—a giving of thanks! Faith moves us to proclaim the Gospel of truth. By faith our confidence is founded on the Word of God. Indeed, the Resurrection itself is the basis for such confidence. We serve a risen Savior. Note the use of the human name, Jesus, the Man who suffered, bled and died, was buried and raised by the glory of God the Father.

Paul picks up this same spirit of faith that defies persecution and death. He has the assurance that the same God and Father who raised up the Lord Jesus from the dead will also raise him and his assistants. And God will present the apostle and his comrades along with the saints in the church at Corinth. This hope in the Resurrection, and being present with those at Corinth for whom he has labored, strengthens Paul. Such inner hope fortifies him against the destruction of the outer, physical man.

Continued deliverance from dangers and perils caused Paul to know the grace of God in a better way. He saw God's grace at work as he preached the Gospel, and people believed and were saved. Here then is what we learn. Paul said: "All that I have gone through as an apostle—the trials, tribulations, tests and troubles—all of the dying daily, have been for you. Why? In order that God's abundant, overflowing spreading grace might be extended more and more, as those who hear the Gospel believe it and accept it. Then they too will join the swelling chorus and give thanks. This increased thanksgiving will redound to the glory of God.

E. THE PREPARATION FOR GLORY (2 Corinthians 4:16-18)

For which cause we faint not; but though our outward man perish, yet the inward man is renewed day by day. For our light affliction, which is but for a moment, worketh for us a far more exceeding and eternal weight of glory; While we look not at the things which are seen, but at the things which are not seen: for the things which are seen are temporal; but the things which are not seen are eternal.

The day we are born we begin to die; the first step we take we begin marching to the grave. Yet we have hope. For although our earthly house is perishing, decaying (NASB), wasting away (RSV), there is the simultaneous action of being renewed daily. The one-a-day vitamin pill we take for our bodies does not compare with the dose of day-by-day Christlikeness for our souls. Our present temporary, light affliction produces something much more valuable.

Paul makes no attempt here to develop a philosophy of suffering, or explain the cause or purpose of affliction.

However, there is expressed a confidence that God is in charge. By calling his suffering "light affliction" the apostle does not imply what he experienced was mild, moderate or frivolous. But in comparison to eternity, the "for the moment" troubles do not weigh enough (the word *worthy* in Romans 8:18 also means weighty). "Spiritual maturity comes as believers allow the trials of life to develop in them a patient spirit" (Hayden).

The things which are not seen are not invisible things. Lack of faith prevents us from seeing some things. When our faith journey is complete, we shall see what cannot be seen now. To "look at" (verse 18) in Greek is *skopeo*, a word readily recognized in telescope, microscope. The stuff that is seen is outside, light, ephemeral, evanescent—here today and gone tomorrow. God wants us to focus our eyes on that which is inside, abiding, eternal, "heavy stuff."

III. Special Features

A. PRESERVING OUR HERITAGE

When the heinous institution of slavery was practiced in the United States, Black Christian slaves emphasized the future, not the present. Of course, they hated slavery, but were powerless to emancipate themselves. They looked forward to a better life, believing that there was a heaven where they would at last enjoy freedom. The emphasis upon preaching and singing about heaven and the after life is called by some scholars, "compensatory." Emphasis on the joyous life in heaven compensated for the miseries of life here on earth.

However, contrary to the beliefs of some liberal scholars, the New Testament does indeed emphasize the life to come. Pity Black Baptists who put all of the eggs in the here and now basket. Vance Havner warned of the danger of getting all tied up with various movements and causes to the point that when the movement collapses, we have nothing to preach.

When future events are viewed properly through the eyes of God, and the Bible is sincerely believed to be His Word, the Lord uses such faith to enable the saint to live better in the present. Knowledge of the future helps us live a better life here and now! So it is that our lesson would seek to re-establish the correct emphasis. What we experience now, that which is temporal, in no way compares with that which is eternal, that which awaits us in glory. And yet there is this paradox, that when our faith matures to this point of view, we enjoy now a foretaste of glory divine. Our slave foreparents could teach us a thing or two about coping with life's afflictions.

B. A CONCLUDING WORD

Today's lesson is placed within the background of the description of the New Testament ministry. In an earlier lesson, we learned that the ministry is triumphant, and that we all are led in victory by Jesus Christ. Second: We were taught that the ministry is accredited. In other words, the life of the new creation in

Christ is proof of the reality of the Gospel. The changed lives of the believers are evidence of the working of the Holy Spirit. "The day-by-day life of every Christian is an epistle (or letter) which other people read" (Pilgrim Bible). Third: The ministry is not one based upon God dealing with believers on the basis of the law. Rather the principles is the working of the Holy Spirit. This means New Testament ministers and all church workers are made sufficient by the enabling work of the Holy Spirit. Fourth: The ministry is honest; it is true. Preachers and church officers must realize that all ministry is to be without hypocrisy and lying. Our lives are to back up what we preach and teach. What we preach and teach is to be supported by the kind of life we live! A true ministry cannot be carried out faithfully where deceit is involved or practiced. Furthermore, the honest ministry exalts the Lord Jesus Christ. In so doing, we are the servants of others.

Watchman Nee said: "If we cling to our pleasures and griefs, grudging to let go of our own interests, we shall be like a room that is too full of furniture to accommodate anything more." The true ministry recognizes that regeneration and the spiritual illumination that accompanies it originate in Jesus Christ. In other words, the true ministry proclaims the true light. And Jesus Christ alone is the Light of the World. Fifth: The Christian ministry involves suffering. Paul said in 2 Timothy 3:12: "All who desire to live godly in Christ Jesus will suffer persecution." Christ said: "In the world you will have tribulation; but be of good cheer, I have overcome the world" (John 16:33). All of us involved in Christian ministry must so adjust our minds to the will of God that we are willing to have the attitude of the Savior reproduced in us. Remember that there is a cross to bear in the service of the Lord, but there is also a crown to wear. For all of the temporal trials we experience produce a far more exceedingly eternal weight of glory.

HOME DAILY BIBLE READINGS FOR THE WEEK OF MAY 14, 2000

THE TRIALS AND TRIUMPHS OF CHRISTIAN MINISTRY

May 8	M.	2 Corinthians 4:1-7, God's Light Shines in Our Hearts
May 9	T.	2 Corinthians 4:8-15, God Raised Jesus and Will Raise Us
May 10	W.	2 Corinthians 4:16—5:10, We Walk and Live By Faith
May 11	T.	2 Corinthians 5:11-21, Reconciled to Be Reconcilers
May 12	F.	2 Corinthians 6:1-11, Open Wide Your Hearts
May 13	S.	2 Corinthians 6:14—7:1, We Are Temples of the Living God
May 14	S	2 Corinthians 7:1—13, Paul's Joy at the Corinthians' Repentance

Eternal God, our Father, You have called us into the vineyard to labor for the cause of the kingdom. Amen.

The Collection for
Jerusalem Christians

Adult Topic—*From Reluctance to Joyful Giving*

·····

Youth Topic—*Joy From Giving*
Children's Topic—*The Joy of Giving*

·····

Devotional Reading—2 Corinthians 8:1-15
Background Scripture—2 Corinthians 9
Print—2 Corinthians 9:1-13

PRINTED SCRIPTURE

2 Corinthians 9:1-13 (KJV)

FOR AS touching the ministering to the saints, it is superfluous for me to write to you:

2 For I know the forwardness of your mind, for which I boast of you to them of Macedonia, that Achaia was ready a year ago; and your zeal hath provoked very many.

3 Yet have I sent the brethren, lest our boasting of you should be in vain in this behalf; that, as I said, ye may be ready:

4 Lest haply if they of Macedonia come with me, and find you unprepared, we (that we say not, ye) should be ashamed in this same confident boasting.

5 Therefore I thought it necessary to exhort the brethren, that they would go before unto you, and make up beforehand your bounty, whereof ye had notice before, that the same might be ready, as a matter of bounty, and not as of covetousness.

6 But this I say, He which soweth

2 Corinthians 9:1-13 (NRSV)

NOW IT is not necessary for me to write you about the ministry to the saints,

2 for I know your eagerness, which is the subject of my boasting about you to the people of Macedonia, saying that Achaia has been ready since last year; and your zeal has stirred up most of them.

3 But I am sending the brothers in order that our boasting about you may not prove to have been empty in this case, so that you may be ready, as I said you would be;

4 otherwise, if some Macedonians come with me and find that you are not ready, we would be humiliated—to say nothing of you—in this undertaking.

5 So I thought it necessary to urge the brothers to go on ahead to you, and arrange in advance for this bountiful gift that you have promised, so that it may be ready as voluntary gift and not as an extortion.

6 The point is this: the one who

sparingly shall reap also sparingly; and he which soweth bountifully shall reap also bountifully.

7 Every man according as he purposeth in his heart, so let him give; not grudgingly, or of necessity: for God loveth a cheerful giver.

8 And God is able to make all grace abound toward you; that ye, always having all sufficiency in all things, may abound to every good work:

9 (As it is written, He hath dispersed abroad; he hath given to the poor: his righteousness remaineth for ever.

10 Now he that ministereth seed to the sower both minister bread for your food, and multiply your seed sown, and increase the fruits of your righteousness;)

11 Being enriched in every thing to all bountifulness, which causeth through us thanksgiving to God.

12 For the administration of this service not only supplieth the want of the saints, but is abundant also by many thanksgivings unto God;

13 Whiles the experiment of this ministration they glorify God for your professed subjection unto the gospel of Christ, and for your liberal distribution unto them, and unto all men.

sows sparingly will also reap sparingly, and the one who sows bountifully will also reap bountifully.

7 Each of you must give as you have made up your mind, not reluctantly or under compulsion, for God loves a cheerful giver.

8 And God is able to provide you with every blessing in abundance, so that by always having enough of everything, you may share abundantly in every good work.

9 As it is written, "He scatters abroad, he gives to the poor; his righteousness endures forever."

10 He who supplies seed to the sower and bread for food will supply and multiply your seed for sowing and increase the harvest of your righteousness.

11 You will be enriched in every way for your great generosity, which will produce thanksgiving to God through us;

12 for the rendering of this ministry not only supplies the needs of the saints but also overflows with many thanksgivings to God.

13 Through the testing of this ministry you glorify God by your obedience to the confession of the gospel of Christ and by the generosity of your sharing with them and with all others.

KEY VERSE

Every man according as he purposeth in his heart, so let him give; not grudgingly, or of necessity: for God loveth a cheerful giver. —**2 Corinthians 9:7**

OBJECTIVES

After reading this lesson, the student should realize that:

1. We cannot beat God giving;

2. There are divinely established principles of giving;

3. Generous givers glorify God; and,

4. Those who receive gifts are led to praise God.

POINTS TO BE EMPHASIZED

Adult/Youth
Key Verse: 2 Corinthians 9:7

Print: 2 Corinthians 9:1-13

—The Corinthians were congratulated for the example they set with their eager response the previous year to the appeal for an offering for the needy Christians in Judea. (1-2)

—Paul urged the Corinthians to follow through on the commitments they had made earlier for giving to meet the needs of impoverished Christians. (3-5)

—Some principles of Christian giving include giving generously, cheerfully, out of commitment, and without compulsion. (6-7)

—God gives to us so that we may continue to share God's blessings with others. (8-10)

—Generous giving by believers results not only in meeting people's needs but also leads people to thank and glorify God. (12-13)

Children
Key Verse: 2 Corinthians 9:7

Print: 2 Corinthians 9:1-8; Acts 11:27-30

—Agabus, a prophet who came to Antioch from Jerusalem, predicted a severe famine. (Acts 11:27-28)

—The disciples determined to send help to the church in Judea. (29)

—Barnabas and Saul took the gift to Judea. (30)

—Paul told the church at Corinth that Christians should give generously and cheerfully. (2 Corinthians 9:6-7)

—God gives to us so that we may share God's gifts with others. (8)

(**Note**: Use KJV Scripture for Adults; NRSV Scripture for Youth and Children)

I. Introduction

A. THE PROSPERITY MOVEMENT

"But this I say: He who sows sparingly will also reap sparingly, and he who sows bountifully will also reap bountifully" (2 Corinthians 9:6); "Do not be deceived, God is not mocked; for whatever a man sows, that he will also reap: (Galatians 6:7); "Give, and it will be given to you: good measure, pressed down, shaken together, and running over will be put into your bosom" (Luke 6:38); "Cast your bread upon the waters, for you will find it after many days" (Ecclesiastes 11:1). The principle of sowing and reaping combines in these four Scriptures to form what is called the law of compensation.

Advocates of the Prosperity Movement often use these four Scriptures to support their motto, "Conceive it, believe, achieve it." They teach that God is rich, God is in you, therefore you should not be poor, but rich. God is well, God is in you, therefore you should not be sick, but healthy. Their philosophy appears to be a "tit for tat," or *quid pro quo* principle, a plan for getting whatever you want in life. However, 1 Corinthians 9:6 is no guarantee of such results. All too often we see wicked folks "blessed" with material goods, physical health, position, power, etc. We have no explanation for this. It is a matter strictly in God's hands. Our basic motivation for giving is not for what we will receive in turn.

We want first of all to be specifically directed by the Lord. Second, we give because we love the Lord. Third, we do not give in order to get. This is not to eliminate the desire for rewards, for we take God at His Word when He promises to reward us. Fourth, we love those in need. Fifth, we are aware that we are blessed spiritually when we obey God's Word. Emphasis then is upon spiritual blessings. Keep Habakkuk

3:17-18 in mind: "Though the fig tree may not blossom, nor fruit be on the vines; though the labor of the olive may fail, and the fields yield no food; though the flock may be cut off from the fold, and there be no herd in the stalls—yet I will rejoice in the Lord, I will joy in the God of my salvation."

B. BIBLICAL BACKGROUND

The Bible has much to say about the stewardship of believers. Those who stress the giving of their time and talent, but who do not think highly of giving money, are reminded that money represents time and talent. Scriptures teach we are to give without SHOW (Matthew 6:1-4). We are not in some money-raising contest to win prizes or the plaudits of men. We are to give without SELF-CONCERN. Acts 20:35 literally states: "Bless it is continuously to be giving than to be taking." We are to give without STEALING (Malachi 3:8-9). If Old Testament folks tithed, surely the New Testament church should not be guilty of "stealing from God" by giving less than ten percent. We are to give without SORROW—sorry the money slipped out of our hands. To give grudgingly or out of necessity is to give out of compulsion, to be forced to give. There is to be no arm-twisting in God's church. Finally, keep in mind that the object of the collection of money is to help the Christians in Jerusalem. Persecution was the main problem there; add to this whatever depression resulted from periods of famine. Relief was needed, so Paul was led to raise funds and thus express Christian love.

II. Exposition and Application of the Scripture

A. PREPARATION TO GIVE
(2 Corinthians 9:1-5)

FOR AS touching the ministering to the saints, it is superfluous for me to write to you: For I know the forwardness of your mind, for which I boast of you to them of Macedonia, that Achaia was ready a year ago; and your zeal hath provoked very many. Yet have I sent the brethren, lest our boasting of you should be in vain in this behalf; that, as I said, ye may be ready: Lest haply if they of Macedonia come with me, and find you unprepared, we (that we say not, ye) should be ashamed in this same confident boasting. Therefore I thought it necessary to exhort the brethren, that they would go before unto you, and make up beforehand your bounty, whereof ye had notice before, that the same might be ready, as a matter of bounty, and not as of covetousness.

The word translated "ministering" in verse one, "administration" in verse twelve, and "ministration" in verse thirteen, is diakonia, from which is derived the word, deacon. Diakoneo means to serve, wait at table and offer food and drink to the guests, to relieve one's necessities by collecting alms (Thayer). Bringing to their attention the matter of providing for the relief of the destitute saints in Jerusalem is called a superfluous (more than necessary) task. Earlier, Paul had exhorted the Corinthian saints to give systematically, proportionately, purposely (1 Corinthians 16:1-2), on the first day of the week. Now he urges liberality and cheerfulness.

He had been boasting to the Macedonians of the Corinthians' generosity, eagerness, enthusiasm, and readiness to give. "It is superfluous" is like saying, "I need not say." Often we use such rhetoric in matters that deeply interest us, and then we go on to have much to say (ICC).

The zeal of the Corinthian saints stirred up or stimulated many others to do as well. Because he did not want his bragging about them to be in vain, he sent some men along with this letter. Having continuously said they were prepared, he did not want the men to arrive at Corinth and find it otherwise. "Paul wants them to see from the results which they find when they get to Corinth that he had, indeed, made excellent preparation" (Lenski). If the money is not ready, it will give a bad impression. Their unpreparedness would be first of all an embarrassment to Paul, and then also a disgrace to them.

The prefix "pro" is used three times in verse five. It is rendered "ahead, beforehand, previously" (KJV), and "before, beforehand, before" (KJV), and "in advance" all three times by Lenski. Such language points to Paul's desire for everything to be prepared on time. Use of the words "bounty" and "covetousness" sets up an interesting contrast. This is because the word translated "bounty" is *eulogian*, from which is derived our English word, "eulogy."

Literally, it means "well-spoken" a "blessing" (Lenski), "beneficence"

(Alford), "gift" (RSV and NIV), "benefit" (Interpreter's). Expositors state the blending of the two ideas (blessing and gift) "arose from the fact that every blessing or praise of God or man was in the East (and is still to a great extent), accompanied by a gift" (Genesis 33:11). On the other hand, the word rendered "covetousness" means "greedy desire to have more" (Thayer); "greediness, insatiableness, avarice" (Arndt). The translations "extortion" (NEB) and "exaction" (RSV) are said to be too strong (Wycliffe).

Paul desired to elevate the act of giving to a high spiritual level. A sparing, covetous spirit that gives no more than it has to, but gives grudgingly misses the joy of the generous heart. Money is not to be squeezed out of us in a demanding and greedy spirit. The proper spirit in which gifts are given is with an honest and sincere desire to be a blessing to others.

B. PRINCIPLES OF GIVING
(2 Corinthians 9:6-7)

But this I say, He which soweth sparingly shall reap also sparingly; and he which soweth bountifully shall reap also bountifully. Every man according as he purposeth in his heart, so let him give; not grudgingly, or of necessity: for God loveth a cheerful giver.

All Christians are farmers and sowers (Psalm 126:5-6). This implies that a harvest is coming. The motivation for giving is not a selfish one. It is an act of faith, taking God at His Word. If He said that we should be blessed, then we have every right to look for and expect a blessing. Note once again the use of the word *eulogian*, this time translated "bountiful," that is, blessings.

Each Christian is to give as he or she had decided in advance. "Purposed" minds are made up already. Furthermore, the giving is not to be done grudgingly, literally, "not from grief." We are not to give out of compulsion, or be forced to give, or with murmuring, or reluctance. What about assessments or quotas? Or compulsory tithing? Is undue pressure put upon non-tithers when we practice having "all tithers come first"? All such is not the will of God. Some of our churches have become quite legalistic in their approach to Christian giving.

Finally, note the word "cheerful." In the Greek it is *hilaros*, from which we get the English word, hilarious. It means "joyous, prompt to do anything, ready of mind" (Thayer); "glad, merry" (Arndt & Gingrich). The word connotes a spirit of genuine enjoyment. All restraints are swept away. However, giving is still to be discriminating; we are not to let our benevolence be misused, wrongly applied. "Giving is not a joke; it is serious business but it is also a delightful experience" (Parallel). Surely Ananias and Sapphira would attest to the seriousness of Christian stewardship (Acts 5:1-11). God loves to see saints so bubbling over with the joy of the Holy Spirit that they desire to share their possessions with others.

C. PROVIDENCE OF GOD
(2 Corinthians 9:8-10)

And God is able to make all grace abound toward you; that ye, always having all sufficiency in all things, may abound to every good work: (As it is written, He hath dispersed abroad; he hath given to the poor: his righteousness remaineth for ever. Now he that ministereth seed to the sower both minister bread for your food, and multiply your seed sown, and increase the fruits of your righteousness;)

The Greek word (*pan*) for "all" is used five times in verse eight: "**all** grace, at **all** times, **all** sufficiency, **all** things, **all** good work." In other words, God has the power to supply you with spiritual and material blessings in abundance—so that you always—can have all that is needed—and can provide others with all that is needed—for all good work, in short, God gives us enough for ourselves and gives enough to help others. "Sufficiency" is the translation of the word (*autarkeia*) that means "a perfect condition of life, in which no aid or support is needed, a sufficiency of the necessaries of life" (Thayer); "competence, enough of everything, contentment, self-sufficiency" (Arndt & Gingrich). Montgomery calls it "being independent of external circumstances" (ICC). This truth is reinforced by Psalm 112:9, and its description of the man who fears the Lord. We learn that the righteousness of reward endures. Righteousness here does not refer to salvation, but to good deeds, right acts. Righteousness leads to prosperity, and prosperity promotes almsgiving.

However, remember we emphasize spiritual prosperity for the New Testament saint, for Paul does not intend to suggest every saint will always be wealthy materially. Almsgiving, for example, is seen as an outward expression of righteousness. God gives us enough, enabling us to give to others. Paul's prayer is that the Lord will take what we give to others, multiply it, and thus increase the fruits of our benevolence.

D. PRAISE AND GLORY OF GOD
(2 Corinthians 9:11-13)

Being enriched in every thing to all bountifulness, which causeth through us thanksgiving to God. For the administration of this service not only supplieth the want of the saints, but is abundant also by many thanksgivings unto God; Whiles by the experiment of this ministration they glorify God for your professed subjection unto the gospel of Christ, and for your liberal distribution unto them, and unto all men.

God enriches the generous giver in everything. Giving to the Lord never impoverishes us. What He give to us in return is way out of proportion to our gifts to Him or to others in His name. NIV clearly states: "This service that you perform is not only supplying the needs of God's people but in also overflowing in many expression of thanks to God." The word rendered "(ad)ministration" means any public service, but has come to signify the service of God. When we serve other people, we actually help ourselves, and in addition such service overflows to God's glory by means of many thanksgivings. In other words, thanksgivings to God are multiplied by our giving to the needs of others.

By their generosity, the Gentile saints proved to the saints at Jerusalem that Christ indeed had done a genuine work in their lives. Their expressions of kindness erased any earlier doubts, demonstrating the reality of the Corinthians' faith. Because the saints at Corinth liberally shared with the saints at Jerusalem, God was glorified. This is true because the needy believers in Jerusalem recognized the gifts as the result of the Corinthians having accepted and obeyed the Gospel of the shed blood of Jesus Christ.

III. Special Features

A. PRESERVING OUR HERITAGE

The deacons are usually in charge of the disbursements of the money held in what is variously called the Poor Saints Offering, Benevolent or Benevolence Fund, Love Fund, Deacons Fund, or the Fellowship Fund. Over the years, hundreds of thousands of dollars have been distributed to the needy members of Black Baptist churches across America. Without such aid, our struggle with racism would have been made all the more difficult.

B. A CONCLUDING WORD

We see the circle involved in Christian stewardship. Out of the wealth of God's abundant grace, He supplies our needs. We express our thanksgiving to Him by liberally sharing what we have with others. Those who receive from us praise God from whom all blessings flow. And the cycle is completed. "Christian giving is the outward expression of a heart already rich in generosity" (NIC).

Indeed, our giving is evidence of obedience to the Gospel. Montgomery (ICC) offers these three motives for joyful, liberal giving: (1) Giving to the needy is done in a right attitude, it is a sowing which is sure of a harvest; (2) God in Christ is able and willing to give us such a spirit and resource whereby we can exhibit such generosity; and (3) What we give not only helps the recipients, but increases their affection for the giver, and then more important, moves them to express thanksgiving to God. Remember, in all of this, attitude or spirit is extremely important (2 Corinthians 8:12).

HOME DAILY BIBLE READINGS FOR THE WEEK OF MAY 21, 2000

THE COLLECTION FOR JERUSALEM CHRISTIANS

May 15 M. 2 Corinthians 8:1-7,   Exceeding Generosity
May 16 T. 2 Corinthians 8:8-15,   Show Your Love by Your Giving
May 17 W. 2 Corinthians 8:16-24,   A Generous Gift Glorifies God
May 18 T. 2 Corinthians 9:1-9,   God Loves and Blesses Cheerful Givers
May 19 F. 2 Corinthians 9:10-15,   Generous Giving Brings Joy to All
May 20 S. 2 Corinthians 16:1-9,   A Collection for Jerusalem Christians
May 21 S. Romans 15:22-29,   Paul Intends to Visit Roman Christians

Know Your Bible

- Our Jesus Christ is called the "Word" because He is the revelation of God Himself. (John 1:18)
- We know that the Gospel is free to all because Jesus Christ, like the light, reaches all persons so that all through Him might believe. (John 1:7, 9)
- The worship that is pleasing to God is that worship which comes from the heart. (John 4 :23, 24)
- The "broken hearted" consists of all those whose hearts are broken or crushed under the burden of godly sorrow for their sin. (Luke 4:18)
- The proof that there is a connection between sin and suffering is indicated in Jesus' warning to the man sick of the palsy to sin no more lest a worse disease or thing should happen to him. (John 5:14)
- Meekness is patience under provocation following the example of Jesus Christ "who when he was reviled, reviled not again." (1 Peter 2:21-23)

O God, we affirm that the earth is the Lord's and the fullness thereof, and that what we possess is only a trust from Thee. By Your grace, grant that we may be ever sensitive to the needs of others as we surrender ourselves as channels through which Your blessings flow. We pray in the name of Him who gave His all. Amen.

Living in the Faith

Adult Topic—*From Confrontation to Growth*

•••••

Youth Topic—*Growth From Confrontation*
Children's Topic—*The Joy of Peaceful Living*

•••••

Devotional Reading—Acts 4:32-37
Background Scripture—2 Corinthians 13:1-13
Print—2 Corinthians 13:1-13

PRINTED SCRIPTURE

2 Corinthians 13:1-13 (KJV)

THIS IS the third time I am coming to you. In the mouth of two or three witnesses shall every word be established.

2 I told you before, and foretell you, as if I were present, the second time; and being absent now I write to them which heretofore have sinned, and to all other, that, if I come again, I will not spare:

3 Since ye seek a proof of Christ speaking in me, which to you-ward is not weak, but is mighty in you.

4 For though he was crucified through weakness, yet he liveth by the power of God. For we also are weak in him, but we shall live with him by the power of God toward you.

5 Examine yourselves, whether ye be in the faith; prove your own selves. Know ye not your own selves, how that Jesus Christ is in you, except ye be reprobates?

2 Corinthians 13:1-13 (NRSV)

THIS IS the third time I am coming to you. "Any charge must be sustained by the evidence of two or three witnesses."

2 I warned those who sinned previously and all the others, and I warn them now while absent, as I did when present on my second visit, that If I come again, I will not be lenient—

3 since you desire proof that Christ is speaking in me. He is not weak in dealing with you, but is powerful in you.

4 For he was crucified in weakness, but lives by the power of God. For we are weak in him, but in dealing with you we will live with him by the power of God.

5 Examine yourselves to see whether you are living in the faith. Test yourselves. Do you not realize that Jesus Christ is in you?—unless, indeed, you fail to meet the test!

6 I hope you will find out that we have not failed.

6 But I trust that ye shall know that we are not reprobates.

7 Now I pray go God that ye do no evil; not that we should appear approved, but that ye should do that which is honest, though we be as reprobates.

8 For we can do nothing against the truth, but for the truth.

9 For we are glad, when we are weak, and ye are strong: and this also we wish, even your perfection.

10 Therefore I write these things being absent, lest being present I should use sharpness, according to the power which the Lord hath given me to edification, and not to destruction.

11 Finally, brethren, farewell. Be perfect, be of good comfort, be of one mind, live in peace; and the God of love and peace shall be with you.

12 Greet one another with an holy kiss.

13 All the saints salute you.

7 But we pray to God that you may not do anything wrong—not that we may appear to have met the test, but that you may do what is right, though we may seem to have failed.

8 For we cannot do anything against the truth, but only for the truth.

9 For we rejoice when we are weak and you are strong. This is what we pray for, that you may become perfect.

10 So I write these things while I am away from you, so that when I come, I may not have to be severe in using the authority that the Lord has given me for building up and not for tearing down.

11 Finally, brothers and sisters, farewell. Put things in order, listen to my appeal, agree with one another, live in peace; and the God of love and peace will be with you.

12 Greet one another with a holy kiss. All the saints greet you.

13 The grace of the Lord Jesus Christ, the love of God, and the communion of the Holy Spirit be with all of you.

KEY VERSE

Examine yourselves, whether ye be in the faith; prove your own selves. Know ye not your own selves, how that Jesus Christ is in you, except ye be reprobates?—2 Corinthians 13:5

OBJECTIVES

After reading this lesson, the student should remember that:

1. Sometimes what is perceived as weakness is in reality strength;
2. Self-examination is always in order; and,
3. The victorious life should be emphasized.

POINTS TO BE EMPHASIZED

Adult/Youth

Key Verse: 2 Corinthians 13:5
Print: 2 Corinthians 13:1-13

—Paul warned the Corinthians that, if necessary, he would deal severely with them in order to resolve the problem that had disrupted the fellowship. (1-2)
—Leaders who follow the example of the crucified Christ may seem weak by human standards, but by the power of God they are strong. (3-4)
—Paul exhorted the Corinthians to examine their own lives for evidence of their faith in Christ. (5-6)
—Paul's concern was not his own success but that the Corinthians do what was right. (7-9)
—Paul hoped that the Corinthians would solve their problem themselves before he came to them so that his time with them could be spent in teaching them more about the Christian life, not in correcting their problems. (10-13)

Children

Key Verse: 2 Corinthians 13:11
Print: 2 Corinthians 13:11; Acts 2:41-47

—Paul urged the church to be agreeable and live in God's peace. (2 Corinthians 13:11)
—Many people who heard Peter preach were baptized and followed his teaching. (Acts 2:41-42)
—All the believers were together and shared their possessions. (44)
—The people sold their possessions and gave to the needy. (45)
—Many people were added to the congregation. (47)

(**Note**: Use KJV Scripture for Adults; NRSV Scripture for Youth and Children)

TOPICAL OUTLINE OF THE LESSON

I. Introduction

A. Examine and Test Yourselves
B. Biblical Background

II. Exposition and Application of the Scripture

A. Sinners Not to be Spared (2 Corinthians 13:1-4)
B. Self-examination Avoids Severity (2 Corinthians 13:5-10)
C. Staccato Summary (2 Corinthians 13:11)
D. Salutation to the Saints (2 Corinthians 13:12-13)

III. Special Features

A. Preserving Our Heritage
B. A Concluding Word

I. Introduction

A. EXAMINE AND TEST YOURSELVES

"Examine yourselves as to whether you are in the faith. Test yourselves" (2 Corinthians 13:5). In the original, the words *examine* and *test* are different words, but both are used interchangeably. For example, the Greek word *dokimazo* is rendered "prove" or "test" in Luke 14:19, and then "examine" in 1 Corinthians 11:28. *Dokimazo* means to test in order to approve. As used in the New Testament, it almost always implies that the proving or testing leads to approval. It is to test and stand the test. The trial is made in expectation and hope that the issue would be successful (Trench). Thus the words "Test yourselves" (NKJV) or "prove yourselves" (KJV) imply having done so, you pass the test, you are accepted, approved.

On the other hand, the verb *peirazo* is also translated "prove" or "test" (John 6:6). It is rendered "examine" in 2 Corinthians 13:5. But it is not perfectly synonymous with *dokimazo*. When told to examine themselves as to whether they are in the faith, Paul used a verb which most often signifies a making trial with the intention and hope of discovering what of good or evil was in them (Trench).Or, where this is known already by the one who administers the test, it is revealed to those who are the ones trying or examining themselves.

Because we humans so often flunk the test, this word has come to mean "**tempt**" – that testing which leads us to fail. In other words, we so often break down under this test that the word has been given a predominant sense of putting to the proof while hoping for disapproval or reprobation.

B. BIBLICAL BACKGROUND

The seeking "proof of Christ speaking in" Paul (2 Corinthians 13:3) gives us a reason for the Epistle as a whole. A major thrust of the Letter is Paul's vindication of his behavior, and assertion of his apostolic authority. What he writes is called an *apologia* or defense of his calling. In 2 Corinthians 12:19, we read: "Again, do you think that we excuse ourselves to you?" The word translated "excuse" is *apologeomai*, to talk one's self off of a charge, to speak so as to absolve one's self (Thayer); speak in one's own defense, defend oneself (Arndt and Gingrich).

It is his reply (apologia) to those who sit in judgment over him (1 Corinthians 9:3). The Corinthians should get it out of their minds that they are judges of Paul's ministry. Paul spoke as one commissioned by the Lord Jesus Christ. This background helps us understand in part the strong language Paul used: "You should be looking at yourselves to make sure that you are really Christ's. It is yourselves that you should be testing, not me" (J. B. Phillips, 2 Corinthians 13:5).

II. Exposition and Application of the Scripture

A. SINNERS NOT TO BE SPARED
(2 Corinthians 13:1-4)

THIS is the third time I am coming to you. In the mouth of two or three witnesses shall every word be established. I told you before, and

foretell you, as if I were present, the second time; and being absent now I write to them which heretofore have sinned, and to all other, that, if I come again, I will not spare: Since ye seek a proof of Christ speaking in me, which to you-ward is not weak, but is mighty in you. For though he was crucified through weakness, yet he liveth by the power of God. For we also are weak in him, but we shall live with him by the power of God toward you.

It appears that Paul already had paid two visits to Corinth. This includes his first trip there in which the church was founded; and then a shorter visit, at which time the members sorely mistreated him (ICC). Now he is about to visit them a third time, but he wants them to have some idea of what to expect from him when he arrives. It is his intention to bring to account those in the church guilty of misbehavior.

Note however that Peter is not the judge and the jury. As it was in Old Testament times, so it was then in the early church—witnesses were needed to establish charges against wrongdoers. The apostle cites the need for two or three witnesses (Numbers 35:30; Deuteronomy 17:6; 19:15). New Testament Scriptures also support this principle (Matthew 18:16; John 8:17; 1 Timothy 5:19). Use of such witnesses indicates also that the local assembly was involved.

Alford states it should be "two **and** three respectively." Where only two witnesses are available, well and good, but if there are three, use them. Two constituted a minimum, three a maximum (Lenski). Obviously, some folks at Corinth continued to misbehave, "to

sin their old sins" (Pilgrim Bible). The Corinthian Church was not an easy field; the city was well-known for its immorality. Paul boldly, solemnly forewarned again, this time by letter, "I will not spare." Evasion is impossible! Where there is evidence of sinful behavior, Paul's authority as an apostle is sure to be exercised, as he would advise and guide the congregation in the matter of discipline.

Verse three gives the reason for the severity. They sought proof that Christ spoke in Paul, or that Paul spoke with divine authority. Any rebellion against a true, faithful minister is rebellion against Him who called and appointed the minister (Numbers 16:28). Paul reminds them of the danger of provoking the Christ by whom Paul spoke. Paul's Commissioner is not weak. Rather, He is strong. In the world's eyes, Jesus Christ is weak, a failure. He allowed Himself to be killed. However, He rose from the grave and lives forevermore.

We Christians live with Him in that resurrection power, although we also appear weak in the world's sight. Though God the Father willed His Son should die an ignominious death, God the Father also raised Him from the dead. Thus the paradox—that which seems contradictory—of strength issuing out of weakness, as demonstrated in the life of Jesus Christ, is also seen in the lives of the servants of Christ.

B. SELF-EXAMINATION AVOIDS SEVERITY
(2 Corinthians 13:5-10)

Examine yourselves, whether ye be in the faith; prove your own selves. Know ye not your own selves,

how that Jesus Christ is in you, except ye be reprobates? But I trust that ye shall know that we are not reprobates. Now I pray to God that ye do no evil; not that we should appear approved, but that ye should do that which is honest, though we be as reprobates. For we can do nothing against the truth, but for the truth. For we are glad, when we are weak, and ye are strong: and this also we wish, even your perfection. Therefore I write these things being absent, lest being present I should use sharpness, according to the power which the Lord hath given me to edification, and not to destruction.

"Here is something more profitable for you to do," said Paul. "Rather than waste time testing me, try putting your own selves to the proof! There is something you should know about yourselves—that Jesus Christ is in you! Do you know that?" Note the two-edged thrust: Are you in the faith (Do you believe the principles of the new spiritual life)? Is Christ in you?

If tested and found false, it means you are disproved, reprobate. It is quite possible to join church, get baptized, sing in the choir, usher, then die and end up in hell! Imagine someone deceiving himself into believing that Jesus Christ lives in us, an assurance given by the Holy Spirit. One result then is godly living, and taking God at His Word. It is possible, you see, for the believer to "give diligence to make your calling and election sure" (2 Peter 1:10).

Time and experience would prove to the Corinthians that Paul was not a phony. The power to inflict punishment would prove this. On the other hand, if the Corinthians test themselves and see that they are for real, then they will know automatically that Paul also is sound. Then there would be no need to administer discipline. Paul really had no desire to use his apostolic power in this way. "Do what is right and I won't have to prove anything!"

Because Paul and his assistants are devoted entirely to the truth, they are not deeply concerned about the Corinthians approving them. What counts is the truth of the Gospel. "Walk in the truth and we shall be at one with you, for we rejoice," said the apostle, "when we are weak." By weakness, he meant having no need to demonstrate apostolic power in discipline. The strength of the Corinthians was their good behavior, making punishment or censure unnecessary. Either way, God's power is effectively shown.

Paul is anxious that all causes of strife and dissension should be eliminated before he comes to Corinth. He hopes the saints there will respond favorably to what he has written. This way, when he does arrive, there will be no need to use his divinely given authority to destroy or punish. Instead, he will be able to build up. The secular world all too often is impressed with the ability to destroy, blow up, to use force and power! It takes the love of Christ to engage in edification. God had given Paul apostolic power to build. Sometimes church members are so intent upon having their way in certain issues that they would rather wreck than build up!

C. STACCATO SUMMARY
(2 Corinthians 13:11)

Finally, brethren, farewell. Be perfect, be of good comfort, be of one

mind, live in peace; and the God of love and peace shall be with you.

Farewell means "fare thee well," or "may things go well with you." We used to sing, "In that great getting up morning, fare thee well." The Greek word means "rejoice" (NASB), "be glad," and is sometimes rendered "hail" (John 19:3). "Cheer up" (JBP). "Be happy" (LB). "Goodbye!" (TEV, Moffatt). There follow four exhortations. (1) Be perfect means become complete, and suggests steady growth in Christlike living. Because of the sinful conduct so evident in the church community, the command is also rendered, "Mend your ways" (RSV, Moffatt), or "straighten yourselves out" (JBP). (2) Be of good comfort means "Listen to my appeals, take to heart what I have told you, pay attention." Literally, it is to keep encouraging one another. The verb (*parakaleo*) has also the meaning of "be comforted, receive comfort through words" (Arndt & Gingrich). (3) Be of one mind means to agree with one another, mind the same things. Here the saints are warned against the chronic tendency of divisiveness at Corinth. Churches today still need this exhortation to be harmonious in thought and deed. This is accomplished by having the mind of Christ. (4) Live in peace; they are exhorted to demonstrate that irenic spirit (conducive to or operating toward peace or conciliation) that become believers.

These exhortations are urged in order to combat the "immaturity, unrest, division and quarreling" prevailing in the church. They are called "staccato injunctions" (NIC) because of their abruptness. Paul promises obedience will result in the presence of God being especially made known to them. One definite article in verse 13: **the** God of love and peace emphasizes they are a unit. The title "God of love" is found here for the first time in Paul's writing, but the title, "God of peace" is found in Romans 15:33, 16:20; Philippians 4:9; etc.

D. SALUTATION TO THE SAINTS
(2 Corinthians 13:12-13)

Greet one another with an holy kiss. All the saints salute you.

The word for greet comes from a verb meaning to draw to one's self. Thus, "embrace one another with the holy kiss" (TDNT). The holy kiss (*philema*) was a sincere and pure expression of comradeship, and mutual confidence, symbolizing Christian fellowship in the early church (Romans 16:16; 1 Corinthians 16:20; 1 Thessalonians 5:26; 1 Peter 5:14). It was a sign of fraternal affection (Thayer) among "members of one family in the Lord, or as specially united in holy love." Later, the custom was restricted because of abuses. "There is reason to believe that, as a rule, men only thus greeted men, and women, women" (ISBE).

III. Special Features

A. PRESERVING OUR HERITAGE

We have no desire to return to the days of slavery, or of rampant, overt Jim Crow. But the question comes, "Did we have more spiritual power under oppression than we have now under relative freedom? Has our push for political clout, financial power, material possessions, enervated us spiritually? Does Christ still speak in the "Black Churches" of America?

The desire to demonstrate what the secular world considers strength may be at the expense of Holy Spirit power. Worldly gain comes at the loss of spiritual might. Would self-examination reveal that we possess a Christlikeness that is untarnished by evil? Are we light in a dark world, salty salt helping to slow up corruption? Thank God for every local church that has not fallen in love with a world-system that is passing away (1 Corinthians 7:31). We are still in the faith, and Christ is still in us.

B. A CONCLUDING WORD

The self-examination we all ought to make does not have as its criteria self-made standards, or rules of humanism, secularism, and homemade philosophy. Paul said those who measure themselves by themselves, and compare themselves among themselves, are not wise (2 Corinthians 10:12). The standard for measurement is the Lord Jesus Christ.

Objectively, we are to be found in the faith; subjectively, Christ is to be found in us. Some men will say it is presumptuous to be assured of salvation. But it is not presumption; it is taking God at His Word, and wearing the helmet of salvation. It is a knowledge given by the Holy Spirit, Who Himself is a down payment of guaranteed Salvation. As we live in the faith, other assurances follow—love of the sanctified life, hatred of sin, love of other Christians!

HOME DAILY BIBLE READINGS FOR THE WEEK OF MAY 28, 2000

LIVING IN THE FAITH

May 22	M.	2 Corinthians 10:1-11, Paul Defends His Ministry
May 23	T.	2 Corinthians 10:12-18, If You Boast, Boast in the Lord
May 24	W.	2 Corinthians 11:1-15, Paul and the False Apostles
May 25	T.	2 Corinthians 11:16-29, Paul's Sufferings as an Apostle
May 26	F.	2 Corinthians 12:1-10, Paul's Visions and Revelations
May 27	S.	2 Corinthians 12:11-21, Paul's Concern for the Corinthian Christians
May 28	S.	2 Corinthians 13:1-13, Live in Faith: Christ Is in You

Our Father and our God, because You have forgiven us through the sacrificial death of Thy Son Jesus Christ, grant that we may search our lives and hearts for any and all un-confessed sins and failures that hinder us from being committed. Teach us how to forgive others as You have forgiven us, so that the fellowship of the faithful will truly become the bond of blessings. Amen.

SUMMER QUARTER

June, July, August, 2000

New Life in Christ

General Introduction

During this quarter, we shall concern ourselves with Paul's letters to the Philippians, Ephesians, Colossians, and Philemon. These letters are traditionally referred to as those which Paul wrote from his prison cell, and speak to various problems that the respective churches encountered that lay heavily upon his heart, along with his personal letter to Philemon relative to the status of Onesimus who had come to embrace the Gospel of Christ under Paul's ministry.

Unit I, *"Living in Christ,"* is presented in four sessions based on the letter to the church at Philippi. Herein, Paul deals with what it means to live in Christ, which includes a mind-set that controls all human relationships. Rather than having a static acceptance of the Gospel, Paul urges that the Christians at Philippi press on toward being more Christlike with joyful anticipation as they mirror His life.

Unit II, *"Called to Be a New Humanity,"* is a challenge to the church at Ephesus to realize fully the spiritual blessings embodied in the faith that encompass the affirmation of oneness in Christ, the use of spiritual gifts for the edification of the fellowship of faith, responsible living as becomes the people of God, and the admonition to stand firm as participants within the new community made possible by the death and resurrection of Jesus the Christ.

Unit III, *"Christ Above All,"* is based on Paul's letter to the church at Colosse wherein emphasis is placed on the supremacy, completeness and righteousness of the Christ. This unit concludes with Paul's personal letter to Philemon concerning the new relationship between Philemon and Onesimus as a result of the extended grace of Jesus Christ.

As we study these lessons, it will be to our advantage to understand the structural setting of the churches to which Paul wrote. The churches that Paul founded did not enjoy the privileges associated with designated buildings dedicated for the purpose of worship, but referenced the faithful followers of Christ who met as a gathered community. Hence, the churches should not be conceived of as bricks and mortar, but all societies or "churches" located in that particular area. For example, the church at Galatia means all of the societies or churches in that country; and we may surmise that the letters cited for our study have to do with the fluid membership that met in houses or other places of convenience.

Think then of the church (at Philippi, Ephesus, and Colosse) as any number of believers who were united in their commitment to the Christ and met for the purpose of worship: to hear the Word proclaimed, to participate in the ordinances properly administered, and to enhance godly living in accordance with the mandate of Jesus Christ as the Head of the church.

Paul's letter to Philemon is clearly a challenge that Christians embrace and relate to each other not in terms of earthly stratifications, but in terms of that essential unity of our new humanity by which our behavior and demeanor are to reflect the life of Jesus the Christ.

The problems that Paul identifies in these letters are those that are indigenous to the human conditions to which the Gospel is to be applied to enable us to live consistent with God's purpose for our lives. In a real sense, Paul writes not to "them," but to us who are also redeemed by the only begotten Son of God.

Living Is Christ

Unit I—*Living in Christ*
Children's Unit—*Living to Please Jesus*

•••••

Adult Topic—*Living Is Christ*

•••••

Youth Topic—*Hope During Hardship*
Children's Topic—*Believing in Jesus*

•••••

Devotional Reading—1 Peter 1:3-9
Background Scripture—Philippians 1:12-30
Print—Philippians 1:12-26

PRINTED SCRIPTURE

Philippians 1:12-26 (KJV)

12 But I would ye should understand, brethren, that the things which happened unto me have fallen out rather unto the furtherance of the gospel;

13 So that my bonds in Christ are manifest in all the palace, and in all other places;

14 And many of the brethren in the Lord, waxing confident by my bonds, are much more bold to speak the word without fear.

15 Some indeed preach Christ even of envy and strife; and some also of good will:

16 The one preach Christ of contention, not sincerely, supposing to add affliction to my bonds:

17 But the other of love, knowing that I am set for the defence of the gospel.

18 What then? Notwithstanding, every way, whether in pretence, or in truth, Christ is preached; and I therein do rejoice, yea, and will rejoice.

Philippians 1:12-26 (NRSV)

12 I want you to know, beloved that what has happened to me has actually helped to spread the gospel,

13 so that it has become known throughout the whole imperial guard and to everyone else that my imprisonment is for Christ;

14 and most of the brothers and sisters, having been made confident in the Lord by my imprisonment, dare to speak the word with greater boldness and without fear.

15 Some proclaim Christ from envy and rivalry, but others from goodwill.

16 These proclaim Christ out of love, knowing that I have been put here for the defense of the gospel;

17 the others proclaim Christ out of selfish ambition, not sincerely but intending to increase my suffering in my imprisonment.

18 What does it matter? Just this, that Christ is proclaimed in every way, whether out of false motives

19 For I know that this shall turn to my salvation through your prayer, and the supply of the Spirit of Jesus Christ,

20 According to my earnest expectation and my hope, that in nothing I shall be ashamed, but that with all boldness, as always, so now also Christ shall be magnified in my body, whether it be by life, or by death.

21 For to me to live is Christ, and to die is gain.

22 But if I live in the flesh, this is the fruit of my labour: yet what I shall choose I wot not.

23 For I am in a strait betwixt two, having a desire to depart, and to be with Christ; which is far better:

24 Nevertheless to abide in the flesh is more needful for you.

25 And having this confidence, I know that I shall abide and continue with you all for your furtherance and joy of faith;

26 That your rejoicing may be more abundant in Jesus Christ for me by my coming to you again.

or true; and in that I rejoice. Yes, and I will continue to rejoice,

19 for I know that through your prayers and the help of the Spirit of Jesus Christ this will turn out for my deliverance.

20 It is my eager expectation and hope that I will not be put to shame in any way, but that by my speaking with all boldness, Christ will be exalted now as always in my body, whether by life or by death.

21 For to me, living is Christ and dying is gain.

22 If I am to live in the flesh, that means fruitful labor for me; and I do not know which I prefer.

23 I am hard pressed between the two: my desire is to depart and be with Christ, for that is far better;

24 but to remain in the flesh is more necessary for you.

25 Since I am convinced of this, I know that I will remain and continue with all of you for your progress and joy in faith,

26 so that I may share abundantly in your boasting in Christ Jesus when I come to you again.

KEY VERSE

For to me to live is Christ, and to die is gain.
—*Philippians 1:21*

OBJECTIVES

After reading this lesson, the student should be informed about:

1. How God uses what men consider bad circumstances;

2. Why Christians preach Christ even in adversity;

3. The advantage of having died in Christ; and

4. The confidence of the believer's faith.

POINTS TO BE EMPHASIZED
Adult/Youth
Key Verse: Philippians 1:21
Print: Philippians 1:12-26

—In spite of imprisonment, Paul was able to influence others to speak the Word of God courageously and fearlessly. (12-14)
—In the early church, motives for proclaiming Christ varied from envy to love, and some wanted to increase Paul's suffering. (15-17)
—Regardless of the motives of others, Paul rejoiced that they proclaimed Christ. (18)
—Paul believed whether he was released or killed, his life would magnify Christ and serve God's purpose. (19, 20)
—Paul desired to be with Christ, yet believed the Philippians needed him. (21-24)
—Paul wanted to visit the Philippians and rejoice in their spiritual growth. (25, 26)

Children
Key Verse: John 20:31
Print: Philippians 1:19-21; Acts 16:11-15

—Paul believed that, whether he was released from prison or killed, his life would magnify Christ and serve God's purpose. (19-21)
—Paul and his missionary party left Troas and came to Philippi. (Acts 16:11-12)
—On the Sabbath by the riverside, Paul preached to the women who had gathered to pray. (13)
—Lydia, a God-fearing business woman, believed Paul's message. (14)
—After she and her household were baptized, she invited the missionary party to stay in her house. (15)

(**NOTE**: Use KJV Scripture for Adults: NRSV Scripture for Youth and Children)

TOPICAL OUTLINE OF THE LESSON

I. Introduction
A. Life and Death
B. Biblical Background

II. Exposition and Application of the Scripture
A. Providential Arrangement (Philippians 1:12-14)
B. Preaching Christ (Philippians 1:15-18)
C. Paul's Expectation (Philippians 1:19-20)
D. Philosophy of Life (Philippians 1:21-23)
E. Present Confidence (Philippians 1:24-26)

III. Special Features
A. Preserving Our Heritage
B. A Concluding Word

I. Introduction

A. LIFE AND DEATH

Philippians 1:21 is the Key Verse or Golden Text of today's lesson: "For to me to live is Christ, and to die is gain." Paul's announcement to the saints at Philippi is strange, for at the time he was not living too well. In fact, he was in jail, guarded by Roman soldiers. How can one have inward joy in the midst of outward persecution? The answer is—Christ! True life is to have Jesus Christ living in us, letting Him live His life in us. But now every philosophy of life must have something to say about death, otherwise it is an inadequate philosophy. The apostle declares that just as the act of living is Christ, so the state after death is an advantage. We learn that to die is gain. The text does not assert that the act of death is gain, for the verb is better translated, "to have died." It thus does not refer to the act of dying, but the state after death. To have died and gone to heaven to be with the Lord Jesus is an advantage. To be set free from the frailties of these feeble frames we now inhabit is gain. To look forward to a new body, a resurrected body is an advantage, for then we shall be like Him, for we shall see Him as He is. To die becomes an occasion for rejoicing. What bliss to fall at His nail-pierced feet, hold His nail-pierced hand, and dwell eternally in His presence! And so, we see Paul's interpretation of life and his definition of death.

B. BIBLICAL BACKGROUND

Paul visited the city of Philippi on his second missionary journey. The trip to Macedonia was made in response to a vision which appeared to Paul (Acts 16:9). Philippi was the chief city of that part of Macedonia, located in the northern part of Greece, a few miles inland from the Aegean Sea. As Paul's first conquest for Christ in Europe, Philippi was a city never to be forgotten. It has been called "the birthplace of European Christianity."

Humanly speaking, the main reason for the Letter seems to be the expression of joy and gratitude to the Philippian saints for their gifts and devotion to Paul. Such expression is all the more remarkable when we remember that at the time Paul was imprisoned. Many of us, at ease in Zion and at home, are so easily upset by adversities that it appears strange to hear of a man in prison bubbling over with joy and thanksgiving. Nonetheless, Paul the missionary expressed joy and gratitude for the support of the saints at Philippi. The mind of Christ is given as the basic underlying theme. Paul's immediate purpose seems to be to express his appreciation for the love and kindness of the saints at Philippi in their gracious generosity by the hand of Epaphroditus. It is thus a letter of joy and love, even as such virtues characterize the mind of Jesus Christ.

II. Exposition and Application of the Scriptures

A. PROVIDENTIAL ARRANGE-MENT (Philippians 1:12-14)
But I would ye should understand, brethren, that the things which happened unto me have fallen out rather unto the furtherance of the

gospel; So that my bonds in Christ are manifest in all the palace, and in all other places; And many of the brethren in the Lord, waxing confident by my bonds, are much more bold to speak the word without fear.

Our lesson begins what is considered the doctrinal section of the Letter. As usual in the epistles of Paul, the doctrinal section is put first, then the practical section last. Remember this pattern, lest we fall into the trap of thinking that doctrine is not very important, and that what counts is what we do. Keep in mind also that false doctrine can lead to false living. So from Philippians 1:12 to 3:21, the emphasis is upon what we should believe. Chapter four stresses what we should practice.

J. H. Jowett calls this part of the lesson, "the Fortune of Misfortune," for the rest of chapter one deals with joy triumphing over suffering. Paul was a prisoner, but his chains were used of God to spread the Gospel. Four times in Chapter 1 (verses 7, 13, 14, 16) the apostle Paul mentions his bonds (KJV), chains (NKJV, NIV), or imprisonment (RSV, JBP, NEB).

The apostle wanted the Philippian Christians to know, and continue to keep in mind, that "the things which happened to him"—mobbed by rioters in Jerusalem, unjustly incarcerated, shipwrecked, etc., and now imprisonment—did not hinder the spread of the Good News. He still was able to pray for others, so that his ministry of intercession was not restricted. He still could witness or evangelize, and could continue his ministry of writing ("the Prison Epistles").

"Furtherance" is literally to cut one's way through heavy undergrowth of a forest. Here it is to cut ahead, beat forward, or step out into unoccupied territory. Paul delights in the fact that the news has reached the entire palace guard concerning his chains in Christ. The word for palace is Praetorium, either the headquarters in a Roman camp, or the official residence of the governor of a province. The Praetorium soldiers protected the palace where the ruler lived.

The God we serve overrules the schemes of wicked men and demons. What seems sure tragedy produces triumph, and beauty is brought out of ashes. A prisoner guarded and in chains propagates the Gospel of Christ. Paul's courage inspired other Christian men to boldly, fearlessly preach and testify for the Lord Jesus Christ.

B. PREACHING CHRIST
(Philippians 1:15-18)

Some indeed preach Christ even of envy and strife; and some also of good will: The one preach Christ of contention, not sincerely, supposing to add affliction to my bonds: But the other of love, knowing that I am set for the defence of the gospel. What then? Notwithstanding, every way, whether in pretence, or in truth, Christ is preached; and I therein do rejoice, yea, and will rejoice.

Men have different motives for preaching. Some preach for money, power, or prestige. Paul stated some preached prompted by envy ("the rottenness of the bones," Proverbs 14:30) and strife (wrangling, contention). Note Paul states, they preach Christ! How strange that sounds. They are not heretics, or Judaizers (legalizers). The apostle considers them "brethren," despite their faults. They were men who wanted the honor which was due Paul.

Some, out of sympathy with Paul's views and methods, were jealous of his influence. This is nothing new! Men with selfish ambition, envious, jealous, nourished feelings contrary to the Gospel. They believed they were right and everybody else was wrong; and hoped their success would annoy Paul. And so you see here two kinds of preachers. Some of good will and others who sought to take advantage of Paul's imprisonment to depreciate him and his preaching, to cause him trouble of spirit. Imagine serving God in the energy of the flesh!

Some preached for love of the Gospel, love and concern for Paul. It is shocking that some men use the name of Christ as a cover or mask for personal and selfish ends. God may use even poorly motivated preaching for His glory. He can even bless insincere preaching. Even hypocritical preaching can be blessed of God. Note I said preaching, not the preacher. There is no blessing for the hypocrite (Job 8:13, 20:5). But somehow God uses the grain of truth that is mixed with error and bad motives. He places no premium upon error or upon pretense. See Paul's reaction: "It doesn't bother me at all," he said, "for I rejoice because Christ is preached." It is not true to say that the preaching of Christ serves no purpose and yields no fruit in cases where it is not carried on in the right way or best spirit.

God is not tied up to give no success to His Word just because the men who speak have wrong motives or belong to denominations of which we may disapprove. "It takes great grace for independent thinkers to acknowledge that truth can flow in channels other than their own" (D. Guthrie). The word rendered "pretense" means to cause to shine before or shine forth. We would say some preaching is a " show." It is a falsely alleged motive (Arndt & Gingrich); in reality, these men have other interests. This is in contrast with the truth; the false motives are condemned, but Paul rejoiced that Christ is preached.

C. PAUL'S EXPECTATION
(Philippians 1:19-20)

For I know that this shall turn to my salvation through your prayer, and the supply for the Spirit of Jesus Christ, According to my earnest expectation and my hope, that in nothing I shall be ashamed, but that with all boldness, as always, so now also Christ shall be magnified in my body, whether it be by life, or by death.

The words "I know" point to Paul's confidence. He rejoices in his victory over suffering, over selfish preachers, over every expression of bad motives. Use of the word "salvation" (*soteria*) must not be interpreted to mean his soul's salvation. All Christians have eternal life already, so this is not the issue. Nor is eternal salvation the issue in Philippians 2:12, where the saints are exhorted to solve their own problem "with fear and trembling." The Greek word means preservation, safety, solution, or deliverance.

Paul expects deliverance from prison. There is of course a wider sense that includes the full enjoyment of the day of Christ. All of us look forward to this day. Two things are cited as reasons for this expectation. One is the prayer of the saints. The second is the supply of the Spirit of Jesus Christ. It is believed Paul coined the word rendered "earnest expectation." Literally, it means to watch from the head, thus to watch with the head erect or outstretched, to direct attention to anything, to wait for in suspense (Thayer). As Paul uses the word, it signifies constant, persistent expectation. It means to look intently into the distance with outstretched head. Paul's attention is entirely occupied with one thing, to the exclusion of others. That something is to glorify Jesus Christ!

D. PHILOSOPHY OF LIFE
(Philippians 1:21-23)

For to me to live is Christ, and to die is gain. But if I live in the flesh, this is the fruit of my labour: yet what I shall choose I wot not. For I am in a strait betwixt two, having a desire to depart, and to be with Christ; which is far better:

To live means to continue in physical life. To die is to have died. The act of living is Christ Himself. But it is the state after death, not the act of dying, which is gain. Gain means advantage, even if my death should be the result of my enemies' scheming and plotting, it will be no shame to me. For Paul, Christ was the essence of life, the model of life, the aim of life, the reward of life. Everything he did or thought, and all that he planned was done in relation to Jesus Christ. Even to die would be gain for him, because in death he would go to Him whom he served. He would be free from the bondage in which he now existed, and would have a liberty of spirit that no man will ever know until he is in the presence of the Lord.

There is no concept of soul-sleep here; there is no intermediate probation. There is no unconsciousness after death. The attempt to prove we are not aware of anything when dead is based upon a wrong interpretation of Ecclesiastes 9:5, 10. Paul openly declared that we enjoy Christ's presence when we are dissolved in death. On this earth Christ was everything to Paul, but in heaven the actual presence of the Lord will be far better. We may be sure that no intermediate state is entertained.

E. PRESENT CONFIDENCE
(Philippians 1:24-26)

Nevertheless to abide in the flesh is more needful for you. And having this confidence, I know that I shall abide and continue with you all for your furtherance and joy of faith; That your rejoicing may be more abundant in Jesus Christ for me by my coming to you again.

Paul desires to finish the work the Lord gave him to do. He had been persuaded in time past, and had present assurance that God would allow him to remain and continue with the saints at Philippi. He was further convinced that seeing them again face to face would result in an overflowing rejoicing or exaltation.

III. Special Features

A. PRESERVING OUR HERITAGE

In slavery, blacks lived on the average to be 39 years old. Their lives were held cheap by slavemasters, their deaths merely a loss of property. But those slaves who believed in Christ considered death a gateway to heaven. They held Paul's philosophy that "to die is gain." Today, life expectancy for Black Americans is approximately 72. However, in recent days the increases in suicide and murder among the black populace have caused great concern.

From our point of view, it is because fewer and fewer blacks can truthfully say, "For to me to live is Christ." And few there are who can sing the Spiritual, "I want to die easy when I die, shout salvation as I fly." Emphasis on the here and now has ill prepared us to enjoy the life we presently live, because such emphasis detracts from the bliss of contemplating future life.

B. A CONCLUDING WORD

With the increase in the population of the elderly, some adults struggle with whether they want to live or die. More and more, we hear talk about mercy killing or euthanasia (Greek: well-dying or a good death), and such terms as "pull the plug," and "quality of life." Where there is a strong hold on Jesus Christ, there is a hope (expectation of good) that senior citizens maintain even in the midst of adverse circumstances.

Not that they are in jail as was the apostle Paul, but faced with loneliness, ungrateful children, crippling arthritis, glaucoma, diabetes, strokes, and a host of other geriatric afflictions, those who have a bold faith in the Lord Jesus discover that their biblical philosophy of life and definition of death serves them in good stead, and gives them joy in their remaining days.

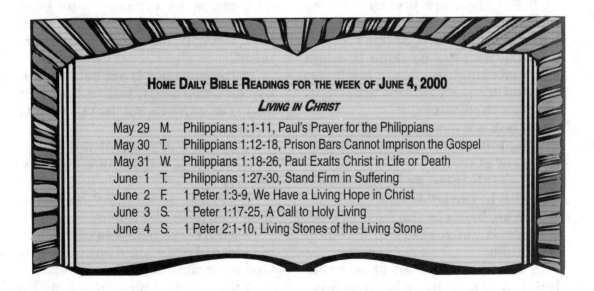

HOME DAILY BIBLE READINGS FOR THE WEEK OF JUNE 4, 2000

LIVING IN CHRIST

May 29	M.	Philippians 1:1-11, Paul's Prayer for the Philippians
May 30	T.	Philippians 1:12-18, Prison Bars Cannot Imprison the Gospel
May 31	W.	Philippians 1:18-26, Paul Exalts Christ in Life or Death
June 1	T.	Philippians 1:27-30, Stand Firm in Suffering
June 2	F.	1 Peter 1:3-9, We Have a Living Hope in Christ
June 3	S.	1 Peter 1:17-25, A Call to Holy Living
June 4	S.	1 Peter 2:1-10, Living Stones of the Living Stone

O God who has redeemed us to live as members of the body of Christ, grant that the consciousness of Your grace may empower us to model the life of Your Son. Teach us Your will as we rise above selfish concerns to live for Him who died for us, even Jesus Christ Our Lord and Savior. Amen.

Having the Mind of Christ

Adult Topic—*Genuine Humility*

•••••

Youth Topic—*Setting Aside Privileges*
Children's Topic—*Being Like Jesus*

•••••

Devotional Reading—2 Peter 3:8-18
Background Scripture—Philippians 2:1-18
Print—Philippians 2:1-13

PRINTED SCRIPTURE

Philippians 2:1-13 (KJV)

IF THERE be therefore any consolation in Christ, if any comfort of love, if any fellowship of the Spirit, if any bowels and mercies,

2 Fulfil ye my joy, that ye be likeminded, having the same love, being of one accord, of one mind.

3 Let nothing be done through strife or vainglory; but in lowliness of mind let each esteem other better than themselves.

4 Look not every man on his own things, but every man also on the things of others.

5 Let this mind be in you, which was also in Christ Jesus:

6 Who, being in the form of God, thought it not robbery to be equal with God:

7 But made himself of no reputation, and took upon him the form of a servant, and was made in the likeness of men:

8 And being found in fashion as a man, he humbled himself, and became obedient unto death, even the death of the cross.

Philippians 2:1-13 (NRSV)

IF THEN there is any encouragement in Christ, any consolation from love, any sharing in the Spirit, any compassion and sympathy,

2 make my joy complete: be of the same mind, having the same love, being in full accord and of one mind.

3 Do nothing from selfish ambition or conceit, but in humility regard others as better than yourselves.

4 Let each of you look not to your own interests, but to the interests of others.

5 Let the same mind be in you that was in Christ Jesus,

6 who, though he was in the form of God, did not regard equality with God as something to be exploited,

7 but emptied himself, taking the form of a slave, being born in human likeness. And being found in human form,

8 he humbled himself and became obedient to the point of death—even death on a cross.

9 Wherefore God also hath highly exalted him, and given him a name which is above every name:

10 That at the name of Jesus every knee should bow, of things in heaven, and things in earth, and things under the earth;

11 And that every tongue should confess that Jesus Christ is Lord, to the glory of God the Father.

12 Wherefore, my beloved, as ye have always obeyed, not as in my presence only, but now much more in my absence, work out your own salvation with fear and trembling.

13 For it is God which worketh in you both to will and to do of his good pleasure.

9 Therefore God also highly exalted him and gave him the name that is above every name,

10 so that at the name of Jesus every knee should bend, in heaven and on earth and under the earth,

11 and every tongue should confess that Jesus Christ is Lord, to the glory of God the Father.

12 Therefore, my beloved, just as you have always obeyed me, not only in my presence, but much more now in my absence, work out your own salvation with fear and trembling;

13 for it is God who is at work in you, enabling you both to will and to work for his good pleasure.

KEY VERSE

*Let this mind be in you, which was also in Christ Jesus.—**Philippians 2:5***

OBJECTIVES

After reading this lesson, the student should be encouraged to:

1. Desire to have a mind like Jesus Christ;
2. Put humility into practice at home and at church;
3. Make meekness and unity a reality; and
4. Exalt Jesus Christ in every aspect of life.

POINTS TO BE EMPHASIZED

Adult/Youth
Key Verse: Philippians 2:5
Print: Philippians 2:1-13

— Paul said his joy would be complete when the believers demonstrated unity in Christ and esteemed others better than themselves. (1-4)

—Paul exhorted the Philippians to follow the example of Christ in humility, obedience, and service. (5-8)

—Because God exalted Jesus and gave Him a name above every name, all creation should worship and reverence Christ as Lord. (9-11)

—Salvation, both God's work in the believer and a personal response to God, enables believers to please God. (12, 13)

Children

Key Verse: Galatians 6:10

Print: Philippians 2:1-8; Acts 16:16-18

—Paul said his joy would be complete when the believers demonstrated unity in Christ and esteemed others better than themselves. (Philippians 2:1-4)

—Paul exhorted the Philippians to follow the example of Christ in humility, obedience, and service. (5-8)

—As Paul's missionary party went to pray, they were met by a girl who cried out that Paul and his companions were servants of God. (Acts 16:16)

—After many days, Paul was grieved and in the name of Jesus commanded the spirit to come out of her, and she was healed. (17-18)

(**NOTE**: Use KJV Scripture for Adults; NRSV Scripture for Youth and Children)

TOPICAL OUTLINE OF THE LESSON

I. Introduction

A. The Kenosis Theory

B. Biblical Background

II. Exposition and Application of the Scripture

A. Exhortation (Philippians 2:1-4)

B. Emptying (Philippians 2:5-8)

C. Exaltation (Philippians 2:9-11)

D. Example (Philippians 2:12-13)

III. Special Features

A. Preserving Our Heritage

B. A Concluding Word

I. Introduction

A. THE KENOSIS THEORY

In Philippians 2:7, we have the words, "made himself of no reputation," (NKJV), "He emptied himself" (RSV), "made himself nothing" (NIV, NEB). The Greek verb (*Kenoo*) means to empty, make empty, to make void (Thayer). "He divested Himself of His privileges" (Arndt & Gingrich). From this verb is derived the word, Kenosis. Unfortunately, some scholars have ignored the context and parallel Scriptures, and have taught that when Christ became a man, He divested or emptied Himself of all divine attributes. However, the idea of God the Son no longer existing as God is an absurdity.

No matter what God does or becomes, He cannot stop being God. It is impossible. We make no attempt to explain how, but we do have something to say about what. Jesus Christ allowed certain manifestations of Deity to be veiled for a moment of time, He emptied Himself of whatever was necessary in order to do what He had come to do. He emptied Himself only of the external and visible indications of the Godhead. At no time did He ever empty Himself of His omniscience, omnipotence or omnipresence.

"At all times His divine attributes could be exercised according to His will" (Scofield). Chafer states, "The subordination of self in behalf of others does not require the discarding of self." Strong says He gave up the "independent exercise of the divine attributes," and used them only at the pleasure of God the Father (John 5:19). It is therefore an error to believe that God the Son can cease to be God. Accept the fact that we do not understand how that at times our Lord appeared limited, i.e., hungry, thirsty, tired, weeping, bleeding, dying. The Incarnation remains a wonderful mystery—God became a Man, but He never stopped being God!

B. BIBLICAL BACKGROUND

In the church at Corinth, a wrong concept of wisdom was a root cause of the carnality and schism there. Here in the church at Philippi pride was a major cause of strife. Still today, pride that manifests itself in erroneous ideas about true wisdom plagues the local assembly. The very fact that the apostle emphasizes the matter of humility indicates the saints in the city of Philippi were not especially humble in character.

There was an undercurrent of contention created by differences of opinion. In chapter 4, two prominent members of the church are mentioned: Euodia (prosperous journey) and Syntyche (good fortune). Evidently, these ladies had a disagreement of long standing. We are not told the nature of their dispute, but Paul heard about their wrangling, and was moved to exhort them to be "of the same mind in the Lord."

II. Exposition and Application of the Scripture

A. EXHORTATION
(Philippians 2:1-4)

If there be therefore any consolation in Christ, if any comfort of love, if any fellowship of the Spirit, if any bowels and mercies, Fulfil ye my joy, that ye be likeminded, having the same love, being of one accord, of one mind. Let nothing be done through strife or vainglory; but in lowliness of mind let each esteem other better than themselves. Look not every man on his own things, but every man also on the things of others.

When we have a conditional clause that assumes the premise is true, the word "if" may be rendered "since." So the "if" here is not that of doubt. Four reasons or blessings are mentioned as to why the saints in the Philippian church should live in close harmony and cooperation. First is consolation in Christ. This means encouragement, strength afforded by our relationship in Christ. It is the persuasiveness of Christ (F. B. Meyer).

Second is comfort of love. This refers to the persuasive incentive (Amplified Bible) furnished by the bond of love; it is the tender care love provides.

Third is communion of the Holy Spirit. Here we see the fellowship, partnership, and mutual concern that is effected by God's Spirit. In other words, it is the work of the Holy Spirit to create a fellowship, both between saint and God, and among the saints.

Fourth is combined compassion and tender mercies ("affection and sympathy" (RSV). The Hebrews regarded the "bowels" (KJV), intestines (the heart, lungs, liver, etc.) as the seat of the tenderer affections, especially kindness, benevolence, compassion (Thayer). Figurative of the seat of the emotions, the belly in our usage is the heart (Arndt & Gingrich).

Here is an appeal to human kindness, the depth of affection (Amplified). When these things are true of us, they put pressure upon us and urge us to harmonious living. Moffatt summarizes: "So by all the stimulus of Christ, by every incentive of love, by all your participation in the Spirit, by all your affectionate tenderness, I pray you to give me the utter joy of knowing you are living in harmony, with the same feelings of love, with one heart and soul."

In verse three, strife implies the formation of cliques within the church. Such groups try to maneuver things their way. Vainglory is pride; it means the ambition of any member to gain position so as to create a following and to minister to his personal vanity. D. L. Moody said, "Strife is knocking another down; vainglory is setting oneself up." The solution to the egotism and party spirit, which destroy the unity so essential to healthy church life, is HUMILITY. It is the power of the indwelling Holy Spirit that enables us "to efface self in order that others might be honored" (MacDonald).

B. EMPTYING (Philippians 2:5-8)

Let this mind be in you, which was also in Christ Jesus: Who, being in the form of God, thought it not robbery to be equal with God: But made himself of no reputation, and took upon him the form of a servant, and was made in the likeness of men: And being found in fashion as a man, he humbled himself, and became obedient unto death, even the death of the cross.

We see that the preeminent social grace is humility. What the Lord desires of us, He has already set the pattern for in Jesus Christ. With this passage begins the great discourse on the Incarnation, strongly affirming Christ's essential deity. The word translated "form" is *morphe*, and means the permanent expression of existence. Thus we have the form of God, the form of an angel, the form of a man, and the form of a beast, all of which are immovable manifestations of being or existence.

The fashion or shape may change, but the form remains. The form is the external appearance by which a person or thing strikes the vision (Scofield). Man's eyes could not look upon His glory. So Christ emptied Himself, divested Himself of the outward glory and lived in human form as a Man on earth. He did not consider equality with God, the exalted rank to which the Father raised Him, a thing to be clung to or grasped. He did not consider it robbery means He was not grasping after something that was not His. After all, He is God. He had glory with the Father before the world began (John 17:5). Instead, He chose the path of humility, suffering and the death of the cross. In verse 6, we see the height from which our Lord descended; in verses 7 and 8, the depth to which He descended.

C. EXALTATION
(Philippians 2:9-11)

Wherefore God also hath highly exalted him, and given him a name which is above every name: That at the name of Jesus every knee should bow, of things in heaven, and things in earth, and things under the earth; And that every tongue should confess that Jesus Christ is Lord, to the glory of God the Father.

In verse nine, we see the height to which God the Father has exalted Him. The day is coming when there shall be a universal outpouring of worship praising the Lord Jesus Christ. This is not universalism, the belief that eventually all human beings shall be saved. There will be those who are forced to acknowledge the sovereignty of Christ! Refusal to confess Him now means compulsion to confess Him later.

There will be universal submission to the Lord Jesus Christ! Those who assert they will not have "this man reign over them" will sing a different song in that day. Scholars are not sure what is meant by the point that the Father has given Jesus Christ "the name which is above every name." Note that what is said of Jehovah in Isaiah 45:23 is said of the Lord Jesus: "That to me every knee shall bow, every tongue shall take an oath."

Some men state that the phrase refers to Isaiah 45:23, so that the name is Jesus, which contains the name of Jehovah (Joshua is Hebrew for Jesus and is a contraction of Jehoshua, Jehovah Saves, Jehovah is Salvation). Another idea states it is just a figurative way of signifying that Christ is Supreme. "The full significance of the name will only be realized when all the world acknowledges the sovereignty of Christ" (Expositor's).

D. EXAMPLE
(Philippians 2:12-13)

Wherefore, my beloved, as ye have always obeyed, not as in my presence only, but now much more in my absence, work out your own salvation with fear and trembling. For it is God which worketh in you both to will and to do of his good pleasure.

Paul went on from here to suggest to the saints at Philippi that they can solve their problem by applying the principle of humility to their own lives. "Put into practice the salvation God has already given you. Continue to work out your own deliverance!" said Paul. And do so "with fear and trembling," which is to say, with a humble frame of mind. Rest assured that verse 12 does not teach salvation by works. Ephesians 2:8-9 plainly teaches we are not saved by works (see also Titus 3:5). Just keep in mind that the word translated "salvation" also means safety, deliverance, preservation (Thayer).

The church had depended too much on Paul and felt helpless in his absence to conduct its affairs or solve its problems. In their perplexity, the church appealed to Paul through the visit of Epaphroditus to the apostle there in

Rome. Paul wrote and reminded them God's presence was with them, and the Lord could and would deliver them no matter where Paul was.

In verse 13, the word God (*Theos*) is put first for emphasis. God alone creates within us both the will and the power. He energizes us to do His will. Here it is His pleasure that there be harmony in the church. Note the paradox, "I yet not I." I will, I decide, I choose, I purpose—yet that which is good I choose only because the Lord Jesus Christ in me moved me to do so.

III. Special Features

A. PRESERVING OUR HERITAGE

Someone has said that wherever we have two Baptists, we have three opinions! Of course, congregationalism is the very heart of the Baptist denomination. Unfortunately, congregations can be wrong, out of the will of God. Numbers do not necessarily insure righteousness. The crowd may be wrong, the majority in error. Democracy, the rule (kratos) of the people (demos) is only as good as the heart of the people who rule.

All too often church leaders, whether pastors, deacons, trustees, auxiliary presidents, and others, become proud, stubborn and filled with unholy ambition. For some, a little power goes to their heads; given an inch they seek to take a mile. The power struggles that occur in Baptist circles are devastating! Psychologists speak of implosion and inform us that because the Black Church plays an important role in the life of Black America, that the potential for explosion or implosion is increased all the more.

You see then how much we need to obey the exhortations of today's lesson. Peace and harmony can be preserved only when we have the mind of the Lord Jesus. But when we want to hold on to offices, titles, prestige, power, and money—and are not willing to "make ourselves of no reputation,"—great harm is done. The cause of Christ is hindered, the church is shamed, our witness lost. And the joy and peace rightfully belonging to the blood-bought escapes us.

Surely, we need to hear again and heed the exhortation, "Let this mind be in you which was also in Christ Jesus." Yea, "Bear ye one another's burdens, and so fulfill the law of Christ...As we have, therefore, opportunity, let us do good unto all men, especially unto them who are of the household of faith" (Galatians 6:2, 10).

B. A CONCLUDING WORD

MacDonald states that the key word in chapter 2 is "others." We are reminded that the Lord Jesus lived for others. So did the apostle Paul, Timothy, Epaphroditus, et al. And so we should live for others. "Esteem others better...Let each of you look out not only for his own interests, but also for the interests of others" (verses 3-4).

Our pattern for such living is Jesus Christ. Recall that it is said of Him: "that though he was rich, yet for your sakes he became poor, that you through his poverty might become rich" (2 Corinthians 8:9). The way to be a blessing to others is through the door of humility. Combined with a heart, soul and mind that are one with Christ, it becomes easy for saints to demonstrate that the Lord lives His life within them.

What is the answer, the solution to the egotism and party spirit that destroys the unity essential to healthy church life? The antidote to these evils is humility. There are those within the church who are Christians, but are proud of their culture, their race, privilege, denomination, tradition, intellect, Bible knowledge, etc. And their pride prevents them from putting God first, others second, and self last.

HOME DAILY BIBLE READINGS FOR THE WEEK OF JUNE 11, 2000

HAVING THE MIND OF CHRIST

June 5 M. Philippians 2:1-11, Imitate Christ's Humility in Your Lives
June 6 T. Philippians 2:12-18, Rejoice in One Another's Faithfulness
June 7 W. Philippians 2:19-24, Timothy, a Faithful Servant of Christ
June 8 T. Philippians 2:25-30, Welcome Epaphroditus in Christ
June 9 F. 1 Peter 3:8-12, Repay Evil with a Blessing
June 10 S. 1 Peter 3:13-22, Suffering for Doing Right
June 11 S. 2 Peter 1:1-11, You Are Participants in God's Nature

Know Your Bible

- It is God who "puts down one king and sets up another" as indicated by the anointing of Hazael by Elisha to be king of Syria. (2 Kings 8:13)
- Jehu showed great zeal for the outward worship of God, but was wicked in other ways. (2 Kings 8:7-21)
- Jehu had all of the worshipers of Baal put to death (2 Kings 10:23-25), in return for which the Lord promised that his children for four generations would sit on the throne of Israel. (2 Kings 10:30)
- Jehu ruled over Israel for twenty-eight years, following which his son Jehoahaz succeeded him. (2 Kings 13:1)

Our Father, You have reconciled us to thyself to live in commitment to Your will. Grant that the mind of Jesus Christ may become the constraining force in our behavior to the end that our every action may reveal the saving power of Your grace by which we are transformed into persons whose quality of life depicts Your presence within the fellowship of the forgiven. In the name of Jesus Christ, we offer our prayer. Amen.

Pressing On in Christ

Adult Topic—*Striving to Be Christlike*

•••••

Youth Topic—*Press Ahead!*
Children's Topic—*Telling the Good News*

•••••

Devotional Reading—Hebrews 10:19-25, 32-36
Background Scripture—Philippians 3
Print—Philippians 3:7-21

PRINTED SCRIPTURE

Philippians 3:7-21 (KJV)

7 But what things were gain to me, those I counted loss for Christ.

8 Yea doubtless, and I count all things but loss for the excellency of the knowledge of Christ Jesus my Lord: for whom I have suffered the loss of all things, and do count them but dung, that I may win Christ.

9 And be found in him, not having mine own righteousness, which is of the law, but that which is through the faith of Christ, the righteousness which is of God by faith:

10 That I may know him, and the power of his resurrection, and the fellowship of his sufferings, being made conformable unto his death;

11 If by any means I might attain unto the resurrection of the dead.

12 Not as though I had already attained, either were already perfect: but I follow after, if that I may apprehend that for which also I am apprehended of Christ Jesus.

13 Brethren, I count not myself to have apprehended: but this one thing I do, forgetting those things which are behind, and reaching forth unto those things which are before,

Philippians 3:7-21 (NRSV)

7 Yet whatever gains I had, these I have come to regard as loss because of Christ.

8 More than that, I regard everything as loss because of the surpassing value of knowing Christ Jesus my Lord. For his sake I have suffered the loss of all things, and I regard them as rubbish, in order that I may gain Christ

9 and be found in him, not having a righteousness of my own that comes from the law, but one that comes through faith in Christ, the righteousness from God based on faith.

10 I want to know Christ and the power of his resurrection and the sharing of his sufferings by becoming like him in his death,

11 if somehow I may attain the resurrection from the dead.

12 Not that I have already obtained this or have already reached the goal; but I press on to make it my own, because Christ Jesus has made me his own.

13 Beloved, I do not consider that I have made it my own; but this one thing I do: forgetting what lies

14 I press toward the mark for the prize of the high calling of God in Christ Jesus.

15 Let us therefore, as many as be perfect, be thus minded: and if in any thing ye be otherwise minded, God shall reveal even this unto you.

16 Nevertheless, whereto we have already attained, let us walk by the same rule, let us mind the same thing.

17 Brethren, be followers together of me, and mark them which walk so as ye have us for an example.

18 (For many walk, of whom I have told you often, and now tell you even weeping, that they are the enemies of the cross of Christ:

19 Whose end is destruction, whose God is their belly, and whose glory is in their shame, who mind earthly things.)

20 For our conversation is in heaven; from whence also we look for the Saviour, the Lord Jesus Christ:

21 Who shall change our vile body, that it may be fashioned like unto his glorious body, according to the working whereby he is able even to subdue all things unto himself.

behind and straining forward to what lies ahead,

14 I press on toward the goal for the prize of the heavenly call of God in Christ Jesus.

15 Let those of us then who are mature be of the same mind; and if you think differently about anything, this too God will reveal to you.

16 Only let us hold fast to what we have attained.

17 Brothers and sisters, join in imitating me, and observe those who live according to the example you have in us.

18 For many live as enemies of the cross of Christ; I have often told you of them, and now I tell you even with tears.

19 Their end is destruction; their god is the belly; and their glory is in their shame; their minds are set on earthly things.

20 But our citizenship is in heaven, and it is from there that we are expecting a Savior, the Lord Jesus Christ.

21 He will transform the body of our humiliation that it may be conformed to the body of his glory, by the power that also enables him to make all things subject to himself.

 **KEY VERSE**

I press toward the mark for the prize of the high calling of God in Christ Jesus.—**Philippians 3:14**

OBJECTIVES

After reading this lesson, the student should strongly seek to:

1. Make Christ likeness the number one priority of life;
2. Keep pressing on to higher heights;
3. Walk without compromising; and
4. Continue looking for the return of the Savior.

POINTS TO BE EMPHASIZED

Adult/Youth
Key Verse: Philippians 3:14
Print: Philippians 3:7-21

—Paul said knowing Christ surpasses everything of worth to him and he suffered the loss of all things for Christ, for personal righteousness does not come by the law but through faith in Christ. (7-9)
—Paul spoke of sharing Christ's suffering and the power of His resurrection in order to attain eternal life. (10-11)
—Paul said that attaining the goal of God's call in Christ requires forgetting past failures and pressing toward the future with Christ as guide. (12-14)
—Paul exhorted mature believers to live changed lives, be steadfast, and to follow his example. (15-17)
—People who worship earthly things and do not follow Christ will be destroyed. (18, 19)
—As citizens of heaven, we expect Christ by His almighty power to transform us into the likeness of His glorious body. (20, 21)

Children
Key Verse: Acts 16:31
Print: Philippians 3:12; Acts 16:19, 24-31

—Paul acknowledged that he was still pressing on toward his destiny in Christ because Christ had made him His own. (Philippians 3:12)
—The owners of the slave girl brought Paul and Silas before the authorities. (Acts 16:19)
—Paul and Silas were put in prison. (24)
—While Paul and Silas were praying and singing at midnight, there was a violent earthquake. (25-26)
—When the jailer asked how he could be saved, Paul and Silas shared Jesus with him. (27-31)

(**NOTE**: Use KJV Scripture for Adults; NRSV Scripture for Youth and Children)

TOPICAL OUTLINE OF THE LESSON

I. Introduction
    A. Perfection
    B. Biblical Background

II. Exposition and Application of the Scripture
    A. The Right Kind of Righteousness (Philippians 3:7-9)
    B. The Power of the Resurrection (Philippians 3:10-11)
    C. The Pursuit of Perfection (Philippians 3:12-16)
    D. The Enemies of the Cross (Philippians 3:17-19)
    E. The Citizens of Heaven (Philippians 3:20-21)

III. Special Features
    A. Preserving Our Heritage
    B. Concluding Word

I. Introduction

A. PERFECTION

In Philippians 3:12, 15, we read: "Not as though I had already attained, either were already perfect...as many as be perfect." The word translated "perfect" is derived from a verb that means to complete, finish, bring to an end, accomplish, and fulfill. It does not refer to absolute sinlessness (Romans 3:23). Keep this in mind when you read that Noah was perfect in his generations (Genesis 6:9). Asa's heart was perfect with the Lord all his days (1 Kings 15:14). Hezekiah walked with a perfect heart (2 Kings 20:3). The men of war came with a perfect heart to make David king (1 Chronicles 12:38). Job was perfect and upright (Job 1:1, 8).

When the Lord Jesus exhorts (Matthew 5:48), "Therefore you shall be perfect, just as your Father in heaven is perfect," He does not imply sinless perfection, but demands complete maturity. It is as if He commands believers to be full grown Christians, fully developed. Here is God's ideal for us, "forever shining before us, calling us upward, and making endless progression possible" (ISBE). "An apple may not be due to ripen fully until October, but may be perfectly developed in September as a September apple" (Pilgrim Bible note).

Lenski points out that the perfect tense is used: "I have already been made complete." Paul cannot say that God is finished or through, and looks at him "like a contractor who has finished a building."

While in verse 12, the apostle denies having attained perfection in body, soul and spirit, he does claim (verse 15) spiritual maturity (or what is called relative perfection).

B. BIBLICAL BACKGROUND

Chapter three begins with a warning against false teachers, in this case specifically against men who are called Judaizers or legalizers. Men have their own ideas about righteousness, but the righteousness of God is found only through Christ. All else is false. Paul's premise seems to be, if you want to rejoice in the Lord, make sure you are holding to and practicing the truth, and not some false religion.

Judaizers followed Mosaic practices but had no real heart for God. They are called "dogs," meaning evil men, a term of contempt. Dogs were scavengers, the eaters of garbage in the streets. To call a man a dog meant he was profane, impure. In the Jewish usage of the word, uncleanness was the prominent idea. Paul uses this insulting epithet on these extreme Judaizers or antagonistic Jews. So it is strong language for false teachers who teach against Christ.

While their character is seen in the term "dogs," their conduct is seen in the phrase, "evil workers." Saints are warned to beware of these opponents described by the words: dogs, evil workers, and concision. This latter word means mutilation of the flesh, with emphasis upon ceremony. This is their creed. They would prefer being called the circumcision, but with bitter play on words, Paul calls them flesh mutilators. They glorified ceremony by insisting there is no salvation unless one is circumcised according to the custom of Moses.

II. Exposition and Application of the Scripture

A. THE RIGHT KIND OF RIGHTEOUSNESS (Philippians 3:7-9)

But what things were gain to me, those I counted loss for Christ. Yea doubtless, and I count all things but loss for the excellency of the knowledge of Christ Jesus my Lord: for whom I have suffered the loss of all things, and do count them but dung, that I may win Christ, And be found in him, not having mine own righteousness, which is of the law, but that which is through the faith of Christ, the righteousness which is of God by faith.

The "gain" or advantageous things of life for Paul are described in verses 5-6. He had given up culture, wealth, prestige, and counted them loss ("damaged goods," Henry Morris) for Christ. Meeting the Lord Jesus on the road to Damascus changed Paul's values. More valuable than anything else is the knowledge of Christ as Savior and Lord. So high or excellent is this understanding of Christ that all else, whatever men boast of, is relegated to the trash can. Whatever the loss, Paul calls it trash. The Greek word (*skubala*) is strong language. It means rubbish (NASB, NKJV, JBP, NIV), animal excrement, dung, refuse (RSV, Moffatt), garbage (NEB, TEV), less than nothing (LB), "that which is worthless and detestable" (Thayer).

What is meant by the words, "to win Christ...and be found in Him"? Paul already had the Lord, but not yet in fullness. The desire to be spiritually profitable in the service of the Lord is a goal to be worked on. In short, the apostle wanted to exhaust (an impossibility!) the unsearchable riches in Christ (Ephesians 3:8). A man found in God's righteousness will not be found in any righteousness of his own, for our righteousnesses are filthy rags. Men still seek to work their way to heaven, but Christ is not gained by keeping laws or doing good works. All personal achievements are discounted. We are in Him by faith, yea, by grace connected with Christ.

B. THE POWER OF THE RESURRECTION
(Philippians 3:10-11)

That I may know him, and the power of his resurrection, and the fellowship of his sufferings, being made conformable unto his death; If by any means I might attain unto the resurrection of the dead.

Paul's desire was to know Jesus Christ, not merely intellectually, but in a personal way. To have experiences with the Lord in increasing measure in life and in service—this was the apostle's goal. The power of His resurrection is to be realized in daily living. It is more than head knowledge that on the third day the Lord rose from the grave. The question is this: How does that resurrection power affect our living? Paul wanted the power that flows from being in Christ, in union with Him, to manifest itself in daily service.

What is called "fellowship of his sufferings" consists of those hardships the Christian experiences for the cause of Christ. Being in Christ involves being hated by the world (John 15:18-19). Are we willing to endure whatever will bring us closer to the Lord Jesus? The expression "being made conformable unto his death" refers to a continual dying out of self. The apostle does not speak of outside show, or what we call "form and fashion," (*schema*) or masquerade. Conformity to the world is prohibited (Romans 12:2). Paul speaks of an inner attitude towards the world that may end in the shedding of blood! This is a far cry from the goal set by some church members today who are at ease in Zion (Amos 6:1).

The words "if by any means" do not express doubt or uncertainty, but humility and self-distrust. To know the Lord Jesus is to be on your way to glory through the resurrection of believers. "He expresses the devout hope of sharing in" the resurrection of the saints (A. T. Robertson). Paul is not afraid of death; it holds no terror for him. He sees death as an open door to a richer fellowship with Jesus Christ.

C. THE PURSUIT OF PERFECTION (Philippians 3:12-16)

Not as though I had already attained, either were already perfect: but I follow after, if that I may apprehend that for which also I am apprehended of Christ Jesus. Brethren, I count not myself to have apprehended: but this one thing I do, forgetting those things which are behind, and reaching forth unto those things which are before, I press toward the mark for the prize of the high calling of God in Christ Jesus. Let us therefore, as many as be perfect, be thus minded: and if in any thing ye be otherwise minded, God shall reveal even this unto you. Nevertheless, whereto we have already attained, let us walk by the same rule, let us mind the same thing.

We are ever obligated to close the gap between doctrine and deed, between our position and our condition, between our standing and our state. We know, however, that we will never achieve such a goal while in these mortal bodies. God has set the standard, and it is our duty to strive in the power of the Holy Spirit to reach the mark. At our best, we are unprofitable servants. Failure to attain is no excuse for not attempting to please the Lord; and we have no excuse not to preach that it is God's will we live a clean life in a dirty age. Paul is very much aware of his deficiencies. He was determined to follow after, press toward, the absolute standard of behavior the Lord had established. Some of us fail to climb Jacob's ladder because we are so busy looking at the faults of others, or even crying over spilt milk in our own lives. With single-minded determination, Paul concentrated on what I call the "Philosophy of one-thing-ness."

Read Joshua 23:14, Psalm 27:4, Ecclesiastes 3:19, Matthew 21:24, Mark 10:21, Luke 6:9, 10:42, John 9:25 and Acts 19:32, 21:34. These verses will help you to develop "one-thing-ism." Forgetting some past experiences in life is absolutely necessary for a successful pursuit of perfection. Some memories are of evils we committed. Although God has cleansed us, and there is now no condemnation, often our minds return to yesteryear, causing ghosts of the past to haunt us and drive us to become melancholy. Another interpretation of the phrase "those things which are behind" is to refer them to verses 4-6, the things in which Paul might have bragged about. "Forbid it, Lord, that I should boast, Save in the death of Christ my God;

All the vain things that charmed me most, I sacrifice them to His blood" (Isaac Watts).

In Philippians 3:14, the "high calling" is the complete and perfect Christian life already begun. The apostle wants it known that he does not feel that he has arrived. Sinless perfection in this life is impossible. However, we are to be watchful, observing the signs that signify we are approaching the finish line. Our ears are open to hear the trumpet blast, and to hear the high calling to "come up hither!" Imagine the joy of hearing the Master say, "Well done!" Those of us who are in training, fit and equipped, are encouraged to move on to a higher goal.

D. THE ENEMIES OF THE CROSS
(Philippians 3:17-19)

Brethren, be followers together of me, and mark them which walk so as ye have us for an example. (For many walk, of whom I have told you often, and now tell you even weeping, that they are the enemies of the cross of Christ: Whose end is destruction, whose God is their belly, and whose glory is in their shame, who mind earthly things.)

Paul's "follow me" is the use of the verb meaning to imitate. It is used always in connection with some specific problem (1 Corinthians 4:16, 11:1, 2 Thessalonians 3:7-9). Christ's command to follow Him uses a verb that means to walk the same road. Figuratively, the command means to follow Him as a disciple: "Follow Me," means, "Be My disciple." So Paul states, "Imitate me when it comes to your walk." They are warned to beware of the enemies of the Cross of Christ. They profess to be Christians but they really

are not. Paul's heart is broken and he is moved to tears to have to use such language about followers of Christ.

Four things are said about these enemies. (1) Their Bottom line is Destruction. "Their destiny is destruction" (NIV), "their future is eternal loss" (LB), "they are going to end up in Hell" (TEV). (2) Their Belly is their God. Belly refers to appetite, bodily desires, and sensual indulgences. A man whose biggest aim in life is to satisfy his own desires is a spiritual pig. (3) Their Boast is their Shame. They are proud of what they should be ashamed of. A. T. Robertson said: "These moral perverts turn liberty into license; they throw moral pride to the winds and become unmoral degenerates." (4) Their Brain is limited. They think only of things that belong to this world system, that are passing away!

E. THE CITIZENS OF HEAVEN
(Philippians 3:20-21)

For our conversation is in heaven; from whence also we look for the Saviour, the Lord Jesus Christ: Who shall change our vile body, that it may be fashioned like unto his glorious body, according to the working whereby he is able even to subdue all things unto himself.

The word "conversation" used elsewhere in the KJV means behavior, conduct, and walk. But the word used in verse twenty means citizenship. In contrast to those who mind earthly things, our commonwealth is in heaven. When Christ returns our humble bodies shall be changed by His power, and we shall receive bodies suited for our new home, heaven!

III. Special Features

A. PRESERVING OUR HERITAGE

I thought it interesting to see what hymns, spirituals or gospels we can relate to the major themes of the Sunday school lesson. As for the Right Kind of Righteousness, I vaguely remember hearing folks sing, "Get right with God, and do it now, Get right with God, He will show you how." How appropriate in this day when we tend to serve God the way we want to serve Him, and thus seek to establish our own brand of righteousness. For the Pursuit of Perfection, one favorite we used to hear is, "I'm pressing on the upward way, New heights I'm gaining ev'ry day; Still praying as I'm onward bound, 'Lord, plant my feet on higher ground'" (Oatman). For the Citizens of Heaven, there is still the popular hymn, "When We All Get to Heaven." What a day of rejoicing that will be!

B. A CONCLUDING WORD

We are encouraged to push, press on, to chase after, attain the goal of God's call in Christ. This means persevering, enduring past failures, accepting God's forgiveness. Pressing on in Christ includes forgetting what we "gave up" or what we could have become! Becoming more like the Lord Jesus Christ is the greatest goal in life! Living the life that pleases the Lord, and doing so in the strength of the Holy Spirit is commendable. And what great motivation we have in knowing that one day we shall see the Lord Jesus for ourselves, and "when he is revealed, we shall be like him, for we shall see him as he is" (1 John 3:2).

HOME DAILY BIBLE READINGS FOR THE WEEK OFF JUNE 18, 2000

PRESSING ON IN CHRIST

June 12	M.	Philippians 3:1-6, Don't Be Led Astray!
June 13	T.	Philippians 3:7-11, The Ultimate Richness: Knowing Jesus Christ
June 14	W.	Philippians 3:12-16, Press on Toward the Goal
June 15	T.	Philippians 3:17—4:1, Our Citizenship Is in Heaven
June 16	F.	Hebrews 10:19-25, Encourage One Another in Christ Jesus
June 17	S.	Hebrews 10:26-39, Hold Fast Your Confidence in Christ
June 18	S.	Hebrews 12:1-13, Live a Disciplined Christian Life

 *Eternal God, our Father, as we embrace the reality of the sacrificial death of Jesus Christ our Lord, grant that the hope of eternal life may become the mode by which our earthly lives are shaped. In Jesus' name. Amen.*

Rejoicing in Christ

Adult Topic—*Deep Joy*

•••••

Youth Topic—*Rejoicing in Christ*
Children's Topic—*Rejoicing Together*

•••••

Devotional Reading—1 Thessalonians 1:2-10
Background Scripture— Philippians 4:4-20
Print—Philippians 4:4-18

PRINTED SCRIPTURE

Philippians 4:4-18 (KJV)

4 Rejoice in the Lord always: and again I say, Rejoice.

5 Let your moderation be known unto all men. The Lord is at hand.

6 Be careful for nothing; but in every thing by prayer and supplication with thanksgiving let your requests be made known unto God.

7 And the peace of God, which passeth all understanding, shall keep your hearts and minds through Christ Jesus.

8 Finally, brethren, whatsoever things are true, whatsoever things are honest, whatsoever things are just, whatsoever things are pure, whatsoever things are lovely, whatsoever things are of good report; if there be any virtue, and if there be any praise, think on these things.

9 Those things, which ye have both learned, and received, and heard, and seen in me, do: and the God of peace shall be with you.

10 But I rejoiced in the Lord greatly, that now at the last your care of me hath flourished again; wherein ye were also careful, but ye lacked opportunity.

Philippians 4:4-18 (NRSV)

4 Rejoice in the Lord always; again I will say, Rejoice.

5 Let your gentleness be known to everyone. The Lord is near.

6 Do not worry about anything, but in everything by prayer and supplication with thanksgiving let your requests be made known to God.

7 And the peace of God, which surpasses all understanding, will guard your hearts and your minds in Christ Jesus.

8 Finally, beloved, whatever is true, whatever is honorable, whatever is just, whatever is pure, whatever is pleasing, whatever is commendable, if there is any excellence and if there is anything worthy of praise, think about these things.

9 Keep on doing the things that you have learned and received and heard and seen in me, and the God of peace will be with you.

10 I rejoice in the Lord greatly that now at last you have revived your concern for me; indeed, you were concerned for me, but had no opportunity to show it.

11 Not that I speak in respect of want: for I have learned, in whatsoever state I am, therewith to be content.

12 I know both how to be abased, and I know how to abound: every where and in all things I am instructed both to be full and to be hungry, both to abound and to suffer need.

13 I can do all things through Christ which strengtheneth me.

14 Notwithstanding ye have well done, that ye did communicate with my affliction.

15 Now ye Philippians know also, that in the beginning of the gospel, when I departed from Macedonia, no church communicated with me as concerning giving and receiving, but ye only.

16 For even in Thessalonica ye sent once and again unto my necessity.

17 Not because I desire a gift: but I desire fruit that may abound to your account.

18 But I have all, and abound: I am full, having received of Epaphroditus the things which were sent from you, an odour of a sweet smell, a sacrifice acceptable, wellpleasing to God.

11 Not that I am referring to being in need; for I have learned to be content with whatever I have.

12 I know what it is to have little, and I know what it is to have plenty. In any and all circumstances I have learned the secret of being well-fed and of going hungry, of having plenty and of being in need.

13 I can do all things through him who strengthens me.

14 In any case, it was kind of you to share my distress.

15 You Philippians indeed know that in the early days of the gospel, when I left Macedonia, no church shared with me in the matter of giving and receiving, except you alone.

16 For even when I was in Thessalonica, you sent me help for my needs more than once.

17 Not that I seek the gift, but I seek the profit that accumulates to your account.

18 I have been paid in full and have more than enough; I am fully satisfied, now that I have received from Epaphroditus the gifts you sent, a fragrant offering, a sacrifice acceptable and pleasing to God.

 **KEY VERSE**

*Rejoice in the Lord always: and again I say, Rejoice.—**Philippians 4:4***

OBJECTIVES

After reading this lesson, the student should be aware that:

1. Joy, gentleness, prayer, and gratitude lead to God's peace;
2. The peace of God leads to joy;
3. Anxiety robs us of peace and joy; and
4. Christ alone is the joy of our salvation.

POINTS TO BE EMPHASIZED
Adult/Youth
Key Verse: Philippians 4:4
Print: Philippians 4:4-18

—Paul said that joy, gentleness, refusing to worry, and diligent prayer lead to the presence of God's peace. (4-7)

—Paul encouraged his readers to set their minds on positive, life enriching attitudes. (8,9)

—Paul expressed joy for the concern the Philippians showed him and said that he had learned to be content with what he had. (10-12)

—Paul recognized his spiritual partnership with the Philippians and affirmed Christ as his ultimate strength. (13,14)

—Paul reminded the Philippians that their support of his work benefitted them as well as him. (15-17)

—The Philippians' gifts to Paul's ministry satisfied Paul and pleased God. (18)

Children
Key Verse: Philippians 4:4
Print: Philippians 4:4-7; Acts 16:32-34

—Paul said that joy, gentleness, refusing to worry, and diligent prayer lead to the presence of God's peace. (Philippians 4:4-7)

—Paul and Silas told the Philippian jailer and his family about the Lord Jesus. (Acts 16:32)

—The jailer took care of Paul and Silas' wounds, and then he and his family were baptized. (33)

—The jailer brought Paul and Silas into his house and fed them. (34)

—Paul, Silas, the jailer and his family rejoiced because they all believed in God. (34)

(**NOTE**: Use KJV Scripture for Adults; NRSV Scripture for Youth and Children)

TOPICAL OUTLINE OF THE LESSON

I. Introduction
    A. The Meaning of Joy
    B. Biblical Background

II. Exposition and Application of the Scripture
    A. The Prescription for God's Peace (Philippians 4:4-7)
    B. The Presence of God's Peace (Philippians 4:8-9)
    C. The Practice of God's Peace (Philippians 4:10-13)
    D. The Participants in God's Peace (Philippians 4:14-16)
    E. The Product of God's Peace (Philippians 4:17-18)

III. Special Features
    A. Preserving Our Heritage
    B. A Concluding Word

I. Introduction

A. THE MEANING OF JOY

There are at least fifteen different verbs rendered "rejoice." Eleven of them are in the Old Testament; four are in the New Testament. D. M. Edwards states, "The idea of joy is expressed in the Old Testament by a wealth of synonymous terms that cannot easily be differentiated" (ISBE). Some of the synonyms are: spring about, exult, shout, cry aloud, sing, enjoy, laugh, shine, leap much, be well pleased, and boast.

In the Old Testament, the Hebrew word (*sameach*) found most often has a root that "denotes being glad or joyful with the whole disposition as indicated by its association with the heart, the soul; and with the lighting up of the eyes" (TWOT). The Lord is the source of religious joy. Perhaps the closest passage to the key verse (Philippians 4:4) in today's lesson that uses this Hebrew word is Psalm 97:12: "Rejoice in the Lord, you righteous, and give thanks at the remembrance of his holy name."

The main verb used in the New Testament (*chairo*) means to rejoice, be glad. In a broader sense, it means to be well, to thrive, as in salutations. With regard to the book of Philippians the words "joy" and "rejoice," or some other forms of these words, are found eighteen times (Pilgrim Bible). "Joy" is the keynote of the Letter. "Christian joy is no mere gaiety that knows no gloom, but is the result of the triumph of faith over adverse and trying circumstances" (ISBE).

Prison did not prevent Paul from enjoying this part of the fruit of the Holy Spirit! He knew the joyous life, the mood of cheerfulness, the calmness of spirit possible only to the soul stayed on God. The present tense command is repeated, suggesting we make it a habit of rejoicing. Saints can be commanded to rejoice because our ground for rejoicing is not in circumstances, but in the Lord. Happiness depends upon what happens! But for the Christian, no matter what happens, nothing is ever to dim our spiritual joy.

B. BIBLICAL BACKGROUND

Chapter four begins with the word "therefore." The last paragraph in chapter three deals with our heavenly citizenship (Philippians 3:17-21). Because of the wonderful hope that saints have in the return of the Lord Jesus, the apostle states, "Since you are citizens of heaven, hold your ground. Show stability. Stand fast in the Lord." Paul himself is an example of steadfastness. He had learned that environmental conditions and earthly circumstances cannot take away the peace of God that we possess through Jesus Christ.

It is clear that the Philippian church that Paul founded was dear to his heart. He calls them brothers, dearly beloved (twice), longed for, and his joy (on earth) and crown (in heaven.). He appeals for harmony between Euodia and Syntyche, two ladies in the church. An appeal is made to help these good women. Then once again Paul strikes the keynote of the Epistle and deals with the life of joy through peace.

II. Exposition and Application of the Scripture

A. THE PRESCRIPTION FOR GOD'S PEACE
(Philippians 4:4-7)

Rejoice in the Lord always: and again I say, Rejoice. Let your moderation be known unto all men. The Lord is at hand. Be careful for nothing; but in every thing by prayer and supplication with thanksgiving let your requests be made known unto God. And the peace of God, which passeth all understanding, shall keep your hearts and minds through Christ Jesus.

Looking at the paragraph (verses 4-7) as a whole, we see that joy, gentleness, lack of anxiety, continuous prayer and supplication, along with thanksgiving are ingredients in the peace of God. The word translated "moderation" (KJV) means forbearance (RSV, Moffatt), gentleness (NKJV, NIV), magnanimity (NEB), courtesy, patience, kindness, yielding, graciousness, reasonableness. Perhaps it is best to see the word meaning "the grace of giving up," thus, not strict about your legal rights, not making an obstinate, determined stand for what is your due, your right.

How do the words "at hand" fit? Does it refer to our Lord's presence or His soon coming? If it is a bridge to verse 6, then it means do not be anxious, for the Lord may come at any moment. Or do not be anxious, for the Lord is present right now. Furthermore, do not fret, do not worry, have no anxiety. What a command this is for this present age so full of anxiety, frustration and fear! The antidote for anxiety is prayer offered in the spirit of thanksgiving. We learn that there is the peace of God from the God of peace available to all who have peace with God. The God of the Bible is the source, origin, and dispenser of this peace. It is a peace that stands guard over our inner life. Human intellect and speculation cannot grasp this peace. Psychiatrists cannot explain it. Men are utterly unable to fathom the peace of God.

B. THE PRESENCE OF GOD'S PEACE (Philippians 4:8-9)

Finally, brethren, whatsoever things are true, whatsoever things are honest, whatsoever things are just, whatsoever things are pure, whatsoever things are lovely, whatsoever things are of good report; if there be any virtue, and if there be any praise, think on these things. Those things, which ye have both learned, and received, and heard, and seen in me, do: and the God of peace shall be with you.

This section of the lesson is likened to a strainer or sieve or filter. Often we are asked, "Is it wrong to do such and such?" Or, "What's wrong with—?" Here is a good passage to sift the matter through. Whatever things are truthful, belonging to the nature or realm of reality. Whatever things are honest, worthy of reverence. Whatever things are just, in accordance with the loftiest conception of what is right and what is wrong before God and before man. Whatever things are pure, not mixed with elements that would debase the soul. Calvin called it chastity in all departments of life.

Whatever things are lovely, things that inspire love. Whatever thing are of good report, or have a good ring to them. We are to meditate on them; let them be our thoughts. A. T. Robertson calls them "high thinking." The present tense command suggests we take these things into account and put them into practice and keep on doing them. This is not the mere flash of thought like the flitting of a sparrow. Deliberate, prolonged contemplation is the issue. By giving our attention to God-approved matters, we shape our minds into the very image of Jesus Christ.

Note the verbs used in verse 9: learned, received (not by word of mouth, but by knowledge of Paul's character), heard, saw. Do these things—keep practicing them! If we reckon on these things, we will at the same time practice them. Thought is to be translated into action. Since Paul was their example he could say, "Be joint-imitators of me." Obey this exhortation and discover that the God of peace will be with you.

C. THE PRACTICE OF GOD'S PEACE (Philippians 4:10-13)

But I rejoiced in the Lord greatly, that now at the last your care of me hath flourished again; wherein ye were also careful, but ye lacked opportunity. Not that I speak in respect of want: for I have learned, in whatsoever state I am, therewith to be content. I know both how to be abased, and I know how to abound: every where and in all things I am instructed both to be full and to be hungry, both to abound and to suffer need. I can do all thing through Christ which strengtheneth me.

The Philippian saints knew it was a blessing to give, and although for a time they were remiss in their obligations, they renewed their aid through Epaphroditus. Paul is very careful lest someone is offended and his motives misunderstood. Misunderstanding comes easily when the subject is money. So he tactfully reminded them of their "lack of opportunity" and having expressed his gratitude for the revival, said he was not unduly anxious.

Note the word "want" in verse 11. It is not the verb to desire, yearn for, long for, or wish. Rather, it means to be deficient, to lack or need. Paul learned to be content with his lot, no matter how meager his means. This contentment is a perfect condition of life, one in which no aid or support is needed, it is a sufficiency of the necessities of life. The apostle points out that he knows how to adjust himself to either being made very lowly or abounding in plenty. Some people do not take prosperity well. Money burns a hole in their pockets.

But Paul realizes he is at all times in the hands of the Lord. The section closes with the very popular verse, "I can do all things through (in) him who strengthens me" (RSV, NASB). God gives us the power to do anything He wants us to do. "Within the circle of His will there are no impossibilities" (MacDonald).

D. THE PARTICIPANTS IN GOD'S PEACE (Philippians 4:14-16)

Notwithstanding ye have well done, that ye did communicate with my affliction. Now ye Philippians know also, that in the beginning of the gospel, when I departed from Macedonia, no church

communicated with me as concerning giving and receiving, but ye only. For even in Thessalonica ye sent once and again unto my necessity.

Here we discover what staying connected to Jesus Christ can do for us, for gifts reveal something about the givers. Paul could see the spiritual value in the sharing or communicating of material gifts. He rejoiced over what he saw in their lives. By no means does the apostle blame the other churches for not having sent him a gift. But he does commend the Philippian church for their liberality.

E. THE PRODUCT OF GOD'S PEACE (Philippians 4:17-18)

Not because I desire a gift: but I desire fruit that may abound to your account. But I have all, and abound: I am full, having received of Epaphroditus the things which were sent from you, an odour of a sweet smell, a sacrifice acceptable, wellpleasing to God.

What was Paul's motive then? It was that fruit might abound to their account. If parents desire their children to grow up and become adults, why should it seem incredible that the minister desire the same thing for the children of God? The saints at Philippi knew their responsibility to God's servant and sent Epaphroditus to aid Paul in prison. There he offered the gifts he brought with him, and devoted himself to Paul's service. Now Paul sends him back with this letter, one of joy and thanksgiving.

Epaphroditus not only brought gifts, but he was himself a gift to Paul. Thus, the apostle abounds as one who has more than enough. Noah built an altar to the Lord, offered burnt offerings on the altar, and the Lord smelled a soothing aroma (Genesis 8:20-21). Here Paul likens the gift of the Philippians to the fragrance of sweet incense. Do we always think of the gifts we offer to the church, to the preacher, as gifts to God? The idea here is of course figurative. "What the old Jewish sacrifices at the temple were, this gift of the Philippians is; it has the same sweet odor for God and is thus acceptable, well pleasing to Him" (Lenski).

III. Special Features

A. PRESERVING OUR HERITAGE

Having studied this lesson, what are your thoughts about gifts and giving in the local assembly? Many of us grew up in churches that spent an inordinate amount of time "raising" money. We had several kinds of offerings—"penny offerings, dime offerings,"—we had Spring Rallies, Fall Rallies, and all kinds of programs that had as their main function the raising of money. And what shall we say of dinners that were sold!

Then auxiliaries would "club" us to death with envelopes begging for contributions. Yes, it is amazing that so many black churches were built out of such hard-earned nickels, dimes, and quarters! And though we may criticize the emphasis and the amount of energy expended, we marvel at the spirit of sacrifice, the love for the church and for the Lord Jesus Christ.

Today, Black Americans have much more money. And yet the per capita giving has not increased proportionately. We wonder whether the "gimmickry of professional fund-raisers who extort by cajolery, pathos or comedy" has robbed us of the joy of having our gifts received by the Lord as a sweet smelling sacrifice. In this day of the megachurch, where millions of dollars are needed to construct huge edifices, our desire for bigness has robbed us of the joy and peace that passes all understanding. Some groups have become legalistic in the demand that their members tithe, even to the point of excluding non-tithers from holding office. Giving then becomes grudging and of necessity.

Finally, although the lesson stops just short of verse 19, note that the promise to supply our need according to God's riches in glory by Christ Jesus is connected to our supplying the needs of the saints of God. When a local assembly is engaged in the liberal support of missions and evangelism, God blesses with peace and joy, and provides for all its needs.

B. A CONCLUDING WORD

Despite redemption from slavery in the land of Egypt, the Israelites were guilty of grumbling, murmuring and complaining. We see ourselves in them, for we too have been redeemed. Through faith in the shed blood of Jesus Christ, God has saved us. And yet it appears so few of us can truthfully say, "I have learned in whatever state I am, to be content."

Evidently, this contentment is a learning process, something to be cultivated. Paul learned by experience to trust in the Lord Jesus. Remember, this Letter was written while in chains in Nero's prison in Rome. Paul had no comforts or luxuries and had no guarantee of what might happen to him. Deprived of many of the barest necessities of life, still he could say, "I'm happy with Jesus alone. Though poor and deserted, thank God, I can say I'm happy with Jesus alone" (C. P. Jones).

HOME DAILY BIBLE READINGS FOR THE WEEK OF JUNE 25, 2000

REJOICING IN CHRIST

June 19	M.	Philippians 4:2-7, Rejoice, and Be Gentle with One Another
June 20	T.	Philippians 4:8-14, Keep On Keeping On in Christ
June 21	W.	Philippians 4:15-23, Paul's Thanks for the Philippian Church
June 22	T.	Acts 2:43-47, Life Among the Early Believers
June 23	F.	1 Thessalonians 1:1-10, Paul's Thanks for the Thessalonian Church
June 24	S.	1 Thessalonians 4:1-12, Lives Pleasing to God
June 25	S.	3 John 1-8, Faithfulness Brings Great Joy

Our Father and our God, we rejoice because You have granted us peace that transcends the temporal trials and tribulations that keep us in bondage with those who fail to turn to You in contrition and repentance. Amen.

Called to Spiritual Blessings in Christ

Unit II—*Called to Be a New Humanity*
Children's Unit—*Living in God's Family*

·····

Adult Topic—*Claim Your Spiritual Blessings*

·····

Youth Topic—*That's the Spirit!*
Children's Topic—*We Are God's Children*

·····

Devotional Reading—Romans 1:8-17
Background Scripture—Ephesians 1
Print—Ephesians 1:1-14

PRINTED SCRIPTURE

Ephesians 1:1-14 (KJV)

PAUL, AN apostle of Jesus Christ by the will of God, to the saints which are at Ephesus, and to the faithful in Christ Jesus:

2 Grace be to you, and peace, from God our Father, and from the Lord Jesus Christ.

3 Blessed be the God and Father of our Lord Jesus Christ, who hath blessed us with all spiritual blessings in heavenly places in Christ:

4 According as he hath chosen us in him before the foundation of the world, that we should be holy and without blame before him in love:

5 Having predestinated us unto the adoption of children by Jesus Christ to himself, according to the good pleasure of his will,

6 To the praise of the glory of his grace, wherein he hath made us accepted in the beloved.

7 In whom we have redemption through his blood, the forgiveness of sins, according to the riches of his grace;

Ephesians 1:1-14 (NRSV)

PAUL, AN apostle of Christ Jesus by the will of God, To the saints who are in Ephesus and are faithful in Christ Jesus:

2 Grace to you and peace from God our Father and the Lord Jesus Christ.

3 Blessed be the God and Father of our Lord Jesus Christ, who has blessed us in Christ with every spiritual blessing in the heavenly places,

4 just as he chose us in Christ before the foundation of the world to be holy and blameless before him in love.

5 He destined us for adoption as his children through Jesus Christ, according to the good pleasure of his will,

6 to the praise of his glorious grace that he freely bestowed on us in the Beloved.

7 In him we have redemption through his blood, the forgiveness of our trespasses, according to the riches of his grace

8 Wherein he hath abounded toward us in all wisdom and prudence;

9 Having made known unto us the mystery of his will, according to his good pleasure which he hath purposed in himself:

10 That in the dispensation of the fulness of times he might gather together in one all things in Christ, both which are in heaven, and which are on earth; even in him:

11 In whom also we have obtained an inheritance, being predestinated according to the purpose of him who worketh all things after the counsel of his own will:

12 That we should be to the praise of his glory, who first trusted in Christ.

13 In whom ye also trusted, after that ye heard the word of truth, the gospel of your salvation in whom also after that ye believed, ye were sealed with that holy Spirit of promise,

14 Which is the earnest of our inheritance until the redemption of the purchased possession, unto the praise of his glory.

8 that he lavished on us. With all wisdom and insight

9 he has made known to us the mystery of his will, according to his good pleasure that he set forth in Christ,

10 as a plan for the fullness of time, to gather up all things in him, things in heaven and things on earth.

11 In Christ we have also obtained an inheritance, having been destined according to the purpose of him who accomplishes all things according to his counsel and will,

12 so that we, who were the first to set our hope on Christ, might live for the praise of his glory.

13 In him you also, when you had heard the word of truth, the gospel of your salvation, and had believed in him, were marked with the seal of the promised Holy Spirit;

14 this is the pledge of our inheritance toward redemption as God's own people, to the praise of his glory.

KEY VERSE

*Blessed be the God and Father of our Lord Jesus Christ, who hath blessed us with all spiritual blessings in heavenly places in Christ.—**Ephesians 1:3***

OBJECTIVES

After reading this lesson, the student should have a deeper understanding of:

1. What it means to be spiritually blessed;
2. The doctrine of election, predestination, and adoption;
3. The mysteries of God's will concerning believers; and
4. Our Holy Spirit guaranteed inheritance.

Adult/Youth./Children
Key Verse: Ephesians 1:3; 1:4-5 *(Children)*
Print: Ephesians 1:1-14

—As one appointed by God, Paul identified himself as an apostle of Christ Jesus by the will of God. (1, 2)

—God chose us as believers to praise Him and do His will. (3-6)

—Paul said that because of Christ we have redemption, forgiveness, and the richness of God's grace. (7, 8)

—With wisdom and knowledge, God has revealed the mystery of His will through Jesus Christ. (8-10)

—In Christ, the people of God become an inheritance so that they might live in a manner that praises and glorifies God. (11, 12)

—In Christ, believers are marked by the seal of the Holy Spirit which is the pledge of their inheritance. (13, 14)

(**NOTE**: Use KJV Scripture for Adult; NRSV Scripture for Youth and Children)

TOPICAL OUTLINE OF THE LESSON

I. Introduction

    A. Positional Truths

    B. Biblical Background

II. Exposition and Application of the Scripture

    A. Salutation (Ephesians1:1-2)

    B. Chosen, Predestined, Adopted (Ephesians 1:3-6)

    C. Redeemed, Forgiven, Enriched (Ephesians 1:7-8)

    D. The Mystery of God's Will (Ephesians 1:9-10)

    E. The Believer's Inheritance (Ephesians 1:11-14)

III. Special Features

    A. Preserving Our Heritage

    B. A Concluding Word

I. Introduction

A. POSITIONAL TRUTHS

Our position or standing refers to the "unchangeable and perfect work of God for the believer" (Chafer). Position is not something we feel, or experience. It is based upon what the Bible says and we accept it. On the other hand, our condition or state refers to the way we are, as we know by experience; it is our expression of life, what we are in actual conduct and behavior. Positionally, we are perfect, for God looks at us through the eyes of Jesus Christ. Faith alone confers standing in God's sight. All Christians have the same standing regardless of what our state may be. We are "in Christ," vitally connected with Christ who is perfect.

Conditionally, we are imperfect. Every experience of life is calculated to make the Christian more like the Lord Jesus Christ. It is the desire of the Holy Spirit to conform our state to what we are in our standing. To this end, the book of Ephesians has much to say. In chapter one alone, we learn that we are "blessed with all spiritual blessings" (verse 3). We have been placed as sons or adopted (verse 5). We are "accepted in the Beloved" (verse 6). We have obtained an inheritance (verse 11). We are sealed with the Holy Spirit of promise (verse 13). The list of references to positional truths continues throughout Ephesians.

B. BIBLICAL BACKGROUND

The Epistle to the Ephesians was written while Paul was in prison, probably in Rome. He had visited Ephesus at least three times. From Acts 20:31, we learn he spent three years there, teaching, "warning everyone night and day with tears." Paul knew the church at Ephesus better than he knew any other local assembly. This intimate acquaintance with the saints at Ephesus may have been one of the reasons the Letter is considered a general or circular letter for the churches of Asia Minor.

The very fact the Epistle lacks personal references and greetings seems to support this. In addition, the words "in Ephesus" are missing in some manuscripts. As our study begins, we see the theme of what Paul calls "the mystery," that which man cannot discover, but which God must reveal. In chapter one, emphasis is upon the fact that God revealed the mystery of His will by describing the believer's exalted position through sovereign grace.

II. Exposition and Application of the Scripture

A. SALUTATION (Ephesians 1:1-2)

Paul, an apostle of Jesus Christ by the will of God, to the saints which are at Ephesus, and to the faithful in Christ Jesus: Grace be to you, and peace, from God our Father, and from the Lord Jesus Christ.

The Letter begins with the usual salutation. Paul never forgot his calling (Acts 9:1-16). It was the Lord's will, not Paul's will; it was not the will of some synod, board or ecclesiastical group that commissioned him. No! His

Damascus road experience was indelibly impressed upon his heart and mind. His calling was accomplished by the will of God. Note that all Christians are saints, holy ones, or set apart ones. This early and very frequently used title signifies that we are separated from the world by God for God.

Grace—the unmerited, undeserved favor of God—always comes before peace. God has shown His grace by sending His Son, who is full of grace and truth, to die for us. If a man rejects this act of grace, he will never have any peace. Remember then, the grace of God demonstrated by the shed blood of Jesus Christ must be accepted first, then there is peace with God. See the one source of the grace and peace, God our Father and the Lord Jesus Christ.

B. CHOSEN, PREDESTINED, ADOPTED (Ephesians 1:3-6)

Blessed be the God and Father of our Lord Jesus Christ, who hath blessed us with all spiritual blessings in heavenly places in Christ: According as he hath chosen us in him before the foundation of the world, that we should be holy and without blame before him in love: Having predestinated us unto the adoption of children by Jesus Christ to himself, according to the good pleasure of his will, To the praise of the glory of his grace, wherein he hath made us accepted in the beloved.

Note in verse three the words "blessed . . . blessed . . . blessing." They have the same root and mean to speak well of. To say "Blessed be the God and Father" is to say, "Praise Him." This was surely David's intention in Psalm 103:1-5. "We speak well of God when we say what He is and does in His attributes and His works" (Lenski). We bless the Lord when we ascribe to Him the honor that is due Him.

Next we see that He whom we call "blessed" has indeed blessed us—with spiritual blessings. Unfortunately, there are church members more interested in material, economic, civic, political, social and racial gains than in spiritual blessings. We are not to be unmindful or even ungrateful for material blessings. But true spiritual blessings benefit both body and soul. Spiritual blessings (the fruit of the Spirit: Galatians 5:22-23) are more important because they deal with our born again, regenerate spiritual nature or the new man or new woman in us.

The phrase "in the heavenly places" is found five times, occurring only in Ephesians (1:3, 20, 2:6, 3:10, 6:12). It signifies the spiritual sphere where we fellowship with God. It is not heaven, but the phrase is literally "in the heavenlies." Rather, it is the sphere where Christ is, which is heavenly in nature and privilege (Scofield). Because God the Father blessed us in the heavens also, we are to see our blessings as infinitely superior to anything this old earth affords us here below.

God the Father also chose us for Himself. We were elected in union with Christ before the foundation of the world. No reasons are given why He chose us. The purpose or goal of this election is that we should practice holiness and blamelessness before God. Sanctification is the goal. In love, He predestinated us. Predestination is defined as the effective exercise of the sovereign will of God by which things before determined by Him are brought to pass. Those chosen in Christ in eternity before the world began were marked out to the place of sons and daughters. This is the meaning of adoption.

C. REDEEMED, FORGIVEN, ENRICHED (Ephesians 1:7-8)

In whom we have redemption through his blood, the forgiveness of sins, according to the riches of his grace; Wherein he hath abounded toward us in all wisdom and prudence.

The word rendered redemption signifies a setting or loosing or freeing, and gives us the picture of a slave or POW who is delivered by payment of a ransom. We were released from the penalty of sin through the blood sacrifice of Jesus Christ. He paid the full ransom for our release. Not only by faith do we have redemption, but also we have forgiveness or remission of trespasses. In other words, the forgiveness rests upon the redemption. When we accept His shed blood, our sins and guilt are removed. Ransoming and remission are according to the riches, the magnificence, and the greatness of God's unmerited favor. Such great grace abounded, overflowed for us in all wisdom or judgment and understanding or discernment. Such is available to us to apply to every situation in life.

D. THE MYSTERY OF GOD'S WILL
(Ephesians 1:9-10)

Having made known unto us the mystery of his will, according to his good pleasure which he hath purposed in himself: That in the dispensation of the fulness of times he might gather together in one all things in Christ, both which are in heaven, and which are on earth; even in him.

What has Christ done for us? In Him, we have redemption and forgiveness. We learn from verse nine that He made known to us the mystery of His will. This is true wisdom. A mystery is a design hidden in God's counsels until revealed to mankind in and by Christ. It has to be revealed by God, otherwise we would never know. Men cannot search out God's design of sovereign grace. God moves in mysterious ways His wonders to perform, and men cannot know what he does not want them to know. The mystery here is the whole gospel, now preached by believers throughout the world.

What is God's purpose? It is that when the time is ripe, He will gather us all together to be with Him in Christ, eternally. God's program is to be carried out in connection with the Lord Jesus Christ. The word "dispensation" is literally "house rule" (*oikonomia*, economy), the management of a household, an arrangement, order, or plan. Jesus Christ is God's administrator or manager, under whose administration during what is called the fullness of time, all things in heaven and earth shall be gathered together, summarized or focused in Christ.

E. THE BELIEVER'S INHERITANCE (Ephesians 1:11-14)

In whom also we have obtained an inheritance, being predestinated according to the purpose of him who worketh all things after the counsel of his own will: That we should be to the praise of his glory, who first trusted in Christ. In whom ye also trusted, after that ye heard the word of truth, the gospel of your salvation: in whom also after that ye believed, ye were sealed with that holy Spirit of promise, Which is the earnest of our inheritance until the redemption of the purchased possession, unto the praise of his glory.

We have redemption, forgiveness, and knowledge of the mystery and finally, an inheritance. In Christ, we were made a heritage. Literally, we were assigned a lot or allotment under the

Lord's administration. "Already in eternity, God determined the lot he assigned to us in time" (Lenski), "for as part of God's sovereign plan we were chosen from the beginning to be His, and all things happen just as He decided long ago" (LB).

Verse twelve tells us why we were given a lot. God's intention was that by our hoping in advance, we who were the first to hope in Christ should be for the praise of His glory. We have learned that the Father blessed us, chose us, and predestinated us; that the Son ransomed us, remitted our sins, informed us and gave us an inheritance. Now we consider the work of the Holy Spirit. That which the Father plans and the Son provides, the Holy Spirit bestows. All that the Spirit does is in connection with Jesus Christ. The hearing and believing of the message of truth, the gospel of our salvation, leads to sealing. At the moment we come to faith, the sealing takes place.

Now we seal things for several reasons: (1) Authentication. We seal a thing to make it valid. (2) Security. Matthew 27:62-66 tells of the sealing of our Lord's tomb. (3) Concealment.

We seal up our first class mail, hiding the contents or the message. (4) Marking. A seal may also be for marking and identification. (5) Ownership is the main idea in our lesson. By the bestowal of the Holy Spirit, the Lord marked us as His very own. The Spirit is a living seal, and we are sealed once and for all. We remain that way as long as the Holy Spirit lives. God promised the Spirit and so the Holy Spirit is here called the spirit of Promise. He is the Gift promised by God.

The word "earnest" means pledge (NEB), guarantee (RSV, NKJV), deposit guaranteeing (NIV). It is pledge money, first installment, a down payment, that pays a part of the purchase price in advance and thus secures a legal claim to the article in question, or makes a contract valid. It obligates the contracting party to make further payments (2 Corinthians 1:21-22). The Holy Spirit is the first down payment of our inheritance. He guarantees us, that is, His presence in us guarantees us that in due time the full inheritance will be ours. The sealing of the Spirit is a matter of certainty for the believer (1 John 3:24, 4:13).

III. Special Features

A. PRESERVING OUR HERITAGE

The Letters of Paul generally follow God's method of putting doctrine first, then practice second. There is no suggestion of either/or, but both. It is doctrine and practice. With regard to the book of Ephesians, the doctrinal section begins with chapter 1 verse 3. The practical section starts with chapter 4. So basically, the first three chapters are doctrinal. We learn by this arrangement that God is concerned that we believe the right thing, then put what we believe into practice.

What we practice is our walk (how about our talk?). Our walk is our conduct, behavior or deportment. All we want to keep in mind is the priority, for there are those who would say, "It doesn't matter what you believe so long as you treat other people right." On the other hand, Black Americans are well aware of those who stress doctrine but have unscriptural, racist concepts of dealing with other people.

Our concern here, however, is the fact that far too many black churches manifest a lack of interest in doctrine. Prior to today's lesson, did you know the meaning of election, predestination, adoption, or redemption? Were you acquainted with the definitions of such words as acceptance, dispensation and inheritance? Doctrine is meat. Some of us have been drinking milk and eating baby food for many years. Perhaps today's lesson will prick our consciences and stir us up to learn more about our spiritual blessings in Christ.

B. A CONCLUDING WORD

We see in today's lesson the work of the Godhead—God the Father, Son and Holy Spirit. Groups that deny the truth that the One God exists as Father, Son and Holy Spirit would destroy the teaching of the Bible, and find it all the more difficult to understand today's lesson. We see the work of the Triune God as follows: (1) The Father blessed us, chose us and predestinated us. (2) Jesus Christ the Son of God (God the Son) ransomed us, remitted our sins, informed us and made us a heritage. (3) The Holy Spirit sealed us.

HOME DAILY BIBLE READINGS FOR THE WEEK OF JULY 2, 2000

CALLED TO SPIRITUAL BLESSINGS IN CHRIST

June 26	M.	Ephesians 1:1-6, God Has Blessed Us in Christ
June 27	T.	Ephesians 1:7-14, God's Grace Lavished on Us in Christ
June 28	W.	Ephesians 1:15-23, Paul's Prayer for the Ephesian Christians
June 29	T.	Romans 1:1-7, Called to Belong to Jesus Christ
June 30	F.	Romans 1:8-17, The Gospel: God's Power for Salvation
July 1	S.	Galatians 5:16-26, Bear the Fruit of the Spirit
July 2	S.	Galatians 6:1-10, Bear One Another's Burdens

Know Your Bible

- The prophecy of Jonah to the city of Nineveh is also cited in 2 Kings 14:25 during the reconquest by Jeroboam. (2 Kings 14:15-25)
- God forbid that we should continue in sin just because He is merciful and forgiving. (Romans 6:1-2)

Our Father, You have called us to spiritual blessings in Jesus Christ. May we understand ourselves as instruments of Your will. Amen.

Called to Oneness in Christ

Adult Topic—*Claim Your New Status*

•••••

Youth Topic—*All for One!*
Children's Topic—*Members of God's Family*

•••••

Devotional Reading—John 17:1-11, 20-23
Background Scripture—Ephesians 2
Print—Ephesians 2:8-22

PRINTED SCRIPTURE

Ephesians 2:8-22 (KJV)

8 For by grace ye are saved through faith; and that not of yourselves: it is the gift of God:

9 Not of works, lest any man should boast.

10 For we are his workmanship, created in Christ Jesus unto good works, which God hath before ordained that we should walk in them.

11 Wherefore remember, that ye being in time past Gentiles in the flesh, who are called Uncircumcision by that which is called the Circumcision in the flesh made by hands;

12 That at that time ye were without Christ, being aliens from the commonwealth of Israel, and strangers from the covenants of promise, having no hope, and without God in the world:

13 But now in Christ Jesus ye who sometimes were far off are made nigh by the blood of Christ.

14 For he is our peace, who hath made both one, and hath broken

Ephesians 2:8-22 (NRSV)

8 For by grace you have been saved through faith, and this is not your own doing; it is the gift of God—

9 Not the result of works, so that no one may boast.

10 For we are what he had made us, created in Christ Jesus for good works, which God prepared beforehand to be our way of life.

11 So then, remember that at one time you Gentiles by birth, called "the uncircumcision" by those who are called "the circumcision"—a physical circumcision made in the flesh by human hands—

12 remember that you were at that time without Christ, being aliens from the commonwealth of Israel, and strangers to the covenants of promise, having no hope and without God in the world.

13 But now in Christ Jesus you who once were far off have been brought near by the blood of Christ.

14 For he is our peace; in his flesh

down the middle wall of partition between us;

15 Having abolished in his flesh the enmity, even the law of commandments contained in ordinances; for to make in himself of twain one new man, so making peace;

16 And that he might reconcile both unto God in one body by the cross, having slain the enmity thereby:

17 And came and preached peace to you which were afar off, and to them that were nigh.

18 For through him we both have access by one Spirit unto the Father.

19 Now therefore ye are no more strangers and foreigners, but fellowcitizens with the saints, and of the household of God;

20 And are built upon the foundation of the apostles and prophets, Jesus Christ himself being the chief corner stone;

21 In whom all the building fitly framed together groweth unto an holy temple in the Lord:

22 In whom ye also are builded together for an habitation of God through the Spirit.

he has made both groups into one and has broken down the dividing wall, that is, the hostility between us.

15 He has abolished the law with its commandments and ordinances, that he might create in himself one new humanity in place of the two, thus making peace,

16 and might reconcile both groups to God in one body through the cross, thus putting to death that hostility through it.

17 So he came and proclaimed peace to you who were far off and peace to those who were near;

18 for through him both of us have access in one Spirit to the Father.

19 So then you are no longer strangers and aliens, but you are citizens with the saints and also members of the household of God,

20 built upon the foundation of the apostles and prophets, with Christ Jesus himself as the cornerstone.

21 In him the whole structure is joined together and grows into a holy temple in the Lord;

22 in whom you also are built together spiritually into a dwelling place for God

*Now therefore ye are no more strangers and foreigners, but fellowcitizens with the saints, and of the household of God.—**Ephesians 2:19***

OBJECTIVES

After reading this lesson, the student will know:

1. The broader meaning of the word salvation;
2. What we were before we were saved;
3. Jews and Gentiles are one body in Christ; and
4. The church is a temple of the Holy Spirit.

Adult/Youth/Children

Key Verse: Ephesians 2:19; 6:19 *(Children)*
Print: Ephesians 2:8-22

—Paul taught the Ephesians that salvation through faith is God's free gift of grace and does not derive from human effort; yet God's intention for believers has always been that they do good works. (8-10)

—Paul reminded his Gentile readers that they formerly were not a part of God's people, but that now in Christ they were included in the family of God. (11-13)

—Through the Cross, Jesus broke down the hostility between Gentiles and Jews and made in himself one new humanity, thereby proclaiming peace to all persons both far and near. (14-17)

—Through Christ all believers have access in one Spirit to God. (18)

—Gentiles are no longer strangers, but members of God's family, built on the foundation of the prophets and apostles, with Christ as keystone. (19, 20)

—In Christ God's household is joined together and grows into a holy temple in the Lord. (21,22)

(**NOTE**: Use KJV Scripture for Adults; NRSV Scripture for Youth and Children)

TOPICAL OUTLINE OF THE LESSON

I. Introduction

A. Three Aspects of Salvation
B. Biblical Background

II. Exposition and Application of the Scripture

A. One Way (Ephesians 2:8-10)
B. One Position (Ephesians 2:11-13)
C. One Body (Ephesians 2:14-18)
D. One Church (Ephesians 2:19-22)

III. Special Features

A. Preserving Our Heritage
B. A Concluding Word

I. Introduction

A. THREE ASPECTS OF SALVATION

The study of salvation, called Soteriology, is all the more interesting when we consider its threefold aspects. In other words, salvation may be seen as past, present, and future. First of all, the genuine Christian can say, "I have been saved." In Ephesians 2:5, 8, a perfect passive participle is used, giving us in English, "you have been saved." The Greek is literally, "By grace are you having-been-saved ones." Passive means we did not save ourselves, an outside force saved us. Salvation is not achieved. It is God's gift. Perfect means it happened in the past but is having (participle) the present result of maintaining the salvation. We were saved and continue to be so (Expositor's). The past act of salvation (Justification) deals with sin's penalty.

Second is the truth that Christians are being saved. This verb tense is used in 1 Corinthians 1:18: "For the message of the cross is foolishness to those who are perishing, but to us who are being saved it is the power of God" (NKJV). This aspect of salvation (Sanctification) deals with the power of sin in our lives.

The third aspect of salvation is the wonderful assurance that we saints shall be saved (Glorification). Romans 10:9 uses the future passive, "you will be saved" (Romans 13:11). This aspect of salvation points to the rapture at which time we shall receive new bodies and the very presence of sin will be no more (1 John 3:2; Philippians 3:20-21). Even so, come, Lord Jesus.

B. BIBLICAL BACKGROUND

Ephesians chapter two deals with the doctrine of Salvation. There is no break in thought with chapter one, for the power of the Resurrection mentioned in the last paragraph of chapter one is the power put forth in salvation. To better define and understand salvation, we should consider what we were and what we did in the condition we once were in. The verses immediately preceding our lesson describe our state before we were saved.

We were dead in trespasses and sins. We were alive physically but dead spiritually, and ready to die physically and remain forever spiritually dead. Second, we walked in the world's way, the way of depraved mankind, a way which is in complete disharmony with God's way, a way which is tuned to the mind of Satan who is the prince of the power of the air. Third, we lived in the lust of our flesh, in disobedience. Fourth, we were by nature the children of wrath, the sons and daughters of disobedience. The list continues in Ephesians 2:12 which is a part of today's lesson. Thus, knowing what we were heightens our appreciation of salvation.

II. Exposition and Application of the Scripture

A. ONE WAY (Ephesians 2:8-10)

For by grace are ye saved through faith; and that not of yourselves: it is the gift of God: Not of works, lest any man should boast. For we are his workmanship, created in Christ Jesus unto good works, which God hath before ordained that we should walk in them.

The sentence, "For by grace you have been saved through faith," uses the perfect tense that suggests "the past act of rescue plus the resultant condition of safety." This is an enduring state so that we should have no fear of losing salvation or being "unsaved." God saved us from the death we deserved. The gift is not earned; if it were, it would not be a gift. It is free; it is of grace. Works do not save us!

How the old nature despises this truth. Men constantly and consistently seek to save themselves, or help God save them, or do something to stay saved.

Thus, we find people insisting that we worship on certain days only, eat certain foods, or visit certain religious shrines. Some say we must speak in tongues, or have pronounced over us at baptism a special formula. And so it goes. Boast we would, if works saved us. By works, we mean self-directed human efforts to get right with God or stay right with God, efforts which may take direction in a thousand and one different forms.

Faith is a gift, so that we do not get any credit for believing. If you were drowning and someone threw out a life line to which you clung and were drawn in safe to land, would you later boast, "Man, did you see the way I reached out and grabbed that old life line?" You would have been foolish not to grab it. The glory and praise go to the One who threw it out to you and pulled you in and who, by the way, gave you presence of mind and the energy to reach out and hold on.

God's purpose in saving us is that we should walk in good works. We are saved to good works. This means we are not saved to sit down in a rocking chair, fold our hands, nod, rock and sleep. Too many professed Christians get on the Salvation Train at Justification, sleep through Sanctification and expect to wake up in Glorification. The Christian life is not morally indifferent. Good works are the product of what the Lord made us to be when by grace He created us anew. He thus made us to do good works, and whatever good works we Christians do, they are the result of God's saving work in us.

The good works we are to walk in are those that God made ready beforehand. Do not let the world determine for us what "good works" are! The world is superficial in its judgment, and often it can see no further than its nose. It seeks, stresses, and strives all too often for that which at best is temporal; it is short-lived, passing away and headed for the fire. But our God has prepared the good works in which He wants us to walk. He created us in Christ, and prepared in advance the good works. All we are to do is walk in them.

B. ONE POSITION
(Ephesians 2:11-13)

Wherefore remember, that ye being in time past Gentiles in the flesh, who are called Uncircumcision by that which is called the Circumcision in the flesh made by hands; That at that time ye were without Christ, being aliens from the commonwealth of Israel, and strangers from the covenants of promise, having no hope, and without God in the world: But now in Christ Jesus ye who sometimes were far off are made nigh by the blood of Christ.

Before conversion, we were many things; presently saved and in Christ Jesus, we are but one thing, we have but one position—brought near to God by the blood of Christ. Before our conversion: (1) At one time we were Gentiles in the flesh, and were called the "Uncircumcision." Having the foreskin is equivalent to being a Gentile; to the Jew or the Circumcision, the foreskin was the sign of impurity and alienation from God (Thayer). (2) We were without Christ, separated from Him. (3) We were excluded from the commonwealth of Israel; in short, we were not Jews. The true and living God had made Himself known to Israel in a unique way, a way that hitherto the Gentiles had not known. Thus alienated, the Gentiles dwelled in darkness. (4) We were strangers from the covenant of promise—unilateral contract made by God between Himself and Israel. We did not have in our bodies the sign (circumcision) of the covenant. (5) We were without hope. A man without God in his life is a man without hope (the expectation of good). (6) The word translated "without God" is *atheoi* (atheists). Hostile pagans often called the Christians *atheoi* because the Christian refused to worship the gods of their neighbors who were also the gods of their ancestors. The pagans were not atheists, for they worshiped a multitude of dead, imaginary, lifeless divinities (1 Corinthians 8:4). (7) Finally, we were far off, completely out of fellowship with God. Prior, then, to being born again, we were all these things. What are we presently? We have been brought near to God by the blood of the Lord Jesus Christ.

C. ONE BODY (Ephesians 2:14-18)

For he is our peace, who hath made both one, and hath broken down the middle wall of partition between us; Having abolished in his flesh the enmity, even the law of commandments contained in ordinances; for to make in himself of twain one new man, so making peace; And that he might reconcile both unto God in one body by the cross, having slain the enmity thereby: And came and preached peace to you which were afar off, and to them that were nigh. For through him we both have access by one Spirit unto the Father.

Here we learn that Christ brought converted Jews and converted Gentiles into one body, the church. They were put on an equal level. In the temple in those days, there was a court of the Gentiles. They could draw no nearer. The next nearer court was for the Jews. A partition separated the two. But in the church there was no barrier. The blood of Christ is the objective means whereby we are brought near. The blood means the sacrificial death of Christ, for the life is in the blood. Ours is a blood theology at the very heart of the Gospel.

Note that peace is a person. Peace is not found in "peace movements," hypnosis, pills, or tranquilizers, etc. Christ is our peace (verse 14); He made peace (verse 15); and He preached peace to the Gentiles and to the Jews (verse 17). Paul stressed here the actual removal of the awful barriers between Jews and Gentiles. In the time of the apostle, the Jews utterly despised the Gentiles and considered them vile, dirty, and unclean dogs. Of course, the Gentiles felt the same way about them. They hated the Israelites because of their arrogance, their separation, and their peculiar religious habits. So the hatred was mutual.

But the Lord Jesus Christ took the two groups—the far away Gentiles and the nearer Jews—and reconciled them both to God in one body, the church. How? By His own death on the Cross! At Calvary, He put enmity to death. Men may seek to reconcile hostile human beings to one another through unity days, common cause, economic advantage, survival, etc., but only Jesus Christ brings harmony out of estrangement, alienation, and hatred. Finally, in this section, note the work of the Trinity. All three Persons of the Godhead share in the work of salvation. Our access in prayer to the Father is through Jesus Christ, and in the power of the Holy Spirit.

D. ONE CHURCH
(Ephesians 2:19-22)

Now therefore ye are no more strangers and foreigners, but fellowcitizens with the saints, and of the household of God; And are built upon the foundation of the apostles and prophets, Jesus Christ himself being the chief corner stone; In whom all the building fitly framed together groweth unto an holy temple in the Lord: In whom ye also are builded together for an habitation of God through the Spirit.

The word "therefore" recalls the fact that all hostility and enmity are past. Accordingly, we are no longer strangers, aliens (verse 12) or foreigners, outsiders (Lenski), sojourners (RSV). Instead we are (1) fellow citizens of the saints. The Greek word rendered "fellow citizens" means "possessing the same citizenship with others." It is spoken of Gentiles as received into the "communion of the people consecrated to God (saints)." (2) And we are family members of God, "belonging to God's household, that is, to the Theocracy" (Thayer).

Paul advances from dwelling in the house to believers constituting the house. God placed the Ephesian believers "upon" the foundation of the apostles and prophets. There are several interpretations of these words.

One idea is that the foundation itself is composed of or consists in the apostles and prophets. A second interpretation has the foundation laid by them. This would include the Gospel they preached and taught.

The question has arisen also as to whether the prophets are Old Testament, and the apostles New Testament, or whether the term prophet is to be applied to Christians only. Expositor's deems it best to see the Gospel of Christ preached by the apostles to be the "foundation" upon which their converts were built up into the spiritual house. In 1 Corinthians 3:11, Jesus Christ is the foundation stone on which the building rests.

But He is also the Chief Cornerstone; the stone from which all dimensions are measured (NIC). This is the stone placed at the summit of the edifice as its crown and completion. There is not a single line or angle in this building not determined by this Stone. God puts each one of us (living stones) exactly where He wants us to be. With Him, there are no misfits. Unfortunately, there are church members who hold positions they have hard sought and long fought for, disregarding the fact that they may be altogether out of God's will.

The word "temple" is sanctuary, for it is set apart for the Holy Spirit. In the Old Testament, the Lord dwelt with His people; in the New Testament, He lives in His people. The lesson closes by bringing to our attention once again the work of the Trinity. In Christ, all believers are fitted and formed into one building by the Holy Spirit, Who regenerates and indwells us so that we are a dwelling place for God.

III. Special Features

A. PRESERVING OUR HERITAGE

In these days considered by some as Post-Christian, it is sad to see Christians of different races unable to get along. Sometimes, we wonder at the power of God. It seems that Uncle Sam (I.R.S.) forced some Christian schools to do what they should have done anyway. In spite of the tremendous differences between Jews and Gentiles, Christ made them one. Today, we meet some people who are able to give us glowing accounts of how Christ saved them from their sins. These saints can relate how terrible habits were taken away by the Holy Spirit.

Too often, when it comes to proper race relations, their God is weak and powerless, a respecter of places, faces and races. Evidently, there are middle walls of partition, barriers of dividing, walls of myths of racial superiority, walls of tradition and social customs, walls of pride, political power which must be broken down in the lives of saints who contend that they stand for the once-for-all delivered faith. "The cross is God's answer to racial discrimination, segregation, anti-Semitism, bigotry, and every form of strife between men" (MacDonald).

B. A CONCLUDING WORD

The call to oneness in Christ is an act of grace exercised towards us that prepares us to walk in God's way. We are to tread the pathways He prepared ahead of time. Thus, we work out what God works **In** while working **On** us. Make sure you are where the Lord wants you, doing what He wants, holding the office He has given you, teaching the class He created for you, and doing good works in His name! We are saved to serve.

HOME DAILY BIBLE READINGS FOR THE WEEK OF JULY 9, 2000

CALLED TO ONENESS IN CHRIST

July 3 M. Ephesians 2:1-10, Saved and Made Alive by Grace
July 4 T. Ephesians 2:11-16, One Body in Jesus Christ
July 5 W. Ephesians 2:17-22, God Dwells in You
July 6 T. John 17:1-6, Jesus Commits Disciples to God's Care
July 7 F. John 17:7-13, Jesus Prays for the Disciples' Protection
July 8 S. John 17:14-21, Jesus Prays for the Disciples' Unity
July 9 S. John 17:22-26, May God's Love Be in Christ's Disciples

Eternal God, You have created us in Your image and likeness as unique persons on whose hearts are stamped our individuality. May our respective identity point toward Your majesty. Amen.

Called to Use Your Spiritual Gifts

Adult Topic—*Claim Your Ministry*

•••••

Youth Topic—*Use Your Gifts!*
Children's Topic—*Grow Up in Christ*

•••••

Devotional Reading—Ephesians 3:14-21
Background Scripture—Ephesians 4:1-16
Print—Ephesians 4:1-16

PRINTED SCRIPTURE

Ephesians 4:1-16 (KJV)

I THEREFORE, the prisoner of the Lord, beseech you that ye walk worthy of the vocation wherewith ye are called,

2 With all lowliness and meekness, with longsuffering, forbearing one another in love;

3 Endeavouring to keep the unity of the Spirit in the bond of peace.

4 There is one body, and one Spirit, even as ye are called in one hope of your calling;

5 One Lord, one faith, one baptism,

6 One God and Father of all, who is above all, and through all, and in you all.

7 But unto every one of us is given grace according to the measure of the gift of Christ.

8 Wherefore he saith, When he ascended up on high, he led captivity captive, and gave gifts unto men.

9 (Now that he ascended, what is it but that he also descended first into the lower parts of the earth?

10 He that descended is the same

Ephesians 4:1-16 (NRSV)

I THEREFORE, the prisoner in the Lord, beg you to lead a life worthy of the calling to which you have been called,

2 with all humility and gentleness, with patience, bearing with one another in love,

3 making every effort to maintain the unity of the Spirit in the bond of peace.

4 There is one body and one Spirit, just as you were called to the one hope of your calling,

5 one Lord, one faith, one baptism,

6 one God and Father of all, who is above all and through all and in all.

7 But each of us was given grace according to the measure of Christ's gift.

8 Therefore it is said, "When he ascended on high he made captivity itself a captive; he gave gifts to his people."

9 (When it says, "He ascended," what does it mean but that he had

also that ascended up far above all heavens, that he might fill all things.)

11 And he gave some, apostles; and some, prophets; and some, evangelists; and some, pastors and teachers;

12 For the perfecting of the saints, for the work of the ministry, for the edifying of the body of Christ:

13 Till we all come in the unity of the faith, and of the knowledge of the Son of God, unto a perfect man, unto the measure of the stature of the fulness of Christ:

14 That we henceforth be no more children, tossed to and fro, and carried about with every wind of doctrine, by the sleight of men, and cunning craftiness, whereby they lie in wait to deceive;

15 But speaking the truth in love, may grow up into him in all things, which is the head, even Christ:

16 From whom the whole body fitly joined together and compacted by that which every joint supplieth, according to the effectual working in the measure of every part, maketh increase of the body unto the edifying of itself in love.

also descended into the lower parts of the earth?"

10 He who descended is the same one who ascended far above all the heavens, so that he might fill all things.)

11 The gifts he gave were that some would be apostles, some prophets, some evangelists, some pastors and teachers,

12 to equip the saints for the work of ministry, for building up the body of Christ,

13 until all of us come to the unity of the faith and of the knowledge of the Son of God, to maturity, to the measure of the full stature of Christ.

14 We must no longer be children, tossed to and fro and blown about by every wind of doctrine, by people's trickery, by their craftiness in deceitful scheming.

15 But speaking the truth in love, we must grow up in every way into him who is the head, into Christ,

16 from whom the whole body, joined and knit together by every ligament with which it is equipped, as each part is working properly, promotes the body's growth in building itself up in love.

But unto every one of us is given grace according to the measure of the gift of Christ.—
Ephesians 4:7

OBJECTIVES

After reading this lesson, the student should remember that:

1. Our conduct should be in line with our calling;
2 Christians are perfectly united in their position;
3. God gives the church what it needs; and
4. God's gracious gifts edify the church.

POINTS TO BE EMPHASIZED
Adult/Youth/Children
Key Verse: Ephesians 4:7; 4:15 *(Children)*
Print: Ephesians 4:1-16

—Paul pleaded with the church at Ephesus to be humble and gentle, to be patient and tolerant, and to make every effort to maintain the unity of the Spirit. (1-3)

—God's people exist as one body governed by one Spirit and called into one hope; they participate in one baptism and serve one Lord. (4-6)

—Christ gives believers exactly the right amount of grace and gifts they need to build up the church the way He desires. (7-8)

—Christ conquered sin and death by descending into the grave, rising from the dead, and ascending into heaven. (9-10)

—God provides different spiritual gifts to build up the church in unity and maturity. (11-13)

—Believers must grow spiritually to become like Christ, who is the Head of the church and who promotes the church's growth in love. (14-16)

(**NOTE**: Use KJV Scripture for Adults; NRSV Scripture for Youth and Children)

TOPICAL OUTLINE OF THE LESSON

I. Introduction

   A. The Key Verse
   B. Biblical Background

II. Exposition and Application of the Scripture

   A. How to Walk Worthy (Ephesians 4:1-3)
   B. A Perfect Unity (Ephesians 4:4-6)
   C. Gifts From on High (Ephesians 4:7-11)
   D. The Purpose of Christ's Gifts (Ephesians 4:12-16)

III. Special Features

   A. Preserving Our Heritage
   B. A Concluding Word

I. Introduction

A. THE KEY VERSE

Ephesians 4:7 is the key verse for today's lesson: "Each of us was given grace according to the measure of Christ's gift." No believer is omitted or overlooked. In verse eight, we read that Christ gives gifts; then in verse eleven, we are told He gave gifts. So there is an emphasis upon giving. The diversity of gifts to individual believers and the diversity of gifted believers to the church are calculated to be motives to unity.

Whenever and whatever the Lord tells us to do, He gives us the power to do it. Thus, all His commands include His enabling ability. Someone has said: "The will of God will never lead you where the grace of God will not sustain you." This includes not only the physical strength, but also the financial needs. He supplies all our needs according to His riches in glory by Christ Jesus (Philippians 4:19).

Acceptance of this key verse eliminates envy of others. There is no need to cry the blues over what we do not have or wish we had; no need to be jealous of what others possess. Every good and perfect gift comes from the Lord, so that it is foolish for the one gifted to act haughty, and folly for me to envy him. The thing to do is take what Christ has given us and turn it over to

the Holy Spirit for Him to use for the glory of Christ, thus benefiting the church as a whole.

B. BIBLICAL BACKGROUND

Today's lesson begins the second half of the Ephesians Letter. The first half basically concerned itself with doctrine. Now we consider practice. Keep this order in mind: Doctrine, Practice. Do not fall for the world's order that suggests it does not matter what you believe so long as you do what is right. When doctrine has the proper effect on our hearts, we act like it. In other words, our actions conform to our relationship with Christ.

Ephesians chapter four begins the "acting-like-it" section. To walk means to behave or conduct yourself; to walk in a manner worthy of the calling with which you have been called is to live in such a way as is in accord with what you profess to believe. Our belief fixes the trend of our footsteps. We are what we believe (Hodge).

III. Exposition and Application of the Scripture

A. HOW TO WALK WORTHY
(Ephesians 4:1-3)

I therefore, the prisoner of the Lord, beseech you that ye walk worthy of the vocation wherewith ye are called, With all lowliness and meekness, with longsuffering, forbearing one another in love; Endeavouring to keep the unity of the Spirit in the bond of peace.

Paul wrote this Epistle while in prison, but no matter where we are, we can witness for Christ. We are prisoners of the Lord together, but we must

recognize and realize that our situation as His prisoners does not prevent us from fulfilling our position. Paul states, "I entreat, urge, beg of you, based on what we learned earlier (about predestination, adoption, position, redemption, grace, access, reconciliation, prayer, etc.), that you walk worthy of the calling to which you were called."

A number of virtues are essential to the worthy manner of walk. One virtue is lowliness; this is humility. Humble mindedness is not a false feeling, but is a knowing who you are yet content to be treated as if you were less than you really are. Second is meekness, a word connoting gentleness and mildness. A third virtue is longsuffering. This signifies a slowness to get even with folks who step on your toes in church! It is the ability to hold up under a load of vexations dumped on us (Trench). It is showing a steady, even temperament in the face of adversity and persecution (Wycliffe Bible Commentary). A fourth virtue is the forbearing of one another in love. "Show your love by being tolerant with one another" (TEV). Make allowance for each other's faults because of love (LB).

Note we are NOT told to make or manufacture this unity. It exists already! We are to study, make haste, give diligence, be busy, and endeavor to maintain, continuously preserve, and guard that which already exists. Peace is the bond in which the unity is kept. The bond consists of peace. Take vigilant care that we ourselves avoid troubling this unity of the Spirit, and at the same time resolve difficulties and dissension that threaten this unity from any external source.

B. A PERFECT UNITY
(Ephesians 4:4-6)

There is one body, and one Spirit, even as ye are called in one hope of your calling; One Lord, one faith, one baptism, One God and Father of all, who is above all, and through all, and in you all.

Note that the sevenfold (perfect) unity is grouped around the three Persons of the Godhead. The church or body owes its very existence and unity to the Holy Spirit (verse 4). The one faith by which men believe unto salvation belongs to the Lord Jesus Christ (verse 5). And God the Father (verse 6) is the source of this unity.

The supreme source of unity is this one God who exists as Father, Son and Holy Spirit at the same time. We praise the One God from whom all blessings flow. He is unique. He is one in essence, one in purpose, has one mind to all; owns one heaven, prepared one hell, desires our undivided attention and singleness of devotion. He has one plan of salvation for everybody, for He sent His one and only begotten Son to die once upon the Cross of Calvary for our sins.

C. GIFTS FROM ON HIGH
(Ephesians 4:7-11)

But unto every one of us is given grace according to the measure of the gift of Christ. Wherefore he saith, When he ascended up on high, he led captivity captive, and gave gifts unto men. (Now that he ascended, what is it but that he also descended first into the lower parts of the earth? He that descended is the same also that ascended up far above all heavens, that he might fill all things.) And he gave some, apostles; and some, prophets; and some, evangelists; and some, pastors and teachers.

Here we learn that the gifts bestowed by the Lord Jesus Christ are for every saint. His gifts are for the church, and every believer in the body of Christ, the church. So all gifts are for us. The gifts bestowed are for the unity and growth of the church. Two interpretations are offered for verse 8. (1) The "captivity" was made up of the enemies of Christ: death, Satan and sin. This means the verse announces victory over such evil powers. (2) The "captivity" was composed of redeemed Old Testament saints who were removed from the confines of Sheol to be with Christ.

It is believed that prior to the resurrection of our Lord, all deceased went to sheol or hades, the unseen place, the nether world, also called hell. But the place was divided. One section was for unbelievers, the other for believers. And a great gulf divided the two sections (Luke 16:26). When Christ died He descended into hell, into the section of the faithful, then gathered them out of this section (Abraham's bosom or paradise), and carried them to heaven with Him. From that point on, believers who die no longer descend into hades, but go immediately to heaven. Thus, to be absent from the body is to be present with the Lord. However, the unsaved dead continue to descend into sheol.

Now four gifts are mentioned. (1) An apostle is one sent with a commission, who has seen the Lord, and was inspired of God and worked miracles. Apostles were given for a specific purpose and time. Technically, there are no apostles today, although some men are wont to call themselves such. The original twelve disciples spoke with special authority, having received a message from God for the entire church. (2) Prophets were those who spoke forth, who proclaimed the Gospel. They were the inspired teachers and revealers of the will of Christ. Frequently, they were grouped with the apostles as having particular authority. Perhaps today we would call them evangelists.

(3) Evangelists preached the Gospel to the unconverted; they were the itinerant preachers. To this group belonged the task of evangelism, missionary work, principally among unbelievers. They were the missionaries of Paul's day. They did not serve any one congregation or area, but moved from place to place as they found opportunities to preach the Gospel. (4) Pastors and teachers are to be taken as dual titles for a single office, reflecting the twofold task of the settled ministry. Thus every pastor should be a teacher also ("apt to teach," 1 Timothy 3:2). In other words, the phrase "pastors and teachers" refers to one person (Wuest).

D. THE PURPOSE OF CHRIST'S GIFTS (Ephesians 4:12-16)

For the perfecting of the saints, for the work of the ministry, for the edifying of the body of Christ: Till we all come in the unity of the faith, and of the knowledge of the Son of God, unto a perfect man, unto the measure of the stature of the fulness of Christ: That we henceforth be no more children, tossed to and fro, and carried about with every wind of doctrine, by the sleight of men, and cunning craftiness, whereby they lie in wait to deceive; But speaking the truth in love, may grow up into him in all things, which is the head, even Christ: From whom the whole body fitly joined together and compacted by that which every joint supplieth, according to the effectual working in the measure of every part, maketh increase of the body unto the edifying of itself in love.

First of all, we see that the gifts of our Lord help the church to mature.

He gave us apostles, prophets, evangelists, and pastors who are also teachers in order that they might perfect saints for the ministry. They are to equip the saints for the work of service. The gifts are calculated to inspire every member to serve. Perfecting means to fit out, equip for service, coordinate, complete, and mend. The church is not left an orphan, to make out the best it can by underhanded tactics, manipulation, politics, psychology, unholy alliances and inflated titles.

Indeed, the message directed to us is, GROW UP! It is God's desire that His children become mature, adult spiritual saints. The exhortation is be children no more! Note the words "sleight of men." The Greek word is *kubia* (kubeia), referring to cubes or dice. Because of the cheating of dice players and gamblers in general, the expression means the trickery or fickleness of men, men with no firm principles to guide them. Cunning craftiness means deceitful scheming, deliberate plan or system of error.

We learn that the immature Christian is easy prey to spiritual slickers and church charlatans. They are tossed to and fro, easily carried about by all kinds of teachings. Whatever new philosophy is announced, whatever phony with a silver tongue or healing hand comes along, they are swept up with him. They are immature, carnal, weak, unsettled, unsteady, erratic, flighty, temperamental, ignorant of their own makeup and the fact that the old nature is still within them. They are ignorant of the old nature's willingness and readiness to go astray; and finally, they are ignorant of the devices of the Devil.

God's Word commands, "Be no longer babes. Grow up." A mature Christian's emphasis is internal, not external; it is eternal, not temporal; it is heavenly, not mundane and worldly; it is spiritual, not carnal. We must resist all attempts to make it otherwise. Jesus Christ has supplied that which we need in order (1) to escape the danger of remaining dwarfed, stunted children, (2) to grow up in all things, governed by Him who is our Head, and (3) to receive from Him that which enables the whole body to rightly function and build up itself in love.

III. Special Features

A. PRESERVING OUR HERITAGE

One of the thrilling studies of the development of the church among Black Americans is the story of how God raised up preachers and missionaries within a slave society. Despite white hypocrisy and despite blacks who sought only to use Christianity as a means to escape slavery or the cruelty and rigors of such an evil institution, there were those slaves who were genuine believers.

The Holy Spirit broke through language barriers, disease, poverty, ignorance, illiteracy, carnality, animism, and whatever else was attached to chattel bondage. God used those who were genuine in their faith. And the gifts He bestowed—for He is no respecter of places, faces or races—He used to build up His church. Today, we enjoy the fruits of their labor in Christ.

B. A CONCLUDING WORD

It is interesting to note that Paul does not mention any local officers in the church. The apostle was led to stress those who serve the whole church at large. Just as we did not arrange our body members the way we desired, so it is also true we had no say in arranging the church. Since the church belongs to God, He orders it as it pleases Him. There should be no quarrel or jealousy over offices. Just as the organs within our bodies are to work together for our good, so it is in the church.

We may not know what every part in our bodies does, but we have no desire that any part be cut out in order to discover how we would be affected. So each saint has a particular function to fulfill in the organic life of the church, in the body. You can see the folly of claiming to be a Christian yet not a member of any local assembly. We are spiritually endowed, gifted by God to do a specific work in the body. But today's lesson deals with the gifted individuals given to the church in order to strengthen the church as a whole. God the Father gave His Son, the Son gave His life. As the Head of the church, the Son has given all of us gifts, then He has given those gifts to the church in order that the members may be trained and use their gifts to edify the church, win the lost and glorify God.

HOME DAILY BIBLE READINGS FOR THE WEEK OF JULY 16, 2000
CALLED TO USE YOUR SPIRITUAL GIFTS

July 10	M.	Ephesians 3:1-6, Gentiles Are Fellow Heirs in Christ
July 11	T.	Ephesians 3:7-13, Gentiles Receive the Gospel's Riches
July 12	W.	Ephesians 3:14-21, Paul Prays for the Ephesian Christians
July 13	T.	Ephesians 4:1-10, Unity in the Body of Christ
July 14	F.	Ephesians 4:11-16, Grow to Maturity in Christ Jesus
July 15	S.	Ephesians 4:17-24, Live in Righteousness and Holiness
July 16	S.	Ephesians 4:25-32, Live a New Life in Christ

Know Your Bible

- Jehoahaz was a wicked king and the Lord punished Israel by delivering them into the hands of the king of Syria, but he prayed to God for deliverance, and the Lord heard his prayer. In spite of this, idolatry still continued in the land. (2 Kings 13:2-8)

O God, by Your grace we have been empowered with gifts by which to enrich the lives of others; may we not appropriate Your blessings for selfish gains; but like the Christ, sacrifice our lives for the welfare of those for whom Christ died. Amen.

Called to Responsible Living

Adult Topic—*Claim Your Responsibilities*

•••••

Youth Topic—*A Place for Me!*
Children's Topic—*Love One Another*

•••••

Devotional Reading—Ephesians 5:6-20
Background Scripture—Ephesians 5—6:4
Print—Ephesians 5:1-5, 21-29; 6:1-4

PRINTED SCRIPTURE

Ephesians 5:1-5, 21-29; 6:1-4 (KJV)

BE YE therefore followers of God, as dear children;

2 And walk in love, as Christ also hath loved us, and hath given himself for us an offering and a sacrifice to God for a sweetsmelling savour.

3 But fornication, and all uncleanness, or covetousness, let it not be once named among you, as becometh saints;

4 Neither filthiness, nor foolish talking, nor jesting, which are not convenient: but rather giving of thanks.

5 For this ye know, that no whoremonger, nor unclean person, nor covetous man, who is an idolater, hath any inheritance in the kingdom of Christ and of God.

•••••

21 Submitting yourselves one to another in the fear of God.

22 Wives, submit yourselves unto your own husbands, as unto the Lord.

23 For the husband is the head of the wife, even as Christ is the head of the church: and he is the

Ephesians 5:1-5, 21-29; 6:1-4 (NRSV)

THEREFORE BE imitators of God, as beloved children,

2 and live in love, as Christ loved us and gave himself up for us, a fragrant offering and sacrifice to God.

3 But fornication and impurity of any kind, or greed, must not even be mentioned among you, as is proper among saints.

4 Entirely out of place is obscene, silly, and vulgar talk; but instead, let there be thanksgiving.

5 Be sure of this, that no fornicator or impure person, or one who is greedy (that is, an idolater), has any inheritance in the kingdom of Christ and of God.

•••••

21 Be subject to one another out of reverence for Christ.

22 Wives, be subject to your husbands as you are to the Lord.

23 For the husband is the head of the wife just as Christ is the head of the church, the body of which he is the Savior.

saviour of the body.

24 Therefore as the church is subject unto Christ, so let the wives be to their own husbands in every thing.

25 Husbands, love your wives, even as Christ also loved the church, and gave himself for it;

26 That he might sanctify and cleanse it with the washing of water by the word,

27 That he might present it to himself a glorious church, not having spot, or wrinkle, or any such thing; but that it should be holy and without blemish.

28 So ought men to love their wives as their own bodies. He that loveth his wife loveth himself.

29 For no man ever yet hated his own flesh; but nourisheth and cherisheth it, even as the Lord the church.

Ephesians 6:1-4

CHILDREN, OBEY your parents in the Lord: for this is right.

2 Honour thy father and mother; which is the first commandment with promise;

3 That it may be well with thee, and thou mayest live long on the earth.

4 And, ye fathers, provoke not your children to wrath: but bring them up in the nurture and admonition of the Lord.

24 Just as the church is subject to Christ, so also wives ought to be, in everything, to their husbands.

25 Husbands, love your wives, just as Christ loved the church and gave himself up for her,

26 in order to make her holy by cleansing her with the washing of water by the word,

27 so as to present the church to himself in splendor, without a spot or wrinkle or anything of the kind—yes, so that she may be holy and without blemish.

28 In the same say, husbands should love their wives as they do their own bodies. He who loves his wife loves himself.

29 For no one ever hates his own body, but he nourishes and tenderly cares for it, just as Christ does for the church.

Ephesians 6:1-4

CHILDREN, OBEY your parents in the Lord, for this is right.

2 "Honor your father and mother"—this is the first commandment with a promise:

3 "so that it may be well with you and you may live long on the earth."

4 And, fathers, do not provoke your children to anger, but bring them up in the discipline and instruction of the Lord.

 **KEY VERSE**

*Submitting yourselves one to another in the fear of God.—**Ephesians 5:21***

OBJECTIVES

After reading this lesson, the student should be better informed that:

1. God's children are to walk in love and live in the light;
2. Submissiveness is a key to responsible living;

3. Husband-wife relations portray Christ and the church; and

4. Parent-child relations also illustrate the church.

POINTS TO BE EMPHASIZED
Adult/Youth/Children
Key Verse: Ephesians 5:21; 1 John 4:7 *(Children)*
Print: Ephesians 5:1-5, 21-29; 6:1-4

—Imitate God in your behavior, just as children would, and be subject to one another out of love for Christ. (1-2)

—Paul said that impure actions and improper speech are unacceptable behavior for believers, but a grateful spirit is edifying to the kingdom of God. (3-5)

—Paul instructed the believers to submit themselves to one another out of reverence for Christ. (21)

—Wives are subject to their husbands as the church is subject to Christ. (22-24)

—Husbands love their wives in the same spirit that Christ yielded Himself to establish the church. (25-29)

—Paul said children are to submit themselves to their parents in obedience and parents are to guide and discipline their children in the Lord. (6:1-4)

(**NOTE**: Use KJV Scripture for Adults; NRSV Scripture for Youth and Children)

TOPICAL OUTLINE OF THE LESSON

I. Introduction

A. Submissiveness

B. Biblical Background

II. Exposition and Application of the Scripture

A. Imitating God (Ephesians 5:1-2)

B. Avoiding Improper Behavior (Ephesians 5:3-5)

C. Wives and Submissiveness (Ephesians 5:21-24)

D. Husbands and Love (Ephesians 5:25-29)

E. Children and Parents (Ephesians 6:1-4)

III. Special Features

A. Preserving Our Heritage

B. A Concluding Word

I. Introduction

A. SUBMISSIVENESS

The key verse for today's lesson is Ephesians 5:21: "Submitting yourselves one to another in the fear of God." Note that this verse connects directly with what precedes (verses 18-20), not with what follows. In this key verse, every Christian is to subject himself or herself to every other Christian. To do so is one of the results of being filled with the Holy Spirit. In what follows (5:22-6:9), the command to submit refers to family and marital relationships, and bondservants. There is to be always that willingness to obey God's Word and maintain the order He has established.

Submissiveness is a major ingredient in the life of the Christian who is filled with the Holy Spirit. Living in a responsible manner is possible only through the Spirit of God. The verb that is used has two parts to it. *Tasso*, the root of the verb, means to put in place, to station, arrange in a certain order, appoint, or to assign. With the prefix *upo*, which means "under," we get *upotasso*, signifying to put under, subject, subordinate, obey, submit to one's control, or yield to one's control, or yield to one's admonition or advice. As a military term, it means to line up under.

B. BIBLICAL BACKGROUND

The Christian WALK is a major theme in Ephesians. Remember that our walk is our conduct or behavior. Saints are exhorted to walk in good works (Ephesians 2:10). Only those who have divine life can produce that which is well pleasing in God's sight. We are also to walk worthy of our heavenly calling (Ephesians 4:1), remembering that we have been quickened, raised and seated in Christ, and made members of the household of God. Such a calling carries with it the responsibility of high practical daily living.

As we begin our study of chapter five, we learn that to walk as God's dear children means to walk in LOVE (verse 2), as Christ also has loved us and given Himself for us an offering and a sacrifice to God for a sweet smelling savor. We are also to walk in the LIGHT (verse 8). Once we were "darkness," but now we are "light" in the Lord. What is more, the light is in us. And since light and darkness cannot mix, we are exhorted to have no fellowship with the unfruitful works of darkness. Then we are told to walk LOOKING (verse 15), to be careful how we walk. We are to "pick our way," looking all around (circumspectly).

II. Exposition and Application of the Scripture

A. IMITATING GOD
(Ephesians 5:1-2)

Be ye therefore followers of God, as dear children; And walk in love, as Christ also hath loved us, and hath given himself for us an offering and a sacrifice to God for a sweetsmelling savour.

The lesson begins with the command, "Be or become at all times imitators of God." Copy God. The noun rendered "imitators" refers to likeness and similarity, not to complete duplication. That would be impossible anyway. To copy God is to fully depend upon Him in all we do. Thereby, we let Him do what needs to be done, and we are to do it as "beloved children." Let those who love the world copy other men and women as they seek to keep up with them in the latest fashions, fads, novels, dance steps, hairstyles, hit tunes, etc. We Christians are called upon to copy God.

The first characteristic of the saint who walks as God's dear child is to walk in love. This love is first of all directed to the Lord. It is our relationship to Him that keeps us from all ugly and unloving and unlovely living. We show our love for the Lord by reading and taking Him at His Word. Now Christ's offering and sacrifice of Himself to God was as a fragrant aroma. The words "offering and sacrifice" remind us He was both the Priest and the victim. He brought the offering and He was the offering.

B. AVOIDING IMPROPER BEHAVIOR (Ephesians 5:3-5)

But fornication, and all uncleanness, or covetousness, let it not be once named among you, as becometh saints; Neither filthiness, nor foolish talking, nor jesting, which are not convenient: but rather giving of thanks. For this ye know, that no whoremonger, nor unclean person, nor covetous man, who is an idolater, hath any inheritance in the kingdom of Christ and of God.

Does it seem strange to talk about loving God in one breath, then exhort against filthiness in the next breath? Lenski asks: "Can we, who were made God's beloved children by this sacrifice on our part return to a life that is reeking and stinking with vile odor?" Indeed, there are some things not to be even named among those who walk in love. There should not even be a suspicion of such evils existing among us.

Fornication is immorality, and includes prostitution in all its forms. Uncleanness is every form of impurity.

Covetousness is greed, grabbing for more. Filthiness is indecency. Foolish talking is silly talk. Jesting is flippant banter, off-color wittiness. These things are not fitting, suitable or proper. They do not come up to the mark God has set for us; they are far beneath us. What then is proper? The answer: the giving of thanks. How strange that sounds. Filthy habits are on one side, thanksgiving to God on the other side. What a contrast! The thought is that we are so blessed by the Father and our hearts so full of gratitude that these dirty practices will not be named among us.

Paul then reminds the saints of what they already know. They grasped intellectually the fact that not everybody is going to inherit God's kingdom. When you live in a society where there is constant temptation to commit sexual immorality, there is need for just such a reminder. Paul also mentions the covetous man, the money-grubber, literally, an "over-reacher," a grabber, exploiter, one who worships gold instead of God. Any one who practices any one of these things has no inheritance in the kingdom of Christ and God. Only one definite article is used in the phrase "the kingdom of Christ and God." This suggests we have the fullest justification for considering "Christ and God" as One Person.

C. WIVES AND SUBMISSIVENESS (Ephesians 5:21-24)

Submitting yourselves one to another in the fear of God. Wives, submit yourselves unto your own husbands, as unto the Lord. For the husband is the head of the wife, even as Christ is the head of the church: and he is the saviour of the

body. Therefore as the church is subject unto Christ, so let the wives be to their own husbands in every thing.

We dealt earlier with verse twenty-one in our Introduction. Verse twenty-two begins the actual exposition of the passage dealing with wives. This is not to say what is exhorted is not good advice for all married women, but we recognize that God gives the Christian power to do what He commands. Deeds done in His strength glorify Him. Deeds done in human strength alone glorify man. What is commanded of the Christian woman is to be done "as to the Lord," that is, for His sake. This makes a world of difference between the believer and the unbeliever. The married life of the believer illustrates Jesus Christ and the church.

The husband is the head of the wife. This headship was established by creation, for God made man first and put him in charge. This leadership was further enforced by the Fall. God said to Eve after their disobedience, "Your desire shall be for your husband, and he shall rule over you" (Genesis 3:16). Paul was led also to write later "the head of the woman is man" (1 Corinthians 11:3). There can be no misinterpretation with these Scriptures.

Because Jesus Christ is the Head of the church (and He is the Savior of the body, the church), the church is subject to Him. Therefore, in similar manner, wives are to be subject to their own husbands in everything. Keep in mind that subordination does not imply inferiority. Submissiveness is a matter of authority, responsibility, and function. It speaks of what is called the division of labor. The man has his job;

the woman has her job. Efficiency calls for one head, not two.

Furthermore, being the head is not license to tyrannize or enslave the wife. The husband is no "demanding domestic despot" (Parallel Bible Commentary). What Paul wrote was not simply the product of a male-dominated Jewish society. What God has decreed is for our own good, and is not to be countermanded by our concepts of equality or what we think is right. And as we shall see in the next section, the husband's obligation is just as binding. Remember, God designs the way that humans are to conduct themselves.

D. HUSBANDS AND LOVE
(Ephesians 5:25-29)

Husbands, love your wives, even as Christ also loved the church, and gave himself for it; That he might sanctify and cleanse it with the washing of water by the word, That he might present it to himself a glorious church, not having spot, or wrinkle, or any such thing; but that it should be holy and without blemish. So ought men to love their wives as their own bodies. He that loveth his wife loveth himself. For no man ever yet hated his own flesh; but nourisheth and cherisheth it, even as the Lord the church.

The command to love (*agapate*) is a present tense imperative meaning to love and continue to love. Imagine telling sinful, fallible men that their love for their wives resembles the love of Christ shown when He gave Himself on Calvary for the church. In contrast to normal sexual desire, this love is unselfish. Christ's love for the church is to be the pattern of the Christian man's love for his wife.

The Lord Jesus gave Himself for His bride (the church) in order to accomplish a number of things. (1) He wanted to sanctify or set apart or separate the church from the world-system (2) He desired to cleanse her with the washing of water by the Word (3) He yearned that He might once for all present her to Himself. Note that the positional description of the church is not its condition! To think otherwise is to grossly misinterpret the Bible.

The church without spot, wrinkle or any such thing is that church that is changed and snatched up by the Lord when He returns. Presently the visible church is full of wrinkles, spots, blemishes, and "other such things." Do not be fooled into thinking otherwise! One author well states that the church as the Bride of Christ is the special object of His affection with which He is preparing to share His reign and His glory. For when He comes to the earth, we shall come with Him. What a wonderful way to look at the local assembly.

With all of our faults, foibles and failures, the Lord still speaks of us with endearing words of love. How these words must grip the hearts of pastors, deacons, officers and members of every local church! This is a terrific motivation for husbands to pattern their marriages after Christ's relation to the church. To see the church through the eyes of Christ is to "revolutionize our life and ministry" (MacDonald).

We ought to love our own wives, as we love our own bodies. This makes even more sense as we realize that a husband and wife are one flesh (Genesis 2:24), so that a man who loves his wife literally loves himself. And as Christ nourishes (to maturity, nurtures, rears) and cherishes (literally, keeps warm; figuratively, to foster with tender care) the church, so ought Christian men nourish and cherish their own bodies, for no one ever hated his own flesh.

E. CHILDREN AND PARENTS
(Ephesians 6:1-4)

Children, obey your parents in the Lord: for this is right. Honour thy father and mother; which is the first commandment with promise; That it may be well with thee, and thou mayest live long on the earth. And, ye fathers, provoke not your children to wrath: but bring them up in the nurture and admonition of the Lord.

Note especially the words "in the Lord" in verse one. These words do not refer to the religious status of the parents at all! The verse is directed to Christian young people and tells them to be obedient in the Lord, that is, in His strength, in communion with Him. "In the Lord" is the sphere in which the action is to take place (Colossians 3:20). We are not taught that the child is responsible for deciding what commands are in keeping with the mind of Christ, as if to say, "Obey parents insofar as their commands are compatible with your duty to Christ." No. It refers rather to the whole spirit in which obedience is to be rendered. Long life was the promise given to those who obey and honor their parents. Fathers are particularly warned not to irritate the child by vexatious commands, uncertain temper and unreasonable blame.

III. Special Features

A. PRESERVING OUR HERITAGE

Black American women who get involved with black men who are Muslims should take a second look before becoming even more deeply committed. Christian women of course have no business becoming intimate with Muslims anyway. Believers are not to be mismated with unbelievers (2 Corinthians 6:14). Keep in mind that the Koran permits polygamy, although the practice is not legal in the U. S. black women should study the conditions of married women in countries where Islam is in charge. They will discover that Islam has given no evidence or proof whatever of raising the standards of women.

B. A CONCLUDING WORD

Because the family is the basic unit of all society, it is imperative that there be a right relationship between husband and wife, and between children and parents. Failure means disaster. The worst thing that can happen to any society is the disruption and disintegration of its homes and family life. We live in an age of rebellion against authority, and this entire section on submission has come under fire. God grant that Bible loving, Spirit-filled Christians (Ephesians 5:18) will submit first of all to the Word of God. And then, let that submissive inner life show itself in our relationships to all that are in authority over us. In this way, we will exhibit to the world the proper picture of the church as the body (and bride) of the Lord Jesus Christ.

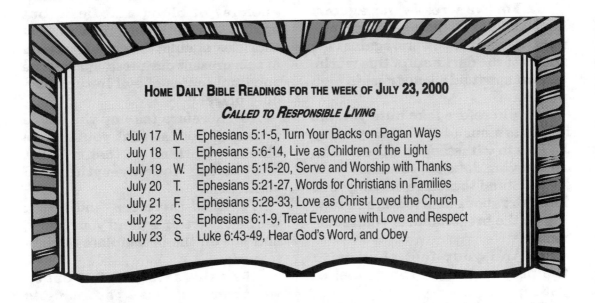

HOME DAILY BIBLE READINGS FOR THE WEEK OF JULY 23, 2000

CALLED TO RESPONSIBLE LIVING

July 17	M.	Ephesians 5:1-5, Turn Your Backs on Pagan Ways
July 18	T.	Ephesians 5:6-14, Live as Children of the Light
July 19	W.	Ephesians 5:15-20, Serve and Worship with Thanks
July 20	T.	Ephesians 5:21-27, Words for Christians in Families
July 21	F.	Ephesians 5:28-33, Love as Christ Loved the Church
July 22	S.	Ephesians 6:1-9, Treat Everyone with Love and Respect
July 23	S.	Luke 6:43-49, Hear God's Word, and Obey

O Thou who has given us freedom as the ground for responsible living, implant within our hearts and minds the reality that we are only free as we surrender our lives to Thee. Amen.

Called to Stand Firm

Adult topic—*Claim Your Power Base*

•••••

Youth Topic—*Stand Firm!*
Children's Topic—*Be Strong!*

•••••

Devotional Reading—John 14:15-27
Background Scripture—Ephesians 6:10-24
Print—Ephesians 6:10-24

PRINTED SCRIPTURE

Ephesians 6:10-24 (KJV)

10 Finally, my brethren, be strong in the Lord, and in the power of his might.

11 Put on the whole armour of God, that ye may be able to stand against the wiles of the devil.

12 For we wrestle not against flesh and blood, but against principalities, against powers, against the rulers of the darkness of this world, against spiritual wickedness in high places.

13 Wherefore take unto you the whole armour of God, that ye may be able to withstand in the evil day, and having done all, to stand.

14 Stand therefore, having your loins girt about with truth, and having on the breastplate of righteousness;

15 And your feet shod with the preparation of the gospel of peace;

16 Above all, taking the shield of faith, wherewith ye shall be able to quench all the fiery darts of the wicked.

Ephesians 6:10-24 (NRSV)

10 Finally, be strong in the Lord and in the strength of his power.

11 Put on the whole armor of God, so that you may be able to stand against the wiles of the devil.

12 For our struggle is not against enemies of blood and flesh, but against the rulers, against the authorities, against the cosmic powers of this present darkness, against the spiritual forces of evil in the heavenly places.

13 Therefore take up the whole armor of God, so that you may be able to withstand on that evil day, and having done everything, to stand firm.

14 Stand therefore, and fasten the belt of truth around your waist, and put on the breastplate of righteousness.

15 As shoes for your feet put on whatever will make you ready to proclaim the gospel of peace.

16 With all of these, take the shield of faith, with which you will be able to quench all the flaming

17 And take the helmet of salvation, and the sword of the Spirit, which is the word of God:

18 Praying always with all prayer and supplication in the Spirit, and watching thereunto with all perseverance and supplication for all saints;

19 And for me, that utterance may be given unto me, that I may open my mouth boldly, to make known the mystery of the gospel,

20 For which I am an ambassador in bonds: that therein I may speak boldly, as I ought to speak.

21 But that ye also may know my affairs, and how I do, Tychicus, a beloved brother and faithful minister in the Lord, shall make known to you all things:

22 Whom I have sent unto you for the same purpose, that ye might know our affairs, and that he might comfort your hearts.

23 Peace be to the brethren, and love with faith, from God the Father and the Lord Jesus Christ.

24 Grace be with all them that love our Lord Jesus Christ in sincerity. Amen.

arrows of the evil one.

17 Take the helmet of salvation, and the sword of the Spirit, which is the word of God.

18 Pray in the Spirit at all times in every prayer and supplication. To that end keep alert and always persevere in supplication for all the saints.

19 Pray also for me, so that when I speak, a message may be given to me to make known with boldness the mystery of the gospel,

20 for which I am an ambassador in chains. Pray that I may declare it boldly, as I must speak.

21 So that you also may know how I am and what I am doing, Tychicus will tell you everything. He is a dear brother and a faithful minister in the Lord.

22 I am sending him to you for this very purpose, to let you know how we are, and to encourage your hearts.

23 Peace be to the whole community, and love with faith, from God the Father and the Lord Jesus Christ.

25 Grace be with all who have an undying love for our Lord Jesus Christ.

*Finally, my brethren, be strong in the Lord, and in the power of his might.—**Ephesians 6:10***

OBJECTIVES

After reading this lesson, the student should have knowledge of:

1. The power of the Christian warrior;
2. The description of the armor given the Christian soldier;
3. The character of the Christian's enemy; and
4. The nature of Christian warfare.

POINTS TO BE EMPHASIZED

Adult/Youth/Children
Key Verse: Ephesians 6:10
Print: Ephesians 6:10-24

—Paul told the Ephesians that believers who get their strength and power from God battle against spiritual enemies, rather than physical ones. (10-12)

—Paul told believers to arm themselves with God's power and with truth and righteousness stand firmly against evil. (13)

—Paul told the Ephesians to arm themselves with truth and righteousness in order to witness to the good news of peace. (14-17)

—Believers are to pray in the spirit in supplication for all saints and also for Paul's boldness in proclamation. (18-20)

—Paul concluded his letter to the Ephesians with a personal word of encouragement and a benediction. (21-24)

(**NOTE**: Use KJV Scripture for Adults; NRSV Scripture for Youth and Children)

TOPICAL OUTLINE OF THE LESSON

I. Introduction
  A. God's Word is a Sword
  B. Biblical Background

II. Exposition and Application of the Scripture
  A. The Christian Soldier's Power (Ephesians 6:10)
  B. The Christian Soldier's Persecutor (Ephesians 6:12)
  C. The Christian Soldier's Panoply (Ephesians 6:11, 13-17)
  D. The Christian Soldier's Prayer (Ephesians 6:18-20)
  E. The Christian Soldier's Postscript (Ephesians 6:21-24)

III. Special Features
  A. Preserving Our Heritage
  B. A Concluding Word

I. Introduction

A. GOD'S WORD IS A SWORD

The Hebrew word for sword is found over 400 times in the Bible, pointing out the importance of the sword as a weapon throughout Old Testament times. The sword continued to be of importance in Roman times in the New Testament. Yet, it is our task in the church age to transfer the use of the sword from a carnal, physical or material use to a spiritual one. The only offensive weapon we have is the sword, God's Word, written and spoken. However, it is true that it may be used defensively to parry thrusts. Recall that our Lord did this with "it is written" (Matthew 4:4, 7, 10).

But in the panoply described in today's lesson, all of the other pieces of armor are basically defensive. In Ephesians 6:17, we are plainly told that the sword of the Spirit is the Word of God. Hebrews 4:12 informs us that "the word of God is living and powerful, and sharper than any two-edged sword." It pierces the conscience, slays self-righteousness, discerns and lays bare the heart. With respect to the whole armor, the sword held an inferior place with Greek soldiers.

The particular Greek word rendered sword here was a small, short sword or dagger. It differed from the large double-edge sword (Luke 2:35). God encourages us as soldiers to properly wield our swords. We are to be prepared to say, "It is written." This will work or wreak havoc in the ranks of the enemy. May we use the Bible intelligently, prayerfully, studiously, quickly, necessarily, and appropriately. And rejoice as victorious saints in the battle of life.

B. BIBLICAL BACKGROUND

Why were military figures of speech so popular with the apostle Paul? What influenced him? It seems quite likely that Paul's Hebrew background and knowledge of the Scriptures influenced his choice. Perhaps this should be put another way. His inclination for the life of discipline and the love of the military were fed by the numerous references to war and the things of war in the Old Testament Scriptures read by Paul.

A more important influence, one more easily seen and readily accepted, would be Paul's environment. Here we assume that the origin of most of Paul's military figures of speech is found in his life and experience. Because of his several imprisonments, presumably near army camps, Paul was very familiar with the military. Those to whom Paul wrote were likewise familiar with soldiers. The apostle not only had experience with soldiers but as a soldier. The labors, stripes, imprisonments, beatings, shipwrecks, stoning, weariness, pain, hunger, thirst, perils and dangers experienced were all physical evidences of a soldier's zeal in a spiritual warfare (2 Corinthians 11:23-28). He knew that God was his Supply-Sergeant, if one may so speak, and provided him with armor—the whole armor.

II. Exposition and Application of the Scripture

A. THE CHRISTIAN SOLDIER'S POWER (Ephesians 6:10)

Finally, my brethren, be strong in the Lord, and in the power of his might.

Religious and moral strength comes from the Lord, "in the Lord," connected with Him. Thayer renders this phrase, "the might of his strength." It is God's strength, not ours. Our Lord supplies not only the pieces of armor but also the strength needed to fight. We are made powerful in Him. Unfortunately, some of us seek to battle in our own strength, with our own weapons and strategies, and we are defeated.

B. THE CHRISTIAN SOLDIER'S PERSECUTOR (Ephesians 6:12)

For we wrestle not against flesh and blood, but against principalities, against powers, against the rulers of the darkness of this world, against spiritual wickedness in high places.

Life is a spiritual battle. Christians must be aware of the fact that our struggle, our wrestling is not with flesh and blood (other human beings), but with evil spiritual forces. It is a war that began ages ago when Lucifer fell and became the Devil (I think his name should be capitalized!) So far as man is concerned, the battle started in the Garden of Eden, and God announced, "I will put enmity between you (the Devil) and the woman, and between your seed and her seed; he shall bruise your head, and you shall bruise his heel" (Genesis 3:15).

Satan is evil, cruel, a wicked tyrant, who seeks to devour. He cares nothing for the weapons of man raised against him. Spiritual weapons must be used in a spiritual warfare. Note the four different terms by which our antagonists are identified. (1) Principalities: "the term is transferred by Paul to angels and demons holding dominions entrusted to them in the order of things" (Thayer). It is a word used "also of angelic and demonic powers, since they were thought of as having a political organization" (Arndt & Gingrich). (2) Powers: the Greek word means

authority. (3) Rulers of the darkness of this age: the word for ruler is *kosmokrator*, literally, world-ruler. (4) Spiritual hosts of wickedness in the heavenly places; Thayer limits this place to the lower heavens or the heaven of the clouds. Satan is the prince of the power of the air (Ephesians 2:2). Air here refers to that atmosphere in which the Devil moves and rules. These terms indicate spiritual, angelic, demonic powers. The Devil has a political organization and hierarchy, well organized and computerized.

Finally, note the words "wrestle against," "fight against" (JBP, NEB), "contending" (RSV), "struggle" (Moffatt, NIV, NASB). The verb to "wrestle" signifies personal grappling. Paul pictures hand to hand fighting, a close-up struggle. His purpose was to show the "personal, individualizing, nature of the encounter" of the Christian with the forces of evil (Ellicott). Each evil foe must be dealt with individually, for the preposition "against" is repeated five times.

C. THE CHRISTIAN SOLDIER'S PANOPLY (Ephesians 6:11, 13-17)

Put on the whole armour of God, that ye may be able to stand against the wiles of the devil. Wherefore take unto you the whole armour of God, that ye may be able to withstand in the evil day, and having done all, to stand. Stand therefore, having your loins girt about with truth, and having on the breastplate of righteousness; And your feet shod with the preparation of the gospel of peace; Above all, taking the shield of faith, wherewith ye shall be able to quench all the fiery darts of the

wicked. And take the helmet of salvation, and the sword of the Spirit, which is the word of God.

Pan means whole, all, full (panorama, Panasonic). *Hoplos* means tool, weapon. Thus panoply means the whole armor. To successfully contend with evil, the Christian warrior must put on all the equipment that God provides. Only in this way can the saints hold their ground against the "wiles" of Satan. We have derived the word method from the Greek word (*methodeias*) rendered "wiles." It means schemes or plans, and suggests the crafty methods by which Satan tries to deceive even Christians into thinking that he and his plans are quite all right. In 2 Corinthians 2:11, a different word is used as Paul warns that we are not to be ignorant of Satan's "devices" or thoughts and purposes.

First in the panoply is the Belt of truth (uprightness). In order to be unimpeded in movement, people would bind their long and flowing garments closely around their bodies and fasten them with a leather girdle (Thayer: Jeremiah 1:17, 1 Peter 1:13, Isaiah 11:5).

Second is the Breastplate of righteousness that protects the back, breast, neck, stomach, but primarily protects the heart within the breast or thorax (*thoraka*). Purity and uprightness of character are produced by the Holy Spirit, and defend the heart against the assaults of the Evil One.

Third are the shoes or sandals of the gospel of peace. The feet represent action, behavior or conduct. Christians are to enter the conflict with minds that are occupied with peace. How strange to consider the gospel of peace as a part of the armor of war! Peace in the heart shows itself in the readiness of the feet.

Fourth is the Shield of faith, to be taken on all occasions ("above all"). Our faith must reach out and accept the protection offered by the Lord. The darts of fierce temptations lose their fierceness when we depend entirely upon Christ. To go into battle without faith is foolish! Step out on God's Word and see the fierceness of temptation extinguished.

Fifth is the Helmet of salvation. The salvation of which Paul speaks is past, present, and future. It is suggested that believers who engaged in spiritual conflict but do not believe they are eternally secure in Christ have defective helmets! God wants His soldiers to know they are saved. As Conybeare and Howson said: "The head of the Christian is defended against hostile weapons by his knowledge of the salvation won for him by Christ."

The sixth piece of armor is the Sword of the Spirit. Some church members do not handle their swords well. A member who looks for the book of Romans in the Old Testament, or who looks for the book of Isaiah in the New Testament is evidently not familiar with the sword. Skilled use is not developed overnight, but the Holy Spirit our Teacher gladly tutors us in using the Bible as an effective tool against the Devil. *Rhema* is the Greek term for the "word" here. It certainly includes the words of the Bible, but also includes the spoken word, "that which is uttered by the living voice" (Thayer).

Finally, note the admonition to stand. The basic verb is used four times: "stand (verse 11) ...withstand... stand (verse 13) ...stand (verse 14)."

With the prefix *anti*, the verb is rendered "withstand" in verse 13. It means to set one's self against, to resist, or oppose. In each instance the Christian soldier is exhorted to hold his or her ground. We are to maintain our position. In other words, the implied opposite is not flight but defeat. To not stand is to be defeated. Thus we are never to retreat or fall in the struggle. To stand means to be victorious, successful!

D. THE CHRISTIAN SOLDIER'S PRAYER (Ephesians 6:18-20)

Praying always with all prayer and supplication in the Spirit, and watching thereunto with all perseverance and supplication for all saints; And for me, that utterance may be given unto me, that I may open my mouth boldly, to make known the mystery of the gospel, For which I am an ambassador in bonds: that therein I may speak boldly, as I ought to speak.

Some commentators have made prayer a piece of the armor solely for the purpose of saying there are seven pieces of armor thus constituting the perfect panoply, and giving us perfect protection. However, it is better to consider prayer as backing up the use of the full armor. Christian warriors are to pray always, without ceasing (1 Thessalonians 5:17). We are to pray at every season, on all occasions, including public meetings, private closet, at home, at church, etc. We are to pray in all places, at all times and for all things.

The words "all prayer" are interpreted to mean all forms: confession, humiliation, adoration, praise, thanksgiving, petition or supplication, and intercession. It appears that the word

Spirit refers to both the Holy Spirit and the human spirit. None of us prays in spirit save by the Holy Spirit's help. We are responsible to pray for all the saints. "Watching" is to accompany the praying. We are to persevere—keep on asking, seeking, and knocking (Luke 11:9), and remain steadfast. Paul also asks for prayer for himself. His request is not to be released from prison, but that as an ambassador in prison, he might have freedom of speech and boldly proclaim the church as the one body composed of Jews and Gentiles in Christ.

E. THE CHRISTIAN SOLDIER'S POSTSCRIPT (Ephesians 6:21-24)

But that ye also may know my affairs, and how I do, Tychicus, a beloved brother and faithful minister in the Lord, shall make known to you all things: Whom I have sent unto you for the same purpose, that ye might know our affairs, and that he might comfort your hearts. Peace be to the brethren, and love with faith, from God the Father and the Lord Jesus Christ. Grace be with all them that love our Lord Jesus Christ in sincerity. Amen.

Tychicus is mentioned five times (Acts 20:4; Colossians 4:7; 2 Timothy 4:12; Titus 3:12; and Ephesians 6:21). As the bearer of this Ephesians letter, it was his purpose to inform the saints of Paul's situation, and encourage them not to worry. The Epistle opened with grace and peace. Now it ends with peace and grace, extended to all who love the Lord (Deity) Jesus (Humanity) Christ (Savior) "with never diminishing love," and with incorruptible sincerity. True Christian love is like a flame that is never extinguished.

III. Special Features

A. PRESERVING OUR HERITAGE

The military spirit is seen in the spirituals. Study War No More, Heav'n Boun' Soldier, Joshua Fit de Battle of Jerico, Singin' wid a Sword in Ma Han', Keep on the Firing Line, My God He Is a Man of War, are examples. We are called soldiers of de cross in We Are Climbin' Jacob's Ladder. Lovell points out (*Black Song*) that the symbolism of the believer at war appealed very much to the slave. The terms of the Christian warfare were adapted to the slave's everyday war. God grant that we sing in truth, "I'm On the Battlefield for My Lord."

B. A CONCLUDING WORD

We are commissioned to fight the forces of evil all the days of our lives, remembering that we are fellow-soldiers. "Christians should fight shoulder-to-shoulder and knee-to-knee" (Parallel Bible Commentary). We are not alone in the battle, nor are we weak and defenseless. We wage war while wearing the whole armor of God. In His strength we defend the Gospel, pray for each other, and proclaim boldly the unsearchable riches of Jesus Christ.

"Stand up, stand up for Jesus, Stand in His strength alone;
The arm of flesh will fail you, Ye dare not trust your own:
Put on the gospel armor, Each piece put on with prayer;
Where duty calls or danger, Be never wanting there." (George Duffield, Jr.)

HOME DAILY BIBLE READINGS FOR THE WEEK OF JULY 30, 2000

CALLED TO STAND FIRM

July 24 M. Ephesians 6:10-15, Be Strong in the Lord
July 25 T. Ephesians 6:16-20, Pray Always in the Lord's Spirit
July 26 W. Ephesians 6:21-24, Grace, Peace, and Love From God
July 27 T. John 14:15-27, God's Spirit Will Strengthen You
July 28 F. John 15:1-11, Abide in Christ, and Bear Fruit
July 29 S. John 15:12-27, We Are Chosen by Christ
July 30 S. John 16:16-24, Your Pain Will Turn to Rejoicing

Know Your Bible

- King Uzziah, Amaziah's son, was sixteen years old when he ascended the throne. (2 Kings 15:1-2)

Eternal God, our Father, may we respond to the pressures of this present life with the power to stand firm in the faith by which we are saved. In Jesus' name, we pray. Amen.

The Supremacy of Christ

Unit III—*Christ Above All*
Children's Unit—*Jesus Is Over All*

•••••

Adult Topic—*The Source of Life*

•••••

Youth Topic—*The Image of God*
Children's Topic—*Jesus Is Over All*

•••••

Devotional Reading—John 1:1-5, 9-18
Background Scripture—Colossians 1
Print—Colossians 1:15-28

PRINTED SCRIPTURE

Colossians 1:15-28 (KJV)

15 Who is the image of the invisible God, the firstborn of every creature:

16 For by him were all things created, that are in heaven, and that are in earth, visible and invisible, whether they be thrones, or dominions, or principalities, or powers: all things were created by him, and for him:

17 And he is before all things, and by him all things consist.

18 And he is the head of the body, the church: who is the beginning, the firstborn from the dead; that in all things he might have the preeminence.

19 For it pleased the Father that in him should all fulness dwell;

20 And, having made peace through the blood of his cross, by him to reconcile all things unto himself; by him, I say, whether they be things in earth, or things in heaven.

21 And you, that were sometime alienated and enemies in your mind by wicked works, yet now hath he reconciled

Colossians 1:15-28 (NRSV)

15 He is the image of the invisible God, the firstborn of all creation;

16 for in him all things in heaven and on earth were created, things visible and invisible, whether thrones or dominions or rulers or powers—all things have been created through him and for him.

17 He himself is before all things, and in him all things hold together.

18 He is the head of the body, the church; he is the beginning, the firstborn from the dead, so that he might come to have first place in everything.

19 For in him all the fulness of God was pleased to dwell,

20 and through him God was pleased to reconcile to himself all things, whether on earth or in heaven by making peace through the blood of his cross.

21 And you who were once estranged and hostile in mind, doing evil deeds,

22 He has now reconciled in his fleshly body through death, so as to present you holy and blameless

22 In the body of his flesh through death, to present you holy and unblameable and unreproveable in his sight:

23 If ye continue in the faith grounded and settled, and be not moved away from the hope of the gospel, which ye have heard, and which was preached to every creature which is under heaven; whereof I Paul an made a minister;

24 Who now rejoice in my sufferings for you, and fill up that which is behind of the afflictions of Christ in my flesh for his body's sake, which is the church:

25 Whereof I am made a minister, according to the dispensation of God which is given to me for you, to fulfil the word of God;

26 Even the mystery which hath been hid from ages and from generations, but now is made manifest to his saints:

27 To whom God would make known what is the riches of the glory of this mystery among the Gentiles; which is Christ in you, the hope of glory:

28 Whom we preach, warning every man, and teaching every man in all wisdom; that we may present every man perfect in Christ Jesus.

and irreproachable before him—

23 provided that you continue securely established and steadfast in the faith, without shifting from the hope promised by the gospel that you heard, which has been proclaimed to every creature under heaven. I, Paul, became a servant of this gospel.

24 I am now rejoicing in my sufferings for your sake, and in my flesh I am completing what is lacking in Christ's afflictions for the sake of his body, that is, the church.

25 I became its servant according to God's commission that was given to me for you, to make the word of God fully known,

26 the mystery that has been hidden throughout the ages and generations but has now been revealed to his saints.

27 To them God chose to make known how great among the Gentiles are the riches of the glory of this mystery, which is Christ in you, the hope of glory.

28 It is he whom we proclaim, warning everyone and teaching everyone in all wisdom, so that we may present everyone mature in Christ.

KEY VERSE

*For it pleased the Father that in him should all fulness dwell; And, having made peace through the blood of his cross, by him to reconcile all things unto himself; by him, I say, whether they be things in earth, or things in heaven.—**Colossians 1:19, 20***

OBJECTIVES

After reading this lesson, the student should have a better knowledge that:
1. Jesus Christ is God the Creator;
2. Jesus Christ is the Head of the body, the church;
3. Jesus Christ maintains the work of reconciliation; and
4. Christ in us is the hope of glory.

POINTS TO BE EMPHASIZED
Adult/Youth
Key Verse: Colossians 1:19, 20
Print: Colossians 1:15-28

—Jesus Christ is the eternal image of God in whom all things were created and through whom all things are held together. (15-17)

—Jesus Christ, the Head of the church and the firstborn from the dead, has preeminence in all things. (18)

—God was pleased to live fully in Jesus Christ and reconcile the world through Him. (19-22)

—Paul exhorted the Colossians to remain established and steadfast in the faith. (23)

—Paul rejoiced in suffering as a servant of God in order to make the Word of God fully known. (24-28)

Children
Key Verse: Acts 17:24
Print: Acts 17:22-27

—Paul told the Athenians that it was clear that they were very religious, but that they worshiped unknown gods. (22-23)

—God who made the world is Lord of heaven and earth and does not live in shrines made by human hands. (24)

—God gives to all, life and breath and all things. (25)

—God wants all to search and find Him. (27)

(**NOTE**: Use KJV Scripture for Adults; NRSV Scripture for Youth and Children)

TOPICAL OUTLINE OF THE LESSON

I. Introduction
A. Reconciliation
B. Biblical Background

II. Exposition and Application of the Scripture
A. Christ the Creator (Colossians 1:15-19)
B. Christ the Reconciler (Colossians 1:20-23)
C. Christ the Indweller (Colossians 1:24-28)

III. Special Features
A. Preserving Our Heritage
B. A Concluding Word

I. Introduction

A. RECONCILIATION

We are born the enemies of God. We came into the world dead in trespasses and sins, idolatrous, in revolt against God's authority, uncircumcised of heart, and walking in craftiness. By nature we were children of wrath, walking in ways of wickedness, hateful and hating one another, living in malice and envy, serving various lusts and pleasures, having no hope, and without God in the world. The need for a change in our condition is called reconciliation. In other words, reconciliation means to change thoroughly, or completely. It is to restore to a right relationship or standard. To reconcile is to make peace where there is hostility and war. It is giving up an old position and accepting a new one in agreement with someone else. It is the removal of enmity. Reconciliation is the transferal from a certain state or condition to another which is quite different, hence a restoration of favor.

B. BIBLICAL BACKGROUND

The apostle Paul during his first imprisonment in Rome wrote the letter to the Colossians. Moved by the Holy Spirit, he dealt with the Person of Jesus Christ. Paul's purpose was to combat the heresy that set up intermediaries between God and man, making the Lord Jesus Christ but one step along the way—or one step up the ladder. This dangerous philosophy eventually became known as Gnosticism.

The Greek word *gnosis* means knowledge. We see it in such words as diagnosis, prognosis, and agnostic. The Gnostics believed that knowledge came from spiritual insight, rather than from scientific study (World Book Encyclopedia). Gnostics considered flesh evil. Thus, God could not become flesh as Christians described the Incarnation. Gnostics taught that "the divine Christ came upon the human Jesus at his baptism and departed shortly before" the Lord died, or, the Lord "only had the appearance of flesh" (Thiessen). Paul taught that Jesus Christ is incomparable, the only Mediator, the Head of the church, and that in Him the fullness of the Godhead dwells bodily.

II. Exposition and Application of the Scripture

A. CHRIST THE CREATOR
(Colossians 1:15-19)

Who is the image of the invisible God, the firstborn of every creature: For by him were all things created, that are in heaven, and that are in earth, visible and invisible, whether they be thrones, or dominions, or principalities, or powers: all things were created by him, and for him: And he is before all things, and by him all things consist. And he is the head of the body, the church: who is the beginning, the firstborn from the dead; that in all things he might have the preeminence. For it pleased the Father that in him should all fulness dwell.

Our lesson begins with one of the great passages in the Bible dealing with the Person of Jesus Christ. The word rendered "image" has given us the word, icon. It means representation, and is used also in 2 Corinthians 4:4. In Hebrews 1:3, Christ is described as "the express image of his (God's) person." Here the original word for image is not *eikon*, but *charakter* (character, the precise reproduction in every respect). The thought between icon and character is certainly related.

Unfortunately, certain groups that deny the Deity of Jesus Christ have seized upon the words "the firstborn of all creation." They teach in error that Jesus Christ was the first thing Jehovah created. However, the word (*prototokos*) translated "firstborn" means He is the One by whom all creation came into existence. Satan is very clever in pushing people to believe the very opposite of what a Bible verse really says. Firstborn then is not first created. Firstborn speaks of priority in time, sovereignty in rank (Psalm 89:27), and supremacy or superiority of position.

Now there are these three things we learn from Colossians 1:16-17. First, Jesus Christ who is God Almighty is the GROUND of creation. By this is meant He alone creates all things: viruses and microbes, tiny mosses to giant redwoods, molds to mountains, snails to elephants, small stones to huge planets. He made the earth and the heavens and He also prepared hell. "All things were made by Him; and without Him was not anything made that was made" (John 1:3). And this includes men and angels.

Note again that the "all things" includes the spirit powers that the Gnostics exalted. It appears that the five groups of these invisible entities are (1) thrones (2) principalities (3) authorities (4) powers and (5) dominions. Whereas it is difficult to construct any type of hierarchy here, it is believed they represent the highest orders of the angelic realm (Bruce).

Not only is Christ the Ground of creation, but He is also the GOAL. All things were created for Him. He contains within Himself the reason why creation exists at all, and why it is the way it is. Second, He is the Object of creation; it was created to glorify Him. This is what the twenty-four elders said, "You are worthy, O Lord, to receive glory and honor and power; for you created all things, and by your will they exist and were created" (Revelation 4:11).

Third, Christ is the GLUE of all things. He is before all things, so that no matter how far back we may imagine, Jesus Christ was already there. He is the great I AM (John 8:58). The word rendered "consist" is the translation of a Greek word meaning to cohere, subsist, hold or stick together, put together (Thayer), continue, endure, exist (Arndt & Gingrich). Christ upholds all things by the word of His power (Hebrews 1:3). He holds all things together, so that "we have a cosmos, not a chaos" (Parallel Bible Commentary).

In Ephesians, stress is placed upon the church as the body of Christ. Here in Colossians, emphasis is upon Christ as the Head of the church, that body composed of all true saints regardless of denomination. As such, He directs the church. He is the brain, the boss. The pastor and deacons are not. All are to take their orders from Christ the Head and from His Word, the Bible. This is emphatically stated—He alone, no one else!

The word "preeminence" is used three times in the KJV. In Ecclesiastes 3:19, it means profit, plenty, abundance, superiority. In 3 John 9, the word translated "preeminence" means to love or desire to be first, fond of striving after first place. In Colossians 1:18, "preeminence" means simply to be first in rank, hold the first place, to stand out before, to rise above. Thus it speaks of excellence, superiority, being outstanding! This is exactly what Jesus Christ is; His ranking is number one or first place. Why does He hold this rank?

For several reasons: As the beginning, He is the source, the origin. He is the leader, the active cause, the one by whom anything begins to be; he is the Alpha (Revelation 1:8, 11). Furthermore, He is the firstborn from the dead. Others were restored to life, but died again. Only Christ was resurrected and lives forevermore.

Finally, we learn that in Christ all the fullness of the Godhead was pleased to dwell. The word "dwell" speaks of permanent residence, not simply a temporary visit. Whereas the false teachers at Colosse used the word "fullness" to describe the supernatural powers that supposedly controlled the lives of men, the truth is that the sum total of all power is in Jesus Christ our Lord.

B. CHRIST THE RECONCILER
(Colossians 1:20-23)

And, having made peace through the blood of his cross, by him to reconcile all things unto himself; by him, I say, whether they be things in earth, or things in heaven. And you, that were sometime alienated and enemies in your mind by wicked works, yet now hath he reconciled in the body of his flesh through death, to present you holy and unblameable and unreproveable in his sight: If ye continue in the faith grounded and settled, and be not moved away from the hope of the gospel, which ye have heard, and which was preached to every creature which is under heaven; whereof I Paul am made a minister.

Note that verse 20 is part of verse 19. The fullness of which Paul spoke is manifested not only in creative work, but also in reconciliation. We see that all creation is involved—the sun, moon, animals, oceans, earth, angels, etc. Sin has cosmological consequences. Because of sin, we were alienated, estranged, turned away. Thus, we were at enmity with God. Our entire bent of mind was against Him, and naturally our deeds as expressions of that mind were against Him.

Christ established peace by paying the penalty for sin, satisfying the righteous justice of God. We were brought into a unity. This is to say we were reconciled or thoroughly changed. God has always loved us, but sin had clouded His face. This reconciliation was accomplished through His blood, His bodily physical death at Calvary. In this way we were presented, once for all, holy or separated unto God and Christ. We were presented blameless (faultless, without blemish, without blot or defect); and were exhibited above reproach in His sight. Men may think what they please. What really counts is what God says about us! Grounded and founded when hounded— the Colossian saints are warned to stick with the Gospel. Though troubled by phonies, false prophets, and bad doctrine dispensers, they are to remember that perseverance is the test of reality. Steadfastness in the faith is what counts! This section closes with Paul's assertion that as the apostle to the Gentiles, he has been assigned the task of preaching the Gospel for the benefit of all men everywhere.

C. CHRIST THE INDWELLER
(Colossians 1:24-28)

Who now rejoice in my sufferings for you, and fill up that which is behind of the afflictions of Christ in my flesh for his body's sake, which is the church: Whereof I am made a minister, according to the dispensation of God which is given to me for you, to fulfil the word of God; Even the mystery which hath been hid from ages and from generations, but now is made manifest to his saints: To whom God would make known what is the riches of the glory of this mystery among the Gentiles; which is Christ in you, the hope of glory: Whom we preach, warning every man, and teaching every man in all wisdom; that we may present every man perfect in Christ Jesus.

Paul desired to know more fully the fellowship of the suffering of Jesus Christ. By bearing adversity on behalf of the saints, he entered into the fellowship of Christ's suffering. Of course, our afflictions add nothing to the finished work of the Lord. We cannot take part in that suffering. However, there is a certain amount of suffering that we suffer, what we may call "the leftovers" which result from the world's hatred of Christ and His redeemed (Lenski). The apostle wanted to bear all he could so that other believers might have less to suffer. He felt that this was his God-given ministry or stewardship (dispensation, order, or responsibility).

A mystery in the biblical sense is that which man cannot discover, but which must be revealed to him by God. The mystery in today's lesson is that Jesus Christ lives in believers. The Lord had promised to dwell in His own (John 14:20, 17:23). We have eternal life because He lives within us. The lesson closes with a threefold purpose of the church.

First, we are to Evangelize the Cosmos—the Sinners. It is not God's desire that any one should perish. Note the phrase "every man" is used three times in verse 28. This repetition speaks of universality.

Second, we are to Edify the Christians—the Saints. God's desire is for the Christian to be complete, spiritually mature, fully developed, grownup, and adult—not babes.

Third, we are to Exalt the Christ—the Savior. Unbelievers are to be won to Jesus Christ. Believers are to be edified, made perfect or mature in Christ.

III. Special Features

A. PRESERVING OUR HERITAGE

It appears that in some of our churches it is no longer true that everything that goes on in church is for the edification of the saints. Paul, like every true preacher of the Gospel, was jealous of the soul welfare of all whom God put in his charge. God wants the best for every one of us. This is why Paul's ministry was one of preaching Christ, warning, and teaching.

I was in West Virginia serving as a Bible teacher when the preacher for the day said to me, "You know the motto of the Baptists, don't you? It's WIN 'em, WASH 'em, and WORK 'em." We laughed, but the more I thought about it, the sadder I became. It is true that some pastors make it their policy to keep members "busy." They point out the fellowship and cohesiveness provided.

But all too often what is called fellowship is not. The spirit of competition, raising money instead of being taught how to give, often demonstrates a restlessness that we attempt to cure by keeping folks "busy." A. W. Tozer said the word "program" as we use it in the church was borrowed from the stage and applied with sad wisdom to the type of public service that now passes for worship among us. All too often, we are clubbed to death! Unfortunately, tradition has blinded some of our churches to their real purpose.

B. A CONCLUDING WORD

F. B. Meyer said, "In all His people Christ is present. In some He is prominent. In a few He is preeminent." Which is He for you? May it be that all of us will cry out, "Have first place, Lord!" He who is preeminent is also the Eminent One whose coming is imminent. And when He comes, we will be changed. He has first place because He is the head of our lives, our King eternal, our Boss, Employer, Lord, Savior, Sovereign, Owner. Christ is above all!

HOME DAILY BIBLE READINGS FOR THE WEEK OF AUGUST 6, 2000

THE SUPREMACY OF CHRIST

July 31	M.	Colossians 1:1-8, Paul Gives Thanks for the Colossians
Aug. 1	T.	Colossians 1:9-14, Paul Prays for the Colossian Christians
Aug. 2	W.	Colossians 1:15-20, The Fullness of God Dwelled in Christ
Aug. 3	T.	Colossians 1:21-29, God's Mystery Revealed to the Saints
Aug. 4	F.	John 1:1-9, Jesus Christ: God's Word and Light
Aug. 5	S.	John 1:10-18, God's Word Lived Among Us
Aug. 6	S.	Hebrews 1:1-14, Christ Is Superior Even to Angels

Know Your Bible

• King Uzziah prospered during the times when he sought the Lord. (2 Chronicles 26:1-5)

O God, who revealed Yourself in the person of Jesus Christ, grant us the desire to surrender to the supremacy of Your will as embodied in His life of love and service. Amen.

A Complete Life in Christ

Adult Topic—*The Fullness of Life*

.....

Youth Topic—*A Full Life in Christ*
Children's Topic—*Jesus Wants Us to Be Faithful*

.....

Devotional Reading—Romans 8:31-39
Background Scripture—Colossians 2:6-19
Print—Colossians 2:6-19

PRINTED SCRIPTURE

Colossians 2:6-19 (KJV)

6 As ye have therefore received Christ Jesus the Lord, so walk ye in him:

7 Rooted and built up in him, and stablished in the faith, as ye have been taught, abounding therein with thanksgiving.

8 Beware lest any man spoil you through philosophy and vain deceit, after the tradition of men, after the rudiments of the world, and not after Christ.

9 For in him dwelleth all the fulness of the Godhead bodily.

10 And ye are complete in him, which is the head of all principality and power:

11 In whom also ye are circumcised with the circumcision made without hands, in putting off the body of the sins of the flesh by the circumcision of Christ:

12 Buried with him in baptism, wherein also ye are risen with him through the faith of the operation of God, who hath raised him from the dead.

Colossians 2:6-19 (NRSV)

6 As you therefore have received Christ Jesus the Lord, continue to live your lives in him,

7 rooted and built up in him and established in the faith, just as you were taught, abounding in thanksgiving.

8 See to it that no one takes you captive through philosophy and empty deceit, according to human tradition, according to the elemental spirits of the universe, and not according to Christ.

9 For in him the whole fullness of deity dwells bodily,

10 and you have come to fullness in him, who is the head of every ruler and authority.

11 In him also you were circumcised with a spiritual circumcision, by putting off the body of the flesh in the circumcision of Christ;

12 when you were buried with him in baptism, you were also raised with him through faith in the power of God, who raised him from the dead.

13 And you, being dead in your sins and the uncircumcision of your flesh, hath he quickened together with him, having forgiven you all trespasses;

14 Blotting out the handwriting of ordinances that was against us, which was contrary to us, and took it out of the way, nailing it to his cross;

15 And having spoiled principalities and powers, he made a shew of them openly, triumphing over them in it.

16 Let no man therefore judge you in meat, or in drink, or in respect of an holy day, or of the new moon, or of the sabbath days:

17 Which are a shadow of things to come; but the body is of Christ.

18 Let no man beguile you of your reward in a voluntary humility and worshipping of angels, intruding into those things which he hath not seen, vainly puffed up by his fleshly mind,

19 And not holding the Head, from which all the body by joints and bands having nourishment ministered, and knit together, increaseth with the increase of God.

13 And when you were dead in trespasses and the uncircumcision of your flesh, God made you alive together with him, when he forgave us all our trespasses,

14 erasing the record that stood against us with its legal demands. He set this aside, nailing it to the cross.

15 He disarmed the rulers and authorities and made a public example of them, triumphing over them in it.

16 Therefore do not let anyone condemn you in matters of food and drink or of observing festivals, new moons, or sabbaths.

17 These are only a shadow of what is to come, but the substance belongs to Christ.

18 Do not let anyone disqualify you, insisting on self-abasement and worship of angels, dwelling on visions, puffed up without cause by a human way of thinking,

19 and not holding fast to the head, from whom the whole body, nourished and held together by its ligaments and sinews, grows with a growth that is from God.

KEY VERSE

As ye have therefore received Christ Jesus the Lord, so walk ye in him: Rooted and built up in him, and stablished in the faith, as ye have been taught, abounding therein with thanksgiving.
—*Colossians 2:6-7*

OBJECTIVES

After reading this lesson, the student should know that:

1. God desires that believers guard against deception;
2. There are no rituals required for salvation; and
3. All the Christian needs is found in Christ.

POINTS TO BE EMPHASIZED
Adult/Youth
Key Verse: Colossians 2:6-7
Print: Colossians 2:6-19

—Paul exhorted the Colossians to live their lives in Christ and to remain faithful to Him. (6-7)

—Believers were cautioned against allowing themselves to be deceived by philosophies that are contrary to Christ's teachings. (8)

—Christ is the Head of every ruler and authority, and everything needed for religious life can be found in Him. (9-10)

—God's forgiveness, through Christ's death and resurrection, brings new life. (11-15)

—Ritual practices should not interfere with loyalty to Christ from whom all nourishment comes. (16-19)

Children
Key Verse: 2 Timothy 1:7
Print: Colossians 2:6, 7; 2 Timothy 1:3-8, 13, 14; 3:14, 15

—Paul exhorted the Colossians to live their lives in Christ and remain faithful to Him. (Colossians 2: 6, 7)

—Paul told Timothy that he prayed constantly, thanking God for him and desiring to see him. (2 Timothy 1:3, 4)

—Paul reminded Timothy of his heritage of faith going back to his grandmother and mother. (5)

—Paul urged Timothy to use his spiritual gifts without fear or shame but with power, love, and self discipline. (6-8)

—Paul exhorted Timothy to maintain, with the help of the Holy Spirit, the purity of the faith entrusted to him. (13, 14)

—Paul charged Timothy to continue in his beliefs, knowing that he learned them from the sacred writings as a child. (3:14, 15)

(**NOTE**: Use KJV Scripture for Adult; NRSV Scripture for Youth and Children)

TOPICAL OUTLINES OF THE LESSON

I. Introduction
A. Circumcision
B. Biblical Background

II. Exposition and Application of the Scripture
A. Caution: Danger (Colossians 2:6-8)
B. Completeness: Doctrine (Colossians 2:9-15)
C. Criticism: Direction (Colossians 2:16-19)

III. Special Features
A. Preserving Our Heritage
B. A Concluding Word

I. Introduction

A. CIRCUMCISION

Physical circumcision is not in view here. However, it is interesting that the very day this lesson was prepared, the American Academy of Pediatrics issued a strong statement saying there were too few medical benefits to justify recommending circumcision. It was admitted that there are "some potential medical benefits," but they are not considered "compelling enough to warrant recommending routine newborn circumcision." However, religious and cultural customs that favor circumcision should be maintained. And remember, there are some physical benefits for circumcision.

With respect to the ritual of circumcision, the apostle divides mankind into three groups. One, the uncircumcised are the Gentiles. Two, the Jews are those circumcised in the flesh. Three, the Christians are the circumcision made without hands. In Jewish society, the baby boy's flesh was cut when he was eight days old. This custom was instituted as a sign of God's covenant with Abraham (Genesis 17:9-14). In time, men began to depend more on the cutting of the flesh than on obeying God's will. Hear God saying, "Therefore circumcise the foreskin of your heart, and be stiffnecked no longer" (Deuteronomy 10:16).

Reference to circumcision of Christ (verse 11) is a reference to His death. This circumcision does not pertain to the physical body of Christ (Colossians 1:22) or of the believer. Rather this is a spiritual reality, "an ethical circumcision in which the sin nature which is found in the flesh" of the believer is put to death (Chafer). It is as if the foreskin represents man's Adamic nature, that which is a hindrance to spirituality, and so it is cut loose. Christ's death is seen as judgment of the believer's sin nature.

B. BIBLICAL BACKGROUND

The saints at Rome were warned, "Note those who cause divisions and offenses, contrary to the doctrine which you learned, and avoid them. For those who are such do not serve our Lord Jesus Christ, but their own belly, and by smooth words and flattering speech deceive the hearts of the simple" (Romans 16:17-18). The saints at Corinth were told that Paul's speech and preaching (heralding) were not with persuasive words of human wisdom (1 Corinthians 2:4), or as Simon Peter said, with feigned words (2 Peter 2:32).

Note Paul's concern lest the saints at Colosse are "beguiled with enticing words" (KJV) or "deceived with persuasive words" (NKJV). The apostle speaks of cheating or deceiving by false reason (James 1:22), and the use of plausible (but false) arguments in speech adapted to persuade, and lead others into error (Arndt & Gingrich). As the Church age draws to a close, there will be more and more false doctrine spread within Christendom. Obviously, Satan's strategy from the very beginning has been to deceive. You can see why the apostle Paul was led of the Holy Spirit to emphasize teaching true doctrine, while warning against that which is false.

II. Exposition and Application of the Scripture

A. CAUTION: DANGER
(Colossians 2:6-8)

As ye have therefore received Christ Jesus the Lord, so walk ye in him: Rooted and built up in him, and stablished in the faith, as ye have been taught, abounding therein with thanksgiving. Beware lest any man spoil you through philosophy and vain deceit, after the tradition of men, after the rudiments of the world, and not after Christ.

Paul encourages the saints to continue in the same way they began, the way of faith. As we received Christ by faith, so we are to live (walk). Our conduct must match our talk. The word received speaks of a personal appropriation, a "taking hold of" Christ Jesus the Lord (His full salvation title). If Christ has been truly received, then go walk forward. Step out on Him. Paul's admonition to the saints at Colosse is for them to continue in the transmission of the Christian faith.

How strange it sounds to be told to keep walking rooted! "Having been rooted" is the proper rendering. We have been firmly grounded, fixed firm, anchored by the deep roots of faith, and we are thus able to survive the strong winds of adversity. Paul mixed his figures of speech. Exhorted to walk as living men, take root like a tree, now he exhorts, continue built up like a house! A fifth verb is "established" and the command is to continue being strengthened, confirmed, or consolidated with respect to what we believe.

"You are being established in the faith which you were taught." What Epaphras taught and they believed is constantly divinely confirmed. This shows that the doctrine is genuine, complete in every way. Finally, there is the seventh verb, "abounding." We are to continuously overflow in thanksgiving. Understand then that this aspect of the fullness of life in Christ involves these seven verbs: receiving, walking, being rooted, and built up, established, taught and abounding.

Another danger is having our faith spoiled through philosophy (the love of wisdom) or what J. B. Phillips calls "intellectualism," and vain deceit, which Phillips calls "high-sounding nonsense." Reject whatever man offers contrary to the Scriptures or that disregards the Lord Jesus Christ. Do not let man-made philosophies take you captive. There are many different ideas about the meaning of the phrase, "rudiments of the world," or "basic principles," (verse eight). MacDonald suggests they are "Jewish rituals, ceremonies, and ordinances by which men hoped to obtain God's favor." Pilgrim Bible states they are "religious rites."

B. COMPLETENESS: DOCTRINE
(Colossians 2:9-15)

For in him dwelleth all the fulness of the Godhead bodily. And ye are complete in him, which is the head of all principality and power. In whom also ye are circumcised with the circumcision made without hands, in putting off the body of the sins of the flesh by the circumcision of Christ: Buried with him in baptism, wherein also ye are risen with him through the faith of the operation of God, who hath raised him from the dead. And you, being dead in your sins and the uncircumcision

of your flesh, hath he quickened together with him, having forgiven you all trespasses; Blotting out the handwriting of ordinances that was against us, which was contrary to us, and took it out of the way, nailing it to his cross; And having spoiled principalities and powers, he made a shew of them openly, triumphing over them in it.

We are complete in Christ. We need not add baptismal formulas, speaking in tongues, a trip to Mecca, worshiping only on Saturdays, circumcision, etc. In Christ, we are justified, sanctified and glorified (Romans 8:30). This is what being complete means. Use of the perfect passive tense means that at some time in the past we are completed, we are so right now, and we continue to be so by the power of God. Furthermore, we are fit for heaven right now, for no matter what condition the believer is in he or she will have to be changed anyway to enter God's heaven! (1 Corinthians 15:51-52).

In connection with Jesus Christ we have been made full, complete, made exactly what we ought to be. No religious rites are needed. Christ needs no supplement. What the Judaizers and Gnostics claim essential means absolutely nothing so far as salvation is concerned. Deity in its totality is in Christ. There is no element of the divine nature absent in Christ. The adverb "bodily" emphasizes the manner of the indwelling. He is still a human being and will be for all eternity. He is still the God-Man. Thus, the Incarnation is asserted.

Circumcision is not needed to make us complete. The fullness of Deity is corporately in Christ. Baptism puts us into the body of Christ, but water baptism is only symbolic of what the Holy Spirit has done already. When Christ died, we died. When He was buried, we were buried. And when He rose from the grave, we also rose. Consequently, we live as people upon whom the great initial blessing of forgiveness has been bestowed already.

The principalities and powers in Colossians 2:10 may be good angelic beings. But in Colossians 2:15, the "spoiled principalities and powers" are evil angels, wicked spirits. There is joy in knowing that the Law observances were abolished in Christ. Neither Jew nor Gentile could keep the law of conscience in their hearts. But the Mosaic Law lay even heavier upon the Jew. So here the certificate of debt presumably refers to the written Law of Moses, including the Ten Commandments, as well as ceremonial laws.

By dying on the Cross, Christ took care of the penalty for disobeying, blotting out, wiping away, erasing, obliterating, and canceling it as one does when paying a debt. Indeed, these are expressions of forgiveness, for our sins were nailed to the cross, and we bear them no more. Christ spoiled, disarmed or put off these forces. In Old Testament times, captives were stripped of most or all of their clothing. Nakedness symbolized defeat, disgrace, and the result of God's judgment. One stripped naked is devoid of all authoritative power. This is the idea seen here. Not only were the principalities and powers conquered, but their cover was blown also. Christ makes a show of them openly; He pulled off their cover! At Calvary, the Lord publicly and boldly disgraced the powers of evil, bearing away the sin which was their claim and hold on man.

C. CRITICISM: DIRECTION
(Colossians 2:16-19)

Let no man therefore judge you in meat, or in drink, or in respect of an holy day, or of the new moon, or of the sabbath days: which are a shadow of things to come; but the body is of Christ. Let no man beguile you of your reward in a voluntary humility and worshipping of angels, intruding into those things which he hath not seen, vainly puffed up by his fleshly mind, And not holding the Head, from which all the body by joints and bands having nourishment ministered, and knit together, increaseth with the increase of God.

As has been said before, "therefore" is there for a reason. Here the word refers to verses 14 and 15. Because Christ canceled the bond against us, because Christ triumphed over all evil powers, therefore let absolutely nobody judge you in the following matters:

(1) Food and drink. Literally, the word for food is "eating." On this matter, read Acts 10:9-16 and 1 Timothy 4:3-5. Paul pleads for liberty, for the kingdom of God is not food and drink. His desire for the saints at Colosse is that they will not make a religious obligation out of rules concerning what to eat and drink or not eat and drink.

(2) Observance of festivals, holidays, new moons or sabbaths. Just what the heretics at Colosse demanded with respect to these matters is not known. Paul wanted it known that these things are not to be demanded as aids to the Christian life or as a basis for salvation. All rites and ceremonies men would add to improve Christianity are useless. As someone has said: "The dirty rags of legalism

add nothing to the silk robe of liberty in Christ."

Sabbatarians or Christians who insist on keeping the Sabbath or Saturday as the special day of worship, and who teach it is a sin not to observe it, are cut down by Colossians 2:16. Such observances are mere shadows of what is to come. Why chase after the shadows when the substance is Christ?

Paul next warned against false mysticism—insight or knowledge of God attained through intuition, inner light, visions, etc. Verse 18 is a difficult one. The verb rendered "beguile you of" or "keep defrauding you of" is used only here in the New Testament. In verse 4, a different word is used, and it means to try to cheat or trick. In verse 18, it is let no one "deny you the prize." What prize?

The prize of being honored and esteemed as good Christians because you do not pose as humble creatures or worship angels! All such is false humility and false worship that tends only to inflate empty minds. Imagine people pretending to be so humble that they dare not approach God directly! Finally, see the effect of such false religion. They let go of Christ, the Head. If He is not your Head, you are not in the body.

Spiritual growth comes from God. Inner spiritual growth comes from Christ. The Head has supplied us with the written Word, and from it we gain sustenance and become more like Jesus Christ. So pay no attention to those who criticize you because of what you eat or drink or because you fail to keep or observe certain days. Since the Savior has come the symbol is not needed.

III. Special Features

A. PRESERVING OUR HERITAGE

Have you ever wondered why Black Americans seem prone to allow themselves to be deceived by philosophies that are contrary to the teachings of Christ? Is it because of the racism we experience, so that we join racist-minded cults? Unfortunately, some of the most theologically conservative schools have been guilty of segregation.

Is it because of lack of doctrinal preaching and teaching in our churches? Is there still a slave mentality that goads us into thinking we can work our way to heaven? Has our low position on the economic totem pole moved us to emphasize the here and now, so that the group that offers material goods attracts us?

What do you think? Inasmuch as the lesson repeatedly warns us to "beware," let no one "beguile" you, what steps should we take to remain steadfast in the calling wherewith we have been called, and seek to live a complete life in Christ?

B. A CONCLUDING WORD

The teaching that Jesus Christ is but one rung among many on some imagined ladder to God is false. Paul wants it known that in Jesus Christ the fullness of the Godhead dwells bodily permanently. So that, there are no go-betweens, no intermediaries by whom man must enter into the presence of God as proclaimed by those eventually called Gnostics. Jesus Christ is the One Mediator between God and men (1 Timothy 2:5).

HOME DAILY BIBLE READINGS FOR THE WEEK OF AUGUST 13, 2000

A COMPLETE LIFE IN CHRIST

Aug.	7	M.	Colossians 2:1-5, Paul Commends the Colossian Christians
Aug.	8	T.	Colossians 2:6-10, God Dwells Fully in Jesus Christ
Aug.	9	W.	Colossians 2:11-16, Dead to the Flesh, Alive in Christ
Aug.	10	T.	Colossians 2:17-23, Hold Fast to Christ, Our Head
Aug.	11	F.	Hebrews 8:1-7, Jesus: Mediator of a New Covenant
Aug.	12	S.	Hebrews 9:11-15, The Blood of Christ Purifies Us
Aug.	13	S.	Hebrews 10:11-18, Christ Perfected Those Who Are Sanctified

O God, who has created us for thyself so that our hearts are restless until they find rest in Thee, grant that we may come to know the completeness that is found in Jesus Christ our Lord who by love has created us anew in Your image and likeness. In Jesus' name. Amen.

The Way to Righteousness

Adult Topic—*The Way of Life*

•••••

Youth Topic—*Life on a Higher Level*

Children's Topic—*Jesus Tells Us How to Live*

•••••

Devotional Reading—Mark 12:28-34

Background Scripture—Colossians 3:1-17

Print—Colossians 3:1-3, 5-17

PRINTED SCRIPTURE

Colossians 3:1-3, 5-17 (KJV)

IF YE then be risen with Christ, seek those things which are above, where Christ sitteth on the right hand of God.

2 Set your affection on things above, not on things on the earth.

3 For ye are dead, and your life is hid with Christ in God.

•••••

5 Mortify therefore your members which are upon the earth; fornication, uncleanness, inordinate affection, evil concupiscence, and covetousness, which is idolatry:

6 For which things' sake the wrath of God cometh on the children of disobedience:

7 In the which ye also walked some time, when ye lived in them.

8 But now ye also put off all these; anger, wrath, malice, blasphemy, filthy communication out of your mouth.

9 Lie not one to another, seeing that ye have put off the old man with his deeds;

10 And have put on the new man, which is renewed in knowledge after

Colossians 3:1-3, 5-17 (NRSV)

SO IF you have been raised with Christ, seek the things that are above, where Christ is, seated at the right hand of God.

2 Set your minds on things that are above, not on things that are on earth,

3 for you have died, and your life is hidden with Christ in God.

•••••

5 Put to death, therefore, whatever in you is earthly: fornication, impurity, passion, evil desire, and greed (which is idolatry).

6 On account of these the wrath of God is coming on those who are disobedient.

7 These are the ways you also once followed, when you were living that life.

8 But now you must get rid of all such things—anger, wrath, malice, slander, and abusive language from your mouth.

9 Do not lie to one another, seeing that you have stripped off the old self with its practices

10 and have clothed yourselves with the new self, which is being

the image of him that created him:

11 Where there is neither Greek nor Jew, circumcision nor uncircumcision, Barbarian, Scythian, bond nor free: but Christ is all, and in all.

12 Put on therefore, as the elect of God, holy and beloved, bowels of mercies, kindness, humbleness of mind, meekness, longsuffering;

13 Forbearing one another, and forgiving one another, if any man have a quarrel against any: even as Christ forgave you, so also do ye.

14 And above all these things put on charity, which is the bond of perfectness.

15 And let the peace of God rule in your hearts, to the which also ye are called in one body; and be ye thankful.

16 Let the word of Christ dwell in you richly in all wisdom; teaching and admonishing one another in psalms and hymns and spiritual songs, singing with grace in your hearts to the Lord.

17 And whatsoever ye do in word or deed, do all in the name of the Lord Jesus, giving thanks to God and the Father by him.

renewed in knowledge according to the image of its creator.

11 In that renewal there is no longer Greek and Jew, circumcised and uncircumcised, Barbarian, Scythian, slave and free; but Christ is all and in all!

12 As God's chosen ones, holy and beloved, clothe yourselves with compassion, kindness, humility, meekness, and patience.

13 Bear with one another and, if anyone has a complaint against another, forgive each other; just as the Lord has forgiven you, so you also must forgive.

14 Above all, clothe yourselves with love, which binds everything together in perfect harmony.

15 And let the peace of Christ rule in your hearts, to which indeed you were called in the one body. And be thankful.

16 Let the word of Christ dwell in you richly; teach and admonish one another in all wisdom; and with gratitude in your hearts sing psalms, hymns, and spiritual songs to God.

17 And whatever you do, in word or deed, do everything in the name of the Lord Jesus, giving thanks to God the Father through him.

 **KEY VERSE** *And whatsoever ye do in word or deed, do all in the name of the Lord Jesus, giving thanks to God and the Father by him.—**Colossians 3:17***

OBJECTIVES

After reading this lesson, the student should better appreciate:

1. The Christian's position or standing in Christ;
2. What the new life in Christ means;
3. Why God reminds us of what we used to do; and
4. Ways in which Christians can get along with each other.

Adult/Youth/Children
Key Verse: Colossians 3:17
Print: Colossians 3:1-3, 5-17; Colossians 3:8-17 *(Children)*

—Paul told the Colossians that life in Christ means lifting the conduct of life to a higher level, for they were one with Christ. (1-3)

—Christians must put aside sinful behavior and live as new creations in Christ. (5-11)

—As the Lord has forgiven them, the Colossians should forgive each other and live with compassion, kindness, humility, meekness, and patience. (12, 13)

—Practice love which produces harmony, so that the peace of Christ can rule in the hearts of Christians. (14, 15)

—Christians should teach and admonish each other in wisdom and sing praises to God. (16)

—Paul exhorted that whatever the Colossians say or do, it should be done in the name of Jesus and in gratitude to God. (17)

(**NOTE**: Use KJV Scripture for Adults; NRSV Scripture for Youth and Children)

TOPICAL OUTLINE OF THE LESSON

I. Introduction

A. Thanksgiving
B. Biblical Background

II. Exposition and Application of the Scripture

A. Union With Christ (Colossians 3:1-3)
B. Living for Christ (Colossians 3:5-11)
C. Forgiven By Christ (Colossians 3:12-14)
D. Thanksgiving for Christ (Colossians 3:15-17)

III. Special Features

A. Preserving Our Heritage
B. A Concluding Word

I. Introduction

A. THANKSGIVING

In Colossians 3:15, we have the command, "and be thankful." Use of the present imperative makes it, "be ever thankful." The same word is used in Colossians 3:17, "thanking God the Father" through Jesus Christ. The Greek word is *eucharisteo*. Literally, it means well-graced or well-favored. *Charis* means grace. One who is grateful is thankful. Note that to say grace before eating is to give thanks. The word *Eu* is a prefix meaning noble, good, well, happily, rightly. We see it in such words a Eugene (noble birth, well born). Eulogy (praise or well-spoken of), and euthanasia (good death). Eucharist is a word with a special meaning that came about because in the "Holy Communion the Church embodies her highest act of thanksgiving for the highest benefits which she has received of God" (Trench). In Roman Catholicism, the Eucharist is the sacrament of the Lord's Supper or Holy Communion. Baptists do not use the term, nor do we believe in what are called "sacraments." For us the Lord's Supper is an ordinance.

For our present study, we see thanksgiving as a part of prayer that expresses "grateful acknowledgment of past mercies, as distinguished from the earnest seeking of future." In verse 15, we are to be ever thankful that the peace of God or peace of Christ acts as umpire in our hearts assuring us we are God's beloved. In verse 17, we learn that "the favors for which thanks are given and the gratitude which prompts the thanks are due to Christ, through Him, and by Christ's help" (Thayer: Romans 1:8, 7:25). We ever revel in the sunshine of gratitude to our Father in heaven through Jesus Christ in whom all good words are spoken and deeds are done.

B. BIBLICAL BACKGROUND

Once again, the matter of positional truth is important in understanding our lesson. When Christ died, we died, for we were in Him. Likewise when He rose, we rose. That is why we have a life that may be hidden with Christ in God. Obviously, we did not die physically, so that what we have here is a positional truth.

Our relationship with the old order or the Adamic self was terminated. It was slain. This is our position, the way God the Father sees us. This is our standing in His sight, for He looks at us through the eyes of Jesus Christ. Consequently, the things of this world-system no longer affect us the way they used to. The old life and all that belonged to it do not move us anymore. Why? Because we died to them.

This is why the apostle exhorts us to seek and mind things above, where Jesus Christ is seated at the right hand of the Father. We are to be heavenly-minded because we died to earthly things; the things here on earth filled our thoughts, consumed our energy, controlled our activities, and guided our passions. To all such things God has declared we died!

II. Exposition and Application of the Scripture

A. UNION WITH CHRIST
(Colossians 3:1-3)

If ye then be risen with Christ, seek those things which are above, where Christ sitteth on the right hand of God. Set your affection on things above, not on things on the earth. For ye are dead, and your life is hid with Christ in God.

It is a fact that the genuine Christian has been raised with Jesus Christ. When He rose from the grave, we rose.

The word "if" is better rendered "since." As Ephesians 2:6 points out, we have been raised up together, and made to sit together in the heavenly places in Christ Jesus. This positional truth moves us to say goodbye to the old way of life, and hello to the new life in Christ. Our outlook on life is no longer earthbound. Rather, we are seeking continuously those things that are above. As C. A. Tindley put it: Nothing between my soul and the Savior. Naught of this world's delusive dream; I have renounced all sinful pleasure; Jesus is mine; there's nothing between. Nothing between my soul and the Savior, So that His blessed face may be seen; nothing preventing the least of His favor, Keep the way clear! Let nothing between.

Our eyes are upon the Lord Jesus who sat down at the right hand of the majesty on high (Hebrews 1:3), having cleansed away our sins once for all. The right hand of God the Father signifies a place of power and authority; Christ is seated exalted there. The Christian is exhorted not only to practice seeking spiritual things, but also to keep on thinking about heavenly things. Be heavenly minded! See and think about life through the eyes of God and according to His Word. Observe things in the light of eternity. The statement that our lives have been hidden with Christ in God means that the world cannot see or understand the believer. What we truly are will be made manifest to the world at a later time (Romans 8:18). Our spiritual life is hidden to the sin-blinded eyes of the world. While we exist in the world, our true life is centered around heaven. There, is located not only our treasure, but the very basis of our being.

B. LIVING FOR CHRIST
Colossians 3:5-11)

Mortify therefore your members which are upon the earth; fornication, uncleanness, inordinate affection, evil concupiscence, and covetousness, which is idolatry: For which things' sake the wrath of God cometh on the children of disobedience: In the which ye also walked some time, when ye lived in them. But now ye also put off all these; anger, wrath, malice, blasphemy, filthy communication out of your mouth. Lie not one to another, seeing that ye have put off the old man with his deeds; And have put on the new man, which is renewed in knowledge after the image of him that created him: Where there is neither Greek nor Jew, circumcision nor uncircumcision, Barbarian, Scythian, bond nor free: but Christ is all, and in all.

The verb (*nekroo*) translated "mortify" means to put to death, to slay. We have derived the word necromancy from it. God hates necromancy (Deuteronomy 18:11), seeking signs from corpses, and attempting to communicate with the dead. Mortify is an English word with Latin roots, and we see the "mort" in mortician, another word for undertaker.

Our "members" are our bodily organs, attitudes and actions. Now if the believers are dead already, why must they mortify their members? It is because God wants us to see the implications of our new position. All positional truths have practical implications. Such truths are to be made objectively true. There is no real dichotomy or split between ethics and doctrine or deeds and beliefs. Doctrine is the basis for ethics. What a man believes does determine to a large degree what he does.

Consider now the thing that should be put to death, and keep in mind that there is a tremendous emphasis on sexual sins. Sexual immorality was the cardinal offense of the pagan world in Paul's day (MacDonald). First is fornication (*porneia*) or illicit sexual relations in general. Our word pornography is seen here. As a figure of speech, fornication means idol worship (Revelation 14:8), but here in Colossians 3:5 it is literally sexual immorality.

A second sin is uncleanness. Morally it is "the impurity of lustful, luxurious profligate living" (Thayer), or what Arndt and Gingrich call "impurity, dirt; immorality, viciousness, especially of sexual sins."

Third, inordinate affection is called passion (NKJV), especially of a sexual nature (Arndt & Gingrich). The Greek word pathos. Used in a bad sense it means depraved desire or passion.

The fourth word is evil concupiscence (Latin for strong desire) or evil desire (NKJV), or the craving or lust for something forbidden (Thayer). Covetousness, which is idolatry, is the fifth item. The Greek word means "eager to have more." When we strongly desire to possess a thing, that thing to some degree actually possesses us, and becomes an idol or false god.

God's wrath or vengeance and terrible judgment are still on the divine schedule; sin is not regarded with indifference. God is not mocked by unbelievers or "sons of disobedience." Certainty and imminence are denoted (John 3:18, 36) by the use of the present tense, "is coming." And we Christians are reminded of our former estate also (verse 7); the imperfect tense speaks of the time when we "used to live" in such vices. Constant conduct is implied.

We are to take off the following evils, as we would disrobe from dirty clothes. First mentioned is anger, or uncontrolled temper, or deep-seated emotion of resentment that we call a slow burn; wrath or boiling agitation is that explosive, fiery outburst of temper or violent fit of rage. Put off malice, that vicious disposition to harm the person or reputation, accompanied by rejoicing in evil to others. Blasphemy is slander, evil speaking or what we call "bad-mouthing." Finally, in verse 8, there is filthy language out of our mouths. We daily hear such obscene speech; dirt that comes out of the mouth has a dirty heart as its source.

Saints are told to stop lying (present tense imperative or command forbids continuing an action that is going on). Often liars in the Bible caused the deaths of those they lied on. We are to obey these exhortations because we have put off the old man with his deeds. The old man is the unregenerate nature, unrenewed, and corrupt. He is old because he is derived from Adam by way of our natural birth. The old nature is the inborn, inherent, congenital sinful nature with all of its sinful thoughts, motives, emotions and volition.

The new man is "new" (*neo*) in existence (Colossians 3:10) and "new" (*kainos*) in quality or difference also (Ephesians 4:24). Positionally, we have disrobed the old man forever. Experimentally, he remains in us and can be controlled only by the indwelling of the

Holy Spirit. The new man is constantly being renewed, daily growing and developing, becoming more like the Lord Jesus Christ. In Christ, all believers stand on level ground. National, cultural, social, racial and economic differences mean nothing. The God of the Bible is no respecter of faces, races or places. Christ is all and in all!

C. FORGIVEN BY CHRIST
(Colossians 3:12-14)

Put on therefore, as the elect of God, holy and beloved, bowels of mercies, kindness, humbleness of mind, meekness, longsuffering; Forbearing one another, and forgiving one another, if any man have a quarrel against any: even as Christ forgave you, so also do ye. And above all these things put on charity, which is the bond of perfectness.

Having been told what to put off, now we are told what to put on. As the elect of God, chosen in Him before the foundation of the world, we are told with a sense of urgency to clothe ourselves at once with tender mercies. The bowels (viscera) were regarded as the seat of the affections; thus the phrase means a "heart of pity." Put on kindness, humility or modesty, and meekness which is not weakness but is the opposite of arrogance and self-assertion; and longsuffering which is patience under provocation, a restraint that enables you to put up with insult without seeking revenge.

The Holy Spirit in us enables us to put up with the idiosyncrasies of fellow saints. Even as Christ freely forgave us of our faults and follies, we should forgive one another. Christians learn to disagree without being disagreeable. As we discovered earlier, the Greek word for forgiveness here has in it the root meaning grace and the unconditional bestowal of favor. Finally, love is described as the belt or outer garment that binds all the other virtues together.

D. THANKSGIVING FOR CHRIST
(Colossians 3:15-17)

And let the peace of God rule in your hearts, to the which also ye are called in one body; and be ye thankful. Let the word of Christ dwell in you richly in all wisdom; teaching and admonishing one another in psalms and hymns and spiritual songs, singing with grace in your hearts to the Lord. And whatsoever ye do in word or deed, do all in the name of the Lord Jesus, giving thanks to God and the Father by him.

Christ's peace acts as an umpire in our hearts. When occasions of dispute (quarrels or complaints) arise in the local assembly, the peace of Christ is to give the decision, the final say. It has been said, "Darkness about going is light about staying." So if you have no peace about a certain matter, then don't do it! In all of this a thankful spirit is important. Furthermore, saturate your heart and mind with the Word of Christ, the Bible. Teach and admonish (warn, exhort, literally, "put in mind") one another in psalms, hymns and spiritual songs. Do everything as in the presence and will of Jesus Christ. "In all relations of life, act as His representative, obeying His Word, trusting in His power, and devoted to His service" (Parallel Bible Commentary).

III. Special Features

A. PRESERVING OUR HERITAGE

The phrase "Greek nor Jew" refers to culture and religion. "Circumcision nor uncircumcision" points out the opposition between Jew and Gentile. Greeks called all people who did not speak Greek, barbarians (strangers, aliens). Scythians were uncivilized people who lived in Scythia, north of the Black Sea. Scythian is also the climax of barbarism, a savage. The Greeks despised the Jew; circumcision despised foreskin; a barbarian scorned a Scythian; and those who were free despised slaves.

What the apostle teaches (Colossians 3:11) is that racial, religious, and cultural differences are transcended in Christ. This seems a difficult thing for some American Christians to realize today. Is the Holy Spirit capable of removing barriers between black and white believers? Repeatedly, we are told that God is no receiver of faces. For in Him the old man is abolished and the new man has been created. In Him, all Christians are brothers and sisters.

B. A CONCLUDING WORD

Rejoice, believer, in the Lord, Who makes your cause His own;
The hope that's founded on His word Can ne'er be overthrown.
Though many foes beset your road, And feeble is your arm,
Your life is hid with Christ in God,
Beyond the reach of harm. (John Newton)

HOME DAILY BIBLE READINGS FOR THE WEEK OF AUGUST 20, 2000

THE WAY TO RIGHTEOUSNESS

Aug. 14 M.   Colossians 3:1-6, Revealed With Christ in Glory
Aug. 15 T.   Colossians 3:7-11, Put on the New Self
Aug. 16 W.   Colossians 3:12-17, Live Faithfully, Joyfully, and Give Thanks
Aug. 17 T.   Colossians 3:18—4:1, Love and Honor All People
Aug. 18 F.   Colossians 4:2-6, Live and Speak in Christian Love
Aug. 19 S.   Colossians 4:7-11, Paul's Faithful Support Community
Aug. 20 S.   Colossians 4:12-18, Paul's Final Greetings to the Colossians

O God, give us the grace to walk in the path of righteousness as set forth in Your Son Jesus Christ's suffering and death. Free us from the selfish bondage that imprisons us to the desires of the flesh that we may embrace that style of living revealed in the life of Your Son by whom we are saved. Amen.

Welcoming Others in Christ

Adult Topic—*The Grace of Life*

•••••

Youth Topic—*A Plea for Acceptance*
Children's Topic—*Jesus Wants Us to Be Friends in Christ*

•••••

Devotional Reading—James 2:1-13
Background Scripture—Philemon
Print—Philemon 4-21

PRINTED SCRIPTURE

Philemon 4-21 (KJV)

4 I thank my God, making mention of thee always in my prayers,

5 Hearing of thy love and faith, which thou hast toward the Lord Jesus, and toward all saints;

6 That the communication of thy faith may become effectual by the acknowledging of every good thing which is in you in Christ Jesus.

7 For we have great joy and consolation in thy love, because the bowels of the saints are refreshed by thee, brother.

8 Wherefore, though I might be much bold in Christ to enjoin thee that which is convenient,

9 Yet for love's sake I rather beseech thee, being such an one as Paul the aged, and now also a prisoner of Jesus Christ.

10 I beseech thee for my son Onesimus, whom I have begotten in my bonds:

11 Which in time past was to thee unprofitable, but now profitable to thee and to me:

Philemon 4-21 (NRSV)

4 When I remember you in my prayers, I always thank my God

5 because I hear of your love for all the saints and your faith toward the Lord Jesus.

6 I pray that the sharing of your faith may become effective when you perceive all the good that we may do for Christ.

7 I have indeed received much joy and encouragement from your love, because the hearts of the saints have been refreshed through you, my brother.

8 For this reason, though I am bold enough in Christ to command you to do your duty,

9 yet I would rather appeal to you on the basis of love—and I, Paul, do this as an old man, and now also as a prisoner of Christ Jesus.

10 I am appealing to you for my child, Onesimus, whose father I have become during my imprisonment.

11 Formerly he was useless to you, but now he is indeed useful

12 Whom I have sent again: thou therefore receive him, that is, mine own bowels:

13 Whom I would have retained with me, that in thy stead he might have ministered unto me in the bonds of the gospel:

14 But without thy mind would I do nothing; that thy benefit should not be as it were of necessity, but willingly.

15 For perhaps he therefore departed for a season, that thou shouldest receive him for ever;

16 Not now as a servant, but above a servant, a brother beloved, specially to me, but how much more unto thee, both in the flesh, and in the Lord?

17 If thou count me therefore a partner, receive him as myself.

18 If he hath wronged thee, or oweth thee aught, put that on mine account;

19 I Paul have written it with mine own hand, I will repay it: albeit I do not say to thee how thou owest unto me even thine own self besides.

20 Yea, brother, let me have joy of thee in the Lord: refresh my bowels in the Lord.

21 Having confidence in thy obedience I wrote unto thee, knowing that thou wilt also do more than I say.

both to you and to me.

12 I am sending him, that is, my own heart, back to you.

13 I wanted to keep him with me, so that he might be of service to me in your place during my imprisonment for the gospel;

14 but I preferred to do nothing without your consent, in order that your good deed might be voluntary and not something forced.

15 Perhaps this is the reason he was separated from you for a while, so that you might have him back forever,

16 no longer as a slave but more than a slave, a beloved brother—especially to me but how much more to you, both in the flesh and in the Lord.

17 So if you consider me your partner, welcome him as you would welcome me.

18 If he has wronged you in any way, or owes you anything, charge that to my account.

19 I, Paul, am writing this with my own hand: I will repay it. I say nothing about your owing me even your own self.

20 Yes, brother, let me have this benefit from you in the Lord! Refresh my heart in Christ.

21 Confident of your obedience, I am writing to you, knowing that you will do even more than I say.

KEY VERSE

That the communication of thy faith may become effectual by the acknowledging of every good thing which is in you in Christ Jesus.
—*Philemon 6*

OBJECTIVES

After reading this lesson, the student should realize that:

1. Christian brotherhood transcends slave-master relationships;
2. In Christ there are no classes, castes or colors;
3. Paul's actions do not show approval of slavery; and
4. Paul's actions sowed seeds for slavery's dissolution.

POINTS TO BE EMPHASIZED

Adult/Youth/Children
Key Verse: Philemon 6
Print: Philemon 4-21; Philemon 8-22 *(Children)*

—Paul wrote to Philemon expressing his thanks to God on hearing of Philemon's love for all Christians and his faith in the Lord Jesus. (4-5)

—Paul expressed his appreciation for Philemon's Christian love and faith. (6-7)

—Paul asked Philemon to welcome Onesimus back as a brother, rather than as a slave, even as he would welcome Paul. (8-17)

—Paul offered to right any wrong and repay any debt owed by Onesimus. (18, 19)

—Paul was confident that Philemon would do as expected and give reason for Paul to rejoice in the Lord Jesus. (20-21)

(**NOTE**: Use KJV Scripture for Adults; NRSV Scripture for Youth and Children)

TOPICAL OUTLINE OF THE LESSON

I. Introduction

    A. A Word About Slavery
    B. Biblical Background

II. Exposition and Application of the Scripture

    A. Thanksgiving Offered (Philemon 4-7)
    B. Intercession Made (Philemon 8-14)
    C. Relationships Noted (Philemon 15-20)
    D. Confidence Expressed (Philemon 21)

III. Special Features

    A. Preserving Our Heritage
    B. A Concluding Word

I. Introduction

A. A WORD ABOUT SLAVERY

It is estimated that the slave population in the Roman Empire at the time of Paul's ministry was sixty million. Life for slaves was difficult, for they were but chattel in the sight of the law; they were put on the same level with wagons and the animals that drew them. Slave masters had absolute power over their property; law offered the slaves no protection from the cruelty of their owners.

Slaves had no conjugal rights, although cohabitation was allowed at the master's pleasure. Those with families were liable to be split up at will and sold. Their owners could whip them, brand them, crucify them, and throw them to the wild beasts in the arena—do whatever they pleased. Men captured in wars, criminals, debtors—these were the main constituents of the vast slave population, in addition to those who were indentured servants or under voluntary contracts. Keep in mind that race or skin color, religion and education were not factors in determining who would be made slaves.

B. BIBLICAL BACKGROUND

The comments about slavery also serve as an introduction to the lesson. Paul wrote Philemon while he was imprisoned in Rome; five times in this brief letter he makes mention of his incarceration (verses 1, 9, 10, 13, 23) or bonds. Note the interesting titles in the introduction of the letter. In verse one, we find Paul's title as a prisoner of Jesus Christ. In this way he establishes his authorship of the epistle. Timothy is called a brother. Philemon is a beloved friend and fellow laborer.

This latter title is one used of those who labored with Paul in the spreading of the Gospel of the shed blood of Jesus Christ. Philemon had come to Christ by way of Paul's ministry, probably in Ephesus, and was used of the Lord. Apphia is a woman's name; she may have been the wife of Philemon. Archippus, "a fellow soldier," may have been their son.

From verse two, we see that the church began in private homes; it was not until several centuries later that separate buildings for worship were erected. There are scholars who suggest that once persecution begins to increase in America, Christians will once again be forced to meet in private homes. The salutation closes with Paul's usual greeting. Grace always comes before peace. Failure to accept the grace of God demonstrated in the Cross of Jesus Christ means that it is impossible to have peace with God. Both grace and peace are from God, our Father, and from the Lord Jesus Christ. Combining these titles in this way points to the Deity of our Lord.

II. Exposition and Application of the Scripture

A. THANKSGIVING OFFERED
(Philemon 4-7)

I thank my God, making mention of thee always in my prayers, Hearing of thy love and faith, which thou hast toward the Lord Jesus, and toward all saints; That the communication of thy faith may become effectual by the acknowledging of every good thing which is in you in Christ Jesus. For we have great joy and consolation in thy love, because the bowels of the saints are refreshed by thee, brother.

This section of thanksgiving is characteristic of Paul, for thanksgiving played a large part in Paul's prayer life. The apostle rejoices upon hearing of Philemon's love and faith for all the Christians. He is delighted to write these words about him, and thanks the Lord every time he mentions Philemon's name in prayer. The Christian grace and the devoted activity of Philemon provide a firm basis and warm encouragement for thanksgiving and rejoicing.

Surely such a person as Philemon would respond favorably to the request the apostle is about to make of him. Paul prays also that those helped by Philemon might acknowledge Philemon's good works as done for the Lord Jesus. Through this believer many saints had been refreshed. Evidently, Philemon had shown kindness to other slaves, and thereby stirred up the "tender compassions of the saints by the Christian love he exercised in fellowshipping slaves as brethren" (Lenski).

Philemon's faith was not an empty faith. We have too much of that empty-head, empty-heart, empty-hand type of faith today. We are warned in the Bible that the time would come when religious people would have a form and fashion of godliness, but deny the power of it (2 Timothy 3:5).

B. INTERCESSION MADE
(Philemon 8-14)

Wherefore, though I might be much bold in Christ to enjoin thee that which is convenient, Yet for love's sake I rather beseech thee, being such an one as Paul the aged, and now also a prisoner of Jesus Christ. I beseech thee for my son Onesimus, whom I have begotten in my bonds: Which in time past was to thee unprofitable, but now profitable to thee and to me: Whom I have sent again: thou therefore receive him, that is, mine own bowels: Whom I would have retained with me, that in thy stead he might have ministered unto me in the bonds of the gospel: But without thy mind would I do nothing; that thy benefit should not be as it were of necessity, but willingly.

As an apostle appointed by the Lord, Paul might have commanded Philemon to carry out his order. However, rather than command, Paul on account of love entreats Philemon. He lays aside his authority and relies only upon the persuasive power of love. He calls his request "that which is fitting," or befitting a believer. Paul had been in the work a long time, and even then suffered because of the work. He was probably between fifty and sixty years old, worn by persecutions and labor (Lenski).

Here Onesimus is named for the first time (verse 10). It appears Onesimus was a slave who ran away from his master, Philemon. We are told Onesimus may have "wronged" Philemon (verse 18). Possibly he stole some money or had run away because he disliked being a slave. We are not sure what Onesimus did, but it seems certain that Philemon was not a cruel, heartless master. As God would have it, the runaway slave somehow came in contact with Paul the prisoner, and was converted under Paul's ministry.

Because Paul had been instrumental in the conversion of Onesimus, he refers to him as his spiritual son, "begotten in my bonds." The name Onesimus was not an uncommon one for a slave in that time and region. It means useful, helpful, or profitable. Reflecting on the meaning of the name, the apostle in humor points out that he whose name means "useful" was formerly "useless," but now to both Paul and Philemon he is "useful." Once useless, he ran away. Now he is useful, for Paul is returning him. Paul's inclination was to keep Onesimus with him in order that Onesimus in behalf of Philemon or in Philemon's place might minister to Paul in the bonds of the Gospel. But he determined not to do anything without Philemon's consent in order that the latter's goodness (or benefit or favor) might not be of necessity or compulsion.

C. RELATIONSHIPS NOTED
(Philemon 15-20)

For perhaps he therefore departed for a season, that thou shouldest receive him for ever; Not now as a servant, but above a servant, a brother beloved, specially to me, but how much more unto thee, both in the flesh, and in the Lord? If thou count me therefore a partner, receive him as myself. If he hath wronged thee, or oweth thee aught, put that on mine account; I Paul have written it with mine own hand, I will repay it: albeit I do not say to thee how thou owest unto me even thine own self besides. Yea, brother, let me have joy of thee in the Lord: refresh my bowels in the Lord.

The word "perhaps" in verse 15 suggests God's providential purposes are veiled. Note the delicate description of one who may have been a runaway thief: "Perhaps he took a brief vacation that you might take him back for good."

To be a Christian is to be a brother or sister to other believers. Christian brotherhood (sisterhood)—not race, nationality, education, gender, wealth or poverty—should be the determinative factor in all other human relationships.

Consider the words "no longer as a slave" (verse 16). The words "no longer" are the translation of a word that means no more, no further. Whatever his prior condition, it was no longer. But this needs to be explained. Paul did not write "no longer a slave," but "no longer as a slave." Onesimus is still a slave! But now as a Christian brother he will no longer be regarded as a slave, or be treated as a thing, a tool, a mere possession. He is now to be received in an altered, transformed relationship— as a "brother beloved."

Christ makes the difference! "There is enough dynamite packed in that simple statement to blow every form of slavery to pieces" (E. Stanley Jones). Onesimus is now "above a slave," or "beyond a slave." Yet both levels must be carried on simultaneously, a slave but not as a slave. Onesimus was now both a brother and a slave. And Philemon was both a brother and a slave master. Their common relation to Christ made them brothers, now and evermore.

Surely when Philemon thinks of this purpose of providence he cannot be harsh with his slave who is now so wonderfully changed. And now Paul calls Onesimus his (Paul's) dearly beloved brother. He does not leave Philemon with much choice! Receive Onesimus as if it were I that you are receiving unto yourself. If Onesimus wronged you—did an injustice, injured, caused loss, or mistreated Philemon—

put that on my account. Perhaps Paul knew what Onesimus had done, but graciously avoided bluntly naming it.

When Stephen was dying he cried, "Lord, lay not this sin to their charge" (Acts 7:60). Now we read Paul saying, "Put that on my account. I will repay it." But this was to Philemon for Onesimus, by Paul. Here we have a perfect picture of what is called imputation. It is an act "of God whereby He accounts righteousness to the believer in Christ, who has borne the believer's sin in vindication of the law" (Schofield).

We read of this when God accounted Abraham's faith to him for righteousness (Genesis 15:6). "Imputation is another way of expressing the idea of crediting something or charging it up. When God saves a sinner, He charges up to the sinner's credit His perfect righteousness in Christ" (Pilgrim Bible Commentary).

Paul reminds Philemon that he owed his conversion to Paul's ministry. He thus owed a double debt to the apostle: (1) not only his conversion (2) but now the return of a runaway slave who is a better slave than he had lost. Understand then that Paul did not want anything on Philemon's mind that might hinder him from genuinely receiving Onesimus.

D. CONFIDENCE EXPRESSED
(Philemon 21)

Having confidence in thy obedience I wrote unto thee, knowing that thou wilt also do more than I say.

Paul expresses confidence or trust in Philemon's obedience—this hearing and heeding. He states he knows that Philemon will do more than Paul says. More what? Possibly he could manumit or set Onesimus free. In this way Onesimus could freely serve in the Gospel ministry and thereby refresh Paul's heart. To receive Onesimus back was the bottom line; to emancipate would be "more."

III. Special Features

A. PRESERVING OUR HERITAGE

There are those who would condemn Paul's action and accuse him of compromising with the status quo. There are those who would not advise Onesimus to return to slavery. They would sing, "Before I'd be a slave, I'd be buried in my grave, And go home to see my Lord." In fact there are those who would seek to overthrow slavery by all means necessary, but especially by violent means.

What some people miss is the fact that Paul's method—obey your masters, be a good slave—sowed the seeds for the disruption of the slavery system. But it was the slow way, as God's ways often seem to men. Remember that the Lord Jesus also lived on this earth at a time when slavery was widespread. And He did not lead any crusade to abolish this evil.

We should not be unmindful of the fact that had our Lord or the apostle Paul attempted to overthrow slavery, it would have caused an insurrection, possibly anarchy, untold misery, disruption of the entire Roman economy, terrific loss of life, and disastrous defeat by the Roman army. Society would have been torn virtually to shreds.

And the purpose for which the Lord Jesus came—to seek and to save that which was lost—would have been rendered impossible. The purpose for which Paul was apprehended on the road to Damascus likewise would have been nullified. Can you imagine God allowing the attempt to eliminate slavery in this manner betray the character of the Gospel, and proscribe His grander purpose for His Son and for His Son's servant, Paul?

No, God would not allow His only begotten Son to be used to make a mockery of the promises in God's Word! Keep in mind that the Gospel of the Christ that Paul preached, slowly destroyed the abuses of slavery. In time, Christians learned that slavery was incompatible with the claims of Christ. As for the letter to Philemon, Paul did not consciously seek to overthrow or maintain slavery. His primary objective was to improve spiritual relationships between two Christians, one of whom was a slave, the other a slave owner.

B. A CONCLUDING WORD

In Christ both Philemon and Onesimus have the same God as their Father. They are both indwelt by the same Holy Spirit, and cleansed by the same blood of the only Lamb of God. Being in Christ transforms relationships. Whatever our different physical, educational, social and political standings are, however varied our physical characteristics, in the Lord we are on equal footing. Whatever Philemon and Onesimus were "in the flesh," whatever their relationship in that sphere, it did not disappear, it did not cease. There is at the same time a relationship called "in the Lord," which now existed by virtue of their union to Jesus Christ.

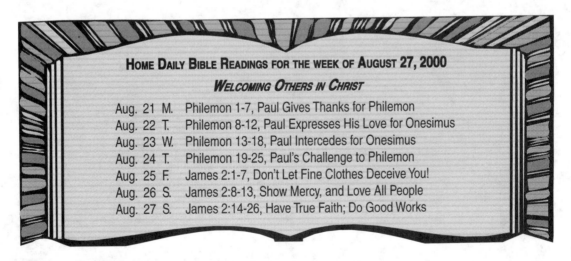

HOME DAILY BIBLE READINGS FOR THE WEEK OF AUGUST 27, 2000

WELCOMING OTHERS IN CHRIST

Aug. 21	M.	Philemon 1-7, Paul Gives Thanks for Philemon
Aug. 22	T.	Philemon 8-12, Paul Expresses His Love for Onesimus
Aug. 23	W.	Philemon 13-18, Paul Intercedes for Onesimus
Aug. 24	T.	Philemon 19-25, Paul's Challenge to Philemon
Aug. 25	F.	James 2:1-7, Don't Let Fine Clothes Deceive You!
Aug. 26	S.	James 2:8-13, Show Mercy, and Love All People
Aug. 27	S.	James 2:14-26, Have True Faith; Do Good Works

Eternal God, our Father, we affirm that You have loved us in spite of ourselves. Grant us the grace to accept others because of Your love for us. May the sacrifice of the Christ become the example by which we place personal desires on the altar. Amen.

Personal Notes and Reflections

Personal Notes and Reflections

Personal Notes and Reflections